THIS THING OF DARKNESS

THIS THING OF DARKNESS

EISENSTEIN'S IVAN THE TERRIBLE
IN STALIN'S RUSSIA

JOAN NEUBERGER

CORNELL UNIVERSITY PRESS
Ithaca and London

Cornell University Press gratefully acknowledges the support of the Office of the President at The University of Texas at Austin, which provided funds toward the publication of this book.

First published 2019 by Cornell University Press

Printed in the United States of America

Library of Congress Cataloging-in-Publication Data

Names: Neuberger, Joan, 1953– author.
Title: This thing of darkness : Eisenstein's Ivan the Terrible in Stalin's Russia / Joan Neuberger.
Description: Ithaca [New York] : Cornell University Press, 2019. | Includes bibliographical references and index.
Identifiers: LCCN 2018035596 (print) | LCCN 2018036651 (ebook) | ISBN 9781501732775 (pdf) | ISBN 9781501732782 (epub/mobi) | ISBN 9781501732768 | ISBN 9781501732768 (cloth; alk. paper)
Subjects: LCSH: Ivan Groznyi (Motion picture) | Eisenstein, Sergei, 1898–1948—Criticism and interpretation. | Stalin, Joseph, 1878–1953—Influence. | Ivan IV, Czar of Russia, 1530–1584—In motion pictures. | Motion pictures—Political aspects—Soviet Union.
Classification: LCC PN1997.I77 (ebook) | LCC PN1997.I77 N484 2019 (print) | DDC 791.43/72—dc23
LC record available at https://lccn.loc.gov/2018035596

This thing of darkness, I acknowledge mine.
　　　　　　　　　　—William Shakespeare, *The Tempest*

CONTENTS

ILLUSTRATIONS

ACKNOWLEDGMENTS

Some time ago, I decided to take a break from studying the worst things human beings do to each other and focus on the best things we can do. This book is about making art in difficult times, because making art in difficult times is one of those things. Its subject is something Bertolt Brecht knew all too well: that in dark times, "There will be singing. About the dark times." It is also a salute to Toni Morrison, whose words have buoyed many of my friends in our own dark times, and who wrote that "this is precisely the time when artists go to work. There is no time for despair, no place for self-pity, no need for silence, no room for fear. We speak, we write, we do language. That is how civilizations heal." I don't know if *Ivan the Terrible* healed anyone, and I'm sure Eisenstein took some time out for despair, but he also understood that in such times, "the main thing is to do. To really get down to it." It probably killed him, but he got down to it, and he left us this beautiful, inspiring thing.

I am grateful for the support I received to research and write this book from the National Council for Eurasian and East European Research and the International Research and Exchanges Board. The University of Texas (UT) at Austin provided numerous research and travel grants for which I am immensely thankful. I would like to thank everyone at the Russian State Archive for Literature and Art (RGALI) who made my research there such a great pleasure.

My colleagues have made the UT History Department an ideal community for me for almost three decades now. I want to thank our current and former chairs, Jackie Jones and Alan Tully, for their many forms of support, including Alan's visionary fund raising (at a university with no sabbaticals), which made possible two crucial semesters at our Institute for Historical Studies. Judy Coffin probably doesn't remember this, but among the many, many things that I'm grateful to her for, she told me I should write a book about Eisenstein, so I did. Erika Bsumek and Louise McReynolds have each been indispensable friends, especially during some hard times, for which I am genuinely eternally grateful.

Retraining myself as a film scholar took longer than I expected, but it has brought me many new friends in an extraordinary international community. It is impossible for me to express how deeply I appreciate everyone who has contributed to making my study of Eisenstein so much fun. For their friendship, conversation, and invaluable criticism (and gracious responses to my criticism), and for invitations to contribute to their publications or present portions of this research at their institutions, it hardly seems adequate to simply list you, but I sincerely thank Ada Ackerman, Luka Arsenjuk, Kevin Bartig, Masha Belodubrovskaya, Laurie Bernstein, Vince Bohlinger, David Bordwell, David Brandenberger, Oksana Bulgakowa, Phil Cavendish, Katy Clark, Julie Cassiday, Ian Christie, David Crew, Marina Frolova-Walker, Darra Goldstein, Julian Graffy, Hubertus Jahn, Lilya Kaganovsky, Michael Kunichika, Susan Larsen, Joanne Meyerowitz, Rachel Morley, Anne Eakin Moss, Anne Nesbet, Simon Morrison, Stephen Norris, Ana Olenina, Serguei Oushakine, Natasha Riabchikova, Vera Rumiantseva, Masha Salazkina, Barry Scherr, Irina Schutzki, Marian Schwartz, Yana Skorobogatov, Antonio Somaini, Mark Steinberg, Matthew Stephens, Ron Suny, Richard Taylor, Kristin Thompson, Gleb Tsipursky, Yuri Tsivian, Julia Vassilieva, and Bob Weinberg.

Additional thanks go to Marina Alexandrova for assistance with some tricky translation questions and to two of my graduate students who provided superlative research assistance, Margaret Peacock and Rebecca Johnston. I owe a special debt of thanks to Karla Oeler and Kevin Platt for their thorough, engaged reading and insightful comments on the manuscript. And I especially want to thank Mahinder Kingra, Roger Hayden, and Carolyn Pouncy at Cornell University Press.

I was finally able to finish this book because two people generously arranged for me to take research leave at their institutions. Emma Widdis made it possible for me to spend a semester at the University of Cambridge, where she provided everything I needed: friendship, collegiality, solitude, and cake. Val Kivelson has been at my side since I began this project, and I could not ask for a better companion—in Moscow, at home, at ASEEES, on Skype, at our institute in Los Angeles—and I cannot list all the ways her friendship and cousinship has enriched my entire life. Then, in addition to all that, she opened her house to me (thank you, too, Tim), and gave me the refuge I needed to write. Every aspect of this book has benefited from our travels together.

Naum Kleiman: I feel incalculably lucky to consider you my friend. It is no exaggeration to say that some of my very happiest hours have been spent in your company among Eisenstein's books at the apartment on Smolenskaia Street. I cannot thank you enough for everything you have done for Russian film studies, for your brilliant conversation about our favorite topic, and for your unmatched kindness and generosity. I hope this book returns at least some of my debt to you.

Last but not least, it is customary for authors to thank their family members for putting up with the obsessions and distractions of writing a book; I thank Charters Wynn for putting up with me, period. All I can say is that I hope you agree that the whole of our spiraling journey has been worth the wayward parts. For proof, our amazing boys. Max and Joel: you are the best children, the best company, and the most lovely young men anyone could wish for. We should have left you a better world; we tried, but not hard enough, it turns out.

Transliteration, Translations, and Citations

I follow Library of Congress rules for transliteration from Russian with exceptions for names given in anglicized forms: Eisenstein, Kurbsky, Mosfilm (Eizenshtein, Kurbskii, and Mosfil'm in the notes and bibliography). I cite widely available English translations whenever possible; when I cite the original Russian publications, the translations are my own. The first citation of an archival source gives the abbreviated name of the archive and the fond, or collection, in which the document is found. Thereafter I give only the numbers of the *opis* (inventory), *ed. khr.* or *delo* (file), and *list* (page), separated by a forward slash, and a date if I have it, in brackets. Citations without a *fond* number are documents from Eisenstein's personal papers at RGALI, f. 1923. Titles cited in the notes without an author were written by Eisenstein.

Eisenstein often underlined and double-underlined text in his notes and manuscripts. These are underlined or **underlined and bolded** here. Eisenstein often used ellipses in his notes to convey emphasis. To avoid confusing these with punctuation meant to show words have been left out of a quotation, I give Eisenstein's ellipses as em-dashes. When I quote a text he originally wrote in English, I reproduce the English in italics, with its errors and idiosyncrasies intact. I also italicize text that appeared originally in French or German but marked with an additional note.

Some of the research that produced this book appeared in the following publications, reprinted here with permission: "Not a Film But a Nightmare: Revisiting Stalin's Response to Eisenstein's *Ivan the Terrible*, Part II," *Kritika: Explorations in Russian and Eurasian History* 19, no. 1 (2018): 115–42; "Another Dialectic: Eisenstein on Acting," in *The Flying Carpet: Studies on Eisenstein in Honor of Naum Kleiman*, ed. Joan Neuberger and Antonio Somaini (Paris: Éditions Mimésis, 2017): 255–78; "Sergei Eisenstein's *Ivan the Terrible* as History," *Journal of Modern History* 86, no. 2 (2014): 295–334; "The Music of Landscape: Eisenstein, Prokofiev, and the Uses of Music in *Ivan the Terrible*," in *Sound, Speech, and Music in Russian Cinema*, ed. Lilya Kaganovsky and Masha Salazkina (Bloomington: Indiana University Press, 2013): 212–29; "Eisenstein's

Cosmopolitan Kremlin: Drag Queens, Circus Clowns, Slugs, and Foreigners in *Ivan the Terrible*," in *Ours and Theirs: Outsiders, Insiders, and Otherness in Russian Cinema*, ed. Stephen Norris and Zara Torlone (Bloomington: Indiana University Press, 2008): 81–95; and *Ivan the Terrible: The Film Companion* (London: I. B. Tauris, 2003).

Ivan the Terrible was released on DVD by Criterion Collection in 2003 in the boxed set *Eisenstein: The Sound Years*. This version also contains footage for Part III, some deleted scenes, and other material. In 2017, Mosfilm released a newly restored HD version, which is available with English subtitles online. Time codes to these videos are given in parentheses throughout the text for easy viewing while reading. As of this writing, it can be found here: http://cinema.mosfilm.ru/films/film/Ivan-Groznyj/ivan-grozniy-1-ya-seriya/ and here:

Part I: https://www.youtube.com/watch?v=jJmsV10MTJE&t=3306s
Part II: https://www.youtube.com/watch?v=i5g-Ss9BDR4&t=1039s

ABBREVIATIONS

EC	S. M. Eisenstein, *The Eisenstein Collection*
IK	*Iskusstvo kino*
IP	S. M. Eizenshtein, *Izbrannye proizvedeniia v shesti tomakh*
KZ	*Kinovedcheskie zapiski*
NN	*Nonindifferent Nature*
NP	*Neravnodushnaia priroda*
RGALI	Rossiiskii gosudarstvennyi arkhiv literatury i iskusstva
RGASPI	Rossiiskii gosudarstvennyi arkhiv sotsial'no-politicheskoi istorii
SW	S. M. Eisenstein, *Selected Works*

THIS THING OF DARKNESS

Introduction

"We're not beginning to . . . to . . . mean something?"
—Samuel Beckett, *Endgame*

At the beginning of 1941, Sergei Eisenstein was feeling defeated. Three years had passed since he had completed a film and, on January 2, he confided to his diary that he felt like his broken-down car, lethargic and depressed. A few days earlier, tired of waiting for the film administration to approve his latest proposal, he had written directly to Iosif Stalin, requesting him to intercede. When the phone rang on January 11, it was Andrei Zhdanov, secretary of the Central Committee and member of the Politburo's Committee on Cinema Affairs, calling to say that no one was interested in his most recent pitch, but that they should meet to discuss the film Stalin wanted him to make. We don't know exactly what was said at that meeting, but immediately afterward Eisenstein began reading and thinking and jotting down ideas about Ivan the Terrible. By January 21, the possibilities for the project had captured his imagination and would not let him go. He was writing about *Ivan the Terrible* when he died, at age fifty, only seven years later.[1]

Those seven years would be the most productive of Eisenstein's life. Two major works of theory, unpublished; notes for at least four more books, unfinished; an eight-hundred-page book of memoirs, unpublished; diaries, letters, speeches, articles, newspaper articles; hundreds of production notebooks; thousands of drawings. They were also years of war: invasion, evacuation, an incomprehensible scale of death and destruction, and, after victory, a difficult reconstruction. It was in this tense but intellectually and artistically fertile context that he made his extraordinary film *Ivan the Terrible*, no less a masterpiece for itself being unfinished.

The film Stalin commissioned was expected to celebrate Ivan (1530–1584) as a progressive and visionary leader, the first autocrat who unified Russia and founded the modern Russian state, whose vicious reign of terror against his own people would be justified as necessary for preserving that state. Stalin, who didn't like surprises, got much more than he bargained for. Eisenstein's film ranged far from the official commission and was controversial even before it hit the screen. *Ivan the Terrible* was not only a shrewd critique of Stalin and Stalinism, but it raised profound questions about the nature of power, violence, and tyranny in contemporary politics and the history of state power more broadly. Eisenstein's film used Ivan's story to examine the psychology of political ambition, the history of absolute power and of recurrent cycles of violence. It explores the inner struggles of the people who achieved power as well as their rivals and victims.

The process of thinking seriously about biography and history for the first time also opened up possibilities for Eisenstein to develop new ways to approach fundamental artistic problems of depiction and communication. To explore the political, historical, and psychological conflicts posed by Ivan the Terrible's story in the context of the 1940s, Eisenstein devised a style that grew out of his lifelong study of montage cinema. Because the details of Ivan's biography and his uses of power corresponded to many of Eisenstein's evolving ideas about art, the film became a laboratory for developing new cinematic methods and testing them in practice. Those methods both incorporated and challenged the prescribed conventions of Stalinist cultural production. Eisenstein was an omnivorous reader, and he drew on artistic practices from all over the world, from the earliest recorded societies to contemporary European modernism. *Ivan the Terrible* embodies Eisenstein's wide interests, complex thinking, bold originality, and experimental approach to filmmaking.

This book is the first to analyze Eisenstein's great masterpiece by combining historical, political, cinematic, and cultural approaches, which, I argue, is the only way to understand its sweeping achievements. *Ivan the Terrible* is much more than a movie: it contains a theory of history, a theory of political violence, and a theory of artistic production and perception. It represents one of the world's greatest filmmakers and one of the twentieth century's greatest artists experimenting with every element of film art in the service of telling a story about Russia's most notorious and bloody ruler(s) on the screen. Eisenstein depicted violence not as an attribute of "the enemy" but as a universal impulse rooted in human psychology and history. And he didn't exonerate anyone: not Ivan, not Stalin, not the Russian people, not himself. As Shakespeare's aging magician Prospero said of his own project, Caliban, "this thing of darkness, I acknowledge mine."

Art and Politics: The Interrogative Mode

Eisenstein was a sharp observer of the world around him, and *Ivan the Terrible* reflects not only his artistic thinking but his historical experience and political acuity. He came to this project after witnessing some of the worst episodes of violence in modern European history: World War I, the Russian Revolution, the Russian Civil War, and the Stalinist reign of terror, and he made the film during World War II. He saw class animosity and ritual humiliation produce a revolution that replaced one horrific regime with another. The creation myths he invented for that revolution in his first films in the 1920s made him world famous, but then he watched as the revolution degenerated into a dictatorship in the name of an idealistic and increasingly empty abstraction. The historical narrative that Eisenstein composed for *Ivan* is based on his reading of historical sources through a filter of his experience, intuition, and preconceptions, together with his vast reading in world cultures to show how such cycles of human tragedy could perpetuate themselves so destructively.

Eisenstein constructed his portrait of Ivan and his examination of power by posing several key questions: How does an innocent, vulnerable child become a sadistic, bloody tyrant? To what extent is Ivan like the people around him and, by extension, like us? When is killing justifiable? Do Russian rulers and, by implication, all Russians differ from their contemporaries in the West? When are we responsible for our own actions, and when can we blame circumstances? Each scene raises these questions in some form, so the audience is constantly being invited to wonder, compare, evaluate, and judge. Underlying these moral-political issues is a set of related questions concerning human emotions. In general, *Ivan* asks us to consider what role emotions play—in relation to reason and logic—in motivating us to act. More specifically, Eisenstein asks what happens when love, affection, sexual attraction, grief, loneliness, hate, distrust, and the desire for revenge enter into politics. How are political affections and rivalries gendered? What happens when we are asked to love a ruler like a father? What role does affection play in a political brotherhood? These are questions that Eisenstein had been exploring since the beginning of his career as a director. In *Ivan the Terrible*, the persistent homoeroticism and fluid gendering with which Eisenstein poses these last questions played a major role in the film's narrative, form, and politics. These are not the typical structuring devices of the Stalinist biopic. Soviet film biographies of this period were supposed to depict a "usable past" and provide a model of behavior for viewers with characters who could be "guides to life." Individuals in film biographies, whether cult figures or ordinary people, were to undergo some transitional improvement, make a heroic contribution to their community, and offer moments of inspiration and motivation.[2] Eisenstein's moral, political, and aesthetic questions made a mockery of these conventions, while superficially complying with their demands.

Eisenstein's interrogative mode was a radical gesture in the Stalinist world of verities and positive role models. By raising these questions and by structuring the film around questions, Eisenstein works against the didactic, the simplistic, and the one-sided. The opposite of enforced certainty, however, was not amoral relativism. The ambiguities of the interrogative deny viewers a neutral vantage point and challenge us to reclaim our authority to make meaning from observation and experience. *Ivan the Terrible* is a difficult film because it continually presents us with contradictions and questions, and because it denies us a hero to identify with or a villain to hate. It is a great film because it creates a portrait of power that resists simplification and provokes us to engage with hard questions, precisely the hard questions the artist was supposed to suppress. And it's funny. Despite its violent and tragic subject, *Ivan the Terrible* is, at times, shockingly comical. A sly smile and an ironic grimace lurk just below the surface. Eisenstein used humor to question the performative seriousness with which Soviet rulers often presented themselves and to contrast with moments of profound pathos and tragedy. These are all anti-mythmaking moves by the director who brought us the original Soviet mythmaking films.

Ivan the Terrible was not Eisenstein's first film about a Russian ruler, of course, and its focus on an individual rather than the collective hero has made some viewers link it with *Alexander Nevsky* (1938) as a repudiation of Eisenstein's earlier revolutionary films and the radical cinema they have come to represent. Unlike Nevsky, however, the historical Ivan's biography offered Eisenstein opportunities to align the film narrative with his interests in psychology, history, and sensory perception. Rich sources about Ivan's childhood, his piety, and late-in-life remorse allowed Eisenstein to see the Terrible Tsar as a man riven by inner contradictions and unable to escape the trauma of his own past, psychological and historical-biographical structures central to Eisenstein's understanding of human nature. These contours of Ivan's life gave Eisenstein an unprecedented opportunity to explore the nexus of interior thought and feeling with exterior behavior and action, both on paper and on the screen. Eisenstein's writing of the 1940s—*Nonindifferent Nature* and

Method—investigates the ways in which artistic form, individual experience, historical patterns, and political realities mutually constituted each other. And *Ivan the Terrible* is, in fact, a continuation and development of Eisenstein's earlier works. It displays the stage of Eisenstein's thinking in the 1940s but also shows that he was incorporating artistic and theoretical ideas he had been developing since the beginning of his career in the 1920s. Undaunted by his experiences with censure, censorship, and repression, he explicitly resurrected avant-garde practices and made a defiantly modernist, experimental film.

This book looks at the entirety of *Ivan the Terrible* in the context of Eisenstein's entire career, his wide-ranging reading, and the largely unknown writing of his last decade. Understanding *Ivan the Terrible* requires a global approach because the film reflects Eisenstein's extraordinarily wide range of interests and because he was thinking in global terms. His subject was political power and violence, and his sources were political and art history from all over the world: from Machiavelli to Disney; Euripides to Shakespeare to kabuki; Pushkin, Tolstoy, and Dostoevsky; the Russian historians Karamzin, Kliuchevsky, and Soloviev; El Greco, Daumier, Piranesi, and Picasso; East Asian landscape scroll paintings, indigenous Mexican architecture, and pre-contact Peruvian ceramics—to name just a fraction of the artists and writers in play. Examining *Ivan the Terrible* together with the book-length manuscripts Eisenstein wrote while the film was in production and with the books he was reading and art he was viewing shows how his ideas about montage and meaning evolved through the 1930s and into the 1940s. Eisenstein was one of the first writers to explore in depth the importance of sensory-emotional responses to art and the ways in which structures of mind and physiology are essential to understanding our methods for deriving meaning in art and life. His writing about visual, aural, synesthetic, and cognitive perception places him among the great thinkers of the early twentieth century: Walter Benjamin, Mikhail Bakhtin, Aby Warburg, and Sigmund Freud. Even more important, Eisenstein is the *only* major theorist of this period who was a major artist as well, putting theory into practice and developing theory derived from practice. In order to represent the history and psychology of power, in order to convey the inner life of the powerful in a way that would touch, move, and change people, Eisenstein employed a profusion of new cinematic methods meant to activate and intensify the spectator's sensory, emotional, and intellectual experience of watching a film. Much of *Method* and *Nonindifferent Nature* examined the role of story and character alongside his earlier preoccupations with composition and form in conveying an author's ideas to an audience. His extensive production notes (more about those in a moment) addressed details of Ivan's biography in conjunction with cinematic methods for telling Ivan's story. In general, his writing during this period concerned the particular ways in which cinematic storytelling could maximize the impact of the filmmaker's ideas and feelings on viewers. To some extent, these issues have been treated in the literature on *Ivan the Terrible*, but usually only in fragmented or speculative fashion. One of the contributions of this book is its systematic integration of Eisenstein's major writing of this period into an analysis of the whole film. Looking at *Ivan* in light of Eisenstein's intellectual preoccupations together with his biographical experiences shows that the historical and political aspects of his work are integral to understanding the aesthetic, psychological, and philosophical (and vice versa).

Eisenstein worked on *Ivan the Terrible* for five years, from January 1941 until February 1946, completing only two-thirds of the projected three-part film. Part I of the trilogy was completed in December 1944 and went into general release in January 1945; Part II was submitted in February 1946; it was banned in March and released only in 1958; Part III remained unfinished at Eisenstein's death in February 1948, but the scenario, some notes, and some footage has survived. Although the film became about much more than Ivan as a progressive proto-Stalin, Eisenstein's work was nonetheless haunted by Stalin himself. Like other artists of the period, Eisenstein stopped short of drawing direct comparisons between Stalin and Ivan in his public pronouncements.[3] But there is no doubt that while Eisenstein was thinking broadly about power and artistic method, his Ivan was always at least partially a portrait of Stalin. Stalin remained a critical presence in the production process as well, and Eisenstein appealed to him directly during sticky moments in production, going above the heads of film industry officials and his other Politburo patrons. Stalin was not involved in day-to-day decision making about the film, but his response to each finished part determined the censorship, release, and public reception of both Part I and Part II.

By emphasizing history and politics and by addressing Stalin's role in the making of *Ivan the Terrible*, I risk giving readers the impression that this study will center on Stalin, perhaps as a counterweight to most existing commentary on *Ivan*, which typically avoids politics and focuses on film form. But Eisenstein did not make *Ivan* with that kind of divide in mind. On the contrary, he consistently conceived visual, sensory filmic composition to be an instrument—a method—for constructing a coherent narrative, for producing an intellectual and emotional experience for viewers, and for conveying the author's ideas and feelings about the subject to the audience. The enduring importance of *Ivan the Terrible* is to be found in Eisenstein's multilayered or, as he put it, "polyphonic" treatment of the life of Ivan the Terrible. By approaching Eisenstein's dynamic theories of history, visual perception, and cultural evolution in relation to one another, this study uncovers a decisive piece: Eisenstein didn't only want to show the tragic depredations of absolute rule or the universality of power hunger, and he didn't only want to create a moving emotional experience for viewers. He also wanted to show how individuals, societies, and cultures change over time to become bloody tyrannies over and over again. And he tried to convey those ideas about cycles of change in a film structured to create a similar experience of change—recurring feelings of illumination and transformation—in its spectators.

Reception

A whole raft of assumptions have typically prevented viewers from appreciating what Eisenstein was trying to do in *Ivan the Terrible*. Politics and ideology have always interfered in the reception and analysis of this film, often to simplify or dismiss the political in favor of formal analysis. Those who expected to see Soviet triumphalist propaganda were distracted from the film's remarkable narrative structures and its psychological and political challenges. Those who wanted another *Potemkin*, the film in which Eisenstein first showed the possibilities of montage editing, have failed to appreciate *Ivan's* quite different but related uses of montage and formal innovation. Ideologically colored expectations have also hampered viewers' willingness to open up to the film's sensory-emotional effects and its overall strangeness. Underlying many of these distortions is the unsystematic publication and translation history of Eisenstein's writing, which obscures the many ways in which his work of the 1940s grew out of earlier writings and films.

In the United States, *Ivan* has been relegated, for the most part, to the museum of film studies: acknowledged as a masterpiece but rarely watched in general film history classes. One goal of this book is to reverse that trend and make *Ivan the Terrible* watchable and watched again. In the 1960–1970s, Eisenstein was seen as a socialist radical who was forced into conformity under Stalin; as either a discredited renegade or a discredited Kremlin lackey. Later observers have seen him as an apolitical artist or a political opportunist. In the 1990s, a shift began to take place among Eisenstein scholars, with the publication of his later writing as well as definitive versions of earlier publications, edited by Naum Kleiman and others at the Eisenstein Center and Cinema Museum in Moscow. These new sources have complicated Eisenstein's political and theoretical positioning and make possible new inquiries into what he thought he could accomplish and what he did.[4]

Ivan has not been neglected by scholars who specialize in Russian film. Valuable new research has appeared to complement older works on

Eisenstein's aesthetic, theoretical, and cinematic practices in connection with *Ivan the Terrible*.[5] Excellent studies have appeared recently on specific facets of Eisenstein's thinking,[6] or on single elements of form such as music and camerawork.[7] Published documents on the film industry and Soviet cultural life more broadly have been extremely important in helping understand Eisenstein's work in the larger cultural context.[8] The few specialized historical studies of Eisenstein's *Ivan*, while certainly valuable, suffer from a piecemeal approach to specific limited problems or an incomplete reading of the published and archival sources.[9] Understanding of *Ivan*'s politics and artistry has also been obscured by the fact that most reviewers and scholars have assumed that the film had to be either apolitical or politically conformist. Eisenstein's official Soviet biographer, Rostislav Iurenev, presented him as dutifully toeing the ideological line, as do many other Soviet, Anglophone, and émigré film scholars, though for a variety of different reasons.[10] Alexander Solzhenitsyn set the tone by having a character in his novel, *One Day in the Life of Ivan Denisovich*, denigrate Eisenstein by saying: "You can't call him a genius! Call him an ass-kisser who followed orders like a dog."[11] Many early critics and some recent scholars assumed that Eisenstein had no choice but to comply with given political conditions. Oksana Bulgakowa agreed but for different reasons: Eisenstein "never understood his mission in a political sense. He succumbed to the images of his future film as an artist and visionary."[12] For ten years after his death, little was written about Eisenstein, and in the Soviet Union he was a figure in disgrace. But the 1958 release of Part II and the publication of Eisenstein's six-volume collected works in the 1960s–1970s led to a new appreciation for *Ivan*'s complexity and a reevaluation of its political stance.[13] Part II came to be seen as a serious, perhaps even suicidal, critique of Stalinist despotism. The earliest expression of this view can be found in the works of two great Russian film scholars, beginning with Naum Kleiman's appendix to volume 6 of Eisenstein's collected works.[14] Leonid Kozlov developed this argument in a series of articles about *Ivan* published in the mid-1970s, but Kozlov, like many viewers, saw a critical disparity between Parts I and II.[15] As Neia Zorkaia put it in 1966, "Eisenstein produced the official version of *Ivan* in Part I, and the tragic truth of the epoch in Part II."[16] This bifurcated view, while still quite popular,[17] is not sustained by close reading of the archival materials for *Ivan* or by examination of the films in their unfinished entirety. James Goodwin, who examines *Ivan* as a whole, is correct in concluding that from the beginning, Eisenstein had no interest in justifying violence or praising tyranny.[18] Based primarily on published sources, Bernd Uhlenbruch and Evgeny Dobrenko show that the film's Kremlin was indeed a mirror of Stalin's: "a cryptogram of the internal state of the Party in the 1930s and 40s," but not in a way that was intended to praise Stalin.[19] The possibility that Eisenstein conceived of and produced a thoroughly critical film from beginning to end, nonetheless, has been stubbornly resisted by some.[20]

To survey the literature on *Ivan the Terrible* this way, narrowly focused on its political stance, does a disservice to the rich scholarship on the film (including the works cited above), but existing treatments have left fundamental questions unresolved: What does *Ivan the Terrible* have to say about Russian history, with its cycles of revolutions, its recurrent tyrants, and its particular relationships between rulers and ruled? How did Eisenstein draw on historical and other sources in making *Ivan*? How did Eisenstein get away with making such an unconventional and challenging film? Why did Eisenstein choose to make such a strange-looking film, and how does its cinematic form convey or produce meaning? How did theory and practice inform one another in the last, highly productive decade of Eisenstein's life? Who, ultimately, is Eisenstein's Ivan? And who is *Ivan's* Eisenstein? These and many more questions can only be answered by understanding that the film was conceived, produced, watched, and censored by people with specifically Soviet historical experience who were engaging with the world in which they found themselves. *Ivan the Terrible's* better-known formal innovations served specific functions and are inseparable from the time and place where the film was made and can be better appreciated when we see how Eisenstein deployed the biography and autobiography; the history and cultural politics; the embedded visual, dramatic, and intellectual history; and the evolving film theory to tell a story by raising questions.

The interrogative mode, however, makes my project a tricky one. Today we tend to favor arguments that privilege contingency and open-endedness, but we also know that Eisenstein wanted to shape the way audiences received his work and that he cared about viewers processing and understanding his ideas and feelings. We can only understand *Ivan* and its contradictions if we remember that both impulses are at work in this film, that Eisenstein embraced contradiction as a fundamental human trait, and that those contradictions follow identifiable patterns. Eisenstein shared with Walter Benjamin a conception of the open-endedness of history that did not simultaneously lead him to "disavow the act of judgment"; in fact, history "insistently poses the question of interpretation."[21] *Ivan the Terrible* continually raises questions, but in doing so, it also answers them. While posing questions about the personal and the political, the sensory-emotional and the logical-rational, the individual and the collective, the past and the present, the moral and the expedient, Eisenstein offers an explanation of the unredeemable dangers and inevitable violence of absolute power. He shows that the contradictions inherent in the exercise of absolute power are both inevitable and monstrous.

Ivan's Eisenstein

The making of *Ivan the Terrible* isn't a romantic story about choosing between heroic resistance and cowardly compliance. It is a story of observation and adaptation, of risk taking and risk aversion, of winning sometimes and losing sometimes. Understanding the choices Eisenstein faced in making *Ivan the Terrible* gives us a revealing, in-depth portrait of the Stalinist artist at work, both within and against Stalinist structures of power. Eisenstein was capable of making a film of sublime beauty and profound thinking, not only because he was a privileged artist (though he certainly was exceptional) or because he was a dissident or martyr. Eisenstein was able to make a film that engaged with the deepest political and cultural and subjective issues of the Soviet experience of the mid-twentieth century precisely by operating within the constraints of Stalinist culture and politics. Stalin exercised his power by alternately rewarding and punishing artists, but policy and Kremlin decision making never acquired total control over artistic production and individual creativity. In this arena, for all his privilege, position, and talent, Eisenstein was like every other Soviet artist: interpreting directives and working within a system. Eisenstein had resources no one else had, and *Ivan* was a prestige project that kept him in Stalin's spotlight, but ultimately Eisenstein was able to make *Ivan* such a challenging and transgressive work because he was willing to take risks, because he was good at gaming the system, and because he found himself in circumstances that made those risks possible. What makes *Ivan the Terrible* so extraordinarily important and revealing is that Eisenstein not only negotiated official institutions and structures of power but also used his film to examine precisely those systems of decision making and constraint. There are undoubtedly some readers who still believe that Eisenstein was incapable of making a film that challenged Kremlin policy, either because he didn't care about politics or because he was the Face of Communist Film or because Stalinist subjectivity precluded thinking like an individual subject. This study of the film and the documents recording Eisenstein's interaction with arts institutions, all the way up through film studio administrators to the Politburo and to Stalin himself, show that Eisenstein worked as a creative individual within and outside the system; with just enough calculation, at times defiant and at times compliant, to create an enduring masterpiece but not enough to finish it or physically survive the process. Understanding what Eisenstein thought he could do as an artist shows us the Stalinist cultural system in practice.

In 1941, when work began on *Ivan the Terrible*, Eisenstein was the most famous filmmaker in the Soviet Union, with an international reputation that literally circled the globe, and he was one of the country's most important cultural figures. But Soviet fame and power were fickle and insecure. Eisenstein's debut on the cultural scene was a spectacular one, and it brought him enduring international renown, but he had a checkered career in the Soviet Union that included as much heartbreak and failure as success.

Between 1924 and 1929, he made four feature-length films on revolutionary themes and with revolutionary cinematic techniques: *Strike, Battleship Potemkin, October,* and *Old and New*. *Potemkin* made Eisenstein famous, but at the same time, he became embroiled in polemics—increasingly rancorous—with other members of the Soviet film community over the *purpose* of cinema in "the building of socialism."[22] Eisenstein never joined the Communist Party, but he remained committed to some form of democratic socialism and utopian collectivism throughout his life. In this early part of his career, Eisenstein believed that cinema should serve society and help build socialism. Such views would become petrified in the following decade and be used to criticize Eisenstein himself for failing to understand exactly how the Soviet state wanted to use cinema to serve society.

Eisenstein missed the transition from the relative artistic freedom of the 1920s to the increasing state control of the 1930s because he was traveling abroad. In 1929, he went on an extended trip with his cameraman, Eduard Tisse, and his assistant director, Grigory Alexandrov. The trio went to Europe and the United States in search of new sound technologies and with hopes for a lucrative Hollywood contract to bring revenue for the Soviet film industry. In Paris in early 1930, Eisenstein signed a contract with Paramount Pictures and then slowly made his way to California with detours through London, Paris, New York, and Chicago. In Hollywood, Eisenstein and his friends hobnobbed with the film world glitterati—including Charlie Chaplin and Walt Disney—but none of his three film projects went into production. Rescue seemed to be forthcoming in an offer from the wealthy socialist writer Upton Sinclair to fund a film about Mexico, *Que Viva Mexico!*

Eisenstein's year in Mexico was one of personal and artistic fulfillment. Mexico City in the 1930s was an international cultural center, as important and exciting as Paris, with expatriate artists from around the globe. Eisenstein found the environment extremely congenial and stimulating. His old interest in anthropology was revived by his fascination with Mexican culture. He began to draw again, a practice that he would continue for the rest of his life.

But Mexico was too much fun. Sinclair became disgruntled with filming that ran months over schedule, and he was disturbed by rumors of sexual escapades. When Stalin threatened to banish Eisenstein permanently if he did not return to the Soviet Union, Sinclair seized the opportunity to pull the plug on *Que Viva Mexico!* Eisenstein never recovered the year's worth of footage, and for the rest of his life he was haunted by the loss.

The Moscow Eisenstein found on his return in May 1932 was more constricted and impoverished than the city he had left. Exhilarating ideas about art serving society had become the rigid guidelines of artistic institutions that were ultimately run by Communist Party bureaucrats.[23] A paradoxical situation emerged. Eisenstein's numerous projects and proposals were turned down, but he remained the representative of Soviet cinema for the international film community. Eisenstein was criticized for being out of step, old-fashioned, and "formalist," which is to say he cared more about cinematic form than making films "accessible to the masses." The 1930s were years of repeated frustration and humiliation at the hands of the film industry, in particular its chief, Boris Shumiatsky, who loathed Eisenstein. During the thirties, Shumiatsky decided which kinds of films best served Soviet society, and he saw to it that few of Eisenstein's proposals went into production.

By nature, Eisenstein was a deeply private and cautious man. He could be charming and charismatic in social situations as well as serious and demanding while working, but these were public masks; he guarded his private life. People familiar with Eisenstein through his published works and silent films are always surprised to learn that he was famous among friends for his pranks and dirty jokes. As a result, his intimate relationships have been the subject of speculation, gossip, and wishful thinking. He had sexual relationships with both men and women, but these were rare and short-lived. In 1934, just after a law was passed making male homosexuality illegal in the Soviet Union, Eisenstein married his good friend and assistant, Pera Atasheva. Records of his relationships with men are scarce, and no one who knows more is talking. He consulted with psychoanalysts about his bisexuality in the 1920s and 1930s, he had one known sexual relationship with a man in Mexico, and *Ivan the Terrible* is so suffused with homoeroticism as to indicate more than a passing interest in the subject. It is hard to know what Eisenstein's sexuality might have been if he had had more freedom to choose, but it is fair to say that sex was a source of dissatisfaction for him and his private life in general brought him considerable pain. He suffered from periodic bouts of depression, and from the 1930s on his health was regularly threatened by heart disease and other maladies.

The political attack on the director culminated in 1937, the height of the Great Terror, which saw the mass arrest and execution of prominent intellectuals, political leaders, and other citizens—men, women, and children. In that year, after many delays, Eisenstein was finally nearing completion of *Bezhin Meadow*, his first film since returning from abroad. Shumiatsky had the production halted, but he did not stop there. He denounced Eisenstein to the Central Committee (the highest party institution in the Soviet Union), and then directly to Stalin. This was no petty squabble among artists and bureaucrats over the interpretation of a film. Everyone involved knew that they were playing a game of life and death. In the hopes of distancing himself from the firestorm, Eisenstein left Moscow for Kislovodsk (a resort in the Caucasus), and it turned out that he had just enough support among party members in the film industry and, more critically, on the Central Committee (whose decisions could be capricious). The highest authorities decided that Eisenstein was reliable enough to allow him to continue to make films, and that Shumiatsky had overstepped his own authority (and possibly outlived his usefulness). Shumiatsky did not accept defeat gracefully and refused to back down. In a horrifying, but typical, Stalinist reversal, Shumiatsky was arrested in the following year and subsequently shot.[24]

After writing the required self-criticism, Eisenstein was given the opportunity to make another film. *Alexander Nevsky* became his most popular film, with its heroic battle against German invaders, but Eisenstein was ashamed of it. In 1937, Shumiatsky's attack on *Bezhin Meadow* had plunged Eisenstein's reputation to its lowest point and put his career as a filmmaker in mortal danger. Then, suddenly, the success of *Alexander Nevsky* catapulted him to the highest of inner circles. He had finished *Nevsky* in record time, he had made a film that was patriotic, and he wrote obsequious articles for major newspapers about it. In 1939 he won the Order of Lenin, and in 1941 *Alexander Nevsky* won the newly created Stalin Prize. In a restructuring of the film industry that brought more artists to positions of authority, Eisenstein was made artistic director of Mosfilm, a prestigious and powerful job. But, as if to underline the capriciousness of these decisions and the fragility of his own position, *Alexander Nevsky* was rarely shown after Stalin signed a nonaggression pact with Nazi Germany and then returned to circulation and celebrated when the Nazis broke the pact and invaded the Soviet Union in June 1941.

Eisenstein often said that writing and drawing carried the same weight as filmmaking in his artistic profile.[25] On one hand, his drawings are beginning to attract the attention they deserve, and they played a major role in his preparation for *Ivan*.[26] On the other hand, while Eisenstein's writing has long been appreciated, the scattershot publication of his texts has made it difficult to trace the development of his ideas and the junctures of thinking, writing, drawing, and filmmaking. Here I want to outline a few of the elements of

Eisenstein's writing in the decades before 1941 that would have an impact on his work on *Ivan the Terrible*, *Method*, and *Nonindifferent Nature*.

Eisenstein's writing was eclectic, unsystematic, and experimental. His thinking often coincided with or drew from contemporary discourse, but it always exhibited extraordinary independence of mind and reflected the staggering diversity of sources he consulted. Although we can see shifts in his interests, his style, and his arguments, I see Eisenstein's writing as essentially accumulative. The "Kino-Fist"—the direct assault on the sensibilities of the audience that he proposed in 1925—became less pugnacious as his understanding of spectator response evolved, but his primary underlying question was always how to reach, touch, and change the audience by stimulating an intense sensory-emotional experience. We can find the origins of many of his later ideas, such as the pre-logical and montage "within the shot," in some of his earliest notes and essays.[27] Like many of his contemporaries in the early Soviet avant garde, he adopted ideas about feeling and sensation in the body from both psychologists and physiologists. In the early 1920s, he thought he could direct audience response the way Ivan Pavlov trained dogs, but he soon realized how difficult that would be.[28] He believed that images had to possess a balance between opposing forces—intellectual and emotional, interior and exterior, invisible and visible—in order to have the greatest conditioned response. Montage at this time meant juxtaposing and superimposing visual images that commented on each other in such as way as to do more than simply move the story along. Montage collisions were intended to produce a startling experience and an awareness of new sensations or ideas.

Montage was always about more than editing, and from this period onward, it would accrue meanings and functions. In a collection of important transitional essays written around 1929, Eisenstein would add three key components. First, he expanded the meaning of montage by exploring "montage within the shot." The collision of all kinds of elements within each frame could produce the same kind of startling and generative effects as those earlier juxtapositions between shots. If originally montage involved combining shots, it would soon go beyond elements within the shot to elements of the entire process of producing and perceiving art, but it always was directed toward having the greatest effect on the viewer. Second, while the purpose of montage was ideological, directed toward raising the viewer's class consciousness, Eisenstein expanded those goals to include a much broader range of effects, which in turn aroused his interest in a broader range of artistic structures, genres, media, and more complex forms of reception. Montage collisions could produce something ephemeral, perceived more as a feeling or a sensation, perhaps only barely acknowledged, an image that did not necessarily resolve itself into words or ideas—the equivalent of an "overtone" in music. Third, he began to write about the collisions that produced these more complex responses and elusive overtones in terms of dialectics. Everywhere he looked, Eisenstein saw the world in shifting binaries that collided, resolved themselves in a synthesis of some kind, and fragmented again into new binaries. Within a particular shot there might be numerous such dialectical collisions: between thought and feeling, sound and silence, visible and invisible, movement in different directions, narrative and stylistic elements, or between what one sees on the screen and what one had previously seen, felt, or thought.[29] These accretions to his early theory of "montage of attractions" have confused observers to this day. Eisenstein spent the last two decades of his writing career refuting those who thought he was finished with montage after the 1920s. As Jacques Aumont wrote, "what is at stake in Eisenstein's work is not the elaboration of *methods* of montage, nor the formulation of one single concept of montage, but a kind of ongoing and even somewhat systematic study of the principle of montage (or the phenomenon of montage)."[30] After 1929, montage and dialectics would be the foundation for all Eisenstein's film theory and practice.

In the 1930s, Eisenstein expanded the meaning and uses of montage and dialectics under the influence of his travels abroad. Already before leaving Russia, Eisenstein was struck by the survivals of the past in present; the revolution had not eradicated everything that came before it and, unlike many of his peers, Eisenstein was unwilling to "throw Pushkin, Dostoevsky, Tolstoy, etc., etc., overboard from the Ship of Modernity," in the words of the notorious Futurist manifesto.[31] His year in Mexico, where he saw even starker survivals of the past in the present, not only confirmed the importance of this historical dialectic but joined it to research on perception he had begun back in Moscow with the psychologists Lev Vygotsky and Alexander Luria and in Paris, when he encountered the ethnographer Lucien Lévy-Bruhl and his concept of the pre-logical.[32] Lévy-Bruhl argued that in "primitive" societies, people thought and responded to the world in less rigidly structured, less rationally differentiated ways than in the "modern" world. He called this kind of thinking "pre-logical," and it included antirational elements of magic, feeling, and shape-shifting of various kinds. But Eisenstein rejected Lévy-Bruhl's belief in linear evolution from primitive to civilized. He saw attributes associated with so-called primitive peoples in his own society and psyche. The human capacity for the pre-logical (and its dialectical tension with the logical) would become the focus of *Method* but this work came to fruition only during the production of *Ivan the Terrible*, where it would have a decisive impact (and will therefore be discussed later). During the 1930s, Eisenstein collected material and began writing drafts on the artistic implications of the pre-logical, and its corollary, sensory-emotional thinking (*chuvstvennoe myshlenie*), but when he spoke about this work at the 1935 state-sponsored conference on cinema, convened to establish Socialist Realism in film, he was roundly ridiculed and criticized. His subsequent writing in the late 1930s addressed the roles of sensation, feeling, perception, and sociocultural history in terms of montage. During and after the Stalinist Terror, publishing or even acknowledging his work on magical and sensory-emotional thinking seemed impossible.

Eisenstein did not stop asking fundamental questions about art that led him to fundamental questions about human perception and creativity. What makes a work of art enduring and universal? How does an artist turn an idea or concept into a story about seemingly real people? How does art work on us? And how can artists produce works that tap into our fundamental sensory-emotional and intellectual capacities and intensify our responses? To answer these questions, Eisenstein read a phenomenal number of works on art and theater history, psychology, ethnography, philosophy, and physiology, as well as fiction, drama, history, and biography. Eisenstein was passionate about books, and he collected a large library. In his memoirs, he discusses more books than people, and he rhapsodizes about bookstores he visited in cities around the world and about the books he found in them. "They fly to me, run to me, cling to me," he wrote with a collector's ardor, "so long have I loved them . . . I can steal them. I could probably kill them." His self-image was at least much book-oriented as film-oriented, and he animated his books with uncanny powers: "currents flow from small cells of grey matter of the brain, through the cranium and the sides of bookcases . . . into the hearts of the books . . . and, in response to the flow of thoughts, they hurl themselves at my head."[33]

For all that passion for books and ambition to discover universal patterns in artistic production and reception, he could be an opportunistic reader and fuzzy thinker. These qualities have opened him to criticism, but I prefer to characterize his writing as practice-oriented and experimental. He cherry-picked ideas that appealed to him and tried them out in the process of developing methods for powerful, memorable, emotionally moving works of art. In his writing of the 1930s and 1940s, he constructs arguments about universal patterns by giving examples from an astonishing range of artistic genres, periods, and cultural traditions, as well as from psychology and ethnography, which took him into the roles of sex and violence, politics and history, magical thinking and the sciences of the mind. The montage essays of the late 1930s are exploratory examinations of the ways in which art conveys an artist's intentions and ideas through disassembly and reassembly of visual and other sensory and cognitive elements, now including sound and color, feeling and thought, movement and rhythm. He shows how this montage process takes place dialectically. Individual fragments of an artist's ideas are materialized on the screen in a depiction or picture (*izobrazhenie*); these depictions collide with each other within the shot, between shots, and across the time-space of the film, until they can be reassembled by the viewer in a coherent synthesis that produces some new, higher, and deeper level of understanding, an awareness that Eisenstein (confusingly) calls the "generalizable image" (*obraz*) or "montage image." Elements of character, appearance, types of movement, material objects, music, lighting, mise-en-scène, and so on are reassembled in ways that trigger our awareness and imagination in increasingly intense emotional and intellectual contradictions to produce an image that is abstract enough to be generalizable (*obobshchaiushchii*)—that is, more abstractly or broadly applicable—in a way that allows viewers to take a leap to a new level of consciousness or understanding. The generalizable image, however, is never an endpoint: as soon as one dialectical synthesis and comprehensible transformation has taken place, the image is disassembled in new ways that produce new dialectical tensions that lead to new forms of knowledge and experience. Montage and dialectics: these processes are directed by the artist, but the combination gives viewers powerful tools for their own independent responses, as they reconstruct the fragments into meaningful images and new, transformative levels of understanding.

The montage essays explore the concepts and structures Eisenstein used to think about the production and reception of the arts; his film-school lectures from this period show how he would put these ideas into practice. In the chapters that follow, we see how this practical and theoretical work finds its way into the first chapters of *Nonindifferent Nature* and then how Eisenstein combines his studies of montage structures of art and mind with his interest in the dialectic of logical and pre-logical in *Method*. And we see how those ideas are once again reshaped as Eisenstein processes them through the historical and biographical issues connected with *Ivan the Terrible*. Both of these important works evolve alongside and in dialogue with the making of the film. Many of the ideas that we now associate with *Method* and *Nonindifferent Nature* began as diary entries or production notes connected with making *Ivan*.

Diaries, Production Notebooks, and Other Sources

At the heart of this story is Eisenstein's gargantuan archive: sources that give us rare entry into the artistic process of writing, directing, and producing a film. Eisenstein kept diaries throughout his life and often took notes on his reading and viewing, but his private writing during the making of *Ivan* is unusually expansive. Repeated delays connected with the war allowed Eisenstein to explore ideas, stories, characters, and sources in more detail than is usually the case with film production. Central to my study are the more than one hundred folders in Eisenstein's archive with notes connected to *Ivan the Terrible*. Some of these are relatively coherent notebooks. Some are collections of notes he scribbled on scraps of paper and used as bookmarks. Naum Kleiman tells the story that when Eisenstein's papers were given to the state archive, the people who came to collect his books nonchalantly turned them upside down and shook all the bookmarks into boxes, later to be collected in folders, where the scraps float free, detached from their referenced texts, often obscuring their point. Even the original, intact notebooks are far from straightforward. They contain notes on readings, drawings and doodles, lists of things to be done, streams of consciousness. Some of the notebooks (or individual pages in notebooks) are marked "dn" for *dnevnik* or diary, but these usually contain more reflections on reading than personal revelations. Other notebooks (or passages in notebooks) are marked *metod* (method), meaning that they are sketches or ideas to be included in that manuscript.

These notes are remarkable for another reason. Although primarily written in Russian, long passages in the notebooks were written in Eisenstein's fluent but imperfect English, German, and French. Curiously, each language is coded. More or less consistently, he reserved German for notes on philosophy and psychology (or books he read in German); French was for romance, feelings, and fiction; and when he wrote something he wanted to keep secret or considered taboo, he wrote in English. The notes cover a wide range of material. The long study of Walt Disney that has become well known as a manuscript in its own right (or as a section of *Method*) was initiated and developed in direct relation to work on *Ivan*. Several folders and a large number of pages are devoted to Eisenstein's reading of historical sources. Other folders contain pages of passages from histories of art and theater, or the names of books with images he wanted to adapt to characters and scenes in the film. These included everything from an instructional handbook on Orthodox monks' rituals to *Life Magazine*. He reflected on key resonances between *Ivan* and Shakespeare, Ben Jonson, Pushkin, and Dostoevsky. Quotes from the Marquis de Sade unexpectedly address the writing process; a biography of Machiavelli takes him beyond *The Prince* to Napoleon, the loneliness of power, and the moral hypocrisy of political rulers. Freud is ever-present, often unacknowledged or as the object of criticism. Eisenstein returned to favorite artists—El Greco, Piranesi, Daumier, Van Gogh, Degas, Serov, and Leonardo da Vinci—with updates based on thinking about *Ivan*. He recorded conversations with his friends in the film business—Grigory Kozintsev, Viktor Shklovsky, Mikhail Romm, Esfir Shub—and conversations with actors about their roles in *Ivan*—Pavel Kadochnikov, Andrei Abrikosov, Serafima Birman, and crucially with Andrei Moskvin, his main cinematographer for *Ivan*. An entire folder is devoted to correspondence and conversations with Sergei Prokofiev. Eisenstein noted the devastation of the war, while still in Moscow and then in evacuation in Alma Ata, and as rumors brought horrific stories from Leningrad and the front. And he noted down his thinking about difficult problems in writing the script for *Ivan*, and later in casting and filming it. Many notebooks contain sketches for ideas about psychology and ethnography as they related to his evolving ideas about mind and body, and feeling and sensation in the production and reception of art. The range of these notes and the collage of media and mentality that they represent is impossible to reproduce in this introductory summary, but I will cite the notes often, hoping to trace both the sources of Eisenstein's work as well as development of his ideas.

For anyone who has encountered Eisenstein's writing primarily through published articles, the notebooks come as a refreshing surprise. In place of bombastic, coy, and often impenetrable prose, the notebooks are passionate, inquisitive, and intellectually unguarded (somewhat). Despite the scarcity of intimate revelations, they allow us to see Eisenstein's personal and eccentric ways of thinking. Historians of Soviet subjectivity have argued that people in the Soviet Union did not make the sharp division between a private, authentic self and a public persona required by the unrelenting surveillance of the totalitarian state; that totalitarianism left no space for a private, individual persona; that people didn't remove in private the masks they felt the need to wear in public; and that many people chose voluntarily to integrate themselves into the Stalinist collective.[34] Eisenstein's notes tell a different story. His writing style and the subject matter in the notes is freewheeling and far more open about things he treated cautiously or in code or not at all in public. Eisenstein was so cautious about revealing himself in public that he felt the need to conceal his authentic thoughts about himself in what he imagined was a little-known language even in a notebook meant for his eyes alone: *"There are so few English reading people in this country here so that I can write what ever I think of myself in—this language."*[35] Not surprisingly then, Eisenstein rarely abandoned his natural caution in his notes—there are precious few comments on contemporary politics, for example, or on intimate relationships or even friendships—unlike in his more personally revealing diaries from the late 1920s. Eisenstein organized his writing behavior and his sense of self in a language-coded, multilayered scheme meant to protect his privacy from prying eyes. As Juliane Fürst has put it, "in a society such as the Soviet Union, where borders between utopian fiction, propaganda, and factual reality habitually blurred, the subjective perspective was of crucial importance in determining an individual's reality. For a critical Soviet subject there was no objectivity except one's own."[36] This is important for understanding the main sources of my study but also for understanding the film at its center: not only does Eisenstein wall off his private from his public life, but the divide between public and private, the performativity of Stalinist culture, and the masks worn by ordinary people and public figures alike make up the main conflicts explored in *Ivan*. The revolutionary remaking of the Soviet subject was a major topic of public discussion in political as well as artistic publications in the first decades of Soviet rule.[37] Eisenstein participated in debates about the role of art in shaping the new Soviet persona in the 1920s; his manuscripts and unfinished or interrupted film projects of the 1930s show his continued interest in the issues, especially the nature of the socialist collective; and *Ivan the Terrible* puts performance and the conflict between public and private at the heart of Ivan's triumphs and tragedies.

We have other extraordinary sources for examining this film: industry documents and correspondence with Mosfilm administrators about production, Eisenstein's letters and telegrams, memoirs written by cast and crew, records of the pre-release screenings, and deliberations of the Stalin Prize committee. This body of sources gives us an unusually detailed record of a filmmaker's thinking, problem solving, negotiating, and shepherding his work along that bumpy road of Stalinist Socialist Realism and in a country at war.

The notes also give us a chance to examine in detail the interaction of theory and practice. As a classic "auteur," Eisenstein certainly embraced the role of the director as a visionary puppet master. He had unusual control over his film with a hand in writing, casting, cinematography, production design, costumes, soundtrack, and more—but he was also eager to give credit to his collaborators.[38] Not everybody loved working with Eisenstein, but many did, including a host of actors and crew members as well as Nikolai Cherkasov, the actor who played Ivan; the cinematographer Andrei Moskvin; and, some of the time, Sergei Prokofiev. Those working relationships and the balance Eisenstein created between control and collaboration are a critical ingredient in understanding how this particular film came to be. In addition, the active role he played as producer of the film reveals crucial facets of the institutional practices central to Soviet filmmaking, including the entire censorship review process from screenplay to industry review to Stalin's view; to release, reward, and ban.

Eisenstein was as mercurial and contradictory as the characters he created. He could run from taciturn to garrulous, from compassionate to quick-tempered, from sexually repressed to sexually adventurous, and much in between. His defiance and even recklessness in the studio was matched by extreme circumspection and compliance in public. His experiences in the terrifying late 1930s when he and so many people he knew were threatened by, or subjected to, arrest and death during the Stalinist Terror; his close call in 1937 when his film *Bezhin Meadow* was shelved and he was denounced; and his resurrecting success with *Alexander Nevsky* in 1938 led him to publish articles praising Stalin and accept the role of leading Soviet artist, with the shame and the privileges that came with it. I am bringing up a few of these temperamental contradictions to emphasize that the goal in analyzing both Eisenstein and Ivan is not to judge whether they were good or evil, or even good *and* evil, but to understand something about how they behaved in specific conditions, how those conditions combined with experience and temperament to produce their behaviors, and to understand what they thought they could and should do. Eisenstein wasn't thinking about Ivan in theologically inflected categories and neither should we. My goal is not to determine good or evil but to explain what people do with the circumstances they are given.

Eisenstein's *Ivan*

Eisenstein's *Ivan the Terrible* is a film about the specific mechanisms of change. The notion of cinema as transformative was not unique to Eisenstein; in the 1920s and into the early 1930s, film was considered an ideal medium for remaking Soviet subjectivity by virtue of film's ability to transform spectators' emotional and sensory abilities.[39] Change was also central to the master narrative of Marxism and to the master narrative of Socialist Realism. But Eisenstein explored the mechanisms of change in more detail and in more contexts than anyone else: in every aspect of making a film, in thinking about making a film, in watching a film; in history and politics, in biography and autobiography, and in modes of thinking, moving, and representation. In *Ivan*, Eisenstein employed ideas he had been developing since his own works of the 1920s to explore processes of transformation in new spheres and in new, more complex forms. *Ivan* is about understanding and depicting those fleeting moments of transformation, when everything changes and yet retains traces of what came before: ephemeral and material at the same time.

Ivan the Terrible is structured to highlight transformative moments. Part I begins with a lavish display of wealth and power at Ivan's coronation. Aged seventeen, he is young, androgynous, and vigorous—as well as angry and suspicious. His suspicions are echoed among members of the audience: boyars (that is, the Muscovite elite), clergy, and foreign dignitaries. Ivan's coronation speech infuriates just about everyone. His plan for making Russia great is to centralize power at the expense of the Church and the elite, reclaim territories on its borders, and establish the Great Russian State. The rest of Part I shows Ivan going about the business of establishing his rule and fulfilling his mission, while his enemies (that is, everyone) conspire in whispers and gestures in darkened corners and doorways. Part I was supposed to begin with a prologue about Ivan's traumatic childhood. It was removed during the pre-release screening, but because Eisenstein considered it so important for understanding Ivan's life, he reinserted it as a flashback in Part II. In The Prologue, the boyars murder Ivan's mother and are seen selling off Russia's wealth to foreigners for their own personal gain, which together shaped Ivan's lifelong hatred of the boyars and his sense of mission. His coronation and subsequent wedding to Anastasia, meant to be celebratory events, are shadowed by betrayal and conflict. His two best friends, Andrei Kurbsky and Fedor Kolychev, prove to be disloyal. Kurbsky is seen flirting with Anastasia, and Kolychev tells Ivan that he'd rather retreat to a monastery (as the priest to be known as Filipp) than serve a tsar who seeks absolute power at the expense of the boyars. The wedding is interrupted first by fires of revolution, then by threats from foreign enemies. The revolutionary rabble intending to attack the tsar are so impressed by Ivan's clever and threatening demagoguery that they are transformed into his loyal servitors. Their loyalty is confirmed by Ivan's victory over those foreign enemies, a victory that establishes Ivan's transformation into a powerful tsar.

Each time Ivan asserts his supreme power—often by solemnly intoning the word "Tsar"—the next scene sees him brought low in some way. Returning from battle, Ivan becomes deathly ill. The majority of his courtiers openly (or secretly) betray him. Just when everyone thinks he's dead, he comes back to life, more powerful and terrifying than before. For the rest of Part I, Ivan is torn between impulses: private and public, revenge and forgiveness, move forward or give up, go it alone or make alliances. Should he continue his campaign to centralize power and make Russia great despite the opposition, or should he give up? Each resolution changes him; each makes him more powerful, more manipulative, and lonelier. His wife, Anastasia, is murdered, and his boyars betray him again on the battlefront, sending him into a vortex of despair. Ivan does not realize that his wife's murderer is his aunt Efrosinia, acting on behalf of her childlike son, Vladimir, who, despite being utterly ill-equipped for the role, is next in line for the throne. Ivan is rescued from despair by new supporters, Maliuta Skuratov and the father and son Aleksei and Fedor (Fedka) Basmanov, who lift his spirits by reminding him that the common people support him and urging him to forge them into his own iron band of brothers, known in Russian as the *oprichniki*. Ivan caps his dark resurrection by rising up above Anastasia's coffin as the leader of this mob-turned-royal-guard and announces that he is abdicating his throne. He retreats from Moscow to his nearby regional palace in Alexandrova and waits for the people and boyars to prove their loyalty by calling him back to reign over them. They do so, and he rises even higher (and bigger). Part I ends with an extreme closeup of Ivan looming over his people.

In addition to The Prologue, another critical scene was cut from Part I. Eisenstein filmed a scene in which the oprichniki pledge an oath to Ivan, placing their loyalty to state and tsar above love for their family and friends. At the pre-release screening, there was a great deal of criticism of The Oath of the Oprichniki for its sinister portrait of Ivan, but Eisenstein was not required to delete it.[40] Nonetheless, when the final cut of Part I was screened for the Artistic Council of the Committee on Cinema Affairs in December 1944, The Oath was gone. According to the editor, Esfir Tobak, the scene was simply, quietly, mysteriously removed from the film before the final screening.[41] These two scenes were so central to Eisenstein's conception of the film that I discuss them (and other censored scenes) in detail.

Part II is the story of Ivan's transformation into the Terrible Tsar as he repeatedly chooses to respond to the opposition with violence in his efforts to found the Great Russian State. Each step in his transformation recalls his own vulnerability as a child and offers Ivan a choice between violence and conciliation, murder or forgiveness. Afterward, these decisions spark crises of conscience, but revenge and ambition win each time and set him back on his path to establishing the Great Russian State at all costs. Ivan returns to Moscow and reiterates the division of the realm between his own stylish, black-clad oprichniki and the old-fashioned bearded boyars in their cumbersome brocade cloaks. (In the released version, this is where The Prologue is inserted as a flashback.) Ivan is powerful but lonely, so when his old friend Filipp shows up to denounce him, Ivan sees only the beloved friend, not the opposition leader, and begs for his support. Filipp agrees when Ivan promises to spare his family (suspected of treason) and promote him to metropolitan. Next, Maliuta persuades Ivan to betray his promises to Filipp and murder Filipp's family, as a Machiavellian display of force. In one of the strangest scenes in the film, Ivan, seeing the corpses that Maliuta has slain, and recalling his wife's murder, calls for more corpses: "Too few!"

Were these murders a necessary sacrifice for Russia's greatness? Boyar leaders don't think so and plot to overthrow Ivan both as revenge and as sheer ambition. Filipp persuades Efrosinia to postpone plans to assassinate Ivan, so that he can try first to shame the tsar into dropping his violent, satanic campaign. He stages a liturgical play that dramatizes the martyrdom of three innocent boys at the unfeeling hands of the Babylonian ruler Nebuchadnezzar. That fails to sway Ivan. Next, Ivan's main rival for power, his aunt Efrosinia, and the former Metropolitan Pimen together plot to murder Ivan. The climax of Part II comes during a prolonged banquet and murder scene, in which various characters are transformed into each other, merging the powerful and powerless, the child and the adult, the murderers and the victims. Ivan gets everyone drunk, Fedor dances in drag as Anastasia, and the oprichniki dance around him/her, singing songs of mayhem. Ivan flirts with Vladimir to get him to spill the plot and when this makes his oprichnik lieutenants jealous, he puts them in their place. Tipsy, chatty Vladimir is torn between not wanting the responsibility of being tsar and wanting to dress up in the tsar's robes. Ivan tricks him into sitting on the throne, crowned and dressed as the tsar, recalling both Ivan as a child and Ivan at his coronation, as vulnerable and powerful despite himself. Ivan propels Vladimir, still dressed in the tsar's costume, to enter the cathedral, where the assassin kills him instead of Ivan. Efrosinia loses her mind on discovering that her assassination plot has backfired and taken her son. Part II ends with an epilogue in which Ivan announces that he is now entirely free from constraints and will deal with all his enemies as he sees fit.

We do not know how Eisenstein would have handled the filming of Part III, but the screenplay can be summarized. After subduing all internal strife, Ivan turns to external enemies, to punish the traitors led by his erstwhile friend Kurbsky and defeat those who prevent Russia from claiming access to the Baltic Sea. He still has to deal with more betrayal at home, now from his own oprichniki. In one of the most horrific episodes that Eisenstein wrote, Ivan discovers that Aleksei Basmanov has been embezzling to enrich his own family, so he has Fedor kill his father to prove his loyalty to the tsar; then he has Fedor killed for his willingness to turn on his own father. Ivan discovers that a German mercenary, Heinrich von Staden, who was serving as an oprichnik, was in fact a spy for Kurbsky and the Livonians who blocked Russia's campaign to reach the sea. In another horrific scene (that we have as unedited footage), Ivan toys with von Staden, threatens him with death, and then, claiming to have trusted him all along (what a fun game!), has von Staden released, leaving the mercenary dazed and confused. Ivan discovers a conspiracy in the city of Novgorod and has everyone there massacred. He feels absolutely terrible about that and in a fit of anguished remorse begs God's forgiveness, banging his head on the floor of the cathedral before a gigantic fresco of the Last Judgment. But when God is silent, Ivan reasserts his own will and rededicates himself to the Great Russian State. He finally defeats the traitors and the Livonians and reaches the sea. Maliuta, his last loyal servitor, has died, and Russia lies smoking in ruins behind him. Was he right to sacrifice so much for national greatness?

Eisenstein often called *Ivan the Terrible* a tragedy, but what kind of tragedy was this? A conversation between Eisenstein and Prokofiev, in 1942 before the score was written, provides an essential key for understanding how Eisenstein conceptualized *Ivan*. His notes on the conversation record Prokofiev summarizing what he saw as Eisenstein's four themes: Ivan embodied as a threatening storm; Ivan as God (Sabaoth); Ivan's wracking remorse as Lucifer, the fallen God; and the "ironic-sarcastic-sardonic" theme. Eisenstein corrects Prokofiev, saying that what Prokofiev sees as four separate themes are really four facets of Ivan that grow out of one another or take more prominence at various moments: "The Storm [Ivan] *rises* (when necessary) to become a God—and *falls* from the highest point [like Lucifer]—Irony and sarcasm flow from the tragedy."[42] This kind of tragedy shares qualities with all the major European tragic traditions—Greek, medieval, Elizabethan, modernist—but in *Ivan*'s case, tragedy always has a specifically political dimension rooted in Ivan's own interior, human, dialectical conflict. Eisenstein's Ivan is primed by experience and position for extraordinary ambition and superhuman morality. But, as a flawed and divided mortal, he both questions that ambition and amorality and repeatedly overcomes his doubts to reach for God-like power. Lucifer's choice is inherently ironic and doomed, eliciting both pathos and contempt.

Eisenstein's importance has always been measured in terms of cinematic innovation and pioneering film theory. As a comprehensive study of *Ivan the Terrible*, this book gives us a new and more radical view of Eisenstein in the 1940s and an original reading of the film based on his own extensive writing. My study of Eisenstein's role as political figure, historical actor, and public intellectual establishes the importance of his interconnected interest in politics, history, psychology, and aesthetics. From that combined perspective, I offer an exploration of power by one of the most important artists of the Stalinist period and an original dissection of Stalinist cultural production, reception, and censorship practices. This book reveals Eisenstein's often reckless moral courage and acknowledges his insight into the nightmare world of Stalinism and the everyday mechanisms on which it functioned. *Ivan the Terrible* is not only a great work of art; it was a courageous political and artistic act of will.

CHAPTER 1

The Potholed Path

Ivan *in Production*

Ivan the Terrible was heavily stamped by the historical context in which it was made. Understanding *Ivan* first of all requires us to recognize that Eisenstein was both the exceptional, willful, privileged auteur who is familiar to us as well as an embattled Soviet citizen functioning under the everyday restrictions of life and work in Stalin's Russia during a devastating war. His access, power, and talent were undoubtedly exceptional, but his experience of Stalinist hypertrophied power, its unpredictable judgments, its uncertain boundaries between public and private, its corrupt and corrupting forces in everyday life—these were the conditions in which everyone lived. And like filmmakers everywhere, Eisenstein would have to realize his artistic vision within the confines of social and political imperatives and local institutional practices, where many financial and artistic decisions were beyond the control of even the most powerful auteur filmmaker.

It took almost four years to complete Part I of *Ivan the Terrible* and another year to finish Part II. During that time, the Soviet Union was invaded and occupied by Germany. Thousands of towns and cities were destroyed by the Nazis, tens of millions of people were killed, and many millions more had their lives uprooted and transformed. During the war, while Leningrad was under siege and Moscow under attack, the Moscow and Leningrad film studios were evacuated to Alma Ata in Kazakhstan, where most of *Ivan the Terrible* would be filmed. By the time Part I was released at the very end of 1944, the Red Army had turned the tide of the war and was pushing the Nazis out of Eastern Europe and back to Berlin. But the social and institutional turmoil of the war years did not end with military victory. Demobilization, reevacuation, and repatriation as well as physical and emotional recovery from bombing and loss all impeded the resumption of stable, everyday life and complicated the completion of Eisenstein's film.[1]

Making any film anywhere requires the coordination of multiple institutions and personalities reaching decisions about funding, equipment, location, transport, and many other smaller matters, independent of the artist's vision. In the Soviet film industry, high-stakes ideological demands and the official cultural policy known as Socialist Realism added several more layers of complication and oversight. During the 1930s and 1940s, the Soviet government tried to control artistic production in a variety of ways, both for ideological purposes and for profit. Artworks of all kinds were considered important media for cultivating socialist values and behavior. Soviet officials at the highest levels, including Stalin himself, took an interest in the artistic embodiment of state ideological goals.[2] As in other creative ventures, filmmaking was subject to an array of official decisions intended to produce films that carried proper political messages. Ideology was always prioritized over profit, insuring that Soviet filmmaking would never repay the state's financial investment, much less make a profit, and studio chiefs worried about money constantly, if ineffectively. Centralized planning in the absence of adequate investment meant that technology and training in all areas of production failed to keep up with demand.[3] These kinds of failures did not lessen the government's obsession with ideological control but rather made it seem all the more imperative.

In the broadest sense, ideological control was successful. It limited production to films that neither challenged Soviet power directly nor openly praised alternative ways of life. But the process was cumbersome and often counterproductive. After proclaiming Socialist Realism as the reigning ideological model for all the arts in 1932–1934, officials in the administration of each of the arts, from the lowliest critics up to Stalin himself, discovered how difficult it was to organize artistic production by command. To make matters more complicated, the ideological requirements were never clearly articulated.[4] At the First Writers' Congress in 1934, Andrei Zhdanov and others made speeches intended to end debate about the definition of Socialist Realism. Socialist Realist art was supposed to be "accessible to the masses" and show socialist reality "as it should be," or as it would look after the successful building of communism. Socialist Realism, it was often said at the time, quoting a popular 1920s song, was supposed to "turn fairy tale into reality."[5]

Literature and the visual arts were to be positive and optimistic rather than critical or cynical. Soviet art was to embody loyalty to Party (*partiinost'*), to ideology (*ideinost'*) and to the people and the nation (*narodnost'*). These vague and open-ended concepts raised innumerable problems of implementation.

In practice, Socialist Realism was an official rejection of the formal experimentation of the modernist avant-garde in the 1920s, which people with mainstream tastes in all classes found difficult and alienating. Peasants, workers, and party functionaries all wanted art that enlightened and uplifted without being too challenging.[6] Vague as such instructions seem, Maksim Gorky applauded the open-endedness of the policy, optimistically stating that "the method of collective work will allow us to understand socialist realism better."[7] That left artists and arts administrators to figure out whether any individual work of art met state ideological requirements. Since no one knew exactly what Socialist Realism was, every artistic project was a gamble. On one hand, artists never knew whether their work would be approved or not, because party watchdogs decided whether a work met the requirements of Socialist Realism on an ad hoc basis. On the other hand, the lack of clear directives gave artists room to continue to experiment and an ability to negotiate the approval process.

Socialist Realism was a two-pronged transformation of arts production in the Soviet Union and, contrary to the way it is usually studied, its institutional structure was by far more radical and damaging than its aesthetics and poetics. As a way of telling a story, Socialist Realism has much in common with other, politically neutral genres. Formulaic narrative and style may have marked Socialist Realism as inferior to literary fiction and serious art but placed it in the company of other popular formulaic genres like adventure, romance, and mystery. And to some extent, the realism of its aesthetics was a continuation of earlier trends that paralleled contemporary international movements and drew on preconstructivist aesthetics.[8] But where formal and storytelling guidelines revived earlier realist styles, Socialist Realism was a policy carried out by a government determined to control the message of works of art. Socialist Realism is most significantly distinguished by the institutional structures that attempted to control its production.

In the film industry, the implementation of Socialist Realism produced an accretion of committees for oversight and criticism, the structure of which changed every few years.[9] The system's vagaries put not only artists in a vulnerable position but also the people charged with patrolling the borders of acceptability. Required to protect the Soviet people from dangerous ideological messages and the Soviet government from any hint of criticism, arts administrators had to guess how a work would be interpreted not only by audiences but also by successive layers of critics, including Stalin himself, who took a growing personal interest in the film industry.[10] Since political loyalty remained the highest value, it would always be safer for officials to argue that a film failed to meet ideological standards in case someone higher up the chain of command came to that conclusion after they had approved a work.

During the 1930s, Boris Shumiatsky, as head of the Main Cinema Administration (whose form, name, and functions changed repeatedly between 1932 and 1946), instituted increasingly rigid and punitive practices to ban suspect films. Screenplays (also in short supply) went through ideological reviews. The screenplays themselves were written in two stages: first as a "literary treatment" or scenario (*literaturnyi stsenarii*), and then as the "director's screenplay," which included dialogue and specific technical instructions. Both had to be approved by studio administrators before going into production. Films were then reviewed in the form of rushes, and again when finished, often resulting in additional shooting, editing, and cutting. But even in this carefully monitored context, viewer response was no more predictable in the Soviet Union than it is in Hollywood. Each year, films made it through the gauntlet of preliminary committees, only to provoke controversy once completed.[11]

Artists, even those more or less aligned with state ideology, generally responded to these formal and institutional restrictions with a large dose of skepticism. Film offered artists more latitude than fiction or painting because the semantic ambiguity of visual images combined with the temporal progression of narrative offered more room for interpretation and experimentation. Technological changes like the coming of sound and color and the continual improvement of cameras and lenses gave filmmakers the tools to innovate.[12] Filmmakers approached this obstacle course in various ways. No one was free to pitch a film that would be entirely outside the boundaries of Socialist Realism, so everyone practiced some degree of self-censorship. But because many of the modernist directors of the 1920s remained active and powerful in the 1930s, modernist practices remained visible even in films with conventional forms and plots. And since the parameters of Socialist Realist film were ill-defined, even the most orthodox-seeming projects could get caught in the political crossfire if someone somewhere along the line worried that it contained something suspicious. These failures of planning and complications of ideological control should make it clear that film censorship was a negotiated process rather than a unilateral imposition of restrictions from above. The word "censorship" itself is a misleading label for the multidirectional, negotiated process that led to the release of a Soviet film.

Those negotiations were part of a larger system of patronage. One of the things that makes *Ivan the Terrible* such an extraordinary project for its time is that Eisenstein did not stop at *imagining* a transgressive portrait of absolute power and its consequences; he succeeded in making the film he imagined—or at least he made two-thirds of it. In order to protect his *Ivan the Terrible* and get it released, Eisenstein exploited (or tried to exploit) the patron-client system that operated in the film industry. In the Stalinist film industry, as in the institutions that administered the production of music and painting, the patronage system seems to have been more or less institutionalized.[13] Ivan Bolshakov, the film industry chief at the time, played a complicated dual role in this system as both patron to his filmmakers and as client of Stalin's patronage. Bolshakov was responsible to Stalin for providing acceptable films, but he was also responsible to his clients for giving them the resources and feedback they needed to make their films acceptable. Almost anyone could write directly to Stalin and call on him to be a patron, and Eisenstein took full advantage of this loophole. But ultimately it was Bolshakov's job to move films through the production and approval process. In Eisenstein's case, he proved to be a loyal patron through to the end. Despite the extraordinary political difficulties *Ivan* presented, Bolshakov promoted the film that he had invested with time, state resources, and enormous effort over the five-year period of its gestation, and he intervened with Zhdanov and Stalin on Eisenstein's behalf. Bolshakov undoubtedly had a hand in the censorship decisions that made Part I politically successful; decisions that have had an enormous effect on the way Part I has been seen, even to this day. He did not, however, succeed in persuading Stalin to approve Part II.

This system put the head of the Committee for Cinema Affairs (as it was called from 1938 to 1946) in a vise. Constant pressure from above to produce more films and constant artistic, organizational, and ideological challenges from below created recurrent crises, three of which occurred during the production of *Ivan the Terrible*, in 1941, 1943, and 1946. In the spring of 1941 before the Nazi invasion, when Eisenstein was writing the literary scenario for *Ivan*, Zhdanov called a meeting with Bolshakov and leading filmmakers to try to resolve the chronic bottlenecks in production. When Bolshakov had taken his position in 1939, he tried instituting reforms, such as bringing directors into administration with the introduction of artistic directors—Eisenstein was made artistic director of Mosfilm—but in 1940 and 1941 a large number of films were still being banned.[14] Bolshakov wanted to expand his reforms, but Zhdanov had other ideas, including the counterweight of greater political oversight. The invasion temporarily distracted officials, but the slow pace of production put Bolshakov under the microscope again and again.[15]

The production of *Ivan the Terrible* offers an especially prolonged and demanding example of working within this system. In some ways, *Ivan the Terrible* was a typical product of its time. The literary scenario underwent several rounds of formal and informal review. Negotiations over financing, casting, and material issues were recorded in sometimes flaming telegrams and memos. Both Part I and Part II were screened several times by film industry committees, by the central Committee on Cinema Affairs, and by Stalin before decisions were made about releasing them. All of that was more or less the norm. At the same time, everyone involved knew that *Ivan the Terrible* was a prestige project with Stalin's personal investment, so at various stages it underwent extra scrutiny, and at other times Stalin's role gave Eisenstein extra latitude.

The production story in general outline has been told before; here I want to focus on specific moments that illustrate Eisenstein's ideas and strategies and that help resolve the controversies about *Ivan the Terrible* that have preoccupied previous writers and viewers. I will show how Eisenstein was able to make such a transgressive film, both in terms of the inner development of his ideas and his outer manipulation of the rules of Soviet filmmaking. We can never know exactly what Eisenstein was thinking, but we don't need to, nor do we need a finished three-part film to see how Eisenstein worked within this system. The choices he made in writing, filming, and revising Parts I and II show us how he negotiated the limits marked by the concepts and institutions of the Socialist Realist system, the hierarchy of committees, the material realities, and the knowledge of Stalin's ultimate gaze. We can see where state intervention occurred, what forms it took, and how Eisenstein responded. We can see when and how Eisenstein tried to elude those controls and when he called on his own position or the film's prestige or worked with his patrons, up to and including Stalin, to protect his vision. And we can see when those strategies worked and when they failed.

Eisenstein gives us insight into the wily determination and artistic commitment with which he approached working in politically complicated circumstances in a letter he wrote to Maksim Shtraukh in 1931 when he was filming in Mexico. He was irritated with the passivity he saw in Shtraukh and his wife, Iudif Glizer (both actors and both good friends of Eisenstein's), as cultural life was becoing increasingly restrictive. He wrote:

> I am very dissatisfied with what you and Ida are doing. One must apply pressure, pull strings, debase oneself, *be diplomatic, crafty, cunning, and again press*. The main thing is to *do*. To really get down to it. You have what it takes: real force. You have to drop the Oblomov act. . . . One

more thing. *Learn to find a place where you can apply what it is you want to do.* Go to the club. Organize something for yourself and Idka. Find materials. Playing small roles, even with Meyerhold, is *not* work.[16]

Leonid Kozlov once argued that Eisenstein decided early on to make the film he wanted to make—to push to make it as personal and creative as he thought he could get away with—while still producing a film that could be approved and released.[17] The production history invites us to rework that argument. He certainly tried to make the film he wanted to make, but obstacles to his plan arose at every step and required constant adaptation. It is more accurate to say that Eisenstein took advantage of the circumstances in which he found himself to work the way he wanted to work: slowly and methodically and with extraordinary attention to specific details. If we compare the production of *Ivan* with that of his other films, it is most like his work on *Que Viva Mexico!* In both cases, far from Moscow and from studio control, he took his time. He became immersed in history and theory and practice. He revised and refined. He filmed scenes and even individual shots over and over again until they satisfied him. To do all that, he knew he was not working in an artistic vacuum and would need every diplomatic skill he had. To work the way he wanted to work, Eisenstein "really got down to it."

Reading and Writing: The Scenario and the Director's Script

As soon as Zhdanov conveyed Stalin's commission, Eisenstein had to decide what kind of film he wanted to make. He was unhappy with the compromises he had made in *Alexander Nevsky* and unhappy with himself for making them: *"It is the first film where I gave up the Eisenstein touch . . . You ought to be ashamed of your self, dear Master of Art!"*[18] *Alexander Nevsky* was his ticket back into the good graces of the authorities. More controversial projects followed. He accepted a commission to produce Richard Wagner's *Die Walküre* just after the Nazi-Soviet nonaggression pact was signed, and his film about the Soviet modernization of Central Asia reached the production stage in 1939 before being shelved.[19] Now he had to decide how to present the biography of a tsar who was best known for a savage rampage against his own people.

Zhdanov very likely gave Eisenstein at least a general outline of Stalin's views on the history of Ivan the Terrible and the approach he expected the film to take. For several years previously, also under Zhdanov's guidance, historians had been rewriting the history of Ivan's reign in accordance with Stalin's wishes. Historians praised Ivan for uniting Russia into a single, powerful nation and justified the harsh measures he used by the importance of the result. In the chapters that follow I discuss Eisenstein's specific ideas about Ivan and the course of Russian history. Here I want only to point out that his first notes about the project reveal the broad outlines of his approach and the kind of strategies he was considering. Those notes show that within a week of receiving the commission, he decided to make a film that would be unconventional by Soviet standards in both form and content. His first thoughts were not about Ivan as a wise ruler or great hero of Russian history, or about telling Ivan's story in a way that would exhibit his greatness or justify his cause. Rather, Eisenstein's first notes concern Ivan's interior life: his feelings as a vulnerable, grieving child and an anguished, remorseful old man, as an individual whose childhood memories both drove and tormented him. These first notes show Eisenstein thinking primarily about plausible psychological motives for a man who became a bloodthirsty ruler. These same notes show that he rejected the representations of earlier artists who focused on melodrama and madness. From the very beginning, he aimed for historical as well as psychological plausibility.[20]

He also imagined, consistently from the beginning, a modernist structure for conveying Ivan's inner life. One of his earliest notes, from January 18, says, "scenes follow each other with a sharply ruptured rhythm—the rhythm of unsystematic, emotionally disproportionate childhood memories."[21] He took notes on reading about the secrets and lies in Ivan's earliest experiences, specifically noting that the historical boyar, Andrei Shuisky, whose power rested precariously on Ivan's youth, punished another boyar for telling Ivan about the great power his grandfather had enjoyed, thereby creating in the child a sense of conflict about his right to rule and resentment toward the boyars who blocked his power.[22] In early February, Eisenstein jotted down a number of fragmentary ideas. One establishes that "Ivan's tragedy" is that he was "tormented by doubts—is he taking the right path?"[23] Another refers to *"the effect of daring*. He doesn't entirely believe in himself, *but dares."* Eisenstein adds a memory of his own here, noting that he personally identified with Ivan's overcoming self-doubt to dare to speak in public.[24] Another note links what he later called "the poetry of revenge" with specific narrative structures: "Movement (eye-for-eye). The whole time—tit-for-tat. Growing in scale and cruelty. First [the boyars]. Then the boyars and the Church. Then the boyars and the Church and Novgorod. And then abroad."[25] Taken separately, any one of these notes appears to be nothing more than a half-baked thought, but when read together, they show Eisenstein developing a conception of Ivan in terms of personal and psychological explanations for his behavior that correspond to historical events and a nonlinear, nonrealist narrative style. He also began

Figure 1.1 Early drawing. "Into this scene, right after the return of the oprichniki to Moscow (their first)—the wolves' heads and brooms (seen for the first time) enter like a black cloud. Presentation of the program of the oprichnina. *And first meeting with Philippe and his first opposition to what John's doing.* (and the first meeting—just arrived, and the first declaration, "Silence, Archbishop" (Filipp isn't metropolitan yet). Then they remain alone, just the two of them, to talk. And beyond the walls, they are already taking the heads of the boyars." RGALI, 1923/2/1666/4 [Feb 9, 1941]. Used with permission.

FIGURE 1.2 Ivan's Confession

to picture sets, camerawork, and visual strategies for telling Ivan's story, as a number of drawings made in early February 1941 attest.[26]

When read in the context of his thinking process, these notes also help explain some of the most often quoted and least understood comments Eisenstein made in public about his concept for the film. When he was getting ready to publish the scenario in 1943, he wrote an essay about his initial thoughts on *Ivan* called "A Few Words about My Drawings."[27] In "A Few Words," Eisenstein revealed that the first image to occur to him after talking to Zhdanov was the famous scene that takes place at the climax of Part III, Ivan's Confession.[28] Although the footage for this scene was destroyed, its dramatic central image is familiar from published photographs of Nikolai Cherkasov, the actor who played Ivan, sprawled on the cathedral floor before a gigantic fresco of the Last Judgment.

According to the scenario, after having ordered the annihilation of Novgorod in 1570, Ivan beats his head bloody on the floor at the foot of the fresco, in a paroxysm of remorse.[29] The tsar begs God's forgiveness for his violent orgy of vengeance—without exactly admitting he had sinned. Devastating, self-lacerating guilt does not prevent Ivan from rationalizing mass murder as selfless commitment to the establishment of the Great Russian State.[30] In the previous year, Eisenstein had been sketching out a film about the great Russian poet Alexander Pushkin that would feature scenes from Pushkin's play about Boris Godunov, another tragedy about an early modern

Russian tyrant. In this scene, Eisenstein transposed both visually and themati-cally ideas developed for his conception of Godunov.[31]

The second image came to him at the Bolshoi Theater, a week after receiv-ing the commission, where he was attending a performance on the anniver-sary of Lenin's death. This image was the poisoning of Ivan's mother, Elena Glinskaia, which occurred in 1538 when Ivan was a child. In the film, Glin-skaia's murder at the hands of rival boyars was the event that precipitated Ivan's lifelong hunger for revenge against the boyars. The third image was the candle used to ignite the explosives that Ivan had ingeniously planted under the fortress at Kazan in 1552. That explosion made possible Ivan's conquest of Kazan in 1552, Russia's first imperial victory and, in the film, Ivan's only unchallenged moment of tsarist power and legitimacy.[32]

It is not possible to tell whether these scenes, intended for crucial turn-ing points at the beginning and end of the film, and central to Eisenstein's conception of Ivan as man and ruler, were derived from the previous days' reading or from memories of reading Russian history as a student or from his musing about stereotypical images of Ivan. These first images together with articles he published in 1941, 1942—and again in 1945 when *Ivan*, Part I, was released—make it clear that he was aware of such stereotypes: "Ivan the Terrible! Who has not, since childhood, been troubled by this romantic, mysterious, and at times sinister figure? Numerous historical tales, stories, and dramas, familiar to all since childhood, are devoted to portrayals of Ivan the Terrible. The figure of this powerful Muscovite tsar of the sixteenth cen-tury seems familiar to us."[33] At the very least Eisenstein wants us to believe that these were landmark moments in his initial conceptualization of Ivan, and later notes confirm that they do indeed represent key moments in his thinking.

Each of these first images—revenge, remorse, and explosive transformation—presents Ivan as a man of sharp contradictions. A few weeks later Eisenstein wrote: "Let this be characteristic for Ivan—*everything he sees from two angles. Essential, by the way, in the ironic attitude*—culminating in the scene of the con-fession!"[34] The poisoning of Ivan's mother when he was a child conveys both Ivan's vulnerability and his decisive response to powerlessness. It also displays the failure of revenge to expunge Ivan's desire for revenge. The candle at Kazan signifies the moment when Ivan's victory marked his coming of age as a ruler, the explosion itself triggering the transformation. The confession dis-plays Ivan's capacity for remorse even after trying to justify his worst crimes as necessary for the Great Russian State. Each image complicates the common stereotypes about Ivan by providing a dialectical pair and an explanation: Ivan was murderous *and* remorseful, vulnerable *and* powerful, a ruler who both respected the bounds of legitimate authority and exceeded them disastrously. These first images show that, from the very beginning, Eisenstein found Ivan to be a man of contradiction and inner division.

Ivan's abandonment and confession are also profoundly human moments in the tsar's life. Eisenstein understood as well as anyone the nature of historical mythmaking, but these initial ideas for *Ivan*'s screenplay mark a turn away from the mythical toward a human Ivan. He explicitly rejected mythmaking in connection with Ivan on numerous occasions, including an often quoted article published in 1942 that begins with a reference to the horrific legends associated with Ivan. He dubbed the torture and mass murder of suspected enemies as "the cruel jokes of literary tradition and legend."[35] Without disputing those "legends," he declared:

> It is not my intention to whitewash him or to turn Ivan the Terrible into Ivan the Sweet. . . . The fundamental aim of the film was to show Ivan in the whole range of his activity and the struggle for the state of Muscovy. And it should be said straight away that this activity and this struggle were colossal and bloody. But I do not intend to wipe one drop of blood from the life of Ivan the Terrible. Not to whitewash, but to explain.[36]

This article and "A Few Words" demonstrate Eisenstein's ability to maneuver in the Stalinist political-cultural labyrinth. They show how he could publicly conform to the official line in a way that made possible a veiled, more complex inquiry into the nature of power and the psychology of the powerful. He accepted the official goal of presenting Ivan in a positive light but was able to sidestep having to justify the bloodletting by finding other positive ways to approach the tsar's biography: "not to whitewash, but to explain." In an early notebook, sometime in mid-February 1941, he wrote (in English) that *"the secret of the whole thing is to humanize, explain the most atrocious things!"*[37] Showing that Ivan had plausible human, psychological motives for forming the oprichniki, murdering his boyars, and laying waste to Novgorod was a rejection of simplistic myths about Ivan, both Stalinist and populist. Humanizing and seeking explanations for Ivan's turn to violence could serve the purpose of explaining the tsar's actions, but without automatically justifying those actions. The task Eisenstein set himself was more difficult. To "explain the most atrocious things" required an understanding of how Ivan evolved as a person. The first images from "A Few Words" are stepping stones in Eisenstein's understanding of that individual evolution. At the end of the tsar's life, after founding the Great Russian State, Eisenstein's Ivan is equal parts proud and remorseful at his accomplishment and the methods he used to achieve it. The origins of that pride and remorse were to be found in his response to childhood trauma suffered at the hands of the boyars. Ivan asserted his power as tsar, first over the boyars and then over Russia's national enemies, and he took revenge on those who had humiliated him and exploited Russia in its weakened state. These first images linked key historical events with key psychological moments in Ivan's life. Eisenstein's plan was to look beyond myth and stereotype to find a plausible psychology for explaining a complicated man and his legacy for Russian history.

The evidence of Eisenstein's early thinking in "A Few Words" changes the way we read the literary scenario. It is possible, of course, to read it as corresponding to the official expectations and Socialist Realist narrative conventions. Ivan's childhood is marked by the perfidy of the boyars and the foreigners who seek to exploit Russia's wealth for their own purposes. When he becomes tsar, Ivan announces his intention to centralize power in Russia in order to undermine the power of the Church, the greedy boyars, and the foreigners who controlled Russian trade and circumscribed Russia's power. He overcomes all the obstacles they pose, with extreme measures when necessary, and is victorious in the end, centralizing power, reaching the Baltic Sea, and reestablishing Russian power there. But the complexities of guilt and responsibility, the depictions of power and violence and their consequences, the murderous father-son dynamics and homoerotic gender play, and above all the entirely unexpected visual universe of the film are camouflaged in the scenario. On the surface, only the unusual choice to write the script in verse hints at Eisenstein's departure from Socialist Realist conventions of form. Eisenstein knew he could have made a relatively simple film glorifying the Russian ruler and confining his creative energy to aesthetic elements of the film. But as he confessed in his diary in April 1941, when he was becoming overwhelmed by "the volume of Ivan," he was tempted to write a realistic, conventional script, but he resisted because of "the guilt of not sticking [his] neck out!"[38]

How then did he both try to stick his neck out and still make a film that would win the approval of all his patrons, and how do we know? One clue comes from notes that pop up all over Eisenstein's manuscripts: examples of people defiantly hiding things in plain sight.[39] At the end of one of the most revealing chapters of his memoir, written in June–July 1946, he shifted from a memory of the school gym to bigger things:

> Squashed between the bars and the wall, with my back against the window, I looked straight ahead with bated breath. But perhaps this is where my second tendency comes from. To rummage, rummage, rummage.

To work my way into every fissure of a problem; to break inside and dig, trying always to penetrate it more deeply, to get ever closer to its core . . . what I find I do not hide; I bring it out into the open—in lectures, books, magazines, newspapers. And . . . did you know, the most effective way of hiding something is to put it on display?![40]

Similarly, in a series of notes intended for *Method*, Eisenstein related several folktales about cunning tactics simple folk used to outwit Ivan the Terrible.[41] Or consider this ghoulish anecdote about a simple but devious stonemason that Eisenstein scribbled on a piece of paper and stuck at the end of a notebook devoted to the paradoxes of representing sixteenth-century history and political life. At the top of the page he wrote, "In the Crosshairs," and then:

Images are always represented in terms appropriate to their own epoch or context. So, for example, the famous story about one of the builders of St. Paul's Cathedral in London (the same cathedral having just now suffered under German bombardment). The builder was denied permission to bury his dying wife in the cathedral. He smiled slyly and said that her soul would be buried in the building one way or another. Then he cremated his wife's body, mixed her ashes in the mortar, and spread her into the walls of the cathedral![42]

This concrete Aesopian gesture (so to speak) is classic Eisenstein—defiant, secretive, and slightly gory—and he adopted the stonemason's tactics in making his film the way he wanted to make it. Eisenstein constructed a surface narrative that was politically acceptable, with recognizable elements of Socialist Realist narrative, and then proceeded to saturate that narrative with misdirection, contradiction, and a visual style that continually invites the viewer to look beyond appearances, until the surface orthodoxy becomes another one of the dialectical contradictions that shape our understanding of Eisenstein's Ivan.

On April 8, 1941, Eisenstein finished the first draft of the scenario.[43] He spent the next few weeks showing it to friends, including the documentary director Esfir Shub and the screenwriter and literary critic Viktor Shklovsky. Shub (who later confessed that she did not understand it very well) made a number of suggestions. Eisenstein underlined one of Shub's questions that would long plague him: "Why do the people love Ivan"?[44] Shklovsky noticed many of the things that would make the movie controversial: the historical distortions and anachronistic details. He wanted Eisenstein to remove the anachronistic moments like Fedor Basmanov's masquerade in drag at

The Feast of the Oprichniki and reduce the number of murders. Eisenstein dismissed Shklovsky's suggestions.[45] He didn't ignore warnings about these issues; he kept them in mind for more than a year until he thought he needed to act on them. But on May 1, 1941, he had a draft of the scenario ready to submit for approval, and he fully expected to be filming by the end of the year.

In the meantime, Eisenstein prepared his diverse audiences for his particular approach to Ivan the Terrible. In March and April 1941, he published articles in the official film press and in the central state media about the Stalin Prizes just announced, including his own prize for *Alexander Nevsky*, and about the new project on Ivan the Terrible. These articles accomplished several things in several different moral registers. Articles in response to the Stalin Prizes cemented Eisenstein's position as the official face of Soviet film. As the artistic director of Mosfilm, he expressed the film artists' gratitude for government recognition and their determination to continue to make films that were "worthy of the Stalinist epoch."[46] He placed his own film in the protective circle of Stalinist patronage by linking *Ivan* with his Stalin Prize winning film, *Alexander Nevsky*, and then by linking Ivan the Terrible's unification of the state with Stalin's. One article ends, "We recall Ivan the Terrible in these days when the dreams of the best minds of humanity about a united, multinational socialist state are becoming a reality; an unprecedented victory, led by the great genius Stalin."[47]

In the more substantive articles that appeared in more prominent publications (the popular illustrated magazine *Ogonek* and the state newspaper *Izvestiia*), Eisenstein offered a very limited depiction of his approach to Ivan. Two particular refrains emerge here: Eisenstein's Ivan will differ from that of earlier artists and his depiction of the infamous sixteenth-century tsar will be based on historical documents rather than myth and legend. In an interview in *Ogonek*, Eisenstein emphasized the historical basis for his image of Ivan and, diametrically at odds with what we find in his notes and the scenario, the "skillful and visionary" politics of the young tsar in comparison with more familiar and frightening images of the tsar in old age in works by the sculptor Mark Antokolsky, the painters Ilya Repin and Viktor Vasnetsov, and the novelist and playwright Aleksei Tolstoy.[48] The longest article of the bunch, in *Izvestiia*, again began by distinguishing Eisenstein's conception of Ivan from the frightening images made by other artists, and he again explained his approach to those popular ideas by referring to historical sources. Most of what we know about Ivan and about the "horrors of the oprichniki," he said, came from the slander of foreign travelers' accounts and the disparaging history written by the traitor Andrei Kurbsky (this was the standard Stalinist historiographical position). He wrote, "the task standing before me is to reconstruct 'the poet of the state idea,' as he was called by one of the historians of the past."[49] In "The Heirs and Builders of Culture," Eisenstein celebrated Soviet artists for continuing "to advance the cause of world culture" in their unique position outside the turmoil engulfing the rest of Europe. It also credited "the wisdom and foresight of the Soviet government and Comrade Stalin," for making the Soviet Union the only country in the world where artists could still work in peace—an obvious but unstated reference to the Nazi-Soviet nonaggression pact of 1939.[50]

Some Soviet artists were able to avoid such public statements of support during this period, but Eisenstein chose compliance, at least in public. He knew all too well what state violence had done to people in 1937. His own life hung in the balance in that year of mass arrests and dead-of-night disappearances of prominent intellectuals and party members. In 1941, he knew what it would take to retain the support he needed to make a film about bloody tyrants. The cost to his conscience and reputation was high, as we will see, but *Ivan the Terrible* went forward. In these published articles in 1941, Eisenstein chose to advertise his work on the film within an orthodox framework, replete with reference to Stalin's "genius." Yet Eisenstein's approach to Ivan was not, as Kozlov put it, "in complete accordance with the official—that is—Stalinist—point of view."[51] His public statements clash sharply with his notes, his memoirs, and his other writing. The published articles say nothing about Ivan's personal trauma, his hunger for revenge, his essential irony; there is no "sticking one's neck out" and no hint of "the most atrocious things." Nothing here suggests Eisenstein's refusal to "whitewash" Ivan. He avoided the subject of violence altogether. Yet, the articles were not entirely empty rhetoric. They show us that Eisenstein insisted on demonstrating that his portrait of Ivan was historical and verifiable rather than mythic. He would return to this position repeatedly to defend his unorthodox and contradictory conceptualization of Ivan as unjustifiably violent and tragic but historically accurate.

A year later, in May 1942, while still waiting for filming to begin, Eisenstein published "*Ivan the Terrible*: A Film about the Russian Renaissance in the Sixteenth Century."[52] The war gave Eisenstein a different tyrant to use as a foil, and this article was his first public discussion of the film to suggest its deviation from the proscribed historical narrative and the difficulties associated with that approach. He made four main points. First, he took the position that while Ivan's unification of the government was a historically progressive act, it was carried out with extreme violence. Second, Eisenstein placed Ivan in the context of other Renaissance rulers who centralized their governments around the same time and who carried out these same modernizing, progressive policies with great violence, identifying that violence as historically necessary. Third, he made it clear that he had no intention of ignoring or excusing Ivan's violence, but that he distinguished past from present: what was acceptable in the sixteenth century was not acceptable today: "Obscurantism and bloodthirstiness are two charges that will be leveled against anyone who, in the great age of the democratic freedoms of the twentieth century, uses the devices of the medieval feudal scoundrel dishonestly to seize power from his people."[53] Fourth, he claimed that the fact that violence was necessary historically did not automatically justify it morally—not in the past and not in the present. He argued that the necessity of violence for the purpose of carrying out historically progressive policies did not make it any less horrific or inhumane. In fact, it forced us to question any justification of violence. "And this image [of Ivan], which is frightening and attractive, charming and terrifying—tragic, in the full sense of the word, in his inner struggle against himself, a struggle that he waged that was inseparable from the struggle against his country's enemies—becomes an image that is close and comprehensible to today's audience."[54] Eisenstein's Ivan is a tragic figure because his bloodletting, so progressive and necessary, was in conflict with his inner humanity; this conflict was at the very heart of Eisenstein's purpose: "not to whitewash but to explain." And just in case his contemporary parallel was not understood, he made an analogy with an unnamed demagogue, easy enough to read as Hitler, because who would dare to think in 1942 that it was a public critique of Stalin: "For today, at a time of war, it is obvious as never before that anyone who invites ruin upon his homeland deserves death; that anyone who crosses over to the side of his motherland's enemies deserves punishment; that those who open up their country's borders to the enemy must be ruthlessly dealt with."[55]

I see this article as a real tour de force that shows us Eisenstein's ability to exploit the rhetoric of Soviet speech to challenge simplistic moral and political categories and raise complex questions about Soviet public life and political rulers. His Ivan will not be simply a good Ivan or a bad Ivan; nor will he be simply a metaphor for Stalin or Hitler or any single figure. Eisenstein's Ivan was an ambitious ruler and a complex, troubled man, whose public responsibilities conflicted with his private beliefs, a portrait that addressed some of the most important and intractable issues of life in Stalin's Russia. And by the time Eisenstein published this article a year after finishing the first draft of the scenario, he had figured out ways to make his sinister, tragic view of Ivan even more dramatic and complex.

Production Limbo

Eisenstein spent the late spring of 1941 preparing for production with the expectation that he could soon begin shooting the film Stalin had ordered. He was at his dacha outside Moscow on June 22, 1941, when news of the German invasion reached him. Sergei Prokofiev, staying nearby, joined him as people all over the Soviet Union gathered with friends and family to prepare for war. All the major film studios held emergency meetings on that day to decide how best to support the war effort. The Soviet government had always regarded film as an important instrument of political persuasion, and during the war filmmaking was considered essential for maintaining public morale. As artistic director, Eisenstein led the discussion at Mosfilm, where it was decided to make a series of short films with clear antifascist messages as quickly as possible. Older writers and directors threw themselves into this work, while younger crew members and actors gave up their jobs to join the army, often opening up positions for women. Some young actors and technicians were commanded to stay behind to make movies. Pavel Kadochnikov, who would later be cast as Vladimir Staritsky in *Ivan the Terrible*, found it humiliating to be shooting films far to the rear while other men and women of his generation were facing live ammunition, but film was war work and the studios were given quite remarkable resources during a time of great deprivation to continue production. Galina Ulanova, the prima ballerina, recalled after the war that everyone who wasn't on the front felt the need to work as hard as they possibly could to honor those fighting.[56]

Eisenstein spent the rest of the summer on official duties at the film studio, producing morale-boosting shorts while awaiting approval of his scenario. His diary records unnerving, nighttime trips to the bomb shelter and a gnawing fear that he had been wasting his life.[57] He copied these lines from Thornton Wilder's *Our Town* in his diary: "'*That's what it is to be alive. To move about in a cloud of ignorance . . . to spend and waste time as though you had a million years. To be always at the mercy of one self-centered passion or another . . . ,'*" and wrote alongside them: "*But how true! And how!*"[58] Returning to work on the scenario in September hardly helped his mood: "individual episodes and narrative threads in *Ivan* are turning out fine, but *as a whole* it just limps along."[59] In early October, Bolshakov promised to relieve Eisenstein of his duties at the film studio (after he'd skipped some important meetings) to let him get back to work on transforming the scenario into a director's script and preparing for filming.[60] But work on *Ivan* was interrupted almost immediately, when, with the German army getting dangerously close to Moscow, the capital was evacuated.

As essential personnel, artists were among the privileged populations put on the first trains for cities in the Caucasus, Siberia, and Central Asia. Eisenstein departed for Alma Ata, in Kazakhstan, on October 14, 1941. According to Rostislav Iurenev, an entire train car was requisitioned to transport Eisenstein's books, a considerable exaggeration. Eisenstein himself claimed that he took only five books with him, probably an exaggeration in the other direction.[61] The evacuation was an enormous undertaking. Train journeys were slow as they passed through stations filled with mobilized soldiers and hungry refugees of all ages.[62] In Alma Ata, food and fuel were scarce even before the city was deluged with thousands of artists, intellectuals, and workers for the factories that turned out war materiel. The film actors, crew members, and staff were housed in hotels, dormitories, or barracks. The actor who played Fedor Basmanov, Mikhail Kuznetsov, recalled that "the times were hard. We were hungry, cold, and disoriented."[63] Eisenstein was given an apartment in a small building nicknamed the "Laureatnik" because most of its inhabitants were prizewinning artists. His Moscow housekeeper, Aunt Pasha (Praskovia Petrovna Zaborovskaia), came later and slept in the hallway.[64] The weather was balmy in October but soon turned cold and dreary and then unbearably hot. Eisenstein's film was again put on hold while more immediate tasks were given priority. In Alma Ata, he busied himself constructing new studio space, transferring and reopening the Central Film School (VGIK), and producing other people's films.

The Soviet intellectuals who were dispersed to various cities in Siberia and Central Asia during the war would remember those years with deeply contradictory feelings. For many, evacuation was isolating, disorienting, and dispiriting. Others hoped that the war would overthrow the Stalinist regime. Some—despite terrible deprivation and loss, German atrocities and Soviet repressions—remembered World War II as a time of relative freedom of expression and of a genuine, uncoerced, collective effort in the fight against fascism. Dmitri Shostakovich wrote that "the war brought great sorrow and made life very hard. Much sorrow and many tears. But it had been even harder before the war, because then everyone was alone in his sorrow."[65] Eisenstein shared the populist patriotism, but his experience of the period was deeply conflicted. He hated the climate in Alma Ata, was frustrated by the rough conditions and repeated delays, and suffered especially from a sense of isolation and displacement. To friends who stayed behind in Moscow or who returned there sooner, he complained in frequent letters, begging them to write more often and to send books. His diaries are marked with sad entries about friends and acquaintances who were killed at the front and with the trickle of news from the terrible siege of Leningrad. He endured serious illness, exhaustion, and bouts of the depression that had often plagued him in the past. Those who worked with Eisenstein in Alma Ata remembered a man who could be cantankerous and demanding, as well as generous and funny. Everyone remembered him as passionately committed to his work. And he clearly enjoyed the relative artistic freedom he found—or seized—far from the center of power.

When he wasn't holed up in his room or at the studio working, he seemed to enjoy the company of his fellow film artists. If memoirs are to be trusted, many people who knew him in Alma Ata found him to be congenial, hospitable, and supportive. Gleb Shandybin, the prop master on *Ivan*, recalled that at the Laureatnik, Eisenstein's "door was open to everyone. And how many people came to see him! For advice, to share happiness and sorrow, or simply to sit and talk. Sergei Mikhailovich found a kind word or piece of advice for everyone; more than once he shared his last kopeck."[66] Esfir Shub wrote that Eisenstein was always cracking jokes, even when he returned from the studio long past midnight.[67] Elizaveta Telesheva, the Moscow Art Theater (MKhAT) director and actress with whom he was romantically involved in the late 1930s, remembered things differently. Eisenstein invited Telesheva to Alma Ata to serve as acting coach, a role she had played for *Alexander Nevsky* and *Bezhin Meadow*.[68] She spent several weeks there in August and September 1942 and described Eisenstein's social life in a letter to his mother.

> He has again fallen into that unhealthy circle from which I worked so hard to extricate him. Pera [Atasheva] and [Esfir] Shub, according to the people around him, have taken over. He received a lot of money for the screenplay and has nothing at all . . . Shub is living in the room he offered to me. Everyone is unhappy about this because she's not a Laureate and has no right to live there. . . . The two of them have completely turned him around again. And the main thing is that he is surrounded by that unhealthy atmosphere of flattery and adulation that was so harmful for him and that he so enjoyed.[69]

Telesheva concluded disapprovingly that all this made Eisenstein "imperious, impatient, and intoxicated with himself."[70]

Telesheva had arrived in Alma Ata after months of trying unsuccessfully to contact Eisenstein. From evacuation in Saratov, she wrote him desperately lonely letters, begging him to respond. He ignored her entreaties almost entirely. Mikhail Nazvanov, whose own letters to his wife back in Moscow are among our best sources for this period, observed Eisenstein's sorrow when Telesheva died of cancer less than a year later, in July 1943, but even in her last months Eisenstein rarely wrote to her, and he didn't go to Moscow for her funeral.[71] Eisenstein's neglect, the war, and the much harsher evacuation conditions she had been experiencing in Saratov all understandably depressed the former favorite, Telesheva. So to find a world of gossip, love affairs, and people taking advantage of Eisenstein's reckless hospitality was sure to upset the much more proper and exhausted Telesheva.

There is more at stake here, however, than sorting out the worshipful from the jealous. Telesheva's letter inadvertently contains clues to Eisenstein's spirit in evacuation. For all his complaints—legitimate and otherwise—it is clear that he enjoyed a sense of release in Alma Ata. The breathing space he found far from Moscow gave him a degree of independence he hadn't enjoyed since his year in Mexico—independence that was personal, political, and sexual. More important, Telesheva unintentionally linked the self-intoxication she saw in Eisenstein with his attitude toward his work: "The scenario is good, but there are various "buts" . . . And in the atmosphere in which he finds himself— reminiscent, by the way, of *Bezhin Meadow*—he will not listen to anything."[72] What looked like imperiousness and arrogance to Telesheva was actually the director's unimpeded, even fierce determination to make a film with all the "'buts'" included. That "arrogant" determination was apparent as early as the fall of 1942, while he was casting and working on the director's script.

Despite, or perhaps because of wartime conditions in Alma Ata, Eisenstein remained remarkably busy even before *Ivan* went into production. During the day he saw to his studio and teaching responsibilities, and at night, sometimes *all* night, he continued thinking about and developing ideas for *Ivan the Terrible*.[73] In December 1941, he finished revising the literary scenario (again) and once again began preparing the director's script for production. When the approval process was delayed again by the war in 1942, Eisenstein continued his intensive work on character, plot development, and shot composition, turning the wait into an extraordinarily fertile period artistically. In the first half of 1942, he had some of his most important insights, and he made many of the remarkable drawings that he used to illustrate every shot and work out the visual style of the film at that time.[74] He also sent his assistants to Moscow with long lists of costumes, weapons, and other objects of Muscovite material culture to procure or to photograph so that he might reproduce (or borrow) authentic museum pieces to use in the film.[75] Throughout his life, Eisenstein continued to mine his previous works for ideas, long after they were finished. In the case of *Ivan the Terrible*, the production delays caused by war, evacuation, politics, and other disagreements allowed Eisenstein to perform this sort of ruminative analysis while waiting for production to begin. Between 1942 and 1944, he filled literally scores of notebooks with thoughts and drawings, pushing himself to extend and clarify his conceptualization. However frustrating the delays were for him, and even more so for his cast and crew, the delays undoubtedly deepened the film's narrative and enriched its formal structure and visual effects.

On February 11, 1942, while still finalizing the shooting script, Eisenstein wrote two letters about the narrative content and portrait of Ivan that help us see his developing political strategy. The first letter was to Bolshakov, whose responsibilities included getting necessary approvals and signing off on pre- and postproduction decisions.[76] A prolonged correspondence followed. In June 1942, Eisenstein met with Bolshakov to discuss the revised version of the scenario and director's script, and Eisenstein wrote a response to Bolshakov's comments. There would be another exchange in September 1942. Bolshakov sent another detailed round of comments to Eisenstein, who then obstinately defended the script as he wrote it.

The letter to Bolshakov was a preemptive, and conciliatory, gesture. Eisenstein wrote that because the scenario had not been changed since before the war started, it was in need of some corrections. His list of suggestions sought to moderate issues that would trouble readers and censors throughout the approval process, together with a few items that appeared in this letter and never again. He proposed including something about the domestic reform program the historical Ivan initiated early in his reign, when he was at his most prudent. He offered to clarify the positive role of the oprichnina; to highlight Ivan's genius in faking his abdication and forming the oprichnina as a way out of a seemingly unresolvable political conflict with the boyars; to minimize the theme of Ivan's loneliness; and, in light of the ongoing war, to shift the focus in military scenes from conflict with Livonia to conflict with Germany, and to introduce the theme of Ivan's Anglophilia.[77] The second letter was to Andrei Zhdanov. In that letter, Eisenstein thanked Zhdanov for the opportunity to work on such a "fascinating" topic and asked his advice on how to proceed with the theme of Russia's relations with England, now made more sensitive by the war.[78] He didn't send that letter directly to Zhdanov but asked Bolshakov to forward it.[79] The message to Zhdanov seems designed to revive the high party official's investment in the film. Eisenstein's effusive thanks and request for advice might seem entirely gratuitous, if not for the film industry's reliance on patron-client relations. Eisenstein sought to engage Zhdanov by asking a question, "whose answer I can receive only from you,"[80] on a subject—Russia's relationship with England—that was politically sensitive. It was just at the time that Stalin was waiting, with increasing impatience, for his Western allies to open a second front. It is possible that Eisenstein never intended to trouble Zhdanov personally but only to encourage Bolshakov to clear this subplot with his own boss.

These letters help us understand Eisenstein's thinking about the project a year after starting it in conditions that had changed drastically. Lev Roshal argues that the unusual step of suggesting corrections on his own initiative, without waiting for the Cinema Committee or the studio, or even Stalin, to comment on the scenario shows that Eisenstein was willing to make these particular concessions to the official interpretation of Ivan in order to protect the psychological complexity and the historical tragedy central to his conception of the film. Roshal also notes, almost incidentally, that the letters show Eisenstein's awareness of the possibility that the literary scenario might be read as too negative.[81]

Roshal is certainly correct to see Eisenstein making concessions to protect what mattered to him, but I want to draw attention to Eisenstein's concern that the scenario might be seen as too dark a portrait of Ivan and his circle. Viewers who wish to see *Ivan* (especially Part I) as a conformist film that glorifies and celebrates the image of Ivan the Terrible might read Eisenstein's preemptive self-corrections as submission to his Kremlin handlers and the demands of Socialist Realism or as attempts to make the portrait more positive and therefore more flattering to contemporary rulers. But other documents make it clear that while Eisenstein was consistent in his efforts to "rehabilitate" Ivan, as he put it, he also stuck to his promise to refuse to "whitewash" him or his role in Russian history. He didn't intend to change the direction of his thinking, but he may have understood that he wouldn't be able to proceed with the project if film authorities read the scenario as too negative. These concerns show that he knew the script contained the textual basis for the visual, psychological, and political complexity he was already in the process of imagining and planning; and that he was prepared to meet potential criticism on all those grounds. And it is possible that he wrote these letters because he already had ideas in mind that would be even more alarming to his patrons and official viewers.

Eisenstein followed these apparently conciliatory gestures not by softening his portrait or removing the elements that already troubled his readers and critics, but, on the contrary, by digging into the most sinister and twisted dynamics within his characters. The period between February and May 1942—that is, between writing obsequious letters to his patrons and receiving a response—was the first of three periods of extraordinarily intensive and creative work on *Ivan*. Within days of writing to Bolshakov and Zhdanov, Eisenstein worked out many of the most interesting and fundamental, but unspoken, details of the political, historical, and tragic (and tragicomic) trajectory of the film. To give just a few examples here of topics I discuss in detail in the following chapters, he wrote long entries in his production notebooks on the convoluted motives and horrific betrayals of the Basmanovs and on the moral and political degeneration of Ivan's circle modeled on the degeneration of the Russian Revolution in the decades after 1917. He established Ivan's role as a demagogue who tricks the people into supporting him. He worked out Ivan's motives for allowing Maliuta to carry out the tsar's bloody executions—keeping Ivan's hands deceptively clean. He realized that the homoerotic subtext that he had included more subtly in the scenario had to be brought to the surface: both Maliuta and Fedka Basmanov would love Ivan, mixing personal jealousy with political revenge and complicating everyone's motives. And he realized that he could make Maliuta a bit of a clown—the merry executioner—a combination of traits that thoroughly delighted Eisenstein and saved him from removing the clownishness of the Russian people altogether.

Then the stakes were raised even higher.

Just a month after Eisenstein wrote to Bolshakov and Zhdanov, his assistant, Lev Indenbom, wrote from Tashkent to report on his meeting with the academic historians hired to evaluate Eisenstein's screenplay as well as Aleksei Tolstoy's play about Ivan the Terrible, also a Stalin commission. Indenbom reported that Militsa Nechkina, a powerful official historian, though not a specialist on the early modern period, was "ecstatic" about Eisenstein's scenario. Ironically, Nechkina considered Eisenstein's Ivan far more decisive than Tolstoy's, who, she thought, did nothing but vacillate and seemed unable to execute anyone. But at the same time, she thought that there were "too many executions" in Eisenstein's scenario and that he should "subtract some." In response to this, Eisenstein wrote in his diary: "I am very afraid of this kind of observation from above. To do that is to lose the 'bared teeth' of the epoch (of both!)."[82] Fear and caution competed with defiance and determination. I am not the first the report this comment, but viewing it in chronological context makes it that much more revealing. Eisenstein's notes and drawings for the rest of March and April show that he continued not only to bare the sharpened teeth of both epochs but to file them even sharper. He refused to subtract corpses. Instead he piled them up and simultaneously complicated everyone's motives for murder. For the rest of the spring and summer, Eisenstein's notebooks develop the critical themes of revenge and violence, the links between personal feeling and political action, and the role of personal responsibility in state violence in ways that raised pointed questions about power.[83] The reformist period early in Ivan's reign, broached in his letter to Bolshakov, disappeared, never to be mentioned again. After this, Eisenstein never wavered in his commitment to exploring Ivan's darkest motives and actions and trying to explain the tsar's behavior, but he knew he had to do so in ways that wouldn't alarm his studio and state patrons.

In June 1942, Eisenstein responded to Bolshakov's critique of the scenario. He defended the length of the film and his request for a large amount of film stock by insisting that he could not make the film any shorter without sacrificing his "conception and fundamental interpretation of things." The film might seem long but, Eisenstein insisted, to include all the corrections Bolshakov himself suggested, the film could not be cut.[84] Bolshakov's detailed response to this came in a letter dated September 5.[85] Whatever they had discussed in June, Bolshakov now told Eisenstein to remove the entire subplot concerning Queen Elizabeth and England's support for Ivan's Russia because his treatment of this scene wasn't historically accurate. The timing of this instruction is critical. Between June and September 1942, Crimea had fallen to the Nazis, and fighting had intensified all throughout the southern USSR as the Germans approached and then arrived at Stalingrad. On August 12, British Prime Minister Winston Churchill came to Moscow to tell Stalin that there would be no opening of a second front in Western Europe in 1942. Onscreen friendship with England was no longer possible, so the suggestive drawings and campy screen tests Eisenstein shot of the director

FIGURE 1.3   Mikhail Romm playing Elizabeth I

Mikhail Romm playing a flirtatious Queen Elizabeth in drag would never have a chance to be realized.[86]

Eisenstein's response to Bolshakov's September directive was defiantly insistent, even regarding issues on which the director would later concede. In mid-September, he wrote to Pera Atasheva that he had finally finished negotiations over the script and that Bolshakov had approved everything except the English support for Ivan's Russia. But *"I see no objection to that,"* he wrote.[87] The Committee on Cinema Affairs had not in fact "approved everything" but only offered approval of the director's scenario on September 5 on the provision that Eisenstein cut or revise several more scenes, all of which had been discussed before and all of which had sensitive political overtones. Bolshakov instructed Eisenstein to make his representatives of the Russian people less foolish and more dignified, to limit attention to religion and Ivan's religiosity in particular, to revise a scene in which Maliuta Skuratov spoke openly to the tsar and seemed "on an equal footing" with him. He ordered Eisenstein to stress the positive aspects of Ivan's reign and, finally, to minimize the theme of Ivan's loneliness, on one hand, and his demagogic manipulation of the people, on the other. Bolshakov's memo also included two full pages of individual lines, shots, and words to be changed or removed.[88]

Eisenstein adamantly defended his script against Bolshakov's charges that some scenes were historically inaccurate. The subject of historical accuracy had come up repeatedly now and would loom even larger when it became clear that Stalin was especially invested what he called historical accuracy and in his ability to detect historical errors. But Eisenstein maintained his ground in that area. Despite telling Atasheva that he was willing to scrap the English scenes, his letter to Bolshakov cited historians who discussed English support for Russia, and letters between Ivan and Elizabeth that proved their alliance to be based on historical documents.[89] He also insisted that he did not simply imagine the scene between Ivan and Maliuta but included it to establish an important psychological relationship between the tsar and his entourage. To Bolshakov's criticism that the theme of Ivan's loneliness was still too prominent, Eisenstein protested that it was just right. He argued that loneliness was not a sign of political weakness but merely an absence of close friends. He agreed to remove the "clownish" verses—*chastushki*—sung by representatives of the Russian people, but he pointed out that the song in the script had been written in "precise correspondence with countless pieces of evidence of Ivan's taste for exactly that kind of entertainment."[90] And then, despite his promise, he shot some of these scenes anyway: the assertive adviser, the lonely tsar, and the foolish people were all filmed. The people ultimately were cut, but the rest remained.[91]

These negotiations over the screenplay are important because they show the extent to which the Cinema Committee was involved in script approval, the numerous stages that approval had to go though, and the extent to which Eisenstein felt he could fight or even defy official instructions. He consistently emphasized the historical accuracy of his depiction of Ivan and his reign as well as the importance of the psychological profile he was developing. The correspondence also reiterates the presence of dangerous political themes in Eisenstein's conception of *Ivan* from the very beginning of the project and in the earliest scenes of the film and his knowledge of how these ominous themes were likely to be received. Official readers—just like his friends Shub, Shklovsky, and Telesheva—read in the script an Ivan who was demagogic, tragic, indecisive, overly religious, and psychologically vulnerable, and they found a portrait of the Russian people as easily manipulated fools. Bolshakov and his assistants wanted Eisenstein to tone down the director's script in order to make a film that could be approved for release, but Eisenstein did not oblige, or at the very least he did not buckle under. Ivan's loneliness, for example, remained one of the film's central explanatory psychological factors and a major theme linking the personal and the political. And the shifting power relationship with Maliuta remained one of the key illustrations of Ivan's identity in the film. In April 1942 (after Eisenstein's February conciliatory letter to Bolshakov but before Bolshakov's September response), Eisenstein rewrote the scene with Maliuta and Ivan:

> This is the *beginning* of the executions. It is the sword that leads to judgment. It is the beginning of the bloody epic. It is—a moment of doubt in a man about to put his hand to a terrible deed. The preparation of the doubt is the scene with Filipp [where Ivan confessed an agonizing loneliness dating back to his childhood]. The apogee of doubt [is when Ivan says]: "by what right do you judge—when it is God's place to judge?[92]

And this is, of course, what we see in the finished film. The religious culture of his court and Ivan's own religiosity—at one point in the notes, Eisenstein refers to Ivan's "ironic religiosity"[93]—would also be visible from the beginning of the film to the end. The tsar's repeated return to moral questioning rooted in religious belief was the source of the vacillation that disturbed official readers at this scriptwriting stage and irritated Stalin and his circle when they saw the completed Part II in 1946. In Part III, Ivan would nearly strangle his confessor, Evstafy, with the chain that held his crucifix.

The fate of the film's portrait of the Russian people, another target of criticism here at the script stage, was more complicated or, at least, more difficult to solve satisfactorily. "Ivan and the people is *very* interesting and *not at all* simple," Eisenstein wrote in April 1942.[94] But popular support for Ivan was a key element in the Stalinist historiography, so this was another problem Eisenstein had to solve in a way that challenged the party line from an oblique angle.

In his obstinate correspondence with Bolshakov, Eisenstein defended his portrait of the tsar in much the same way he presented it to the public in his newspaper articles of 1941–1942. He didn't hide Ivan's bloodletting, but he didn't justify it either. Instead he sought to explain Ivan's descent into mass state violence on the basis of what he considered psychologically accurate historical evidence. Throughout the correspondence over the scenario, he continually insisted on his right to make this film the way he wanted to make it. Roshal argues that Eisenstein hated being treated like a subordinate by Bolshakov—like a child—but that he often had to suppress or camouflage his defiant instincts. Certainly, Eisenstein courted Bolshakov's favor at times, as in February 1942, and he ignored Bolshakov's directives at other times, carrying on the way he wanted to, but there were also numerous occasions, as in the letters of June and September 1942, when Eisenstein openly fought back. In this case, he explicitly defended his portrait as correct and his scenario as "just right." He didn't always win, but he chose when to bend and when to stand. And he chose to stand, in direct defiance of official criticism, rather often.

In May 1942, while the director's scenario was still undergoing revision, the Alma Ata studio received provisional approval of the literary scenario and a green light to begin planning for production.[95] One result of that decision was that casting *Ivan the Terrible* could begin in the spring of 1942, even though filming would not, in fact, begin until the following year. Even before this, Eisenstein invited Nikolai Cherkasov, who had played Alexander Nevsky, to play Ivan. They finalized the agreement on a train station platform in Alma Ata when the actor's train stopped for forty minutes en route to Novosibirsk where he had been evacuated with his wife and child.[96] The role of Ivan's adoring servitor and last loyal friend, Maliuta Skuratov, was offered to Mikhail Zharov, a popular, versatile, larger-than-life actor (though Zharov originally wanted to play the traitor Andrei Kurbsky).[97] The role of Kurbsky would be filled by the stately stage actor Mikhail Nazvanov, who was at the time making his first film as the romantic lead in what would become one of the most beloved Russian war films, Alexander Stolper's *Wait for Me* (1943). Nazvanov's career had not always been so successful. In 1935, when he was a twenty-year-old novice actor at the Moscow Art Theater, he was denounced to the police for telling a political joke. He served five years of hard labor in exile before being released at the beginning of the war.[98] Each of these actors would play their roles partially against type, reversing or complicating previous roles:

after heroic Nevsky, Cherkasov played Ivan as a tsar tormented by remorse and doubts; after the good-hearted servitor Alexander Menshikov in Vladimir Petrov's *Peter I* (1938), Zharov played Skuratov as a clownish murderer; and Nazvanov turned his romantic hero into a weakling and a fool as Andrei Kurbsky.

The young Ivan was played by Erik Pyriev, the son of another well-known Soviet director, Ivan Pyriev, who, ironically, would be one of the people most critical of the finished films. Eisenstein wanted his friend and rival filmmaker, Vsevolod Pudovkin, for Metropolitan Pimen, leader of the Orthodox Church, but Pudovkin suffered a heart attack during the screen tests.[99] Later Pudovkin was cast as the snarling "Holy Fool" Nikola, and Eisenstein invited Alexander Mgrebov, a stage actor in evacuation in Novosibirsk, to come to Alma Ata to play Pimen. He didn't know that Mgrebov was deathly ill with tuberculosis and malnutrition. Mgrebov later claimed that the invitation saved his life, because when Eisenstein saw the condition he was in when his train arrived in Alma Ata, the director used all his influence to provide Mgrebov with good medical care.[100]

The young men in the film, Fedor Basmanov and Vladimir Staritsky, were played by actors of diametrically opposed look and temperament. The devilish, dark-haired Mikhail Kuznetsov, who played Fedor, was one of the Stanislavsky-trained actors who clashed most sharply with Eisenstein over acting method.[101] Pavel Kadochnikov, blond and lighthearted, became a favorite of Eisenstein from the start. He would also play one of the Chaldei clowns in The Fiery Furnace and was slated to play Evstafy, Ivan's confessor, in a key scene of Part III.

It proved much more difficult to cast the female parts—Ivan's wife, Anastasia, and Ivan's major rival for power, his aunt Efrosinia Staritskaia. Neither role was filled until more than six months of filming had already gone by. When Eisenstein's first choice for Anastasia could not get permission to travel to Alma Ata, he tried to persuade the ballerina Galina Ulanova to take the role. Ulanova had the graceful, regal bearing of a dancer and a soulful, self-possessed face that would have given real depth to the character. Ulanova herself was intrigued, if a bit intimidated, by the possibility of a film role, and she agreed to pose for a series of screen tests. Ulanova admired Eisenstein, but to his great disappointment she declined the role, unwilling to sacrifice her dancing career for the amount of time the filming would take.[102] This occurred at the end of 1943, when the shooting of Anastasia's scenes could no longer be delayed. The role was finally offered, at the very last moment, to Liudmila Tselikovskaia, who had none of Ulanova's presence or grace of movement but happened to be Mikhail Zharov's wife and available.

Efrosinia proved even more problematic. Eisenstein wanted the great, outspoken, comic actress Faina Ranevskaia to play Efrosinia and got as far as shooting screen tests, the photographs of which show a face of great power and malevolent expressiveness, with an ironic undertone. Eisenstein, always the dialectian, was drawn to people who possessed the combination of wickedness and humor he saw in Ranevskaia, and in costume she bore a marked resemblance to the wicked stepmother in Disney's *Snow White*. But when Bolshakov (who had final approval of casting choices) looked at those same photographs, he saw only Ranevskaia's "Jewish" features and, in a renewed atmosphere of official antisemitism, deemed her ineligible to play a "Russian" boyarina.[103] A rancorous correspondence ensued. Eisenstein continued to demand Ranevskaia and gave up only after a full year of arguing and stalling. When Bolshakov finally lost patience, he sent Eisenstein a telegram, saying, "Your request [concerning] Ranevskaia manifests an intolerable lack of discipline and dissolute willfulness [*raspushchennost'*]. I suggest that you waste no more time refusing to carry out my orders."[104] The loss of Ranevskaia infuriated the director (and the actor). Another MKhAT stage actor, Serafima Birman, was finally, reluctantly, offered the role.

Birman was an unpopular choice, and her arrival on the set was inauspicious to say the least. Here's how she put it years later:

> The moment [Moskvin, the cinematographer] set eyes on me, he seized his head in his hands and stood as if turned to stone. . . . The waving of his arms, the javelins his eyes hurled into the director's face, the whisperings that turned at times into rumblings, at times into shouts,—all this was as good as a curse upon Eisenstein and a death-sentence for me. This happened long ago, but to this day I can feel the searing pain of it. Eisenstein was discredited by the dreadful impression I made. . . . But impelled by his compassion for me or to quell his own perturbation, he disguised his feelings and kept a tight leash on his smile to keep it from running away.[105]

Only the skilled work of the makeup artist Vasily Goriunov gave Birman a passable look, and only on his third try.[106]

After successfully collaborating on *Alexander Nevsky*, Eisenstein was eager for Sergei Prokofiev to write the score for *Ivan the Terrible*. Eisenstein had written to Prokofiev very early on, in December 1941, to say that the script was almost finished and that the composer would have considerable freedom writing the music.[107] In March 1942, Eisenstein sent Prokofiev the finished literary scenario, and when Prokofiev was able to travel to Alma Ata, they worked on the score together, but little music was actually written during their meetings in 1942–1943.[108] They conversed in depth about what Eisenstein wanted, but only two pieces were completed in Alma Ata: The Oath of the Oprichniki for the sinister, deleted scene in Part I, and a foreshadowing lullaby, "Ocean Blue-Deep Blue Sea" for the deleted Prologue. While in Alma Ata Eisenstein wrote several glowing articles about Prokofiev's contribution to *Ivan*, but if the resulting score was highly satisfying, the process thoughout production was extremely difficult to coordinate and was responsible for some critical delays (as we will see).

Hopes that filming might begin soon after the director's script was approved in September 1942 were soon dashed. Through the end of that year, Eisenstein continued to read and write about various things, some related to *Ivan*, some not. He finished articles on Charlie Chaplin and Prokofiev. He read Steinbeck, Shakespeare, and a lot of psychology: Freud and Le Bon on crowds and the medical psychologist Ernst Kretschmer on hysteria and the physiological manifestations of emotions. He worked on synchronizing the score with the text of the scenario. He wrote about the painters Van Gogh, El Greco, and Hans Holbein.[109] And he was painfully aware of the desperate fighting that made the winter of 1942–1943 the darkest days of the war: "The war is becoming epic. . . . *Life's lousy, Hell with it. Mais c'est passable.*"[110] He noted the deaths of friends and relatives of friends and the terrible loss of life in Leningrad, then under siege. He took the death of a student very hard.[111] In November, he noted that he was continuing to get work done—"feverishly," as if on hashish—even without electricity and despite "melancholy," and his own "loneliness."[112] But at the same time, in November 1942, he began a romance that would last until the end of 1943 with Liubov Dubenskaia, a young actress who also lived in the Laureatnik.[113] This was a tumultuous affair and a surprise (and possibly the reason he noted that wartime was *"passable"*—in French, his language for romance and feeling). He wrote to Pera back in Moscow: *"Just my luck! Am leading family life . . . not my kind of it. Just imagine how I feel. Expect to have it over in a couple of days."* But a few weeks later he wrote again: "Strange to say: things are best in the emotional sphere!"[114] And she wrote back, *"If you can't be good, be careful, Romeo!"*[115]

In April 1943, after several additional postponements, more than two years after Eisenstein began work on *Ivan*, filming finally got underway. Within a few weeks, a new problem arose. Since his very first feature in 1924, Eisenstein had worked with only one cameraman, the renowned Eduard Tisse. Tisse had accompanied Eisenstein to Hollywood and Mexico, and his own career had been tied to Eisenstein's for twenty years. But even before shooting began, Eisenstein was considering a new look for *Ivan*, and in mid-1942, he was seen taking long walks with Andrei Moskvin, another of Russia's most acclaimed cinematographers. Eisenstein and Moskvin quickly found a common language, both intellectually and temperamentally. Esfir Shub recalled that "Eisenstein felt differently with him, than with anyone else, often conferring, asking his advice, and joking around."[116] The difference is immediately apparent in Eisenstein's letters to the two cameramen. After twenty years, the tone of his correspondence with Tisse is friendly but detached and professional (even before this break), while his letters to Moskvin are immediately warm and playful.[117] But the situation was delicate and needed to be handled with care. Eisenstein was especially concerned because during the war anyone with a Germanic-sounding surname was vulnerable to arrest, and Tisse, though not German, had already been threatened by the police.[118] Keeping him employed on the production was essential. Two months after filming began, Moskvin was officially brought in as cinematographer for all interior scenes, and effectively became the director of photography; Tisse was retained for outdoor filming, but it was clearly a demotion. "With Tisse, everything was and is still very painful," Eisenstein would write to Pera back in Moscow.[119]

Like Telesheva, Tisse believed that Eisenstein had fallen under the influence of harmful people, in this case the Leningrad directors Friedrich Ermler and Leonid Trauberg, who were also in Alma Ata and who pushed him into "aestheticism."[120] Tisse is correct that Eisenstein was returning to many of the ideas and practices of the old Leningrad avant-garde of the 1920s (just as he may have responded to the willful encouragement of the longtime friends Telesheva disapproved of) but both his will and his thoughts about style and production design were apparent in his notes long before Eisenstein reached Alma Ata and long before he began shooting *Ivan*. I have much more to say about cameramen, camerawork, and style below, but for now it is worth emphasizing that Eisenstein consistently pursued an unconventional visual plan for this film even though it meant sidelining his oldest collaborator.

Between April 1943 and July 1944, when the production moved back to Moscow, Eisenstein shot scenes from both Parts I and II at the same time as well as several key scenes from Part III. Until May 1944, he was still trying to shoot the film in two parts and he intended to film all of *Ivan the Terrible* in Alma Ata and release both parts at the same time. But it became apparent that wartime priorities, conflicts with the film administration, the actors' schedules and illnesses, as well as *Ivan's* complexity and Eisenstein's perfectionist commitment to it, would all conspire to delay completion. By all accounts, *Ivan the Terrible* was shot under conditions that would have seemed catastrophic had the rest of the country not been at war or under siege and occupation. A shortage of electricity in Alma Ata meant that indoor filming

FIGURE 1.4   On the set in overcoats. RGALI, 1923/2/130/6. Used with permission.

mostly took place at night, when the available fuel was not being used for industrial production. From six in the evening until eight in the morning, or sometimes longer and sometimes for weeks at a time without a day off, the crew and the actors were forced to stay on the set in their heavy medieval costumes and elaborate makeup. The studio was blisteringly hot in the summer and freezing in the winter (in some shots the vapor from the actors' breath is visible). The less prestigious actors were often hungry, because food was rationed and scarce. And Eisenstein was an exacting director, making the actors take the awkward poses depicted in his drawings while he shot and reshot each scene.

Eisenstein could be demanding and disagreeable, but most of the cast and crew ultimately believed his demands were motivated by the deepest artistic commitment. Though Nazvanov, Birman, Kuznetsov, and others complained about Eisenstein and many aspects of the production, the cast and crew unanimously agreed that Eisenstein inspired them to believe that they were engaged in a project of great significance. Most of the actors describe working on *Ivan the Terrible* as the chance of a lifetime: Mgrebov remembered that Eisenstein "inspired everyone to believe in the importance of the project. Everyone spoke about him with a smile. He didn't make himself scarce, Eisenstein was always on the set, always available. To work alongside and together with him was nothing but pleasure. As an artist and as a man

Eisenstein warmed me."[121] The director worked harder than anyone, visibly placing the value of the work above his own individual comfort.[122] Oleg Zhakov, who played Heinrich von Staden, remembered that Eisenstein "could be sharp when the shoot was interrupted or one of the actors got out of hand [*kapriznichit*]," but also that "whenever things became too difficult he would interject a funny story."[123] Cherkasov's wife, Nina, also reported that Eisenstein was good at using jokes to diffuse problems on the set. Eisenstein and Cherkasov both loved the circus and practical jokes and enjoyed calling each other funny names and making fun of each other.[124] As an observer, Shub wrote that the atmosphere on the set was always "festive." During the filming of some scenes, such as The Coronation, it could even become "triumphant."[125] Even Birman, the most difficult member of the cast, was impressed by the loyalty and commitment Eisenstein inspired in his crew, though she frequently complained that he seemed cold and unsympathetic toward her.[126] It is, of course, possible that these memoirs, mostly written much later, polished their authors' views of the famous director, but their memories corroborate one another in reporting both Eisenstein's irritability and his charm and in confirming his almost obsessive commitment to the project.

Unlike the retrospective memoirs that emphasized the positive, Nazvanov described the year of filming as painfully and unnecessarily drawn out. His letters to his wife, the actress Olga Viklandt, lack the sheen of retrospection or the bitterness of rejection, making them a particularly useful source. He reported that days often went by without any apparent progress. The actors had to get into full makeup and costume and then sit for eight or nine hours waiting to be called. Birman got on everyone's nerves. She thought nothing of telling the other actors how badly they were performing their roles, but Nazvanov thought she was often terrible in her own part, and Birman's memoirs inadvertently confirm Nazvanov's portrait of her as disagreeable and narcissistic. One of several actors who found Eisenstein's directing method incomprehensible, Birman pestered Eisenstein about performing her role the way she wished.[127] Late in the process, in March 1944, during a period of intensive shooting, Nazvanov wrote to his wife:

> Today they finished "The Cathedral" (ten days of shooting and reshooting and all possible artistic caprices of S. M.). He filmed an enormous quantity of shots that will not be included in the film but were necessary for the montage (or so it seemed to him!). He made dozens of variations of one shot, as if chewing on and relishing his own artistry. Moskvin delayed things with the lighting, which was especially difficult on the large and complex set of the "Dormition Cathedral." Birman

delayed things terribly with her endless conversations, proposals, and rehearsals.[128]

Later in April, he wrote that Eisenstein reshot scenes in order to get every little detail right and that once when Cherkasov was howling and weeping hysterically, even fainting, Eisenstein coolly looked on while eating his dinner. Cherkasov confirmed that Eisenstein painstakingly set up each shot, carefully attending to every detail of mise-en-scène, costume, design, body placement, and then looked through the camera lens repeatedly until everything was set up exactly as he wanted. Nazvanov wrote, "O Lord! When will this Golgotha come to an end?" And while Nazvanov also reported the director's ability to lighten even the most difficult moments with a joke or a prank, he considered Eisenstein to be for the most part distant and cryptic. "In general, the atmosphere is cold, unfeeling, and, alas, unproductive."[129]

But in the end, even Nazvanov was pleased with the result: "My God, how I have grown into the role this year and how everyone and everything has grown! Not excluding Eisen, Cherkasov, Moskvin, and Goriunov."[130] At three in the morning on February 12, 1944, after months of frustration, terrible weather, and not enough food or sleep, Nazvanov wrote to Olga that the scenes he had just shot showed the film to be "a magnificent spectacle."[131] Earlier that night, he wanted to curse everything connected with the film:

> And yet, in fact! The man is creating the work of a lifetime. A historical-artistic dissertation in the form of a film. He is taking his time, clearly betting everything he has on this work. He tries things, experiments, tries variations, shoots, shoots again, and clearly scorns everyone who attempts to interfere with the pace and deliberation of his work. From his point of view, he is deeply justified. For a director, such creations as *Ivan*—especially if you take into account the fact that he is the writer and artistic director of the film—are a testament to their maturity.[132]

By the end of the shoot in Alma Ata, in May 1944, Nazvanov concluded that, on one hand, the filmed material was magnificent, that Eisenstein was happy with his acting, with his close-ups, with all his scenes, and he came around to admire the director's ambition and commitment. On the other hand, he wondered if anyone would understand a film so visually stylized and lacking the usual narrative and emotional cues. And he never got over what he saw as Eisenstein's egotistical and selfish demands. "I curse this picture with the most magnificently obscene curses, but I have to admire Eisenstein's iron tenacity as he literally tramples people's hearts and even their bodies in striding toward his goal, in creating, in such hellish conditions, a monumental work of art."[133]

Conflicts between Eisenstein and the authorities over the pace and expense of production flared up repeatedly. Throughout the production process, Eisenstein had to fight with Moscow for funding, equipment, and permission to keep his crew paid, fed, and on the set. Most of all, he had to fight for time. The studio was frustrated with Eisenstein's pace, but he ignored the increasing pressures to hurry. He carried on as if he knew he had enough clout to make the film the way he wanted to make it, regardless of missives from Moscow, pleading from actors eager to return home, and scheduling conflicts with Prokofiev and others. Even before shooting began, Bolshakov was unhappy with Eisenstein's ambitious budget and production schedule, and at that early point Eisenstein was still predicting he would deliver the finished film within a year (that is, by the summer of 1944).[134]

In late 1943, when Eisenstein fell ill and the film was still unfinished after nine months of filming, Bolshakov demanded that he speed up production or lose *Ivan* to an assistant director. In response, Eisenstein wrote directly to Stalin, this time to get Bolshakov off his back.[135] The letter shows Eisenstein appealing to Stalin's personal investment in the film and the prestige Stalin lent to the whole project. Just a few months earlier, in September 1943, Stalin had personally approved the screenplay, noting that Eisenstein had "managed the assignment" and dealt with the historical issues "not at all badly."[136] Eisenstein's letter to Stalin explained in detail that while the obstacles to production could not begin to compare with the challenges facing the Red Army, the problems were significant and the entire company was committed to "an entirely uncompromising attitude toward quality," so it was necessary to resist rushing.[137] The day after he wrote the letter to Stalin, Viacheslav Molotov (deputy premier and minister of foreign affairs), sent a telegram to the set asking why things were taking so long. And two days later, word came down from Moscow to send clips of the material that had been filmed so far. Nazvanov wrote to his wife that everyone expected a scandal or worse.[138] But apparently the letter to Stalin worked and the clips were approved, because production was allowed to continue at the director's painstaking pace and with less interference from Moscow.

Kozlov has argued that at this critical juncture in the production of *Ivan the Terrible*, during the fall and winter of 1943–1944, the director abandoned the caution he had displayed in making Part I to "to turn the film into a tragedy" in Part II. "The contradiction 'between Parts One and Two' or more accurately between the artist and the man who had given the order—increased as the artist came to grips with his project."[139] Until that point, Kozlov's Eisenstein believed he could make the film he wanted to make within the parameters defined by Stalin's commission, but Stalin's approval of the script had sent

Eisenstein into a moral and artistic crisis. He supposedly resolved that crisis by throwing all caution to the wind.[140] The main problem with this influential analysis is that Eisenstein actively sought Stalin's approval in order to protect his project, either directly as in January 1944 or indirectly, as when he wrote to Zhdanov in 1942. And later, in 1945 and 1946, Eisenstein wanted and fully *expected* to win Stalin Prizes for both Parts I and II. It seems more likely that he read Stalin's approval of the script as a positive sign. Eisenstein enlisted Stalin to play the role of his patron, repeatedly writing to him for intervention and protection—even in the midst of World War II.

Given how much attention has been devoted to this question, it is necessary to state that there is no sign Eisenstein decided to use one strategy for Part I and a new strategy for Part II. Throughout 1943–1944, he was shooting scenes from the entire film, and not in chronological order. The scenes he reshot in early 1944 were from both Part I and Part II. His did a great deal of writing during the winter of 1943–1944, both on characters in *Ivan* and on his manuscript for *Method*, and these texts did not differentiate at all between parts of the film. A key piece of evidence on this issue comes again from Nazvanov, who resented the slow pace of production but understood that there was another reason for it:

> and that reason is significant and insurmountable. S. M. didn't want to release the two parts *separately*, because he considered Part I to be explication—the foundational dramaturgical, psychological core of all the actors' scenes in Part II. Besides that, *the image of the elderly terror familiar to everyone*—Tsar Ivan—only appears in Part II. If the first part were released individually, it might seem pale and ruin the reputation of the film and, with it, his personal reputation.[141]

Many people warned Eisenstein that releasing Part II without the uplifting Livonian victory in Part III would be political suicide. But Eisenstein wasn't worried about Part II being too dark; he was worried that people would see Part I as too *tame*—and of course they did. Eisenstein saw Parts I and II as inextricably and logically connected. Around this time, he wrote to Romm that, "in principle, I am <u>categorically opposed</u> to releasing Part I by itself. Both in terms of narrative and in terms of ideas, this is <u>two halves</u> of one film, <u>not two films</u>."[142]

He eventually did receive permission to make the film a trilogy in 1944, but this did not indicate a sudden desire to make Part II more "tragic." He had considered making *Ivan* a trilogy on and off all along. As early as 1942, he had written in a notebook: *"It is a very great pity that I'm obliged to make a two-series film and not the one that is planned in the scenario in-extenso . . . In form of a trilogy it is much better composed and themes and problems personal and non-personal—adamant.*"[143] In the spring of 1944, his desire to make the film a trilogy was as much practical as political. He didn't think he could finish filming everything that came after what became Part II in Alma Ata, but he did think that he could finish what became I and II by the end of the summer once he got back to Moscow. That would allow him to release I and II at the same time, then finish what would be Part III (some of which had already been shot in Alma Ata). He underestimated the chaotic state of postwar conditions at the Moscow film studios and did not foresee the difficulties he would have keeping the cast together or getting Prokofiev to write and record the soundtrack. His commitment to keeping Parts I and II together and released at the same time was only very reluctantly abandoned.

In the meantime, in 1943 Eisenstein was also involved in negotiations to publish the literary scenario for *Ivan*. Like everything else connected with this high-profile, high-stakes movie, the negotiations were complicated. In September 1943, Eisenstein learned that Goskinoizdat would publish the scenario in an abridged form approved by the Cinema Committee. He wrote to the editor of the journal *Novyi mir,* which was also publishing the scenario, to request that they publish the entire text, including the scenes deleted by the Cinema Committee censors. Eisenstein wanted to accompany the publication of the scenario with some of his drawings for the film and the essay discussed earlier, written expressly for this purpose, "A Few Words about My Drawings." At the same time, he sent to both *Novyi mir* and Goskinoizdat an eighty-three-page manuscript, "Historical Commentary on the Film *Ivan the Terrible,*" with expectations that it would also be published alongside the scenario and the drawings.[144] The Historical Commentary was a compendium of lines from the scenario annotated with the historical sources that proved their authenticity. The journal promised to publish the Historical Commentary but then reneged without telling Eisenstein. When he learned in November 1943 that Goskinoizdat also refused to publish the Historical Commentary, Eisenstein sent a telegram to Goskinoizdat demanding that the scenario be published only if it were accompanied by the Historical Commentary, but he was ignored. In the end, both the book publisher and the journal published the abridged version of the scenario in 1944 without either accompanying text.

The winter of 1943–1944 was the second period of Eisenstein's intensive thinking and writing about the film and its underlying structures. In addition to the daily preparation and nightly filming, Eisenstein was writing some of his most important analytical passages about *Ivan* while also linking his work on this film with theoretical concepts he had been developing. After a month of round-the-clock work, heart disease and collapse earned him ten days of quiet solitude in a sanatorium in the mountains above Alma Ata. His diary from that intermission contains several notes that might explain, if not the catalyst, at least the motives for his renewed commitment to *Ivan*, the only thing that did shift during that winter. After a bit of melodramatic complaining ("torment. . . . serenity. . . . nerves, nerves, nerves. . . . *a bout of hatred. Hatred of Ivan the Terrible*. Then ambition."),[145] he wrote that the thing that tormented him most was that he was almost forty-six years old and still hadn't finished the book he'd been writing for more than a decade. But, he goes on to say, he can finish it now because *Ivan* provided the "last necessary link" in his thinking about a universal artistic method. When Eisenstein returned to work, Nazvanov reported that he seemed even more determined that each scene be perfect.[146]

As winter turned to spring and spring to summer in 1944, wartime necessities continued to hamper efforts to finish shooting and Eisenstein continued to take his time, meticulously fixing details in each shot. As Eisenstein pushed the actors to their limits, one after another of them fell ill, further delaying completion. In April, the head of the film studio in Alma Ata, N. M. Kiva, took his turn to chastise Eisenstein for dragging his feet and failing to fulfill his work plan. Clearly irritated by Eisenstein's willful disregard for his "concrete, personal instructions," Kiva demanded a new plan and threatened that the Cinema Committee would hold Eisenstein personally responsible for fulfilling it. Within a month, even his loyal and supportive assistant director, Lev Indenbom, was trying to impress on Eisenstein the dangerous forces he was tempting by ignoring the entreaties and threats of studio and committee chiefs.[147]

As more people began returning to Moscow, Eisenstein was torn: he didn't want to remain in Alma Ata, but he hadn't finished filming. According to Nazvanov, Eisenstein was in no hurry to return production to the capital. The sets as well as all the workshops and crew were in Alma Ata, so moving the production would be a major, disruptive undertaking. In May, Indenbom was dispatched to Moscow to report on the situation there and solve some immediate production problems. He received permission to keep Moskvin as cinematographer until the entire film was finished and obtained enough American film stock to shoot one more major scene in Alma Ata. He also got final official approval to divide the film into three parts. However, Indenbom reported that all this was contingent on Eisenstein's finishing Part I by June 25, a point he reiterated in capital letters: "THIS IS MANDATORY." In the same letter, Indenbom described the general situation at the Mosfilm studios. Having suffered serious destruction from bombing, the studio structures were a wreck. The roof was full of holes; rain leaked all over three of the film stages and half the editing rooms, as well as the director's office and most of the hallways. No one there wanted Eisenstein or *Ivan the Terrible* back in Moscow, where supplies and space were so limited. Furthermore, Indenbom reported, "those who keep their noses carefully attuned to the way the wind is blowing, unanimously warn that all new films will have to be optimistic and show positive Russian people. And unfortunately, all your latest scenes show Ivan crawling on his knees."[148] As much as Eisenstein hated living in Alma Ata, he had good reasons to stay.

In late July1944, Eisenstein at last transferred the production of *Ivan the Terrible* back to Moscow.[149] Unlike many less privileged evacuees, Eisenstein was able to return to a job and a place to live.[150] Bolshakov ordered him to finish both Parts I and II by the end of that year and to provide a detailed plan for doing so. Given that Prokofiev had yet to record the score for all of Part I or even write the score for the second half of Part II (and had nowhere to live in Moscow); that several key scenes in Part II had not yet been shot and Eisenstein was still revising the director's scenario for those scenes; the physical state of the film studio and the need to construct new sets; and the massive social disruption caused by bombing, evacuation, and return, this outcome was highly unlikely.

The biggest obstacle was the soundtrack. Since January, Eisenstein had repeatedly postponed meeting with Prokofiev, who finally got tired of waiting and went to work on other projects at an artists' retreat in Ivanovo. To Eisenstein's urgent request that he return to Moscow to prevent even more delays, Prokofiev kindly but firmly refused to interrupt the work he was doing until late August.[151] At that point, Prokofiev finished and recorded the score for Part I, and Eisenstein edited it into the film.

In August, October, and November, Part I was given its official screenings before the Mosfilm Artistic Council and the Artistic Council of the Cinema Committee, which imposed successive rounds of direct censorship. Before this point, Eisenstein had received almost universally positive responses to the filmed sequences that he showed studio executives in Alma Ata or sent to Moscow. The same people who were furious at him for taking so long and spending so much money and generally flouting the rules that everyone else had to follow praised both the scenario and the film excerpts they saw. Eisenstein worried every time he sent off another batch of rushes, but each time the response was positive, even ecstatic.[152] One very telling experience had to give him confidence that his strategy was working. On August 29, 1944, he wrote to Moskvin (who was back in Leningrad) about Bolshakov's response to the rough cut of Part I, saying that his assessment was "highly favorable."

Eisenstein was especially happy that Bolshakov didn't cut the scene in the chapel where Kurbsky declared his love for Anastasia while Ivan was in the next room dying. A year earlier, Eisenstein told Nazvanov they would film the scene even though Bolshakov "categorically forbade" it. Most of the scenes with Foma and Erema, the comic representatives of the Russian people, however, did not survive: "Sacrific[ed] on the altar of the fatherland," Eisenstein wrote, "oh well—to hell with them [*khui s nimi*]!"[153] Eisenstein had chosen to film the scenes he wanted to film, the way he wanted to film them, defying both indirect and direct orders from the highest authority in the film industry. He lost some of these battles, but he won enough of them to make the gamble worthwhile. As Iurenev pointed out, Eisenstein responded to the criticism of Part I and recommendations for revisions with an attitude both "serene and businesslike."[154] And as Eisenstein himself wrote to Pera Atasheva: "The work is difficult, but in my opinion it will turn out to be interesting."[155]

On the night of December 25–26, after several rounds of screening and revisions, *Ivan the Terrible*, Part I, was screened for Stalin and his inner circle. On December 31, it was officially approved for release. Its public premiere in Moscow was on January 20, 1945, and within a few days, *Ivan the Terrible*, Part I, was being shown in other cities, on the front, and around the world. Critics throughout Europe and the United States found it to be a brilliant piece of film art, though at times too stylized and too cerebral. International reviewers generally either considered the character of Ivan to be incomprehensible or saw what they assumed to be Soviet political propaganda.[156]

As the Soviet people celebrated victory and then began the turbulent transition from war to peace, it took all of 1945 for Eisenstein to complete Part II. The approval and release of Part I (along with Bolshakov's unbending support throughout the censorship process and Stalin's approval) seems to have given Eisenstein some confidence in the success of his tactics. In 1945, he continued making Part II the way he wanted to make it, knowing that he would probably have to accept some changes during the approval process. His behavior in 1945, during the long completion of Part II, shows him intent on facing down every challenge to his pace, his budget, and especially his personnel choices. Even as pressure from the studio and the Cinema Committee was increasing, Eisenstein ignored deadline after deadline and worked at his own pace. A new production plan was developed in February 1945, and in March outdoor winter shooting took place at Kolomenskoe, then on the outskirts of Moscow, with horses and riders provided by the Red Army. But much more remained to be done. Approximately one-third of Part II still had to be filmed, including many key scenes: Efrosinia's Lullaby, Sigismund's Palace, The Refectory, and The Feast and Dance of the Oprichniki. Since actors and crew members had gone to work elsewhere during *Ivan's* delays, special requests had to be filed to enable each one of them to return to Moscow at the same time for filming the final scenes. In April, Indenbom had to submit requests to the studio to retrieve Moskvin from Tashkent (and later from Kazan), mak up artist Goriunov from Leningrad, and actors from Kiev, Alma Ata, and cities all over the empire. Special requisitions had to be made to reserve hotel rooms for the out-of-towners and to round up costumes and props from the Historical Museum, the Hermitage, and the Red Army. A month later, similar requests were sent to the studio along with revised scheduling as one person after another fell ill or continued their responsibilities elsewhere.[157]

The plan that Eisenstein signed called for filming to run from May 15 to July 29 with submission of the completed Part II on October 3, 1945. In fact, filming began forty days late, on June 26. By July 10, *Ivan* was fifty-one days behind schedule, primarily because Eisenstein's two indispensable collaborators, Moskvin and Prokofiev, were unavailable. Eisenstein had always known that he had Moskvin on borrowed time. Officially assigned to the Leningrad film studio, Moskvin was able to work on *Ivan* only because the two studios were combined in Alma Ata and Moskvin was temporarily free. Despite agreements with Bolshakov in 1944 and Lenfilm in 1945 that would allow Moskvin to shoot both Parts II and III of *Ivan the Terrible*, he went back to work after the war for the Leningrad directors with whom he had worked throughout his career, Grigory Kozintsev and Leonid Trauberg. Mosfilm tried to force Eisenstein to use a different cinematographer. Eduard Tisse was available, for example, but to the studio's great annoyance, Eisenstein refused to work with anyone except Moskvin.[158]

In the spring and summer of 1945, Prokofiev was too sick to compose. He had suffered a concussion in January and was still forbidden to work. In August, when the sets and shooting plan were in place to film The Dance of the Oprichniki, Eisenstein wrote to Prokofiev begging him to reconsider composing the music for The Dance. Despite serious concern for his health, Eisenstein wrote that postponing the score for several more months would be "catastrophic."[159] In September, when Prokofiev still hadn't recovered, he (and Mosfilm) asked the composer Gavriil Popov to substitute, but Eisenstein wouldn't hear of it. Apparently Popov wasn't keen to replace Prokofiev either. In October, Prokofiev was just well enough to write the score for what became two of the greatest scenes in the film.[160]

Threatening and increasingly angry memos from Bolshakov and Mikhail Kalatozov, who had become head of Mosfilm, made it clear that they considered Eisenstein to be acting extraordinarily irresponsibly. The director continued to respond with calm, if not arrogant, messages reminding his superiors that he was moving as quickly as he could given the complications of producing a film in postwar Moscow. In these negotiations with film chiefs over production troubles, he took the same determined stance he had taken when insisting on casting Faina Ranevskaia in the part of Efrosinia in 1943 and when he set up and shot as many takes as he wanted in Alma Ata in 1944. In 1945, he prevailed. Even after Moskvin and Prokofiev were back on board in the fall, material and other obstacles continued to impede completion, and Eisenstein continued to resist pressures to rush. A handwritten note in the Mosfilm archives from November 1945, when his bosses were furious at him, reads: "Very unfortunately, I am compelled to inform you that *no acceleration of any kind is possible* given the absence of screening rooms. Editing is held up by *half a day* as a result of the overuse of the only one at the studio."[161]

All these setbacks proved to be a windfall, if one can speak of war booty in such a positive way. The delays allowed Eisenstein to obtain some Agfacolor film stock, sent to Moscow by Soviet forces in occupied Germany. Long intrigued by the possibilities of film color, Eisenstein used the explosive Dance scene to experiment with color and created one of the most dazzling and memorable segments of the entire film.

But Eisenstein was still recording music and shooting scenes as his extended December deadline passed. The studio blamed "this absolutely abnormal situation" on Eisenstein's inflated sense of entitlement. Of the 184 working days since May 15, only 59 were taken up with rehearsing, shooting, editing, or recording music. A full 125 days were lost to illness or the unavailability of cast and crew, to Eisenstein's obstinate refusal to accept substitutes for Prokofiev and Moskvin, and to other brazen demands. The conductor Abram Stasevich "with Eisenstein's support" accepted only his chosen musicians, and Eisenstein refused to record the music without Boris Volsky or stage The Dance of the Oprichniki with anyone other than the choreographer Rostislav Zakharov. On top of all this, well into December, Eisenstein insisted on enlarging the set for Sigismund's Palace to accommodate the gigantic, painted "Gobelin" tapestries of two knights on horseback behind the king's throne, which had the domino effect of delaying another film that needed that studio.[162] On December 21, Kalatozov told Eisenstein that if he didn't turn in a finished cut of the film on January 5, 1946, he would ask the Cinema Committee to take *Ivan* away from him.[163] This time, Eisenstein complied, though it would again require round-the-clock work. The plan he submitted was feverish.[164] And it took until February 2, 1946, for Eisenstein to send the completed film to the Cinema Committee for approval.

No one at the time realized the toll all this work was taking on Eisenstein's health. Throughout 1945, he was also still writing as well as teaching. He was devoted to his students, as one of them noted in his memoir. In the harsh post-war months, as Stanislas Rostotsky recalled, Eisenstein always knew which students lacked food or a warm coat and took the time to use his position to find them what they needed.[165] During the last months of the year, the delays and the pressure from above were extraordinarily stressful, and when there was work, the pace was frenetic. The very night that Eisenstein submitted the finished Part II—February 6, 1946—he went to a celebration for the Stalin Prizes just recently announced. While dancing at the party, he suffered the heart attack that landed him in the hospital and from which he barely recovered.

The next day he received a congratulatory note from the studio:

Dear Sergei Mikhailovich!

The Directorate of the Mosfilm Studio has viewed Part II of *Ivan the Terrible*. Congratulations on the outstanding work. This film is an enormous achievement of Soviet film art and above all of your directorial work. At the first opportunity we will relate our elation in more detail to you.

Congratulations on finishing the film!

We wish you the speediest recovery.

With your permission we wish to show the film to the Artistic Council of the Cinema Committee in order to speed its final approval (all the more so, since the situation is extremely unique and opportune).

We shake your hand.

Kalatozov
Alexandrov

Contrary to this cheery note written to the very sick director, ministry and studio officials were already worried about the fate of *Ivan*, Part II.[166] I come back to the official reception of *Ivan the Terrible*, Parts I and II, below, but on February 2, 1946, the production of *Ivan* came to an end. The film we have today is the same film in the same form as when Eisenstein submitted it. Almost: from his hospital bed, Eisenstein instructed Moskvin to correct the color print of the color scenes in Part II, which he completed by February 14.[167] After that, Eisenstein did no more work on Part II, and he did not finish shooting Part III. For two months he wasn't even allowed to sit up. He spent most of 1946 recovering his health and writing his memoirs. He spent 1947 and the early part of 1948 writing a number of theoretical works, many of which included important analyses of *Ivan the Terrible*. He was at work on an article about the tragic theme in *Ivan* on the night of February 10–11, 1948, when he suffered another heart attack, this one fatal.[168] Eisenstein was barely fifty years old when he died.

The Potholed Path

Eisenstein and Moskvin jokingly referred to their work on *Ivan* as "stumbling down potholed paths of evil,"[169] and the day-to-day production record shows just how hard it was. Let's be clear: making *Ivan the Terrible* in Alma Ata was not as hard as survival in a frozen Gulag labor camp or in a Belarusian village under Nazi occupation. But in the sideshow to the war, in the world of art and politics where *Ivan the Terrible* was made and where we usually judge such work, making a film as ambitious and challenging as *Ivan the Terrible* incurred serious obstacles and cost its makers. Compromises could have been made, and Eisenstein made some. He wrote sanitized articles about Stalin's "genius" and produced a work that he expected to earn a Stalin Prize. But he was constitutionally incapable of simply making a film that would please the ruler. *Ivan the Terrible* is an edifice that deceived enough viewers—the right viewers at the time—but Eisenstein laced the mortar that held its bricks together with his own blood and ashes like the devious St. Paul builder he admired in 1941. From the beginning and throughout the process, in the face of heavy pressure from film and political authorities, Eisenstein chose to write, cast, shoot, score, and edit the film he envisioned. In February 1942, he offered to make a slew of narrative concessions and then immediately turned around and found ways to make each character and each scene more complicated, sinister, and critical. At the end of 1945, he rushed to finish Part II under unavoidable threats and turned in a film that he considered not quite finished. The result is a work that would have been unthinkable and impossible to make in the years that preceded or followed. Eisenstein both submitted to and defied the institutional practices of Stalinist Socialist Realism.

Eisenstein's many encounters with politically motivated criticism and the subsequent required self-criticism shaped the strategy he would use to complete *Ivan*, knowing all along that missteps could be perilous, either to himself or to his film. He chose an approach to the subject, and although he used the repeated periods of wartime delays to refine and deepen his conception of Ivan, he stuck with his initial approach from beginning to end. Part II is not more challenging or radical than Part I: there was no changing of horses in midstream. He took calculated chances and then chose when to bend and when to resist. He clearly wanted to play cat and mouse with the masters of the game, even as the game often tormented him and knowing that he would lose a few rounds. The making of *Ivan the Terrible* shows us how Eisenstein worked when he thought he had the freedom to work as he liked. He followed the advice he gave his friend Shtraukh in 1931 almost to the letter: "One must apply pressure, pull strings, debase oneself, *be diplomatic, crafty, cunning, and again press.*" The production history shows us what kind of film Eisenstein thought he could make and the methods one artist used to test the limits of the Stalinist systems of patronage and cultural production. When *Ivan*, Part I, won the Stalin Prize, Mikhail Kuznetsov called Eisenstein on the telephone to say, "Hooray, Sergei Mikhailovich, our cause was right!" and Eisenstein replied, in a voice Kuznetsov remembered as strangely serene and sad: "No, Misha, our cause was left, but by chance it appeared to be right."[170]

CHAPTER 2

Shifts in Time

Ivan *as History*

Academic historians tend to be suspicious of historical films, and for good reason. Filmmakers don't share historians' concerns with evidence, and they have different goals as well as different audiences. *Ivan the Terrible* will never be mistaken for a historian's rendering of the past, but Eisenstein's immersion in the primary and secondary sources on Ivan's Muscovy and his repeated insistence that his portrait of Ivan was based on historical documents indicate an approach that is far from cavalier. Film scholars have long known that Eisenstein read a substantial number of historical sources to prepare for making *Ivan the Terrible*, but no one has taken his historical preparation seriously enough to ask what he did with this material, how it shaped his understanding of Ivan IV and the Russian past, or how it shaped his ideas about artistic production and political reality in the Soviet present.[1]

Eisenstein did more than skim the main books in the field. He read a sizable number of the major works on Ivan and sixteenth-century Muscovy and many minor or specialized ones as well. He took detailed notes and linked what he read with works on psychology, ethnography, and literature to compose his portrait of the tsar and develop his approach to history. His notes on sources, his attempt to accompany the publication of his screenplay with his annotated Historical Commentary, and the choices that we ultimately see in his scenario and film show an artist and thinker struggling to understand a complex actor and controversial events in explicitly historical—and contemporary—context. When Eisenstein decided not to make another simplistic political parable like *Alexander Nevsky*, the necessity of telling Ivan's story over time intrigued him and led him to contemplate patterns of individual evolution in the context of social and historical development. As he began to read the history, he discovered that Ivan's biography offered attractive possibilities for experimenting with ideas on the art and psychology of filmmaking and on the nature of change over time that already interested him. Although he had made historical films before, his work on *Ivan the Terrible* marked the first time that he elaborated his ideas about how societies and individuals changed over time, then integrated those ideas into his filmmaking and writing. As Leonid Kozlov once said, "*Ivan the Terrible* isn't a film *about* history, it's a *theory of* history."[2] Eisenstein had made historical films before, and he wrote detailed notes for a history of cinema later, but it was here, while writing the scenario and preparing to shoot *Ivan*, that he fashioned his "theory of history."[3]

But what kind of historian was he? Those few studies that have addressed the historical content of his films have paid little attention to Eisenstein's own writing about history. James Goodwin saw Eisenstein as a profoundly historical director, but lack of access to archives limited him to enumerating *Ivan's* distortions of the historical record and studying the ways those distortions shaped the film's political narrative. Two recent studies that examine Eisenstein's historicism imagine him as a kind of postmodern skeptic of historical narrative. Evgeny Dobrenko proceeds from the position that historical representations are constructed to suppress lived experience and legitimize authority but, in the case of Eisenstein, to do precisely the opposite. Kevin Platt claims that *Ivan the Terrible* neither supports nor subverts a Stalinist reading of history but questions our ability to understand the meaning of history and our own place in it, because Eisenstein saw historical meaning as an entirely mutable construct.[4]

The notes Eisenstein wrote about history in connection with *Ivan* and the historical thinking that pervades his book *Method*, especially the key chapter titled "Shifts in Time," show that he assumed the existence of a "literal past" and the value of historical sources for understanding the past. He wanted to construct a "truthful" depiction of the tsar's life based on those sources.[5] Eisenstein did see meaning—the meaning of history and of anything else—as mutable and socially and culturally constructed, but he incorporated those contingencies into his historical thinking by taking seriously the different ways people read sources in different contexts and putting them in dialogue with each other. One of his core beliefs was the continued relevance of experiences and ideas from the past for constructing meaning in the present. His approach to history was to find a way to plausibly explain the course of events and the significance of those events to contemporary viewers by depicting the threads that connected Ivan with the present. Far from questioning historical narrative, one of his main goals in reading history was to discover what Russians call *zakonomernost'*—the regular patterns or laws that determine change over time and, among other things, explain the persistent role constructions of the past play in constructions of the present.

When *Ivan the Terrible* was commissioned, it was one of a number of projects in a state-sponsored campaign to rehabilitate individual tsarist rulers (rejecting the collective, mass heroes of early Soviet historiography and culture) and to use Russian history to bolster the legitimacy of the Soviet state and Stalinist rule. Under Stalin's direct guidance, with Zhdanov's assistance, historians in the late 1930s developed a new, official interpretation of the reign of Ivan IV.[6] Stalinist historiography promoted Ivan as the heroic founder of Russia's modern state and its establishment of one-man rule (*edinoderzhavie*), which was "progressive for its time." Initially, Soviet historians minimized the tsar's most violent excesses, carried out during the period known as the *oprichnina* (1565–1572), when Ivan formed a personal army, the oprichniki, and unleashed a campaign of mass violence. In the 1940s, however, even this legendary, horrific episode was justified as necessary for defeating the boyars, the aristocrats who obstructed Russia's national destiny by clinging to the power and wealth they possessed as a feudal elite.[7] All the art works commissioned to portray Ivan the Terrible were expected to conform to this historiography, and all the artists involved struggled with their commissions. Eisenstein alone produced a work of enduring artistic value.

The director, however, wasn't interested in parroting Stalinist historiography or justifying terror. He didn't see Ivan as a ruler without merit.[8] Instead he aimed to discover, and then depict, the ways that historical patterns produced a ruler who could conceive of using bloody retribution as a basis for political power and legitimacy in the sixteenth century and again in the twentieth. Eisenstein believed that sociohistorical change shared structural and semantic patterns with the process of change in individual lives, and he came to believe that works of art only acquired enduring appeal if they were properly inscribed with those same structures of social and individual change over time. He argued in *Method* that in order to make a historical film meaningful to a modern audience, the film must use the shared structures of human perception and historical change that link people in the present with people in the past, while at the same time acknowledging change. A historical film should tap into both archetypal processes and the consequences of changing social and cultural beliefs. *Ivan the Terrible* poses questions about the ways that the past, both individual and collective, continues to play a role in the present. Every "progressive" step that Ivan takes toward the founding of the modern Russian state is linked with the violent conflicts of his own past, raising questions about his mission and his motives, and ultimately undermining his potential for success. Reading history in preparation for making *Ivan the Terrible* led Eisenstein to construct the film as a history of a potentially progressive movement that could neither eradicate the conflicts of the past nor prevent people from reenacting the most savage chapters of their own individual and collective histories.

Eisenstein also had a strategic reason for his avid attention to history. During the historiographical revisions of the 1930s, Stalin made it known that he considered himself a historical expert. He took a personal interest in writing new histories, often line-editing drafts of texts important to him like the new history of the Communist Party that he commissioned.[9] Eisenstein's notes repeat phrases associated with official state historical views (Ivan as a "progressive hero," his policies as "progressive for his time," for example), which has made some previous scholars assume that he shared those official views.[10] Given how far Eisenstein's historical thinking departs from the official historiography, it is more likely that when Zhdanov presented Eisenstein with the commission, he reminded the director of Stalin's expertise and gave him the outline of the historical interpretation that they had been pressing historians to adopt. Eisenstein used regular references to historical accuracy as a shield to protect his own vision of Ivan and the Russian past and went out of his way in public statements to claim that his portrait of Ivan was historically accurate. A closer look at the Historical Commentary that Eisenstein wanted to publish as an addendum to the scenario for *Ivan* supports this reading.

The Historical Commentary is a list of 272 excerpts from the scenario, each annotated with its specific historical sources.[11] The extensive and diverse list of sources includes such primary documents as sixteenth-century chronicles and foreigners' accounts of life in Muscovy during Ivan's reign, and secondary sources include, for example, modern historians' studies of the period and the works of Marx and Engels.

At the very least, Eisenstein's insistence on publishing the commentary with the scenario indicates a desire to show that he did his homework, and did it thoroughly, echoing his insistence all along, to Bolshakov and in print, that his approach to Ivan the Terrible was historically accurate. No matter how peculiar his portrait of Ivan might seem in the scenario and in the film, these notes were evidence that his Ivan was based on historical documents and was supported by a wide range of historians.

Significantly, as Table 2.1 shows, Eisenstein associated lines in the script with primary sources far more often than with the secondary historical works

Table 2.1   Historical Commentary: Primary and Secondary Sources

Type of Source	Primary				Secondary	
	Chronicles	Other Primary	Foreign Author	Songs/ Folklore	19th- Century	20th- Century
No. sources cited	14	23	15	8	18	18
No. excerpts from scenario	59	78	55	15	35	30

Compiled by Rebecca Johnston from "Istoricheskii kommentarii k fil'mu 'Ivan Groznyi,'" *KZ*, no. 38 (1998): 173–245.

written in the nineteenth and twentieth centuries, most of which had been criticized by Stalin or revised by official Stalinist historians. In an assessment of the Commentary from the 1970s, M. I. Andronikova suggested that the scenario offered a view of the tsar that was subjective and controversial, but the Historical Commentary skewed that view in a positive direction by placing Ivan alongside other important rulers, like Peter the Great.[12] Eisenstein wrote the draft of an introduction to the Historical Commentary that also supports this reading. That text compared his own *Ivan* with the image of the tsar in the popular songs and stories published in the nineteenth century by the literary critic Vissarion Belinsky and others. Unlike the Ivan in his film, Eisenstein pointed out, theirs was a fairytale figure—fantastic and larger than life—based on tall tales rather than historical documents. But, he conceded, sometimes one had to "play with the facts," and therefore he was publishing his sources to show the factual basis of the film overall.[13] This has to be seen as another anti-mythmaking gesture on his part.

Most important, though, is that his insistence on historical documentation corresponded with Stalin's preferences. In 1946, when Stalin publicly criticized *Ivan the Terrible*, Part II, along with other films made during the war, he emphasized both the necessity of historical accuracy and the failure of directors to research their films properly. Stalin's claim to historical expertise was regularly conveyed to the historians rewriting history on his command, so it is quite possible that Eisenstein knew that providing proof of historical research and accuracy would help protect his film with the critic who counted the most. In a scribbled note attached to his draft introduction he wrote that the Historical Commentary should "answer all questions that might arise from reading the scenario."[14] Ultimately, it is hard to know exactly how Eisenstein balanced pressure from above and his own interest in history, but his notebooks and his publications show that history written by historians and history written into great works of art mattered to Eisenstein for both creative and strategic reasons.

Today, the issue at stake is not the historical accuracy of Eisenstein's portrait of Ivan, but the concept of history inscribed in the filmmaker's depiction of sixteenth-century Muscovy and the ways that historical thinking framed his own understanding of Ivan as a ruler, as well as the political and cultural uses of Ivan's portrait in Stalinist culture. As a result, and despite the film's almost comically egregious historical distortions, Eisenstein's serious and nuanced approach to history can help us understand the film's discourses on power and the ways tyranny and terror could be conceived in the Soviet Union in the 1940s. *Ivan the Terrible* gives us a rare Stalinist-era meditation on the cycles of violence and despotism in Russian history that should be of interest to all modern viewers. What follows is not intended to be a comprehensive survey of Eisenstein's treatment of historical events and characters. Rather my goal is to explain Eisenstein's uses of history in *Ivan the Terrible* and the role history played in his thinking about Ivan and the overall composition of the film.

Reading History

First of all, *what* did Eisenstein read? The answer is: he read a lot. The production notebooks contain detailed notes on dozens of historical works. Lev Indenbom helped with the initial research, piling up 130 archival sheets of notes, heavily marked with Eisenstein's colored pencil.[15]

Their combined reading list includes all the major histories, travelers' accounts, and published documents available in Moscow in 1941 in the months preceding the Nazi invasion. These included popular and scholarly histories, published Muscovite documents and chronicles, foreigners' accounts, and academic articles on a variety of specialized topics. Eisenstein took his most extensive notes on the first books he read in early 1941 and on those he came back to the following year, during that intense period of work in the winter and spring of 1942. The books he recorded in most detail include the German mercenary Heinrich von Staden's chilling contemporary report on his life as one of Ivan's oprichniki, Ivan's correspondence with his treasonous general Andrei Kurbsky, Kurbsky's history of Ivan's reign, two classic nineteenth-century histories by Sergei Soloviev and Vasily Kliuchevsky, the canonical Stalinist work Robert Vipper's *Ivan the Terrible*—as well as Alexander Pypin's two-volume *History of Russian Literature* and Igor Grabar's monumental anthology on Russian visual arts, both published in the early twentieth century.[16] When a specific detail or topic piqued his curiosity, Eisenstein followed up on Indenbom's summaries of the works of other major nineteenth- and twentieth-century historians—including Nikolai Karamzin, Sergei Platonov, and M. N. Pokrovsky—as well as Marx, Engels, Lenin, and Plekhanov. He also read

FIGURE 2.1   Lev Indenbom. RGALI, 1923/1/2950/1. Used with permission.

and took notes on works about the folklore, folk songs, and popular memory of Ivan and on West European history and culture, with special attention to the reign of Elizabeth I and the plays of Shakespeare and his contemporaries. Then, in addition to these, he read specialized literature on such topics as Muscovite sacred painting, theater history, liturgical drama, military weaponry, early modern engineering, and Orthodox ritual.

Second, *how* did he read? Always self-conscious about his working practices, Eisenstein described his evolving historical method in numerous notes. Early in the project, he scribbled "for me" next to a quotation from Vipper's history of Ivan about how researchers are most responsive to sources that reinforce their own preconceived ideas.[17] Months later, in October 1941, when he was revising the first draft of the scenario, he wrote that "the **most** trustworthy creative principle" was to begin by developing a feel for the characters and events and only then go back to the documents to see if the original intuition was historically possible.[18] He would note with satisfaction the many instances when his "intuition" about an image or a character was later confirmed by documents.[19] But he took equal satisfaction when his treatment seemed psychologically trustworthy or historically plausible even when some of their details were contradicted by the documents.[20] Once Eisenstein developed his basic images of Ivan, Ivan's circle, and the consequences of their actions, he continued reading for material to support those ideas and figure out how to depict them on screen. He was willing to abandon the documentary evidence when it served his purposes, but he continued to read sources to flesh out and verify his characterizations well into production.

Eisenstein gave a more sustained explanation of the principles underlying his thoughts about history in 1940 at the annual industry conference on "The Problems of Historical and Historical-Revolutionary Film," just a few months before he began work on *Ivan*.[21] The first priorities of the historical film, he explained, ought to be historical truth and contemporary significance. The filmmaker should depict historical events and characters, not as "solitary fact[s]" isolated from the present in some distant past but as a contemporary film, with "individual characters elevated to major historical generalization."[22] The concept of "historical generalization" is the historical equivalent of the generalizable image, so central to Eisenstein's overall thinking and aesthetics during this period and explored at length in the essays on montage that he wrote in the late 1930s.[23] He distinguished his own use of montage from that of D. W. Griffith, the American montage pioneer, for its ability to evoke more than the heightened drama and emotion found in Griffith's works. The purpose of Soviet montage, and of historical film as well, was to produce a new, broader and deeper understanding of the subject that should be true to life, even if some of its details were fictional.[24] The generalizable message of *Battleship Potemkin*, he went on to say, was the essential victory of the Russian people in uniting with the sailors to fight against tsarist tyranny. Historical fact may show that the mutiny was crushed almost immediately, but if the overall generalization that arises from the depiction—popular unity against the tsar—is essentially correct, the filmmaker can skew the short-term outcome of the mutiny. In composing his portrait of Ivan the Terrible, Eisenstein would translate these principles into practice by creating a generalizable image of the tsar's evolution from young, energetic, revolutionary leader to vengeful, murderous tyrant in a way that was intended to resonate with contemporary audiences. He sought to balance documentary accuracy with psychological accuracy in creating a general, truth-ful idea. The generalizable idea is sometimes described as "abstract," but it is important to note that Eisenstein didn't think the generalizable idea could res-onate with audiences unless it was firmly grounded in the historical record, in the local context, in real, everyday experience and psychology. In discussing Ivan's attempt to win back Filipp's friendship despite their political differences, Eisenstein wrote that the scene may not have occurred exactly as he depicted it, but by drawing on Ivan's specific memories of childhood "it is psychologi-cally truthful . . . not through actual fact but through the emotional memory of analogous conditions in another age and other objective circumstances."[25]

Third, and most important: how did reading about the historical Ivan the Terrible contribute to Eisenstein's own portrait of Ivan and history of the events of the period? More specifically, how did reading history shape Eisen-stein's interpretation of Ivan's reign and his development as a ruler? And how did Eisenstein join that reading with his other interests to create a new general-izable image and a "theory of history" that would resonate with contemporary viewers? When Eisenstein began research in January 1941, he found that his reading spurred curiosity about his own autobiography and the ways that indi-vidual lives evolve. It led him back to books on cultural evolution and psychol-ogy that he had read in the 1920s and 1930s, in particular while living in Mexico and working on his film about Mexican cultural history, when he first began thinking seriously about patterns in history.[26] He settled on the film's specific characters, scenes, and themes remarkably quickly during the spring of 1941. Then, during the prolonged delays in production, Eisenstein continued read-ing and deepening his ideas. It was during this period, from his evacuation to Alma Ata in October 1941 until production began in April 1943, that he devel-oped his understanding of history by exploring the correspondences among his theoretical, aesthetic, cultural, biographical, and historical ideas. Bringing these disparate sources together created a portrait of Ivan the Terrible as he developed as an individual and as a historical actor, and as a figure from the past who resonates with people in the present. That dynamic generalizable image contains factual distortions but succeeds in showing remarkable insight into the roots of violence, the results of revolutionary change, the evolution of the authoritarian personality, and the cyclical consequences of one-man rule.

From Intuition to Books: The Political Is Personal

Since Eisenstein proceeded from preconceptions to the sources to the depicted image, we can discern the shape of his historical thinking by identifying his earliest thoughts and tracking his next steps through his reading. We have three main sources for Eisenstein's initial ideas about Ivan: his reading notes, his first outlines, and the essay discussed earlier: "A Few Words about My Drawings." The first images from "A Few Words" are milestones in Eisenstein's understanding of Ivan's personal history. As discussed previously, at the end of Ivan's life, after founding the Great Russian State, the tsar is filled with equal parts pride at his accomplishment and remorse over the methods he used. The origins of that pride and remorse were to be found in his response to childhood traumas he suffered at the hands of the boyars. He asserted his power as tsar, first over the boyars and then over Russia's national enemies, and he took revenge on those who had humiliated him and exploited Russia in its weakened state. These first images linked key historical events with key psychological moments in Ivan's life. "A Few Words about My Drawings," together with Eisenstein's published articles, show his determination to look beyond myth and stereotype to find a plausible psychology for Ivan. His earliest notes and outlines help us understand the ways he proceeded from these early images and crude understanding of the generalizable expressed in 1940s to a more elaborate "theory of history."

Eisenstein's first notes show that Ivan's politics were personal and the past is never past. He dated his first outline (written in English) January 21, 1941, the same day as the Bolshoi event that brought him the vision of the boyars murdering Ivan's mother.

Possibly start with frightened boy
Shadows running passed him
Door opens
Out rushes
Queen Helen Glinskaya
Dying "poisoned"
Beware of poison
Dies
Rushes after her.
Queen's lover
And is stabbed
Here before his eyes
Explaining who and why.

Slightly more grown up
Scene with boyars
In bed room
Fight of groups
Shuisky

Friendship with Kurbsky
Marriage
  Happiness
    Kazan
Friendship with Kurbsky
  Something very effective

Kazan gives him basis for views
Starting his plans
Break with K
Oprichnina
  Bishop
    Phillippe
Novgorod
Livonia[27]

I have quoted this in full (even if the particular events are unfamiliar to many readers)[28] to convey Eisenstein's emphasis on personal and emotional issues. But it is also important to observe that Eisenstein had the narrative arc of the entire screenplay, from childhood trauma to adult massacre and triumph, fully worked out only a week after meeting with Zhdanov. The next outline, dated January 26, was similar if a bit more balanced (and in Russian):

I.   Childhood
       Poisoning of Glinskaia
       Fights with Boyars
       Andrei Shuiskii
       Friendship with Kurbsky

II. Marriage (500 virgins) Ivan-tsar
       Kazan
       Fake death

III. Kurbsky's Betrayal (1564)
       Oprichnina
       Filipp (recalled) + 1568

IV. Novgorod (confessor 1570)
       Livonia (Kurbsky tragique)

V.   The Sea. 1576.[29]

Except for deleting the "500 virgins,"[30] and adding scenes that would dramatize the developments hinted at here, these are the signposts that Eisenstein would use to portray Ivan's life story. Iurenev claims that these initial thoughts demonstrated the director's conception of Ivan as "striving for one-man rule, which was undoubtedly progressive for that time, and opposed to the obsolete feudal will of the boyars."[31] Iurenev's characterization aligns precisely with the official historical narrative, but it is hard to discern in these sketchy outlines from the notebooks or in the images Eisenstein discussed in "A Few Words." At the other end of the interpretive spectrum, Kozlov found that these early ideas showed "the tragedy of autocracy" and "the dreadful price paid for progress," a portrait of Ivan that already exceeds the commission's parameters.[32] Eisenstein's humanization of Ivan linked the autocrat's personal tragedy with fundamental human attributes, on one hand, and the price everyone in the country would have to pay for Ivan's ambition and methods, on the other. The full text that Iurenev only partially quoted turns out to include a sardonic comment on writing to prescription, though it requires some interpretation of Eisenstein's cryptic, multilingual note:

Apparently
The path is as follows . . . ?
A strong state internally is the foundation for a strong state internationally.
Therefore, must end with Livonia—the reaching of the sea.[33]

Rather than the statement of purpose Iurenev suggests, I read this as Eisenstein trying to supply events to conform to a narrative imposed from without. The passive voice, the ellipsis and question mark, and the underlined prescription lack the characteristic style of Eisenstein's other notes on sources or on developing plot and character. And as the historian Isabel de Madariaga points out, there is no evidence of Ivan's obsessive drive to the sea in the sources.[34] I believe that Eisenstein was figuring out here how to abide by the commission's strictures while simultaneously distancing himself from its message. But in order to accomplish this, to humanize Ivan and understand him without praising or justifying his actions, Eisenstein must conglomerate characters, misconstrue some events, and leave others out altogether. The ending with a victory over Livonia is a case in point. The war that Ivan fought in Livonia, as Eisenstein well knew, ended in defeat for Russia; it took another century and a half before Peter the Great would secure the country's hold on the Baltic Sea.[35] A few weeks later, he noted: "Very important, Livonia as a screen [*Livonia kak zaslon*]."[36] This note suggests that Eisenstein ended his narrative with the victory not to justify the harsh measures Ivan has taken against internal enemies but to question that justification.

Similarly, Eisenstein chose characters that he could use to show the tsar's personal inner divisions and gave them attributes associated with multiple historical figures. For example, Eisenstein quickly gravitated in his notes toward two historical priests, Pimen and Filipp, who rose to become metropolitans and were associated with conspiracy, betrayal, and execution. These two were less significant historically than Metropolitan Makarii or the priest Sylvester, who were active during the more benign period of Ivan's reign, before the oprichnina, and were believed to have had some moral influence on the tsar. Early on in his reading Eisenstein discovered that Filipp was one of the most vocal critics of Ivan's savagery during the oprichnina and that both Filipp and Pimen were linked to the opposition that arose in Novgorod.[37] Stalinist historiography defended Ivan's bloody devastation of Novgorod as an effort to protect the newly centralized state from a conspiracy of boyar opposition to Ivan, allowing Eisenstein to neatly construct a narrative that linked boyar perfidy with clerical treason.[38] But Filipp is also given some attributes associated with Sylvester, who, evidence shows, made every effort to persuade Ivan to abandon his cruel ways.[39] And in order to intensify the sting of their betrayal of Ivan, he made both the oppositional Filipp and the treasonous Andrei Kurbsky Ivan's childhood friends.[40]

The choice of these particular characters also shows that Eisenstein decided immediately to focus on Ivan during the period of the oprichnina. The absence of any reference in the film to the reform program of the 1550s (despite the brief gesture at inclusion in February 1942) is important. If Eisenstein wanted to portray Ivan as a "wise and just" tsar, why not include Ivan's most rational and progressive reforms (even if Stalinist historians had by then dropped the reform period as evidence of Ivan's wisdom)? Nonetheless, Eisenstein's Ivan never descends into "madness." Though he acts with melodramatic vehemence at times and is seized by debilitating doubts, his cunning never abandons him.[41] I can only speculate here, but insanity was not in the Kremlin's rulebook on Ivan, which makes sense if the goal were to justify, rather than just excuse, state terror. But Eisenstein didn't need it either: to make Ivan insane would make any other explanations—historical, psychological, or political—superfluous.

Eisenstein quickly limited the characters he would use to dramatize Ivan's life to a small circle of people: Ivan's first wife, Anastasia; his loyal servitor Maliuta Skuratov; the friend and traitor Andrei Kurbsky; the other friend and clerical opponent Filipp, eventually metropolitan of Moscow; the enemy, Metropolitan Pimen from Novgorod; Efrosinia and Vladimir Staritsky, Ivan's

aunt and cousin and his main rivals for power; and the founder of the oprichnina, Aleksei Basmanov, and his son Fedor. Each of these figures is associated
directly with the oprichnina and the mass murder it spawned, even Anastasia, whose murder was said by some historians to be the event that triggered
Ivan's paranoia and descent into violence and despotism. Important people
from the more positive decades of Ivan's reign, such as his advisers Aleksei
Adashev and Sylvester, are hardly mentioned in the notes, and people from
later in the tsar's life after the oprichnina was dissolved, as well as the son
he killed in a fit of rage and the rest of his wives quickly drop out of Eisenstein's sight. One can reasonably conclude from this that the oprichnina was
at the center of Eisenstein's conception from the beginning; that he chose to
examine Ivan primarily as a ruler who subjected his friends and allies, his own
servitors, and his country to a devastating campaign of mayhem and violence.

Even the narrative about defeating Russia's western enemies and reaching
the Baltic Sea, which played a larger role in the literary scenario than in the
film, could be partially jettisoned because of its lack of connection to the terror.[42] As discussed above, Eisenstein took notes about the wars in Kazan and
Livonia with some interest, saying at one point that everyone "must be sea-
frenzied through the whole film."[43] But this scene disappears, and not only
because Part III was unfinished. The theme of "sea-frenzy" was to have been
set up by a lullaby about the sea that Ivan's nanny sings to him as a child. The
scene was shot, and the music was commissioned. Prokofiev composed two
versions of it, and Eisenstein singled out "Ocean Sea, Deep Blue Sea" as an
example of Prokofiev's talent for writing musical montage.[44] But if, as I am
suggesting, Eisenstein was primarily interested in explaining Ivan as the ruler
of oprichnina and mass terror, then the role of the "Ocean Sea, Deep Blue
Sea" as an indication of childhood aspiration and a political justification for
Ivan's violence could be filled by other, more sinister things. When Eisenstein
reinserted The Prologue into Part II as a flashback, he chose not to include
the lullaby. Its absence removes the one note of warm feeling from Ivan's
unhappy childhood. The effect of the cut was to remove the national security
justification for Ivan's actions, to sharpen the focus on Ivan's suffering and
vulnerability in the childhood flashback scenes, and to emphasize his resulting
desire for revenge, considerably darkening the film.

The notebooks show that Eisenstein devised the main narrative soon after
beginning to read the history. The first books he read included a turn-of-the-
century popular history of Ivan's reign by Kazimir Valishevsky (Kazimierz
Waliszewski) and Sergei Soloviev's *History of Russia since Ancient Times*.[45] We
don't know much about Valishevsky's impact, but Soloviev was a major source.
Writing in the mid-nineteenth century, the heyday of European nation-state

formation, Soloviev was the first historian to offer a positive assessment of Ivan's efforts to establish central state power. As Indenbom summarized Soloviev's argument for Eisenstein, "he considered Ivan's era to be the period of the definitive triumph of the state over the clan."[46] The liberal Soloviev was no apologist for Ivan, however. He argued that Ivan should have carried out his statist political reforms with less turmoil and cruelty, but that his traumatic childhood made him incapable of controlling his instinct for violence.[47] S. F. Platonov, whose work appears briefly in Eisenstein's notebooks and Indenbom's notes, continued this line of argument, emphasizing the class nature of the oprichnina, as Ivan sought to destroy the power of the feudal elite with the support of the common people.[48] This argument is also the basis for the official Stalinist line, although with less emphasis on the class conflict and a less positive view of Ivan's violent state-building methods. Eisenstein publicly rejected the works of prerevolutionary liberal historians in his 1942 article, but in fact he found the structure and themes that he wanted in their work, rather than in the Soviet historiography. With the exception of Vipper's biography, Soviet historians appear rarely in his notes, and at one point he mentioned that he read Vipper only after his major decisions were made: "*Post*—confirmation of intuitive decisions."[49]

Soloviev provided an overarching political explanation for the two elements of the Kremlin-required narrative: state building and the oprichnina. But he also pointed to Ivan's childhood as a psychological explanation for his behavior, which Eisenstein found a congenial starting point. Ivan's correspondence with Kurbsky reinforced the impression that his painful youth determined his later behavior. In his first letter to Ivan, Kurbsky attacked the tsar's cruelty and tyranny, in part to explain his own defection. Ivan's response to this letter was an eighty-five-page rant rejecting Kurbsky's charges and enumerating the evils done to him, beginning in his traumatic childhood. Ivan bitterly denounced the boyars who usurped his power when he was too young to fight back. Many other historians, drawing from the correspondence and the chronicles of the period, have treated Ivan's childhood as a critical, formative chapter in his life and have relied on these descriptions of Ivan's childhood to explain his personality, his ideology, and his later behavior.[50]

These outlines and notes show an emphasis on formative emotional experience, adult conflict, and violence, followed by aged victory and hollow validation. Within days after deciding which events and characters to include, Eisenstein's reading notes and ruminative entries became more detailed and began to consider characters' psychology, motivations, and ways to use the historical evidence to explain Ivan's development. Historical films typically explore personal experiences to which historians have little access, and

Eisenstein saw his project in such terms. But these notes make it clear that for Eisenstein the political is a direct result of personal experience (and he could base this view on documents and historians' uses of these documents). In order to "explain" and humanize Ivan, Eisenstein wrote that the audience would have to see him as the victim of cruelty, first in childhood, and later in the conflicts he faced as the ruler: *"each of the first scenes form him: each his action as RE-action to something done to him by others."*[51] This comment follows a sketch of The Prologue that lists the personal issues that culminated in a key political move.

1. *poisoned mothers*
2. *patterns of tsar caracter*
   Vorontsoff's picture of his grandfather
3. *hateful behavior of boyars towards his friend Vorontsoff, ruthlessness*
4. *Double-crossing attitude of boyars and reception of ambassadors*
5. *Foretaste of <u>forever</u> in this scene*
6. *New attitude towards boyars as Andrew Shuisky killed as <u>personal</u> incident*
7. *Attack upon his life as contre-coup, and his reaction towards whole bulk of friends and family of Andrew's as <u>political</u> measure and expropriation*
8. *caracter formed: decision of <u>absolutism in form of tsar</u> (he is but seventeen!)*[52]

Eisenstein was taking note here of Ivan's suffering at the hands of the boyars, who poisoned his mother, trampled on his parents' reputation, nearly beat his friend Vorontsov to death, and took advantage of his youthful inability to exert his power as grand prince to benefit themselves. Ivan's response was revenge. Eisenstein's Ivan marks his first assertion of power by having a leading boyar, Andrei Shuisky, seized and killed. Eisenstein's primary explanation for Ivan's insistence on absolute power, power *over* the boyars, is revenge, "a *personal* incident." Eisenstein decided that revenge, "increasing in scope and cruelty," would continue to motivate Ivan (and everyone else) throughout the rest of the film.[53] This raises one of the fundamental sets of questions Eisenstein asks us to consider. If Ivan's behavior was entirely determined by harm done to him, was he responsible for his actions? What makes people do what they do? What role do childhood trauma, desire for revenge, and the web of personal relationships play in forging a ruler's reign of sadistic violence? In order to answer these questions and figure out how to dramatize them, Eisenstein developed the connections between the personal and the political in Ivan and in all the characters around the tsar. He would look more deeply into the literature on politics and violence, and he would return to two favorite topics, patricide myths and the Elizabethan revenge drama, to deepen his understanding of the relationship between the personal and the political and the questions of agency it poses.

First, though, he spent the rest of March and April 1941 fleshing out the personal. From Soloviev, Ustrialov, and the Kurbsky documents, Eisenstein developed the personal sources of conflict between Ivan and the circle of characters who would appear in the scenario. Von Staden's memoir about the oprichniki gave him a vivid, graphic picture of the ruthless violence perpetrated by Ivan's allies and opponents. Soloviev gave him the portrait of an unstable but determined state builder, countered by Vipper's highly flattering depiction of a ruler trying to maintain order domestically while under the pressure of fighting a war. The correspondence between Ivan and Kurbsky was of prime importance in unlocking Ivan's experiences and ruling ideology. But none of the sources give much evidence of the relationships between people and, thinking like an artist rather than a historian, Eisenstein wanted a backstory.[54] So in March 1941, he invented the illicit romance between Kurbsky and Anastasia. After playing around with a few other ideas, he made Kurbsky Ivan's oldest and most loyal friend and used his covert attraction to Anastasia as the root of disloyalty among Ivan's two most loyal followers: *This does give a certain personal touch: his crime must start from some personal moment which entangles him further.*[55] Eisenstein conveys the climate of betrayal around Ivan and shows that the desire for revenge, first triggered by the boyars' poisoning of his mother, was reinforced by Kurbsky's personal duplicity. At the same time, he proposed a subtext of homoerotic feelings between Ivan and his friends Kurbsky and Filipp, and between Ivan and Fedor Basmanov. On Ivan and Fedor, Eisenstein would have had not only references in historical sources but explicit depictions of their homosexual relationship in earlier films about Ivan.[56] Personal experiences of loyalty, betrayal, and desire are fundamentally responsible for the political crises to come, but at this point Eisenstein was just beginning to sketch in those feelings and their consequences.

In April 1941, weeks of frustrating inactivity were followed by a short period of productive work. This is when Eisenstein confessed in his diary that he was feeling overwhelmed by the "volume" of Ivan.[57] In the very next entry, he said that something about the scenario had been nagging at him—"the lack of generalizable relationships among the characters." Then, as so often happened, a book came to the rescue.[58] He happened to buy John Masefield's *William Shakespeare* (1911), which contained just the formula he needed. Masefield had written that *Henry IV* is "about a son [Hotspur] too brilliant to be understood and a son [Prince Harry] too common to understand."[59] Whatever one thinks of this characterization of *Henry IV*, it gave Eisenstein "a clue" for constructing a film around an individual. *Ivan the Terrible* was his first "personal drama," a departure from the two kinds of "depersonalized" film he already knew how to make: the collective drama of *Potemkin*, and the patriotic drama in *Nevsky*. This personal drama would contain "a confrontation of the position 'for oneself' with the position 'for the state.' Ivan is 'for the state,' all of his opponents are 'for oneself' in all of its nuances."[60] Just as Hotspur masked his personal ambition with his "brilliant" devotion to honor, Ivan's opponents justified their actions with abstract or ideological rationalizations about tradition, legitimacy, family, or the proper exercise of power, a false collectivism that masked their solely self-interested motives. Hotspur's "brilliance" here seems to mean a talent for deception. "The main *clash* is still between Ivan and Kurbsky. The rest are like Kurbsky's 'chorus.' I just need to stir in the nuances: from Filipp's philosophical noble position, the personal side of feudalism, to the Basmanovs' simple greed. The power-loving [Efrosinia] Staritskaia. Ambitious Kurbsky. The synthesis of all these features in Pimen."[61] Eisenstein wasn't finished with these characters or these issues, but Masefield helped him nail down one of the major themes and one of the major structures of his approach: the clash between abstract ideas and emotional realities, between false collectivism and bald self-interest that differentiated Ivan as the only actor selflessly committed to the Great Russian State. The primary inner conflict at the root of Ivan's tragedy and the national disaster is caused by a conflict between his own selfless devotion to duty and the personal feelings underlying his compulsion to punish those who wounded him. Ivan would be tragic not only because loneliness was the result of choosing duty over feelings, but because of the ways he dealt with this conflict by embracing an image of selflessness that involved eradicating his emotional connection to others. Masefield offered him Shakespeare's solution to representing this archetypal inner contradiction of rulership: projecting it onto two competing characters.

When Eisenstein returned to work in September, these thoughts about biography and history led him to write about himself: some of the first sketches that he would write for his memoirs date from this period. And he read a lot of books. On September 22, he noted that:

> It took only 3 months to invade and seize Kiev. In the past few days I bought a whole pile of American and English books. Today I was skimming through (relevant to Ivan?) Harold Lamb's *The Crusades* vol. 21 *The Flame of Islam* about the assassins (Marx called the oprichniki—Ivan IV's assassins). There is a resemblance. Fr. Hackett, *Henry Eighth*—of course <u>our</u> boy in comparison with Henry VIII.[62]

And then he added, like a child faced with homework: "Kurbsky is not coming together for me yet. Now I will sit down with his 'works' and with S. M. Soloviev."[63] He did, in fact, get back to work on *Ivan*, but that month he also sat down with Shakespeare, Freud, Thornton Wilder, Sinclair Lewis, Gordon Bachelard, Alexandre Dumas, Arkady Averchenko, John Galsworthy, J. B. Priestley, Havelock Ellis, Henri Bergson, Voltaire, Samuel Johnson, Jonathan Swift, William Thackeray, Gustave Flaubert, Guy de Maupassant, Ernest Hemingway, J. W. Beach on the modernist novel, and a book on Peruvian pageantry.[64] Apparently the combination of homework and belles lettres worked (together with pressure from the studio to keep at it), because during these weeks in September and October, Eisenstein made important conceptual breakthroughs and embarked on lines of thinking that would lead to key concepts later on. On September 30, for example, he read Freud on the fetal position and the similarities between sleeping and prenatal life in the womb. Prenatal life was a subject that was becoming central to his understanding of human nature, perception, morality, and change and would eventually play a role in his portrait of Ivan.[65] This is the context in which he began developing the relationships among the characters around Ivan into a web of ironic contradictions, betrayals, and mirrors of Ivan's behaviors. Responding to Beach's discussion of shifting point of view in modernist novels, Eisenstein noted, "for us it is not the point from which a character sees, but the *theme through which* we see a leading character in a given place . . . This is undoubtedly the next step in my 'Bach-like' manner: the theme running through everything and its eternally changing variations."[66] Eisenstein would use this structure—the projection of Ivan's inner conflicts on his conflicts with other characters—to dramatize the inner divisions he discerned in Ivan from the beginning.

Ivan's inner divisions, his "unity of opposites,"[67] made him a perfect character for Eisenstein to explore in dialectical terms. When he turned from theory to the historians, however, he discovered that there was more than one way to skin this dialectical cat. His notes on Indenbom's research show that Eisenstein was dissatisfied with the explanations for Ivan's contradictions in the standard liberal and Marxist histories. Karamzin "did not understand the laws of history [*zakonomernost'*]," and Kliuchevsky "saw only irrationality" in Ivan.[68] He discovered the model he was looking for in a book review by the nineteenth-century founder of modern Russian literary criticism, Vissarion Belinsky:

> Karamzin presents [Ivan the Terrible] as some kind of "double" [*dvoinik*]
> . . . whose two halves are visibly stitched together with thread. Polevoi
> [the subject of the review] takes a middle position; his Ivan is no genius,

only a remarkable man. With this we cannot agree . . . We understand this madness, this animal bloodthirstiness, these unprecedented evil acts, this pride, and along with these, the scalding tears, the tormenting contrition, the humiliation, in which all of Ivan's life manifested itself.[69]

This was an important passage for Eisenstein. He printed "MOTTO?" underneath the citation in his notebook. He copied it twice, it appears later in *Nonindifferent Nature*, and it is key to understanding his conceptualization of Ivan. The "unity of opposites" did not mean Ivan alternated between "good" and "evil," or that his reign was divided into "good" and "bad" periods. On the contrary, from his first public steps to his last, Eisenstein's Ivan embodies the coexistence and mutual influence of good instincts and bad, revenge and remorse, duty and pleasure, pride and self-pity. Ivan possessed conflicting impulses always and these would determine how he would rule. Later Eisenstein characterized this dualism as "reciprocal interaction" (*vzaimodeistvie*) rather than a "link" (*a ne—sviaz'*) between the two sides.[70] Belinsky captured not only the specific qualities Eisenstein imagined from the first—evil, bloodthirsty cruelty and Ivan's awareness of the consequences of his acts—but also the correct kind of dualism. Everyone knew that Ivan was a cruel tyrant; Eisenstein wanted to understand how his inner divisions interacted reciprocally to produce the man who became that tyrant. His initial thoughts and the historical reading gave him a vulnerable child, a powerless all-powerful young tsar, and a spiteful, remorseful old man, but his own view of human nature was dialectical and evolutionary, not linear or strictly sequential. So he continued looking for the right mechanism to get Ivan from vulnerable child to remorseful adult. He was just beginning to concentrate on the crises in Ivan's childhood when real world crises intervened and Moscow was evacuated.

In Alma Ata, Eisenstein resumed his study of history as he worked on the characterizations in *Ivan*. That Eisenstein was thinking about history during that prolific spring of 1942 can be seen in the ways he developed two characters: the traitorous friend, Andrei Kurbsky, and the founder of the oprichnina, Aleksei Basmanov. His work on both these characters shows how he began with historical literature and sources, in particular von Staden, Soloviev, Kliuchevsky, and the Kurbsky-Groznyi letters, but then expanded on them with psychology, ethnography, literary history, and ancient myth.

On February 20, 1942, he started a notebook on Kurbsky, the primary purpose of which was to collect his scattered reading notes to understand why a man would betray his country and defect to the enemy and how this reflected on Ivan as man and ruler, so that he could decide how to portray him. In the historical documents that Eisenstein read, Kurbsky blamed the tsar, claiming that mistreating his servitors and usurping their power was responsible for their treason. In Stalinist historiography, the boyars were an obsolete class who opposed Ivan because they were greedy individuals desperately defending traditional power and feudal landholding against the progressive state-building ambitions of the autocrat.[71] In his notebook, Eisenstein recorded a different approach altogether, departing significantly from the prescribed "path." According to Kliuchevsky, Kurbsky didn't oppose Ivan's centralization of state power and wasn't committed to defending feudal power. On the contrary, Kliuchevsky argued, Kurbsky wanted to be tsar; he wanted to replace Ivan: "tsar and boyars made mortal enemies of each other in the name of one and the same general political program."[72] A. A. Kizevetter, another major nineteenth-century historian, called their conflict "more pantomime than drama."[73]

In a long passage that follows these notes, Eisenstein worked out what he wanted to do with these arguments. Kliuchevsky's point was that Ivan was self-destructive and foolish (if not insane) to attack boyars who shared his goals. Eisenstein turned that around. His Kurbsky is as "progressive" as Ivan and opposes Ivan for purely dynastic reasons, which is to say that he wants to place his own princely line in power. Eisenstein decided to invest Ivan with the characteristics other historians had associated with Kurbsky, but in personal rather than political form: "Preserv[e] inside Ivan, not in the form of a *progressive program*, but, most important, in *personal* terms, as an atavistic attachment to his own clan."[74] Kurbsky's attachment to his clan is political: he wants the tsar's power for himself and his family. Conversely, Ivan's attachment to clan is personal, emotional, and backward-looking, and this has numerous far-reaching consequences. As a personal attachment, family doesn't (or shouldn't) get in the way of Ivan's "progressive" campaign to establish the Great Russian State, but it does. He can't bring himself to attack his relatives, the Staritskys, even when he suspects that they killed his wife. And the attachment to clan, considered a reactionary or feudal characteristic, was shared by most of the main characters in the film. Every character is internally divided between emotional forms of personal attachment and ideological forms of impersonal politics—that is, between their identities as individuals and as members of the collective; private desire versus public service. In dramatic terms, at the level of plot, emotional attachments complicate politics, making it difficult for the characters to know what motivates them and difficult for viewers to distinguish between the personal and the political.

Both Kurbsky's betrayal and Ivan's violence are motivated by something other than the political revolution taking place—the replacement of feudal with modern centralized power—prescribed by party-line historiography.

Each wanted the new modern kind of power, one-man rule, but each was attached to the old form as well: feudal, clan-based power. Kurbsky and the other characters around Ivan wanted power for themselves and their relatives, and Ivan wanted revenge. The violence that resulted from these conflicts was not rooted in a political revolution or a progressive movement of any kind, but in the opposite, emotional attachment and personal desire. Their motives are political, but it is a politics that is personal. And Ivan was as guilty of this atavistic attachment to clan as everyone else.

Now we see the long fuse of some of Eisenstein's early intuitions producing sparks. Eisenstein invented the Kurbsky-Anastasia romance to give Kurbsky a personal, instinctive source of animosity and envy. The personal issues that fuel Kurbsky's envious betrayal of Ivan are both doubly personal: romantic and dynastic. To make matters more complex, personal issues don't matter solely for political reasons, but for historical reasons as well. The old feudal structure that was overthrown by the new centralized autocracy was fundamentally personal. It was clan-based and kin-oriented, and it was being replaced by a modern, impersonal, abstract state. To be clear, historians no longer think that the transfer of power from boyar aristocracy to one-man rule (*edinoderzhavie*) occurred in this schematic way, Marxist or otherwise, but rather that autocracy retained significant elements of personal status and kin-based rule.[75] It turns out to be more difficult than expected, however, to jettison the personal. Even while Ivan justifies all his actions as being for the good of the state, he cannot seem to escape his individual feelings, his personal attachments and enmities. This is an example of the way in which Eisenstein depicted a conflict with an interrogative—was Kurbsky justified in committing treason? were the boyars justified in attacking Ivan? was Ivan justified in attacking the boyars?—while at the same time implicitly offering an answer that directly challenged elements of Stalinist rule, in this case, the cult of the leader as selfless servant of the people who overturned the power of the feudal boyars. The answers to these questions also comment on ideologically charged categories of individual and collective: here Eisenstein makes it clear that no political revolution can eradicate all vestiges of the past. The feudal clan-collective may be reshaped into a socialist classless collective, but personal, individual feelings and motives remain. In April 1942, Eisenstein wrote, "the motif of the struggle between the landlord [*votchinnik*] and the state still within Ivan (*There is some tragic stuff*)."[76]

The Basmanovs' story gives Eisenstein another way to show the consequences of a politics based on personal-political conflict and another dimension to Ivan's inner conflict. In Eisenstein's telling, Aleksei Basmanov, as a member of the middle-service class (noble elite but a step below the boyar aristocracy), feels powerless and humiliated before boyars like the Kurbskys and Staritskys. These personal feelings of vulnerability underlie his political ideology and his role in the establishment of the oprichnina. He recommends that Ivan form the oprichnina in order to surround himself with new men whose loyalty is only to the tsar, circumventing the existing hierarchy. When he offers his son to Ivan as the first oprichnik, Aleksei is proud to sacrifice his paternity for the good of the state. But his sense of honor is corroded when Fedor's loyalty to Ivan partially displaces his loyalty to his father, a conflict that ultimately destroys the whole family.[77] The fact that Fedor has a homoerotic attachment to his political father further inflames the tension with his biological father.[78] A scene Eisenstein never filmed but that appeared three times in his notes and remained in the scenario, exemplifies this clash of personal and political. Aleksei finds his son Fedor wearing earrings, which Eisenstein explicitly linked to homosexuality. Aleksei is enraged. He admonishes his son to recall the great "principles of the oprichnina" and then boxes Fedor in the ear. In this exchange, ideology is made to eclipse desire, leaving Fedor humiliated and seething with animosity toward his father, which ultimately sows the seeds of patricide.[79] For Aleksei, that desire painfully twists his own tangled loyalty to Ivan and painfully distances himself from Fedor, leading him to hit his son. Both father and son suffer from their lack of power in relation to the other. By giving his son to Ivan, Aleksei sacrifices both his paternal and ideological power over Fedor, but Fedor suffers as well from his father's demeaning and physical admonition.

In all these cases, violence results not from the prescribed clash between modern state power and the obsolete feudal elite but from compensation for feelings of powerlessness connected to the most intensely personal, emotional ties. Ivan, Aleksei, Fedor, Efrosinia, and Kurbsky (as well as Maliuta Skuratov) all hate those with power over them. Those hatreds are the result of personal affronts or personal attachments brought about by asymmetrical power relationships. Everyone wants power. Everyone is motivated to fight for power and to seize power not only for abstract ideological goals but to compensate for vulnerability, humiliation, and jealousy. Marxist class struggle is recast here in purely emotional and individual terms. Stripped of its progressive ideology and egalitarian goals, Eisenstein's class struggle is reduced to something dangerous and shameful.

The linking of the political and the personal in this way raises another one of the fundamental questions of the film: why do some rulers exceed acceptable norms of violence and resort to mass terror? Eisenstein's study of the past found characters who experienced inner divisions between the past and the present and the personal and the political. The next step toward the answer is that because they feel small and powerless, they begin to compensate by becoming and possibly outdoing their powerful tormentors.

From Myth to Psychology and History

It is no coincidence, nor is it trivial that Eisenstein insisted on reinserting the scenes of Ivan's childhood in Part II after prescreening censorship cut them from Part I. The Prologue, Eisenstein stressed, contained the origins of everything important that happens in the film.[80] In addition to the letters and chronicles discussed above, Eisenstein took extensive notes on Kliuchevsky's *Lectures in Russian History*, repeatedly revisiting the lectures about Ivan's childhood. He was struck by the contrast between the messages conveyed to Ivan: that he was the all-powerful tsar but as a child lacked real power to rule. Kliuchevsky's explanation for the adult Ivan's cruelty emphasized Ivan's sense of victimization as a child and his "instinct for self-preservation." Kliuchevsky viewed the tsar's extremes of self-pity and lack of self-awareness as irrational, abnormal traits that led to irrational, idiosyncratic, and extreme behavior.[81]

Eisenstein departed from Kliuchevsky in his understanding of the ways in which Ivan was affected by this contrast between power and powerlessness. Eisenstein's Ivan is likewise motivated by hunger for revenge against the boyars who poisoned his mother, lied to him, treated him with contempt, and ruled in his name, but he was motivated by a psychology that the director attributed to a universal human trait. He saw violence as a fundamental and natural aspect of human behavior, as a ubiquitous human instinct, and he saw this instinct as a return to our most primal, wordless impulses. He found examples of the instinct for revenge and violence like Ivan's everywhere in ancient European myths and in the kinds of cultural practices recorded by James Frazer and Lucien Lévy-Bruhl and attributed to "primitive" peoples. Eisenstein gravitated to stories, fables, folklore, and ethnographic descriptions that he applied to historical change over time. He interpreted stories about people exchanging clothing, taking on the form of animals, and crossdressing as ways of coping with threatening moments of sharp differentiation and vulnerability in the face of powerful enemies and forces by enacting sameness.[82] In connection with *Ivan the Terrible*, the subject that most interested him was the way these exchanges intersected with the violence that seemed to accompany transitions between stages of history and stages of individual development. He often returned in his notes to the Greek Titan, Saturn, who castrated his own father and, fearing the same treatment from his children, ate them, but who then gave way to the Olympian gods Zeus and especially Dionysus, who challenged both the gods and the Titans.[83] And, of course, Eisenstein wrote about Oedipus, who similarly kills his father in order to make the transition to adulthood, though lacking certain critical information (though he gave far less weight to the Oedipus story than Freud did). Eisenstein anointed just one other passage in his voluminous notes with the label "Motto"—a quote from Georgy Plekhanov's *On the Materialist Understanding of History*: "The role of violence is very great in the transition from one set of institutions to another. But that violence does little to explain the possibility of such a transition, or its societal results."[84] This jumbled collection of examples scattered throughout the notebooks for *Ivan* start to make sense when we place those notes in the context of the film narrative and the texts he was writing at the same time for *Method*.

Eisenstein's Ivan resorted to violence as a vulnerable child when his own powerlessness in the face of the corrupt boyars frightened him. He took his first step toward real power when he ordered the boyar Andrei Shuisky seized for insulting the young tsar and selling Russia's wealth to foreigners. Eisenstein wrote about this act as a key transformation for Ivan: a rite of passage from innocence to experience, from child to man, from unarmed to armed.[85] It also marked an important set of transitions in the film and in Eisenstein's thinking about history and power. In a diary note written in January 1944, Eisenstein claimed (only slightly facetiously) that despite reading Durkheim, Freud, Frazer, and others on totemism, he only came to understand the origins of Ivan's violence by playing a game of "bear and wolf" with Varia Vasilieva, a child who lived in his building in Alma Ata.[86] Eisenstein would growl "somewhere between a bear and a wolf," and Varia would pretend to be a frightened little girl. What fascinated him was that when Varia began to fight back, she didn't do so as a brave little girl; she became a wolf. She howled just like her stronger, predatory enemy. The prey overcame the predator by imitating him, by becoming him. And every time she imitated him out of fear and desire for revenge, her strength and confidence grew.[87]

Eisenstein found confirmation for his understanding of these transitional, transformational states in the research of a contemporary psychiatrist, Ernst Kretschmer, whose work he often cites in *Method*. In *Medical Psychology*, Kretschmer explored the reflexive responses to stimuli in the behavior of simple aquatic organisms and in children, hysterics, and even adults, all of whom found release, safety, and sometimes pleasure in regressing to states of purely physical, instinctive reflex. A young woman who sees no logical escape from a stressful situation and goes into a faint is similar to a grown man who lashes out when he becomes irrationally angry (despite the obvious gender coding). When faced with such situations, people freeze or panic. A minuscule aquatic infusorium frantically swims from side to side of its petri dish when surprised by an unseen sensory stimulus. All are exhibiting what has become incorporated in contemporary psychology as a "fight or flight response." Unable to access the rational thought processes that help us escape from danger, we revert to defensive instincts that originate as a physical reaction and produce some physical act. Kretschmer also claimed that those reflexive states come about through a kind of dialectic: intense feeling (panic) in response to stress leads to the overproduction of physical movement and then the renunciation of all intention in enacting automatic movements free from stimulus. Even plants show this on-off alternation of compression and release, intensity and automatic reflex, thought and pure physical sensation. Eisenstein thought we replicated this dialectical "on-off" as societies, during periods of transition, and as individuals, during moments of transformation, and as human organisms while responding to art.[88]

Not all people who go through this transition become violent, bloodthirsty tyrants like Ivan the Terrible. For ordinary people, the transition from prey to predator is imaginary or unconscious—stories we tell ourselves to explain the violent impulses we share as human animals, but stories that we usually don't enact. However, if some people freeze in their reactive flight from panic, others put their impulses to more productive or destructive use and fight back. Those who act out their animal instinct for tyranny and violence, Eisenstein explained, were motivated by a combination of ambition and compulsion: "Cruelty comes from the compulsion to be the first in line, the ruler—the father—for them this is not metaphorical, it is the identical fear, the identical pain that comes with castigation."[89] Here Eisenstein added "(but definitely not—*castration*; à la Freud!)." This is an important caveat. Eisenstein agreed with Freud that people are driven throughout their lives by impulses formed in infancy, but he believed Freud exaggerated the role of sexual desire at the expense of our other impulses, including violence.[90] When a person is under attack and feeling vulnerable, the desire for revenge can take the form of a violent merger (or imitation or interpenetration) of the prey with the predator that transforms the prey into something more powerful and violent than the original threat. This form of imitation and interpenetration defined the character Aleksei Basmanov.

Historically, Eisenstein wrote, Basmanov was "the author of the oprichnina project," but, he added, "his real motif ought to be—the creation of a *new feudal* group."[91] In Eisenstein's conception, the oprichniki were ultimately no different from, and no better than, the class they had replaced: "It is important to bring out that [Basmanov] is struggling against the appanage and clan system, so that he himself can establish a 'new feudalism,' with property for the clan of the Basmanovs and their successors."[92] In the censored Oath scene, the oprichniki swear to place their loyalty to Ivan and to the Great Russian State above their ties to their mothers, their fathers, and their families.[93] So when it turns out that Aleksei Basmanov is more interested in securing position and wealth for his son Fedor and his future clan, his material greed is not only a betrayal of his oath to the tsar; it is a betrayal of oprichnik "principle" as well.[94] Eisenstein clarified this numerous times in his notes: "The neo-feudalism of the oprichniki. They themselves are guilty of that which they were called forth to destroy. The rebirth of the elite: in contradiction of that which they were called forth to oppose. This theme makes Basmanov-the-clan-destroyer—into a clan-founder."[95]

Still, in February 1942, just two days after Eisenstein wrote those conciliatory letters to Bolshakov and Zhdanov, he told his notebook that he didn't yet have the "general approach" he wanted for Basmanov Senior.[96] Then he stumbled into a solution in the course of writing a diary passage that started to be about something else. A new Aleksei Basmanov emerged from Eisenstein's thinking about the ways a dramatist has to lodge hints or shards of ideas deep in a viewer's consciousness, allowing them germinate slowly so that later they seem to appear out of the blue, the way potatoes sprout roots in a warm kitchen.[97] The rebirth of the elite, personified by Aleksei Basmanov, began to work for Eisenstein only when he could link it to the two key transitions discussed above: when the powerless, vulnerable child makes the transformation into the predatory, powerful tsar; and when Ivan struggles to eradicate his emotional attachment to family in favor of an abstract attachment to the state. Just as little Varia became a wolf in order to protect herself from a wolf, Basmanov and the other oprichniki murdered the boyars to compensate for their feelings of vulnerability, and when they acquired power for themselves, they became the same or even worse than those they had overthrown.[98] Eisenstein included in the Historical Commentary confirmation of this phenomenon that he found in the German oprichnik von Staden's memoir: "The violence carried out by the oprichniki . . . no worse than the boyar traitors."[99]

Eisenstein's conception of Basmanov's "new feudalism" and of the conflict between public and private loyalties directly challenged Stalinist historiography and pointed to an essential contradiction in Stalinist values more generally. The mix of class jealousy and powerlessness, together with ineradicable personal feelings and attachment to family, created an impossible moral-political situation in which betrayal was inevitable. All the main characters, including Ivan, experience a conflict between "consciousness (programmatic) and instinct (personal-animalistic-family). And this dissonance leads to real risk . . . To raise it means to bring it out. Not simply to allow for something patiently awaited to occur, but to give a hard push into action. The only possible action is betrayal."[100] Ivan's (and Eisenstein's) oprichnina failed both to eradicate class hierarchy and to subordinate individual, personal attachments to collective, public commitments. In this film, the tsar who was "progressive for his time," and the "progressive" history, evolving by stages from primitive feudalism to advanced communism, continually reinvent their own most primitive, "atavistic," violent, and backward-looking features. And they do so because separating the personal from the political is impossible.

In the Soviet political context, it would have been heretical for Eisenstein to openly portray the oprichnina as a new elite when it was supposed to be a revolutionary force of the people, yet this contradiction between ideal and reality had been central to Communist Party culture and practice since the early 1920s. As Arch Getty notes, "party members thought of themselves as some version of the elect, the privileged, those with special knowledge and mission."[101] But until after World War II, they avoided public acknowledgment of this kind of elitism. Not that no one else had noticed. As early as 1929, ordinary people in the Soviet Union were complaining that the Communist Party leadership had become a new elite, who lived "like lords, go[ing] round in sables and with canes with silver handles."[102] Even the Stalinist government, with its typical punishing contradictions, used the privileges officials acquired against those officials when they were purged during the late

FIGURE 2.2   Maliuta: the prey becomes the predator

1930s.[103] Instead of depicting this theme explicitly in dialogue, Eisenstein represented the oprichnina's neofeudal rebirth visually. The carrier of the visual markers of neofeudal rebirth is not the founder of the oprichnina, Aleksei Basmanov, but its leader, Maliuta Skuratov.[104]

We first meet Maliuta at the beginning of Part I, when a crowd of rebellious commoners enters the tsar's palace, aiming to overthrow Ivan. At the head of the mob, Maliuta is dressed in a dirty, frayed, simple homespun caftan. He and the rest of the men are immediately overwhelmed by the awe-inspiring figure of the tsar. Falling to his knees, Maliuta allows Ivan's wit and authority to win him over completely. After proving his loyalty to Ivan by directing the explosives operation during the battle at Kazan (lighting that first candle), Maliuta is promoted to the important position as "the tsar's eye," skulking around the palace as a spy. His political elevation is marked by an entirely new outfit: a long, black robe, with over-long black sleeves and rounded shoulders that is a forerunner of the oprichnik's black robe and caftan. Later, as oprichnik leader, his black caftan acquires a fur collar, and soon all the oprichniki are wearing elegant fur-trimmed hats with the puffy-sleeved black robes. The key transition in Maliuta's neofeudal dress occurs at the same moment that he carries out Ivan's first executions. Reading the order of execution, we see that Maliuta's black robe covers an oprichnik-style caftan, but instead of oprichnik black, the caftan is now made out of boyar, gold-stitched, brocade. As he tosses off the black robe, he carries out the execution with brocade caftan in full view. The next real transition comes in The Feast of the Oprichniki, the climax of Part II, where Ivan manipulates Vladimir Staritsky into becoming the victim of the assassination plot meant to kill Ivan. Here Maliuta not only wears a hybrid boyar-oprichnik brocade caftan, but now even his outer robe, with its oprichnik rounded shoulders, is also covered in luxurious brocade. The oprichnik and the boyar are fully blended. He has become what he was called forth to overthrow.

Eisenstein is not assigning moral responsibility here for the perpetuation of violence. Instead he shows us how cycles of violence are perpetuated historically, and how they doom revolutionary change to repeat the violence in ever more complex conditions, producing systems as bad or even worse than those they had overthrown. Basmanov's creation of a new elite with all the same greed, jealousy, and corruption as the old is rooted in his own past jealousies and his personal process of compensating for powerlessness. He hates the feudal families for the same reason that Ivan hates the boyars: they made him feel powerless. Ivan's lingering ties to the feudal elite infuriate Basmanov, whose jealousy comes to the surface in The Feast of the Oprichniki, when he sees Ivan cozying up to Vladimir Staritsky (II: 56:07). Aleksei brazenly tells the tsar that he shouldn't be consorting with the enemy. Ivan, the cruel predator toying with his prey, responds, "Know your place, Alyosha," using the diminutive childish version of his name. If class animosity planted the seed of Basmanov's neofeudalism, this new humiliation at Ivan's hands germinates that seed.[105] And just as Ivan lost his mother and wife to the boyars, Basmanov lost (gave) his son to the tsar, to Ivan. He gave his son away in a moment of political loyalty ("the first oprichnik!"), but when Ivan takes Fedor as his son, and then his lover, Aleksei feels the loss even more acutely. This twisty path of loyalty, betrayal, and love for father and tsar, and love for family and state was to grow into full, tragic flower in Part III.

But Ivan's evolution is even more convoluted and revealing than Aleksei's or Maliuta's. The tsar's "atavistic" feelings for his aunt Efrosinia and her son, Vladimir, hamper him from acting against them, despite the fact that Vladimir is Ivan's main rival for power and Efrosinia harbors murderous hatred toward Ivan. His feelings of kinship prevent him from believing that Efrosinia poisoned his wife, even when all signs point to her, even after Fedor tells him she did it. When Ivan can no longer sustain the belief that Efrosinia is blameless, he finally discards those atavistic feelings and severs his personal ties with her and the rest of his clan.

This crucial transformation occurs in Part II during Filipp's production of *The Fiery Furnace*, an allegory about a tyrant and three innocent victims (II: 32:44). The play, which was widely performed in Russian churches in Ivan's time and is depicted in several surviving frescos, derives from a story in the Book of Daniel that itself derives from the history of the Jews' Babylonian exile.[106] After Nebuchadnezzar captured the city of Jerusalem and destroyed its Temple, he forcibly relocated much of the Jewish population to Babylon, a period of legendary anguish for the Jewish people. In Daniel's version, three Jews are thrown into a furnace and executed for their refusal to worship idols, and not just any idols, but a huge golden statue of the king, who had declared himself to be like God. As in *Hamlet* and Thomas Kyd's *The Spanish Tragedy*, a play *en abîme* is staged to shame the king into repentance—Filipp wanted Ivan to disband the oprichniki and give up his murderous persecution of the boyars—but the plan backfired: Efrosinia's "unmasking" leads to Ivan's "unmasking." In an important note, Eisenstein labels this moment "masks off!" and he characterizes it as the culmination of previous turning points in Ivan's life: Anastasia's cup of poison and Ivan's call for more corpses "(Too few!)."[107] There is no new evidence in this scene, no visible sign, no change at all to alert Ivan to Efrosinia's guilt. He looks at her, sees through her mask, and removes his own. When he can no longer pretend that the boyars support him, he just stops pretending that he didn't know she was guilty. And looking into these mirrors and seeing himself as the wicked Babylonian King Nebuchadnezzar, Ivan not only does not repent; he embraces revenge and asserts himself: "I will be what you call me: I *will* be Terrible." Acknowledging Efrosinia's guilt frees Ivan to protect himself and act against Efrosinia and Vladimir. The trouble is that this also frees him from all human ties. As Eisenstein told Prokofiev, "the Storm *rises* (when necessary) to become a God." Another diary comment tells us that at this moment Ivan becomes *predel'no krut* —"ruthless in the extreme."[108]

This is a scene of intense dialectical tension: visual, moral, and political. While the performance is beginning, a long shot of the audience in the cathedral shows the startled boyars jumping back as the hooded oprichniki force their way forward; an ominous intrusion. Scored with the triumphant tsar's theme, a cut shows Filipp and his entourage entering from another direction, moving toward a confrontation. When the other priests see Ivan, all except Filipp turn back and flee. A medium shot shows the boy martyrs conferring before standing to sing the most defiant lines of the song, which they direct to the imagined audience of the play, the boyars in the cathedral and the audience in the Soviet movie theater: "Why, shameless Chaldeans, do you serve this lawless tsar . . . this devilish, blasphemous, despotic tsar?" That gets Ivan's attention. When he bows to receive Filipp's blessing, Filipp increases the tension by remaining silent, and one of the boys turns to glare straight at Ivan, singing, "the earthly Lord will be humbled by the Heavenly Lord." Filipp not only refuses to bless the tsar; he calls Ivan a "bloodthirsty beast." To add insult to injury, the laughing child in the audience spots Ivan and strips all pretense from the spectacle by pointing and calling him "the terrible, pagan tsar." Ironically he is the only person in the room to think that the play is *only* a play but in simultaneously erasing the boundary between spectacle and reality, he shows everyone else that it is *not* only a fiction. The child is laughing, but this is only funny while viewers think they are watching a play and not reality. The adults around the boy, though, recognize Ivan as the real tsar and cower in terror, all except Vladimir (half-child himself), who laughs too until he realizes no one else is laughing. At this point, when the laughing boy unmasks the tsar, Ivan momentarily crumples into Fedka, then rises up, leans back, bends forward threateningly, and then a jump cut to a close-up of Ivan shows him glaring off-camera toward where the boy, Efrosinia, and Vladimir had been. Growling from beneath the hood of his black oprichnik-monk's robe, he declares "I will be Terrible." Without moving his head, his eyes circle round to look at the camera, to look at us.

Numerous binaries are juxtaposed and overcome in this scene—reality and spectacle, laughter and fear, good and evil, heaven and earth, the past and the present. There is more sinister laughter and a sharper contrast between humor

FIGURE 2.3   Ivan asserts his power

and threat in this scene than in any other in *Ivan the Terrible*. Ivan interrupts the deadly serious play as he enters the cathedral, laughing loudly off-screen. The tsar is laughing at Maliuta for being humiliated by Efrosinia in a scene that was scripted and shot but is no longer extant. The evil tyrant's henchmen, the Chaldean guards who escort the boys to the furnace, are dressed and made up to resemble clowns (and boyars, with their patterned tunics and long beards). Their awkward cartwheels and the strange circus-like score blends laughter with horror (II: 34:31). A menacing sequence of cross-cut close-ups shows one Chaldean clown asking if it is indeed the tsar's order to burn the boys to death, if the boys had indeed disobeyed the tsar, and if they are really to throw the boys into the furnace and burn them for disobeying the tsar. With a series of twisted grimaces, the other affirms each question. This conversation is intercut, not with horrified faces of the boyar spectators, as might be expected, but with a shot of two smiling women as if from the audience—the repetition of a shot from Ivan's Coronation—and then a shot of the little boy, laughing as the clowns talk about the vicious murder about to take place. All this mingling of laughter and violence intensifies the dialectic resolved by Ivan's final statement and prepares viewers to understand that the tsar's very humanity was at stake.

Ivan's childhood trauma and humiliation activated his desire for revenge and inflamed the forms it took, but before he declared himself "The Terrible" those atavistic personal ties had kept him human. This is what Eisenstein meant when he wrote that he saw Ivan as rising to become like a God; as "superhuman."[109] The tragedy of this story derived not from Ivan's sadism or his crimes of violence but from the literally impossible conflict between his selfless commitment to the Great Russian State and the human costs of that commitment: his friends, his family, the devastation of his whole country. The superhuman position he sought (and claimed here at the end of The Fiery Furnace) would always be at odds with his messy, contradictory needs as a human being. Their elimination created something much worse. When Ivan rose above the flawed and dangerous realm of human feelings, when he ruled only in the name of an abstraction, the Great Russian State, when he became all-selfless and all-powerful, he became truly monstrous. His human feelings made him less great and more flawed, but also less Terrible.

Ivan's selfless, willful, and ruthless pursuit of centralized power, has led numerous observers to assume that Eisenstein saw Ivan as a kind of Machiavellian prince.[110] Eric Shmulevich argued that Eisenstein's Ivan subordinated morality to politics and justified the resulting cruelty, which made the film a Machiavellian allegory, justifying Stalin's own cruelty and murderous terror.[111] Machiavelli was certainly on Eisenstein's mind as he was writing the scenario. He read The Prince shortly after accepting the commission and, rereading it later in 1941 alongside Pasquale Villari's classic Life and Times of Niccolò Machiavelli, provided "renewed momentum" for his work on the film at the end of the summer of 1941. Eisenstein knew that The Prince had been interpreted and applied in contradictory ways, and he cited pages in Villari that explore some of these contradictory applications of its lessons. At times, Eisenstein's Ivan does seem to fit Machiavelli's prescriptions. As has often been noted, Eisenstein was taken with Konstantin Kavelin's characterization of Ivan as a "poet of the state idea," a ruler who pursued centralization for the good of the state.[112] Eisenstein, however, made it unequivocally clear that he did not see Ivan as a Machiavellian ruler. On the contrary, Eisenstein wrote, it was an "entirely different program of thought that dictated his program of action."[113]

Machiavelli believed that ordinary human weakness and contradictory desires for freedom and order made it necessary for rulers to be authoritarian, even cruel, in order to protect state stability. Machiavelli deplored violence but recommended its use as a political virtue if it brought "unity . . . order and obedience." He considered it legitimate for a prince to come to power "by crime" rather than "fortune" or "prowess," if political stability were the result and if the prince's cruelty were tempered with "greatness and nobility of mind."[114] Ordinary morality could be sacrificed for the good of the state, which in turn would provide for the good of the people: the ends justified the means. Machiavelli's prince also must be willing to be more feared than loved. He would have to tolerate the loneliness and isolation required of his position, again for the good of the state. On the surface, these qualities sound like Eisenstein's Ivan. He sacrificed his personal life for his political mission and came to understand that loneliness was his fate. Ivan repeatedly says that his efforts are not for himself but for the good of the Great Russian State. But there are critical differences. Ivan's motives were never purely rational. His underlying motivation was rooted in revenge against the boyars who murdered his mother and his wife and lined their own pockets. And equally important, since *Ivan the Terrible* was a study in modern power as much as it was a historical biopic, Eisenstein subjected to critical scrutiny Machiavelli's prioritizing of rationality over emotion and state stability and security over freedom.

Eisenstein's portrait asks us whether it is possible to put state interests above personal needs, and whether sacrificing personal happiness is ultimately for the good of the Great Russian State. Ivan's efforts succeed but they also produce instability, illusory unity, and senseless destruction. Eisenstein showed the tsar's choices as having tragic consequences for Ivan personally and for the whole country. By the end of the film (according to the scenario and the notes), the state was an empty shell, the towns of the kingdom annihilated, the population utterly devastated, and a historical pattern of cycles of resurrection and destruction in subsequent Russian history set in motion. Already before the end of Part I, Ivan had begun to make choices, such as establishing the oprichnina, seeking vengeance for his wife's death, and manipulating the people through deception and demagoguery, that initiated the means (unjustifiable violence) that would destroy the end (the state). The risky defiance and impetuousness of his early years together with his insatiable hunger for revenge eventually mutates into sadism, a distinctly un-Machiavellian trait. Eisenstein described Ivan as "sadistic" at the end of Part I, when he was looking out over the procession of people who have come to Alexandrova to beg him to return to Moscow and to the throne he has abandoned—when he was observing the success of his patently Machiavellian "trick."[115]

Neither did Eisenstein intend Ivan to be seen as a ruler who thought it was better to be feared than loved. First of all, Eisenstein, the ironic dialectician, rarely made that kind of either/or distinction in thinking about individuals. Accordingly, he showed how the desire to be feared and loved, rather than being opposed to one another, intersect as the twin impulses of any true ruler. Ivan's need to be loved—by his wife Anastasia, by his friends Kurbsky and

Filipp, by Fedka Basmanov, even by Maliuta who was far beneath him, and crucially by the Russian people—was central to both his individual feelings and to his political motivations and historical fate. Ivan was devastated by the betrayal of his friends. Eisenstein refused to relinquish his depiction of Ivan as a deeply lonely man and ruler in the face of strong and unrelenting opposition from political officials and film studio chiefs. And his "trick"—the abdication and retreat to Alexandrova—was meant to inspire the people to recognize how much they loved and needed Ivan. When they come to ask him to return to Moscow, they come in fear mixed with love. The painful sense of betrayal and need for support was critical to understanding the source of his desire for vengeance and his willingness to resort to violence. Ivan tried to keep "morality and politics being things apart," as Machiavelli advised, but the inability to disentangle them, this inherent unity of opposites, was one of the key determinants of his actions and the tragedy that followed.[116]

The inextricably political and personal, the suprahuman power and deeply human need for love were, ironically, central to the discussion in Villari that Eisenstein found most interesting. He copied out long passages that characterized Napoleon as a true Machiavellian prince in ways that resonated with Ivan's loneliness: "But after all, is a man of state made to be understood by others? Isn't he a completely eccentric person, always alone, off to one side with the world on the other."[117] Reading Machiavelli's *Prince* and Villari's political biography clarified for Eisenstein the internal contradiction between wanting power to serve a higher cause and wanting it for self-aggrandizement. Machiavelli also clarified the ways those two—the moral and the political, the selfless and selfish—can be difficult to distinguish. Eisenstein saw the ruler's isolation not as a rational necessity but as a human and moral catastrophe.

Eisenstein found Villari especially useful for the book's discussions of modern rulers who followed Machiavelli's instructions with disastrous results. Villari goes into some detail identifying rulers who were false Machiavellians; those who claimed to condemn Machiavelli's amorality while following his amoral prescriptions to further their own aims. The "antimachiavellianism" in words and "machiavellianism" in deeds helped Eisenstein define the character of Ivan's main rivals for power, Efrosinia Staritskaia and Andrei Kurbsky. "Must introduce into the character of Kurbsky the same cruelty, ruthlessness, and *hypocrisy*" as the Machiavellian prince.[118]

Eisenstein developed his own critical reading of Machiavelli in the context of contemporary politics. Violence might be an inevitability, but it was never a useful or controllable political instrument. Rulers, like all people, were subject to emotional triggers that interfered with even the most positive, rational plans. And seeking power for the most selfless possible purposes can be as dangerous and destabilizing as seeking power for one's own interests. Eisenstein's *Ivan the Terrible* may not be an illustration of Machiavellian rationalist politics, but its mixing and matching of Machiavellian prescriptions challenged the audience to think about specific questions with historical and contemporary significance: When is violence acceptable, and when is it excessive? Is violence the result of rational choice or uncontrollable feelings? Is it possible to place loyalty to abstract ideals over loyalty to friend and kin? What happens when rulers rise above the rest of us? Nietzsche made that point more clearly for Eisenstein than Machiavelli had because Nietzsche recognized the isolation of the extraordinary as morally autonomous. "Nietzsche," he wrote, "*was* about Ivan the Terrible." In casting off his "atavistic" attachments to his friends and kin, and in believing that ordinary constraints did not apply to the modern state-building autocrat, Ivan became a Nietzschean "superman." In Eisenstein's view such rulers could become selfless "poets of the state idea" like Ivan or self-serving egotists like Haiti's Henri Christophe, England's Elizabeth I, or Muscovy's Kurbsky, Efrosinia, Pimen, and others surrounding Ivan.[119] But this, too, left Ivan both entirely alone and beyond the ordinary judgment of contemporaries. Eisenstein singled out another quote of Napoleon's found in Villari along these lines:

> The acts of the statesman, which considered individually are so often blamed by the world, form an integral part of a great work, afterwards to be admired, and by which alone they should be judged. Elevate your imagination, look farther before you, and you will see that the personages you deem violent, cruel, and what not, are only politicians knowing how to master their passions, and expert in calculating the effect of their actions. I have shed blood and it was my duty. I may perhaps shed more but without anger and merely because bloodletting is one of the prescriptions of political surgery. I am the man of the State. I am the Revolution.[120]

Eisenstein's Ivan shared Napoleon's political justifications but not his emotional detachment; in fact, his attempts to rise like a God above human complexity and attachments led to his tragic fall. Half a century ago, the historian Michael Cherniavsky attempted to explain the historical Ivan's excessive violence, "the savagery, the incredible, blasphemous cruelty, the vengefulness," in similar terms. He noted that there were contemporaneous Muscovite sources for the kind of pragmatic politics Machiavelli recommended, including Ivan IV himself. Ivan Peresvetov, among others, claimed that human sinfulness and immorality required that rulers govern with a heavy hand. Cherniavsky pointed out that Machiavelli (but not Ivan) saw political rule as independent of sacred morality or divine intervention, which may have accounted for the excessive violence some of these rulers practiced. But Cherniavsky also saw in the Renaissance the same discourse that Nietzsche and Napoleon represented for Eisenstein. Renaissance rulers could be cruel and just at the same time—inspiring both awe and terror—because it was accepted that "he had both the need and the right to live and act beyond the boundaries of human laws and rules." The Renaissance ruler was *"terribile,"* in Petrarch's formulation.[121] The Renaissance "legitimated in one person absolute political power with no limitations except his own interests, and the untrammeled human personality fulfilling itself by exceeding all human limitations. The result frequently was awe-inspiring and monstrous."[122] I don't know if Cherniavsky knew Eisenstein's *Ivan the Terrible* or was thinking of Eisenstein's Renaissance prince when he wrote about the dangerous fusion of Machiavelli's political autonomy with Petrarch's personal autonomy, each a seemingly liberating precept of modern humanism. But it was this formulation—the catastrophic, tragic consequences of morally autonomous power—that Eisenstein put to the test by contextualizing his psychological profile of Ivan the Terrible in a dynamic model of change over time.

Revenge Drama and the Laws of History

The narrative traced from the abandoned child to the power-seeking, isolated, suprahuman ruler represented Eisenstein's understanding of Ivan as a man driven to found the Great Russian State, but doomed by psychology, politics, and history—by his own humanness and the circumstances he was given—to isolate himself from the rest of humanity and destroy not only his enemies but the country he sought to unite. The thread that tied all these themes together— state enemy and personal enemy, revenge and remorse, the child in the man, the deadly violence, the hunger for power, and the revolution that failed—is what Kozlov called Eisenstein's "theory of history." The shape of his thinking about history took three related forms, each primarily concerned with the mechanisms of historical change. First, he understood historical change as a dynamic with identifiable patterns—*zakonomernost'*—with specific socio-moral consequences; second, he believed that that dynamic was replicated in individual, biographical change; and third, he believed that powerful works of art must reproduce those same patterns in order to tap into our instinctive responses to change, to show the persistence of the past in the present, and to create a powerful effect on spectators.

Eisenstein elaborated his ideas on historical *zakonomernost'* in a series of notes (many of which show up later in *Method*) that joined the reading in history, ethnography, and psychology discussed above with Elizabethan and

Jacobean revenge drama. Eisenstein was interested in the revenge dramas by Shakespeare and his contemporaries when writing and filming *Ivan* because they helped him develop his thinking on form, story, and historical and biographical change. Eisenstein called revenge "monstrously ubiquitous," and the "most basic of themes," and he understood the attraction to revenge as an exemplary mode of the primal instinct for violence that people could never eradicate or overcome, no matter how advanced they or their societies became.[123] In the film, revenge dominated Ivan's personal motives and raised the most important questions about the role of emotions in personal and political actions. English revenge tragedies also offered a special kind of plot structure for depicting these issues: the vestiges of the past in the present and the consequences of the personal in the political.

Eisenstein wrote this series of notes on *Ivan* and early modern revenge dramas during those two periods of remarkable productivity in the spring of 1942 and the winter of 1943–1944. He was interested in the fact that the genre flourished during a period of collisions between stages of history when new ideas and behaviors were replacing traditional socio-moral norms. *The Merchant of Venice, Romeo and Juliet,* and *Hamlet,* all of which featured the revenge plots so popular on the early modern London stage, "discredit" eye-for-eye systems of retribution—"the principle of mechanical, physical *tit-for-tat.*" Eisenstein was aware that they were written and staged at the same time as more humane, individualistic, institutional, and abstract concepts of justice associated with Renaissance humanism were coming into practice; when Protestant reformers and state authorities were actively seeking to substitute expanding state legal powers for private aristocratic clan violence.[124] In these notes, Eisenstein showed no particular interest in the thematic issues at stake: neither in Renaissance humanism as a moral or political ideology, nor in institutionalized justice as a civilized practice, nor in feudal collectivism and clan ideology as political organizing principles.[125] He was primarily interested in the dynamic of historical change itself and the ways in which it was represented on stage.[126] The key point here is that Eisenstein saw the Renaissance as a progressive shift toward institutionalized, rational justice replacing the mechanical exchange of physical eye-for-eye revenge, but he believed that Renaissance legal progress was incapable of eradicating earlier, cruder, physical forms of revenge and so stood in dialectic tension with it: progress and regress together. Here we see two dialectical lines of thought come together. In *Ivan*, progress never leaves the past behind, and politics is personal. Renaissance humanism, the Great Russian State, and the modern Russian revolution may have been progressive for their times, but they never resolved the conflicts of the past, and those conflicts were never purely rational or collective or impersonal.

The chapter in *Method* that discusses revenge tragedy, historical film, and historical *zakonomernost'* begins by explaining that in making *Ivan the Terrible* Eisenstein had to expand his penchant for theorizing about form to recognize subject, plot, and character as key elements for materializing his ideas and intentions.[127] But, he wrote, the chosen historical and biographical facts must be arranged in specific ways in order to effectively move people, to change them, and to achieve the status of great art.[128] The contradictions between formal and narrative elements—form and content— are resolved for him by historical change. The choice of story elements must represent the author's intentions, but they have to be organized in such a way that the plot and characterizations bring out the specific historical conflicts in which they are embedded. The sharper the conflicts between the past and the present, between the resonances of those shifts inside the characters, and their presentation of those shifts, the greater the emotional and intellectual impact on the audience.[129] In this way, studying historical and biographical *zakonomernost'* added a new layer to Eisenstein's film theory and practice.

A significant shift takes place here in Eisenstein's thinking about the processes of history and about film form. Before making *Ivan the Terrible,* Eisenstein's conception of the historical film largely revolved around issues of veracity: one might "play with" the facts of individual depictions as long as the ultimate, generalizable image represented a larger truth. In formal terms, dialectical montage could bring together the various elements at play (depictions) to produce that larger truth (the generalizable image) In 1942 and afterward, he was arguing that the historical film also had to be structured according to the discernible patterns of historical change and their analogues in individual development in order to speak to the audience undergoing its own conflicts over individual and historical change. The chapter in *Method* called "Shifts in Time" is devoted to explaining those patterns of social, cultural, political, and individual evolution in their connection with sensory-emotional thinking, dialectical change over time, and artistic methods.

Eisenstein's original purpose in *Method* was to explore the structures of mind and body that produce and respond to art. What happens when we watch a film or read a poem or walk through a building? What does that do to us? Is it like anything else that goes on inside us? And how can those effects be produced by the artist to reach the audience with the greatest impact? He discovered that the relationship between word and image, and thought and feeling, were connected to the links between past and present. Eisenstein believed that art puts us in a receptive state that taps into what he called the "pre-logical" by activating our "sensory-emotional thinking." In a 1944 note, he called this "magic."

> Magic is no empty turn of phrase here. For art (true art) artfully / artificially [*iskusstvenno*] returns the viewer to a stage of sensory-emotional thinking . . . [to] a stage of magical interaction with nature. When you have achieved, for example, the synesthetic fusion of sound and image—you have placed the perception of the viewer in a state of sensory-emotional thinking, where synesthetic perception is the only possibility—there is no differentiation of perception (of the senses). And your viewer is "transformed" [*perestroen*] according to the standards not of today, but of primordial perception—"returned" to the conditions of the magical stage of apprehending the world through the senses.[130]

The pre-logical, then, is a condition of pure sensation and feeling, an instinctive, nonverbal state where boundaries between things, animals, and people are blurred or "undifferentiated." Great art stimulates the pre-logical as one side of a dialectic, where the pre-logical or sensory-emotional thinking—perceiving with our bodies and feelings—is in dialectical opposition to thinking-thinking—or thinking with our intellect.[131] Art has special powers for giving us access to this state, and we cannot understand how art works on us without understanding the pre-logical experience of sensory-emotional thinking. *Method* is Eisenstein's search in world history, literature, ethnography, psychology, medicine, and biology for examples of sensory-emotional thinking and explanations of its powerful appeal for us. It explores the ways conscious and unconscious modes of perception are joined in the production and perception of art forms of all kinds. Eisenstein was keenly attuned to the qualities of nonverbal images and art forms, and he came to believe that our structures of mind are constructed similarly to the natural and social worlds where we live, as we move through time. The same feeling / thinking dialectic that operates in the production and perception of art is at work in the fundamental laws that govern change over time in nature, history, and individuals. Along with montage, this is Eisenstein's key contribution to aesthetics, and it underlies everything he wrote from about 1932 until the end of his life.

This investigation grew out of his very earliest work in the theater and his early writing on expressive movement, that form of acting and actor training that Meyerhold developed, linking body movement, thought, and feeling. What began for Eisenstein with the links between physical movement and sensory-emotional responses led him to study people whose culture seemed to be focused more on the nonverbal and nonintellectual than on the logocentric rationality of modern European culture.[132] Since the early 1930s, when he saw the survivals of traditional ways of life in modern, urban, postrevolutionary Mexico, Eisenstein had been fascinated by the presence of the past, in all its forms, in our individual and collective lives, examples of which he found seemingly everywhere he looked.[133] Eisenstein's interest in the past in the present led him to develop the links between history and biography, on one hand, and the production and reception of the arts, on the other, and he found pre-logical, sensory-emotional thinking to be fundamental elements of them all.

Like Lucien Lévy-Bruhl, who coined the term, Eisenstein associated the pre-logical with premodern peoples and a premodern structure of mind. Unlike Lévy-Bruhl, he did not believe that modern people left the primitive behind when they matriculated into a more advanced, civilized state. On the contrary, rational, advanced modern people have a continual desire for, and ready access to, this undifferentiated, instinctive, wordless, sensory, creative and destructive, pre-logical state of being. He believed that premodern peoples had special access to a visceral, emotional, and direct physiological mode of interacting with the world that circumvented word, text, and logical thinking. Most of his subjects came from classical European myth and ethnographic studies of "primitive" peoples of Asia, indigenous Americans and Latin Americans, Africans and Pacific Islanders. Like other modernist artists, Eisenstein was fascinated by the art and ritual and descriptions of peoples brought back to Europe by modern imperialists, and he was drawn to what he saw as the elemental, authentic, and creative in "the primitive." Like his contemporaries, Eisenstein used a Eurocentric terminology of hierarchy, progress, and European superiority, but in fact his views of progress and European civilization itself were highly attenuated. While Eisenstein articulated his aesthetic, psychological, and philosophical studies in the Eurocentric historical idiom of his day, his thinking was fundamentally anti-Eurocentric, and he was deeply skeptical of historical progress toward "civilization." He didn't celebrate the premodern pre-logical for its recovery of something European civilization had lost à la Joseph Conrad, or its alterity and exoticism as in the work of the orientalist painter Jean-Léon Gérôme. Rather he saw the pre-logical as unquestionably inscribed in *modern* life and of no less value than the logical. He believed that those physiological and psychological impulses are in constant dialectical tension—a creative tension—with our advanced, complex, intellectual ability to reason. He believed we always have access to and desire for our instincts for the pre-logical no matter how advanced societies become. And he considered both of equal importance in understanding human perception and human creativity, as well as the human penchant for revenge and violence. The denigration inherent in his Eurocentric terminology should not be underestimated, but neither should it obscure his critique of Eurocentrism and colonialism or his rejection of the valorization of logocentric rationality. His placement of nonverbal, nonrational processes of perception at the heart of his view of human nature and his theory of artistic production and reception marks a fundamental challenge to the logocentrism and claims to progress of Soviet culture and ideology. And he took it further than anyone else did at the time, seeing in the pre-logical both the origins of our instinct for violence and self-destruction, on one hand, and a conduit to the richest possible sensory-emotional experience with the potential for transcendence, transformation, and liberation, on the other. Perhaps most important here is that Eisenstein understood our response to art to be more than an intellectual exercise; art also touches us directly through our senses and speaks directly to our emotions.

Many readers of *Method* who discover Eisenstein's fascination with the pre-logical and his tireless pursuit of examples of the pre-logical in world cultures and history neglect the other side of this dialectic. The pre-logical is central to our perceptive practices and evolution as individuals and societies, but it is always in dialectical conflict with the logical, rational, and intellectual. These contradictions, so apparent in revenge dramas—the continual pull of primal violence despite social and intellectual progress—allowed Eisenstein to locate these conflicts within his overall thinking about the dialectics of historical change. He came to believe that one of the central operations of human psychology involved an inexhaustible desire to relive the primal, originary, instinctive feelings of our earliest experiences, both as individuals and as societies. These views of the "eternal return," the "return of the repressed," and the cyclical nature of time played a critical role in his historicism and his composition of Ivan.

Like Freud, Eisenstein saw perceptions of difference as fundamental to the formation of the psyche, but rather than privilege gender difference, Eisenstein believed that the more primary distinction was between the logical, rational, and intellectual, on one hand, and the instinctive, sensory-emotional, pre-logical, on the other. Following Freud's student Otto Rank, author of *The Trauma of Birth*, Eisenstein believed that a pure, blissful state of "undifferentiated" experience in the womb, where we are nothing but feeling and sensation, is traumatically ruptured by the experience of birth, our first critical transition. That change in our condition forces us to begin differentiating, thinking, and reacting.[134] For this harsh, outside world, we need our wits, we begin to differentiate, we begin to think. Afterward we are forever subject to a dialectic of sensory-feeling, on one hand, and reason, on the other: pre-logical and logical, undifferentiated and boundaried, connected and isolated, all freeing and constraining us: "the central trauma on the path of development toward consciousness—this is, of course, the transition from the stage of sensory-emotional thinking, pre-logical thinking, thinking *with images*, to differentiated thinking and structured *logic*."[135] Eisenstein's understanding of dialectics in works of art was rooted in the constantly growing tension between the instinctive and the intellectual, or the undifferentiated and the differentiated, and in the automatic revisiting of childhood trauma each time individuals took a step toward mastery in adulthood. When this dialectic reaches a kind of emotional intensity that he called *pathos* and an acute, no longer bearable tension, it explodes in synthesis, which we experience as what he calls *ekstasis*. This *ekstasis* is not just any old dialectical synthesis but a transcendent, out-of-body transformation—a moment of pure sensation and feeling, returning us to the state of being in the womb but at a higher, deeper stage, based on all the knowledge acquired since birth together with the fireworks of ecstatic liberation.

The dialectic of pre-logical and logical is the very motor of history for both individuals and societies and exploring these dynamics is the one of the main goals of *Method*. Individually and historically, progress comes about as the result of conflicts between ways of thinking and behaving, dialectically producing new stages and new conflicts, whether "about love, ethics-justice, the problem of jealousy, the institution of vengeance."[136] But progress (toward humanism, socialism, or whatever) is never linear and never purely progress, because we are always pulled to the sensory-emotional, physiological, social-moral elements of our past.

Eisenstein envisioned this combined backward-forward historical process in the form of a three-dimensional spiral: picture history as a spiral staircase. As individuals and societies move forward (or upward) through time (toward something progressive), we repeatedly, inevitably circle back to our most primal experiences, but at incrementally higher stages of consciousness, in more complex circumstances, with progressively elaborated explanations or ideologies. The spiral, "as the reflection of the struggle accompanying the displacement of one structure by another, is 'eternal,' as 'eternal' as the formula of dialectics. Eternal, not in time, but in its *omnipresence*, that is, it is always on hand."[137] Eisenstein was not the first to imagine the course of history in this form. He knew that Hegel, Marx, and Lenin had all discussed movement in history as a spiral and, among the Russian avant-garde in the 1920s, the spiral had been a popular sign of liberation and progress.[138] But more than his predecessors and contemporaries, Eisenstein had serious doubts about the linear progress inherent in such incremental advances in history. He made (and was tolerant of) contradictory statements about historical progress, and as early as the 1920s he distinguished idealist and materialist dialectics from his own "ironic" dialectics. He did not believe that we ever leave the irrational behind in our perfection of the rational; we never expunge our primal violent instincts as we make advances in social and political consciousness, either as adults or as progressive societies. On the contrary, history is a spiral not only for structural reasons but because with each advance to a "higher" stage of development we return to and revive original traumas, experiences, and drives.[139] As conflicts intensify, heading toward dialectical synthesis and displacement, we reach further into the primal past, toward our pure, unalloyed feelings and earliest experiences. In fact, Eisenstein's historical *zakonomernost'* not only departs from Marxist teleology; he explicitly linked his repudiation of the Marxist conception of progress with Stalin. In a scribbled note from June 1942, he contrasted "Stalin's collective farmer," a social category that should be eradicated by progress toward communism, with characters in literature that Eisenstein identified with the backward-forward spin of his own conception of the historical spiral. And in *Method*, he wrote that, unlike Stalin, he didn't find it necessary to see moving forward as inherently superior to the tendencies that resisted progress.[140]

Eisenstein was interested in the structures of historical change because the parallel individual and social contradictions shaped by the laws of history helped him answer one of the questions he began with: how to make a historical film (and a great work of art) that would resonate with contemporaries. He believed that works of art become "great" (which he defined here as "universal" and "immortal") only when they conformed to biological and psychological structures of perception and cognition.[141] This correspondence between artistic and biological structures is one of the main themes of *Nonindifferent Nature*, and there are a number of passages in *Method* that address the connection between historical change, historical drama, and structures of mind and feelings. In November 1941, soon after arriving in Alma Ata, he addressed part of that formula in discussing the "interpenetration" of the archetypal and the contemporary in connection to the logical and pre-logical: "when contemporary material doesn't sit in the saddle of the ancestral (pre-logical) context, it won't grip the emotions, that is, a 'great' work won't be realized."[142]

Eisenstein saw revenge tragedy as an ideal genre for bringing together the fundamental structures of thinking and feelings, and the forward-backward spiral pattern of historical and individual change, with changes in artistic forms. Eisenstein thought that what gave Shakespeare's characters their "invariable, inherent appeal," could be found in his ability to capture the parallels between the inner conflict his characters experienced and the contradictions produced by the historical conflicts taking place. The "new moral demands" of Renaissance humanism denaturalized and denigrated the legitimacy of ancient forms of physical vengeance, while at the same time confirming their hold on people.[143] Eisenstein praised Shakespeare for the alignment in his revenge dramas among character, plot, theme, and form when the "'shifts' in time" were marked by "intense collisions between divergent social forms of consciousness."[144] Their inner divisions, moral dilemmas, and political conflicts were shaped by the historical changes taking place around them, so they each possessed "dabs of complimentary tones from opposite palettes," and they acted on impulses from both sides of the historical-psychological divide.[145] *The Merchant of Venice* dramatized these shifts at the level of plot: because Shylock stubbornly insisted on a form of physical vengeance that was no longer socially or morally acceptable, he appeared to others as immoral. But even Shylock recorded the external changes. His dawning awareness of the new morality gave him access to the social conscience of his era and at times even produced a flash of remorse.[146] And Hamlet—"as opposed to unconflicted Laertes and Fortinbras"—shared the dialectical contradictions Eisenstein saw in Ivan.[147] *Hamlet* dramatized the overcoming of our "passive, reflexive instincts" for revenge by the advent of "'humanism' or humanistic consciousness," but at the same time *Hamlet* exhibited the continuation of these primal instincts in what Eisenstein called the "extremely cruel product of the 'humanistic Renaissance.'"[148] Eisenstein cites Hamlet's devious little speech on the inescapable leveling inherent in cycles of life and death as an example of that cruelty inherent in humanism. "Nothing but to show you how a king may go a progress through the guts of a beggar," Hamlet says to the king, meaning that death makes all of us wormfood.[149] "*This is very far-reaching and important,*" Eisenstein wrote, not because he himself was conflicted over the issues involved in Renaissance humanism, but because *Hamlet* offered him a model for synchronizing the structures of individual, historical, and contemporary contradiction inevitable during periods of historical change.[150]

Stalin was right to call Eisenstein's Ivan "Hamlet-like," as he famously did, because Ivan reflects, vacillates, doubts, and externalizes his inner struggle over avenging the murder of his mother. Eisenstein appreciated Shakespeare's psychological innovations, which he characterized in his own terms as Hamlet's "unity of opposites," but he saw the very different plays by Thomas Kyd and Ben Jonson as well as Christopher Marlowe, Thomas Middleton, and John Webster as offering dramatic models he also wanted to follow.[151] All the early modern revenge tragedies depicted conflicts set in the past to explore the shifts taking place in the lives of the contemporary audience. But Eisenstein recognized the differences between the ways in which Shakespeare and the other playwrights portrayed those conflicts. As a character, Ivan is defined by his inner conflicts like Hamlet, but he also projected parts of himself on other characters who often represented fixed types as in plays by Kyd and Jonson where external conflicts among the characters provide the drama, and deeds counted more than words. From Kyd's archetype, *The Spanish Tragedy* (first performed in 1587), to Middleton's *The Revenger's Tragedy* (1606), revenge was depicted as physical punishment exacted on the body by characters performing as types rather than as modern realistic characters with an inner life. Eisenstein considered the collision of such types in plays like Jonson's *Volpone* to be "characteristic for the construction of *pathos* effects by the direct charging of elements ecstatically exploding into each other with constantly increasing intensity."[152] In her lectures on these plays, Emma Smith notes that Shakespeare's psychological innovations didn't negate the merits (or the popularity) of other early modern plays. Smith points out that the reflexive soliloquys in *Hamlet* may have no greater power to move us than the rougher conflicts we see dramatized in *The Spanish Tragedy*. Heronimo's "traumatized, almost unbearable, mood swings and unpredictability may be designated crude but they actually have the power to affect an audience potentially numbed by witnessing [*The Spanish Tragedy's*] horrific cruelties."[153] In composing his Ivan, Eisenstein found uses for the dialectical, internalized psychological conflicts Shakespeare introduced in part by contrasting them with the externalized physical conflicts between types that made Kyd's *Spanish Tragedy* the most popular play of its time.

Another facet of the revenge tragedy makes it possible to show yet another, deeper connection between the two fundamental historical-biographical features of Eisenstein's Ivan—that is, his transition from prey to predator and his unquenchable, atavistic attraction to blood vengeance. As Deborah Willis points out in her study of trauma and *Titus Andronicus*, there is an element of self-delusion at the heart of revenge that applies to all the Renaissance revenge tragedies, though less *Hamlet* than *Titus Andronicus*. All the characters seeking revenge in those plays claim to be seeking justice. They call revenge an equal trade: an eye for an eye. Avenging the death of a loved one by taking the life of someone close to the murderer was supposed to exact justice and return balance to the social order. But Willis argues that these symmetrical acts of violence are not so symmetrical after all. The revengers who claim to be seeking social justice and balance are additionally motivated by the grievous harm done to themselves personally, by their inconsolable grief. The *language* of revenge is symmetrical and social, but the *act* of revenge is doubly motivated by the social traumas of loss and the personal trauma of grief. Such doubling and self-delusion made the acts of revenge "exceed rather than equal the original wrong."[154] Ivan's childhood trauma, to which he cannot resist returning, is not only the loss of his mother but the grief he suffered as a result of her murder. The false belief that revenge is an equal exchange means that revenge can never *feel* adequate. Avengers will continually, eternally, obsessively spiral around to return to the original act of violence and the feelings that motivate their need for revenge in seeking an elusive, illusory sense of balance.

Eisenstein constructed *Ivan the Terrible* as a spiral history and biography: "the drama with Tsar Ivan sits firmly in the pre-logical saddle."[155] His portrait of Ivan exemplifies the same collisions dramatized by Shakespeare and the other revenge tragedies: Ivan vacillates between enacting violent, physical, eye-for-eye revenge and doubts about his moral right to do so, culminating in the dramatic display of remorse and recommitment in The Confession scene in Part III. Ivan's every progressive move toward a modern unified state is complicated by a return to his earliest formative experiences and his primal feelings of vulnerability and grief. Every step toward ideologically progressive displacement of feudal clans and feudal political structures is mirrored by Ivan's "atavistic" attachment to his own clan, also producing doubts and remorse. Neither ideological advance nor political or military success can exhaust Ivan's primal, raging need to avenge the deaths of his mother and, later, his wife. Just as the early modern plays acquired their intellectual relevance and emotional power through the restaging of ancient, archetypal narratives of historical transitions, Ivan-the-preyed-upon becomes Ivan-the-predator, replicating similarly widespread and archetypal revenge dramas.[156] Like his rival Vladimir, like his ally Aleksei Basmanov, and like little Varia playing bear and wolf, Ivan draws on the atavistic instincts that progress is supposed to eliminate by reaching into his deepest, animal instincts to turn vulnerability into power, and in doing so makes himself as dangerous as those he overthrows. All the early modern English revenge plays show that cycles of revenge fail to extinguish the desire for revenge and do more harm than good. They show that the violence motivated by revenge recurs because intellectual and judicial progress don't keep us from reliving our most primitive, pre-logical desire for relief from our pain: "Where words prevail not, violence prevails."[157]

Epilogues

By the time Eisenstein was shooting and editing *Ivan the Terrible*, his thinking about history had evolved beyond looking for ways to fuse sources with intuition to create historical verisimilitude and a generalizable image. At first, he read the sources to find characters and events to dramatize the story he set-tled on fairly quickly: an antimyth that portrayed Ivan as a conflicted human being, whose personal feelings and desire for revenge helped him found the Great Russian State but also made opposition and violence inevitable. During this period Eisenstein developed an understanding of historical patterns of change that integrated individual inner divisions into transitions in social and political history as a dynamic backward-forward moving spiral. These ideas about historical *zakonomernost'* were also incorporated into his exploration of the enduring appeal of great works of art. The patterns of historical contra-diction and change, of the spiral's inevitable return, had to be reproduced in the structures of the film's narrative and aesthetics in order to convey the art-ist's ideas and feelings to the audience. "Thinking with images" is inherently ambiguous not only because images lack the specificity of texts, but because they engage us dialectically—plunging us into pre-logical feeling while stim-ulating our most complex ideas—producing chains of associations that can proceed in multiple, not always logical, not always consistent, directions. For Eisenstein, history moved in a regular but unpredictable fashion, following discernible, but not deterministic, patterns. In Ivan's case, the historical spiral challenges us to consider questions that arose in all the early modern stage tragedies: If history follows laws, are individuals responsible for their own actions? Or are they only reacting to circumstances?

Naum Kleiman's study of Eisenstein's film endings offers a way to understand this conundrum at the heart of Eisenstein's "theory of history." Part III of the published screenplay ends with Ivan striding triumphantly down the beach to the sea, as trumpets sound, the sea roars, and even the waves come forward to pay homage to the tsar. As Kleiman points out, however, this was the politically safe ending but only one of several alternative finales that Eisenstein considered. The terrible cost of Ivan's triumph is conveyed by the juxtaposition of two drawings: the "Apotheosis of Ivan," with huge waves rising up to greet the tsar at his com-mand, and the somber "Alone? . . . ," made the same day, depicting a weary, bent Ivan, not striding but trudging along the shore of a quiet sea.[158]

In an early note, Eisenstein also considered showing an aged Ivan, contem-plating his achievements and failures while envisioning "Ermak—the people, the future." Ermak Timofeevich was a Cossack adventurer and explorer who was associated with Russia's conquest of Siberia during Ivan's reign, but Ivan associates him with the Russian people. In another scenario, Ivan is dying alone in a dark corner, having murdered his son in a fit of rage; an act Eisen-stein calls a suicidal gesture that destroys all Ivan has achieved. In yet another idea, a dying Ivan is back in the Kremlin, having lost Russia's hold on the Baltic weeks after winning it, when he has a vision of the future Peter the Great

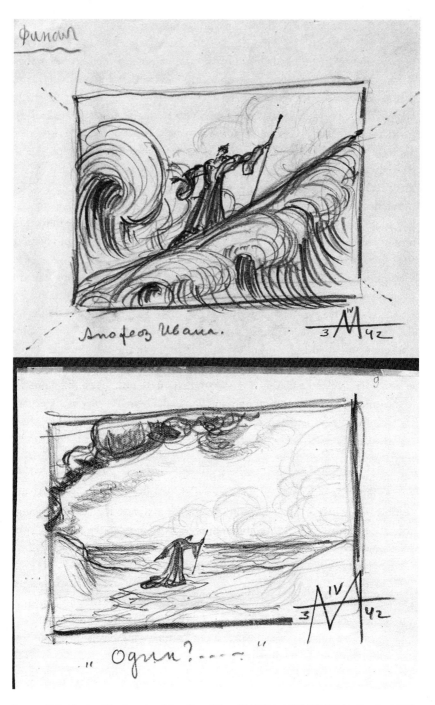

Figure 2.4 Finale: "Apotheosis of Ivan" or "Alone?" RGALI, 1923/2/1702/6 [Apr 3, 1942]; 2/1702/9 [Apr 3, 1942]. Used with permission.

securing the Baltic for good.[159] We will never know whether these contradictory futures would have found their way onto film, but the contrasts are stark. Each of these imagined Epilogues superimposes images of divergent historical paths: illusory triumph, victory overturned, raging violence, and, intervening between Ivan's time and ours, future historical victories with similar patterns of triumph and tragedy as the Russian Empire expands westward to the Baltic and eastward across Siberia. One can interpret these as the prescribed justification for Ivan's violent methods or, alternatively, as the tragic cost of autocracy, or as both: a dialectical evasion of any historical or moral judgment. It is more in line with the spiral shape of Eisenstein's thinking to understand these multilayered Epilogues as components of a theory of history that is both regular (*zakonomerno*) and open to the dialectical possibilities of triumph and tragedy. History does not predetermine recurring waves of terror, but it regularly creates conditions in which some people cannot resist the primal allure of revenge. And in Eisenstein's film, as Tsivian noted in his comment on Kleiman's finales, there was plenty of drama to come after Ivan reached the sea; the ending was not intended to furnish closure but to provide an exit to the next phase of the historical spiral.[160]

Multiple, indeterminate possibilities for the subjects of Eisenstein's *Ivan* do not exhaust the dialectical shape of his thinking about history. He also believed, as he did when conceiving the spherical book, that perspectives on the past shift. Not only do we understand the past differently from people who came before us, but all these shifts in time and perspective must be incorporated in a work of art to make it effective for audiences in other cultures and times. The spherical history book has a core and a surface: *Ivan the Terrible* is difficult in part because Eisenstein tried to incorporate changing perspectives with shifts in cultural mores and historical change over time in composing his portrait of Ivan. As Anne Nesbet put it, "when traveling the spiral of image-based thinking, it is difficult to know whether one is outbound or inbound, digressing or honing in on the essential."[161] Eisenstein believed—and Ivan embodied this belief—that people often hold contradictory positions; that we are all bundles of contradictions and "unities of opposites." But he stops short of a postmodern suspicion of historical reality and individual coherence. Shifts in perspective and inner contradictions are not the only things that matter. Whatever we believe, our actions have consequences. Ivan was conflicted, remorseful, ironic, "Shakespearean," but he repeatedly overrode his doubts and divisions and consistently chose "Jonsonian" action: revenge, the state, inhuman ambition, and violence. Eisenstein viewed documented historical events in dialectic dynamic with changing views of those events across time. He studied the documents and the secondary sources, and he sought to depict the multiple ways in which the past could be understood. Then he depicted the role played by experience, feelings, circumstances, ideology, inner divisions, and outer conflicts and showed how all those competing forces produced actions that had consequences.

Eisenstein's theory of history refutes those who read *Ivan the Terrible* as a justification for Stalinist dictatorship and terror: the film challenged Stalinist historicism on both the specifics of prescribed historiography and in the larger frame of historical ideology. In Eisenstein's ironic, dialectical, historical spiral, there was nothing to prevent advanced state ideology from coinciding with primal, horrific state violence. The film's portrait of absolute power showed the violent consequences of absolute rule, even when the ruler is motivated by progressive or revolutionary ideas. Each higher stage of historical development enabled a spiral return to originary fear, trauma, and violent reaction. Centuries after Ivan centralized Russian rule, Soviet leaders, whose own revolution was defined by hopes for egalitarian justice based on a progressive ideology, proved equally capable of plunging into the deep well of vengeance and violence and of offering justifications based on selfless promises.

CHAPTER 3

Power Personified

Ivan *as Biography*

Viewers in the 1940s assumed that *Ivan the Terrible* would be about Stalin. To what extent the film does, in fact, portray Stalin has been the subject of controversy ever since. Eisenstein's Ivan is far too complex to be reduced to nothing but contemporary political commentary, and while it is undoubtedly true that the film is not only about Stalin, it can no longer be denied that Ivan = Stalin at least part of the time. One of the rare explicit references to politics in Eisenstein's notes not only confirms that he saw Stalin in his Ivan but shows how the identification of Stalin with Ivan shaped his conception of the film. In October 1942, in a notebook largely devoted to historical and political notes, Eisenstein turned to complaining about Soviet restrictions on artistic expression. He lamented that his thoughts about Russian history and the endurance of the past in the present were, "Alas! Much broader than one is permitted to think." Switching into his fluent but slightly woolly English, as he often did when discussing subjects he considered sensitive, he went on:

> Our art not outgrowing of a conviction of one's own subject but out of prescribed love or hatred! Up to a certain age—progressif. What lacks in the works of today—is the inner conception of ideas (not so in "Mexico"—my theme). "John" [meaning *Ivan the Terrible*, the film]—good—because personal avant tout—a mixture of one's own self and the leading figure of our time.[1]

The imperfections of Eisenstein's English cannot hide the fact that he conceived of Ivan through a filter of his own experiences combined with his view of Stalin and that the film's perspective on Stalin would be "personal *avant tout*" rather than the officially "prescribed love or hatred." His observations of revolutionary and Stalinist Russia, his experience of personal power dynamics, and his subsequent study of Ivan gave Eisenstein a finely tuned awareness of the varieties and uses of power. He knew that his political conception of the film challenged acceptable public discourse and that his depiction of Ivan was far more complex and critical "than one is permitted to think." At this stage, in October 1942, his conception of *Ivan* pleased him because he managed to construct a story that was faithful to history *and* to his own "inner conception of ideas," rather than official prescription.

Watching *Ivan the Terrible* today, many viewers see the echoes of Stalin's crimes and sadistic practices, especially in Part II, and numerous authors have listed the parallels between the film's Kremlin and Stalin's.[2] Ivan's paranoia, manipulation, capriciousness, demagoguery, and cruelty together with his shrewdness, cunning, and his cloying performance of avuncular charm are all reminiscent of Stalin and are all on display from the very beginning of Part I. Eisenstein's shadowy Kremlin is a world of suspicion and surveillance that eerily evoked Stalin's. Much recent literature on Stalin's inner circle shows it to have been a company of competitive insiders, much like Eisenstein's portrayal of Ivan's circle of servitors, each hungry for the ruler's approval and jealous of everyone else.[3] And historians today often portray Stalin and his inner circle as extremely insecure, even paranoid, about their hold on power.[4] A decade after Stalin's death, the Yugoslav Communist leader-turned-dissident Milovan Djilas described for the first time the all-night, all-male drinking feasts organized by Stalin in the years after World War II to pit members of his inner circle against one another.[5] I don't know how much Eisenstein knew of these events, but his Feast of the Oprichniki captures the deadly fun that the manipulative, paranoid Stalin stage-managed at his own feasts.

Eisenstein wanted us to see Stalin in *Ivan*, but which Stalin? Many viewers expected the wise statesman and military genius depicted a few years earlier in Vladimir Petrov's *Peter the First*. The film historian Efim Levin tells us that most Russian viewers expected a "progressive state actor, wise politician, visionary, and great reformer, who, no one disputed, was cruel and spilled a lot of blood, but for a holy and historically understandable and justifiable cause."[6] Yet others undoubtedly thought they would see the terrified and terrifying madman depicted in Ilya Repin's well-known painting of Ivan, unhinged by remorse after killing his son. Stalin himself expected to see the Ivan he approved in the screenplay: "progressive for his time," unburdened by psychology, and unembellished by art. Stalin's progressive hero would have been relatively easy for Eisenstein to portray and would have required no subterfuge, no conflict between official prescription and "inner conception of ideas." But Eisenstein chose to "stick his neck out."

An important formulation for understanding the film's politics can be found in *Nonindifferent Nature*, where Eisenstein emphatically stated that the main theme of *Ivan the Terrible* "first stated by one voice and then subsequently imitated by all the others . . . is *the theme of power*."[7] Eisenstein didn't only want to create a portrait of power, he wanted to dissect power, to show all the contradictions power and the universal hunger for power produced in actual, living people. Placing a deindividualized concept of power at the center of attention shifts focus from any single absolute ruler to questions concerning the acquisition and uses of power at a given time in a given context. Focusing on power itself opens up political and moral questions rather than setting blame in some fixed way on simplistically, ahistorically demonized individuals. Yet *Ivan the Terrible* is about much more than the uses of power. Thinking about Ivan and his times and thinking about power allowed Eisenstein to draw on his own ambition as well as attributes of the other authoritarian figures in his life to deepen his portrait of Ivan as a man and a ruler. Ivan is more than an abstract container for thoughts about power. In his stated effort "not to whitewash Ivan, but to explain," Eisenstein created a portrait of power that is capable of elucidating distinctions among tyrants without simplifying the historical challenges they confronted, their responses to those challenges, or the complexity of our responses to them.

Eisenstein's various political strategies, as it turned out, coincided with his artistic methods. Given that Stalin and everyone else expected Eisenstein to use the story of the sixteenth century to comment on the twentieth, Eisenstein could have made those links much more explicit or less mired in complexity and contradiction. But because he chose not to take that path, he realized he needed to hide or partially hide his "inner conception of ideas." Concealing his secrets in the mortar of the cathedral walls was only one of his tactics for hiding in plain sight. Throughout the notebooks for *Ivan* and his manuscripts of this period, he also discussed methods for gradually exposing ideas and feelings for the film's audience to reconstruct in a "generalizable" whole. Eisenstein wrote numerous notes about exploiting cinema's essential temporality: to *partially* conceal ideas in such a way that viewers would become aware of them subconsciously, instinctively, in their bodies, before dislodging them from their subconscious and processing them intellectually and emotionally: "Must hide, but not completely, just the opposite—hint at, lodge in the perception, but as if in passing, so to speak, *not in the foreground*, not frontally."[8] He used this method for conveying meaning and shaping audience experience both to shield his vision of Ivan from censors and to give viewers the clues to construct an image of Ivan over time. The *Montage* essays were devoted to explicating these processes of dropping "depiction" fragments, disassembled, in the consciousness for viewers to reassemble in meaningful "montage images."

Central to *Ivan the Terrible* is an examination of the absolute ruler as individual subject: the ruler's experience of the unification of power, of the inevitable isolation, and of the excesses of absolute power. Notes written in July 1947 show that Eisenstein saw these issues—self and other, ruler and ruled—running through all his projects, whether filmed or canceled or banned.[9] In fact, Ivan the Terrible wasn't Eisenstein's first tyrant. During the 1930s, he became interested in the late eighteenth-century Haitian slave rebellion and planned a film with Paul Robeson as Henri Christophe.[10] He also considered a film about Nero based on a novel by Lion Feuchtwanger.[11] These projects come up again in his production notes for *Ivan*, but more than either of these, the tyrant who haunted *Ivan the Terrible* was Boris Godunov, Ivan's eventual successor, who also was believed to have murdered his way into power. Eisenstein spent much of the year before he began *Ivan* outlining a film about Alexander Pushkin that featured a long segment on Pushkin's play *Boris Godunov*. Eisenstein returned often to Godunov in his production notes for *Ivan* because his treatment of Pushkin's play, as Håkan Lövgren has shown, focused on similar issues of tsarist power and the tragic fate of a great artist under a despotic regime.[12]

In addition to these historical-political figures, it is well known now that Eisenstein identified Ivan with other authority figures, beginning with Eisenstein's artistic mentor, the monumental Vsevolod Meyerhold. The two men had a competitive, love-hate, father-son relationship that is reflected in Eisenstein's troubled writing about Meyerhold and in the fact that Eisenstein took considerable risks to preserve his great teacher's papers after Meyerhold was arrested. In the middle of the war, Eisenstein asked Pera Atasheva to send the signed photograph of Meyerhold that he'd left behind, hidden, in his apartment to Alma Ata.[13] Eisenstein's father, Mikhail, was another formative and formidable figure in Eisenstein's life and he figures prominently in the notebooks and memoirs of this period as another kind of overbearing authority figure. Eisenstein drew on all these shifting and contradictory associations to create various depictions, partly hidden and gradually revealed that together would eventually produce a generalizable image of men in power.

Previous writers have discussed the particular associations of Ivan with various authority figures, the centrality of power as a theme, and the montage of depiction and image, but the key political questions remain unanswered. What kind of ruler did Eisenstein create in drawing on all these models of authoritarian rule? How is power personified in a single ambitious man bent on power, state building, and revenge? How is power personified in a single character? Eisenstein's notes and manuscripts on power, his various father figures, and his image of Ivan in the world allow us to understand the specifically political elements in his portrait of Ivan. As we have seen, for Eisenstein politics was always personal: his composite figure of Ivan was both an extraordinary man in an extraordinary position of power and an ordinary man subject to the same human impulses as anyone else. Eisenstein makes power personal not only because he is interested in the psychological profile of his characters, but because he sees personalized internal conflicts as central to understanding the nature of subjectivity, power, and the consequences of absolute power and one-man rule.

In his autobiography, Eisenstein tells a relevant anecdote about how he chose to construct his own life story. When he was teaching at the All-Union State Institute of Cinematography (VGIK), he asked the students what they wanted him to discuss. One of them said "shyly but not obsequiously" that they didn't want lectures on montage or directing or production; they wanted to learn "how to become an Eisenstein." Flattered, and disingenuously self-effacing, he used the story to tell us what the book would be about: "it was hard to understand who might want to become [Eisenstein]. However, here it is. Here is precisely how I became what I am. And if anyone is interested in the result, then here are scattered notes about how that very process works."[14] This little story bookends the film—it occurred a few years before Eisenstein made *Ivan the Terrible* and was recorded immediately after work on *Ivan* was halted—and it tells us something about how Eisenstein thought about narrating a life. It is safe to say that when Stalin commissioned artists to represent Ivan as the first autocrat of the modern Russian state, he wasn't interested in Ivan's development as an individual or even as a ruler, much less a *tragic* ruler. But Eisenstein wanted to tell a different kind of story. He not only wanted to challenge established myths; he wanted to understand the psychology of violence, revenge, and remorse. He wanted to understand the ways in which great ambition, power, and doubt shaped Ivan and everyone else as well. He wanted to understand how people change over time and how Ivan became the kind of ruler he became. He also wanted to find new ways to depict a life on screen. He wanted to show "how that very process worked."

The pivotal concept in answer to all these questions was the dialectic of the logical and the pre-logical. Eisenstein organized Ivan's biography along roughly the same lines as the backward-forward historical spiral discussed in the previous chapter. Each key transition in Ivan's life is signaled by some form of regression to the originary experiences of childhood, when he witnessed traumatic violence and suffered traumatic abandonment. We see Ivan repeatedly imitating his more powerful foes, transforming himself from prey into predator. The film shows Ivan moving forward through these two dialectical structures: regression and repetition, and imitation and change. At the same time, Eisenstein uses visual and other sensory cues to trigger the viewer's memory of Ivan's earlier stages and to trigger our own similar experiences, so that we can sense and feel Ivan's trauma, tension, and transformation in our own bodies while we watch him struggle with his ambition and doubts. Eisenstein specifically used objects—props, costumes, and frescoes, for example—to create unconscious and conscious awareness of links and conflicts between characters and ideas and raise questions about Ivan's state of mind and his behavior.

In this chapter I examine, first, the key transitions in Ivan's life to show how Eisenstein adapted the historical spiral to the biography of the individual ruler; second, how he used stage props and production design to create dialectical links and comparisons among multiple characters and ideas; and third, how these complicated narrative structures raised questions about power, subjectivity, and biographical change over time that were mirrored in Eisenstein's own life and led him to call *Ivan the Terrible* a self-portrait and a tragedy.

Narrating a Life

To understand how Eisenstein organized Ivan's biography as a dialectical spiral, we need to take another excursion into theory. Like Freud, Benjamin, Jean Piaget, and many others beginning with Aristotle, Eisenstein believed that the laws of sociocultural evolution were paralleled in individual human evolution: ontogeny replicates phylogeny. As an evolutionary idea, this has been thoroughly refuted, but what Stephen Jay Gould called "the most durable analogy in the history of biology" was fundamental to Eisenstein's thinking when he was making *Ivan the Terrible*.[15] What began as the pursuit of a universal theory of artistic perception and production led Eisenstein to find parallels between historical *zakonomernost'* and biographical *zakonomernost'*, and these patterns produced new insights into the function of power and its representation in art.

Eisenstein believed that as we move forward in life, our desire for the undifferentiated, pre-logical, originary state of being resurfaces regularly, especially at moments of great stress in our individual lives or during historical periods of great change. The "shifts in time" that took place during the Renaissance, the Enlightenment, and the modern sociopolitical revolutions had analogies in moments of personal change such as sexual awakening and confrontations with major moral choices.[16] At such crossroads, as inner conflicts become more pronounced, we are drawn back to our animal selves or primitive selves, our childhood selves or even our prenatal, womb-dwelling selves. As we move onward and upward, we become smarter and more experienced and more complex, but we regularly circle back to these early experiences and to this instinctive, sensory-emotional way of perceiving the world. The essentially spiral process as it applies to individuals—moving forward and returning to the beginning—always contains the attractive but frightening allure of our early, pre-logical selves.

Now, if we have, as a basic structure of mind, a pull backward to the pre-logical in its sexual and violent and emotional and womb-ish forms and if art is one of the things that also can put us into a pre-logical state, then it is the artist's job to compose the story on the screen (or stage or canvas) to tap into those originary cognitive and emotional processes in spectators. One of Eisenstein's fundamental principles was that art is most powerful and most successful when it mirrors not only the historical shifts in time but also the structures of mind and body of the artist producing it and the people perceiving it. Ivan's dialectical upward-tracing spiral biography shows him advancing and evolving while the feelings he experienced at the beginning of his life continually return to him and motivate him. Eisenstein wanted us to feel Ivan's changes from the inside, so he used sensory and cognitive cues to prompt us to feel Ivan's feelings and sense his changes in our own bodies as we in the audience observe the spiral process of biographical change.

According to Eisenstein, no one understood the pre-logical better than Walt Disney, and his work on Disney was directly related to his work on *Ivan* in ways that have not been appreciated. At two critical junctures—just after arriving in Alma Ata and again during the winter of 1943–1944, Eisenstein wrote major passages on Disney for *Method* that illuminate the ways he thought about the spiral, the dialectic, and his understanding of Ivan the Terrible as a man and a ruler. Eisenstein was a passionate admirer of Disney's early animated films.[17] In the first part of the manuscript, written in 1940–1941 (before *Ivan*), Eisenstein rhapsodically described Disney's ability to capture *ekstasis*. Disney's animated creatures and things embodied the spontaneous and pleasurable in art, distilled to its essence. He wasn't talking about princess stories with happy endings. He meant the cognitive pleasure we take in watching the dynamic, graphic transfiguration of forms. In Disney, a fish turns into a tiger and roars with a lion's voice, octopuses turn into elephants, a steamboat consumes a pile of wood as if it were a plate of pastries.[18] This shape-shifting ability perfectly captured the undifferentiatedness of the pre-logical. The boundaries that separate us from animals or animals from plants or one thing from another are not fixed. Disney characters embody and enact the freedom from form—undifferentiatedness—that can be found in both the pre-logical and the dialectical, synthetic, transcendent, ecstatic state that replicates the pre-logical at moments of transformative synthesis. As Rachel Moore puts it, the "cartoon awakens and momentarily satisfies the human desire to become something else."[19]

Eisenstein was especially taken with several recurrent details in Disney's films that turn out to be of consequence for *Ivan the Terrible*. The magic of transfiguration and the liberation of *ekstasis* are things we experience in art and crave in life, but the real change that we long for, the path to real transformation, is hard. Mickey Mouse and many other Disney characters—horses, ostriches, cows, cats, and even plants—signal the difficulty of pushing against their biological forms by stretching their necks, tails, and limbs out toward the limits of the physically possible before returning to their natural forms. For Eisenstein, this stretching of limbs against the limits of form captured something essential in the human psyche about change. As the up-and-down troubles Alice suffered in Wonderland show us, you have to work hard to stretch out of yourself or squeeze yourself through tiny doors for change to occur. Eisenstein ended this section of the manuscript by saying that the kind of transfiguration whose representation Disney perfected can be found in art from all over the world: from Alice to early modern European fables to medieval ornament to Harlem nightclub snake dancing. But for Eisenstein, what's most interesting about these examples is not their universal occurrence but what he called their universal appeal (*pritiagatel'nost'*). This stretching against form is so "omni-appealing" because it promises not just change but a liberation from all preordained forms at the moment of change, a "rejection of the constraint of eternally fixed forms, freedom from ossification, the ability to dynamically take any form."[20] This was proof for Eisenstein, the best kind of proof, that people long for, take pleasure in, and have access to their primitive, pre-logical selves. In Disney, Eisenstein found the appeal of the undifferentiated, the appeal of freedom from form, the desire for freedom from the limits of the body, and freedom from all the conflicts of the world when our nameless feelings are tempered and constrained but also enhanced and enriched by thought and expression. And he found the same processes of stretching, disassembling, and reassembling in the dynamic, multisensory, changing forms of cinema.[21] If Eisenstein thought artists could take advantage of their audiences' capacity to be magically entranced into a state of infinite

sensory-emotional receptivity, he believed that, when confronted dialectically with thought, the result was absolute, if temporary, freedom.

Eisenstein was working on the Disney section of *Method* when Moscow
was evacuated. After arriving in Alma Ata, he picked up where he left off,
but without the original manuscript, which he'd left behind. He began the
new version by reminding himself that Disney "not only knows the magic of
every technical device, but he also knows all the most secret strands of human
thought, images, ideas, feelings . . . He creates somewhere in the realm of
the very purest and primal depths. Where we are all children of nature. He
creates on the conceptual level of humanity not yet shackled by logic, reason, or experience."[22] Throughout the Disney manuscripts, Eisenstein noted
ways in which animation captured a fundamental method of cinematic montage. As Nesbet pointed out, stretching body parts to the point of dismemberment, freed from all physical bounds and rules until they become parts
(*pars*) that need to be reconstructed and reanimated, was a process that Eisenstein's montage was intended for, to intensify audience agency and engagement.[23] Eisenstein's appreciation for Disney's ability to stretch the human
form beyond its physical limits has led Nesbet and a number of scholars to
explore the self-dissolution this involved, as a kind of the death that leads to
life.[24] I'm interested in another aspect of this impossible stretch into *ekstasis*:
where form meets content and where the pre-logical meets the logical, which
Eisenstein explored in texts written later during his break from the filming of
Ivan in December 1943–January 1944. These later Disney texts shift tone and
subject matter, reflecting the work done on *Ivan*. They are no longer about
the general appeal of transfiguration and freedom from form but address the
process of transformation in specifically biographical terms and with biography placed in historical and evolutionary context.

The Disney texts of 1943–1944 weren't all fish and butterflies. The charming difficulties of change in the earlier texts here become a violent process of
threat and domination. The painful and pleasurable animated transfigurations
in early Disney films started Eisenstein thinking about totemism or the various ways in which people identify themselves with animals, plants, and things,
including, for example, the bulls in his own *Old and New* (1926–1929). That
film featured an ecstatic merger, depicted as a wedding of bulls, all dressed up
in wedding finery, and another ecstatic transfiguration in the form of collective farm bulls whose image floated over the farm in looming double exposure
before dying and being reborn as tractors. He wrote about other terrifying
magical creatures from literature who crush, destroy, eat, and symbolically
castrate their humans.[25] Here Eisenstein takes a Freudian move and Disney-
fies it. In these cases, as in his earlier writing, the process of transfiguration is

difficult, but now it really hurts. The story he told about Varia, transforming herself into her bigger, stronger adversary in order to overcome her enemy's power, is one of many such examples of people and creatures that Eisenstein discovered who transform themselves into other creatures at moments of stress and change in order to dominate.[26] For Eisenstein, the mimetic ability to become and dominate the other is enabled by the pre-logical property of undifferentiatedness and the dynamic animated ability to transfigure that Disney captured so exquisitely. These examples proved to him that we desire pre-logical undifferentiatedness not only for the pleasures of freedom but for the necessity of domination—for power to vanquish our enemies and then rise above them, to take the next step on our life spirals.[27]

These are the twin mechanisms of change that Eisenstein used to shape Ivan's biography. Every major step in Ivan's life is depicted in the film with one of them: transitions are visually and physically prefigured by an unbearable, physical stretch or a depiction of merging with the other or a return to an earlier stage in life, before circling around to leap into the new. Many of these changes are dramatized as an intensification of dialectical tensions that explode into an ecstatic, synthetic, "leap to a new quality," an aspect of transformation he would focus on in *Nonindifferent Nature*. Eisenstein layered this repertory of change in increasingly complex ways to narrate Ivan's life. Each regression and each moment of transformation give us clues about the way Ivan's childhood shaped his progression from vulnerable child to powerful, vengeful, violent adult.

Becoming Ivan

The Prologue begins with shot of a very young Ivan huddling on the floor in a dark chamber. Eisenstein described the scene as taking place "in the complete darkness of the subconscious, light penetrating into these bowels" (II: 10:56)[28] The only light that isn't shining on Ivan is dimly illuminating the frescoes painted on the wall and columns that surround him. The columns are so tall and Ivan is so small that we can see only the long dangling legs of a horse and a figure in a fresco stretched down toward him. Ivan is all alone, a tiny spotlighted dot in a loose white tunic, nervously looking around, eyes wide with fear. A door opens, a beam of light appears, and his mother, Elena Glinskaia, enters. With a melodramatic gesture she cries out: "I'm dying! I've been poisoned! Beware the boyars."

The gesture is so stylistically out of place, we want to laugh at it, even as it announces the murder that initiates Ivan's most painful experience. The combination of laughter and fear make this moment an unforgettable image for

FIGURE 3.1   "I'm dying. Beware the boyars."

us, as fear and grief make it unforgettable for Ivan. Mother and son embrace before she is dragged away by three women. A terrifying scene of a different nature (shot but not included in The Prologue flashbacks) showed boyars capturing Glinskaia's lover, Ivan Telepnev, and throwing him down from a ledge into a crowd of ax-bearing boyars as a petrified Ivan looks on. These scenes are the originary experience that Ivan can never resist or expunge. Images, objects, and gestures from these scenes will recur throughout the film, to spiral Ivan back to childhood, to link his actions to childhood fear and abandonment, and to revive, intensify, and explain his desire for revenge against the boyars who poisoned his mother and left him an orphan.

The next scene in The Prologue shows Ivan making the leap from prey to predator (II: 12:23). He sits uncomfortably on the throne, in ill-fitting clothes, listening to two powerful boyars, Belsky and Shuisky, fight over how best to profit from giving Russia's wealth away to foreigners. A flash of anger momentarily breaks through young Ivan's forlorn and passive powerlessness. Then, in an oddly poignant gesture, a close-up of his disembodied little leg shows it stretching down toward the floor (recalling the frescoes in the first dark scene). Variations of those dangling legs and that little stretch will repeatedly signal memories of childhood and presage some momentous change to come. It is a strangely touching moment, drawing our attention to Ivan's too-smallness: his feet don't touch the ground, his royal clothes are too big, and the crown threatens to slide off his head. In a note about costumes, Eisenstein identifies the royal garments with power and position: here in the Golden Hall, the child tsar should wear clothes that were *"too big for the Boy: Power overwhelms him."*[29] His throne adds to his discomfort by making him all too aware of his powerlessness. The stretched-out foot and ill-fitting clothes make us feel Ivan's discomfort and vulnerability. This is another Shakespearean reference and a typically generative dialectical image. One of Eisenstein's favorite books, Caroline Spurgeon's 1935 study of visual imagery in Shakespeare, shows that Macbeth is identified with the repeated trope of ill-fitting or borrowed clothes. Clothes overwhelm, embarrass, and degrade Macbeth to convey the illegitimacy of his power. Spurgeon's Macbeth is both great—courageous, passionate, and ambitious—and small: "a poor, vain, cruel treacherous creature."[30] His large clothes and small frame make the inner contradiction visible in precisely the way Eisenstein worked. Ivan's clothes are not, however, symbols of illegitimacy, but rather are meant to make us see the disparity between his symbolic and real power and *feel* his discomfort.

After the ambassadors leave, Ivan and the boyars go into a bedchamber to get comfortable and debrief (II: 14:48). Servitors remove Ivan's heavy regalia, another repeated trope in the film that often signals a switch between public and private life that Eisenstein deployed as both the vulnerable shedding of royal power and a removal of the burdens of rule. The boyars continue to belittle Ivan. When he tries to assert himself, they laugh. Stretched to the limit of humiliation when Shuisky insults his dead mother, Ivan turns on the laughing boyar. He leapfrogs his fear and the boyars' power over him and orders Shuisky seized: the prey becomes the predator. The conflict between his symbolic power and real powerlessness, and the inner conflict over his right to exercise power, is intensified to a point of dialectical synthesis and transformation. Ivan turns to the camera, to us, and says, "I will rule alone without the boyars. *I* will be *tsar*." Remembering his poisoned mother, feeling his own extreme vulnerability, and regressing to that pre-logical, animal, undifferentiated, sensory-emotional state, he asserts his power as tsar for the first time. It is important to emphasize that Ivan's desire to establish Russia's independence from greedy foreigners and greedy boyars—the political goal—is connected here with personal experience, memory, and animosity. The only way to achieve his goals is to assert the independent power of the tsar from and above his own people. Ivan had to assert not just *samoderzhavie*, meaning *sovereign* rule, which is the common modern term for Russian autocracy or absolute rule, but *edinoderzhavie*, literally, *one-man* rule.

There is one other small but significant device to notice in this scene. Just before his transformation from powerless to powerful, Ivan recoils briefly in fear. This is a favorite Eisenstein directorial touch, the reverse movement (*otkaznoe dvizhenie*), that draws special attention to what is to come by first gesturing to its opposite.[31] This quick, sometimes barely perceptible movement away from the main direction of action was featured in Eisenstein's first publication in 1923, and its use as a dramatic gesture remained important to him for the rest of his life; he wrote a new essay on reverse movement in *Method* in 1943.[32] Here, at Ivan's first major transition along the path from vulnerable to powerful, we see all the mechanisms of change—the spiral regression around to the primal fear, the imitation of the enemy, the brief reverse movement before leaping to the next level and rising above the enemy—Eisenstein used throughout the film to inaugurate the major turning points in Ivan's life, the changes that make him the "caracter" he became. As the film circles back to images from these and other scenes, it will accumulate new associations that further explicate and intensify Ivan's political and moral conflicts.

The next three scenes—The Coronation, The Wedding, and The Rebellion—don't show Ivan making major changes but rather set up and incrementally intensify the dialectical conflicts that will lead to the second *ekstatic* transformation that occurs after the victorious battle of Kazan. Eisenstein uses this pattern throughout: scenes of dialectical setups leading to scenes of synthetic changes, followed by scenes that break down into new and repeated conflicts. If The Prologue initiated what Eisenstein called "the whole bloody epic," The Coronation moves Ivan's conflicts into the open with "the effect of daring" (I: 2:09).[33] Everyone is there: the various boyars who support and oppose him; the sneaky Livonian ambassador who exists only to stir up trouble; Ivan's main rivals for power, Efrosinia and Vladimir Staritsky; leading clergy including Metropolitan Pimen; and Ivan's two best friends, both of whom will soon betray him—Andrei Kurbsky and Fedor Kolychev. After crowning himself, Ivan announces that he plans to make Russia great again by centralizing power in the person of the tsar, by subordinating the Church and the boyars to the tsar, and by defeating Russia's foreign enemies who block access to the sea. This defiant speech makes everyone angry, except Anastasia, who will become his wife in the next scene, and a group of unnamed adoring women (whom we see here in the shot that is repeated in The Fiery Furnace). There, underneath displays of celebration, anger simmers in conspiracy among the boyars and foreigners, which we will see again in cut-aways from the wedding.

The policy announcement leads Kolychev to abandon Ivan's service to become a priest, taking the name Filipp, and it explodes in a popular uprising fomented by Efrosinia. The people, in the form of an angry mob led by

Maliuta Skuratov, flood into the palace to interrupt the wedding and challenge Ivan (I: 21:20). He subdues them with the majesty of his position as tsar and a wily combination of humor and threat, which they both like and fear. That scene is also interrupted, this time by messengers from Kazan threatening Muscovy from the east (I: 26:30). Ivan rallies the people, now his supporters (that was quick!), to go defeat the Tatars: "To Kazan!" In these three scenes, we see Ivan as young and vigorous, a loving husband and a daring ruler, establishing policy and confronting challenges to his rule. Inner conflicts that will later become unbearable are depicted here as fleeting, suspicious shadows: the flash of paranoia that crosses Ivan's face during The Coronation (and recalls Ivan's vulnerability looking around in fear in the dark womb-y hall before his mother is killed), Kurbsky and Anastasia flirting behind the throne at the wedding, Fedor/Filipp's criticism and defection, and Efrosinia hiding in dark doorways scowling.

The conquest of Kazan ends with another stage in Ivan's ascent to power following a metaphorical and literal explosion. The people who were in rebellion in the previous scene are completely subdued here, cannon fodder snaking across the battlefield and moving weaponry into position (I: 28:33). This scene features the clearest example of justifiable, even glorious, killing: on the battlefield in the service of Russian power and security. But Ivan's military is a killing machine that denigrates its soldiers by equating their individual lives with the coins used to count the living before and after the battle to calculate their losses. Conflict with Kurbsky comes to the surface here over both his inhuman treatment of Tatar prisoners and his obvious jealousy of Ivan, a conflict Eisenstein characterizes as "intelligent cruelty" versus "senseless cruelty." There is also Eisenstein's trademark comic relief: phallic cannons and clownish cannoniers, Foma and Erema, whose silliness Bolshakov prohibited, but Eisenstein defiantly filmed anyway.[34] The battle scene ends with Ivan surrounded by billowing clouds of smoke, asserting, "Now, I will truly be Tsar, recognized as Tsar by all Muscovy, as Sovereign [*samoderzhets*] of all Rus" (I: 39:41).

Rise, then fall: in what Eisenstein "calls one of the central scenes in Part I," Ivan returns home from his triumph at Kazan only to sink to a new kind of vulnerability: betrayal and despair (I: 39:59). [35] The next major transition is set up here when he falls ill, appears to die, and comes back to life. After twice asserting his power as tsar, now Eisenstein asks us to consider what kind of ruler Ivan will be: savior or destroyer, Christ or Anti-Christ? In another dark, womby chamber, Ivan, dying, begs the boyars to pledge allegiance to his infant son while Efrosinia openly pursues their allegiance to her own son, the adult but childlike Vladimir. One boyar after another responds to Ivan's pleas by turning away in silence. Ivan, stretching his body back on his knees and then rising and stretching up, curses them and falls back onto his bed, seemingly dead. In the meantime, Efrosinia tempts Kurbsky to betray Ivan, Kurbsky tempts Anastasia to join him and betray Ivan, and Maliuta, keeping his eye on everybody, skulks around the palace, looking for traitors, presumably on Ivan's orders. To everyone's surprise, Ivan revives. He gets some new allies in the Basmanovs and promotes Kurbsky (who pledged allegiance to Ivan at the last moment, after Anastasia rejected him), while pushing him down onto his knees. This is a key transition and bears prominent marks of the spiral regression. Ivan is dressed in a white nightshirt, and he entreats the boyars to support him while kneeling on the floor, recalling both his dress and his gestures in The Prologue. In this turn of the spiral, Ivan regresses back beyond childhood and, in leaping from death back into life, he emerges not more powerful but more knowledgeable about the opposition he faces and more divided between despair and anger at the boyars' rejection and betrayal.

In this scene we are given a number of contradictory cues that ask us who Ivan is: whether he is indeed ill or whether he's faking it to test the boyars, whether he is motivated by fear or cunning, whether he is reborn as Christ or Lucifer. An icon featured in this scene shows the Holy Fool Nikola, who was associated with popular opposition to Ivan and seen as a voice of Ivan's conscience, and there are signs of heretical cult behavior in the strange blessing ritual where Pimen and the other priests stand in a circle around a mysterious source of intense light coming from below. Does Ivan die from despair and abandonment with no ulterior motives, or is he trying to display his superhuman abilities to his opponents? At this point in the film, Ivan is still more or less evenly divided; he seems suspended between possible directions. Eisenstein connects this suspension with a psychological condition described by Ernst Kretschmer, a contemporary psychologist Eisenstein liked in part because he studied the connections between psychological states and physical behavior. Kretschmer observed the ways people panicked and froze when confronted with new stimuli. They enter a purely "instinctive" state (which Kretschmer calls the opposite of the rational), a kind of *Totstellreflex* (*Immobilisationsreflex*)—they "feign death." Eisenstein only read Kretschmer's *Über Hysterie* in 1942 after he finished the scenario, so for him this was another confirmation that his understanding of Ivan's psychology and of sensory-emotional thinking was correct. "Ivan's strength," he wrote, "was in mastering *both*: the *animal-instinctive* characteristics and the ability to find an exit in increasing governing-political *schrewdness* [sic]. Extraordinarily acute instincts are the strength of childhood trauma."[36]

Ivan, meanwhile, goes back to work (I: 1:08:45). In this connection, we see him moving forward, seeking to assert his power in the international arena in an alliance with England's Queen Elizabeth. He dismisses the boyars from his stateroom under enormous shadows of his head that prefigure the close-ups at the end of Part I and project his inner conflicts on the walls. This scene showing Ivan doing the ruler's work is another setup, less about stretching or leaping into the new than it is about revealing the multilayered significance of his inner divisions, the divisions all rulers face in having to balance their private lives and public duties. The shadows that loom over the large, light, open space are so visually striking that they have been often discussed. Here I want to emphasize their multivalent role in this transitional scene. By separating from Ivan and projecting aspects of his personal and inner self on the walls, the shadows show Ivan in a state of conflict: they offer diverse possible paths forward but also offer the possibility of reversal. Their size suggests extraordinary power, but they are ephemeral, dependent, changeable. The physical division (self and shadow-self) suggests this scene to be moving along the dialectical spiral path and heading toward, but not yet arriving at, transformation. Numerous objects and images convey the dialectic of division and unity or division and interpenetration (more on this below). The shadows show Ivan divided; the black-and-white chessboard and the unbroken circles of the armillary sphere suggest forms of competition and alliance. As he leans back in contemplation at his desk, he is and isn't the little abandoned boy. In the bright light of the white-walled hall, he is alone, but he hasn't been abandoned, exactly, because he was the one who sent everyone scurrying away and, equally important, because intercutting to scenes of Anastasia's bedchamber shows that he still has a companion. Yet it is the presence of this companion that creates the new critical inner division now coming to the fore as the conflict between Ivan's public and private identities intensifies. When he rises and exits the hall, he is conspicuously wearing his royal fur cloak, associated with rulership, slung over one shoulder, half on half off. At the same time, as he approaches the portal connecting his public office to his private rooms, his giant shadow shrinks back to human proportions and rejoins with his body, reinternalizing his alter-egos, momentarily whole, just as he crosses the threshold.

After a long day at the office, Ivan heads up to Anastasia's bedchamber where the previous intercutting showed Efrosinia eyeing Anastasia threateningly (I: 1:14:33). More skullduggery follows as this scene intensifies Ivan's internal and external conflicts and clarifies the stakes. Ivan's enemies, led by Efrosinia, have decided that the only way to stop Ivan is to murder his wife. Now we get to watch Ivan regress to childhood again, before tragedy propels him toward the next major transformation in the following scene.

Confessing his loneliness and inability to trust anyone—a mix of public and private feelings—Ivan places his head on Anastasia's chest. Ivan's affect here is as suggestive of child to mother as husband to wife, and Anastasia is costumed in all white, recalling Glinskaia. A messenger brings the news of Kurbsky's military defeat and possible treason: in the background, Anastasia faints with suppressed fear and desire, another mix of the political and the personal. Ivan leaps up to find her something to drink, but he can no more save his wife than he could save his mother. Efrosinia places a poisoned chalice just where Ivan will grab it to inadvertently carry out the murder of his wife on behalf of the boyars. In this scene, Ivan's dialectical inner conflict is conveyed in visual depictions. Sharp contrasts of light and shadow, characters and their shadows, white and black costumes, deep focus that thrusts characters forward and then sees them retreat into darkened or smoky depths, sharp musical contrasts in rhythm and instrumentation, and architectural structures that divide the picture frame all reiterate the sharpening conflict. Efrosinia and Anastasia seesaw up and down in a kind of visual division-interpenetration, and Ivan merges with Efrosinia when he takes the chalice with the poison and hands it to his wife. These moral tensions, played out in gender terms, place Ivan on the precipice of another major explosion of synthesis and change.

Cut to Anastasia's coffin in the cathedral, where Ivan's doubt and despair, followed by ecstatic recovery, are the events that Eisenstein chose to explain his dialectical-ecstatic method in *Nonindifferent Nature* (I: 1:19:45).[37] Eisenstein dramatized one of Ivan's most important transformations here by composing a scene by El Greco (elongated self-portrait) and Picasso (disassembled cubist body) and animated by Disney (regress to the pre-logical). To depict Ivan as stretched beyond reason by despair and therefore deeply divided over whether to move forward with his mission to create the Great Russian State or retreat, defeated by the opposition, Eisenstein draped Cherkasov in a variety of positions on the disproportionately large and strangely tilted coffin and filmed his enervated body and spirit from a variety of discontinuous angles. On the soundtrack, Ivan's division is expressed in a dialectical antiphony of voices that threaten to drown each other out. Ivan's enemy, Metropolitan Pimen, reads selections from the Sixty-ninth Psalm, a desperate cry of abandonment in the face of God's silence (which gestures back to Ivan's childhood and forward to Ivan's confession in Part III). At the same time, Ivan's loyal servitor Maliuta reads out the names of boyars who have betrayed Ivan and gone over to the enemy, including his closest friend, now confirmed as a traitor, Andrei Kurbsky. Pimen evokes Ivan's childhood feelings to force him to surrender to doubt while Maliuta calls on Ivan's current source of despair for the opposite reason, to spur him to action. Analysis of Eisenstein's use of

FIGURE 3.2 "Ivan decides to completely annihilate the feudal landlords (good height for the vaulting)." RGALI, 1923/2/1677/10 [Feb 14, 1942]. Used with permission.

the Sixty-ninth Psalm shows that he deleted lines that address God directly.[38] The edited psalm highlights Ivan's refusal to submit to God's judgment, even while magnifying his despair after the loss of his wife, his servitors, and his best friend. When the tension reaches the breaking point, Ivan literally leaps up and (following the same gesture that preceded his most recent resurrection—beard pointed straight up as if dead), he reasserts his will and makes plans to rise to even greater power. He rejects passivity and despair and turns to new allies— the Basmanovs, Aleksei and Fedor. And he makes it clear that he will continue to centralize power in the unified state.

A number of complicated transactions take place here as Ivan casts off the old and embraces the new, all prepared by the personal and political dialectical conflicts in previous transitional scenes. He trades his old disloyal boyar allies for Aleksei Basmanov and Maliuta Skuratov, and he trades his old, dead wife for Fedor (or, affectionately, Fedka) Basmanov. He trades a measure of private life for public life. He forms the oprichnina as a protective "iron ring" and reaffirms his commitment to establishing the Great Russian State, now as its single, all-powerful ruler. He decides to trick the Russian people into supporting him by withdrawing to his palace outside Moscow at Alexandrova (repeating his attempt to trick the boyars into supporting him when he was on his sickbed). This scene ends with a mirror of its beginning: another post-mortem rebirth. Ivan rises up above the coffin, arms outstretched, in what Kristin Thompson dubbed his "power gesture," surrounded by a crowd of his new supporters, an image of assertion and determination.[39] But now when he rises above Anastasia's coffin to seize a new, higher power, he does so in the company of men Eisenstein calls demons and fallen angels.[40]

The Oath of the Oprichniki was intended to follow here, after Ivan and his new "iron ring" guard arrived at his palace at Alexandrova. We have the text in the original scenario, its sources in the Historical Commentary, and a few stills and drawings, but the original footage has disappeared. The removal of The Oath robs Part I of its full effect by concealing Ivan's growing menace and the specific source of that menace, so it is worth examining in some detail here.

The scene shows the oprichniki, dressed in hooded black robes and led by the "demonic angel," Fedor Basmanov, vowing to place their loyalty to the tsar and the Great Russian State above all earthly and kinship ties. It is a sinister scene, as the young men kneeling before Ivan cast off their human attachments and vow to destroy anyone who doesn't join them.

Eisenstein based the pseudoreligious nature of the ritual and the visual blending of the monastic and the political partly on foreigners' accounts and partly on details in an Orthodox monastic rulebook that conceptualized

FIGURE 3.3 The Oath of the Oprichniki: <u>Chancery of the Oprichnina</u>. <u>The Oath of the Oprichniki</u>. Recited <u>in unison</u>. He himself [Ivan] moves his lips silently. RGALI, 1923/2/1686/9 [Mar 12, 1942]. Used with permission.

FIGURE 3.4   The Oath of the Oprichniki, Fedka in halo/crown of knives. RGALI, 1923/2/137/12. Used with permission.

monks as angels on Earth. The foreigners reported that Muscovites considered Ivan's adoption of monastic ritual and monastic dress to be blasphemous, a tension Eisenstein would use to great effect throughout the film: he conceptualized the oprichniki as "literally fallen angels." Here I would argue that the effect was not so much to raise questions about the morality of the oprichniki but rather to highlight their "sins" through contrast. Just as Eisenstein used humor to underscore tragedy, dressing the oprichniki as monks underscores the human contradictions inherent in the oath that made it such an impossible demand.[41]

The Oath scene was meant to be terrifying. A still shows Fedka, his head encircled by a halo of long, sharp knives, gazing up at Ivan in fear and awe, while he recites:

Before God I swear
A true oath
A grave oath
A dreadful oath

For the sake of the "Great Russian State," each oprichnik pledges:

To destroy the enemies of the state
To renounce my kin and my clan

To forget my father . . . and my own mother
My true friend and my blood brother
FOR THE SAKE OF THE GREAT RUSSIAN STATE.[42]

These lines resurface at the end of Part II after the murder of Vladimir Staritsky, Ivan's cousin. As "fallen angels," dressed in demonic-monks' robes, the oprichniki file into the cathedral in a mock funeral procession, chanting the lines that were supposed to be introduced here in Part I.[43] The scenario foreshadows that convergence of holy and blasphemous at the end of Part II, as does the score for Part I, as the musicologist Katya Ermolaev discovered. It wasn't ultimately shot this way, but the screenplay and Prokofiev's score have the recitation of the oath at Alexandrova merge with the singing of the people snaking through the snow on their way to beg Ivan to return to Moscow and rule over them. The people sing the hymn "Save, O Lord, Thy People," at the same time the oprichniki call for the bloody destruction of Ivan's enemies and the elevation of the tsar above all earthly beings.[44] The oprichniki carry knives; the people trudging out from Moscow carry icons and crosses. Together the two strains elevate Ivan to new heights as one portion of the Russian people pledges a kind of inhuman loyalty to Ivan and another portion makes a holy pledge. But The Oath of the Oprichniki is double-edged, and the two strains are unevenly balanced: not only do the oprichniki pledge loyalty to Ivan, they threaten to destroy anyone whose loyalty is found wanting.

The sixteenth-century sources that provided Eisenstein with the oath of the oprichniki waste no time identifying it as divisive and demonic.[45] The Livonian knights Johann Taube and Elbert Kruse emphasized the way the oath bound men to isolate themselves from others—just as the word *oprich-nina* signified a separate realm, a realm apart—and to identify themselves with threatening clothing and totems: brooms and severed dogs' heads. Another of Eisenstein's major sources, Andrei Kurbsky's history of Ivan's reign, identified the oath as satanic *because* it required the oprichniki to sever their social ties, to break with their parents and siblings: "The tsar instead of well known and good and honorable men of distinction gathered around himself wretched people, full of evil, and in addition bound them with terrible oaths, forcing the cursed ones not only to cut themselves off from their friends and brothers, but even from their parents, and to please him alone in all things."[46] The historical Filipp agreed, describing one of the oprichniki as resembling "the very image of Satan."[47] In the seventeenth century, Valerie Kivelson argues, the sentiments expressed in the oath were understood as "unambiguously evil."[48]

As Eisenstein undoubtedly also knew, Jesus made the same demand: "If anyone comes to Me and does not hate his own father and mother and wife and children and brothers and sisters, and furthermore, even his own life, he cannot be My disciple" (Luke 14:25–26). This dual source for the oath of the oprichniki suited Eisenstein's image of Ivan as a "unity of opposites." The binary source, together with the binary costuming and the counterpoint score, ask us to consider, not for the first time, whether Ivan is Christ or Antichrist, redeemer or destroyer. As in earlier scenes, we see signs of both, yet here Eisenstein, like his early modern predecessors, is unequivocal. He called the oath of the oprichniki the "dark oath," and he considered it the "origin of all the sins of the oprichniki."[49] Eisenstein was delighted to find one of the sources for the oath in von Staden's memoir: "namely, a *spy* and *traitor* recites the *sacred* oath." The irony that infuses everything in the film could not be sharper: the most important thing about the oath was its inherently inevitable entrapment in betrayal. "But what's really *great*," Eisenstein noted, "is that in the end Ivan's line turns this in on itself." Fedor Basmanov was unable to resist the temptation of ties to his brothers and particularly to his father, placing these bonds above his "sacred" oath to the tsar. Eisenstein labeled this impossible conflict of loyalties the "whole theme of the oprichnina." And Ivan will see to it that the Basmanovs pay for their divided loyalties.[50] The Oath showed that the "triumph" of Ivan's emergence from his despair, his rising above the death of his wife, and his formation of the oprichnina was, in fact, a step into the darkness: rise, then fall.[51]

The oath and its historical context also have analogues in Soviet political culture and ethics. Revolutionary asceticism has a long history in Russia, dating back to the most popular novel of the nineteenth century, Nikolai Chernyshevsky's *What Is to Be Done?* In the Soviet period, especially under Stalin, the notion of self-sacrifice was deformed into something like the version encapsulated in the Muscovite oath. Katerina Clark described the place of the Stalinist Great Family in her book on Socialist Realist literature: "The state was prior. If there was any conflict between the state's interest and the nuclear family, citizens were urged to jettison their sense of family, based on blood ties, and replace it with a higher one, based on political kinship."[52] Yuri Slezkine argues that the Bolshevik revolutionaries who became the Soviet ruling class in the 1920s valued comradeship as a higher virtue than marriage ties, family loyalty, and affection for parents and children. Bolshevik parents loved their children, but, Slezkine argues, it wasn't clear to them how legitimate those feelings were.[53] Celebrated heroes like Pavlik Morozov, who was said to have denounced his own father and images of Stalin as a doting father to all children created a public culture that encouraged people to place the state (or the collective or the public) first. Eisenstein's depiction of this cultural trope shines a light on its dark underside. The Oath of the Oprichniki is a turning point in the film (or would have been) because it begins to offer more definitive answers to the questions raised by Eisenstein's binaries and contradictions. Those answers increasingly characterize Ivan as a threatening, dangerous, and violent ruler who creates impossible conflicts of loyalty for his friends and followers. Those conflicts are also ultimately the origin of Ivan's tragedy.

The last scene of Part I opens with a glimpse of the end of the deleted Oath scene in the background as Ivan waits uncertainly for the people to call him back to Moscow to rule (I: 1:31:29). It ends with the most famous shot of *Ivan the Terrible*, his first apotheosis. An extreme close-up shows Ivan's head disproportionately large in the foreground with the lines of people snaking across the snow far below him—one of many images that simultaneously refute Ivan's loneliness but emphasize his distance from others. He has achieved the highest power, like Pushkin's Boris Godunov, but he has done so through trickery and manipulation. Eisenstein tells us we should see sadism in Ivan's eyes in this scene, the same sadism Ivan will put into words and deeds later on.[54]

Part II multiplies the structural and audio-visual resonances with details of scenes from Part I, creating a remarkably intricate network of narrative, visual, and semantic associations that point to Ivan's cycles of regress, rebirth as a higher power, and subsequent fall. Part II begins twice. First we see Kurbsky pledging his loyalty to King Sigismund of Poland (and grand duke of Lithuania) in a court that is in many ways the audio-visual opposite of Ivan's court (II: 2:16). Cut then to the oprichniki speeding back to Moscow through the snow on their black horses; cut again to Ivan entering his own throne room, the Golden Hall, just as he had in the second part of The Prologue when he sat on the too-large throne as a child (II: 6:45). We finally see The Prologue, intercut into this scene, which is set in the same room. Ivan has the nervous boyars lined up on one side of the Golden Hall, and the sinister oprichniki lined up on the other, a visual dialectic (this is the scene illustrated in Fig. 1.1). He's in the middle of explaining just how great the new system is, with the realm divided between the boyars' part and the tsar's part, when his old friend Fedor Kolychev shows up, now as the priest Filipp. Just as Ivan is saying that he is carrying out God's plan, Filipp shouts, "No!, this is not God's plan, but the Devil's." Ivan ignores the accusation and greets Filipp first as an old friend and then as tsar, alternately begging for his friendship and his loyalty. But Filipp is steadfast, stiff-backed even, in his opposition to Ivan. At least, he remains steadfast until Ivan tempts and corrupts him by offering to promote him to metropolitan if he will remain a loyal servitor and friend. In this scene, Ivan flips back and forth between his personal and public roles. Flashbacks to The Prologue add this conflict between public and private to Ivan's current conflict between political commitment and personal loneliness. Repetition increases the tension in preparation for the big leap that occurs next. The clash between Ivan's desire for friendship and his desire for power is melodramatically amplified here. It produces contradictory feelings of sympathy and scorn, and it produces a contradictory political situation for Ivan, who promises to save the lives of boyars in the opposition that he must eliminate in the name of state stability.

In the following scene, the setup for the next transition continues (II: 20:56). We hear Maliuta speak before we see him, a disembodied voice enumerating the contradictions of the previous scene as he had at Anastasia's coffin. Maliuta convinces Ivan that he can keep his promise to Filipp as a friend and still eliminate Filipp's family as the political opposition. All Ivan has to do is let Maliuta carry out the murders for him: the "beginning of the whole bloody epic." He agrees, but this is a new level of deviousness for Ivan. He decides that he needs to start killing people to achieve his goal, the Great Russian State, but he lets Maliuta do his dirty work. Rulership requires deception and betrayal, apparently, but Ivan is not quite ready to fully accept the deals he just made with Filipp and Maliuta. First, his conscience assails him with new doubts. He rises up from the throne and asks dramatically, "By what right do you judge, Tsar Ivan?" When he leaves the throne room, his fur cloak remains behind, recalling the earlier inner conflicts it signified, as if the murders about to be committed were motivated not by state needs but by personal ones. He hears a cry off-screen and turns and flees. Where? To Anastasia's bedchamber, his private refuge (more complicated now given everything that's happened there.)

Fedka materializes to remind Ivan that he's not really all that guilty because the boyars initiated the chain of revenge killings by murdering his mother and his wife (II: 25:37). Not only that, but Fedka points out that Ivan was the one who gave Anastasia the poisoned chalice, which implicates Efrosinia and identifies the death as murder. This is a neat twist: Fedka reassures Ivan that he's not guilty of murdering Anastasia even though he handed her the poison; Efrosinia is still guilty of that murder. But by extension that means that Maliuta Skuratov isn't really guilty of executing the Kolychevs because Ivan gave him the order.[55] These two conversations (with Maliuta and Fedka) take place in locations that recall mother love and the deprivation of mother love in Ivan's lonely childhood. Ivan allows Maliuta to caress him like a child when he's feeling the loneliness of Filipp's rejection, and he embraces Fedka in Anastasia's bedchamber when he's feeling the loss of Anastasia, which itself circles back to his loss of his mother. Tellingly and mysteriously, Eisenstein includes a shot here of Ivan's bejeweled hands stretching out on the furry

FIGURE 3.5   "Too few"

white bedclothes (defamiliarizing the things in a way that focuses on the stretch and the touch) and signaling the major transformation close at hand. The scene with Fedka takes place while Maliuta is busy preparing to decapitate members of the Kolychev clan in the Kremlin courtyard just below the chamber where Ivan and Fedka "consummate" their alliance over the revelation of secrets and crimes.

They are about to run off when Ivan stops to watch the scene below through a little window (II: 27:31). When he emerges, he seems unbearably, physically shaken by his decisions and their consequences and torn between horror and determination looking at the corpses. He could put an end to the bloodshed here and begins to cross himself. Instead, Ivan's next major transitional leap occurs at precisely this moment when he interrupts the sacred gesture, leans back, points at the dead, and decides, "Too few" (II: 29:39). This statement, "Too few," is the "sadism in words" that Eisenstein told us was prefigured by the sadism "without words—in his eyes" on the staircase at the end of Part I.[56]

Eisenstein explicitly links this decision and the interrupted gesture with both the spiral biography and the transition from prey to predator: "'Too few'—the first time he saw blood. It acted on him as it would on a tiger cub raised in a zoo." But this "awakening of the actively beastly principle" in the predator—the "trauma of first blood," is a more conscious state than the more purely intuitive act of the prey.[57] More blood, more corpses: Ivan's decision here results from the inescapable circle back to his innocent childhood, the murder of his mother, and his desire for revenge, which in turn pushes him forward to real blood, real corpses, and a conscious decision to call for more.

Efrosinia, Pimen, and Filipp are mourning, outraged and infuriated (II: 30:20). This scene takes place in a dark subterranean chamber, lighted with black candles and designed with images from Apocalypse icons both painted on the ceiling and enacted by a group of men reaching out as if from the bowels of hell. Filipp doesn't want to get involved—he fled to a monastery to avoid confrontation—but he cannot resist the atavistic pull to avenge his kin any more than Ivan can. Filipp reaffirms his Kolychev and boyar identity and agrees to get his hands dirty by staging *The Fiery Furnace*, one of the great high points of *Ivan the Terrible,* a brilliant indictment of tyranny, and the source of Ivan's final, sensational transformation in Part II (II: 32:43). That transformation is cued with multiple overlapping markers of dialectical opposition, spiral regression, the pre-logical, Ivan's childhood, and reminders of every scene since that first catalyst of revenge tragedy in The Prologue. Here the spiral back to childhood abandonment and vulnerability is represented in ways that have accrued numerous layers of meaning connected with Eisenstein's fundamental questions concerning the motivations for violence and revenge. What kind of ruler is he?

The removal of all masks and stratagems, triggered by the child's laughter, strips away Ivan's intellectual and ideological justifications and returns him to an originary, pre-logical state, unencumbered by adult complexities: the end is the beginning. Reabsorbed in the pure feelings of loss and rage originally experienced in childhood frees Ivan to rise to the terrifyingly amoral and tragic new level of superhuman power we have seen. Filipp's production of *The Fiery Furnace* reinforces the spiral regression by filling the stage with children. We have a child who sees the reality behind the pretense of the dramatic fiction without realizing that the art was a shield to protect the accusers, who can only stage their accusation as performance. And we have a childlike adult, Vladimir, who sees even this as a joke. But Ivan takes the child's laughter seriously, and realizing that everyone sees through his mask, he feels abandoned again by everyone around him. His recognition of himself in the children—the martyrs, the laughers, the clueless, and the seers—propels him to his biggest leap yet. Unmasked but neither shamed nor humbled, this is when he snarls, "I will be what you say I am. I will be Terrible" (II: 40–59).

But there are no simple masked/unmasked binaries in The Fiery Furnace, nor are there simple, deceptive surfaces that conceal true meanings: every

unmasking reveals yet another field of division and interpenetration. Eisenstein shows us how truth itself is masked, how we deceive ourselves, how pain
can be made to seem funny, and how laughter can be used to depict the deadly
serious. The final revealing irony of The Fiery Furnace scene resides in the
mirrored laughter with which it begins and ends. Ivan's hearty but forced theatrical laugh on entering the cathedral announces his supremacy by disrupt-
ing the sacred atmosphere of the play. If laughter defies power, then a confident, laughing Ivan should have had no trouble defying Filipp, the Church,
and the play's moral lesson. Yet Ivan's strategic performance of laughter pales
in comparison with the ecstatic, Chaplinesque, natural laugh of the little boy.
In typical Eisensteinian dialectic, the Terrible Ivan asserts his claim to submit
to no one just when he has been forced to submit to a child's laugh.

In response to Ivan's challenge, the boyars in the opposition ratchet up
their own plans for revenge by deciding they have to kill Ivan and put the
reluctant Vladimir on the throne: the prey is forced to become the predator
(II: 41:21). Efrosinia is at her creepiest in this scene but also her most human.
She throws off her black robe to reveal a white one underneath, linking her
with the other women in Ivan's life, his white-clad mother and wife. Vladimir
lays his head on her lap, and she sings her son a dark lullaby about hunting
down a beaver, a metaphor for killing the tsar. Gesture and costume make
this Madonna and child an eerie inverse of Ivan and his mother. But Efrosinia
becomes just a little bit human, and Vladimir becomes just a little bit grown
up: in this scene he has even sprouted a beard (II: 45:35).

The scenes that follow set up the final cascade of ecstatic transformations
at the end of Part II with a series of multilayered, dialectic, advancing-regressing spirals. Maliuta shows up at Efrosinia's palace with an invitation from Ivan
for Vladimir to come to a feast (II: 51:10). At the feast, Ivan and his men—
Maliuta Skuratov, the Basmanovs, and the oprichniki—reveal themselves to
be as manipulative, violent, and demonic as the forces they were meant to
replace: the prey have fully become predators. While the leaders feast, the
men dance around Fedka in drag (made to look like Anastasia) and sing a song
of murder (mirroring Efrosinia).

Now it is Vladimir's turn to circle back to childhood in Ivan's place as he
fast-forwards toward the murder that was to put him on the throne. Ivan,
suspecting a conspiracy, gets Vladimir drunk so that he will confess, which
he does (II: 55:44). Ivan sets up the almost entirely innocent Vladimir (he did,
after all, agree to the conspiracy, however reluctantly). Ivan stages a mock
Coronation, dressing Vladimir, twin of the innocent young Ivan, in the tsar's
robes (which are as large for him now as Ivan's were when he was a child on
the throne) (II: 1:03:44). Ivan stages this scene as a kind of commentary on,

or reversal of, The Fiery Furnace. Vladimir is being punished for laughing, for confessing, for conspiring to assassinate Ivan, but his punishment is being staged as a game, in which he gets to play the role of tsar as a drunken party stunt. The oprichniki stand around watchfully, and as soon as Vladimir reveals that he likes being tsar after all, decisively undoing his innocence, Ivan sends him to his doom. In the scenario, the oprichniki sing lines from the oath, as they follow him to his death, that seem to accuse Vladimir of favoring kin over state.[58] The assassin sees Vladimir dressed as the tsar, mistakes Vladimir for Ivan, and kills him (II: 1:13:08). Efrosinia goes out of her mind when she realizes what happened, and she's dragged away, just as Ivan's mother was dragged away in The Prologue.

Eisenstein instructed Moskvin to shoot the cathedral to resemble a womb, both so that Vladimir can return to the womb to be reborn into his death, penetrated by a knife, and so that Ivan, costumed in his most phallic black hat, can penetrate the cathedral "like the father penetrates the mother" (II: 1:14:06).[59] This transition to absolute power—the last leap of Part II—is preceded by one of the most primal and universal dialectics: the interpenetration of male and female, phallus and womb, sex and violence. Eisenstein also wanted this scene to be deadly serious, but for that to occur another dialectical, ecstatic synthesis interpenetration was required: "it is always necessary to have its ironic (more often than not: obscene, and even—crudely phallic) *counter-part.* *Cf. The phallic drawings concerning John* for Cherkasov *and analogous.* This has to be in the filming. And between *shots.* . . . NB. Mlb [*mutterleib or womb*] *treatment* of the murder of V.A.: *phallic black tsar.*"[60] After Ivan has put his servitors in their place and eliminated the entire opposition, he celebrates this rebirth with a deeply "ironic" pseudoreligious ritual (II: 1:18:40). Recalling The Oath of the Oprichniki, Ivan leads his demonic monks, his fallen angels, through the cathedral intoning the oath in the background, the color returning to black and white as they file behind him. Ivan stops at an altar to answer the question he asked just before executing the Kolychevs: "By what right do you judge, Tsar Ivan?" Looking up but covering his eyes, he answers: "For the Great Russian State."

Eisenstein closed Part II with an Epilogue that had not appeared in the approved scenario (II: 1:19:50). Filmed in color, it shows Ivan on his throne before an apocalypse-themed fresco. He announces that his hands are now completely free to do whatever is necessary to protect the Great Russian State.[61] This last, unscripted scene might be read as triumphant, but only if one ignores everything that has come before, everything we now know about Eisenstein's thinking, and everything but the dialogue. Can one watch this scene without wondering whether victory was worth the cost? Whether Ivan had better choices? Or whether, in rising up to God's height he fell lower than ever before, as Lucifer fell into hell? At The Fiery Furnace, Ivan rose above human morality and accepted the epithet "Terrible," and what did he do next? He had Filipp executed (off-screen, by Maliuta) and he methodically toyed with, then slaughtered, an innocent (almost innocent) version of his younger self—a murder-suicide. Kleiman argues that these are the gestures of a secular ruler trying to replace God, like Pushkin's Boris Godunov, "achieving the highest power," which would have to be accompanied by his fall.[62] Here Ivan doesn't fall to his knees as he did at his deathbed and at Anastasia's coffin, but he falls all the same. The claustrophobic throne room is filtered in red—only the fresco of God on his Apocalypse cloud is blue—and the lighting from below is conventionally demonic, repeating the demonic lighting and gestures Ivan made between flashbacks in the The Prologue. Ivan speaks not like someone free to do what he wants but like someone still angry at his enemies, still paranoid, and still bent on revenge. Through much of the scene, his body appears weighted down from above: he hunches and slouches and stands awkwardly. For all his threatening assertions of absolute power (and he doesn't make his "power gesture" here, only God is depicted with two arms flung open above his head), he does not appear free. He is Lucifer, still needing to rise again, still wanting to be God.

In Part III (based on the scenario, existing stills, and a few minutes of footage), Ivan uses the power he crafted in Part II to subdue the rest of Russia, conquer the lands separating Moscow from the Baltic Sea, and avenge himself on the traitor Kurbsky, the German spy Heinrich von Staden, and all his remaining enemies. He does all this in particularly cruel fashion, each time spurred on by memories of childhood vulnerability and the revenge it inspired. As in Part II, each new increase in ambition and power finds him sprawling in despair. Each repetition of revenge is more violent and devastating than the last. When Ivan reaches the sea, he is triumphant but alone. Each return to his childhood, each return to the womb to be reborn, has led Ivan to embrace harsher and more deceptive measures, greater and more brutal violence, and to reach for ever emptier justifications for the actions necessary to found the Great Russian State. The last turn of the spiral takes Ivan decisively back to his initial childhood loneliness just as he reaches his "Apotheosis" as ruler of the Great Russian State: the perfect dialectical unity of opposites. There the screenplay ends.

This condensed recounting of the narrative, emphasizing the spiral repetitions and regressions, just scratches the surface of the enormous complexity of intersecting networks of image, sound, and rhythm that Eisenstein constructed to show Ivan moving forward, circling back and moving forward again along his biographical spiral. *Ivan the Terrible* is a massive, fluid network of interlinked dialectics of connecting narratives, images, objects, sounds, and gestures colliding in various directions forward and backward in time, and across motifs and themes. Every scene and episode, every image and gesture, contains a multitude of associations with other scenes, images, and gestures, the connections increasing in number and resonance across the time frame of the film, as the story circles back to the past to swoop up old connections and make them new. As Tsivian puts it, "what matters is not what we see at any given moment, but how what we are seeing now relates to what we have seen a moment ago: in other words, our response to contradictory clues."[63] The viewer can enter the feeling and thinking stream at almost any point and proceed in any direction to find a network of related, but not quite symmetrical, patterns of dualism, repetition, and conflict that construct our image of Ivan and address the basic questions of power. From biography to history to politics to psychology to aesthetics, *Ivan the Terrible* is composed of layers of dialectical cycles that intersect each other repeatedly to represent—in as many ways as possible—the divisions within Ivan and the quandaries he faced as he founded the Great Russian State, centralized the government, and reestablished Russian power on the Baltic Sea: Forward or backward? Public or private? Revenge or compromise? Most narrative films cue us to think about such conflicts with dialogue and action that are supported tacitly but directly by nonverbal cues like facial expressions and soundtrack. Eisenstein leads us to think about and feel Ivan's conflicts with visual and other sensory cues organized in this dense, multilayered, interconnected universe that he would come to call "polyphonic montage." Later in the book I discuss other forms and uses of this "symphony of voices." Here I want to focus on the way Eisenstein mobilized—or animated—props and set design to give meaning to the spiral dialectic of Ivan's life story as a set of questions concerning power and revenge.

Animated Things

One of the ways in which Eisenstein sought to invest every thing on screen with significance was by eliminating objects of everyday use, the collection of things surrounding characters that convey the texture of everyday life in conventional films. The production design of *Ivan the Terrible* alternates between relatively spare and claustrophobically full sets. In place of historical realism, Eisenstein uses things—alone and in combination—to give a sense of living in Ivan's world. He animates those things by creating multiple, overlapping webs of connection and by focusing on individual things in the kinds of close-up that make them take on a life of their own.

The sets *appear* to be overflowing in part because the actors' bodies, especially individual body parts, are treated like autonomous or animated things. Eyes, hands, feet, Ivan's beard, and everyone's shadow all seem to have an independent life of their own. Eisenstein calls this "eccentric" acting. "The eccentric smashes the habitual organic mechanism of movement into separate pieces, which are then reconnected arbitrarily through montage. . . . They are **torn** from their habitual, <u>organic</u>, rational, logical interconnections and balanced in a different, new way. But in an unexpected, unaccustomed, and <u>deliberately **not** organic</u> way."[64] Drawing attention to body parts like this and then repeating their movements so profusely—the stretched-out foot, raised hand, sliding eyes, enlarging and shrinking shadows—creates richly suggestive but laconic, nonverbal networks of meaning. Repeated gestures incrementally form a kind of shadow language; a pre-logical, nonverbal syntax of repeated gestures and things. Architectural details are profuse, distorted, surprisingly empty, and surprisingly overflowing. A number of scenes are set in spaces whose walls are crowded with religious iconography and folkloric ornamental design, all slightly distorted in scale and contour. The spaces that lack paintings and wall coverings have marked architectural detail: prominent interlocking patterns of ceiling ribs and archways, the inexplicably small portals in the Kremlin, or the checkerboard floor and gigantic tapestries in the Polish court. Repetition, reversal, and exaggerated or unexpected gestures make things and bodies seem bigger and more numerous and more prominent than they are. In all these cases, Eisenstein makes individual objects or gestures stand out from the rest. The eccentric, he says, is the thing that stands out from everything around him or it. At the same time the production design accentuates networks of visual connections among objects and images, a profusion of motifs that Kristin Thompson called "insistently systemic," while only gradually revealing the meaning those connections accrue.[65] Eisenstein's nonverbal storytelling makes meaning elusive in unfamiliar but carefully plotted ways and for a specific purpose. The things we see on screen are enlivened (*odushevlennyi*, literally "ensouled") in order to trigger our thoughts and feelings. In a pre-logical state, things can speak to us directly; we register their voices—without having to think about them—with our intuitive senses and feelings. The escalating emotional intensity and complex sensory-intellectual process of reassembly make it seem as if we are seeing more things more randomly utilized than we really are. Eisenstein wants to stimulate our instinctive connections and our intellectual abilities to make sense of things; to make us aware of these processes both unconsciously and consciously at the same time. Standing out and interconnecting form one of the primary visual dialectical "mechanisms" for speaking directly to our senses while providing material to be reconnected intellectually through montage.[66]

Eisenstein's ideas about the production design and the use of things on screen originated amid lively interest in these subjects by Soviet artists and filmmakers in the 1920s, as Christina Kiaer and Emma Widdis have shown in their studies of socialist things and the filming of socialist things. In 1926, the director Abram Room wrote that "real cinema is emotionally saturated," and Shklovsky argued that cinema could form new affective relations between people and things. Widdis shows that filmmakers of all kinds were exploiting cinema's capacity to activate emotional and sensory responses, to awaken a new sense of proximity to things, and to remake an "emotionally saturated" relationship to the world. Even the language of "primitive" experience—its direct encounter with the world and the conceptualization of film as producing embodied knowledge in viewers—was part of cinematic discourse in the 1920s and 1930s.[67] Eisenstein, however, took these concepts and placed them in dialectical relationships that exposed ambiguity and multivalency to interrogate the dynamics of power relationships and individual and cultural evolution. The Kino-Fist that he proposed in opposition to Dziga Vertov's Kino-Eye in 1925 was the first step in this direction, making cinematic images that resonate in the body and ultimately have the power to generate new ideas and transform consciousness. He wrote specifically about the abilities of cinema to effectively stimulate feelings in viewers with the proper use of objects—the "affective expressivity of objects"—in late 1925 or early 1926 in notes for an article on "the play of objects."[68] In *Ivan the Terrible*, Eisenstein used these visual, intellectual, and sensory-emotional strategies to film specific things that could be perceived both instinctively and consciously, that could signal the spiral return to the beginning, convey Ivan's ideas and feelings, and raise questions about Ivan's motives and the implications of his actions for power and tragedy.

Eisenstein wrote about the power inherent in objects in the Disney manuscripts, which I'll come back to, but he also wrote about animated things in a group of texts on the psychology of art. In November 1940, his long-time friend, the eminent psychologist and neurobiology pioneer Alexander Luria, asked Eisenstein to write something on the psychology of art. The war and *Ivan the Terrible* interrupted the project, but in November 1947 Luria returned with another request, this time for a series of lectures.[69] Eisenstein's death in February 1948 prevented him from giving the lectures, but as he noted the day after Luria phoned, "Not yet having made up my mind to do it, I *naturally* start planning this morning while in bed *how* I would present such a series."[70]

The first manuscript from December 1940 (with references to many earlier texts) addressed one of the primary questions about artistic production that he had often written about: "neither theme nor content, but how this theme or content becomes, from an object of reality—an object of art. How an 'event' becomes a 'work.'"[71] The answer he gives is a list of half a dozen moments from works of art that represent a variety of methods for using things—or choosing particular things—to make art from reality. A dangling pince-nez is all that is left of the doctor who sparked the mutiny on the *Potemkin* by declaring the sailors' maggoty meat edible. The howling of a storm blends, with "equal rage and in tone," into the storm of King Lear's "anger and fury." John Steinbeck invests Tom Joad's horse and wagon with a lifetime of feelings about work and family. A vibrant, starry summer sky in Pushkin's *Poltava* becomes a claustrophobic prison dungeon when the poet transforms the stars into mocking eyes and gives the trees "judgmental" voices. Finally, Lev Tolstoy literally gives voice to his condemnation of modern greed and materialism by inventing a wise, talking horse who reveals the semiotic slippage between things and the words that name them, marking them as property.[72] In his discussion of each of these examples, Eisenstein points to our ability to respond to the things around us with a intuitive, nonverbal, sensory-emotional experience. Tapping into this capacity, creating images on screen that trigger it, and joining it to the complex, highly evolved, intellectual response is at the heart of what he thinks makes cinema powerful, even transformative.

Each of the examples given in the draft of "The Psychology of Art" combined ideas about montage that Eisenstein had explored in the 1930s with ideas about the pre-logical. The pince-nez is his favorite instance of his own use of synecdoche or, as he preferred, the more precise *pars pro toto*. "The montage segment (especially a close-up) is a part (*pars*). . . . By the law of *pars pro toto*, that part stimulates the mind to complete the construction of *a certain whole*. . . . For *pars pro toto* is also a means of compelling the mind to generate the image of an event without depicting the event itself."[73] The emotional charge of such images is intensified by the viewer's action of filling in the blanks, of imagining the whole: "it is a *toto* that each individual spectator has, *in his own way*, seen, and has in his own way created. It is quite obvious that the degree of intensity with which *such an image is experienced* is far greater than a *depiction* that is created and executed by some one else."[74] Even more complex and intensely engaging is the experience of constructing a whole from the fragmented depictions of things when it occurs over time: "Galloping hooves, the rushing head of a horse, a horse's rump disappearing into the distance. These are three depictions. Only when they are combined in the mind does there arise an imagistic *sensation* [*obraznoe oshchushchenie*] of a galloping horse."[75] Eisenstein claimed that this method of generating emotion—breaking things down into fragments, leaving some out, allowing (or compelling) the audience to recreate from the visible and invisible pieces—is present in art work of every culture on every continent stretching back to earliest recorded times.

If *pars pro toto* activates the viewer's imagination, the sight of the pince-nez and the process of apprehending its connection with the doctor, the doctor's fate, the injustice, and the mutiny, it is also capable of returning us to the pre-logical experience of apprehending the world purely through sense and emotion. The raging storm, the talking horse, and the watchful sky are examples of ways Eisenstein linked montage to the pre-logical through *pars pro toto*. *Pars pro toto*, he believed, was typical of the pre-logical. In that open sensory-emotional state we lack differentiation between part and whole, a key ingredient in the totemistic affinity with things. A man wearing a bear tooth around his neck feels himself to be not only courageous *like* a bear but to be in possession of the whole bear. He shares the bear's feelings of courage and strength. He *becomes* the bear.[76] Eisenstein's favorite example of this more extreme form of transfiguration and undifferentiatedness comes from the Bororo people of Northern Brazil: "The Indians of this tribe—the Bororo—maintain that, while human beings, they are nonetheless at the same time also a particular species of red parrot that is found widely in Brazil. They do not mean by that they will turn into these birds after death, nor that their ancestors were once parrots. Nothing of the sort. They assert directly that they really are these very birds."[77] Ever since these Bororo statements were published, they have divided anthropologists, many of whom questioned the direct identification with red parrots that Eisenstein accepted as authentic.[78] But his point here is not whether the Bororo really did believe themselves to be parrots or whether modern children and people in nonindustrial societies do not distinguish clearly between parts and wholes, or themselves and the things of the world as Eisenstein argued, but that we continue to have a desire for such intense, transformative, sensory-emotional thinking. Eisenstein was ridiculed for talking about the Bororo when he lectured about them in 1935, but he believed that our ability to imagine becoming other beings and even merging with things was a form of the pre-logical that was absolutely central to human experience and artistic composition.

At this point in "The Psychology of Art," he writes: "Stop joking! Do you really mean to say that the method of art is a reversion of our enlightened, modern intellect to the twilight stage of primitive thought?"[79] Of course, he argues yes. In fact, he writes that we often acknowledge how prone we are to similar kinds of intuitive, antirational thinking about the things that we live with. Sometimes stars *are* eyes and sometimes we feel that we *are* the storm without and within. Writing about Disney, Eisenstein observed that the humanization of animals in his cartoons is akin to the "mythological personification" of natural phenomena: identifying a forest with a wood goblin, or a house with a house spirit was to invest things with personal feelings, which gives them enhanced status and meaning. When we animate things, which we do all the time, we also invest them with *their own* feelings. You stub your toe on a heavy chair in the dark, Eisenstein wrote, and "you regress to the stage of sensory-emotional thinking: you curse the chair as though it were a living being."[80]

Our deep human connection to objects and creatures, our awareness of the undifferentiatedness of organic and inorganic forms, and our desire to animate things and merge with nonhuman species seem to be lessons that, as rational modern people and scholars, we resist. Jane Bennett, one of the leading proponents of a new animated "thing theory," felt the need to begin her recent book by imploring readers to rethink "an idea that runs fast through modern heads: the idea of matter as passive stuff, as raw, brute, or inert."[81] Examples of our desire to animate things and merge with nonhuman species are more than the strange ramblings of an idiosyncratic mid-twentieth-century thinker. They are, in fact, all around us, from serious scholarship to serious bestsellers. In 2005, the historian of material culture Leora Auslander introduced theories about our emotional investment in things with examples that could have come straight out of *Method*. She discussed ordinary transitional objects like a child's blanket that "literally embodies the absent parents until the child is able to keep them securely present in his or her mind's eye," and a ring that incarnated a woman's father so completely that her memory of him was embodied in her vision of the ring: "it was, it was . . . it was my father, voilà."[82] The naturalist Helen Macdonald, in *H Is For Hawk,* one of the most popular books of the summer when I am writing this, movingly describes the way an overwhelming season of grief allowed her to fulfill childhood dreams of not just training hawks but of becoming a hawk. Afterward she had contradictory feelings about the experience as she came to recognize the psychological dangers that accompanied the satisfactions of these out-of-body experiences. In this connection, she cited a work about the Siberian Yukaghir hunters, who also transfigured themselves into their prey and also considered such transfigurations to be as dangerous as they were irresistible.[83] In *Nonindifferent Nature*, Eisenstein identifies the same process— literal, not metaphorical, transfiguration—in Ovid's *Metamorphosis*.[84]

This belief in the magical power of things, acknowledged or unacknowledged, adds to the emotional impact of the things we see on screen.[85] Eisenstein sought to replicate the affective impact of these experiences of interpenetration or transfiguration by means of extreme close-ups. The wideangle 28mm lens created just the kind of distortion Eisenstein wanted for intensifying sensory-emotional responses and triggering the "magical" sense of *pars pro toto* and undifferentiation. In *Nonindifferent Nature*, Eisenstein wrote that the distortions of the extreme close-up produced by the 28mm lens made it possible for objects to go "beyond" themselves, to leap out of themselves.[86] In *Ivan the Terrible*, Eisenstein used such close-ups to enliven things—the dangling legs, the fur coat, the chalice, the discarded mask, the birds in frescoes—to identify motives and actions, dramatize questions about political necessity and morality, and initiate multiple lines of interpretation of Ivan's actions. The repetition of such enlivened things created networks of significance by stimulating the dialectic of pre-logical openness to unconscious, nonverbal cues and by compelling us to consciously start making sense of the connections.

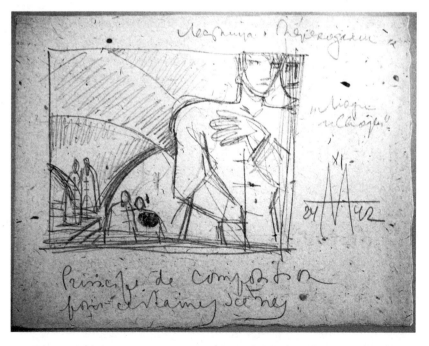

Figure 3.6   *"Principe de composition pour certains scènes.* 'Stairway with Passageways.' 'People and Arches.'" RGALI, 1923/2/1727/12 [Nov 24, 1942]. Used with permission.

These networks followed some discernible patterns of repetition, connection, and allusion. Objects and gestures, first of all, may be repeated in fairly straightforward ways. Like rhymes, visual repetitions can be slightly altered to link characters or actions in unspecified but suggestive ways. Second, Eisenstein liked to drop depictions and fragments of images into the viewer's subconscious, to be dislodged later on and acknowledged more consciously, when they reappear. These cases of circling back before moving forward—the spectator's parallel experience of the spiral—can be relatively simple repetitions or they can be more evocative. Third, connections between objects can start to reveal not only similarities or reversals but also internal conflicts, relationships among characters, motives, and reactions among characters. Finally, some cases of repetition link objects or gestures to systems of meaning outside the film—religious belief, political propaganda, classic novels, psychological theories, existing paintings—that may be suggestive but require analysis and specialized knowledge to understand.[87] All these uses are especially important for articulating what is better left unspoken in a world of surveillance: visual images of things with magical, emotional powers can lead you to conclusions that cannot be articulated in words where words are more closely policed.

The armillary sphere, whose shadow is featured alongside Ivan's head in his stateroom in Part I, shows how Eisenstein used patterns of repetition, connection, and allusion to set up multiple overlapping readings and suggest networks of significance to convey his ideas (I: 1:10:57).

A spherical representation of the universe composed of multiple metal rings, the armillary sphere was an instrument for measuring the relative movement of celestial bodies; it originated in ancient China and Greece and was brought from the Muslim Middle East to Renaissance Europe, where it was often used in paintings as a symbol of wisdom or advanced secular knowledge. Yuri Tsivian and Katerina Clark have identified a number of possible readings of the armillary sphere in *Ivan*, as a projection of Ivan's thoughts about state building and Russia's connection with the West or the larger world, connections that might have signified for Eisenstein Ivan's scientific prowess and political dominance.[88] But, as Tsivian notes, Eisenstein believed that sensory-emotional thinking endows these shadows with autonomy from their literal or historical meaning. In his postwar notes on shadows, Eisenstein began by comparing the explosion of *ekstasis* to the fission of the atom bomb, both of which produce reactions that move centrifugally in all directions. He wanted his shadows to generate the same kind of sensory-emotional fission.[89] He also wanted the projection of Ivan's shadow on the wall to externalize Ivan's inner conflicts so that he could argue with himself. In *Nonindifferent Nature*, Eisenstein identified characters in Shakespeare and Dostoevsky who

FIGURE 3.7   The armillary sphere

did that: Ivan Karamazov, for example, "whose 'second' nature is so intense, that it materializes before his very eyes and enters with him into the most clever casuistry of metaphysical discussion."[90]

In that spirit of fission and externalized dialectic, we can see the armillary sphere as a projection of the inner conflict dramatized in this scene. In contrast with Ivan's anger and cunning in dealing with the boyars and his ambassador Osip Nepeia just moments earlier, his solitary meditation is intercut with shots of Anastasia in her bedchamber: political affairs and private life explicitly juxtaposed. Ivan's meditation takes him past external problems of domestic politics and international ambition to consider a deeper obstacle—inside himself—impeding his path forward. The question he asks himself throughout the film—am I doing the right thing?—is visually suggested here as a conflict between the public and private: the personal pleasures of human connection pull him away from the dangers of human conflict. Enter the armillary sphere as fissioning, dialectical object. Its formal qualities—fusing two-dimensional circles into a three-dimensional sphere—show the potential for an Eisensteinian object to suggest a complex network of associations. As Bulgakowa shows, in the 1920s Eisenstein often associated the circle with a closed space, separated from the world, impermeable and complete, and as a self-contained entity. These closed, isolated forms had ominous connotations in his early theatrical productions, where circles isolated characters from the world.[91] In *Method*, the circle was also closely associated with the pre-logical return to the womb. The womb is a paradoxical space for Eisenstein: safe, protective, and longed-for, but also a return to nonbeing, to the kind of dissolution associated with pre-life and death, as well as the undifferentiation represented in the bisexual body, or that people desire in sex. In contrast to the circle, the sphere in Eisenstein's thinking is associated with openness, the freedom of multiple shifting points of view, and the kind of interpenetration that signals connection with the world. The armillary sphere, then is a projection of both the external political conflict Ivan is pondering in the first part of this scene and the internal conflict that preoccupies him once he is alone. Open or closed? The world or the womb? The state or his marriage? Violence or sex? Power or pleasure? And because Eisenstein didn't think in terms of pure binaries, each of these elements was complicated by containing some measure of its opposite. The happy marriage is marred by betrayal; the progressive political mission is fraught with potential violence. Eisenstein believed that we instinctively respond to such cues as circles and spheres, so that they can trigger fission-like unspecified feelings of inclusion and exclusion, outward and inward, danger and safety, which can then be associated with ideas about Russia and the West or public duty and private pleasure or the experiences of life and death.[92] The armillary sphere is thus not a metaphor or a representation of an idea; its form (circles/sphere) literally embodies the conflicts with which it is associated. It is open and closed, inclusive and exclusive, interior and exterior, all at the same time. Eisenstein expected us to respond to its formal, physical, embodied characteristics in a pre-logical, intuitive, nonverbal way at the same time that we begin to associate that form with ideas and feelings, with content.

The chalice used to poison Anastasia is another animated object that stands out—vibrating with life (and death)—and reaches out of itself to produce networks of associations that raise important questions. Because we see the chalice in numerous settings through the film, we can see how Eisentein used it to accrue resonance and meaning. We first meet the chalice at Anastasia's wedding, where it is nothing more than a simple functional vessel, awaiting its starring role. It reappears later in Part I in medium shot, taken from a niche and half-hidden off screen or under Efrosinia's cloak, but everything in the shot—the line of the candle flames, the angle of the vial of poison, and the spotlighted fragment of Efrosinia's face—points our attention toward it (I 1:17:32). A few frames later, we see the chalice, standing by itself, pushed into position only by Efrosinia's fingers, almost appearing to move on its own. Then briefly, the camera focuses on it in close-up, as if to give it an "independent existence."[93] Finally, we see Ivan grasp the chalice before handing it to Anastasia. These visual rhymes and contrasts highlight the chalice as an animated object capable of evoking strong primal feelings underlying and intensifying its role in this complicated moral, political, and emotional narrative.

Here it also participates in the discourse about agency so central to the questions of power and murder in *Ivan*. One of the political-moral questions raised in the film is whether (and when) murder can be justified for political reasons. A fairly simple example of this occurs at the battle for Kazan in Part I. The battle juxtaposes legitimate wartime killing by Ivan's army with unnecessary, cruel, and vengeful killing in Kurbsky's sacrifice of the Tatar prisoners. Part III was to end with a much more fraught contrast of military slaughter and political murder. In between, both Ivan and his enemies justify murder on the grounds that it serves some greater good. But Eisenstein complicates the question in various ways, including displacing the killings by one degree of separation: Ivan inadvertently carries out Efrosinia's murder of his wife Anastasia, Efrosinia employs Pimen's underling Peter to kill Ivan in Part II, and Maliuta Skuratov volunteers to carry out Ivan's executions to keep the tsar's hands clean. The only person horrified by these arrangements is the childlike Vladimir Staritsky, who intuitively understands that if he ascends the throne because Peter kills Ivan on his mother's orders, he will bear responsibility for the murder even if he never held a knife. Children in *Ivan*, with their natural pre-logical thinking, consistently see through the political rationales for greed and violence: Ivan as a child, Vladimir as a childlike adult, and the children in The Fiery Furnace.

When Ivan takes the chalice to the thirsty Anastasia, it contains not only poison but all of Efrosinia's hatred and jealousy as well as all her ambition and willingness to take risks. When Anastasia drinks from the chalice, her fingers are intertwined around it with Ivan's. He thinks she is the only person left in the world he can trust, but the reason she needs a drink is because she fainted after hearing that the man she truly loves—Ivan's best friend, Andrei Kurbsky—has just been revealed as a traitor (double disloyalties). There follows here a nice bit of typical Eisenstein: to intensify attention and response, Anastasia briefly pauses and the chalice moves in reverse. She momentarily lowers the cup, and a cut shows Efrosinia rising up from behind the ledge, as if she's been summoned by the reverse movement hesitation of the cup that links the two women. Movement resumes; the chalice rises again, displacing Anastasia's face, followed by a shot of Ivan's hand on the chalice still covering Anastasia's face and containing the whole complicated dance going on between rivals and between husband and wife. Who killed Anastasia? Efrosinia? Or Ivan—both by provoking the opposition of the feudal elites and then by handing the chalice to his wife? Or the chalice itself?

The chalice raises these questions in part through its other associations—in particular with the complicated lines of gender, sexuality, and family politics in *Ivan*, a key thematic line that proceeds almost entirely visually. The figure embossed on the chalice, highlighted in its close-ups, is a *sirin*: a sinister, female, birdlike, Russian folklore Siren. An aggressive female creature is a good avatar for Efrosinia, whose power hunger marks her as a male-ish female, responsible for eradicating the last feminine female in Ivan's life. He himself has feminine characteristics that Eisenstein noted, as does Fedka, Anastasia's replacement. Expanding on these explicitly bisexual associations is the blurring of other heterosexual lines. Ivan's address to Anastasia at the beginning of the scene meshes images of wife and mother, which resonates with Eisenstein's belief that sexual desire merged a desire for the *ekstasis* of sexual union with the undifferentiation before birth in the womb. What are the consequences of murder? When Vladimir turns blue at the end of Part II, when he realizes he is about to die (and be reborn in death by entering the womb-like cathedral), he does so below the image of a sirin painted on the wall behind him—collateral damage of unintended consequences.

The chalice appears a third time, just after Ivan has decided to allow Maliuta to execute the Kolychevs (II: 26:03). Ivan runs to Anastasia's bedchamber, the scene of the crime, drawn there by something, loneliness perhaps, but not yet realizing that her death was murder. There Fedka tries to make him realize that Efrosinia is responsible for his wife's death. "Who handed Anastasia the chalice? And where did it come from?" The displacement of responsibility and Ivan's unwillingness to believe that his own aunt would kill his wife give the chalice a kind of autonomous power: Efrosinia couldn't have done it, and Ivan couldn't have done it; for now the chalice itself must have done it.

We see the chalice once more, much later, just before the climax of Part II (II: 51:50). By this point in the film, every object has become more emotionally charged and politically complex. Acting as Ivan's messenger, Maliuta brings the chalice with him when he goes to Efrosinia to invite her son, Vladimir, to feast with Ivan, but we don't know this until the very last moment. For most of the scene, Maliuta carries the chalice concealed beneath a cloth. Under its cover, the chalice is preceded into the room by intensely curious and fearful gazing from Efrosinia and Vladimir, staring at the door as if it were opening by its own power.[94] Even before we see it, before we realize it's the same chalice that poisoned Anastasia, the hidden object has the power to draw all eyes to it and even perhaps to open doors and move people around the room. Before the characters know what's lurking beneath that cloth cover, Eisenstein uses it to evoke guilt and anxiety and to threaten retribution.

FIGURE 3.8 Efrosinia and the covered chalice

Maliuta has absolutely no narrative or logical reason to bring the chalice with him in this scene, except to link the invitation to the feast with the poisoning of Anastasia after Ivan's recognition in the previous scene that Efrosinia orchestrated the poisoning. Only visual clues link these two scenes, such as the movement of the chalice covering and uncovering Maliuta's face and then Efrosinia's and Vladimir's faces in the same way the cup filled the screen and covered Anastasia's face when she drank from it.

The chalice is entirely unnecessary in this scene, but it doesn't block language or preclude meaning.[95] It speaks to us in another, visual and visceral, language. Eisenstein draws our attention to it as a mysterious object, hidden under its cover, in order to make us *feel* as if the chalice itself were moving the story along and foreshadowing the film's horrific demise. Eisenstein considered this kind of metonymy to be a property of pre-logical, sensory-emotional thinking. Like the bear claw, the chalice stands for the entire story of disloyalty, revenge, and murder. It has the power to resurrect the feelings of the past, to return us in Ivan's place to the feelings of that violent event, and the earlier poisoning of his mother, which remind us of Ivan's childhood desire for revenge. We know more by this point in the film, so the chalice has the power to trigger our memories and our accumulated sensations and feelings associated with the two poisonings and to mirror those with the ideas that have been developing in the meantime. This scene takes place in one of the sets that is almost empty. There are only a few other objects in the room—a loaf of bread, a decorative candelabra, a direct mention in the dialogue of Vladimir's clothing, all contained within the visually insistent claustrophobic architecture—but our eyes are riveted on the mysterious covered object as Maliuta and then Efrosinia move it about.

Just when we might expect all this building tension to result in an emotional explosion, Efrosinia raises the temperature of the scene by lowering it. After Vladimir and Maliuta have left the room, we watch her remove the cloth to reveal the chalice, and we see from her point of view that the chalice is empty. This is another suspense-making doubling as we see the cloth whipped away twice. She looks up and, when the threat implied by what she sees should make her scream, she whispers: "Empty?" This is classic Eisenstein irony: the mysterious object that has accumulated so much power turns out to be empty! An intensely contradictory, visual presence is matched by equally emphatic absence. And, wait, why is it empty and why does that unsettle Efrosinia? The emptiness turns out to be full of meaning. The empty chalice not only reminds us of Anastasia's poisoning (she drank it!), it reminds us of Ivan's revenge motive (again) and foreshadows the revenge murder of

Vladimir. And then we get the beat we've been prepared for. The quizzical "Empty?" is followed by a close-up of the chalice and its embossed sirin, accompanied by a loud drumbeat, TA-DUM. Maliuta brought Efrosinia a vessel that speaks. It says that Ivan knows who killed his wife, and vengeance is imminent. Efrosinia has engineered her own undoing. This sirin was ultimately no match for Ivan.

In the midst of the accelerating narrative of conspiracy, this single object has the effect of drawing together all the mysterious, primal fears, hatreds, and jealousies in play. It enacts suspense and elicits wary curiosity in both the characters and their audience. We simultaneously (or alternately) are trying intellectually to follow the complicated narrative of multiple, insinuated, and overlapping disloyalties, when suddenly we are plunged into an intensely visceral moment that seizes our eyes and stirs our feelings, TA-DUM! The reappearance of the chalice in our visual universe, its insistent presence, draws us to it with what Eisenstein called a "swarm" of resonances.[96] Maliuta's soundless presentation of the hidden chalice intensifies its mystery, its power, and its malevolence, and we respond with visceral, unarticulated feeling for its connection to all of *Ivan*'s most important themes and its sinister premonition of what is to come. These little moves, easily overlooked with all the secrets and conspiracies unfolding around them, are themselves an embodiment of the principle of *pars pro toto*, the literal transfiguration. The unnamed object, its repeated close-ups, and the uncovering that reveals ambiguous information refer to violent events in the past and prefigure the failure of violent events to come.

Among the more complicated and inescapable objects that surround Ivan, fulfilling similar functions but with many more sinuous lines of significance in multidirectional networks of visual cues, are the frescoes painted on the palace and cathedral walls and all the other religious objects surrounding and adorning the characters. Orthodox icons feature prominently in *Ivan the Terrible*, appearing in almost every scene in panel paintings, frescoes, murals, tapestries, and even tableaux in which characters enact well-known moments from the Bible. Ivan wears a huge cross throughout, and church leaders play a major role as targets of Ivan's policy and as opponents to his rule. In his production notes, Eisenstein wrote: "all the frescoes in the whole movie, without inordinate *insisting*, should be <u>thematic</u> echoes—obvious or less so—of the ongoing scene. As if they are <u>the working out</u> . . . of all that is going on around them." And this, he believed, "absolutely <u>reflects the spirit of the art of the era of Ivan the Terrible</u>."[97] The frescoes and objects—their subjects, details, placement, style, and so on—speak (like the chalice) both to the characters in the film and to the audience.

FIGURE 3.9   Icons

Sometimes Eisenstein used icons for relatively simple correspondences, as external projections of characters' identities. Metropolitan Pimen, for example, is associated with images of death, Efrosinia appears standing next to devils, the Forty Martyrs look on as Vladimir Staritsky is murdered at the Feast in Part II, and the oprichniki sing and dance beneath images drawn from the apocalyptic Book of Revelation. Some of the icons in the film are remarkably close copies of authentic fifteenth- and sixteenth-century paintings. The large fresco of the Wedding at Cana—a story about a boy and his mother, as well as transfiguration and transformation—which appears on the wall of Eisenstein's Dormition Cathedral, is almost an exact replica of a fresco by Dionisii in the Ferapontovo Monastery. Most, however, are distorted or exaggerated in a cartoonish or folklorish style. Some are made to resemble images found in pre-Columbian Mexican architecture. And a few are radically reimagined, spatially distorted, and conceptually marked, designed by Eisenstein to seize the viewer's attention and lodge in the memory. These images, including the enormous angel that covers the ceiling and part of the walls of the Golden Hall, where two key scenes take place, have a special role to play in Eisenstein's visual construction of Ivan's biography. I have written elsewhere about the "Angel of Wrath" and the ways it and other iconic images are used to produce networks of increasingly complex associations and to prompt affective responses that resurrect pre-logical feelings from earlier stages in life.[98] Here I concentrate on Eisenstein's uses of Orthodox images to convey ideas about montage, the biographical spiral, and the morality of power.

When we first meet Ivan sitting alone in that dark womb of a chamber, he is dwarfed by the huge frescoes (II: 11:01). We have seen how the stretched-out legs we see above him signal an impending transformation, but they have an additional function here. In his production notes for *Ivan*, Eisenstein wrote that the frescoes in this scene should be "especially excessive in scale. In this they should reflect the <u>sensations they produced in little</u> Ivan. In <u>his</u> imagination they are enormous, colossal, threatening."[99] Childhood fear will be one of the main causes of Ivan's lifelong desire for vengeance, and we will see those dangling legs again and again when he feels threatened by the boyars. The dangling feet of the first scene and the poignant stretch that shows the throne to be too big for Ivan also rhyme with feet dangling on the moon behind his throne in the Golden Hall, illustrating lines from Revelation (II: 12:47). Frescoes of dangling feet accompany Vladimir, stumbling through the cathedral to meet his death. This is one of many instances of visual rhyming that joins Ivan with Vladimir, marking Ivan's murder of Vladimir as a kind of suicide and leading to another of Ivan's demonic rebirths. Like the armillary sphere and the chalice from the palace, frescoes are literal embodiments of Ivan's memories (and ours). We can follow the "leg stretch" to threads linking other body parts and signifying meaningful, if slightly different, connections between characters. The frescoes function as memory cues for both Ivan and the film's spectators, underlining over and over again the significance of Ivan's spiral regressions to childhood. Eisenstein's notes tell us that the feelings produced by the "colossal" and "threatening" frescoes from Ivan's childhood reappear at the climax of what would have been Part III, The Confession, which occurs before an enormous fresco of the Last Judgment. "Return to exactly the same thing in the scene of the Last Judgment—where Ivan will again experience the <u>fears of childhood</u>. And—in the scene with Filipp, which, by the way, <u>falls in just the same place!</u>—with the terrifying [*strashnyi*] angel whose face blazes with fire. And it is in just this scene that Ivan takes on the 'childish' fear of loneliness."[100]

Eisenstein's angel, with the blazing head and dangling feet, identified in the screenplay as the "Angel of Wrath, Apocalyptic Angel," performed all these functions and was one of his favorite images. In the spring of 1942, when he storyboarded most of the film, Eisenstein called this "the best graphic image I've made so far."[101] Projecting Ivan's fears onto the ceiling and walls, and insisting that the viewer engage actively with the wall paintings, is one of the ways Eisenstein uses images to draw us into the film. The disproportionate and overwhelming angel, with its disorienting fragmentation that prevents us from ever seeing it whole, places us inside Ivan's perspective and offers us a visceral experience of Ivan's fears of powerlessness (II: 9:24). By making us feel what Ivan is feeling, the filmmaker challenges our safe perceptual distance and forces us both to judge Ivan and to share his feelings when he is judged.

This fusion of child and adult in the spiral biography by analogy collapses the historical distance between the sixteenth and the twentieth centuries, just as the lines between Ivan's past and present and between spectator and character were blurred. Ivan is a child and an adult, we are both in the frame and outside it, Ivan exists in his own time and in Eisenstein's and in ours, whenever and wherever we are watching. This sort of temporal convergence is a principal characteristic of Orthodox iconography. Eisenstein knew that medieval viewers saw not mere illustrations of biblical narratives or divine figures in icons but images that transcended their material form as paintings to link the viewer with the original events of divine history. As Daniel Rowland has written about icons painted in Ivan's time, "[it] would have been perfectly natural to anyone reared in an Orthodox liturgical culture [to imagine] the same cosmic event—the struggle of God's forces against the forces of evil . . . as occurring many times: in the Old Testament, in Byzantium and Kiev, in the sixteenth-century 'present,' and at the Apocalypse."[102] And, one might add, in the Soviet Union in the 1940s. "One version of this struggle was understood as implying the others."[103]

Temporal and other kinds of repetition serve the dual function in *Ivan* of structuring the narrative and structuring our understanding of the narrative. The story "takes place," so to speak, in our reinterpretation of repeated images, with each new piece of accumulating evidence. We understand that Ivan felt lost and powerless, terrified of and furious at the boyars, while sitting helplessly under the angel's fiery face and dangling feet. We understand how these feelings motivate him and affect his judgment and later behavior—not by observing his actions later on or by listening to his speech, both of which can be opaque and contradictory, but by accumulating the evidence of repeated images and resolving or acknowledging their contradictions. The narrative of Ivan's life and our perception of his life proceed in tandem. We see the implications of successive actions accumulate chronologically, as instinct and emotion are layered with increasing knowledge and experience, and simultaneously, as the formative sensations of childhood reappear in the adult. Eisenstein both told Ivan's story and raised questions about it with such linkages and rhythmic repetitions.

He also wrote, and Moskvin filmed, a scene in which we see icon painters at work.[104] Footage of the scene, intended for Part III, is lost, but the text,
some drawings, and a few frames have survived. The text comes almost verbatim from the decisions of the Stoglav Council of 1551, an effort by Ivan
IV's government to regularize and assert central government authority over
some aspects of religious life. One feature of Ivan's rule was the collection of
Orthodox icons from all over the territory of Muscovy and the summoning of
icon painters themselves to work for Ivan, in Moscow, something that Eisenstein noted in several places in his notebooks. The Stoglav prescribed both
what and how they could paint. They were to faithfully follow prescribed
topics and rules for the reproduction of the images of God and were warned
against following their own inspiration under threat of penalties in this world
and the next. There were also behavior prescriptions: painters were not to
be lazy or frivolous, quarrelsome or covetous, and they were to preserve the
purity of body and soul.[105] Eisenstein's scene shows Ivan visiting the painters
as they worked in the Golden Hall. The frames we have show them high up
in the building, working on scaffolds close to the windows that are flooding
the chamber with light. Eisenstein juxtaposes this lyrical, heavenly sight with
Ivan's angry condemnation of the artists. He shouts up from below: "For a
whole hour I've been watching you. You are stupid, lazy masturbators."[106]
There are numerous ways to interpret the prescriptions of the Stoglav, but
Eisenstein chose one that reproduced Stalinist attempts to control artists and
uncannily predicted Stalin's contemptuous treatment of Eisenstein and others in 1946, once the war was over.

In addition to these convergences of time and space, the angel introduces
some of the specific polar elements of Ivan's inner conflicts. Eisenstein's angel
plants these fundamental dualisms somewhere in our perception early in the
film, to be dislodged, connected, and interpreted later: sun/moon, power/
vulnerability, male/female, violence/justice, natural/supernatural, secular/
sacred, sacred/fallen. The head, surrounded by flames, makes a fierce sun,
the feet dangle above a gentle moon. The powerful head in contrast with the
vulnerable feet dangling over the moon are then a "double dialectic"—the
feet embody a second division. First, the angel's feet rhyme with all the other
moments where vulnerability is signaled by dangling feet, and second, they
are described in the screenplay, quoting Revelation, as "trampling the universe," another expression of the angel's overwhelming power. This "double
dialectic" is a key device in *Ivan the Terrible* that Eisenstein uses to show how
our inner struggles constantly present us with choices for action. Ivan is revisited by these infantile feelings of powerlessness throughout his life, and those
feelings repeatedly compel him to act just as he did against the boyars whom

he feared in childhood: decisively and violently. Not only do dangling feet continually remind us that Ivan's power is exercised as an avenging predator who was formerly the prey of his current victims; they remind us of all the other ways that Ivan was internally divided, as a fundamental attribute of being human.

The angel's ambiguous sexuality adds another layer to the inner conflicts and desire for wholeness that reflect Ivan's essential humanness. Sex role differentiation or ambivalence about gender figures prominently in *Ivan*. What Eisenstein called in his notes "b.s." or bisexuality was often less about sexual preference per se, or his own personal sexual ambivalence, than it was a critical issue in his investigation of the "unity of opposites" as an aesthetic and philosophical problem. Life in the womb is sexually undifferentiated and androgynous, for example. The angel is androgynous, a literal "unity of opposites," mirroring Ivan's internal divisions. Bisexuality in this sense was a suitable model for the fundamental dialectic Eisenstein saw between division and synthesis (or merging and interpenetration) in the operation of montage, the structure of dialectics, the composition of art, and, of course, heterosexual intercourse.[107]

The secular and the sacred are also juxtaposed in the nature imagery surrounding the angel: the sun and the moon, the clouds, the birds, and the stars surrounding its head and feet, and the sun and moon obviously connote natural cycles. At first glance, however, these attributes don't resolve themselves as either secular or sacred. Each plays a role in the Book of Revelation, and each can be found in icons from the late fifteenth and sixteenth centuries. Ambiguity and contradiction also attend the angel's possessions. Eisenstein's angel is shown carrying both sword and scales, common symbols of power and justice but an unusual combination in Russian iconography. As Thompson noted, images of justice in the United States include both sword and scales, as do images of Archangel Michael in Western and Mexican icons, but in Russian iconography the sword and scales rarely appear together.[108] It would be typical of Eisenstein to chose disparate symbols and stitch them together in this montage image of the attributes of angels and archangels. The atypical juxtaposition of symbols draws attention to the fraught relationship in this film between power and justice, particularly between earthly power and heavenly judgment. The graphic dualism of the angel draws additional attention to the moral dilemma Ivan faces: by a trick of perspective (and the fact that we never see the angel whole), the angel is both flying above the action as a sacred figure and appears at times to be descending, head first: a simultaneously or sequentially rising and falling angel, like Lucifer and spiral-bound Ivan.

Another way Ivan's dualism is played out is in his struggle between the exercise of power and the judgments he continually invites and usually rejects. The Apocalypse in general and the Book of Revelation in its details provide crucial keys for understanding Eisenstein's own judgment of Ivan and the narrative he constructed. Eisenstein was familiar with the prevalence of apocalyptic imagery in icon painting during Ivan's reign and the ways that imagery was deployed in both Ivan's courts, in Moscow and Alexandrova.[109] Apocalyptic imagery permeated the paintings of the historical Golden Hall, and Eisenstein's Golden Hall is similarly meant to evoke the Apocalypse. During Ivan's reign, the late fifteenth-century frescoes of the Apocalypse in the Kremlin's Annunciation Cathedral were restored, and new paintings on the subject were commissioned for many more important sites associated with Ivan, including the Trinity Cathedral at Alexandrova and the monastery at Sviiazhsk outside Kazan.[110] Fragments of an Apocalypse icon at the Spasskii monastery in Yaroslavl, reproduced by Muratov in a book in Eisenstein's library, were inserted directly into *Ivan the Terrible*.[111] The details of Eisenstein's ceiling—the sun and the moon, the stars, the sword and scales, even the clouds—are all prominently described in Revelation; as are the contest between virtue and vice and the cycles of birth and death. The Book of Revelation can, in fact, be read as one big Eisensteinian, dialectical, montage image. The world is broken apart; good and evil are repeatedly identified and set against one another. Christ battles the traitorous Antichrist and his armies, and in the end, after the Last Judgment, the evil are destroyed and the world is made whole again, reborn on a higher, sacred, transcendent plane in a moment of supreme *ekstasis*. The end is the beginning.

By framing *Ivan the Terrible* with icons of the Apocalyptic Angel in The Prologue and the Last Judgment at the climax of Part III, and by making those images projections of Ivan's interior, Eisenstein cast the film in the shadow of Revelation, which provides Ivan (and the audience) with a standard for moral judgment, to either embrace or reject. As Ivan's power rises and falls, he is tested and judged, he plays *both* Christ and Antichrist. Every decisive action is followed not only by doubt but, significantly, by Ivan's appeal for judgment. The pattern of interior conflict, exterior action, and request for judgment reveals how Eisenstein structured his narrative as a cycle of increasingly complex dialectic confrontations of action and doubt, judgment and silence. Ivan's heroic assertion of power in the drive to establish the Great Russian State is repeatedly countered by the brutal violence with which Ivan treats his political opponents. Time and again, the two collapse within Ivan and create moments of profound transformation. Ultimately the dialectic reaches a climax in the scene of repentance before the fresco of the Last Judgment, where

Ivan reaches the very depths of despair and the heights of his terrible power. At each major transformation in his life, at each assertion that he is tsar, he turns in direct address to the camera, with a guarded, assertive and questioning look. In this way Eisenstein draws us into the film in another role: he implicates the audience in Ivan's judgment. Ivan's first declaration of power as a child and his first "taste of blood" release a cascade of feelings: fear leads to defiance, then courage, then doubt, and back to fear again. But once Ivan has exposed the greed and clownishness of the adults around him, he has no higher authorities to turn to. His parents are dead, and God doesn't speak to him. So he turns to us—we have felt Ivan's fears, now we must decide whether or not his actions are just.

Ivan's desire for vengeance and capacity for remorse in the context of historical judgment brings us to the distinction Eisenstein made between the sixteenth-century tyrant and his twentieth-century counterpart, a distinction that Stalin personally confirmed. Eisenstein very pointedly differentiated the dualism that characterizes Ivan's actions and the analogous bloodletting in his own time: "In spite of the fact that Ivan is a progressive man of the sixteenth century, looking far ahead, he is still a man tied to . . . the superstitions accompanying the religious fanaticism of the epoch. . . . And therefore Ivan's despair creates doubt—and the theme of despair grows into the theme of doubt: 'Am I right in what I am doing?'"[112] Ivan's medieval religious scruples made it possible for him to consider accepting responsibility for the bloodshed he caused. Some viewers might see Ivan's ability to overcome his scruples and renew his commitment to violent state building as Eisenstein's justification for Stalin's crimes. But Stalin himself conformed to Eisenstein's more critical expectations by never experiencing remorse and by being thoroughly disgusted by Ivan's doubts and need for external judgment. Stalin told Eisenstein in their famous conversation in 1947: "When Ivan the Terrible had someone executed he would spend a long time in repentance and prayer. God was a hindrance to him in this respect. He should have been more decisive."[113] Eisenstein's Ivan operated in a culture that saw the Apocalypse as both imminent and real, and his construction of material objects intended as visual reminders of God's terrible Last Judgment compelled him to see both the glory and the horror of Russian power and potential for tragedy in his role as Russia's ruler, a humanizing dualism that Stalin rejected.

In the same way that Eisenstein used the spiral structure of history and biography to show Ivan's movement through time, he used animated things to show the transformation of interior thought and feeling into exterior action in space. Disney's animated things showed Eisenstein how to use the dynamism of visual forms to appeal to the pre-logical and to convey ideas and feelings. Showing the transfiguration of the inanimate into the animate and the merger of the two models, dialectical synthesis and pre-logical undifferentiation, allowed viewers to experience synthesis in their senses, emotions, and thoughts.

Depicting inner divisions by embodying them in exterior visual forms made it possible to show how moving pictures work their magic on us (stimulating sensory-emotional thinking and rational, logical thought) and to project the interior onto the exterior, to make human contradictions and human desire for resolution of contradictions visible. Cinema made it possible to mobilize many kinds of impulses and contradictions for this exteriorization of human dialectics: moral and political conundrums, the cycles of life and death, the proximity of the animate and inanimate, our desire to merge with and distinguish ourselves from things.

The three examples here—the armillary sphere, the poisoned chalice, and the apocalypse iconography—embody successively complex examples of the ways in which Eisenstein made Ivan's inner divisions visible to us by infusing things with fragments of those interior conflicts and the larger questions those conflicts pose. The armillary sphere embodies the dialectic in form—circles and sphere, inner division and unity of opposites—and loosely gestures to themes of cultural difference and the public-private divide. The mobile chalice accumulates associations as it moves from place to place and is much more closely tied to narrative, collecting and beginning to reassemble the contradictory fragments of thoughts and feelings connected with women, love, envy, murder, revenge, and questions of agency and responsibility. The fragments we see of other Orthodox frescoes and the Apocalypse iconography is even more densely suggestive of both Eisenstein's ideas about the process of artistic reception and the process of Ivan's evolution from damaged child to violent adult. The formal distortion of iconic outlines—their cartoonishness—suggests the animated image as well as the way in which animated forms can trigger memory and lead to transformation and action.

The Apocalypse was of special interest to Eisenstein at this time because it embodied aspects of these universal processes of perception and of the generation of action, and because it represented specific narrative themes he wanted to emphasize. The apocalyptic narratives associated with the icons used in *Ivan the Terrible* correspond to the dialectical method that Eisenstein used to construct Ivan's story. The Apocalypse also provided a critical link between the aesthetic and individual, on one hand, and the larger political and historical issues this film addressed, on the other. The Apocalypse provided the narrative of Ivan's life with a framework for moral and political conflict and a continual visual reminder of judgment of all kinds, external and internal. These are also some of the inner conflicts Eisenstein himself experienced that made him perceive Ivan's story as a tragedy.

This Thing of Darkness: Biography as Tragic Self-Portrait

Much has been written about the autobiographical strain in Eisenstein's work on *Ivan*.[114] He often referred to the film as a self-portrait, and all agree that Eisenstein saw himself in Ivan. An impression of himself as an abandoned, emotionally vulnerable child is the departure point for the autobiography he wrote (mostly) in 1946.[115] His identification with the adult Ivan's confessional remorse is more obscure. Eisenstein's own experiences and self-image certainly shaped the story he told about Ivan the Terrible, in particular his persistent awareness of his own childhood. But if his own experiences reinforced his belief in the biographical spiral, he didn't believe that the Freudian "return of the repressed" functioned to eradicate or neutralize childhood fears and neuroses. Those memories of powerlessness and his father's abuse of power, on the contrary, reinforced a profound sense of shame. It is this side of the equation that needs attention in order to understand what Eisenstein meant when he called *Ivan the Terrible* a self-portrait and tragedy.

Eisenstein wrote about fathers in connection with *Ivan* the whole time he was making the film and in the years afterward. Not surprisingly, he associated Ivan's power as tsar with the power of his own father and with fatherhood as a position of power. Eisenstein described his father almost entirely in connection with power, calling him, for example, "a typical bully about the house."[116] He repeatedly identified his father with Ivan, twice catching himself writing "father" in place of "tsar" in his notes, and he explicitly linked his father's tyranny (and totemism) with Ivan's: "my father was a beast, as Tsar Ivan is a beast."[117] Eisenstein also connected Ivan's (and his own) loneliness with his father's emotional coldness. When Eisenstein was working on *Ivan the Terrible*, he realized that "Ivan's loneliness is connected with the favorite expression of *my* father (who was Terrible enough!): '*man is always alone.*'"[118] The important thing here is that he personally identified with the powerless child in these relationships as well as with the powerful fathers, and he defined those father figures in ways that reflected what he saw as the similarities between his own life and Ivan's.

The great drama in Eisenstein's early private life was his difficult and unresolved relationship with his father and the absence of his mother, who left the two for St. Petersburg when Eisenstein was eleven.[119] He remained in his father's house until he was seventeen, when he moved to the capital to study civil engineering and lived briefly with his mother. Two years later, the revolution began and Eisenstein was drafted into the Red Army. His father, a staunch supporter of the old regime, "a pillar of the Church and the autocracy,"[120] emigrated during the revolution and died soon after in Germany, precluding any possibility of softening, much less resolving Eisenstein's adolescent hostility toward him. His parents' rancorous relationship and subsequent divorce left deep scars. In his memoirs, Eisenstein examined his feelings about his parents in some depth, and it seems clear that the unhappy family dynamics of his youth provided a model, or at least confirmed his thinking, about dialectics that he found in other sources. Eisenstein saw himself as the product of a "marriage of opposites" and his family as the origin of his own inner divisions. The animosity between his parents, together with the loss of his mother and his father's cold distance left him feeling alone, powerless, and angry. It is no accident that the particular image of God that Eisenstein chose for his Last Judgment fresco was Sabaoth, God the Father, just as it is no surprise in this context that Ivan's rebellion fails just when it succeeds.

The rebellion of sons against fathers became a subject of fascination for Eisenstein and one that *Ivan* brought to the forefront. The pain the young Eisenstein felt over his inability to break through his father's silence or stand up to his domineering authority would be replicated in Eisenstein's relationship with Meyerhold, and perhaps with Stalin, and would find its way into his portrait of Ivan. Ivan's fear of predatory adults, his desire for retaliation, his own pursuit and assertion of power, and his loneliness all have roots in Eisenstein's early family life as well as in his recurring relationships with authoritarian men. He considered this relationship with his father to be the source of his own lifelong spiral, with its repeated return to feelings of childish inadequacy: "more often, I suffer from the melancholy infantilism of an overgrown child, ridiculous and helpless, pitiable and insignificant in his clashes with life. Eternally tied to Papa and Mama . . . to two people who were sick to death of each other."[121] He began this sketch for his autobiography by listing milestones in his life and noting his recurring feeling of childhood obedience and loneliness at each one.[122] He would always be the good little boy from Riga: "that's how I was aged twelve. And that's how I was when my hair turned gray." But Eisenstein was nothing if not a "unity of opposites." If these experiences forecast a life of submission to authority, they also were "bound to foster rebellion." The paternal bully who worshipped social convention was also responsible for Eisenstein's "contempt for authority" and willingness to challenge every kind of conventionality.[123]

Much of this is well known, at least by people familiar with Eisenstein's work and his writing, but Eisenstein's projection of his own story onto Ivan's has been interpreted in various ways. The philosopher Valery Podoroga argued that Eisenstein's obsession with the unresolved conflicts of his own childhood diverted his work on *Ivan* from the political to the autobiographical and psychoanalytical: "the political theme went by the wayside."[124] Instead, Podoroga argued, Ivan's regression to childhood prevented him from accepting his own role as an authoritative ruler, resorting therefore to homosexual relationships and violence.[125] Such Freudian interpretations obscure Eisenstein's focus on the operation of paternalistic power, the desire for power over others, and his attempt to sort out the inevitable and universal from the pathological and destructive. A note he wrote in 1947, mostly in English and mostly in the third person, linked "autobiographical film" with "unity," another problematic recurring topic for him, and tells us something about how he saw his relationship with his father as a more generally shared experience and as a model for *Ivan the Terrible*. This note, one of many that he called "The Author and His Theme," was written after *Ivan* was finished, and it addressed not only the way tyranny can produce a desire to overthrow the father but can also create immobilizing shame:

> *The Killing of Kids (self portraying the author of his early photographs—the one with parents) as Oedipus inversus.*
>
> *His relationship with his father.*
>
> *(Hate and fight.)*
>
> *Destruction of self-image—is a way of identifying himself with the father who did that to him—becoming father. Also having seen <u>what</u> becomes of marriage in the divorce burlesque drama of his parents. (Additional element, but basic for author's central artistic attitude—ideé fixe upon Unity.) . . .*
>
> The author's infantilism:
>
> Artificial psychological arrest of the self at the stage <u>preceding</u> the schism in the family—the <u>stage of unity</u>.[126]

Eisenstein's response to his powerful father and the trauma of divorce was to harm himself, the prey of a predator, in order to become powerful enough to surpass his father. He internalized the violent impulse, directed it toward himself in self-targeting shame, rather than turning it into aggression. Eisenstein attributed his fixation on unity (synthesis, *ekstasis*) to arrested development and a desire to pave over painful childhood divisions, loneliness, abandonment, and his parents' painful melodrama of a divorce. But he also saw his father's tyranny in dialectical terms, reinforcing that infantilism and abasement before authorities as well as motivating his ability to challenge all authorities. "Becoming father" is key here. When the prey becomes the predator, the results can be contradictory: the transformed prey acquires power to achieve his own success, but the predation and ambition that produced power and the acquisition of power itself entail new problems, new causes for remorse and shame. Eisenstein's Ivan doesn't alternate between power and remorse; the process of obtaining power *causes* remorse.

Eisenstein felt that intertwined, alternating ambition and remorse throughout his life. There is a relevant story in Eisenstein's autobiography that he says had "a profound effect" on him in childhood. The story is often cited because it is unusually self-revealing, briefly lifting the veil he usually kept tightly folded over his private life. A young Persian hero, who felt he was called on to do great things, was forced to abase himself and bide his time in order to accomplish great tasks later on in life. Eisenstein remembered finding the man's story "utterly captivating: his unheard of self-control and sacrifice of everything, including his self-esteem, as he readied himself for the achievements to come." Eisenstein adds that he had Ivan the Terrible abase himself similarly before the boyars when he feared he was dying. But now, he goes on to say, "In my personal, too personal history I have had on several occasions to stoop to these levels of self-abasement. And in my personal, most personal, hidden personal life, this was perhaps rather too frequently, too hastily, and almost too willingly done—and also to no avail."[127] That the self-abasement here is related to the politics of filmmaking is evident from the context. Eisenstein wrote this passage on August 15, 1946, less than a week after Stalin attacked *Ivan the Terrible*, Part II, in his speech to the Central Committee.[128] Writing this passage at that time suggests that Eisenstein felt his efforts had failed: "In the course of time I too was able to chop heads off as they stuck out of their fur coats; Ivan and I rolled in the dust before the gold-stitched hems but accepted this humiliation only in the cause of our most passionate longings . . . For my part, of course, this chopping was metaphorical. And, more frequently, as I wielded the sword above someone's head, I would bring it crashing down on my own instead."[129] All those articles about "Stalin's genius," the self-abasement he recommended to his friend Maksim Shtraukh, and the compromises he made in making films on Kremlin commission seemed at that moment to have been "to no avail." In August 1946, Eisenstein felt that his abasement and sacrifice brought only "pain, and the bitterness of suffering, through which, as through the rings of hell, my personal, all too personal inner world moves from year to year."[130]

He did not always feel quite so fatalistic, however. Diary entries and conversations with his contemporaries give us a larger historical frame for a more nuanced picture of his feelings of shame and the risks it propelled him to take. Going back to September 16, 1941, his diary records a long, sardonic, revealing monologue written in English about all his failures. It follows a season of frustrations with *Ivan*, distractions with studio work, and worries about the war. The passage includes an ironic description of the contradictory mood at a reception he attended for Erskine Caldwell and Margaret Bourke-White, where they consumed champagne and ice cream waiting for the nightly bombing raid. Then he wrote that he'd been reading books instead of experiencing life directly, *"another infantile sparkle of my infantile caracter (fuck it!)."* He is reminded of a humiliating dinner in New York with Sinclair Lewis, where he felt as tongue-tied and self-conscious as Lewis's dull, long-suffering characters.

Sometimes it is just unbearable (is that the way this tragic word is written?)

Gosh, to live a week a day an hour . . . work on John [Ivan] and nevermind

What is appealing in Lewis is the frustration of his heroes—the terrible frustration. I am suffering of—and suffered through the whole of my travels—activities—life as a whole.

There are so few English reading people in this country here so that I can write what even I think of myself in—this language.

I do not do something and then I suffer of not having done it—

And often I do something and then I see I might not have done it. . . .

It would be funny to write a book "My book of shame" where into put down all the suffering one's mean traits of caracter affords one!

Write down shame after shame. Dirt after dirt, vile desire after vile desire. Everything.

One's inadequacy and all tricky credible and incredible, imaginable and unimaginable—to get out of it.

One's meanness and one's still greater meanness not to accept one's meanness.

Pursue it through travel and creation, sex life and business.

It would make the most astounding thing: if everything could be, would be said. Say everything one never does say—even to one's self

And it would represent far more people than the author only!

I think there isn't one mean thing in the world or human caracter I could not find at a given moment in a given situation in myself

Why not try to make it.

Isn't everything I did poisoned by inner suffering . . . ?

Ambition for instance and lack of means to support it.

Suffering at things that are to sniff at.

Humiliation after humiliation.

Lies to cover humiliation (playing up to conceal them from one's self)

It would make a unique study in caracter. Call every impulse by its real name and discover every impulse behind every deed.

From lice caught in Mexico during somber intercourse, up to books stolen from friends and libraries.

> *From being afraid of dogs to lying and plotting to get some smallest thing to fit your pleasure*
>
> *From being corrupted to corrupting somebody else.*
>
> *From morals being nothing to you—to not knowing the simplest things in life, education or f—. . . !*
>
> *Autobiographically would be much more amusing than in fiction.*[131]

This confessional outburst of shame and remorse is worth quoting at length to give us a sense of Eisenstein's mood, his view of himself, and his place in the world as he was settling down to work on *Ivan* a month before his move to Alma Ata. Eisenstein castigated himself for the moral choices he had made, for his choices about taking up agency and responsibility or failing to act: for choosing meanness over kindness, amorality over morality, corruption and corrupting others. And those choices were made in the context of desire and ambition, in art and sex and business. This passage shows Eisenstein in the double self-portrait of an ambitious man, repeatedly thwarted by an authoritarian system—an obedient child and a victim of things done to him and things he did, as someone eternally divided between action and inaction. It also reiterates the dynamic he attributed to his relationship with his father: achieving power, in whatever form, created its own unresolvable problems. This combination of ambition and the unresolvable conflicts of successful ambition is the dynamic at the heart of Ivan's tragedy.

Eisenstein did not see "becoming father" in exclusively Oedipal terms, which I think is especially important, although the film certainly can be and has been read this way. He didn't dismiss the Oedipal altogether, but he explicitly rejected the Oedipal in his discussion of *Hamlet* in *Method* and in his discussion of Freud's relationship with his students.[132] By focusing on the prey becoming the predator, he desexualized the rebellion of sons against fathers. The sexual desire for the woman/mother was conspicuously attenuated in his portrait of Ivan, so the overthrow of the father is entirely about power and position and shame. As a model for understanding generational power conflicts, Eisenstein preferred the myth of Saturn, another *Oedipus inversus,* a father who ate each of his children to prevent them overthrowing him as he had overthrown his own father.[133] Like the Saturn myth, Ivan's story was about the dangers of *edinoderzhavie,* one-man rule: maintaining absolute power is what generated inevitable excesses because it is a position that will always be challenged and can only therefore be maintained by force. This temporary and cyclical nature of absolute power in his own experiences, in the myths Eisenstein cites, and in the rise-and-fall shape of Ivan's life is essential for understanding Eisenstein's view of power and the tragedy of one-man rule.

But what did Eisenstein mean when he insisted that *Ivan the Terrible* was a tragedy? Consistent definition of such a diverse genre is difficult, and as Terry Eagleton has written, the only thing that all tragedies seem to have in common is that they are "very sad."[134] Ivan is certainly sad. He feels lonely, abandoned, and wronged. He sacrifices private pleasures (or they are taken from him) in his commitment to his mission to found the Great Russian State. And Eisenstein expected us to empathize with Ivan. The Prologue paints the child tsar as worthy of sympathy, and its placement in Part II, where Ivan begs Filipp for his friendship by trying to tug on his empathy, shows that Eisenstein expected us to feel Ivan's sadness and fear. But Ivan isn't tragic because he is sad and alone; he is tragic because he is an absolute ruler, and absolute rule creates impossible moral choices for any human being.

All tragedies, Eisenstein wrote in 1947—ancient, Elizabethan, and modern—are rooted in revenge: in the desire to take an "eye for an eye" based on an "innate" desire for justice.[135] The problem, of course, is that the power to obtain justice, or to do great things, creates opposition, which renews the cycles of vengeance, and calls for more violence. So in order to punish the guilty and achieve his great mission, Ivan has to become inhuman or suprahuman. He has to insist on exclusive loyalty—the original sin of the oprichniki—and kill his enemies when they prove disloyal. When that doesn't work, he aims to become a God, only to fall, because after all he isn't God, he's only human. The only way to govern well, to fulfill his great vision, was to become a monster. Absolute rulers can't be human, and they can't be inhuman. Power (or becoming father) didn't solve Ivan's or Russia's problems; it created new ones, tragic ones.

What's striking about *Ivan the Terrible* is not that Ivan isn't an effective father, as Podoroga claimed, but that he has *no* fathers. The boyar enemies of his childhood are easily overthrown (by a child!), as formidable as they seem at first. But the enemies keep coming back, and with escalating violence that Ivan can thwart only with his own escalation of violence. It isn't Ivan's unique position as *edinoderzhavets*—the single absolute ruler, the fatherless father—that deforms him. His tragedy derives from his desire to continue to strive for power, to protect his position as absolute ruler, in the face of continual opposition, to fend off all challengers, and ultimately challenge God himself. That volume of ambition can only be maintained with violence. To form the Great Russian State without the support of the boyars and everyone who had betrayed him, Ivan needs absolute power. His childhood experiences (like Eisenstein's) perfectly prepare him for the challenges to come. "When the emotional impact of a series of childhood traumas coincides with the problems that the adult comes to face, then it is a blessing in disguise. This was the case with Ivan. From that point of view, my life was very fortunate indeed!"[136] But "becoming the father," also necessitated self-destruction, "destruction of the self-image." From that point of view, neither Eisenstein nor his protagonist was very fortunate.

In his essay on the nature and practice of power in Shakespeare, Stephen Greenblatt asks whether the hunger for power in any of the plays can be considered ethical, whether Shakespeare thought that power itself could ever be an "ethically adequate object."[137] Eisenstein was asking the same question in *Ivan the Terrible*, and the answer to that question was no. Eisenstein shared Ivan's desire for power to achieve great things, and they did great things, but like Ivan, Eisenstein discovered that power and success could be maintained only through untenable moral compromises. Ivan repeatedly chose to ignore his conscience and his need for other people in order to maintain and then reach for higher power, tragically succeeding and falling every time. Eisenstein chose, conversely, to acknowledge his compromises. He chose to inscribe his complicity and shame in his film about Ivan the Terrible; to make it a defiant, challenging tragedy about revenge and remorse, and vulnerability and power. Efim Levin, writing in Moscow in the 1990s, described Eisenstein as someone with a profound sense of the imperatives of public and private life in the Stalinist Soviet Union, someone who "understood [that] fate possesses a historical dimension, for every fate is, in one way or another, a model; and that means that everyone should answer for themselves not only as a private person."[138]

Of all the Shakespearean characters who share Ivan's hunger for the "ethically inadequate object," it is Prospero, the magician and exiled duke of Milan, absolute ruler of a tiny island, whose self-knowledge comes closest to and best explains Eisenstein's identification with his Ivan. In some ways, Prospero seems an unlikely analogue, with his fair-minded response to Ariel's injunction to choose virtue over vengeance, to forgive his enemies and put an end to the cycles of revenge. But Ariel is only one of two creatures in *The Tempest* on whom Shakespeare projects Prospero's inner conflicts. Prospero also has to come to terms with his "misshapen knave," Caliban, after he conspired with two servants of the shipwrecked nobles to carry out a farcical rebellion. "Two of these fellows you/Must know and own," Prospero says to the servants' masters, but "this thing of darkness I/Acknowledge mine." Soon he forgives them too, and he takes responsibility for Caliban, at least for owning him or ruling over him, but his fundamental contempt for Caliban never lifts, so he can't quite acknowledge the role he played in Caliban's life. The creature who remains stubbornly immune to Prospero's efforts to educate him doesn't merit even a recognition of fellow feeling, much less the "nobler reason" that allows Prospero to forgive those who have committed much more serious crimes against him. Prospero's incomplete acknowledgment of his responsibility for Caliban, whom he has educated only to enslave, reminds us that his ability to embrace humane reason and forgiveness at Ariel's suggestion didn't erase his own past crimes or enlighten him to their nature or neutralize the contradictions of human feelings. Nobility and callousness go hand in hand in *The Tempest*. From the Olympian height of his throne, Prospero could forgive others' crimes, but he still couldn't fully recognize his own or expunge his past.

Ivan, at the foot of that gigantic fresco with its eternally tormented souls and cartoonish hellmouth, offers God a similarly incomplete acknowledgment. He is crushed by remorse, his conscience activating the knowledge that mass murder is morally unforgivable. But when God responds to Ivan's entreaties for forgiveness with silence, Ivan tries to sneak in an excuse: he wasn't acting out of anger or spite but against sedition and treason; not for himself, not for greed, but for the good of the state.[139] Abandoning his conscience, he tries to use the one thing that made him less reprehensible than the people around him. His selflessness is exposed here as a mere tactic, undermining any genuine acknowledgment of his crimes. Compare this scene with Eisenstein's version of Pushkin's *Boris Godunov*. As in *Ivan the Terrible*, a critical scene takes place when Boris, having achieved the highest power, confesses to God in the same Dormition Cathedral, before the same Last Judgment fresco where Eisenstein has Ivan confess. Boris, like Ivan, receives only silence in response to his prayers. But unlike Ivan, in the face of God's silence, Boris' conscience overwhelms him. His shame is so fierce, it ignites a fire that burns down the cathedral. In sharp contrast, Ivan's anger extinguishes his remorse, and he rises up to try to seize even higher power.

If violence is the result of personal suffering, a desire for justice, and common human conflicts, can it be forgiven? Ivan craves judgment (even when God is silent), but remorse doesn't ennoble his hollow justifications. At this moment of extreme distress, Ivan tries everything: confession, selflessness, protection of the fatherland, the Great Russian State. In his kitchen sink strategy, personal moral responsibility is only one of the options and one he can never fully embrace. Greenblatt argues that Shakespeare's plays—and I think Eisenstein's *Ivan*—"resist the idea of a moralized basic structure of the mind and with it the search for an intrinsically just conception of responsibility." Neither Shakespeare nor Eisenstein were nihilists, but they both recognized the messy complexity of public life and the dangers of packaging political virtue as an abstraction—the Great Russian State—isolated from those infinite human contradictions. Power puts rulers in a morally impossible situation, but to evade responsibility for ruling is even worse. Those who abdicate power only allow the entirely amoral people to take over: the Antonios or the Kurbskys.[140] Eisenstein, therefore, shared Shakespeare's belief in the moral efficacy of earthly judgment. Eisenstein judges himself harshly, and Ivan, even at his darkest moments—especially at his darkest moments—begs for judgment and seems unable to escape it. But every time, Ivan goes on to seek even greater power, rivaling God's, and commits even more violent and arguably demonic acts. Evading judgment altogether is monstrous; seeking and rejecting it is tragic.

Structuring Ivan's tragedy as a conflict between ambition, public commitment, and long-term historical or political goals, on one hand, and personal, human connection and moral responsibility, on the other, challenges us consider whether it is possible to be a decent human being and a decent ruler at the same time. Prospero thought he had managed it until Ariel forced him to acknowledge his human failures.[141] And maybe Eagleton is on to something. *Ivan the Terrible* is a sad movie, whether we empathize with Ivan or not. Decent (if flawed) people are killed after struggling with impossible choices. Every moment of triumph is shadowed by sadness, and every moment of sadness contains something more than sorrow and loss. Tragic sadness, unlike ordinary sadness, is defined by irony and futility. The accidental death of a loved one is very sad. A political murder, one that is motivated by personal compulsion and impersonal, ideological ambition, is tragic because it is intentional and inevitable and yet seems entirely unnecessary. Political murder is tragic because it is justified by an abstraction and because its instrumental motives are so puny compared to the trauma its violence inflicts. This asymmetry uncovers a relevant kind of human darkness. Ivan's flaws and compulsions, his ambition and his beliefs, are political, and his great cause, the Great Russian State, however justified, pales in the light of the scale of its collateral damage. Ivan makes very sad personal sacrifices for the Great Russian State, like Napoleon and all absolute rulers, but those sacrifices cannot be compared with the devastation he visits on his country and its people. Ivan's fate as an individual is sad, but it is also alienating and horrifying. *Ivan the Terrible* is a Russian tragedy, a historical tragedy, not just a personal tragedy about Ivan.

Ivan's spiral biography offers another perspective on tragedy by raising the questions about agency inevitably associated with the genre: if fate or character or *zakonomernost'* determine our actions, can we be held responsible for them? Ivan continually checks himself with remorse and shows us the divisions power cannot resolve, but he still always chooses violence over compromise or retreat. Ivan is a tragic figure not only because responsibility propels him toward loneliness, or because fate propels him toward tyranny and violence, but because he repeatedly responds to his inner conflicts by *choosing* revenge and murder to fulfill his visionary, abstract, historic calling over personal happiness and humanistic (or for that matter, religious) morality. According to Eagleton, many canonical tragic heroes possess the same "ferocious obstinacy," and he cites the classicist Bernard Knox, among many others, who wrote that "there is something monstrous, more or other than human, in such inhuman stubbornness."[142] Choice and fate seem inexorably intertwined in *Ivan*. And Eagleton agrees in part by arguing that modernist tragedy is inherently dialectical: its implicit subjects are always framed by capitalism, which frees and enslaves; or by civilization, which is purchased with barbaric violence.

Eisenstein's tragedy is, of course, similarly dialectical. Although he persists in calling *Ivan* a tragedy, he also insists that founding the centralized, modern Russia state was a matter of "national progress," and that violence is a necessary tool in art and life.[143] Here we can see how history, power, and rulership all conspire to prevent any permanent, synthetic, unified resolution of internal and external conflicts. As another Shakespeare scholar put it, Hamlet "is precisely not a unified subject."[144] This persistent inability to become a unified subject resonates with themes throughout Eisenstein's work: his shame over action and inaction, and the rest of his inner divisions. Unity—Eisenstein's "idée fixe," his "theme"—is always a tenuous, ephemeral object. Associated with his family before his parents' divorce, unity is always something just out of reach, a utopian goal more than a known condition. Perhaps the fleeting nature of unity—political as well as personal, collective as well as individual—is the essence of tragedy for Eisenstein. In his book on *Ivan the Terrible*, Tsivian discusses a text on tragedy that Eisenstein liked because it argued that tragedy was rooted in the ritual dismemberment and collective consumption of the ruler that allowed him to be reassembled and reborn in a higher form, in the body of the collective. As he summarized it, "tragedy replays (and thus revives in our subliminal mind) the ritual killing of the king—a primordial rite whereby the community members were believed to tear into pieces the body of the leader before eating it together as a symbolic act meant to ascertain that the leader's body was now one with the higher body, the body of the collective."[145] Tsivian points out that Eisenstein was attracted to this image because it was precisely how he conceived of artistic composition: the director dismembers the material of the film and presents it to the viewer to be reassembled. But given Eisenstein's unwavering commitment to the model of disassembling-reassembling and given Ivan's perpetual, unresolvable inner divisions and his ironic compulsion to see everything from two sides, perhaps his tragedy resides in his fundamentally human inability to achieve a stable, unified subjectivity. *Ivan the Terrible* is a rare tragedy in which the protagonist doesn't even die; the film ends with Ivan as divided as ever: an apotheosis shackled to loneliness and violence. Emma Smith sees the "ultimate *subject* of Shakespearean tragedy emerg[ing] as less the eponyms of the plays, but rather the contingent, mobile, and evasive notion of 'character' itself."[146] Unified or perennially divided? That question defied Stalin's expectations for a historical portrait of Ivan as an indisputably "progressive ruler for his time," but it also challenges the fundamental premises of a unified, progressive Soviet subjectivity.

As a biography, *Ivan the Terrible* is an implicitly political film, a profound examination of the impossible conflicts rulers face in their own lives and in trying to weigh the terrible costs of change in inevitable violence, opposition, and loss, even when change is carried out in the name of a righteous cause such as national unity or popular justice. Eisenstein used the judgment implicit in Apocalypse narratives and the inner conflicts over responsibility and agency to show Ivan as actively pursuing his mission of the Great Russian State and tragically divided over the methods he chose to carry it out. Those divisions and the remorse they engendered distinguished Ivan and his brutal regime from Stalin and his. Ivan's conscience and his repeated appeals for support and approval do not make him good, nor do they justify the mass violence he visited on his country. Ironically, tragically, it is the Lucifer in him, the fallen angel, the not-God, that kept him tethered, however tenuously, to earth and to his imperfections. His continual overreach, his need for power to free his hands and move into the future, are what make him choose to be inhuman. Critics and scholars have often seized on Eisenstein's comments about unity without acknowledging the emphasis he placed on the ephemeral nature of that unity. Eisenstein's belief in what he called unity was never totalizing because he never saw unified subjectivity as a possibility. He further explored the tragic implications of divided subjectivity in Ivan's relationships with the people around him, his fugue on the theme of power, which is where we turn next.

CHAPTER 4

Power Projected

Ivan *as Fugue*

As Ivan traces his life story up the ever advancing-regressing spiral path and through webs of interconnected signifying objects, he reveals himself to us through confrontation—in Eisenstein's words, "collision" and "interpenetration"—with each of the characters surrounding him. The spiral is a circle of mirrors, and those mirrors are organized like a Bach fugue—with Ivan as the theme and the characters around him as the variations. Like Eisenstein's reading of history, biography, and autobiography, the fugue has often been referenced, but the way in which the form was used to construct and comment on Ivan's persona and actions has never been examined in any depth. The fugue form allowed Eisenstein to dramatize Ivan's inner conflicts about centralized power by projecting them onto his conflicts with the people who opposed and supported him. Each character mirrors some facet of Ivan's inner conflict and provides dramatic situations for revealing the questions Eisenstein wanted to raise about power, about the choices Ivan made, and the kind of ruler he became when those inner conflicts produced actions with consequences. He also used the fugue to show the impact of Ivan's ideology and actions on other people and to raise questions about agency and responsibility as an individual and as a ruler. These questions further cue the audience to think about the ways in which power is exercised and what happens when it is opposed. If the tragic biography discussed in the previous chapter shows us what kind of ruler Ivan was as a person (and a superperson), the fugue shows us what kind of ruler Ivan was in practice. The visual, sensory-emotional, intellectual experience of watching the fugue and the spiral unfold constitute another layer of ashes in the mortar of the Stalinist film: the fugue in all its variations "is the unity of the developing figure of the tsar as he passes through the picture as a whole."[1]

The Fugue: Unity in Variety

Eisenstein came up with the fugue as an organizing principle for *Ivan* very early on, in February 1941, when he was just beginning to work out Ivan's interactions with his opponents.[2] But in *Nonindifferent Nature*, he also referred to the fugue as a "mania that afflicted [him his] whole life."[3] In several of the manuscripts he was writing during this period, he tells the same revealing story about the origin of his attraction to the basic "theme-and-variations" nature of the fugue. While serving as a soldier in the Civil War in 1920, he witnessed the construction of a pontoon bridge over the Neva at Izhora, just outside St. Petersburg. Perched on a bluff above the action, he was mesmerized by the activity of people and machines below: "intoxicated . . . with the charm of the movement of bodies, scurrying in different tempos along a diagram of divided space, the play of their cross-ing orbits, the constantly changing dynamic form of the combination of these paths—running together into momentary fanciful patterns so that they then can again scatter into distant rows that never meet."[4] The scene popped into his head when he was contemplating the fugue for its dynamic, and cinematic, depiction of an immense variety of disparate activities organized for a single purpose.

Note here Eisenstein's emphasis on the variety and the complexity of the scene's organization. Eisenstein repeatedly and emphatically stated that "all my works are always about **unity**."[5] And in relation to the fugue he witnessed at Izhora he specifically tells us, "All my work is a fugue on the theme of unity."[6] Some commentators have gone so far as to argue that his embrace of unity amounted to a "totalizing" or even "totalitarian" complex that erased conflict, difference, and variety.[7] But Eisenstein is at his most misleading when he makes these blanket statements. Unity, whether in the form of an artistic structure or in the form of Ivan himself, is never an objective or end point, and it is always short-lived. Unity is a momentary dialectical synthesis that immediately explodes into new "higher" forms of dialectical division and contradiction. Eisenstein cannot conceive of a unity that doesn't contain "the other." Take, for example, the discussion of a film's rhythm in his article on D. W. Griffith:

> True rhythm presupposes above all an organic *unity*. It is not a succes-sive alternation of opposing themes, mechanically cross cut or spliced

into each other, but above all a unity that reveals its organic pulse in the play of internal contradictions and through the succession of the play of tensions, that lies at the heart of rhythm. It is not the outer unity of plot—the classic image of a chase sequence also has that—but that special inner unity, which can be realised through montage.[8]

Eisenstein's conception of unity always presupposes division, tension, identifying contradictions, and a variety of sensory triggers. This point is especially important for understanding his use of the fugue. "The fugue and the principle of polyphony . . . both strive . . . to realize in a work of art that *principle of unity in variety* that in nature permeates not only phenomena of the same order but also connects all the variety of phenomena in general among themselves."[9]

Eisenstein's approach to conveying meaning in film does not even approximate this level of coherence or "unity," given its constant visual and semantic challenges to unitary meaning. He had an abiding interest in the ways in which all kinds of things—images, shots, objects in mise-en-scène, ideas, historical time periods—could be combined to create something new, but always with significant slippage and incompleteness. Thinking about Izhora he wrote, "I was always fascinated by the way independent lines of action with their detached regularity interlaced with the rhythmic tones of their patterns and the spatial displacements in the one harmonious whole [of mise-en-scène]."[10] The mesmerizing scene at Izhora occurred at just the moment in his life when Eisenstein says he was beginning to shift from thinking about art to making it.[11] And these were not new ideas for him. Remember that he conceived his original plan for a spherical book so that he could provide multiple, shifting points of view on any topic.[12]

Then, while working on *Ivan* in Alma Ata twenty years later, a screening of *Potemkin* in preparation for a class on montage made him realize that the two films were connected in ways that profoundly shaped his thinking about "unity in variety."[13] In *Potemkin*, the underlying force of the battleship as an image of popular unity against the tsarist regime was composed of the voices, faces, and acts of a variety of people coming together to mourn the dead, mutinous sailor and ultimately to face together the bayonets of the tsarist army on the famous steps. Eisenstein conceived of *Ivan* as gathering within himself that same abundance of diverse, contradictory voices.[14] The conflicts Ivan encounters as he sets about building the Great Russian State come from within his own consciousness, even as they are "played" by other characters or voices.

Absolutely—Ivan *en miniature*, that is, in the montage microdrama— absolutely the same principle as in the scenario's macrodrama. Only there: smoke, sky, waves, machines, cannon, etc., in montage polyphony, and here Maliuta, Basmanov, Fedka, Kurbsky, Evstafy in dramatic narrative [*siuzhetnaia*] polyphony. There the image of the battleship is composed of these. Here—the tsar, as a man of his times, the Russian Renaissance. The body of tsarist power as there the body of the mutinous ship. (Funny: "down with autocracy" there and just the opposite here!)[15]

The body he is referring to here is the parallel between the tragic dismemberment of the body of the king and the dismembering process of filmmaking. In *Potemkin* all those different voices came together to join the battleship in a new revolutionary collectivity, "one for all and all for one," whereas Ivan rose from the collective as an individual who carries everyone else within himself—"one against all and all against one." Historically, of course, Ivan the Terrible preceded the Russian Revolution of 1905, and Eisenstein understood the two incidents to represent moments in history when significant shifts occurred in social and political structures. Eisenstein wanted *Ivan the Terrible* to portray all the dangers involved in that individual emerging from and rising above the feudal collective, swallowing up everyone else.

He sketched out *Ivan*'s fugue in April 1941 as a method for making the relationships among the characters depict his ideas about power: "not so much a struggle of equal powers as an active conflict of contradictions within a single theme."[16] But in this film, Ivan did not represent a "type," or someone with a single identifying attribute. Unlike his earlier films that "depersonalized" the main concepts like collectivism (*Potemkin*) and patriotism (*Alexander Nevsky*), *Ivan* would be the "personal drama of a personal epoch." The contradictions of that drama would take the form of a confrontation between acting for one's self and acting selflessly for the Great Russian State. In this way, Eisenstein could raise questions about the legitimacy of ideology or abstract goals as justification for political action. Ivan was always divided between his personal needs and his political mission. Eisenstein externalized that division by making Ivan continually claim that he and he alone was acting for the good of the state, for the people of Russia as well as the Great Russian State, while the other characters were each acting for themselves in one way or another. Each of the other main characters simultaneously represents an external rival and an internal impulse with which Ivan struggles: the "*embodiment* of everything that is raging in the internal battle of Ivan."[17] But to be clear, these are not simple binary oppositions:

a *bifurcated equal-sided struggle* hardly ever lies on my style of films. More often than not there is a strengthening unity under the blows of external assault—be they strides of tsarist soldiers down the Odessa steps, the gallop of the German knights' cavalry wedge, or the serried ranks of the boyar opposition, rushing into battle against the works of Ivan the Terrible. And stemming therefrom not so much a struggle of equal powers as an active conflict of contradictions within a single theme.[18]

Does this mean that Eisenstein saw Ivan's political persona as an entirely individual, personal one? Not at all. Ivan is both an individual man in an extraordinary position of power and the generalized depiction of autocracy, the "montage image" of the unified Great Russian State. The boyars and others who opposed him represented contradictions within the very nature of rulership and within the modern Russian state that Ivan founded (as Eisenstein understood it). In the same way that the significance of the *Battleship Potemkin* could be found in the coming together of the diffuse variety of all the people of Odessa who stood up to defend the mutineers against the tsarist regime, Ivan's significance was to be found in his drawing together inside himself all the voices for and against unification, all the reasons violence could seem necessary and all the reasons violence seemed entirely unjustified. His internal conflicts over power, his internal "unity of opposites," combined the personal crises of conscience and the political crises caused by his actions. Ivan's crises of power, the conflicts within and between his personal and political responsibilities, are the theme that is mirrored in his conflicts with other characters. This is the context in which Eisenstein stated that the basic theme of the the film was power. He goes on to say that power "is 'divided' in the same way into all possible nuances" by projecting it on the other characters.[19] By projecting Ivan's inner conflicts over power onto his conflicts with the characters who opposed his mission to centralize power at all costs, Eisenstein could retain our sympathy for Ivan as a person and make his struggles seem tragic, while at the same time raising questions about how he exercised power and increased his power when he was opposed.

Ivan's Theme

The theme of power—and the risk Eisenstein took in trying to represent it—is at the heart of one of the most commonly quoted excerpts from Eisenstein's notebooks. In September 1941, when he was trying to get back to work on *Ivan,* he wrote that structural and thematic unity (*edinstvo*) was realized in the scenario in two ways: in the film's images of one-man rule (*edinovlastie*) and in Ivan's feelings of isolation or loneliness (*odinochestvo*). These links between the personal and the political, and between structure and narrative, have strong linguistic resonances in Russian that can be lost in translation.

The political concentration of power removes the ruler from ordinary human experience, and, as Eisenstein put it:

> The theme of one-man rule [*edinovlastie*] has a two-sided resolution.
>> One—one-man rule [*edinovlastnyi*]
>> One—alone/lonely [*odinokii*]
> The first gives the theme of state power (progressive at the given historical stage)—the <u>political</u> theme of the film.
> The second gives the personal theme—the <u>psychological</u> theme of the film.
> In this lies the compositional unity of the personal and the social, the psychological and the polit[ical].[20]

The unity of the personal and political in this comment has often been cited as evidence that the tragic nature of the film resides in Ivan's sacrifice of his wife and friends for the sake of national destiny.[21] But while Eisenstein undoubtedly meant for us to see Ivan's lonely sacrifice as the logical—and tragic—outcome of the centralization of power, Eisenstein's portrait goes deeper. He challenges us to consider *why* Ivan is alone, why everyone betrays him. Are the boyars and clerics in his inner circle simply outwitted by Ivan's superior will and cunning and historical necessity? Or did they have good reasons for opposing Ivan? Did Ivan cause his own loneliness by insisting on pursuing centralization and the subordination of all other powers, and by using excessive force when opposed? Or is he the victim of trauma, of destructive early modern state-building politics, or even fate? Does Ivan have the support of the people or not? Who betrayed whom? To understand what Eisenstein was thinking about when he linked unity, one-man rule, and loneliness, we need to examine Ivan as a social being, as someone who operated in a world of alliances and conspiracies and had direct, sometimes familial, relationships with his allies and opponents.

A clue to Eisenstein's perspective on the questions raised by these issues can be found in the continuation of the psychological-political passage just quoted, where Eisenstein links Ivan's actions to the people around him: "in this regard, it is especially interesting to observe that <u>all three</u> decisive episodes [of his rendering of Ivan's life] are <u>wholly</u> the product of <u>creative</u> invention."[22] These "<u>three</u> decisive episodes" in Ivan's biography are neither celebrated victories nor milestones on the path to building the Great Russian State, nor are they moments of significant personal loss. Rather, they are Ivan's politically motivated murders: the patricide-fratricides-suicides of Vladimir Staritsky, Aleksei and Fedor Basmanov, and Evstafy, Ivan's confessor (the last three were meant for the unfilmed Part III).[23] With only the slimmest political justification (none served to further the goal of state building), Ivan ordered each of these murders in response to betrayals that largely resulted from his own violent actions. Just as in childhood (in The Prologue), Ivan resorted to murder to compensate for his own fear of vulnerability. The betrayals were real, and they were both personal and political, linked by the impossible demands of the oath, but they never put Ivan in any real danger. Eisenstein called these murders "decisive moments" because each one displays Ivan's essential nature as a ruler who chooses to murder his opponents to maintain his power. Each of these murders takes place after Ivan has cut ties with his kin and raised himself above the rest of humanity, bringing on even greater power and greater isolation. The ruler who secures his power by violently removing his enemies is increasingly cut off from ties with other human beings and is forced to maintain power through more violence. The portrait of Ivan does not end with tragedy; the tragedy of isolation and loneliness propels him to even greater crimes. Multiple executions were so fundamental to Eisenstein's understanding of Ivan that he refused to relinquish them despite criticism of the scenario: these were *"the bared teeth of the epoch . . . (of both!)"* that linked the tyrant of the sixteenth century with his counterpart in the twentieth.[24]

Eisenstein's depiction of Ivan's reign is curiously far less bloody than either the historical Ivan's or Stalin's. There are, in fact, fewer, not more, corpses in the film than in history. Yet Eisenstein still made murder and the legitimacy of murder as a political weapon the central issue that characterized Ivan's relationships with the people around him. When is murder justified? In the exercise of power? In the name of the people? For the good of the state? To protect one's family? Ivan provoked these questions from the first day of his reign as tsar.

The essential physical brutality of Ivan's actions and the conflict at the heart of the psychology of absolute power might have been more apparent to viewers if they had not run counter to the expectations produced by the film's opening titles. When Part I was released, it began with images of billowing clouds and Prokofiev's dramatic "Ivan" theme, "The Approaching Storm," with its suggestions of thunder and lighting, *groza*. After the credits, a series of opening titles frames the approaching narrative:

This film is about the man
Who in the XVIth century first united our country
About the Muscovite Prince
Who created a united, powerful state out of separate discordant and
    self-serving principalities
About the Commander who spread the military glory of our motherland
    to the east and the west
About the Ruler who, to achieve these great tasks, first took upon himself
The Crown of Tsar of all Rus.[25]

More confusion has resulted from these titles than from any other aspect of the film. With their clear statement of the film's subject and their rendering of the official historiography, these opening lines tell us exactly what to think as they carefully shape our expectations of what is to come. The titles frame our image of the tsar as bold, victorious, majestic, a Russian national hero; they announce the political mode of the film, and they prime us to expect a nationalist epic justifying dictatorship as the path to national unity and international power and security. More than one prominent reviewer has cited them as "the basic ideas that lie at the base of the film and determine its intrigues."[26] However, the film moves in a different direction. We are immediately and permanently distracted from the great cause by the struggle for power within Ivan's entourage and by questions of legitimacy, which soon produce tests of loyalty that almost everyone fails. Betrayals lead to reprisals that quickly turn deadly. In the midst of military glory, instead of unification, we are riveted by terror, murder, conspiracy, treason, accusations, and violent annihilation. Even as early as Part I, the state is not only not united; it is ripped apart. Its tragedy is not exclusively due to the opposition of reactionary, selfish boyars but also to Ivan's own ruthless pursuit of power and his confrontational methods for dealing with boyar resistance. *Ivan the Terrible*, Part I, is anything but "the story of the man who . . . created a unified state . . . spread military glory . . . achieved great tasks." By Part III, it is the story of the man who destroyed every living thing in parts of his country, even the birds. But even Part I shows Ivan as a man who decides to trick his people into submission if they would not choose him to rule over them and a man who creates his own army of inhuman sons without mothers or fathers to terrorize his political enemies.

Why, then, did Eisenstein begin *Ivan* in so misleading a way? Because he was forced to do so, at the very last moment, in order to get the film approved for release. The prescriptive titles that open the film and shape the way generations of viewers have understood (or misunderstood) it, were a late addition and a substitution made for practical political reasons. Eisenstein drafted the new titles on November 28, 1944, only a week before the second pre-release screening was to take place.[27] Up until that moment the film was to begin with the titles printed in the scenario, which placed Ivan in the company of the other bloody despots of his era:

In that same century that saw in Europe
Charles V and Philip II
Catherine de Medici and the Duke of Alba
Henry VIII and Bloody Mary

The fires of the Inquisition and Bartholomew's Night
To the throne of the Muscovite Grand Princes
Ascended the one who became the first Tsar and Autocrat of all Rus
Tsar Ivan Vasilevich the Terrible.[28]

No lofty aims or political justifications here, only references to Ivan's most bloodthirsty contemporaries. The new titles, with their emphasis on national unity and imperial accomplishment, convey an impression opposite to that of the text they replaced and create an entirely different set of expectations. One might argue that placing Ivan amid the "fires of the Inquisition" could have been Eisenstein's way of justifying Ivan's actions as typical of his times or as a revolutionary transcending his times. Even in that case the original titles would still prepare us for the story about violence and power that follows—topics that were far less appropriate subjects for a Socialist Realist epic than unity and glory. But linking Ivan with his West European contemporaries was in line with Eisenstein's plan to explain, rather than justify or "whitewash" Ivan's campaign of violence. As he wrote in his 1942 article about the film, many European rulers at the time employed violence in their modernizing efforts to form centralized governments.

The Renaissance and West European culture more generally play a complicated role in the fugue on the theme of power. Eisenstein doesn't need the other Renaissance rulers for a cosmopolitan frame of reference or as an alternative to nationalist Soviet culture, and he doesn't see Western political ideology as in binary opposition to his own. All his writing during this period draws effortlessly on a wide range of international sources—Asian, Latin American, Pacific Islander, and African as well as European and North American—and he reads the European historical sources on Muscovy, which were criticized in official historiography, in dialectical ways. His published defense of the film in *"Ivan the Terrible:* A Film about the Sixteenth-century Russian Renaissance" focused more on historical comparisons across time than cultural ones across space.[29] This is a tricky article, as I discussed earlier, but it reveals some patterns in Eisenstein's thinking when placed in the context of his writing about other rulers, other tyrants, the nature of one-man rule, and Ivan's characteristics as a ruler.

Even a minor character can illuminate the dialectics of Eisenstein's fugue. As Katerina Clark has pointed out, a note in Eisenstein's archive says that he wanted the Livonian ambassador to resemble Hans Holbein's portrait of Erasmus—the theologian, social critic, and "great hero of humanism."[30] But what seems an odd choice at first—to represent the mercenary, insidious political operative with the face of Renaissance humanism—the combination is emblematic of Eisenstein's dialectical concept of human personality and character representation and is even more interesting and tangled that it seems at first glance (I: 3:14). Eisenstein often used stereotypical binaries to challenge the concept of polar difference itself, to show difference and interpenetration as infinitely mutable categories. He often repeated, in one form or another, Stanislavsky's dictum to "seek in the villain where he is good," and vice versa.[31] Eisenstein made the sneaky Livonian troublemaker look like Erasmus in order to illustrate the two-sided character of Renaissance humanistic culture, the crude and cruel violence under the surface—never eradicated, only suppressed.[32] The original Holbein portrait of Erasmus that still hangs in the National Gallery in London and that Eisenstein very likely saw, is a far more complex image that is often appreciated.[33] Many reproductions of the painting tend to blur the areas around Erasmus's eyes and mouth, softening the "generalizable" impression of his face. The original, far from depicting Erasmus as a man of toleration and compassion, or of any other typical humanistic qualities, portrays him as sneering and haughty, with his gaze coldly averted away from the viewer. I don't know what Holbein thought of Erasmus, but to my eye the portrait captures Eisenstein's dialectical concept of the "cruel product" of Renaissance humanism and makes a perfect model for the clever, arrogant "Humanist-Ambassador" of the enemy West. He and the other ambassadors may dress like Renaissance humanists, but they wear expressions of contempt and they sow discord. *Ivan's* fugue is built on this dialectical understanding of human subjectivity: divided, conflicted individuals (like cultures) confront each other as theme and variations with kaleidoscopic, explosive results.

Part I of *Ivan the Terrible* opens with an ostentatious spectacle of power: the coronation of Ivan IV as tsar in 1547 when he was a mere seventeen years old (I: 2:04).[34] "The theme of the film—the theme of power—is developed from the very beginning as the subject . . . of the monologue on autocracy in the coronation scene in The Dormition Cathedral."[35] We are treated to a sumptuous vision of the coronation ritual, much of which comes directly from historical documents, and a lavish display of the wealth of its participants.[36] Metropolitan Pimen leads a flock of churchmen into a cathedral packed with bowing servitors and guests. Walls and columns are covered from floor to ceiling with stylized Orthodox frescos. Close-ups introduce us to representatives of each of the groups who will become the film's major political players: the clergy, the boyars, and the foreign dignitaries representing Russia's rival European powers. Pimen blesses the crown, and the scepter and orb, and then Ivan takes the crown into his own hands, places it on his head, and turns to face us for the first time. His features are severe and immobile, carefully controlled, but the original scenario tells us that "within all is seething." His eyes betray both internal turmoil and an innate ability to manipulate his audience. He launches into a speech—the "monologue on autocracy"—presenting his view on power. Outlining his plans for consolidating the Great Russian State, he informs the boyars that from now on they will either have to fight in a national army consolidated under his command or financially support the newly centralized state. He declares that power—unified power—resides in the tsar's hands alone. He tells the churchmen that the holy monasteries will also be required to support the new central state with their vast wealth. In response, the metropolitan recoils in shock—literally falling backward, while Efrosinia Staritskaia snarls, "he's challenging the boyars." The foreign dignitaries laugh condescendingly, "amused and mildly curious," as the scenario has it, until Ivan turns to inform them that they too are in for a surprise. The international balance of power is also about to change, because a strong, unified Russian state would be powerful enough to reclaim its ancestral lands, now in the hands of others. Emissaries of the pope, the Holy Roman Empire, and various European powers angrily proclaim that Europe will not stand for this, but the savvy Livonian ambassador says, "If he's strong, they'll accept him . . . He must not be allowed to get strong."[37]

The Ivan of Part I has often been described in secondary literature as a "wise statesman, leader of his people."[38] But what kind of political wisdom is there in immediately alienating the most powerful people in the realm? Ivan undoubtedly would have faced opposition to centralization, but by lashing out so impetuously and defiantly, by allowing his feelings to propel him, he taunted his opponents and stoked their resistance. It is a brute power move that Stalin and, no doubt, some viewers surely approved, but it is hardly wise and statesmanlike. Here at the very outset of his reign, Ivan raises the questions that will define the political, historical, and moral contours of the film. If centralized power was necessary to compete in the early modern European state system and to become a Renaissance prince, how is that power best achieved and exercised? Eisenstein's Ivan acts out of political commitment to Russian power and security but personal, emotionally charged desire for revenge shadows those rational motives. His speech also challenges us to consider what role his provocation plays in the events that follow. If Ivan is responsible for disenfranchising his political opponents, and doing so with such contempt, is their opposition to be seen as nothing but reactionary obstructionism, or is it at least partially justified, at least partially understandable?

In 1941 and 1942, as Eisenstein finished the scenario and then further developed his characters, there is little evidence that he considered Ivan a wise or even responsible ruler. He followed the first images that came to him—Ivan's

late-life confession, his childhood trauma, and his transformation at Kazan—
by fleshing out the attributes that would humanize Ivan's desire for revenge,
explain his path to murder and remorse, and outline the series of explosive
transformations that shaped him as tsar. Ivan's coronation speech, planned in
the earliest stages of Eisenstein's work on the script, was to be delivered with
unbridled passion and daring. Rising to the dais "like a young animal, lithe,
shapely, fervent," Ivan was barely able to contain himself.[39] These first steps
reveal Eisenstein's conception of Ivan as a man willing to take risks and to
exceed his conventional power. His provocative, "undiplomatic" coronation
speech "arouses *everyone* against him . . . the beginning of all the conflicts
of the scenario."[40] His attitude toward the boyars is marked by "*the effect of
daring*; he isn't sure of himself, *but dares*."[41] And he takes growing pleasure in
confrontations with his opponents; the harder they resist, the more he wants
to fight back. Eisenstein linked these notes, probably written some weeks
apart, with his own experiences, speaking out before he had self-confidence
and taking personal pleasure at confronting party and industry officials at
the film studio.[42] Impulsiveness also contributes to several of Ivan's major
transformative moments: he rushes around in a panic when Anastasia falls
ill and snatches the chalice for her without noticing that Efrosinia has poisoned it. Eisenstein explicitly linked that feverishness with the state of mind
Ivan exhibits when, looking at the corpses of the Kolychevs, he calls for more
executions: "Too few!"[43]

Nor did Eisenstein paint Ivan's more deliberate, less impulsive actions as
especially praiseworthy. In his reading notes on Robert Vipper's favorable
biography of Ivan, he marked Ivan's authority and charisma as "traits" worth
remembering, but he also marked a passage where Vipper adds that, despite
his cunning and demagoguery, Ivan lacks insight into the people closest to
him.[44] And even Vipper noted that while Ivan was intelligent, talented, and
boundlessly energetic, he had no sense of limits.[45] What wisdom Ivan possessed often prevented him from taking decisive action.[46] Eisenstein described
Ivan variously as crafty, suspicious, and manipulative.[47] If Ivan's childhood
trauma gave him the necessary emotional tools to fight the boyars' and others' opposition, his reckless, impulsive "daring" was as responsible for provoking opposition as his ideological and political goals themselves.

The Variations

In the spring of 1942, Eisenstein gathered up his notebooks, scraps of paper,
and marginalia from the previous year's work and organized his ideas about
each of the main characters in a series of charts laid out like spreadsheets.[48]

For each character, in each scene, he entered specific actions, the function of those moments in the story, what they revealed about the character's intention and the image (*obraz*) or underlying meaning, the formation of the image and its turning point, the internal ("true") meaning of the particular scene, and the specific traits of the character revealed in that scene. In Ivan's case, Eisenstein never got beyond the first few scenes, as the chart proved too limiting a form for his multilayered ideas. But the charts neatly encapsulate much of the material scattered through the notes about the other main characters, the variations to Ivan's theme. They show the sum of Eisenstein's thinking about the characters, their images, and their meaning just as he was finishing that intensive period of work in the spring of 1942 and as he thought he was about to start filming. Ivan's selfless devotion to the state, which set him apart from and ultimately above the other main characters, was mirrored in the self-serving power hunger embodied in the characters Eisenstein identified as true Machiavellians: his aunt and rival for power, Efrosinia Staritskaia; his loyal but self-serving lieutenant, Aleksei Basmanov; the scheming church leader, Metropolitan Pimen; and the two lifelong friends, Fedor Kolychev/ Filipp and Andrei Kurbsky. There also are a number of characters who love Ivan and betray him anyway: his wife Anastasia, his ersatz son/ersatz wife, Fedor Basmanov, and the Russian people.

Andrei Kurbsky and Fedor Kolychev/Metropolitan Filipp

Andrei Kurbsky is the first of the fugue-like variations that Eisenstein developed, the first of many doubles and alter egos. No betrayal pained Ivan more than Kurbsky's. Eisenstein conceived of Ivan and Kurbsky as similar in almost every way. They shared a belief in the superiority of the centralized state over feudal divisions, but Kurbsky wanted power for himself.[49] One of the first things Eisenstein wrote about him was "Kurbsky—his own interests. Ivan— the interests of the country."[50] And "*Hell* from *ambitions*."[51] In April, he would add: "Kurbsky—the Caesarist idea. Like Ivan. But for himself."[52] Then in October after reading Villari on Machiavelli, he decided, "I do not think that Kurbsky is an **ideologue** of feudalism," and "It is just that **he** . . . wants the role of the absolute ruler, **without** ideals, **without** a program. Power *as such*."[53] This self-serving, unprincipled ruthlessness, the "thesis in words, antithesis in deeds," and the desire for power for its own sake are among the attributes that Eisenstein understood as Machiavellian. In Eisenstein's fugue Ivan is differentiated from these characters by the selflessness of his state-building project (which is, in fact, a Machiavellian prescription), and by the distinctly un-Machiavellian revenge motive underlying his use of violence and his capacity for repentance.

The comparison of Kurbsky and Ivan shows us more than the illegitimacy of Kurbsky's ambition. Like Ivan, Kurbsky is driven by emotions that distract him from political aims, but Kurbsky's passions consistently humiliate him, while Ivan's feelings for his friends and kin are elevated to tragedy.[54] When we see Kurbsky's jealousy of Ivan, we are meant to see it as weakness compared to Ivan's strength. Kurbsky is hurt when Ivan rebukes him at Kazan; his stature is further diminished when the sneaky Livonian ambassador and the conspiratorial Efrosinia Staritskaia play on Kurbsky's jealousy and resentments. And while Anastasia flirts with him throughout Part I, she repeatedly rejects him. When Kurbsky finally does go over to the enemy, he appears at the court of King Sigismund of Poland pledging fealty and bringing intelligence on Ivan, but he is humiliated there too, when his intelligence is proven false.[55] There is a strong strain of coy homoeroticism between Ivan and his best friend, as there is among all the major male characters and especially on display in the Polish court. But Kurbsky's homosociality is primarily played for laughs, diluting the undercurrent of sexual attraction and further undermining the power of someone who might have provided, indeed did historically provide, both comradeship and serious political criticism of Ivan. Kurbsky's treason ultimately turns out to be the least interesting (and most easily ridiculed or defeated) opposition in the film.

The first time we see Kurbsky on screen, he is raining golden coins over Ivan at The Coronation with the tsar's other best friend, Fedor Kolychev, the future Filipp (I: 7:50). This is one of many triangles to come that pairs two characters who mirror and conflict with Ivan in parallel ways. Filipp embodies another kind of commentary on Ivan's selfless devotion to the state. Where Kurbsky mirrors Ivan's ambition and hunger for power but selfishly longs for his own glory, Filipp shares Ivan's selflessness but is passive and lacks Ivan's ambition. At Ivan's wedding to Anastasia, which follows immediately after The Coronation, Filipp (still Fedor then) tells Ivan that he cannot support the tsar's plan to centralize power at the expense of the traditional power of the boyar families. In Filipp's character chart, Eisenstein put his opposition even earlier, making him "unhappy with Ivan's program, given as foretaste" already at The Coronation.[56]

Throughout the film Filipp is outspoken in his opposition to centralization and especially to the murderous oprichniki, but in contrast to Ivan who "dares" and "risks," Filipp chooses not to act on his feelings and instead retreats to the monastery. Now we can begin to see the triangle Eisenstein is building in this strand of the fugue: Filipp's political dissent and personal loyalty are the inverse of Kurbsky's personal betrayal and political alliance. These variations on Ivan's power theme allow Eisenstein to raise more subtle questions about loyalty and betrayal, friendship and alliance, and especially the morality of action and inaction or passivity, without overtly showing his hand. When we first see Kurbsky and Filipp pouring gold coins on Ivan, they appear attentive but dispassionate, unreadable, just doing their jobs. When and how is it appropriate or effective or foolish to act against excessive power? Handsome, passionate, brave Kurbsky leaves Ivan by going over to the enemy, and he is both ridiculed and disempowered for his treachery. Filipp, in contrast, "with his high-minded philosophy," also withdraws from Ivan's service, but he rejects the path of active opposition and tries to live an ethical monastic life even after Ivan has his family executed. He speaks out against Ivan when they both return to Moscow after Ivan's retreat to Alexandrova, but he is pushed into active opposition only when Efrosinia and Pimen pressure him.[57] Both Filipp and Kurbsky end up murdered for their betrayal, but in a film more about questions than answers, the Filipp/Kurbsky variations ask us to consider fundamental questions of political ethics that have strong contemporary analogies. Here Eisenstein uses precisely the kind of structure he promoted in his speech on historical film and in more detail in *Method*: constructing conflicts in the past that subtly resonate with conflicts in the present.

Filipp performs another variation and raises a sharper set of questions in his direct confrontations with Ivan in Part II, beginning in the Golden Hall. That scene takes place just as Ivan is beginning to understand the terrible things he will have to do and the personal price he will have to pay in order to achieve his goal of establishing the Great Russian State. In fact, the confrontation with Filipp articulates the terms of Ivan's "inner contradictions," which have been brewing all along in Part I before transforming them into something more convoluted and dangerous. Just after returning to Moscow from his self-imposed retreat at Alexandrova, when Ivan is explaining the founding of the oprichnina and the division of the realm, Filipp sweeps dramatically into the hall, robes flying and crozier aloft, to proclaim that Ivan's reforms are "from the Devil!" Ivan brushes that off with the wave of a hand and greets Filipp like the old friend he is, or was, leading him away from the world of official state business to talk in private. Ivan is divided: he is determined to retain Filipp's friendship despite their political differences (the human and personal still matter to him), but he is equally determined to seize power from the boyars and establish the centralized autocracy he needs to build the Great Russian State that Filipp has just denounced. Until the very end of the scene, Filipp refuses to allow Ivan's appeal to his feelings to override his principles and his opposition—the political determines the personal. Ivan takes this as a personal rejection. It elicits his sense of loneliness and revives painful memories of childhood abandonment, where the personal determines the political.

Ivan tries to sway Filipp to choose him over the boyars by showing the story of his childhood—here Eisenstein inserts The Prologue that was cut from Part I. He thinks that if he shows Filipp that the boyars murdered his mother and sold Russia's wealth to foreigners, Filipp will both pity him (the personal) and understand why Ivan must usurp the boyars' power (the political). That fails. He tries immobilizing Filipp by grabbing his clothes and appealing to him as a friend: "Devastated by the burden of power. Don't forsake me in my loneliness." That fails too; Filipp remains steadfast. But even when he wants to, Ivan can never separate the personal from the political. He follows this appeal by imploring Filipp to help build the Great Russian State (which Filipp has unequivocally damned). Aching to retain Filipp's friendship but also to win his support to continue his great mission, Ivan sinks to the nadir of despair when he realizes that he cannot have both: if he wants his friend, he will have to give up the Great Cause; if he wants to pursue the Great Cause, he will have to give up his friends. But Ivan also knows that everyone is corruptible, so he offers Filipp a bribe: he offers to promote him to metropolitan if Filipp will drop his opposition to Ivan's plans. Filipp takes the bait with no more than a moment's hesitation but adds, now that he has some leverage, that he wants the right to defend the boyars Ivan is unjustly persecuting. Ivan momentarily lashes out ("no one is innocent!") but quickly concedes. The stalemate ends in compromise, the very last time Ivan would try to balance the personal and the political, the last time he will make a concession to anyone. They kiss and walk out arm in arm. Filipp joyous and Ivan subdued with their mixed victories.

This scene shows how Eisenstein constructed his fugue with complex, subtle shifts in tone to convey a network of interrelated ideas. Here at the beginning of Part II, the Filipp variation brings out Ivan's vacillation between possibilities. Where Kurbsky acted against Ivan and was humiliated and defeated, Filipp briefly gives up his passivity to criticize Ivan and defend his own family, and as a result, he is corrupted. Ivan ends this scene still unsure whether he can pursue the great cause without persecuting his enemies and losing all his friends. Immediately afterward, Maliuta offers him a way forward—"the beginning of the bloody epic"—that also brings Ivan to the critical "moment of doubt as a man lifts his hand to a terrible deed."[58] We will return to Maliuta's offer and to his theme and variations, but first we need to see how Ivan's conflict with Filipp will end.

The turning point of Part II occurs at Filipp's production of The Fiery Furnace, intended to force Ivan to stop killing boyars. By the time he stages the play, the "bloody epic" is well underway. Filipp and Ivan have become mirrored, diametrical opposites (II: 39:22). They face off in the cathedral, Ivan dressed in all black and Filipp in all white, with the play going on in the background, each hoping to shame the other into backing down. For all his passivity and his reluctance to join the conspiracy to stop Ivan's reign of terror, Filipp appears physically imposing and morally implacable in this scene. Filipp is never a figure of ridicule (though he can seem a little overly self-righteous at times). Eisenstein allows him to display his moral authority in refusing to bless Ivan, who is feigning humility in this scene while requesting the metropolitan's blessing. In the performative setting, Ivan cannot make Filipp budge. He wins the showdown, of course, but not by forcing Filipp to go against his conscience; he sidesteps the conflict altogether. Who needs a mere mortal's blessing after severing all human ties and becoming a superman? In the following scene we hear that Filipp has been executed. Eisenstein was planning to shoot a scene with Maliuta strangling Filipp, but in the finished film we never see Filipp again.

Does Ivan lose for winning? Filipp stands defiantly on principle, refusing to bless the tsar-murderer in the face of quite credible glowering threats from Ivan and his little demonic assistant, Fedka Basmanov. Filipp's condemnation of Ivan and the image of his courageous, selfless refusal to back down hang in the air throughout the rest of the film. The most passive figure, the most moral figure, the only character as "selfless" as Ivan, is the only one to stand up to Ivan directly, face to face.

Fedka Has Two Fathers

With his old friends out of the way, the weaving of Ivan's relationships with his new friends is even more knotty and illuminating. Working on Kurbsky and Filipp, Eisenstein was primarily concerned with the issues of loyalty and betrayal and the individual costs of autocratic rule. Thinking about Maliuta Skuratov and the Basmanovs, Aleksei and Fedor, took him much deeper into the psychologies of power and violence. Eisenstein's work on Maliuta and Fedka is generally better known because some of his notes were published in Russian and some were translated into English.[59] In what follows I cover some of the same material found in other studies but with an emphasis on the fugue of power and the off-screen political context so prominent in the way these characters reflect facets of Ivan as ruler. Aleksei Basmanov and his son, Fedor, are among the most complex characters Eisenstein created. They dramatize the conflict between acting based on ideology or in the name of an abstraction, on one hand, and personal, family, or human connection, on the other—one of the key variations on Ivan's tragic conflict between duty and morality or between rational abstraction and personal feeling. Eisenstein constructed his fugue to bring out the political dangers inherent in the conflicted

filial, sexual, homoerotic relationships represented by the Basmanov variations on the theme of power.

Historically, Aleksei Basmanov was one of the founders of the oprichnina,
and that's the role he plays in Eisenstein's film. He lifts Ivan out of despair at
Anastasia's coffin by suggesting that Ivan can circumvent the power of the
boyars by forging an "iron ring" made up of new men who will be loyal only
to him. Foreshadowing The Oath of the Oprichniki, Aleksei describes these
servitors as men who will abandon their own families to pledge allegiance
to the tsar. The actor, Amvrosii Buchma, intones his pledge with a kind of
melodramatic holiness, eyes raised solemnly at Ivan and off into the future
in a conventional Socialist Realist gaze (I: 1:26:10). To cap it off, Aleksei offers
his son, Fedor, to the tsar as the first of these men (I: 1:26:54). In describing
the son who will transfer his allegiance from father to tsar, Aleksei uses two
adjectives with no real equivalent in English that both stress his blood relation to his son: "I offer you my son, my own natal son, my only blood son"
(*syna, rodnogo syna, edinogo, edinokrovnogo, tebe otdaiu*). But what he claims in
words is harder for him to live up to in deeds. The first sign of the conflict
inherent in loyalty that mingles personal and political while at the same time
replacing the personal with the political is conveyed by gesture and lighting
in these shots. Aleksei pronounces this offering with an expression mingling
pride, love, patriotism, and fear and regret. Fedka also seems a little confused
by the transaction. Eyes full of admiration for Ivan, he bows to the tsar, but
whether sadly or solemnly it's hard to tell. Then, on his knees before the tsar,
his face conveys uncertainty until Ivan begins absentmindedly caressing his
hair, which stirs some feeling or sensuality in the face of this angelic demon.

At that moment, Ivan is thinking about Aleksei's "iron ring" and translates
it into the plan to retreat to his estate at Alexandrova in order to trick the
boyars and win the support of the Russian people, who, he seems sure, will
beg him to come back to rule on the throne he is abandoning in Moscow.
The people's appeal, he says, will grant him "unlimited power," to carry out
his "great and merciless mission." Aleksei and Maliuta distrust the tsar's plan
and turn away. This is the first hint of jealousy: Aleksei and Maliuta have
already told us they hate the boyars; now we see that they distrust the people
as well. They want Ivan to sever all dependence on the boyars and to depend
only on them and their select "iron ring." Alone again but for Fedka, whose
beautiful, sensuous face is shown now in close-up, its contours fractured by
shadows both jagged and soft, Ivan has a moment of doubt, wondering about
the wisdom of his plan. He looks to Anastasia for affirmation, but she's still
dead, so he turns to Fedka, a second, parallel transfer of affection. To the tsar's
unspoken question—"am I right?"—Fedka intones decisively, "Right" (*Prav*)

(I: 1:28:34). And with that, Ivan rises up above the coffin and men in black flood the cathedral—the newly hatched "iron ring" of oprichniki.[60]

Eisenstein was very pleased with himself for coming up with this formulation: "Hooray! Hooray! Hooray! The giving of Fedka is very cool [*klassno*] . . . and what a subtext!!"[61] He was pleased because he managed to inscribe several important, related dualisms in this short, triangular exchange. The clash this situation creates for Fedka between his loyalty to the tsar and to his biological father is paramount: Fedka has two fathers. At one point he even wanted Fedka to look a bit like the young Ivan.[62] Eisenstein is explicit about the centrality of the two-father theme to the ideas he wants to convey in the film, but even he was hesitant at first to draw attention to this fraught and obvious reflection of Stalinist family discourse. "If we do the theme of the conflict between fathers, this would be very good. . . . (*If to do it*)."[63] He did "do it," in the end, because it was too important to let go: "The theme of the struggle between fathers—this is the theme of the whole oprichnina—for it is—literally the oath!"[64]

Fedka carries a "double dialectic" that further complicates and reveals his function in the fugue on the theme of power. Not only are his loyalties divided between two fathers, but he also has a dual relationship with his sovereign father as both Ivan's adopted son and as Ivan's "ersatz" wife, the object of the tsar's affection and desire. This is the "subtext" Eisenstein referred to with such delight. He is explicit about the importance of Fedka's homoerotic relationship with Ivan and his unconscious reluctance to introduce it. "I have long known that a little piece was still missing from his role. It is lacking something. Let's dig: Ivan's relationship to him! Damn! (*Verflucht!*) Just the thing that must be avoided. He must love him."[65] The impossibly divided loyalty to two fathers and Ivan's shifting loyalty from female wife to male son/lover are further complicated (as is everything in this film) with a connection to murder. Here's what Eisenstein had to say about "Right," that one-word affirmation of all Ivan was about to do: "I was thinking about how to explain to Fedor [meaning to Mikhail Kuznetsov, the actor who plays Fedor], how to pronounce '*Prav*.' It's not only the idea of rightness, but also the feeling of ecstasy before Ivan. '*Prav*' *drops from the lips by itself*. This is even more intense than the decisive "Tsar" at Kazan."[66] And, not incidentally, Eisenstein links these one-word exclamations, "Tsar" and "Right," with another one-word declaration, "*Malo*" (Too few), Ivan's response to seeing the corpses of the Kolychevs, the first massacre he orders. Power, persistence, and murder are linked by gesture as well. In each scene, a reverse movement precedes a decisive move. Ivan leans back, opens his eyes wide, and looks down from his position above the others as if to say

I am the tsar, I am right in what I'm doing, and I am going to order more murder, if that's what it takes.

The homoerotic relationship with Fedka brings out Ivan's bisexuality, which as we have seen, Eisenstein considered a fundamental human trait. In a long passage written in March 1942, when Eisenstein was working out details of his characterizations and meeting with actors in the hopes that filming was about to begin, he discussed the key roles of Fedka, Maliuta, and the Russian people. The "unfinished" thematics connected with Fedka were still nagging at him.[67] "Dressed like a dandy, Fedka 'slips away' [*iulit*] here, not only in the scene but in the dramaturgy. Meaning there could be something here—but what? What's the theme of Fedka? Of course there's the theme of the choice of fathers—the real [*priamyi*] father—Aleksei—and the sovereign father— Ivan. I already have the whole tragic resolution of that (the ending). I have to *build up* the path that leads there. I already have the love for Ivan (eyes full of tears at the confession) . . . which means for the tragic finale, the *Vorspiel* (prelude) on that very theme." It turns out that Fedka has had that "something" all along, but Eisenstein's writing process was much like his artistic structures: full of holes and muted ideas—"*loose ends*," he wrote in English—that had to be teased out. Such was the case with Fedka in his relationship with Ivan and in the scene in Anastasia's bedchamber.[68]

The sarafan and mask that Fedka wears at The Feast of the Oprichniki were originally (in the scenario) meant as merely a "vulgar travesty [*grubo-eranicheskii*]," but in 1942, when Eisenstein was working on Fedka's character, the costume acquired what he called a new "moral" element. Initially intended only to remind us of the sexual-affectionate transference (The Dance of the Oprichniki is, among other things, a homosocial, ecstatic, vaudeville act), now Eisenstein wanted to be sure to stress the association with Anastasia's violent death. In one note, he referred to a Botticelli painting of a murdered young man, supposedly based on a death mask, and in another, he reminded himself that it might be a good idea to deploy Fedka in a death mask, all the better to show Fedka's malicious jealousy as Ivan cozies up to Vladimir Staritsky.[69] And all the better to show how "frightful and nasty" the scene is by contrasting a ghostly white-faced Fedka / Anastasia against the black-clad oprichniki wildly and semi-threateningly dancing around him / her. Presenting Fedka in a kind of death mask is a reminder that it was Fedka who told Ivan that Anastasia was poisoned by Efrosinia and that Ivan inadvertently handed his wife the poisoned chalice. In these notes, Eisenstein sees that connection and makes it homoerotic: Fedka's revelation takes place in Anastasia's empty bedchamber just as Maliuta is preparing to execute the Kolychevs. That Fedka revealed the truth to Ivan (even if he isn't quite ready to believe

FIGURE 4.1 "Fedka in a sarafan. The top slipping down off the shoulder of his costume." RGALI, 1923/2/1666/7 [Feb 15, 1941]. Used with permission.

it), and that he did so in the very bedchamber where the murder occurred, reinforces the transference from female wife to male lover and revives Ivan's desire for vengeance against the boyars, leading directly to his utterance above the corpses: "Too few."[70] So homosociality, bisexuality, death, murder, vengeance, and moral responsibility all emerge from Eisenstein's thinking about Fedka in Anastasia's sarafan and pale, braided mask. The "vulgar travesty" turned out to contain the central moral questions of the film: which murders are justified and who is responsible for provoking and committing them?

Portraying Fedka as a dancing death mask also foreshadowed his own fate, to be murdered in a cascading chain of betrayal and violence. This sequence of events is the second set of ideas about unity, one-man rule, and loneliness that Eisenstein realized he'd included "intuitively" in the screenplay, which had deeper, more complex and extensive meanings embedded in them. These dual conflicts (from Ivan's and Fedka's perspective as well as from Aleksei's) don't end well. In April 1942, Eisenstein wrote in English and French: "*Now all this is quite great if you read it as it was. Alexi sells Theo [Fedor] to John, expecting to see in him his agent. Destroys him morally. But spiritually Theo remains pure, à donné au roi.*"[71] That purity won't last either.

In what would have been Part III, Fedka threatens to report the German oprichnik von Staden for his rapacious (even by oprichnik standards) plundering of Novgorod, but von Staden informs Fedka that he can't denounce him, because von Staden has something on Fedka's father, Aleksei. Von Staden knows that Aleksei has also been plundering state coffers, but "not for himself," for the good of his own family. Originally, Eisenstein wrote, these "two or three strokes were thrown in to sketch 'the internal atmosphere' of the oprichnina, where the element of 'man is wolf to man' is rather strong," where loyalty doesn't exist, but blackmail and bribes were common. "But now it's clear that this is a very accurate, intuitive introduction of the *true* contours of the theme. That is, *already in this scene*, Fedor violates the 'sacredness' of the oath of the oprichniki."[72] To protect his father, a minor sin, Fedka doesn't denounce von Staden, but then he doesn't denounce his father to Ivan either. He chooses loyalty to his natural father over loyalty to his sovereign father, and that is a major betrayal. As a variation in the fugue, Fedor and Aleksei both choose their ties to kin over their loyalty to Ivan and his mission to found the Great Russian State. They choose biology over ideology and self over state. It marks them as traitors and condemns them both to death, because Ivan inevitably chooses the state over his beloved Fedka.

After forcing them to take an oath they could not help but betray and after discovering that the oprichniki were creating their own "neofeudal" order, Ivan decides to rid himself of their services, but he does so in a particularly devious and sadistic way. At what was to be the climax of Part III, Ivan announces that he has discovered a traitor among the oprichniki.[73] Using only his eyes (just as he did to identify the assassin Peter at The Feast of the Oprich- niki), Ivan pinpoints Aleksei Basmanov as the traitor and selects his son Fedor to execute Aleksei. With this deceptively simple but deeply inhuman act, Ivan forces Fedor to make a final choice between loyalty to his father and loyalty to the tsar. Reluctantly, Fedor does so. Ivan plays on Fedka's complicity, the guilt he already felt for not turning his father over to Ivan when Fedka discovered Aleksei's embezzlement. This is, of course, the sort of guilt the Communist Party relied on in identifying people to carry out the crimes of the Great Terror. To hide their own minor sins of disloyalty, people committed more terrible deeds than they otherwise might have done. Ordinary people and party members alike attacked their coworkers and neighbors to preclude inquiry into their own loyalty.

But compelling a son to kill his father is not terrible enough for Ivan, nor does it satisfy his need to subordinate the entire population to his will. After Fedka kills his father to *prove* his fidelity to the tsar, Ivan uses that murder to *question* Fedka's own fidelity. Ivan sensed that Fedka was willing to murder his own father out of loyalty to the tsar but that he abandoned his oath to the tsar momentarily out of love for and fear of his father. Or maybe Ivan allowed his own feelings of jealousy for Fedka's "other father" to surface. Fedka returns to the banquet hall and immediately senses that Ivan already knows of his short-lived betrayal. With classic Stalinesque maneuvering, Ivan reverses the oath to trap Fedka: "You showed no pity to your own father, Fedor. How will you pity or defend me?" In a final act of irony, gesturing with no more than his eyes, Ivan orders von Staden to murder Fedka. Ivan's personal grief is visible in the drawings Eisenstein made for the scene.

What began as a scene illustrating the cruelty of the oprichnina with its culture of violence "grows through Fedor's drama into the theme of the sacredness of the oath of loyalty to the tsar (*which as a theme* is itself good for the present day as well)."[74] And that scene will continue to grow in Eisen- stein's mind, becoming one of the key depictions of the "theme of power" in the film. He was increasingly satisfied with the shape of the thing as it developed in his notes. During this busy March 1942, in the same set of notes that contained Fedka's mask, he wrote: "Very good. A closed circle. From the dark prologue. To the dark oath."[75] The vengeful, violent denouement of this triangular variation exposes the dangers inherent in the Stalinist family and the convoluted logic of the oath that made these revolutions consume their own children. Aleksei's and Fedka's choice of biological family over sovereign family prevents them from achieving the kind of "greatness" that Ivan sought with his "great and merciless mission," but as demonic as Fedka has become, his ultimate loyalty to his father spares them both from becoming the truly terrible, suprahuman monster that is Ivan. In a classic Eisensteinian twist, their failures keep them human and, even after everything, sympathetic.

And yet, there's more. Eisenstein wrote that before his death, Fedor grows yet closer to Ivan as an "ersatz Anastasia," after "probably something happened" and he acquires a "shadow of familiarity—'of the bedroom.'"[76] But this personal affection gives Fedka power over Ivan, a kind of power that Maliuta exhibits as well. Eisenstein understood that this is a kind of power that no absolute ruler would tolerate and that Ivan should feel compelled to obliterate. Eisenstein ended his March 1942 notes on Fedka as a fallen angel and ersatz wife with this:

> In general, as they say, "The Lord God has entrusted me with a little scene."
> It's turning out well.
> Ivan calls the oprichnina to life.
> The oprichnina becomes a living, autonomous force.
> But it *pressures* Ivan.
> (All three of them: Aleksei, Maliuta, Fedor).
> It begins to push Ivan around.
> To tear itself out of Ivan's hands.
> It wants to direct and dominate Ivan.
> So Ivan reins them in.
> He defies them.
> Breaks them.
> Does not let anyone dominate him.
> (Turned out well—the theme of doubt and remorse.)[77]

In other words, "doubt and remorse" don't just characterize Ivan's conscience but show that Ivan's bouts of conscience, while keeping him human and sympathetic, allow his people to exercise their power over him. Until he, discarding his conscience, "breaks them." We see this dynamic especially clearly in Maliuta's role in the fugue on the theme of power.

Maliuta Skuratov: Tragedy and Comedy

A conversation with Mikhail Zharov, the actor who played Maliuta, led Eisenstein to some important insights about Maliuta's variation.[78] Zharov, first of all, gave Eisenstein an ironic and telling detail about the nature of loyalty and Ivan's need for love and friendship. The one friend who gave him everything, who was loyal to the very end, who literally killed for him, was the friend Ivan valued least of all. And Maliuta, the "loyal cur," hungered desperately for his master's approval. He was willing to do anything to win Ivan's appreciation, even murder for him. But Ivan, who loses friend after friend, barely acknowledges the one who is the most loyal. "*Great, great, great,*" Eisenstein noted.[79] And "extremely important," that Ivan is so mesmerized by his final approach to the sea that he abandons Maliuta, his last individual supporter and his only remaining friend, to die on the battlefield.[80]

To make that theme sharper, Eisenstein says, he made it frightening. Maliuta's function throughout the film is to protect Ivan. At Alexandrova, Maliuta's function is to "*prepare a screen!!!!*" so that if the trick, manipulating the people to support him, fails, Ivan will still be tsar. "Despite all the idealism of his divine judgment of the people, Ivan is also a demagogue." And he will use all the power obtained through this display of popular support to take revenge on the boyars. Here is the fugue in action: "In principle this is terrific because Maliuta is Ivan's other half. And when Ivan decides to make promises to Filipp that he knows he will not keep, that is 'Maliuta traits' in Ivan." But Maliuta's main role as Ivan's screen is to kill the people Ivan wants dead: "Now it's all straightened out. The executions are *an act of will* on Ivan's part. With Maliuta's *hands.*"[81] Eisenstein devoted a great deal of attention to the scene where Maliuta offers to carry out Ivan's murders. It is one of the few moments where Eisenstein wants us to see Ivan's own fear. In his notes, Eisenstein emphasizes that at this moment—when Ivan is considering reprisals against the boyars and Maliuta offers to kill the Kolychevs—Ivan is scared.[82] It should appear as a burden to him both to start the bloody chain of executions and to allow his servitor to take the moral burden on himself. Several things are happening at once here. Ivan is about to embark on "the bloody epic," an ominous task, and he is still not entirely convinced that he is on the right path. When Maliuta offers to take the burden of doubt on his own shoulders, Ivan is grateful, cunning, and terrified. Maliuta may be crouching on the ground below Ivan, but his offer gives him an inverted kind of power over Ivan. Bolshakov saw this in the first drafts of the screenplay, and Stalin and company remarked on it in their criticism of Part II. The lowliest of Ivan's inner circle has the most power over him.

We can get a sense of the moral significance of this interaction from a comment Eisenstein made earlier when reading Machiavelli. Following his note about giving Kurbsky the "*cruelty, ruthlessness and* **hypocrisy**" of the Machiavellian rulers who claimed to be too moral to follow Machiavelli's prescriptions, Eisenstein wrote: "*cf. Dorian Gray—self-illusioned, "becoming good" and bloody stains on hands of portrait.* In other words: Thesis in words— antithesis in deeds."[83] This is a great example of the way the film constructs a contradiction that seems to give us no clue to a clear reading, but the notes offer us a way out. Are we to think that Ivan's hands are clean, and therefore his conscience is also clear and his actions justified? Eisenstein's comment on Oscar Wilde's *The Picture of Dorian Gray* makes it clear that immoral acts are immoral even if a surrogate can be found to bear the markings of responsibility. Ivan "allows" Maliuta to choose to begin the "slaughter" with Filipp's Kolychev relatives, because then Ivan doesn't have to break his promise to Filipp to spare his family. Maliuta personifies Ivan's "impetuous" side. Ivan's "wisdom" sometimes gets in the way of necessary direct action. This is also a great example of the way in which the fugue operates. First a character (here, Maliuta) embodies and acts on a trait of Ivan's (impetuousness). Then that trait is woven back into Ivan's persona, now made more complex by one new attribute and one new inner contradiction (wisdom vs. impetuousness). Ivan has been impetuous since The Coronation, but this turn of the fugue shows us how that impetuousness is intensified through its dialectical conflict with a measure of wisdom and experience.

Maliuta's melody in the fugue also shows us the power dynamics that all the characters participate in, simply by virtue of being in Ivan's inner circle. Everyone is jealous of everyone else, and whenever Ivan gets close to one of his inner circle, it triggers the jealousy of the others. But no one is as jealous as Maliuta. Maliuta is jealous of Fedka because Fedka is Ivan's "soul mate" and Maliuta is only his bodyguard. He is jealous when Ivan mourns for Kurbsky and yearns for friendship with Filipp. He takes pleasure in Ivan's smack down of Aleksei, and he doesn't really mind when Kurbsky goes over to the enemy because that opens up more space for Ivan to notice him.[84] Eisenstein makes Maliuta especially jealous of all the boyars. Maliuta's resentment is class resentment, which may explain why Eisenstein made Maliuta Skuratov a peasant in the film, when historically he was a member of a noble family. Making Maliuta's jealousy "social" makes it that much stronger.[85] He's not just the vicious oprichnik depicted in the sources; he's motivated by the kind of class resentment—class struggle—that fueled class consciousness and led to revolutions. Maliuta wants the tsar to love him, but he, like everyone else, wants to overthrow everyone above him. Maliuta's jealousy together with the pain of Ivan's neglect intensifies the violence with which Maliuta leads the oprichniki after their enemies.[86] At the same time, Eisenstein realizes that Maliuta is associated with Ivan's *"lower self,"* by which he means the pre-logical or sensory-emotional thinking.[87] All this innate feeling—jealousy and frustration—makes Maliuta want to lash out at commoners and elites alike. But the "loyal cur" Maliuta is out of balance: he is too much animal instinct. In a scene that did not appear in the film, where Maliuta leads an assault on the Staritskys' domain, he is crushed by Efrosinia.[88]

Perhaps inspired by Zharov's abilities as a comedic actor or more likely by the need to give Maliuta a set of inner conflicts of his own and his perennial desire to intensify the tragic by interspersing it with humor, Eisenstein made one of history's most despicable villains a clown. When already filming in October 1943, Eisenstein made a note about power inversions that link Maliuta's clownishness to his power over Ivan: *"From internal monologue to actual drama."* Maliuta is the outward manifestation of Ivan's inner struggles; his mixed clownish violence also externalizes his own inner divisions. Eisenstein's interest in comedy went far beyond its function as a foil for tragedy, and his writing about humor's functions in culture and art sheds light on the way he used clowns to subvert conventional hierarchies of power and meaning. His interest in comedy, circus, and clowns goes back to the beginning of his career in theater, but an article on Charlie Chaplin, the study of Walt Disney, and several chapters of *Method*, all written in Alma Ata while he was working on *Ivan*, address rhetorical, visual, and formal aspects of humor.[89] And—like Mikhail Bakhtin, who is better known for it—Eisenstein associated comedy, masquerade, circus, and clowns with reversals of social roles of various kinds and with anarchic freedoms from social and political domination.[90]

In his essay on Charlie Chaplin, Eisenstein claimed that comedy is a form of escape from modernity's suffocating power structures and in a paradoxical note written after completing *Ivan*, he insisted that the one thing that is *"always funny* [is] *the one thing that dares to deny the leading philosophy of its time."*[91] Eisenstein was planning to use Foma and Erema Chokhov this way, as comic, subversive relief. Fedka, too, is at his most frightening when he is playing—that is, dressed as a "phantom Anastasia" during The Dance of the Oprichniki, all in white surrounded by the black-clad oprichniki.[92] Making Maliuta a murdering clown, a noble peasant, and a powerful servant all pleased Eisenstein's sense of irony, his belief in the essential human inner divisions, and his understanding of the dramatic role comedy plays in drawing attention to and deepening tragedy.

Why Do the People Love the Tsar?

Making Maliuta clownish came about because Eisenstein could not figure out what to do with the Russian people. His patrons did not make things easier, giving him mixed messages all along with way.[93] Popular support for the tsar had to be included in the film—"whoever is with the people is not alone"— but it was a challenge.[94] From the time that Esfir Shub read an early draft of the scenario and asked Eisenstein to explain why the people love the tsar to the final pre-release screening, he wrestled with ways to understand what role, if any, popular support played in Ivan's reign.[95] He was not the only one. Historians have struggled for centuries to explain the great corpus of songs and tales that express popular love for Ivan, despite the fact that he did not show them any particular favor; in many ways, just the opposite.[96] Maureen Perrie, who has studied both the original sources and the shifting explanations of the sources, has shown that the positive image of Ivan in folklore seems to correspond to what we know of sixteenth-century views of Ivan: he was both irrationally cruel and rationally just and his justice was often meted out to elites, which made him popular with members of the lower classes.[97] Eisenstein was aware of the sources Perrie studied. Both in his notes and in the Historical Commentary, he cited chronicles and folklore collections that showed popular approval of Ivan. He was also aware of tsarist and Soviet historical analysis of the sources, with their wide range of arguments about the authenticity of the sources' reflection of contemporary attitudes. He knew that some of the same literature that showed Ivan as a demagogue manipulating popular opinion also encouraged peasants to denounce their elite enemies.[98] It would have been easy for him, therefore, to simply follow this line and represent Ivan as a popular tsar: "if not a folk hero, at least a proponent of the people . . . against boyar treason," as A. N. Veselovskii wrote in one of the prerevolutionary works on the topic that was republished in the early Soviet period.[99] Eisenstein did not take the easy path. Instead he represented the people as fools and cannon fodder and made Ivan a cruel demagogue. It can be argued that Eisenstein's Ivan the Terrible was, in fact, that popular tsar of Russian folklore—that the people admired his combination of shrewd manipulation and brutal treatment of his enemies—but if that is the case, who are the people who admired that Ivan?

In 1971, Naum Kleiman argued that Eisenstein never intended Ivan to be "the people's tsar":

> It is not accidental . . . that Eisenstein pointed out Ivan's demagoguery in every instance where the word "people" appeared with him. . . . The director in no way intended to represent Ivan as "the people's tsar"—in his film the people would appear alongside Ivan only when the tsar was carrying out general nationalist tasks (the defeat of the Kazan khans, the Livonian march to the sea), or as victims of oprichnina arbitrariness (reflected in the the lists of the dead [*sinodiki*] in the confession scene).[100]

In Part I we see the people as a collective in three scenes: as rebels interrupting Ivan's wedding by storming the Kremlin, as soldiers in the Kazan campaign, and as supplicants in the finale at Alexandrova. In the first instance, the people exhibit passionate and defiant activism, but they are easily pacified.

In the second instance, the people are introduced as soldiers at Kazan with an image that is passive in the extreme. We see a snaking line of soldiers (echoed in the finale), dropping coins onto a plate. After the battle the coins will be redistributed purely for the purpose of counting up the dead. In the third instance, the people function even more passively than subdued rebels and battleground cannon fodder. They beg the tsar to rule over them, subordinating themselves to his rule. Ivan forces them to kneel and rise with little more than a twitch of his beard.

The finale of Part I shows the entirety of society (peasants, clergy, and boyars are clearly identifiable) coming to the tsar in supplication, falling into his trap (I: 1:32:20). With this act, the people abdicate their own authority in order to submit to the tsar for the purpose of supporting an abstraction, the Great Russian State. "With the trick of his departure, Ivan brings the people over to his side."[101] At the end of Part I, the dream of a unified, independent state (*samoderzhavie*) for the good of Russia and its people has been replaced with the reality of one-man rule, in which the ruler is isolated and his power centralized and unlimited (*edinoderzhavie*). He rules in the name of the people, but he has created the oprichniki as a sinister mirror image of the people: a dark, wolfish, and terrifying iron brotherhood who support Ivan and protect the tsar's power.

The magnificent shot compositions of the finale of Part I emphasize the enormous power of the tsar and the minuscule insignificance of the people (I: 1:34:02). Ivan has been speaking warmly with Maliuta about his fears and hopes as they anxiously wait together for the people to arrive, but when the people finally appear, Ivan drops his familiar persona, puts on his work clothes—the fur cloak and pointy hat—and adopts a regal mask. He performs the role of a detached, impersonal, symbolic figure, an abstraction—the embodiment of the Great Russian State. The positive valence here is political: Ivan *is* the state; he embodies the people and the nation. But in human terms, he is inhuman, set apart, dehumanized (on his way to becoming suprahuman). Eisenstein used repetition in the finale to powerful effect. In twenty-one separate shots, Ivan is viewed from a various positions, with the tiny figures of the people snaking across the snow, obeying his every gesture. Ivan is truly awe-inspiring, an abstract, ritualized, performative image of magnificence.

The finale of Part I is the last time we see the Russian people in their original collective form. In Parts II and III, they are represented only as the wolves and demons of the oprichniki. On the surface, Eisenstein adopted the Soviet historiographical view (which corresponded, without acknowledgment, to a nineteenth-century populist view) that the oprichniki—Ivan the Terrible's murderous private army—arose from among the people to support Ivan in his attack on the elite. In some versions of the final scene of Part III, Eisenstein sees Ivan as utterly alone. In March 1942, his conversation with Zharov led him to conclude in his notebook, "When Maliuta collapsed [just before they reached the sea], Ivan understood that he *was all alone.*"[102] On the whole, his portrait of the people presents them as supporters of Ivan but for questionable reasons. They follow him and become his "effective instrument," as Stalin noted, but they do so blindly or unthinkingly or under coercion. There are no heroes from among the people, nor are they a heroic collective.

Originally, Eisenstein also wanted the people to be represented by individuals. Foma and Erema were going to be based on a pair of fools drawn from Russian folklore. In the film, they appear first among the rebellious rabble and later at Kazan as cannoneers. Eisenstein was repeatedly told by cinema officials that these two fools, who joke and sing and hit each other over the head, weren't dignified enough to represent the Russian people. In his critique of the scenario, Bolshakov told Eisenstein to "give them greater substance . . . their buffoonish song must be shortened especially in the first scene. And remove the places where Foma and Erema are excessively ridiculous."[103] But Eisenstein went ahead and shot two scenes with Foma and Erema anyway, just the way he wanted to, despite all agreements. The scenes are genuinely funny, and Foma and Erema are decidedly undignified, but lovable, fools, so it is not surprising most of this footage did not make the final cut.[104] But these scenes remind us that throughout production Eisenstein held onto his desire to portray the people as both subordinate to the tsar and defiant toward power: their laughter, "*the one thing that dares to deny the leading philosophy of its time.*"[105]

On a darker note, Eisenstein tried to include two scenes with Foma and Erema that showed the theme of Ivan and the people in a more complex light; neither made it into the published scenario, but he argued hard to try to keep one of them, "The Debtors' Punishment" (*Pravezh*). It was to have portrayed Maliuta discovering Foma and Erema being punished for failure to pay their debts and publicly humiliated by being forced to kneel in the snow. Maliuta recognizes them from the Battle of Kazan, so he saves them and turns on the boyars who are tormenting them. The scene ends with Foma and Erema going off to a tavern, Maliuta taking revenge on the boyars, and a crowd of people standing around and laughing. This scene was important to Eisenstein, not only for showing the ties between the fools and the oprichniki, but because it foreshadowed a scene that was to come in Part III, in which Foma and Erema call out to Ivan as he passes by a crowd and ask him to save the people from the wanton violence of the oprichniki; another example of the oprichniki becoming as cruel as the elites they had overthrown.[106]

"No Film without a Woman"

Ivan's wife, Anastasia, and his aunt, Efrosinia Staritskaia, are positioned as rivals, but sweet Anastasia with her big eyes and fairy-tale braids doesn't stand a chance against the determined, power-hungry sirin Efrosinia.[107]

Eisenstein imagined Efrosinia as a prairie eagle: "in makeup, look, strength, determination, crushing power. Devil in a skirt. Satan. In stature: Birman. In malice: Zhikhareva [another actress, who had played Lady Macbeth in 1940 and other evil women]."[108] Anastasia holds her own in their first standoff, when Ivan's illness causes a dynastic crisis and Efrosinia tries to get the boyars to swear allegiance to her weak son, Vladimir (I: 50:27). But Anastasia functions almost entirely passively in the film as Ivan's first and unquestionably loyal supporter of his mission (with her attraction to Kurbsky as her "dab from the opposite palette"). She's tempted by Kurbsky but never gives in to him. Eisenstein wrote almost nothing about her, and, in comparison with the men, he wrote relatively little about Efrosinia either. All the characters in his fugue function to show us who Ivan is and how he exercised power, but the women play fairly minor roles, telegraphed by his ironic note that *Ivan the Terrible* defied the mandatory rules of Hollywood romance: *"no film without a*

FIGURE 4.2   Anastasia and Efrosinia

woman."[109] The women, especially Anastasia, appear to exist only to embody reactions to Ivan—for good and for evil—and as foils to each other as mothers in another set of Eisenstein's interlocking triangles: Ivan-Anastasia-Efrosinia, Anastasia-Efrosinia-Vladimir, Ivan-Anastasia-Fedka, Ivan-Efrosinia-Vladimir. This lack of gender balance, however, would have seemed much less pronounced if Eisenstein had been able to finish Part III, which had a significant role for England's Queen Elizabeth.

One can imagine the ballerina Galina Ulanova as Anastasia, flowing gracefully around Ivan with Faina Ranevskaia as Efrosinia menacing her with a cruel ironic smile (a parallel to Maliuta's clownish executioner). Instead Eisenstein used Tselikovskaia like a doll: woodenly gazing up at Ivan in approval and admiration, innocently (but not so innocently) going to her death surrounded by haloes, white candles, fluffy white bedclothes, and tapestry icons (with Efrosinia in the dark shadows just out of view). Early on Eisenstein planned a scene where Anastasia would be displayed in the ritual of The Bride Show for Ivan to zero in and "seize" on her, as a display of his will. He also considered her murder to be a legitimate catalyst for Ivan's desire for revenge, though ultimately in the film we don't see that particular form of revenge.[110] Anastasia only gets interesting when reprised in demonic form by Fedka and, even there, the mask is cast off at the end of that scene when the farcical reprise of The Coronation takes place, leading to the murder of Vladimir, another sort of innocent.

Efrosinia is almost purely evil, but our first impression is dominated by her depiction as powerful and masculine standing next to her son Vladimir, the heir to the throne, as feminized and infantilized. One of Eisenstein's cardinal beliefs was that reversals of conventional binaries (sex, class, etc.) were all connected as emblems not only of difference but also of interpenetration; not of reason but of merging into an undifferentiated sphere dominated by the senses. The desire to efface difference that people feel in moments of stress or threat are often represented in art and ritual by reversals. Efrosinia is the incarnation of "opposition" as "oppositeness." Eisenstein calls her not only the "Devil in a skirt," but also "Ivan in a skirt." She is Ivan's opposite and his twin, and she plays a role similar to the film's male twins, Kurbsky and Filipp. At the same time, the gender reversal she represents is similar to the power reversal Maliuta represents in the momentary master/slave reversal that takes place when he offers to carry out Ivan's murders. These structural similarities and repetitions in the "melodies" of the fugue are typical examples of Eisenstein's dense network of images meant to trigger awareness in the viewer that is sensory, intuitive, and "not frontal," to be compared and disentangled as "Ivan moves through the film."

Efrosinia and Ivan share numerous traits, though her versions are always inferior to his. They share "reactiveness," a kind of boomerang effect, but while Ivan's reactions are cleverly used to defeat his enemies, Efrosinia's intrigues repeatedly backfire on her. The murder of Vladimir is a (tragic) case in point: she plans it, but Ivan coopts her plan to use against her, and it in fact destroys her.[111] Eisenstein tells us that Ivan loved to use his enemies' weapons against them.[112] But intrigue is Efrosinia's business: she tries to turn Kurbsky against Ivan, instigates the popular riot against Ivan, incites the boyars to act against Ivan, and so on. As Ivan turns each challenge to his advantage and Efrosinia's failures pile up, her frustration compels her to cross the line and poison Anastasia. That also backfires when it leads Ivan to create new alliances with the Basmanovs and found the oprichnina.[113] As with all consequences in this film, Efrosinia's perennial backfires raise the question of personal responsibility and historical causality. When her active, if devious, opposition pushes Ivan to become even more powerful and terrible, is Efrosinia responsible for his ascending violence because she opposed the tsar in the first place? Or is she justified in resisting the centralization of power, especially after it becomes murderous? If he is only acting in reaction to genuine obstacles, is he justified in developing stronger institutions of state power? Or is Ivan ultimately responsible for his own actions, even if they are rooted in childhood trauma and adult conflict? This is what Eisenstein meant early on when he wrote that to understand is to forgive but not to justify.[114]

Just as Anastasia is revealed to have a fatal flaw in her attraction to Kurbsky, Eisenstein sees a limit to Efrosinia's villainy. No one is without inner conflicts, an inherent unity of opposites. In negotiating with Pimen about how to save Filipp after his confrontation with Ivan during The Fiery Furnace, Pimen tells Efrosinia that Filipp will be more useful dead than alive, as a martyr to the cause. When Efrosinia realizes that Pimen will stop at nothing to get back at Ivan, even she is taken aback by the depth of Pimen's cynicism, and this response brings out a few of her positive qualities: loyalty to her comrades and a feeling for her allies.[115] Eisenstein loved to create suspense not with action, dialogue, or narrative information but by increasing the tension between contradictory images or impulses. The scene that follows ratchets up the tension by revealing new depths to Efrosinia's violent impulses while uncovering a surprising measure of maternal love for her son: "a passionately loving mother; and simultaneously a 'Machiavelli in a skirt.'"[116] Visually Eisenstein conveys this with one small gesture. After damning Pimen for his cynical treachery—"white is the cowl, black is the soul"—she tosses off her own black robe to reveal a white gown underneath (with the same gesture Maliuta used to toss off his oprichnik cloak and reveal the boyar brocade) as she prepares to take up her role as mother and sing her son the murderous lullaby (II: 45:36). At the same time, even her maternal warmth has a dark side. Her loving feelings are aroused in a scene where she informs Vladimir that she is plotting to kill Ivan to place him on the throne, and then she fully infantilizes him, a grown man about to become tsar, by treating him like a child. When it's all over, when she realizes that Vladimir is dead and her hopes to see him crowned have collapsed, Eisenstein tells us, she's both a "demon" and "a pitiable old woman."[117]

Vladimir Staritsky: Man-child

At the end of Part II, in The Feast of the Oprichniki, all eyes are on Vladimir Staritsky, at once the least powerful man in the room and the most powerful, as his mother is pushing him to be next in line for the throne. At the same time the power relations among the other main characters are all tested. The old elite, Filipp and Kurbsky, are out of the picture, the first murdered and the second in exile. The new elite, Aleksei Basmanov and Maliuta, sitting around Ivan as his most valued servitors, look on jealously as Ivan seduces Vladimir, drunk and uncomprehending. Ivan reminds both Aleksei and Maliuta of their subordination when they each try to claim a special relationship with him. Anastasia lives on in phantom form as Fedka. The oprichniki dance like they're in on the secret, eventually encircling Fedka / Anastasia and beginning to undress him / her. Fedka puts a stop to this when he sees something suspicious and signals Ivan with his eyes. Vladimir's starring role in the fugue is about to begin. The extended climax of Part II, of the whole of *Ivan the Terrible*, the collision of Ivan and Vladimir (or Ivan and the boyars through Efrosinia and through Vladimir) is laced with interlocking lines of power, history, and imagery, more than I can elaborate here. Ivan's farcical offer to dress Vladimir in royal garments and place him on the tsar's throne (as his mother wishes) travesties the conspiracy itself and recalls all the depredations Ivan suffered as a vulnerable child at the hands of the boyars. The mock Coronation recalls Ivan's Coronation ("the beginning of all the conflicts")[118] and King Sigismund on his throne, another travesty of power. The coronation of the childish, incompetent, drunken fool degrades Ivan, not unlike the laughing child's recognition of his evil tyranny during The Fiery Furnace. On the theme of power, the reversal of power signaled by Ivan bowing to the acting tsar Vladimir is linked with the gender reversal Efrosinia-Vladimir and the class reversal Ivan-Maliuta. And all those reversals rhyme with the ritual exchange of clothing and rings that Eisenstein associated with wedding ritual.[119] And Eisenstein explicitly associates the gender reversal in the wedding ritual exchange with the pantomime of power reversal that the historical Ivan performed during his reign with a subordinate, Semen Bekbulatovich, and that Ivan and Vladimir perform here.[120] Ivan temporarily replaces Fedka (who has replaced Anastasia) as his favorite, with Vladimir in the performance of a wedding as a test for the conspirator, who himself is a stand-in for the conspirators Efrosinia and Pimen. Vladimir fumbles drunkenly with the accoutrements, but then as Ivan observes, to his apparent (or feigned) surprise, even Vladimir, when given a taste of power, "wants it!" (*Khochet!*). And this one-word exclamation is visually linked with *"Malo!"* (and by extension *Tsar* and *Prav*) as Ivan assumes the same position, flinging himself backward, eyes wide and beard thrust out when he pronounces the word. Vladimir has told his mother and then Ivan that he has no interest in being tsar ("It's all conspiracies and executions. I want a humble life of drink and leisure."). And yet, when given the chance, even this passive "wimp" (*triapka*) "wants it." In April 1942, Eisenstein added some lines to the screenplay about this particular moment to emphasize the scene's parody of The Prologue: "The fool likes sitting on the throne. Sweetly, the fool on the throne smiles."[121]

The significance Eisenstein attributed to this realization, "he wants it," can be seen in its juxtaposition with a passage in his diary about accentuating the meaning of an image by mirroring it with its opposite. The tsar and the fool are a power reversal, but the fool is also a link to the people: the fools Foma and Erema and their displaced foolishness onto the clown Maliuta, making the power reversal both farcical and subversive at the same time. Everyone wants power: even the Vladimir variation, least like the fugue's theme, in some ways the opposite of the fugue's theme, shares the desire for power. That Vladimir possessed even a small will to power and a small willingness to participate in subversion showed that everyone is guilty of something. Eisenstein wanted to make sure that the audience saw Vladimir's guilt so that they wouldn't think that Ivan punished someone entirely innocent.[122] Everyone wants power. Even the weakest, most foolish, most unsuitable people want some of the trappings of power and some power over others. Ivan responds to this realization by raising the stakes once more: he decides to have Vladimir remain in the tsar's robes and crown and take the knife meant for Ivan. As he decides this, we might notice, that Ivan is wearing his fur cloak half-on half-off: is it as ruler or as vengeful child-man that Ivan orders Vladimir's execution?

At the end of Part I, Ivan predicted that if his gamble, his trick, paid off and his retreat to Alexandrova went as planned, he would acquire unlimited power. But first he had to defeat the boyars, which he accomplished with even more convoluted trickery in Part II. The drama in Part II has largely been the work of Efrosinia, stirring up resistance to Ivan both to preserve the traditional structure of boyar power and to advance her family interests. With Kurbsky in exile, Pimen out of the way, the boyars cowed by the murders of the Kolychevs and bullying by the oprichniki, Filipp and Vladimir murdered, and Efrosinia defeated, Ivan has achieved his goal. At this point, he doesn't ask "by what right do you judge, Ivan?" Instead, with apparently no remorse, but only a need to protect himself from the heavens, he places his hand over his eyes and answers "for the Great Russian State."

In the unscripted Epilogue we see that Ivan has silenced all the variations on his theme: he has quieted his internal demons by defeating his external enemies. By the end of Part II, his power has become monolithic, unchallenged, and "unified," and as a character he has come into focus. Conflicts with other characters that represent his own inner battle with evil, hypocrisy, demagoguery, intrigue, conspiracy, and betrayal pull Ivan apart into separate pieces as the fugue moves through each of these variations on the theme of power embodied in Ivan. Each conflict and the suppression of each challenge allows Ivan to resolve conflicts and reintegrate the fragmented parts back into himself. The progress of the fugue reassembles Ivan, but at the end of Part II he is more detached from other human beings and from ordinary, flawed, human life with its conflicts and fragmentation, and he is still angry. Power is unified in him (the *edinoderzhavets*), but he is an unbalanced, unstable center, both above humanity and in hell.

Sigismund and Elizabeth: Gender and Power

Eisenstein's understanding of the dangerous instability of unified power that occurs at the very moment of its achievement is nowhere better illustrated than in his theme-and-variations comparison of Ivan with his contemporaries who appear—or were to have appeared—in the film. If the original titles placed Ivan in the company of some of the sixteenth century's bloodiest monarchs, the scenario juxtaposed him with two rulers Eisenstein portrayed as the embodiment of pronounced sexuality, sexual androgyny, and political deception. In the finished film, we see only King Sigismund of Poland, but Eisenstein wrote a scene for Part III that featured a mirror for Sigismund at the other end of Europe, Elizabeth I of England. The scene remained in the scenario even after Bolshakov had banned it and, in addition to the text, we have the screen tests of Romm in the role, as well as many interesting notes and drawings made in the spring of 1942, when Eisenstein was still expecting to include Elizabeth in the film. Both portraits represented monarchical power as a nexus of sexual desire, flirtation, deception, and cruelty, and both rulers mirror Ivan in revealing ways.

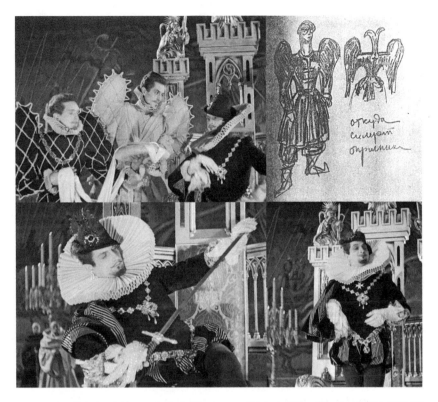

FIGURE 4.3 Sigismund, his courtiers, and the source of high shoulders (drawing: RGALI, 1923/2/ 1714/7). Used with permission.

At the beginning of Part II, we find ourselves in The Palace of the Polish King Sigismund (II: 2:16). Poland is Russia's primary enemy, and the palace provides the location for Andrei Kurbsky to go over to the enemy. Our first view of Sigismund displays him lounging rakishly on his throne, a campy travesty of power that recalls images from earlier in *Ivan* as well as Eisenstein's 1928 film, *October*.[123] Kurbsky is pledging fealty to Sigismund with barely disguised homoeroticism—a coy bit of sexual double entendre that stages this oath of loyalty as a flirtation ritual. Shot from an angle that makes the analogy of proffered sword and erect penis hard to miss, Kurbsky, on his knees, unsheathes his sword and hands it to Sigismund, who examines it suggestively and hands it back for Kurbsky to kiss (II: 2:41). Next, two of Sigismund's courtiers step up to bring the king a medallion for Kurbsky, which Sigismund places around Kurbsky's neck. The courtiers are dressed in what can only be described as bizarrely and conspicuously feminized versions of the black, high-shouldered tunics the oprichniki wore.

Here again Kurbsky is depicted in such a way to suggest a sexual position. He is shot in low-angle close-up on his knees in front of the king with a swoon of desire on his face as Sigismund consummates their alliance by lowering the medallion around his neck.

The Palace scene culminates in Sigismund's speech and is meant to recall Ivan's coronation speech at the beginning of Part I (II: 4:39). Sigismund stands to announce his plans to destroy Russia and isolate it from "Enlightened Europe." This threatening and bellicose statement, however, is delivered from an inviting, conventionally feminine pose: one knee slightly bent, legs close together, one shoulder back, elbows held in, first one arm then the other raised with a little swirl of the hand. Sigismund moves as if dancing a mazurka, not delivering a call to arms. The courtiers respond to the speech with smug satisfaction, until a messenger suddenly arrives from Moscow. The messenger runs into the court to announce that Ivan is not, in fact, the weakling deserter—a bear caught in his lair—that Kurbsky claimed he was. Instead, Ivan has returned to Moscow and is ready to fight. The news leaves Kurbsky embarrassed and useless to Poland. Sigismund turns on his heel with an irritated little flip of his gloves signaling everyone to follow him. The camera tracks back and cranes up, showing us Kurbsky kicking the messenger angrily, with excessive cruelty, in the now empty hall.

Visually and rhetorically, Sigismund's palace is the opposite of Ivan's Kremlin palace in Moscow. Angular geometry and binary alternations dominate the design, with the yin/yang, even/odd patterns that Eisenstein, the dialectician, loved. The design itself was appropriated from well-known prints of European courts and turned into something uniquely his. The checkerboard floor, a huge, stylized tapestry (or a painted wall meant to represent a Gobelin tapestry) of one black and one white knight jousting on the wall above the king's throne, shiny surfaces and clearly marked space with static, rationally placed groupings of people signals a binary comparison that both defines and parodies the conventional rationality and claims to civilization of "the West."[124] In contrast, Ivan's court is all smooth, rounded contours, deep shadowy spaces, strangely proportioned portals, and unsystematically organized crowds. The walls are covered with Orthodox and folk images, where Sigismund's walls sport the two secular, binary knights. Unlike the sexually ritualized and rationalized court of "the West," the Russian spaces are sexually organic. As noted above, Eisenstein instructed his set designer and cinematographer to represent the cathedral as a womb; he made a series of drawings (now lost) that show Ivan's entrance into the cathedral as a phallus.[125]

The contrasts seem obvious: Russia is barbaric, backward, religious, straitlaced, and apparently weak but really strong, while Poland is secular, civilized, advanced, decadent, and apparently strong but really weak. Satirical exaggeration throw all these categories into question and invite us to look under the surface not only to see sameness where difference reigns but to question such abstract and ideological categories in the first place. Eisenstein uses the double binary (East-West and black-and-white checkerboard west) not simply to contrast Russia and the West but to parody the conventions of East-West difference. The markers of Western self-proclaimed civilization and rationality and images of black/white pairing and alternation are superimposed on a scene that also parallels Ivan's Coronation at the beginning of Part I. This sameness-underlying-difference is analogously inscribed in the collapsing of gender difference, which is then also given a comic/tragic spin by collapsing conventional assumptions about gender roles (behavioral and visual markers of feminine and masculine) with sexual roles (male/female and male/ male desire). When apparent difference becomes effaced or muted, underlying sameness becomes viable and vivid, while still in productive tension with difference.

The Polish court is a great example of Eisenstein's use of difference and the blurring of difference. In Eisenstein's style of imaginative appropriation in *Ivan*, seemingly random and seemingly excessive detail have both an anchor in a historical source and a role to play in the complex layers of doubling and redoubling discourse of sameness and difference. Taken all together, these image systems raise questions about the prescribed heroic portrait of Ivan as well as the state's right to dictate artistic production in the first place. The campy, theatrical feminine markers associated with the men in Sigismund's palace did not spring entirely from Eisenstein's imagination. The high shoulders of Sigismund's courtiers' costumes have a historical source: Polish hussars during this period wore wings into battle.[126] Used to frighten their enemies, the courtiers' wings have a similar origin in Russian culture but the opposite effect. The costumes of both the oprichniki and the Polish courtiers' derive from the Romanov double eagle, as Eisenstein shows us in the drawing in Figure 4.3. The wings may also recall Mikhail Kuzmin's well-known 1907 novel, *Wings*, in which growing wings was a sign of acknowledging one's homosexuality.[127] Sigismund's costume was similarly adapted from a relatively common sixteenth-century male dress practice. In numerous Tudor portraits, men wore earrings, lacy cuffs, and elaborately decorated pantaloons. Francis Drake, Sir Robert Carey, and Sir Walter Raleigh were all painted wearing earrings; even Colin Firth, playing the fictional Lord Wessex in *Shakespeare in Love*, gets to wear an earring. Eisenstein makes the association explicit in one of his production notes on how to portray the Polish king: "Sigismund—*absolument efféminé—très gracieux (très Henri III).*"[128]

FIGURE 4.4 "Sigismund—*absolument efféminé—très gracieux (très Henri III) au-denous de cheva-lier de ces proportions*." RGALI, 1923/2/1677/5 [Feb 8, 1942]. Used with permission.

Portraits of the sixteenth-century French king Henri III, who also briefly occupied the Polish-Lithuanian throne and who was widely rumored to be homosexual, portray him wearing an earring and sporting the goatee we see on Eisenstein's Sigismund.

But a man could wear earrings, lace, decorated pantaloons, and high heels with ruffles and still strike a conventionally male-marked pose in the sixteenth century, as can be seen in the portraits of the men mentioned above. Unlike

FIGURE 4.5   Henri III, after François Clouet, c. 1581. Photography by René-Gabriel Ojéda, Musée Condé, Chantilly, France. © RMN-Grand Palais / Art Resource, NY.

all these men, Sigismund's posture denotes him as conventionally effeminate. The pose he strikes is a camp pose; that is, his conventional markers of effeminacy define a man performing as a woman. If this posture isn't marked as explicitly homoerotic, its effeminacy is a conventional marker of homosexuality for mid-twentieth-century Europe when the film was made.[129] Sigismund wields power like Ivan, but the typical male imperiousness and aggression in his speech is cloaked in the come-hither coquettish power of his costume and gestures.

In making Sigismund and Kurbsky effeminate men who act out a ritual of political betrayal that looks like a sexual union, Eisenstein plays with the arbitrariness, and therefore malleability, of gender markers, a hallmark of camp as defined by Susan Sontag in her foundational essay on the subject.[130] Almost everything Sontag said about camp applies to Ivan. Its acting is marked by exaggeration and artifice. Its characters are almost all androgynous. Gender is "convertible," and camp depicts "Being-as-playing-a-role." But according to Sontag, Eisenstein failed at camp because Ivan the Terrible is too successful as art. While Ivan the Terrible juxtaposes the serious and the frivolous, the moral and the aesthetic, and content and style as camp does, camp valorizes the frivolous and the aesthetic, and style always wins over content. If camp style always goes over the top, Sontag argues, the narrative gravitas in Ivan continually weighs it down and keeps it within the realm of the real. Ivan the Terrible may not strictly be a work of camp, but Eisenstein uses the distinctive features of camp—its arbitrariness, its mutable gender markers, its performativity—to point to the arbitrary assignment of sameness and difference in political and cultural hierarchies and to raise questions about the legitimacy and claims to authority of absolute rulers. The very malleability and reversibility of gender markers is mapped onto the malleability and reversibility of cultural markers. So, for example, inasmuch as we see in our enemies a projection of our unspoken fears about ourselves, the homoerotic Polish court is construed as a projection of Russia's fears of weakness, which itself is a commentary on the rhetoric of military strength that was constantly in doubt during World War II and the growing xenophobia that accompanied Stalinist rhetoric at the end of the war (not to mention the echo of discourses related to internal enemies—traitors and enemies of the people—that began in the years before the war). This is one of the ways that Eisenstein prompts viewers to ask questions rather than providing answers. Is Kurbsky wrong to betray Ivan? Who is the real traitor? Is the "West" strong or weak? Is Russia strong or weak? What defines strength? What defines weakness? Russia's conflicts in the face of its enemies are played out here as sharp differences (the insistent black/white, even/odd, us/them visual design and mise-en-scène of the Polish court), but those clearly marked differences are thrown into question by the reversal of conventional gender and sexual roles. When men perform as women and treason masquerades as a comic sex romp, the reversal doesn't just switch conventional differences but blurs the boundary between them; they merge dialectically and transition into something new.[131]

The introduction of camp, dancehall, and circus show that the homoeroticism of these scenes is also meant, at least in part, as comic relief, but as comedy that underscores tragedy. The essence of comedy for Eisenstein was also rooted in the arbitrariness of signifiers (and our willingness to suspend disbelief and accept their normalization). The switching of conventional gender markers throws into question the very nature of power, which has a grotesque effect in relation to Efrosinia, who is manly and powerful and her son Vladimir, effeminate and weak. That gender reversal makes both Efrosinia and Vladimir creepy and unappealing. Though Eisenstein also plays this reversal for comedy at times, the power/gender reversal here adds to the interrogative mode. Does the nature of power depend on who wields it? When we reverse power hierarchies, is the result progressive or comic or tragic?

In his notes Eisenstein makes it clear that homosexuality and visual markers of homosexuality, like effeminate dress and stance, were meant to be funny even if they were subversive at the same time. Sexuality and homosexuality quickly become integrated into the larger picture of the film's overall structure of "polyphonic montage." Eisenstein wrote a scene that begins as comedy but becomes deadly serious, adding another layer to that polyphonic montage dialectic. At one point during the scene where the oprichniki attack the Staritskys' estate, Fedka Basmanov was to be seen chasing down a young woman. When he captures the terrified girl, he says to her, irritably: "No, you fool, it's your earrings I want."[132] These earrings appear a couple of times in Eisenstein's notes and are always marked as comedy. Eventually, though, he writes that it becomes something deeper, the origins of what he calls "the sins of the oprichniki." The *"homo* trait"—occurs first to him *"as comic relief"* but later is associated with "the downfall of the father." He's referring to complicated fate of the Basmanovs, whose loyalty Ivan tests and finds wanting with horrific consequences in the unfinished Part III.[133] This is another example of Ivan forcing Fedka to choose between loyalty to his two fathers. Eisenstein uses sexuality here to highlight and intensify the emotional drama of the questions raised by all the inner divisions we experience over issues of identity, morality, competition, and power.

Eisenstein's representations of Ivan, his court, and the court of his rival ruler as permeated with homoeroticism and homosociality drew on a long and well-known history of such tropes.[134] Kevin Moss has identified an association between politics and sexuality in literary works of late socialism that is useful in this context for understanding how Eisenstein acknowledged and complicated that history. Drawing on Eve Kosofsky Sedgwick's classic, *Epistemology of the Closet*, where Sedgwick examined strategies authors used for surreptitiously drawing attention to homosexuality by marking its secrets and absences, Moss examines the ways authors in late socialist Russia and Eastern Europe used identical strategies to signal political dissidence as well as anti-normative sexuality.[135] The treatment of both these taboo subjects in texts with grammatical constructions that partially conceal and partially reveal them—"mentioned only as unmentionable"—draws attention to the repression inherent in the system that links the closeting of homosexuality with the cloaking of public political critique.[136] The various uses of homoeroticism in *Ivan* function in much the same way. Visually enacted but unacknowledged in dialogue and narrative, homosexuality is both revealed and silenced, drawing attention to the sexual taboo as an open secret at the heart of male rulership. By suffusing *Ivan the Terrible*, Part II, with images of homoeroticism, Eisenstein asserted the presence of homoeroticism or some form of homosociality in the all-male world of the Kremlin, and he claimed the right to depict that presence.

This sameness-underlying-difference seems even more useful and persuasive when we see the mirroring variations Eisenstein used to juxtapose Sigismund with Elizabeth, or Red-haired Bess, as he liked to call her. Sigismund is seemingly strong but really weak, whereas Elizabeth is seemingly weak but actually strong. These reverse paradoxes are represented entirely visually. Where Sigismund is a feminized man, Bess is a masculinized woman: the queen is both a woman in a man's role and (if it had been played by Mikhail Romm), a man in a dress. In her female masculinity, Bess mirrors Ivan's Russian rival, Efrosinia Staritskaia, but where Efrosinia's efforts at trickery and subversion always fail, Elizabeth, like Ivan, succeeds. And like Ivan, Elizabeth's strength is in her ability to deceive.

The dialogue in her scene is contrapuntal, recalling the dialogue between Maliuta and Pimen before Anastasia's coffin, and Eisenstein was extremely pleased with its potential audiovisual montage.[137] While a German diplomat drones on endlessly about the need for England to enter an alliance against Russia, a page is singing a song about Elizabeth's promiscuous sexual appetite and her inscrutable will. Elizabeth herself remains diplomatically motionless through all this until finally responding to the exhausted German emissary by assuring him that "English men-at-arms will be there, in Russia." He hears this as support, though everyone else recognizes it as a ploy. When the German leaves, she breaks out in laughter, takes young Charles Blount onto her lap and begins to teach him the arts of "diplomacy." Drawings of this scene range from illicit (he's a young boy and Elizabeth an adult woman) to explicitly sexual (Elizabeth laughing ecstatically and playing with Charles's erect penis). Eisenstein was amused by the sources that portrayed Elizabeth's court in pornographic terms, and he noted that sources portrayed Elizabeth

FIGURE 4.6 Elizabeth at court. "Queen Elizabeth and young Blount. 'Learn diplomacy, dear boy.'" RGALI, 1923/2/1689/9 [Mar 18, 1942]. Used with permission.

as "vulgar" (*poshlaia*).[138] Eisenstein made numerous drawings that sexualized scenes in the film, like this one that adds sex play to the repeated trope of mother and child, though of course they remained unfilmed.[139]

Elizabeth and Sigismund are not only fugue variations of Ivan as ruler, they are symmetrical mirrors of each other: the masculine woman and feminine man. They share Ivan's success at daring and deception, though their successes are coded as arrogance and corruption. They also mirror an aspect of Ivan that is connected with sex and power or, more precisely, with power rooted in sex. Both Sigismund and Elizabeth use their sexual magnetism and sexual favors to exercise power and forge alliances. Both are sexually aligned with political inferiors and use sex to maintain hierarchies that seem to be of their choosing. Elizabeth succeeds (where Efrosinia fails) by using sex play to appear susceptible and to mask her power play, while Sigismund succeeeds by fusing male power and female flirtatiousness. Each seems to embody a kind of androgynous balance. They are each portrayed as anti-normative and unconventional, but their balance of sexual characteristics is both pre-logical and powerful. Both courts seem to contain a link between the undifferentiated androgynous gender markers of the sensory-emotional and the sexual differentiation and exchange of adult desire and power, a link that for Eisenstein is one of the fundamental ways that we join our instinc-tive, animal selves with our active, rational selves. In comparing Sigismund and Elizabeth, and juxtaposing them to Ivan, Eisenstein used issues of same-ness and difference as related to sex and gender to coincide with—and to mutually reinforce—issues of sameness and difference in the complicated comparisons of Russia and the West, Sigismund and Elizabeth, and Kurbsky and Ivan, comedy and tragedy.

Ivan is similar to Sigismund and Elizabeth in his mixed gender markers, but their courts are entirely different. Eisenstein was aware of the rumors of homosexuality in the historical documents and noted the documents that called Ivan "feminine."[140] When he's a young virile ruler, Ivan has girlish quali-ties: a super smooth face, long eyelashes, and fancily coifed hair. But signifi-cantly, Ivan never displays the kind of gendered mixture in his relationships or in his own body that we see in Sigismund and Elizabeth. Sexuality pervades the Russian courts, both in Ivan's Kremlin and at his oprichnik retreat in Alex-androva, but Ivan is himself largely asexual. His wedding kiss is chaste and ritualistic, the wedding itself is interrupted, and his affection for Anastasia is as maternal as it is wifely. And although Ivan loves Fedka, he is constantly push-ing him away: embracing him to shut him up, ignoring the fact that Fedka is nearly lying on top of him in Anastasia's bedchamber, putting his hand over his mouth to silence him before The Fiery Furnace. Fedka mirrors Anastasia in that he is as much son as lover (and wife-as-masquerade). And of course, in the end, Ivan kills Fedka. Ivan does everything he can to cut himself off from other human beings. The oprichniki have each other, at least, but The Oath and The Fiery Furnace place Ivan above even his own humanity. The Oath of the Oprichniki demands loyalty to Ivan not as a person but as an abstraction, the personification of the state, and during The Fiery Furnace Ivan accepts that inhuman role.

This inner division and Ivan's resolution bring to mind the metaphor for monarchy made famous by Ernst Kantorowicz in his 1957 book, *The King's Two Bodies*. The medieval and early modern monarch was both an individual, mortal, human being who served until he died and a temporary, symbolic figure filling a role in the ongoing drama of dynastic history that superceded any individual. Ivan is perennially divided by the conflict between these two leading roles and between the different moral rules that apply to each, to the personal cares and to the larger historical consequences each implies. But he rejects the first mortal role, or at least he tries to. Even at his most arrogant and grasping, especially at his most arrogant, he is returned to his painful childhood feelings or he falls like Lucifer. It's not that Ivan fails as a ruler, but that the model of leadership that he proposes, embracing the suprahuman at the expense of the human, creates a critical imbalance. Ivan is like Elizabeth and Sigismund in the sexual and affectionate feelings that tie his followers together, but the combination of his oath and the suprahuman powers he embraces in The Fiery Furnace create an unstable, unfunny, unbalanced center of power; Ivan's two bodies are unintegrated.

Sex is not a source of connection to other people for Ivan, and Eisenstein conceptualizes the tsar's sexuality more as depictive attributes or in purely abstract terms, as ontological and phylogenical stages. Eisenstein's phallic caricature of the tsar—the phallus that penetrates the womb of the cathedral at the moment of Vladimir's and Efrosinia's birth into death and madness and Ivan's rebirth—is relevant here as an action that signifies the transition from the stage of the mother, with its related desire to return to the immersion in the womb, to the stage of the father and the desire to pentrate, merge, and dominate as a rational social being.[141]

The Disney manuscripts of January 1944 map Ivan's sexuality onto three different cultural and biographical histories: that of humanity's spiral emergence from pre-logical to logical, the Marxist stages of social organization, and the evolution of Eisenstein's own filmmaking career. Eisenstein uses these schematic processes to understand both the universal urge to regress to the pre-logical and the ways in which individuals and societies develop as they move away from the undifferentiated, instinctive, animal/biological stage, and ultimately to understand the role of artistic production in the context of those stories of human evolution. The writing here is extremely telegraphic and associative, which makes it difficult to interpret precisely, but it builds on themes found elsewhere in *Method* and contains some of the same contradictions. Relevant here is that Eisenstein saw these ontological and phylogenical histories as suffused with sexuality and sexual desire, but he also insisted on de-sexing those elements that are presexual or rational or violent or progressive in order to show how broadly applicable these theories of the pre-logical are.[142]

The Disney manuscripts make a comparison of *Ivan the Terrible* with *Battleship Potemkin* that shows he was thinking about Ivan's unbalanced center in gendered terms and that sheds light on the aspect of Eisenstein's thinking that is fundamentally political and contemporary. Eisenstein discovers that his own path from *Potemkin* to *Ivan* (which he always refers to as "My Epic") replicates the important stages of human history. That this occurred unconsciously convinced Eisenstein that he was on the right track. Those stages are marked by a shift from easy identification with nature, totemism, and shapeshifting to a stage of differentiation, expulsion from the womb, loss of the Mother, and rise of the isolated or distinctive individual, and then a transition from the Mother-as-pre-logical-womb to the Father-as-logical-social-domineering-beast. If all goes well, after that transition, there should be a reintegration into a higher undifferentiated whole of some kind: *"an active return through merger with the creation of the new quality through the unity of opposites flowing together in mutual penetration."*[143] In *Potemkin*, the revolutionary context was marked by a collective social ideal ("one for all and all for one"), while in *Ivan*, the "differentiation of the individual arising from the collective" produced "one against all, all against one and the theme of Ivan's loneliness," which Eisenstein earlier had called "a state of contradiction" (*protivopolozhnost'*).[144] Eisenstein saw this transition as replicating the schematic Marxist stages of history and conceptualized Ivan's rise over the boyars as a kind of feudal collectivism giving way to modern individualism. He also identified the battleship in *Potemkin* as a kind of pre-logical totem: an individual that separated itself from the whole (that is, the fleet) but then wanted to be swallowed back in. The triumph here, Eisenstein says, is that this big metal fish seeks to re-merge with others of its kind not in some primitive form of eating or returning to the womb or sex or domination but in more advanced social terms: in a higher collectivism, in communalism, in uniting the people of Odessa in itself, in its big metal fish body. In this sense, the heroic ship emerged from the feudal collective to become a heroic individual (thesis-antithesis) but then wanted to transform itself through synthesis into a higher social collective. Unlike *Potemkin*, though, in *Ivan*, Ivan the Terrible rose above and chose to stay there. Eisenstein saw this difference as a significant model for understanding the political consequences of personal and cultural evolution.

When any one of these stages or urges dominates another on the backward-forward historical-biographical spiral and pre-logical/logical dialectic, problems arise. Even Disney was susceptible to failure. During World War II, according to Eisenstein, he gave up his pre-logical genius and turned to idea-based productions, resulting in a kind of agitprop. Eisenstein, too, admits that he had a similar problem with his first experiments in intellectual montage—the God and Country sequence in *October*.[145] Sex too can become "malignant" when it is only regressive.[146] His other example?

> *Ivan!!!* where exactly that happens!!! *Potemkin* was the *dissolution into the general* . . . [But in Ivan] the individual broke free from the field of equals and *does not allow itself to be swallowed back in* but, on the contrary, subdues the others to itself. Now *it* swallows, not like a mother, but like *a beast*. And that is—Ivan and—the father![147]

Ivan is a tragedy, not because Ivan as ruler must be dismembered and devoured in order to merge the ruler's body with the higher, collective body, but because once he is reassembled, he stays differentiated, separate, "one against all, and all against one." In *Nonindifferent Nature*, Eisenstein tells us that *Ivan* is a film in which the most diverse possible depictions are synthesized in Ivan in such a way that the particular can rise above the mass and "trample the individual with his feet."[148] *Ivan* is a tragedy, and a political tragedy at that, because Eisenstein's Ivan refuses to be "swallowed back in," and refuses to merge with the higher collective but instead merges with the beast and remains a beast.

One does not need to subscribe to the evolutionary unconscious subplot here or the revolutionary laws of history to understand the social and political implications that it suggests. It is clear in everything Eisenstein wrote—in the plotting of *Ivan* and in all his notes about the demise of the mother, the wife, and the aunt-rival—that the transition from the mother to the father creates a dangerous all-male gender imbalance. This is neither self-hating homophobia nor misogynistic or self-loving homophilia. It does involve conventional gender roles, but this is a conception of gender and power that is tied to the pre-logical/logical dialectic. From his first statement on the subject of reason and instinct in 1935, Eisenstein insisted that balance was essential. Works of art that "tip in favor of logic and theme will be dry, rational, didactic," like agitprop. But emotional excess is equally problematic, making an art work "chaotic, wild, and delirious."[149] Eisenstein wrote that "the role of the father in *Ivan* works absolutely beautifully in Fedka's drama." He is buffeted back and forth between the "blood father" and the "social father," unable to make a successful transition from one to the other or merge the two, and the result was bloody catastrophe, "execution and death."[150] In the other direction, too much male rationality is equally dangerous. The passage in the Disney manuscripts on Fedka's catastrophe of imbalance is followed by a discussion of the necessity for male and female principles (or male and female bodies) to achieve ecstasy in both sex and in art. "But note," Eisenstein wrote, *Potemkin*,

Nevsky, and *Ivan* were all "epics of the father" and all, he emphasized, were commissioned by the party-state: "an order from the Central Committee is a "social order"; it is *rational*, it is formulated."[151] This is a state, he realizes, that is only interested in excessively male, excessively rational "Epics of the Father." Like Ivan, Eisenstein's Central Committee refused to re-merge with the people; it remained a "mouthpiece."[152]

The rulership variations of the fugue on the theme of power show the ways that Ivan deviated from other models of rulership with his inhuman Oath, his imbalanced all-male political and personal life, and his "refusal to be swallowed back in." The conscience that kept Eisenstein's Ivan human and that differentiated him from Stalin was discarded over and over again. Once he decided to be Terrible, he would feel the pangs of remorse only after the most extreme acts of violence, the murder of Vladimir and the annihilation of Novgorod, and even then he rejected the judgment of his conscience and pushed on to establish the Great Russian State at the highest cost. In this male-dominated, Kremlin-commissioned Epic of the Father, Eisenstein explicitly tells us, Ivan trampled individuals with his feet and, like Sabaoth, floated over a sea of blood.

The Spiral and the Fugue: The Mystery of Form

The figure of Ivan the Terrible offered Eisenstein a chance to explore realms of human character and activity that he had not explored before in depth or integrated into his theory or film practice. He wanted to understand power, he wanted to understand how we become the people we become, and he wanted to understand how best to use individual characters and plot to convey ideas and to create his signature vivid, moving, even transcendent experience for viewers. The issues Ivan posed helped him explore who we are—all of us—in our own times and in our own bodies, and how we can transcend our time and individual selves to become meaningful, and to make things that are universally and enduringly meaningful. Or universally and enduringly condemned. Or both.

Because Eisenstein wrote extensively in the 1920s and 1930s about the primary importance of composition, structure, and form in making art, many observers overlook what he had to say about content and ideas or character and plot. His emphasis on form, specifically the importance of his conception of montage and its role in creating structure in art, has compelled some scholars to assume that character and narrative were never important to him. However, as scholars now agree, Eisenstein's film theory and his understanding of artistic creation and reception were always evolving. His production notes and his late theoretical works support that view. Thinking about Ivan as a historical figure located in a specific historical milieu and as a leading character located in a cinematic narrative gave Eisenstein some of the new properties he needed to continue to develop his understanding of artistic method and meaning.

A key passage in *Method*, written during the winter of 1943–1944, tells us how working on *Ivan the Terrible* pushed Eisenstein in these new directions. When the filming of *Ivan* halted due to his illness and exhaustion in December 1943, Eisenstein reached a critical turning point that he described in his diary. Worried that he would never finish his book on artistic method, he wrote: "And only yesterday, under the apple trees, in the company of two rabbits—one white and one gray—did I understand that the time has just about come for *bringing it all together*. . . . And 'Ivan' itself, it appears, is the final, absolutely necessary, connecting link."[153] Then, a few days later, in his manuscript for the book, he elaborated on that last line:

> The "disease" of my theoretical positions is infecting ever-wider realms of inquiry. Gradually it is even shaping up to include what lay outside the boundaries of my direct investigation up until the moment I began work on the screenplay of *Ivan the Terrible*—the question of context, plot, and character [*situatsiia, siuzhet i kharakter*]. Not that these realms are in some way antithetical to the nature of the elements of form. On the contrary, I consider them to be the very elements that embody the intellectual intentions of the author—on the same level with all the other [formal] realms where this occurs.[154]

His earlier films had famously featured mass heroes, and his earlier writing had focused on form, but *Ivan* allowed him to bring narrative and character together with form and method both in making *Ivan the Terrible* and in writing about artistic production and reception.

Though Eisenstein denied it and subsequent critics have exaggerated it, this is a partial break from earlier positions on the role of subject matter or what he calls "the material," so it's worth pausing a moment to remember how extreme his earlier position seemed to be on the subject of plot. When he was first elaborating his theory of montage, he made numerous statements explicitly downgrading the importance of "anecdote" and "allegory." In his notes for a film about Marx's *Capital* in 1928—the height of Eisenstein's materialist, constructivist period—he referred to the subject matter of a film as "banal and humdrum" and "any old trivia taken up and animated."[155] But the break can be overstated. Even in the notes about *Capital*, where Eisenstein emphasized the need to teach workers to think dialectically, he was interested in conveying specific ideas, and he wanted those ideas to emerge from stories rooted in the banal events of everyday life (in this case, bourgeois life). The notes for *Capital* are, in fact, full of colorful and revealing anecdotes, and Eisenstein took pleasure—ironic though it was—in relating them. His youthful ideological commitment to enlightening the proletariat clashed with his own attraction to the same "material" he considered the epitome of banality. By the time he was writing *Method*, he had lost some of his faith in the progressive powers of dialectical materialism and socialist revolution, but he still believed in cinema's ability to educate, move, and transform its audience. His understanding of montage as a dialectical process that stimulated feeling and thinking in viewers by depicting contrasting, colliding images emerged out of these early statements but had come to incorporate a much more complex understanding of perception, social context, politics, and history. Now he was interested in understanding how artists as diverse as Shakespeare, Wagner, Tolstoy, Poe, El Greco, Juan Gris, Walt Disney, Chinese landscape painters, and Mexican architects and muralists, as well as the anonymous creators of image and myth in "primitive" societies, all of whom preceded cinema, conveyed ideas by creating particular characters and stories to embody their ideas. Just before receiving the commission for *Ivan* he had written:

> the most interesting problem in the psychology of art—
> is neither theme nor content, but how this theme or content becomes,
>   from an object of reality—an object of art.
> How an "event" becomes a "work. . . ."
> What is the mystery of the method of art? What is the mystery of
>   so-called form, which distinguishes a phenomenon from its
>   representation in a work of art?
> And a second question: where does the attendant effectiveness of art
>   come from?
> The primal roots of this effectiveness.
> Its meaning.
> And, hence, the eternal tendency of art and something accompanying
>   it which is *greater than* emotionality.[156]

Six weeks after writing this Eisenstein would have a chance to begin answering these questions in practice. The spiral and the fugue were the result. Together the spiral and the fugue form another dialectic that raises the most important question at the center of Eisenstein's investigation of power and violence. The spiral, with its repeated return to the image of Ivan as a defenseless child, repeatedly cues us to sympathize with him as a passive character, the victim of violence, loss, and grief. The fugue, in contrast, translates the revenge born of Ivan's childhood experience into action, as we see him "trample with his feet" (another dialectic: feet both destructive and poignant) each of the characters who question his rationales and challenge his power. The spiral depicts Ivan reaching for power and rising ever further and higher (even as he carries his victimhood with him and even as he falls after each new height) until he becomes altogether detached, while the fugue shows him descending, falling, becoming increasingly demonic and increasingly alone with each victory over the opposition. In part, then, for Eisenstein, a life becomes a work of art when it joins dialectic structures to biographical events and relationships with other people to structure the meaning of those events and relationships as interlocking, dynamic forms that raise the right questions.

In an influential essay, Boris Groys argued that the artists of the Soviet avant-garde in the 1920s, far from being the prime victims of Stalinism, made Stalinist authoritarianism possible through their efforts to establish their power in aesthetic and cultural fields.[157] Following Groys, Alexander Zholkovsky excoriates Eisenstein as a "typical if outstanding example of the avant-garde's metamorphosis into Stalinist culture," and claims that *Ivan the Terrible*'s "merciless poetic machine was indeed part and parcel of the 'totalitarian complex' . . . ; an expression of the director's compensatory desire for total power."[158] But Eisenstein understood some things about the "totalitarian complex." He was well aware of the ways in which one-man rule could disfigure idealistic goals and ideological abstractions could discredit human relationships. He was equally well aware of his own personal attraction to power and the role he had played in producing popular foundation myths for Soviet power. In *Ivan the Terrible*, he used that knowledge not to justify or avoid or whitewash but to dissect totalizing power as immoral and inevitable, both as a symptom of life specific to authoritarian societies and as a universal human attribute. All Eisenstein's models of authority—Ivan, Stalin, his father, his mentor Meyerhold, the boyars, the oprichniki, the Orthodox Church, the Russian revolutionaries, and himself—abused the power they had. In the film, Ivan alone recognized the dangers inherent in power seeking and power having, but this awareness only tormented him. Awareness led him to doubt his choices, to seek judgment and forgiveness, and to never be able to fully acknowledge his own guilt. And, then, to propel him, with "ferocious obstinacy," to greater acts of violence.

CHAPTER 5

How to Do It

Ivan *as Polyphonic Montage*

Eisenstein understood better than anyone else at the time how moving pictures work on us. By the time he made *Ivan the Terrible*, he had written thousands of pages about the process of visual (sensory-emotional and intellectual) perception and the multiple technical means cinema offered to stimulate acts of perception. He studied the visual, aural, spatial, tonal, temporal, and invisible elements of images in every genre and every medium in order to discover the nature of artistic *zakonomernost'*, the patterns of differentiation and merger, or disassembly and reassembly, that artists used to communicate ideas and feelings to their audiences. At this stage of his writing and filmmaking, he referred to these patterns (which mirrored the fundamental structures of human thinking, feeling, and sensing), as "polyphonic montage." Eisenstein thought polyphonic montage could speak directly to viewers—more directly, more deeply, more dynamically—than the realistic or naturalistic methods of conventional storytelling. He used everything he had learned so far to construct the unconventional style he employed in telling Ivan the Terrible's story.

Ivan the Terrible doesn't look or feel like any other movie. It is sometimes compared with German expressionist films or the "eccentric" FEKS films of the 1920s, but in the Soviet context, especially after the advent of Socialist Realism, *Ivan*'s style was absolutely unconventional and transgressive. The actors move in strange, unpredictable ways; space is inconsistently configured;

and portals between spaces are disproportionately sized. Colors are used arbitrarily; religious frescos and other images are cartoonishly, nightmarishly stylized; and the sets are filled with objects that seem to have a life of their own. Sound is a character in its own right, with its own voice, its own shape. Meta-performative acting is juxtaposed with moments of psychological naturalism, and the ratio of these elements is constantly shifting. Even to speak of "a style" is misleading because *Ivan* is a hodgepodge of existing film styles: melodrama, horror, historical biopic, tragedy, and comedy. When Eisenstein wrote in April 1941 that he had to resist the temptation "to just write it out in a realistic framework," he was referring not only to the film's narrative but also to the sensory-emotional method he was considering. Counter-realistic style elements, however, don't fully account for *Ivan's* idiosyncrasy. Socialist Realist films, after all, often included fantastic visual and narrative effects. The heroine of Grigory Alexandrov's *Radiant Path* (1940) has a flying car and a magic mirror. More prosaic collective farm romances and historical biopics distort reality to an improbable, often surrealistic extent. Evgeny Dobrenko has argued that *Ivan*, in fact, shared narrative conventions with other Stalinist-era biopics like *Peter the First* and *Georgi Saakadze*. In the same vein, while arguing for Eisenstein's inventive use of depth-staging and wide-angle shooting, David Bordwell pointed out that distorted close-ups and deep space mise-en-scène were used by other Soviet and Socialist Realist filmmakers years before Orson Welles made them famous in *Citizen Kane*.[1]

These comparisons, valuable as they are, can't account for the radically unfamiliar look and feel of *Ivan the Terrible*. The film's production design, narrative structure, editing, camerawork, lighting, acting, and sound, as well as its bricolage of various theatrical and cinematic genre styles, served a different and more complex purpose than any of these other films, a purpose that Eisenstein fleshed out in his writing. Mikhail Iampolski argues that Eisenstein's theory, while often studied, was never applied, that it was inoperative.[2] But Eisenstein wrote a great deal about how he made *Ivan the Terrible* in accordance with his current theories about art, cinema, perception, and human structures of mind. Conversely, the impact of his experience in making *Ivan* is apparent in pushing his writing in new directions. *Nonindifferent Nature*, *Method*, and other works of the 1940s took his theory several steps beyond the essays on audiovisual montage and the montage image of the late 1930s, as he regularly tells us himself in those works.[3] *Ivan the Terrible* offers us a rare, if not unique, chance to see theory applied in practice and practice translated into theory.[4]

There is a great deal of overlap between Eisenstein's two main written works of this period, but if *Method* was primarily about exploring the characteristics of the pre-logical state of receptiveness in viewers (and its relations to the logical), *Nonindifferent Nature* asked how an artist can use that state of sensory-emotional openness and its dialectical tension with the verbal-intellectual to convey the artist's complex ideas and feelings to an audience. *Nonindifferent Nature* answered this question by examining the underlying artistic structures of *Battleship Potemkin, Old and New, Ivan the Terrible,* and Eisenstein's seemingly inexhaustible supply of visual, literary, dramatic, psychological, and other works to understand the ways that they activate the dialectic of pre-logical and logical by creating what he called *pathos.* Although *Nonindifferent Nature,* primarily written between 1939 and 1947, has been available in Russian and in translation, it has not received the attention it deserves.[5] Like all of Eisenstein's writing, *Nonindifferent Nature* combined obsessive attention to details and the accumulation of examples to demonstrate the omnipresence of the cultural patterns he discovered throughout world cultures and histories. What interests me here are Eisenstein's thoughts on specific methods of composition, the ways those methods represented the artist's intentions, and the effects those methods were supposed to have on viewers.

Nonindifferent Nature picks up from the *Montage* essays to explore the ways in which cinematic images transform the filmmaker's invisible ideas and feelings into visible form on screen that can then be seen, heard, and sensed by the audience and transmuted into a new form inside the mind and body of the viewer. Eisenstein wanted to understand the sensory-emotional and intellectual mechanisms of communication that began inside the artist in some invisible form, are translated into moving images and sound on the film screen, and are then translated a second time as viewers seek to make sense of what they see, hear, feel, and think. His goal was to engage the audience in the active role of making meaning. Eisenstein's purpose had not changed much since his first forays into filmmaking and writing: to move and change people; to open their eyes to new realities; to convey the "generalizable" concepts underlying reality. But he had picked up a number of new tools since 1923 with which to understand the production and perception of art. In *Nonindifferent Nature,* Eisenstein was much more emphatic about what it was he wanted to convey to viewers: that is, the "thoughts, the feelings, the very being and existence of the author."[6]

I am making two related arguments here. First, Eisenstein was not solely interested in providing an intense and transformative viewing experience for his audience. He wanted to convey his own specific ideas and feelings about Ivan the Terrible and all the issues Ivan's life and reign raised. A powerful work of art, he argued, must represent "the author's relationship" to the subject.[7] *Nonindifferent Nature* was Eisenstein's exploration of that process of change—from author's idea to artistic form—in his own work. Second, while *Nonindifferent Nature* explored the ways in which artists convey their ideas and feelings about the subject of their work, Eisenstein's goal was not to impose himself on the audience. He wasn't entirely consistent about this, but to argue that his aim was to deprive the spectator of autonomy and difference is misleading.[8] He did see the director as a magician in relationship to his audience, even a sadist at times, and he always associated filmmaking with power. But he knew as early as 1926 that viewers' responses were unpredictable, idiosyncratic, and socially, culturally, politically constructed, and he gradually moderated his more radical early views. In "Montage 1938," he described the spectator as a creative participant with, not a slave to, the artist in the joint process of producing the generalized image. In early 1943, he reminded himself to be sure to include this concept about the creative role of the viewer in *Method*.[9] By the 1940s, Eisenstein usually understood the director's attempts to direct and control audience response as primarily for the purpose of stimulation, not domination.[10] The purpose of manipulating viewers' perceptions was to provide the sensory-emotional and intellectual tools to achieve their own freedom from form, from their bodies, from the constrictions of everyday life. At the same time, he recognized that viewers respond to visual and other sensory cues in discernible patterns. He sought to understand what those patterns were, how they determined greatness in art, and how to use those methods to maximize the viewer's sensory-emotional and intellectual responses in order to produce a dialectical transformation that included a deeper, new generalizable image.

In this context, it is also important to remember that Eisenstein wasn't working alone. Not only did he have the usual cast and crew necessary to produce a film, but his most important collaborators were also among the greatest artists of the century in their own fields: the composer Sergei Prokofiev, the primary cinematographer Andrei Moskvin, and the actor who played Ivan, Nikolai Cherkasov. All three men were known for their willingness to serve the needs of their directors, and it is hard to imagine anyone more demanding than Eisenstein. However, in all three cases, their contributions to this film were worked out in a deeply collaborative way. Notes, letters, and memoirs record important conversations between the director and Prokofiev, Moskvin, and Cherkasov. Eisenstein gave Prokofiev, Moskvin, and his actors specific ideas, structures, rhythms, poses, and other instructions but fully expected them to use their own creative expertise to implement them.[11] Working relationships were also fused by personal relationships, which were critical for carrying out a project of this scope, in this style, with its particularly challenging and anticonformist profile. Not only did their work contribute to making *Ivan the Terrible* a cinematic masterpiece, but Eisenstein's retrospective writing shows that they each made major contributions to furthering Eisenstein's thoughts about film production and reception.

Although *Ivan*'s style has been studied primarily in formal terms, Eisenstein maintained that form served as an instrument of communication between artist and audience that was about something. He began "On the Structure of Things," the first of four essays that make up the manuscript of *Nonindifferent Nature*, with a statement about the role of form in embodying the artist's ideas and feelings. He identified various problems of using form to convey the artist's intentions, which are among the "most complex problems of the structure of a work of art," and "the most vital aspect" of his work. Up until now, this book has been about Eisenstein's "relationship to the subject" of *Ivan the Terrible*; this chapter looks at his study of form, his theories about the ways in which form conveys the artist's ideas and feelings, and his application of theory in the making of this film. In his memoirs he described his aesthetics as "operational." The question for him was always "How to do it?"[12] Sergei Yutkevich came close to understanding what Eisenstein was trying to do when he wrote in his official review of Part I that *Ivan the Terrible* was

> a symphonic film. Eisenstein . . . puts all his tremendous culture of cinematographic expression into the service of his theme and, as in no other film of his, he achieves a unity of the different expressive means available to the cinematic art. This is not only a brilliant duel of remarks and glances but a passionate battle of sound and silence, light and dark. Brightness and shadow, color and textures—all influence one's mind and feelings.[13]

Not surprisingly, Eisenstein cited this review with approval, but he was not interested in form for its own sake. "Technique, technique, technique. We are interested in the technique of the creation and technique of the composition of works of *pathos*."[14]

From Montage Image to Polyphonic Montage

Eisenstein used specific elements of film form to create a sensory and semantic universe that could activate all the senses at the same time, stimulate the dialectic of the pre-logical and the logical, and move viewers into a state that he called *pathos*. Eisenstein usually defined *pathos* operationally: *pathos* makes something else happen. *Pathos* compels viewers to reach new kinds of awareness of the world through *ekstasis*—the transformational moment of synthesis and transcendence. Or, "put more elegantly, we could say that the effect of *pathos* is to bring the viewer to ecstasy."[15] *Pathos* was associated with a number of qualities that Eisenstein repeatedly found in his study of great art. It produced a "leap to a new quality." It caused the viewer to move, to clap, to cry out, "to be beside one's self." It was a "moment of becoming," moving viewers from "quality to quality," as water becomes ice, or iron ore becomes steel.[16] In other words, *pathos* accumulates in the viewer as the dialectic of pre-logical and logical intensifies and leads to the moment of dialectic synthesis, which Eisenstein refers to as *ekstasis*, or being "beside oneself." But definitions didn't particularly interest Eisenstein here; he wanted to know how to make *pathos* and *ekstasis* happen. At the end of his first essay on *pathos* in *Nonindifferent Nature*, he writes: "Such is *pathos* in life. Such is its reflection in the methods of *pathos* in art. . . . The question remains by what means can the artist pragmatically achieve all these compositional formulas. Is there a recipe? A standard? A prescription? A master key?"[17]

Two underlying ideas shaped Eisenstein's search for a method to reliably produce *pathos*. The first is a principle that permeated Eisenstein's thinking since his works of the early 1920s. He believed that physiology and psychology were linked in such a way that they compelled people to respond automatically or instinctively to external stimuli. Specifically, we reproduce in our own bodies what we see. This theory was a variation on reflexology, which had numerous proponents in Russian intellectual circles in the 1920s.[18] Reflexology was made popular by Ivan Pavlov's experiments with conditioned reflexes in dogs, but it dates back to the nineteenth-century thinkers William James and William Carpenter and their discovery of the physiology of emotions and mimetic muscle contractions.[19] For Eisenstein, the correspondence between watching and responding was essential. When we see actions and emotions performed on screen, we replicate them, in some difficult-to-define way, inside ourselves.[20] In this way the viewer can join with and share the author's "relationship to the subject." The suggestive-reproductive power of what we see and sense underlies all the stylistic compositional methods Eisenstein set in motion in *Ivan the Terrible*.

Second, Eisenstein saw the communication between artist and viewer as more than the sum of formal, compositional elements. Lacking the subliminal, immersive, emotional effects of filmic realism, *Ivan* has often been seen as an overly intellectual, or even sterile, experiment. Many viewers have found it alienating and distancing, but Eisenstein thought that by making the montage process visible and by engaging the viewer in reassembling polyphonic montage fragments he was representing—and stimulating—genuine human feeling, sensation, and movement as well as thought. Effective composition for Eisenstein was not some hermetic intertextual form; it was visceral and "immutably, deeply human."[21] In *Noninidfferent Nature*, for example, he explores the ways that joy and sorrow cannot be conveyed with identical movements, lighting, and rhythm because they are manifested in the body with different sensations. He found support in Bach, who "affirms a similar *deeply human* approach to composition," and who saw the polyphonic fugue as a conversation between identifiable characters.[22] In cases of complex, contradictory subjects—not simple joyful joy, but "life affirming death," for instance—those feelings and personalities are not some random universals but rather originate in the artist's own organic, emotional, and intellectual relationship to the subject represented. In a much larger sense, Eisenstein saw these human behaviors as part of a natural order. The structure of a successful work of art corresponds to the structures of human biology and psychology. And these human functions operate according to the same natural laws that govern the functioning of other species. "The work of art—*an artificial work*—is structured according to the same laws by which *nonartificial* phenomena—'organic,' natural phenomena—are structured."[23] A work of art achieves "organic unity" when "the elements contributing to the work as a whole permeate every feature composing this work."[24] Much of Eisenstein's style can be described as externalized, the creation of a surface, the wearing of masks, but Eisenstein expected that those physiological gestures and surface contours would convey—through *pars pro toto*—the full experience of the character and the ideas and feelings of the author.

Montage was still the fundamental organizing principle in *Ivan*, as it had been in all Eisenstein's film work, and it is still a dynamic and explosive dialectical process that leads from a network of depiction (*izobrazhenie*) to a new, deeper and higher, generalizable understanding, inscribed in the montage image (*obraz*). In *Nonindifferent Nature*, Eisenstein called montage "the most characteristic stylistic sign of cinema." Here and in practice in *Ivan*, as we have seen, montage referred not only to collisions between shots, or even between various formal elements or senses (sound and image, color and movement, etc.), but between far-flung images across the whole of the film and between or among every detail in every frame. Eisenstein rejected a charge made repeatedly, both before and in the years since, that *Ivan the Terrible* was a sharp break from all his previous work. He argued instead that not only did the "unexpected stylistics of [*Ivan's*] montage composition" not repudiate montage cinema, but that "*Ivan* grows completely out of and develops from what was done in *Potemkin*."[25] Much of *Nonindifferent Nature* is given to explaining the evolution of montage: the "center of support of visual montage" moved away "from *the juncture between pieces . . . into the elements within the visual depiction itself.* And the basic center of support is no longer the element between the shots, the juncture, but the elements within the shot, the *accent within the piece,* that is, the constructive support of the actual structure of visual depiction."[26] This is, of course, an exaggeration. Eisenstein would continue to construct scenes whose impact derived from the juxtaposition of shots and the viewers' active response to the invisible in the juncture. But at the same time, he would provide each shot in *Ivan the Terrible* with a dense layering of distinct, related dialectical tensions, details intended to activate emotional and intellectual responses and trigger awareness of connections among disparate narrative threads and visual depictions:

> One or the other thesis or theme, no matter how intellectual-abstract it might be, can be made manifest in a work through any of its elements: through the play of light, through the play of color, through the play of music or sound, through the play of its lines of construction, through a gestural flourish, through the spatial transposition of its dance, through assorted possible complexes of natural phenomena (like landscape, for example), etc., etc.[27]

The ecstatic, synesthetic, and synthetic unity was produced by the same kind of dialectical collisions Eisenstein had been producing since the 1920s, but now including a much more extensive repertory of sensory-emotional and thematic effects.

Polyphonic montage and the uses of synesthesia were not entirely new to Eisenstein in the 1940s. He had been writing about montage "within the shot" from at least 1929 (if not earlier), but he went to some trouble to emphasize the differences between the vertical montage of his essays of the 1930s and his new polyphonic montage.[28] The montage essays unpacked the process he posited at the beginning of his career: that the collision of two concrete visual images could produce something—a new idea, a new consciousness. Vertical montage, theorized when he first began working with music and sound, required the "stacking" of structures like melodic line, rhythm and editing tempo, and the visual contour of action moving on the screen. Even color was prospectively theorized in the montage essays of 1937–1940. Eisenstein referred to the organization of montage units as symphonic or as polyphonic before 1941, but those more complex, multipoint compositions, incorporating both the vertical and the horizontal, were primarily explored later, in works he wrote during and after making *Ivan.* The development of polyphony grew out of his study of the montage organization of image, sound, rhythm, and movement and the realization that depiction within the shot, as well as among shots, included a far wider range of cinematic elements that could be mobilized for the intensification of *pathos* than he had previously appreciated even when he was working with moving image and sound.

Ultimately these multipoint, polyphonic compositions blended sound into image, prompting Eisenstein to incorporate ideas about synesthesia—a multisensory response—that he had also written about for the first time in the 1920s. In *Nonindifferent Nature*, he turned to polyphony and synesthesia to explain how the montage dialectic produced a montage image. Not only does every element of form collide with the others in the montage dialectic, but they also merge into, or interpenetrate, one another. Landscape functions like music in creating mood and conveying feeling; rhythm embodies the montage image of acting; music is acting by other means. In *Nonindifferent Nature*, he began calling this multisensory interpenetration a new form of *synesthesia*: "the ability to gather *into one all the variety of feeling brought from different areas by different organs of sensation.*"[29] The metaphor for this process was no longer a vertical stack of sound and image (as in *Alexander Nevsky*), but a three- (or four-!) dimensional, multicolored, organic, woven fabric or symphony (he used both metaphors). Binary, dialectical montage collisions multiplied with the engagement of multiple voices at multiple emotional, visual, aural, physical, and cerebral levels that produced the intensity of feeling that Eisenstein calls *pathos* until, at moments of unendurable tension on screen and in us, it explodes into that *ekstasis*—that out-of-body leap from quality to quality that produces change in Ivan and in us, the viewers. Polyphonic montage accounts for the extraordinary richness and impact of every shot in *Ivan the Terrible*, as well as the ineffable and abiding *feeling* produced in viewers as sensation, emotion, memory, and idea.

Eisenstein had two related strategies for organizing polyphonic montage. The first is familiar: by disassembling an image into its many constituent details or parts and giving each a "voice," the audience could reassemble the parts into a meaningful whole. In *Nonindifferent Nature*, Eisenstein approached this first strategy from a technical point of view: music, lighting, camerawork, and movement combine with narrative, biographical details, and objects of set design to embody slivers of meaning and feeling for the audience to perceive at various levels of awareness before reconstructing them and sensing them in increasingly intense forms of *pathos* and *ekstasis*. Second, Eisenstein used what he called "ecstatic composition," in which those same disassembled elements of construction model the dialectical process itself. They "grow out of themselves" and are replicated repeatedly but in slightly different form, making viewers aware of the process of interpenetration and incremental, dialectical change. The painters El Greco, Juan Gris, Picasso, and Valentin Serov and the writers Dostoevsky and Shakespeare provided examples for him of the first; the Gothic cathedral, Giovanni Battista Piranesi's etchings of imaginary prisons, and the revenge tragedies by Jonson and Webster exemplified the second.

Architecture brought together Eisenstein's new ideas about *pathos* and ecstatic construction, synesthesia, and the "leap" to a new quality. Great buildings combine line, mass, and material, not unlike the fugue, over time and in synesthetic terms: "at the basis of the harmony of its conglomerating masses in the establishment of the melody of the future overflow of its forms, and in the execution of its rhythmic parts, giving harmony to the relief of its ensemble, lies that same 'dance' that is also at the basis of the creation of music, painting, and cinematic montage."[30] Details of form "grow out of themselves," reaching an emotional pitch that leads to an *ekstatic* leap. A Gothic cathedral represents "the embodiment of ecstasy frozen in stone," by reaching unimaginable heights with forms that seem to grow out of themselves and into one another in a way that can produce ecstatic synthesis in everyone who enters its vaults.[31] Ancient Mayan and Hindu temples, Chinese landscape scrolls, Piranesi's architectural etchings—all depict the same feeling of vast spatial depth. They achieve this with slight spatial distortions as forms "grow out of themselves" and change into something new, reproducing the dialectical conflict between the thing and the "not that thing," which observers then reproduce with their own senses. If properly organized, the accumulation of polyphonic montage stimuli will eventually allow the viewer to construct a sense of the unifying idea underlying the conflict: "suddenly, at a certain moment he is inflamed with the feeling of its unity." Then the unity of opposites grows into the "unity in variety" of the fugue.[32]

One of Eisenstein's favorite architectural models for this process of polyphonic montage, with all its simultaneous minidialectics (including, fundamentally, the dialectic of pre-logical and logical), creating and intensifying *pathos* until reaching a stage of out-of-body *ekstasis*, was Piranesi's series of prisons. Piranesi was an eighteenth-century Italian artist whose sketches of imaginary prisons Eisenstein admired as an illustration of what he called "ecstatic construction." Echoes of the nightmarish, interconnected, archway-divided, deep spaces in Piranesi's series, *Imaginary Prisons*, can be seen in every interior scene in *Ivan*'s Kremlin.

Eisenstein saw the prison etchings as exemplary ecstatic construction for several reasons.[33] The simple lines of realistic architecture are paradoxically multiplied in such a way as to intensify the claustrophobic feeling of confinement. He creates that effect by a counterintuitive expansion of space that makes it seem as if the world is both infinite and at the same time confined by arched portals, endless staircases, and impossible structural beams. Piranesi also creates this effect by breaking down the structural elements of realistic

Figure 5.1 Giovanni Battista Piranesi, *Imaginary Prisons*, 14.

architecture into its constituent parts and repeating them beyond all realistic expectation. Individual elements—stone archway, wooden beam, staircase, rope—are realistically drawn, but their repetition and the way they both break up and expand space create a surreal and intense sense of themselves. The repetition of constituent parts intensifies the sensation of their power and compels the viewers to reconstruct them to make sense of the image. The seeming endlessness and rhyming repetition of the structures makes the confinement seem that much more terrifying. Finally, Eisenstein noticed (or imagined) that the space is broken up in a very specific way: ordinary architectural structures are repeatedly interrupted and reconstituted in a slightly different, usually smaller, scale or shifted orientation. Together these off-kilter renderings of space-defining lines are responsible for that sensation of spatial dynamism and spatial confinement. Chambers grow out of chambers, pillars produce more pillars, staircases lead to more staircases deep into distant space. Piranesi's slightly altered repetitions provide Eisenstein with an illustration of ecstatic composition. By going beyond the limits of realistic depiction, "plane bursts out of plane and, like a system of explosions, plunges into the depths."[34] And "perspective reduction," or the interruption-reorientation-reduction in scale exaggerates the sense of depth and distance. At the same time, these repeated, slightly different, receding shapes depict the way Eisenstein thought organic beings develop. That "telescoping" of stages emerging from the previous stage (in the rising vaults of the Gothic cathedral and the Piranesi prison) is what Eisenstein calls "exploding 'out of itself,'" or ecstatic construction. The depiction of this specially organized recession into the distance gives the viewer not just the idea but the sensation of extraordinary depth and, more important, of shifting from one sense of space to another. That seeming infinity of possibility makes the confining structures of the content—underground prison walls—that much more claustrophobic. Eisenstein recognized in Piranesi his own practice of spatial set design, in which "set design proper seems to be a 'spot in the background' which appears through a system of foregrounds placed like 'wings' attached endlessly in front of it, driving this set design further and further into the distance."[35] He designed Ivan's Kremlin along the same contradictory principles.

Eisenstein's ecstatic composition was not only a representation of a concept; it modeled the process of dialectical escalation toward *ekstasis* that viewers, in accordance with the rules of reflexology, were meant to reproduce in their own feelings and sensations. Ecstatic composition paralleled in form Eisenstein's understanding of the structures of the human mind that determined the spiral processes of historical and biographical change, the dialectics of logic and pre-logic, the dismemberment and reassembling construction of film, and the dynamic, polyphonic, unstable nature of all living things. Because everything in *Ivan* was composed on the basis of a single unifying structural principle, it is not surprising that set design mimics character development. The set functions like a character, with its own unities of opposites exploding in new forms. Conversely, Eisenstein layered one dialectic on another, not in stacks but in dynamic, rhythmic planes intersecting and moving off again at a slightly different scale or angle or trajectory. Characters and objects are elements of design as well as living entities undergoing their own telescoping processes of change. "The last point in this method is the close-up of the actor carried beyond all thinkable limits. Over the actor's shoulder is put the whole space in which can be outlined the set design with all its substructures."[36] The interchangeability of living beings and the objects surrounding them emphasizes difference and interpenetration, both necessary ingredients of *ekstasis*. That interpenetration also brings out the contradictions, the unity of opposites, within both humans and their objects: the liveliness of our things, the death in store for our beings; the accumulation of dialectical experience and the dissolution of parts necessary for artistic communication and for rebirth. These repetitions and contradictions, the divisions and mergers that made up what Eisenstein thought of as the organic unity of the film were also related to the other major concept Eisenstein introduced in *Nonindifferent Nature*: the synesthetic music of landscape.

Working with Prokofiev allowed Eisenstein to join his work on vertical montage with his work on *Method* and take the next step to richer polyphonic montage in *Ivan*. In revisiting *Potemkin* he was particularly struck by the way landscape was the element of film "least burdened with servile, narrative tasks," free therefore to convey pure feeling, and in this way to represent or play the role of music, "with its hazily perceptible, flowing imagery," in a silent film.[37] Freed from character and storytelling, music and landscape share the capacity of *"emotionally expressing what is inexpressible by other means."*[38] When he was first writing about audiovisual or vertical montage in the 1930s, Eisenstein tells us, he had not quite appreciated this degree of the "plasticity" of music or the very intricate ways that such plasticity allowed music to be blended, synesthetically, with lighting, gesture, movement, and other visual elements to create the enhanced, multisensory and thematically rich polyphonic montage. Eisenstein's new appreciation for the background elements of the shot—the landscape broadly speaking—for the interplay among every element of the shot and porousness of boundaries between genres, media, and senses, is a critical ingredient in his composition of the style of *Ivan the Terrible*. This appreciation for the landscape and its expressive qualities gave him a new awareness of the complexity that he could create within each frame between foreground and background and everything in between. And those lively qualities contributed to the animation of things. Nature was not only not indifferent; it was a passionate player in every image. Its ability to carry feeling and everything that could not otherwise be said, animated the full frame and every element in it. Eisenstein's new appreciation for the sensory-emotional valence of the interaction of all the elements in any frame and across frames and his belief that this paralleled the most natural and magical state of awareness for human beings to perceive art, gave him the conceptual framework for maximizing the quantity and intensity of those montage interactions. Prokofiev, Moskvin, and Cherkasov gave Eisenstein the tools to turn concept into form.

Prokofiev and the Music of Landscape

Eisenstein wrote repeatedly about sound and music in cinema, from his contribution to the collective "Statement on Sound," co-authored with Vsevolod Pudovkin and Grigory Alexandrov in 1928, through his discussion of audiovisual cinema and vertical montage in the montage essays of 1938–1940 to his film school lectures on color and sound, his articles on Prokofiev, and his notes on the history of audiovisual counterpoint for his *General History of Cinema*. Each of these built on the previous work and confirmed his original commitment to sound as an active element in film art rather than as a naturalistic underpinning for realism or affect. From his initial insistence on sound "as a new element of montage," Eisenstein developed increasingly complex multimedia, multisensory ideas about the ways sound interacted with visual image to contribute to meaning and experience for film viewers. In fact, Eisenstein's attention to sound in cinema was a consistent factor and probably the primary catalyst in the development of his film theory from early montage to the montage image to polyphonic montage and synesthesia that he used in *Ivan*. Although the arrival of sound in the 1930s contributed to the rejection of avant-garde practices in favor of realism, Eisenstein countered that shift in the films he made, the films he planned, and the theory he was writing throughout that decade.[39] He went beyond the simple counterpoint established in the "Statement on Sound" to explore formal properties of music—rhythm, meter, melody, duration—which then shaped his thinking about cinematic montage and meaning throughout the 1930s. In addition to the simple denaturalizing counterpoint theorized in the "Statement on Sound," Eisenstein made music a critical structural element in *Ivan the Terrible* as well as one of the models for writing about synesthesia and polyphonic montage in *Nonindifferent Nature*. The ability of music to carry emotion and stimulate sensation was key to his study of sensory-emotional thinking and artistic production and reception. As a nonverbal art form, music stimulated Eisenstein's thinking about the ways in which the pre-logical manifested itself in artistic form. And as an art form that shared the elements of rhythm and time with cinema, music was central to his thinking about visual movement on screen, the shape of things seen, and the contours of the visual landscape of a shot.

As many have noted, music plays an especially prominent role in *Ivan the Terrible*. We can see the evolution of Eisenstein's ideas in this period if we compare his pre-*Ivan* writing on audiovisual montage, especially "Montage 1938" and "Vertical Montage," with the essays that became *Nonindifferent Nature* in 1944–1945 and the articles he wrote about Prokofiev during and after making *Ivan the Terrible*, where his ideas about cinematic polyphony and synesthesia emerged.

Eisenstein's essays on vertical montage in *Alexander Nevsky*, his first collaboration with Prokofiev, have been criticized for being overly mechanistic and for proposing too simple a correspondence between listening and looking.[40] But musicologists sometimes miss the advance in Eisenstein's writing from vertical montage to polyphonic and synesthetic montage (or, conversely, they see what he only fully developed later in this earlier writing).[41] While he was still prone to explaining himself in somewhat schematic terms in *Nonindifferent Nature*, his diagrams of "bricklaying," and of the rhythmic editing of sound and shot—for example, like the diagram of vertical montage in *Alexander Nevsky* included as an appendix in *The Film Sense*—should be seen as rudimentary sketches that only hint at a much larger and more complex set of constructions that he describes in his other writings about rhythm, melody, and time duration.

Eisenstein had more control over the direction and uses of the score in *Ivan* than he had in *Alexander Nevsky*. A key difference between the two films and between "Vertical Montage" and *Nonindifferent Nature* was this:

> In the analysis of the "Dawn Scene" in *Alexander Nevsky*, we had a typical analogue to the Chinese picture scroll *unrolled horizontally*. There this can be read as two horizontal, parallel lines of a score—the line of sound and the line of visual depiction—just like the line of air, water, and earth in a Chinese landscape; here then in *Ivan the Terrible*, we apparently have an instance of a roll of film "uncoiling"—so complicated is the interrelationship and interweaving, and so great are the number of elements constituting the general emotional effect.[42]

The final section of *Nonindifferent Nature*, "The Music of Landscape and the Fate of Montage Counterpoint at a New Stage," is devoted to explaining that shift. In that chapter, music is a subject for analysis, but it is also, as the title suggests, the reigning metaphor for Eisenstein's current understanding of the structures of artistic composition. Writing in 1944–1945, while editing Part I of *Ivan the Terrible* and getting ready to finish Part II, Eisenstein developed his earlier thoughts on montage, the montage image, and vertical montage, incorporating many of the insights he gained through work on *Ivan*.[43] In doing so, he developed ways to use sound and music in *Ivan*, and as he was editing, he tells us how well those methods worked out. Here he is on the underlying emotional resonances that make it possible to gather all this diverse material into one unified film: "mainly, it is necessary that everything, beginning from the actor's performance and ending with the play of the folds of his clothes, be equally immersed in the sound of that single, increasingly defined emotion that lies at the basis of the polyphony of a whole multifaceted composition."[44] The key phrase here is the "sound of . . . emotion." Synesthesia is generally understood to be an involuntary neurological condition that activates multiple senses when only one sense is usually stimulated. Some synesthetes perceive numbers to be associated with specific colors, or colors associated with specific feelings. For others, musical tones arouse flashes of specific colors or words trigger tastes.[45] Similar to his use of dialectics, Eisenstein adapted the concept of synesthesia to his own purposes. Throughout "The Music of Landscape," Eisenstein discussed the ways that artists have composed their works to replicate synesthetic responses in viewers. He wrote about the construction of complex montage dialectics by using musical metaphors, for example, to talk about emotions, perception, responses to visual images, and unity in variety: "the sound . . . of emotion." Or, to take another example, in his discussion of unity in variety Eisenstein wrote that great works of art are structured like "a distinctive orchestra of [the] parts independently composing it."[46] He went on to say that such unity is possible only when the diverse pieces are linked "tonally." Each shot has to be perfectly calibrated, in the same way that music "tonally expresses what is inexpressible in words." The word "tonal" can mean numerous things in *Nonindifferent Nature*, linking diverse compositional elements by representing them as constructed of tones. Eisenstein uses tonal modulations to talk about music, light, and color. He also uses tone to describe modulations of shape, contour, and framing: "The changing figure of Ivan is expressed tonally throughout the film by the play of the actor's contour, the framing of the shot, and above all by the miracle of tonal photography of the cameraman Moskvin."[47] In this last example, "tone" represents Andrei Moskvin's subtle manipulation of the gradations of light as if they were notes on a scale, deployed to convey and reproduce in the viewer various registers of emotional response. Moskvin's lighting is itself musical; his "intonations of light" contribute as much as the music to the film's look and feel, "echo[ing], from episode to episode, both the emotional mood of a scene and the emotional state of the tsar-protagonist."[48] In his article on Prokofiev, Eisenstein calls this form of synesthesia "the emotional-imagistic and semantic sensation" of the event (*emotsional'no-obraznoe i smyslovoe oshchushchenie*).[49] As the musicologist Royal S. Brown wrote, Eisenstein conceived of synesthesia not as a set of parallel sensory tracks, but as a setting for each of the senses to answer each other at various paces and rhythms across time.[50] In other words, Eisenstein's synesthesia is the formal equivalent of the narrative fugue in forming the image of Ivan.

Eisenstein explicitly and gratefully acknowledged the critical role Prokofiev played in these developments.[51] Eisenstein's version of their collaboration, however, is so compelling that one can all too easily take it at face value or believe both artists viewed it the same way. New work by the musicologists Simon Morrison and Kevin Bartig allows us to see things better from Prokofiev's point of view.[52] They show that, although the two artists remained good friends until Eisenstein's death in 1948, their collaboration was not always as satisfying as Eisenstein suggests.

Eisenstein and Prokofiev's artistic collaboration succeeded against steep odds. The horrific conditions of wartime and transient exile more than once interfered with production, as did equipment failure and major illnesses suffered by both artists at the worst possible times. Yet the music that resulted is always meticulously well attuned—emotionally, intellectually, and structurally—to the scenes it accompanies and to Eisenstein's overall conception of cinematic polyphonic montage. That attunement allows the music to amplify the emotional impact and thematic development of many scenes while providing emotional and thematic counterpoint to others. In every single scored scene, the music plays a key role in producing the "swarm of lyric visions and representations" that makes up the polyphonic montage image.[53] These two artists' work on *Ivan the Terrible* has to be considered one of the greatest artistic collaborations of the twentieth century.

Eisenstein tells us how he thinks the composer succeeded in writing exactly the music he wanted. Prokofiev, he writes, has a "surprisingly developed" ability

> to "hear" a plastic, visual depiction [*izobrazhenie*] in sounds, [which] makes it possible for him to construct amazing aural equivalents of the visual depictions that fall in his field of vision. . . . In this particular sense, Prokofiev's music is surprisingly plastic, nowhere remaining mere illustration, but everywhere sparkling with jubilant imagicity [*torzhestvuiushchaia obraznost'*]; it reveals in amazing ways the internal movement of a phenomenon, its dynamic structure, which embodies the emotion and meaning of the event.[54]

Before addressing the specific audiovisual theory underlying this statement, it is worth pausing here to notice that Eisenstein is writing synesthetically, using a visual vocabulary to discuss Prokofiev's music: plastic, depiction, illustration, and *obraznost'*. Eisenstein describes Prokofiev's contribution to the score in the same synesthetic terms he proposes to create *Ivan* as a multisensory film. The specific examples he gives are also wonderfully intersensory: the audio and the visual come together to create something more than the sum of their parts. Eisenstein loved watching Prokofiev rehearse the musicians and describes him leading the orchestra in the lullaby that was to have accompanied The Prologue, "Ocean Sea, Deep Blue Sea" (*Okean-more, more-sinee*).[55] The individual musicians in the orchestra literally (to Eisenstein's eye and ear) perform the making of a montage image, and Prokofiev seems to understand the concept perfectly. He tells Eisenstein, "this one is playing light gliding over the waves, that one—the swelling waves, this one, vastness and that one—the mysterious depth."[56] What's key here for Eisenstein is that the music does not attempt to copy nature but rather "[to] re-create, call to life (but not copy from life), and collectively produce a wonderful image of the vast and boundless ocean, foaming like an impatient charger, heaving stormy breakers, or lying placidly, quietly sleeping, its blueness mottled with patches of sunlight, just as the builder of the Russian state sees it in his dream."[57] Prokofiev was capable of composing music that conveyed "ocean blue," not only as a manifestation of nature but also, synesthetically, as the color of Ivan's dream of extending the Russian empire to the Baltic Sea. In this sense, synesthesia is the sensory version of Eisenstein's dynamic process of reassembling depictions into a generalizable image.

This passage helps us understand what it means for a visual artist to "think in images" and to translate that thinking-feeling-sensing into words. Eisenstein found a near-perfect equivalent in Prokofiev's music for what he was trying to effect with synesthesia in moving pictures.[58] The montage image that Eisenstein described above was meant to be the "blueness of the ocean [that] is not merely the color of the sky reflected in its depth, but the color of the dream."[59] Note two things about this statement. First, Eisenstein might have been content to say that the blue of the ocean represented the color of the dream, but he can't resist making a little montage here: the sky *plus* the ocean = the dream. Second, he avoids linking that dream with the overall narrative or even with Ivan's character. This particular piece of music was to be played first when Ivan was a small child; it would only later come to represent his dream of a modern state. As a child, Ivan's future dreams were pure and simple—the blue ocean—but nothing in Eisenstein's story remains pure or simple for long, and soon the "swarm" of associations would begin to come to the surface from the blue depths, releasing the dream of a united, powerful Rus.

Naum Kleiman cites two diary entries from 1938 and 1946 to explain a series of drawings from this period that visually show this transition from the practices of *Nevsky* to those of *Ivan*. The 1938 texts concern the way that music and theme could be synchronized (or a-synchronized) to maximize impact. Eisenstein writes about music and visual images that are "inwardly synchronized in an <u>imagistic</u> *way*. The themes are synchronous: they do not coincide in linear fashion, but [are] co-rhythmic." Or they can be outwardly "synchronized in a <u>imagistic</u> *way*. The themes and the stories—the vehicles of the themes—are both synchronous. The musical equivalent of the imagery has also a pictorial side connected to them, while being independent on the level of plot. Heightened drama." The drawings associated with these ideas show pictorial images in blue pencil with a red line surrounding and behind the figures that seems to trace a countour of the synchronous, rhythmic shape of music.[60]

FIGURE 5.2 *Gedanken zur musik.* RGALI, 1923/2/1384/2 [1938]. Used with permission.

In 1946, though, that musical contour has sunk down beneath the visual surface, into memory and invisible sensory-emotional experience: "Why is there music at all . . . With separation in time, nothing remains but the wave-like outline of the way the course of events oscillates. And so we have the purely musical part of the process. Art, quite apart from the fact that it too is in some sense always a 'memory' and develops according to memory's laws (and the laws of the unconscious: dream, recollection, etc.), needs music to give laws for the work's form and rhythm."[61] Eisenstein was so pleased with the score because he thought Prokofiev was able to transcribe that invisible, underlying, interior "form and rhythm" and give it feeling. He could "read a 'seemingly' random accumulation as corresponding to specific patterns [*zako-nomernost'*]. He interprets this found *zakonomernost'* emotionally."[62] Eisenstein recounts how, after seeing an edited episode of sixty meters only two or three times, Prokofiev composed a piece of music so perfectly timed that the film needed no additional editing. "Moreover, they were arranged not by a crudely metrical *synchronization* of accents but by a complex course of *interweaving* of accents of action and music, where *synchronization* is only a rare and exceptional phenomenon, strictly coordinated by the editing and by the phase of the unwinding action."[63] This is the rhythmic patterning that Eisenstein also called "bricklaying"—that is, the asynchronous arrangement of visual and musical accents, "where the ends of the musical beats and the borders of the pictures do not coincide."[64]

How then did Eisenstein use rhythm, tempo, melody, and tone temporally and colorfully and to what end? In the writing he has established music's ability to carry emotion, to activate memory, to join emotion with form, to join form to content (or theme), to trace the contours of space, to provide an emotional-structural tool for activating the dialectical, synesthetic, polyphonic process of saturating the film with *pathos* and forming the generalizable montage image. Recent musicologists' studies help show how Prokofiev operationalized Eisenstein's ideas about sound in film and about Ivan in this film in ways that made Eisenstein so happy.

Musicologists and film scholars have usually examined the musical contribution to polyphonic montage in two separate ways: thematically and structurally. A number of writers have traced Eisenstein's uses of Prokofiev's musical themes as leitmotifs that reaffirm ideas expressed through words, movement, or other elements. The leitmotif concept is commonplace now, but it was not yet the case in the 1940s, when Eisenstein and Prokofiev adapted the practice from Wagner, who developed it.[65] Unlike Wagner, however, Eisenstein never used leitmotifs to correspond systematically with single characters or even ideas. Bartig calls them "ersatz-leitmotifs" to emphasize Eisenstein's and Prokofiev's use of musical themes to complicate ideas and identities by linking a single motif with characters and situations in diverse, disruptive, and even contradictory situations.[66] Bartig and others have shown *Ivan the Terrible* to be a dense network of "ersatz-leitmotifs," evolving throughout the film, to express what was not stated in words. Brown points out that the leitmotifs often contain disruptive elements that create a sense of doubt. During the deathbed scene when Ivan pleads with the boyars to swear allegiance to his son, a six-note figure (known as *Diabolus in musica*) is repeated at each new entreaty. But although it appears at natural-seeming intervals, "there is not a single point where . . . the harmonic language suggests closure. . . . The six-note figure that acts throughout as a climatic moment always lands on the B-minor chord that all but screams non-resolution."[67] Leitmotifs used in this way stimulate feelings of uncertainty and plant questions in the viewers' minds; questions that activate spectatorship, resist linear narrative clarity, and parallel Ivan's own emotional and intellectual uncertainty. An important addition to the study of leitmotifs is Bartig's historical and intertextual study of musical and thematic antecedents. He contributes to our understanding of the uses of music as commentary by showing that Prokofiev drew on previous Russian musical traditions to link specific characters and ideas with previous representations. Bartig showed that the musical portrait of Efrosinia, for example, incorporated themes from nineteenth-century composers connected with sorcery, contributing to the portrait Eisenstein designated as "the Devil in a skirt."[68]

In the thematic use of leitmotifs, Eisenstein and Prokofiev provided the kind of counterpoint proposed in the "Statement on Sound." Now Eisenstein joined thematic counterpoint to new kinds of synchonization meant to capture the underlying *zakonomernost'* of the sensory-emotional and intellectual dialectic. He claimed that he carried out the synchronization of sound with the various elements of image at a much more microscopic, structural level in *Ivan* than previously. In "Vertical Montage" he had discussed the ways in which meter, rhythm, melody, and tone could be coordinated with visual image, movement, lighting, camerawork, and editing to intensify the effect on the viewer. Judging, as most readers have done, by the diagram that he used to illustrate the coordination of music and depiction, Eisenstein's method seems simplistic and overdetermined.[69] But in the diary passages and drawings cited above, he treated the elements of music with more nuance than the sketches show. Lea Jacobs confirms this discrepancy through detailed analysis of the audiovisual montage in the deathbed scene in Part I that Brown referenced.[70] She also examines the six-note figure, the "Devil in Music," that Brown heard as unsettling. In his own dissection of this scene in *Nonindifferent Nature*, Eisenstein emphasizes three points. First, the most important thing to do before editing sound and picture was to establish the basic "rhythmic development" of the piece. Whether Prokofiev did this first or Eisenstein did, it was never easy. Eisenstein would listen to the recording of the music "endlessly" until the elements of each began to correspond.[71] Second, he was not looking for the simple correspondences between parallel, vertically stacked or horizontally unfolding lines where editing cuts could create the rhythmic articulation of the flow of images. He was looking for "accents" within the shot: "changing light tonality and the change of characters, the movement in the emotional state of the actor, or an unexpected gesture, breaking the smooth flow of the piece."[72] Note that his definition of the visual accent was dynamic and unsettled; it was always related to movement that signified change. And finally, he discussed the laws governing what he called "ligature" (*viaz'*). The accent in the soundtrack and the film must be coordinated precisely so that they neither coincide completely nor fail to coincide at all.[73] Jacobs discovered that the coordination of musical and visual track is even more ingeniously coordinated than Eisenstein conveyed in the " bricklaying" sketches he made for *Nonindifferent Nature*. The density and variety of synchronizing schemes is so complex that she only described what happens in about six minutes of film—forty-three shots and fifty-two bars of music. By examining these shots frame by frame, she shows how precisely Eisenstein varied the uses of coordination, enjambment, and disalignment of musical cues, visual cues within the shot, and visual cues at the cuts. Her major contribution, though, is to show that those disruptions were fully prepared in the rhythm and meter of the score itself. While in some other scenes, Eisenstein edited the soundtrack or chose when to repeat passages of leitmotifs, here the composition seems perfectly timed to be used in the asynchronous "bricklaying" patterns he favored.

Jacobs, however, draws no overall conclusions about the patterns of the "ligature" or what the patterns she discovered can tell us about the ideas and feelings conveyed, about what underlying *zakonomernost'* Prokofiev has transcribed here to convey the author's "relationship to the subject." In his writing about the montage image, Eisenstein emphasized the ways in which each element contributed to the generalizable image of the episode, to something concrete. He wrote about an "emotional-imagistic and semantic sensation," and Prokofiev's ability to capture the "emotion and idea [*smysl*] of the event."[74] In what follows, I expand on Jacobs's study of rhythmic editing of the soundtrack to look at how musical accents and visual accents are arranged with an eye toward what that might tell us about the dependence or independence of the narrative.

The scene in question depicts one of the most profound moments of change in Ivan's life and the beginning of open opposition to his rule (I: 49:11). Ivan is dying. Having received the last rites, he begs the boyars to pledge their allegiance to his young son, Dmitri. Efrosinia defies him and asks the boyars to support a "boyar's tsar"—her son, Vladimir. The boyars reject Ivan, and they think he dies. Kurbsky sees his chance and asks Anastasia to marry him.

We know that Eisenstein imagined an illict relationship between them, and while we saw her in previous scenes pantomime her attraction to Kurbsky, now she looks angry and terrified, which makes sense when she points out that Ivan is alive. Ever the opportunist, Kurbsky pledges to Dmitri just in the nick of time. Life and death, love and fidelity, loyalty and treason. This is an enigmatic scene, typical of Eisenstein's construction of narrative at numerous contradictory levels to compel viewers to question Ivan's motives and tactics, to wonder what kind of ruler he is, and to set up deeper questions that follow. The scene draws out our sympathy for Ivan while planting seeds of doubt: as he's dying, he wants nothing more than support from his servitors, but we see one after another reject him. Can they all be wrong? If everyone in his circle betrays him—his wife, his best friend, his aunt and cousin, and the boyars, is he right to eliminate them for the sake of establishing the modern state? At the same time, contradictory signs make us ask if he's manipulating the whole situation, in total control, or if in his weakness, he is physically and emotionally vulnerable to others. The correspondence of music and image sheds light on these questions and on the visual and spoken narrative. If motifs are used idiosyncratically in this film, is their narrative use aligned with the disruptive rhythm and tempo? Or do musical motifs function to disrupt the disruption and realign sound and image? Let's see how Eisenstein used Prokofiev's repeated six-note figure in this scene to try to answer these questions. I'm looking for "bricklaying" patterns in the synchronization of the six-note figure, in which the "ends of musical beats and borders of pictures do not coincide." If Eisenstein is correct, if he followed his own instructions, the six-note figure of the theme should be timed to coincide with the visual accents but should draw attention to the changes they introduce by indirection, by weaving together disruption and continuity.

The six-note figure is played twenty-eight times in the scene, in fourteen pairs—a highly symmetrical structure. In between the repetitions of those doubled six notes, a shorter three-note motif plays that can signal either suspense, weakness and doubt, or grandeur and power. These three-note intervals are accompanied either by alternating pulsing strings that heighten the sense of anticipation or drawn-out chords that either seem to slow time down or, in crescendo, seem to emphasize anticipation. First I'll look at the alignment of the theme with narrative and character accents and then try to compare that line with the rhythmic editing line.

The sequence begins in silence with a four-second shot of baby Dmitri (I: 49:11). The soundtrack enters with medium high strings, just before a cut to Anastasia, draped at Ivan's bedside, half turned away from us. Ivan is lying perfectly still, while Anastasia makes some hard-to-read movements, quickly reaching out to touch his hand and then slowly, theatrically withdrawing her hand, bowing her head in sorrow. Some horns introduce a bit of melody, three notes that add tension, over the drawn-out, slowly pulsing string chord.

This little passage exemplifies Brown's observation about the lack of closure in the score: the three notes prepare us for a fourth for resolution, but it doesn't come. Just before the backward axial cut, a tremolo sounds over the pulsing low strings that shifts the mood, foreshadowed by the horns, from sorrowful to watchful. And that shift is confirmed visually when the next shot shows Anastasia in a slightly different position, now sitting up a little straighter, as if listening. A louder low bass note sounds on the beat, drawing Anastasia to turn around toward the camera and move forward almost imperceptibly. Another, louder low bass note sounds, again, on the beat, as if prompting her to stand, which she does, looking tensely straight ahead. More strings introduce a new set of slowly unfolding, unmelodious chords just before a another axial cut back, for the boyars to start filing into the chamber. Anastasia stands after her moment alone with Ivan as hulking, nameless boyars follow Efrosinia and Vladimir into Ivan's bedchamber. The score is accented on the down beat, and those three bars of music feel ambiguous and weak, as if they were nothing more than background mood music, a function Eisenstein famously disdained but was not above using as parody. The conventional meter and lack of contrast make the score here transitory, preparatory, rather than emphatic, but it creates suspense. The contrast between the boyars' slow pace, Ivan's immobility, Anastasia's fearful stance, and the suspenseful slow chords feels tense: what next?

These four shots take only seven bars of music and about thirty seconds of screen time with no dialogue. They contain a lot more visual detail than I've included and Eisenstein's characteristic enjambment editing, which is crucial. But for all that, the emotions and information as well as the character motivation here are primarily carried by the music. Enjambment produces a foreshadowing effect that reinforces the score's primary mood, but pulsing and drawn-out strings and truncated, unresolved melodies create their own powerful sense of foreboding jutting into and overtaking sorrow and grief. The music in this introduction prepares us for the complicated polyphony to come by giving us precisely the right register of fear, expectation, and unresolved emotion.

Pulsing strings with the three-note gesture of tsarist grandeur resume just before another off-beat cut brings Efrosinia over to face Anastasia. They bow. Then Efrosinia makes an ambiguous half-bow forward movement that Anastasia interprets as a threat, moving protectively toward Ivan's body. The two women rise and turn away from one another, while a crescendo breaks in and seems to speak for them—anger, danger—and they mime conflict. After another couple of beats Ivan himself speaks. The first iteration of the six-note figure occurs just after he pronounces the order: "I'm dying . . . Kiss the cross to Dmitri," and the camera cuts to Vladimir and Efrosinia. This first sounding of the theme is a rare example of the start of the shot and the theme coinciding. It's not bricklaying, but it's right at the beginning. As the six notes play, Efrosinia pushes Vladimir forward, he looks back in fear, she pushes him some more. Halfway through the repetition of the theme, there's a cut back to Ivan, straining and shifting his head to the right, eyes wide open, as he wordlessly recognizes this challenge to his authority. Whatever doubts he had about his servitors' willingness to remain loyal to him are immediately confirmed. The musical passage, structured like a question and response, goes: conflict → tsarist order → challenge → realization.

The six-note figure here draws a line from Efrosinia to Vladimir to Ivan and back again. The third and fourth iterations of the theme underline the challenge. They accompany a repetition of the eye movements that connect Ivan to Vladimir to Efrosinia, while she still pushes from behind—or maybe Vladimir pulls back a little.[75] But while the third rendition is rhythmically aligned with movements, the fourth is entirely asynchronous rhythmically. The effect is unsettling: order gives way to disorder.

The fifth and sixth renditions emphasize Ivan's shattering realization that no one is following his command. These repetitions come after a few seconds of boyars ignoring Ivan's call to pledge allegiance to his son, then cut back to Ivan, dramatically thrown back against Anastasia in agony, repeating his order, which is turning into a plea: "Kiss the cross." Here it accompanies his distress at the boyars' rejection, but then he leaps to push back at them by rising up and speaking over the musical theme. Editing cuts break up the coordination of music and image, and the score draws a line from Ivan, who is speaking and moving throughout (actively if despairingly) to static close-ups of Dmitri and then the boyars, but this pair belongs to Ivan's reaction.

The seventh and eighth renderings come symmetrically between the first and second three pairs and mark a transition. Unlike any of the other repetitions, they occur together in one, uncut shot. That symmetry, however, is undermined by Ivan's speech, which is not synchronized with the music or by his body movement, which is highly erratic and dehumanized. The speech and the gravity of the situation seem to propel Ivan up from his deathbed, and he approaches the camera with arms outstretched and head back, like a horror-movie zombie cliché. The music itself slows down as he says that the dynasty must continue in order to protect Russia from its enemies—Tatars, Poles, and Livonians. He falls to his knees, then collapses on the floor. During this speech a different musical passage sounds, a repetition of six low bass notes. This is indeed a low moment for Ivan, but things get worse.

The theme plays for the ninth time just as Ivan reaches up from the floor to the first boyar he names, imploring: "Pavlitsky . . . Ivan." No longer in bed giving an order, the tsar is on the floor, pleading for his servitors' loyalty. This iteration of the six-note theme is cut before it ends to a medium shot of Ivan, arm outstretched but now in disappointment after Pavlitsky has turned away from him; then we hear number ten while watching Ivan. The shot again associates the theme directly with Ivan and with his response to the boyars' disloyalty. What began as an unsettling, unspoken, mimed conflict shifts to join its lyricism with the *pathos* of Ivan's loneliness. In contrast, the three-note melody between the repetitions of the theme are played with lower (and sometimes fewer) instruments, feeling like the ominous, threatening storm.

We hear the theme for the eleventh and twelfth times after Ivan rises up and throws himself on another boyar, "Torutan . . . Pronsky." The theme starts not at the cut to Pronsky but a beat later, after Ivan says his name and he looks away. The twelfth repetition comes as Ivan, increasingly desperate, turns around, with the last note coming after the cut to draw attention to what's coming next, the interaction with next boyar. In close-up, Ivan turns to the first of two Kolychevs, asking him to set an example for the other boyars. The Kolychevs are important because they are the relatives of Filipp, who will be executed by Ivan in Part II. Ivan will use their refusal to pledge their loyalty to him here to make an example of them. This is an important transitional moment, as the moving cuts stress. If Ivan was dismayed at the other boyars, he is shocked that Kolychev turns away from him. He leans back, still on his knees (spiraling back to images of Ivan the child alone in the dark), and we hear the transitional three-note suspenseful figure. At that moment Ivan stretches his head back and neck up, with beard extended in the often repeated, strangely exaggerated gesture that always denotes an impending change. Whispering now, he implores another Kolychev, not to "pledge allegiance," but "Why are you silent?"

There is a significant pause before the thirteenth iteration of the theme starts. After Ivan turns from Kolychev and pronounces "Kurletev," we don't hear it again until a second cut shows Ivan pleading, but now in the background of the shot and out of focus, with two large boyars in focus and turned toward us in the foreground. He calls out to "Funikov," who lumbers a few steps away before the thirteenth rendition of the theme even begins. Cut back to Ivan on the floor for the rest of thirteen and fourteen. At this point, halfway through the twenty-eight repetitions of the six-note figure, a major mood shift takes place—signaled by music, movement, and speech—and as

FIGURE 5.3 Deathbed, Part I: Ivan begging, defiant, dead?

Jacobs points out, the tempo and rhythm speed up here as well with a series of short shots.[76] Ivan seems to have suddenly revived completely, regaining strength, clarity, and determination. He damns the boyars and calls them traitors, rising up in sharp focus, with some disjunctive axial cutting to increasingly close close-ups that emphasize his resurrected energy. The soundtrack introduces loud horns that are neither plaintive nor sorrowful nor suspenseful but emphatic and threatening. Then Ivan stretches up and falls back on the bed, appearing to everyone to have died. Anastasia performs a stylized *Pietà* gesture cradling his foot, followed by a cut to Ivan's face, famously modeled on Holbein's portrait of Christ in His Tomb.[77] The theme returns here, at the end of the shot when it passes to Efrosinia, calling for the boyars to support her son, before cutting to a shot of Ivan's out-of-focus close-up.

In this first half of the musical scene, the six-note theme swirls around the room, not unlike a roaming camera eye or like one of the red pencil musical shapes of Eisenstein's *Nevsky* drawings. The accents draw a line from the conflict between the women, moving to Ivan's demand, then to his primary enemies' response, back to Ivan and Anastasia as Ivan realizes something is wrong. Then he gets up and the theme/line follows him from boyar to boyar, landing back on Ivan in despair, just before he rises up and then collapses as if dead. Visual cuts "move" the theme from character to character and propel the emotional and political narrative, and at the same time, their off-beat rhythm keeps the narrative dynamic from becoming static. Eisenstein wrote that this was not crude synchronization but interweaving of music and action.[78]

The six-note figure plays another fourteen times between Ivan's "death" and his resurrection. It is positioned with a similar pattern of symmetry and asymmetry, connecting shots across otherwise disruptive cuts and passing the "question and response" dynamics among the characters. The second fourteen, however, are less associated with the dynastic loyalty crisis than with the marital loyalty crisis. The first of the next fourteen repetitions plays over the close-up of the "dead" Ivan, two play during Efrosinia's scenes, but the other eleven are all Kurbsky's, often with Anastasia in the frame. The strong association of the six-note motif with Ivan and with political loyalty and betrayal makes its more diffuse uses after his "death" seem as if it carries Ivan himself, his crown and his mission, his voice and his all-seeing eye, into these shots even when he's not there physically. There is no music at all when Kurbsky returns to pledge allegiance to the tsar and kiss the cross or when a strange creaking sound makes every one turn around and we cut to Ivan and Anastasia entering through a tiny portal. The contrast between the scored shots and the lack of music during Kurbsky's dramatic and drawn-out pledge to Dmitri also signal a contrast between the complicated braiding of personal and political during the first part of the scene and Kurbsky's purely political, opportunistic pledge.

This analysis of a small thematic motif shows how Eisenstein used the editing of the soundtrack for semantic as well as purely structural or sensory-emotional purposes. The call and response of the first half of the scene associated this motif with Ivan's recognition of the opposition to his rule. Its oddly compelling and dissonant melody gives it a lot of versatility. It can sound movingly lyrical and disturbingly ominous with different instrumentation and synchronized with different images. Its assonant repetition in the second half then carries the associations we've made with Ivan's plight right into scenes that he haunts. In all these cases, the musical bridges that continue over cuts pass the motif from character to character as well as drawing attention to the apparent shifts in the balance of power taking place. The repetition of the motif—14 and 14—provides a structure, a landscape, that organizes the issues in this scene. In the first half, as it moves from Efrosinia and Vladimir to Anastasia and Ivan and then around the room to each of the boyars, it raises questions about all the possible permutations of personal and political power and betrayal by sketching all the possible lines of affection and animosity, selflessness and self-protection. Then in the second half when it moves with Kurbsky to Ivan and away from him, the questions of loyalty and betrayal become concentrated in him. The giant eye of the icon and Maliuta's eye, which we also see in these scenes, would have been enough to convey the feeling of surveillance, but the editing of this motif shows how Eisenstein intensified the feeling of an important piece of information that was better left unarticulated in words. The musical embodiment of the theme, passed across cuts from Ivan to Vladimir to Efrosinia and back again, or from the "dead" Ivan to Kurbsky to Anastasia, moves in time against the static images of Dmitri, for example, or the Giant Eye icon in a way that intensifies the narrative movement, the character complications, and the still inchoate feelings aroused by the unfolding conflicts.

In this scene, Ivan's inner conflict is depicted as balanced between two opposites: manipulative and vulnerable, powerful and vulnerable, living and dying. His servitors are offered a choice: Anastasia and Dmitri or Efrosinia and Vladimir, loyalty or betrayal, or a betrayal that could be seen as loyalty to a different ideology. The visual imagery also presents binaries: angels and demons, Christ and Antichrist, black and white. The musical cues provide another binary, with the repetition of paired melodies underlining the essential binary nature of Ivan's inner conflicts. When Ivan dies and comes back to life, he is changed. Having registered the betrayal of his closest servitors, he is propelled along his path toward manipulation, demagoguery, and revenge. But, Eisenstein tells us, for the moment Ivan accepts self-abasement so that the principle of one-man rule will succeed. Then in the next scene, he offers his disloyal friend Kurbsky a chance to escape his wrath (and prove his loyalty) by promoting him and sending him to the front.[79] In the sections below I discuss the ways camerawork and acting add voices to this polyphonic montage, activating all the senses synesthetically, tracing the spiraling biography, intensifying the *pathos* and the dialectical conflict until the out-of-body experience, *ekstasis*, changes Ivan, signaling a new stage of life for him.

The conflict between the women pantomimed in the deathbed scene comes to a head a few scenes later when Efrosinia poisons Anastasia (I: 1:14:10). Eisenstein's use of Prokofiev's score in this scene shows how he moves past the binary conflict of the deathbed to a more complicated contest that raises fundamental questions about political ethics. At the beginning of the scene the viewer is presented with a number of stark contrasts: Anastasia's and Efrosinia's qualities—light/dark, soft/stony, white/black, luxurious/austere—are associated with conventionally logical musical phrases: flowingly lyrical or harshly syncopated. As the scene progresses and loyalties are called into question, moral uncertainties multiply and at times the musical motifs underscore the reversals or suggest unspoken betrayals. In these narrative contexts, the visual and the musical cues add variations, increasing and decreasing in tempo and volume at the same time, moving up and down their scales both in conjunction with the narrative and against it, all of which has the desired effect of ratcheting up the emotional intensity. At the end of the scene, a number of musical and visual cues effect complete reversals, providing a momentary halt (or reverse movement) that makes the denouement all the more dramatic.

As it happens, this scene raises some of the most profound issues dramatized in *Ivan the Terrible* and the score contributes a sensory-emotional version of that narrative. What appears at the beginning as a clear-cut contrast between good and evil is considerably murkier a short five minutes later. Throughout *Ivan the Terrible*, we are repeatedly asked to consider whether and in what circumstances killing is justified. Both Ivan and his enemies justify murder on the grounds that they are acting in the name of some greater good. These political murders are sandwiched between scenes of warfare at the beginning and end of the film (in Kazan and Livonia, respectively), with their conventional, widely accepted justifications of killing bracketing more debatable political and moral justifications. But even in warfare, we write rules to keep our instinct for violence and vengeance in check, and Eisenstein's Ivan reproaches Kurbsky at Kazan for breaking those rules with unnecessary cruelty. Official Stalinist historiography claimed that Ivan's murder of his own people was justified because the boyars he attacked opposed the establishment of the Great Russian State, which was a historical necessity. Eisenstein was expected to conform to that argument, and on the surface, it appears as though he did. But in this struggle between Efrosinia and Anastasia, relatively early in what was to be a three-part epic, he already complicates the Stalinist political logic.

From the very first scene in which she appears, Efrosinia Staritskaia is Ivan's personal and political enemy. At the beginning of the poisoning scene, she is portrayed as unequivocally evil, a dark *sirin* hungrily watching Anastasia, lurking in the shadows, hiding below ground, scowling, stony, and harsh. It is no surprise that she poisons the tsar's wife, because she has already threatened to do so. What is a surprise is that her victim's innocence is called into question, contributing to her death, when Anastasia faints at the mention of Kurbsky's defeat and possible treason. That Ivan himself hands her the chalice that kills her further complicates the distribution of responsibility for Anastasia's death. In addition, when he threatens to take away the boyars' land, Ivan gives Efrosinia justification for acting against him. If this had occurred at the end of the film, it might be possible to argue that these were mild challenges to the film's moral regime. But they occur near enough to the beginning and mark some of the earliest steps in complicating the political morality of a film that only multiplies such complications as it progresses.

The music in this scene doesn't just reiterate these narrative elements. Its emotional qualities and the ways each phrase is positioned creates a nonverbal, sensory experience that embodies and furthers the moral complexity. After Ivan threatens to punish the boyars, Efrosinia begins to prepare the poisoned chalice, and she is associated with rhythmic, pulsating strings that strike harsh, low, and slightly syncopated beats (I: 1:17:28). The beats seem to slash through the air aggressively, their division of time knifing through space. A lyrical version of Ivan's power themes links him to Anastasia, restlessly lying in her bed, as Efrosinia watches her menacingly. But each of these musical themes is briefly associated with its darker or lighter opposite. This version of "seek in the villain where he is good" has the effect of linking enemies, casting doubt on innocence, and muddying what should have been clear moral and political positions. Eisenstein expected us to register this, even if not consciously. Ivan's lyrical, private "alone" leitmotif from the previous scene is echoed here in more ominous tones and briefly associated with Efrosinia. Her harsh slashing strings alternate with echoes of Ivan's lyrical theme most rapidly at the moment when the two characters are aligned visually as the chalice changes hands. Saintly Anastasia is scored with unambiguously descending notes. A tiny cello phrase of suspense or uncertainty is inserted when evil intention is becoming a deed and there's no turning back. At the only moment when it seems possible that the inevitable will be halted or reversed, Efrosinia gets a brief, against-type echo of Ivan's sweet lyrical theme (a musical reverse movement), but the harsh string beats resume almost immediately to mark the inexorable moral descent. Musical repetition and differentiation make Ivan truly and not just accidentally responsible for Anastasia's death, and that differentiates this poisoning from the poisoning of Ivan's mother. The first murder produced a pure and justifiable desire for revenge, but this time Efrosinia is driven to act against Ivan at least partially because the policies he initiated genuinely threaten her. In this scene Ivan is doubly culpable morally, both directly and indirectly responsible for Anastasia's death yet unable to take responsibility for his actions. Eisenstein links this scene with Maliuta's offer to kill the Kolychevs to keep Ivan's hands clean: "an act of Ivan's *will*. With Maliuta's *hands*. (Seems good. And the nudge from the poisoning of Anastasia is good, and the 'far-sightedness' of Fedka's blue eyes seeing the poisoning.)"[80] The reference to Fedka is to one more repetition of this scene's score that reinforces the lines of complicated responsibility and justification. A unique leitmotif belonging to Efrosinia-as-murderer appears here and only once again—when Ivan revisits Anastasia's bedchamber in Part II and Fedka shows him the chalice that contained the poison that Ivan himself handed to his wife. When Maliuta brings the chalice to Efrosinia under its cover with the invitation to the feast, it is accompanied by a different leitmotif, this one associated with another set of murders: the young Ivan's order to seize the boyar Andrei Shuisky, and Peter's murder of Vladimir. Each theme creates its own network of memories, intersecting with other networks of memory, visual image, and sound, constructing the polyphonic montage. From a political perspective, what matters is that Ivan's justifications all ring hollow in multiple, polyphonic ways by the end of Part II.

The doubled plot and the moral parallels and reversals in the sickbed and the chalice poisoning scenes are configured by the music and the ways it was edited in conjunction with visual and narrative elements to produce polyphonic montage and stimulate synesthesia. The dark, slashing strings; their alternation with lyrical passages (most of which disappear by Part II); the interplay of the music with the lighting, acting, and set design; and the linkage of the melodies as they rise and fall with our responses to ideas about movement all work together to create a multisensory montage image that translates sensory perception into ideas. That polyphonic sensory experience casts a shadow (or traces a shape or rises as a memory) on every political and personal justification for killing, but it does so without drawing attention to the divergence from the official narrative. The synesthesia allows us to register subtle shifts in the film's moral economy, but the number of polyphonic elements alone makes each scene too complicated to comprehend consciously while watching the film. Eisenstein counted on us to take them in intuitively, to register them in our bodies, to apprehend them prelogically, so that at some later point we can join that emotional, preverbal knowledge with our conscious intellectual perceptions. In this way, because music and visual image circumvent language, because of their very plasticity, they can "say" things that cannot be said directly and allow us to register them in our bodies.

In "The Music of Landscape" and "P-R-K-F-V," Eisenstein stressed the difference between mere coordination of sound and picture in conventional films and Prokofiev's ability to reproduce "the structural secret that emotionally expresses, above all, precisely that broad meaning of a phenomenon."[81] He says the same thing about the lighting and acting. Music tonally expresses what is inexpressible in words and "in the same way the changing figure of Ivan is expressed tonally though the film by the play of the actor's contour, the framing of the shot, and above all by the miracle of tonal photography of the cameraman Moskvin . . . the most refined *tonal nuances* of what I would call *intonations of light*, which Andrei Moskvin controls with such perfection."[82]

Andrei Moskvin and the Intonations of Light

Eisenstein went to a great deal of trouble to get Moskvin to film *Ivan the Terrible*. He contrived to postpone shooting (twice) when Moskvin was engaged on other projects. He negotiated with Kozintsev and Trauberg, the directors with whom Moskvin had worked for twenty years. And most difficult of all, as noted earlier, Eisenstein sidelined his own longtime cameraman, Eduard Tisse, the man Eisenstein once called "his eyes," knowing full well the grief and humiliation Tisse would suffer as a result. He kept Tisse employed and on the set, and Tisse shot the famous finale of Part I—the close-up of Ivan presiding above the snowy expanse as the people of Moscow came to beg him to return to rule over them—eight months after Eisenstein began working with Moskvin.

Eisenstein's insistence on working with Moskvin tells us more than is usually realized about what kind of film he wanted to make. Most authors assume that Eisenstein was unhappy with Tisse's work because his remarkable skills as a landscape photographer and his brilliant geometric compositions could not be adapted to the more "psychological" or "interior" profile the director wanted for *Ivan*. This is too simplistic. First of all, as Philip Cavendish has demonstrated, *Old and New* and the surviving frames of *Bezhin Meadow* showed that Tisse had developed an exceptionally sensitive capacity to convey psychological depth with lighting and facial close-ups.[83] Numerous cameramen, including Tisse, had developed deep-focus spatial composition as well as the kind of wide-angle lens foreshortening Eisenstein wanted for close-ups in the late 1930s. Yakov Butovsky, Moskvin's biographer, argues that while Tisse excelled at making "single-meaning shots" that Eisenstein could then edit together into complex montage sequences, Moskvin could foresee the complexity Eisenstein wanted within the shot and in the sequences of shots.[84] Butovsky calls this greater psychological depth and a "monumental

FIGURE 5.4 Moskvin and Eisenstein on set. RGALI, 1923/2/132/12. Used with permission.

lyricism," but while those are the products of Moskvin's contribution to the composition of polyphonic montage, of "ecstatic composition," they don't exhaust Moskvin's contributions or Eisenstein's ambitions. Eisenstein was looking for more than individual psychological depth; he was looking for an entirely different style.

Deep space, like the Gothic cathedral, the Chinese vertical landscape scroll, and Piranesi's prison drawings, creates a pulling-pushing eyeline deep into the farthest spaces and a simultaneous awareness of the layers of foreground that construct depth. Eisenstein made the most of this effect by moving actors toward and away from the camera and by editing sequences of stable shots that move in toward actors on a straight line, which Eisenstein called "perspective reduction" and Bordwell analyzes as the "axial cut."[85] Bordwell rightly sees the axial cut as a central visual device in *Ivan*; a device that unifies the filmic experience, works to bring the viewer into the action on screen, and intensifies drama and *pathos*. It is also one of the devices that ties composition to content and links the worlds on and off the screen. Eisenstein and Moskvin use cutting and lighting to "interrupt" the eye's smooth perspectival advance into depth and slightly shift perspective and scale to replicate the concept of the explosion of *ekstasis* and the leap into a new quality. This slight shift then replicates the process of change in all its forms, along the same lines as Piranesi's prisons. It is a fugue of visual theme and variations in and of itself, and it forms a variation on the theme of *ekstasis*.[86] Axial cutting of close-ups and characters rushing to and from the camera on the lens axis (or slightly off the axis, as is most common) is another variation of the theme that visually, dynamically replicates the spiral process of biological and historical change discussed in previous chapters. It also exaggerates, and in that way highlights, the transitions that were so central to Eisenstein's investigation of artistic practices—the transformation of idea into cinematic depiction and then into montage image inside the body of the viewer. As the camera closes in on Maliuta in axial steps (I: 48:49) or as Efrosinia rushes straight into the immobile camera (II: 30:54), the artist reaches through the screen to grab us.

In "P-R-K-F-V," Eisenstein wrote:

> the structure of the separate pieces shot for any scene is not accidental. . . . If a piece is a truly "montage" one, that is, not disconnected but meant to produce an image together with other pieces, it will, at the very moment it is shot, be infused with elements which characterize its inner essence and at the same time contain the seeds of the structure most suited for the fullest possible revelation of this essence in the finished compositional form.[87]

Moskvin understood the lighting and movement necessary to produce the multipoint polyphonic montage within the frame that Eisenstein wanted for *Ivan the Terrible.*

There is evidence that Eisenstein was already thinking about trying to hire Moskvin when he was still writing *Ivan's* screenplay. Butovsky reports that in the spring of 1941, when Eisenstein became artistic director of Mosfilm, he invited a number of filmmakers associated with the 1920s experimental collective FEKS to transfer to Moscow from Lenfilm.[88] "Come," he wrote, "we will do great, serious, and real things."[89] The Leningraders, exemplified by Kozintsev and Trauberg and their cinematographer Moskvin, were known for their radically nonlinear storytelling and visually carnivalesque style. Moskvin, in particular, was known for innovative, experimental play with light and space, for lyrical, dreamlike use of smoke and soft focus, and for extreme low-key lighting and high-contrast chiaroscuro.[90] If *Ivan the Terrible* looks like any other Soviet film, it looks most like the FEKS classics directed by Kozintsev and Trauberg and shot by Moskvin in the 1920s.

Tisse himself confirmed that Eisenstein wanted to return to the style of the 1920s in the bitter comment that he made to Vsevolod Vishnevsky after the war. Tisse had just returned from ten months in Yugoslavia but, Vishnevsky notes by way of introducing Tisse's reflection, he was still "internally suffering from the pain of his split with Eisenstein."

> I always tried to restrain Eisen somewhat. He is a real inferno. He would send mocking or insolent notes to the administration over trifles. I would intercept them from the couriers and the group's delivery boys . . .—Eisen would cool off. . . .—I tried to protect him from deviations . . . We worked for many years . . .—In evacuation Eisen fell under the influence of the Leningraders—Ermler, the cameraman Moskvin, Trauberg and others. They flattered and worshipped him and dragged Eisen into eccentrism, play with actors and so on. . . .—But Eisen wanted to "prove himself"—The result is *Ivan the Terrible.* When I read the screenplay, I said, "Great. Submit it to the Committee but don't produce it." . . . That's exactly what I said. . . . Then shooting began . . .—I did what I do. Eisen demanded "natural light," that is, candlelight, icon lamps, candelabra . . . He immersed the whole thing in a tone of mysticism . . . I argued, refused . . . I saw that things were going awry . . . the cameraman Moskvin was hired . . .—And now see where Part II has ended up . . . It was all predictable in a "certain" light: the anguish, the lopped-off heads . . .[91]

Tisse, like Elena Telesheva, partially blamed Eisenstein's friends for his regression. They both thought he was too narcissistic to resist their flattery, and they both wanted to protect him from what they considered his worst instincts: his willingness to defy authority and convention. But in fact Eisenstein had never given up experimenting with cinematic form and intended to resurrect the more radical experimentalism and the defiantly disruptive artistic practices he had enjoyed in the 1920s. To that end, he needed people around him who were less conventional, less cautious, and more willing to accompany him on the risky path he had chosen.

Eisenstein pursued Moskvin not only as the cinematographer he wanted but also as a working companion. Butovsky says that Eisenstein was able to talk to Moskvin with an unusual degree of openness about *Ivan*, *Method*, and other matters of art and theory on their long walks around town. And although Moskvin was taciturn with just about everyone else, he was uncharacteristically talkative with Eisenstein, and he had a wickedly ironic sense of humor, which would have suited Eisenstein perfectly.[92] They trusted each other, enjoyed each other's company and conversation, and were both willing to risk making *Ivan*. According to Trauberg, Moskvin was ready to work on *Ivan* by the fall of 1942 but insisted that Eisenstein work things out with Kozintsev, Trauberg, and especially Tisse, before he started.

Moskvin also took some professional risks by going to work for Eisenstein. Having enjoyed extraordinary creative independence as cinematographer for Kozintsev and Trauberg, he nonetheless understood that his job as Eisenstein's cameraman was to bring the director's vision to the screen. Like Prokofiev, Moskvin apparently found that role capacious enough. In preparation for shooting, he devotedly studied Eisenstein's innumerable drawings and engaged in long conversations with Eisenstein about technical and other matters.

An entry in Eisenstein's diary written in November 1943, about six months into the shooting in Alma Ata, shows what kind of instructions Eisenstein gave Moskvin and how his "magical hands" contributed to Eisenstein's thinking about montage. The entry appears to be the draft of a note or letter Eisenstein was writing to Moskvin, summarizing and expanding on a long conversation they had had about fundamental theoretical and technical issues. It begins: *"Do you remember [Souvenez-vous]* that gray and cold morning, when, after the shoot, we sat at my place, ourselves gray with fatigue and shivering from cold. From 6:30 til 9:30 in the morning we drank coffee and I tormented you with questions—where did ideas about method come from—through the drama of Ivan to the systematization of problems of lighting."[93] The rest of the entry gives Eisenstein's ruminating answers to his own questions; his attempt to link the "drama of Ivan" with what he has learned from Moskvin's mastery of light, and finally with his own developing thoughts about polyphonic montage and dialectics.

He begins with a series of typically obscure and elaborate metaphors for his own way of thinking about the structure of things, in this case drawn from Pushkin's *Boris Godunov*. First: "when the shadow of Ivan adopted me, it snuck up on me. . . . But let's move on from pretenders [*samozvanstvo*], the quote from his speech [in *Boris Godunov*] to 'those who are called' [*samo-pri-zvanstvo*]. Dramatists don't appear out of thin air, or out of ardor."[94] In other words, passion and vision—ardor—are not enough. Artists can't be imposters, they're people with a calling, but even so if they want to make the equivalent of a cannon—if they want to materialize their ideas and feelings about a subject—they need a system, science, or as he preferred to put it, a method. He goes on to say that one also needs a detailed, curious, analytical mind, the kind of mind that enjoys things like twenty-kopeck brochures about astronomy, biology, physics, as Eisenstein himself did.[95] This note gives us further evidence that what preoccupied Eisenstein at this stage was understanding the mechanics of the process of making the artist's "relationship to the subject" visible on the screen as a conduit to the viewer's sensory-emotional and intellectual perception: to make a cannon, you can't just "take a long hole and put metal around it."[96]

He continues with what seems at first to be an unrelated thought: "Let's be humble in spirit [*budem nishchim dukhom*]." This biblical phrase had a specific analytical meaning for Eisenstein. As he later wrote in *Nonindifferent Nature*, "you begin to worship even more the great artist whose greatness lies in humility: not in overcoming nature, but in worshipping it." In *Nonindifferent Nature*, that artistic humility was represented by the painter Eugène Delacroix, who treated nature as his ABC, from which he drew all the elements he included in his paintings, and by Vincent Van Gogh, whose every bridge and tree, no matter how outlandishly colored, could be found in his natural surroundings, according to Eisenstein, and above all by ancient Chinese painters, whose artificially composed landscapes, seeming so nonrealistic, were "learned: from nature itself."[97]

The entry's final metaphor for this style of analysis comes directly from Eisenstein's experience working with historical documents on *Ivan the Terrible*: "*And how* at times they bring to life questions of lighting. For example, <u>treatment of history</u> corresponds (apparently) with our treatment of nature and those elements of *nonverity* that create *verisimilitude* [*la vraisemblance*]."[98] Eisenstein drew on historical sources in the same way that Van Gogh could paint bright yellow trees. He felt free to alter the record to create intuitive verisimilitude and insight, but what he created had to correspond to history in the same way that

Van Gogh's yellow tree could be found in nature (at a certain time of day, in a certain light).[99] The artist has to be able to see appearances and represent them in a way that they call to mind the natural essence of the thing.

These wide-ranging references are all a prelude to showing how a series of correspondences are analogous to Moskvin's lighting practices: between nature and art, history and art, good and evil, the sixteenth and twentieth centuries, interior and exterior, and character and plot. The same problems Eisenstein has to solve to create the complex character of Ivan and to devise a depiction that will produce an experience of ecstatic transcendence and access to meaning for the audience watching *Ivan* are problems for lighting, which he needs Moskvin to solve. Eisenstein was telling Moskvin that in the same way that Van Gogh drew from landscape and he drew from historical sources to construct a portrait of Ivan that is both a-historical and deeply authentically insightful about history, Moskvin is to draw on real faces and architectural forms and light them in ways that create effects that appear unreal, like yellow trees, that speak directly to viewers, emotionally and intellectually.

The diary text goes on to cite specific examples from *Ivan the Terrible*. Each one contains conflicts or contradictions that become increasingly complex and intense as they move from an external to an internal setting. The first historical issue is power, in particular the *morality* of power: the "moral exchange: what is good and what is bad (in that day), and within this, what of the history of the sixteenth century is applicable to the present."[100] The dialectic acquires a historical layer: comparative political morality.

He then portrayed Ivan in explicitly (if reductive) Nietzschean terms. In relation to power, Ivan is a "positive" figure—nonegotistical and superpersonal, while those around him (the other characters who represent various internal conflicts within Ivan, various alternatives to Ivan's persona) are "negative." In the narrative of the film this distinction between Ivan, on one hand, and his enemies and entourage, on the other, begins as a set of sharp external conflicts, which gradually "fade" as the conflicts become increasingly internalized. "Is this not," Eisenstein then asks, "the key to the principle of lighting the establishing shot [or medium shot], moving with increasing complexity toward the principle of the portrait?"[101] Here he uses another analogy: "Character and plot—are these not analogous to lighting of a character—the formula: face + application of effect (candles, sunlight, etc.). The revelation stage in *Webster* and *Commedia dell'arte*. Their <u>true</u> reciprocal (but not <u>linked</u>) effect, rather—mutually determining [*vzaimoopredelenie*]."[102]

Here there is no simple, mechanical link between lighting and character or effect and persona—they create each other or determine each other only through reciprocal effects, like the literal exchange of a mask. We have seen this construction in the way Eisenstein composed Ivan's character through weaving his fugue. Ivan's inner divisions are externalized to be represented by conflicts with other characters, through which the internal conflicts are intensified and deepened, resulting in an increasingly complex portrait. The dialectic is by no means sublimated by Ivan's political and narrative dominance; rather his power (and his fatal weaknesses) are both constructed through multiple, intertwined dialectical processes, depicted narratively and visually, with light. And introducing another level of complexity, not only do the exterior, plastic, graphic visual and the interior, moral, emotional create each other and determine each other, but, returning to Ivan's "shadow self," the "shadow side of Ivan's image," that relationship between face and lighting effect has a moral dimension: "Is this not 'looking for evil where one sees good,' and vice versa."[103] As examples, Eisenstein cites "Ivan's *tours de force*—Volynets, the good informer" (Petr Volynets is the assassin who saves Ivan by killing Vladimir, mistaking him for Ivan); "the 'acquittal' of Kolychev" (which is followed by Ivan allowing Maliuta to execute the Kolychev relatives, because technically Ivan's own hands will not be bloodied by their deaths); and "Vladimir's guilt and fall, without which emotionally he could not be 'killed.' Balance."[104] Ivan is saved—by accident, Ivan is innocent—by a technicality, Ivan is exonerated—because his victim is guilty too. This is a revealing kind of "balance."

Here the diary entry ends. Eisenstein has drawn the analogies between lighting and character and plot development, and between lighting effects and the development of his own thinking about contradictions of character. He has described ideas about lighting that will be able to bring out the dialectical montage structure of Ivan's biography and dramatize Eisenstein's exceptionally delicate political morality. But he isn't finished with the subject. In the chapter "The Music of Landscape," Eisenstein explained some of the changes taking place as his conceptualization of montage developed, as he put it, in the "thick of production practices of *Ivan the Terrible*":

> [A] new stage of audiovisual montage, I believe, entered with the sign of an increasing fusion and harmony of montage and polyphony. . . . An increasing number of voices, an increasing number of nuances enter into the primitive polyphonic scheme, and planal interrelationships are replaced by interrelationships of chiaroscuro. . . . The changing figure of Ivan is expressed tonally throughout the film by the play of the actor's contour, the framing of the shot and above all by the miracle of tonal photography of the cameraman Moskvin [who] introduced all those nuances of light that must echo, from episode to episode, both the emotional mood of a scene and the emotional state of the tsar-protagonist.[105]

Based on detailed analysis of lighting and camerawork in several key scenes, Butovsky shows how Moskvin succeeded in translating Eisenstein's visual conception for the film into lighting practices. Butovsky effectively shows Moskvin's ability to capture the "polyphony" of Eisenstein's thinking, but like technical studies of music in *Ivan*, Butovsky stops short of the semantic connections between lighting and meaning.

Moskvin made his mark on the multipoint polyphonic montage that Eisenstein used as the organizing framework for constructing his portrait of Ivan by using wide-angle lenses both to create spaciousness and distort objects closest to the camera, and with lighting setups to create dynamically shifting chiaroscuro. Moskvin used lighting and shot composition, including the creation of the film's justly famous shadows, to depict the complexity of Ivan's inner divisions and outer conflicts polyphonically. He varied lighting and focus to depict what Eisenstein called ecstatic composition: deep space, wide-angle-lens distorted close-ups, low-key lighting and high-contrast chiaroscuro, and dynamic, isolated spotlighting. Each of these, of course, had multiple uses and effects, which themselves multiplied when joined with sound, editing, acting, and mise-en-scène. Let's look at some examples of Moskvin's contribution to the structures of Eisenstein's polyphonic montage by using lighting "intonation" to bring out the internal conflicts of any given shot.

Moskvin used lighting to dramatize the increasing dialectical tensions intended to produce *pathos* and lead to *ekstasis* in several ways, all of which involve variations on structures of friction. The accumulation of different lighting schemes that are all still based on the same ecstatic principle give the film both its strangeness and its unity. Extreme close-ups in front of deep space, for example, soft focus schemes shifting among characters, alterations in lighting between shots, facial shadows that combine and juxtapose conventions (like horror film lighting from below and soft focus side-lighting for reflective dreaminess) or combine effects like the jagged, lacy lighting of Fedka's face looking up adoringly at Ivan when we first meet him at Anastasia's coffin (I: 1:25:32). Butovsky calls this "contingent" lighting that changes from shot to shot and during shots, so that shadows, for example, both reveal and conceal.[106]

Focusing only on spatial constructions, we can see Moskvin's use of lighting and camera position to effect dialectical ecstatic construction in The Fiery Furnace scene (II: 32:44). Through an incremental process of visually narrowing and intensifying dialectical conflict in spatial relationships, Moskvin takes us to that profound moment of transformation when Ivan says "I will be what you say I am. I will be Terrible." The scene begins with complex, visually full, long shots of various groups of people inside the cathedral intercut primarily with medium shots of characters, then medium shots are intercut with close-ups until close-ups are intercut with extreme close-ups. The long and medium shots of the cathedral replicate Piranesi-like effects of what Eisenstein called claustrophobic spaciousness. Frescoes covering every inch of wall space, arched chambers receding deep into the background, and crowds of people crammed into the floor space all make the large hall of the cathedral seem both enormous and confining at the same time.[107]

Geometrically organized mise-en-scène in the long and medium shots is also intercut with shots focusing on more organic subjects—contoured faces and clothing. For example, medium shots of the boy martyrs place them against a background of geometrically symmetrical rounded arches and angled rays of light descending in straight lines from the windows. In contrast, faces are lighted from numerous sources, including spots of candlelight and firelight that emphasize the flickering chiaroscuro lines of contrast between light and dark folds of cloth and skin. Midway into the scene, the contrast between light and dark becomes increasingly pronounced and dramatic as Ivan, in his black hooded cleric's robe, bows in ritual supplication to Filipp, who is all in white. Ivan's performance of subordination to Filipp mutates into a threat, and Filipp's stubborn refusal becomes angry resistance and accusation in a low-angle shot as they lean in to each other head to head. Their heightened emotion and black-white tension is transferred to their audience in the cathedral as onlookers stop chatting and freeze in fear. Close-ups are shot from increasingly sharply canted angles, adding to the tension. When the conflict is close to a breaking point, visually and thematically, the camera cuts from the confrontation between Ivan and Filipp to the little boy who points at Ivan and laughs. Just then, for less than a second, between shots of the boy's two lines—"there's the terrible pagan tsar," and "Mama, look, there's the terrible, pagan tsar"—Eisenstein gives us a visual image of pure dialectical synthesis (II: 40:28). After facing off against each other in increasingly tense conflict, shot in profile, black *against* white, Ivan and Filipp turn in unison to face the boy's voice. They line up next to each other, side by side, black *and* white, leaning backward together at the same slight angle, a synchronized reverse movement. This momentary "synthesis" is then shattered by Ivan's recognition of Efrosinia's guilt and his dramatic transformation: "I will be who you say I am. I will be Terrible."

Moskvin's primary lighting scheme combined low-key, high-contrast lighting with the ubiquitous shadowing patterns. A few scenes are lighted more naturalistically, especially the outdoor shots done by Tisse—in Kazan and Alexandrova, but also the Golden Hall, where young Ivan sits on the throne and where Ivan later confronts Filipp. There polyphonic montage is produced by the visual patterns within the shot: snaking lines of people, the wide-angle close-up distortion of Ivan's head, and matching lines of bodies and architecture, for example.

Low-key and high contrast are conventions used in film noir and horror films because they produce unnatural effects, especially by partially obscuring the space behind characters or drawing on conventions of light as "good" and dark as "evil." Moskvin excelled at using these effects to both create and challenge conventional meanings—"'looking for evil where one sees good,' and vice versa"—in character and plot. Extreme contrast between light and dark, or black and white, divide up the picture plane and draw attention to the contours of the object or face in ways that dehumanize faces and animate objects: a face becomes no more than a canvas for abstract patterning, and an object takes on the organic qualities of a breathing body. Isolating highly lighted figures literally creates multiple visual focal points. Spots of candlelight add to that effect and flickering firelight, or lighting that suggests flames, provides tonal mood-shifting accents. Critical attention to the large shadows in Ivan's stateroom in Part I has obscured Moskvin's ingenious use of shadowing throughout the rest of the film to create striking shot compositions and character studies. Light from natural sources and strong lighting on facial contours represent the shifting inner divisions Eisenstein wanted to bring out. Another dramatic use of shadowing occurs just as Ivan prepares to greet the Muscovite people who have come to Alexandrova to recall him to rule. First we see visual cues of an earlier moment, of conflict between his public and private roles just before Anastasia was poisoned. In a dark hall, now sitting in a throne, Ivan shares a moment of natural affection with Maliuta; then Nepeia, who was sent on his mission to England in the earlier scene, returns to report his success. Ivan rises to reassert his role as tsar, and at that moment (I: 1:32:51), just as he dons his fur coat, a door opens and Ivan is surrounded by a pattern of crosses made by shadows appearing on the wall behind him: projecting both power and imprisonment, his new freedom and new constraints.

Moskvin's camera is exceptionally immobile in *Ivan*. I counted only twenty-six shots in the entire three hours of *Ivan*, Parts I and II, that are panning or tracking shots, less than 2 percent of the total number of shots.[108] Typically, movement takes place in front of a stable camera, and a large number of shots are close-ups of faces and objects. Camera immobility is one source of the peculiar tension in *Ivan* between stasis and dynamism, a favorite kind of revealing contradiction that mimics Ivan's inner conflicts, just as moments of comedy deepen our sense of the tragic. As in all Eisenstein films, editing provides a great deal of the dynamism in *Ivan*. There is not a single moving camera shot during The Dance of the Oprichniki, for example—a scene of unrelenting, frenzied movement, interrupted only occasionally by shots of Ivan seducing the drunk Vladimir. Even in these shots of Ivan and Vladimir sitting at the banquet table, out-of-focus figures move incessantly behind them, dance music continues, lighting flickers across the actors' faces, and the camera alters its point of view between shots (II: 56:07). The swirling, swaying, running, and jumping of the oprichniki is polyphonically intensified by cutting, camera angle, and changing camera placement as well as music, lyrics, and the now complex networks of meaningful associations. Interrupting the freeform swirling with a stagey line dance combines visual dialectic (swirling and lining up) with the kind of comic relief that draws attention to the violence and brutality of the song lyrics.

Given the infrequent use of tracking and panning, it is worth pausing to look at the moments they do appear. In Part I, there are only five tracking shots and one pan. The first two are relatively conventional: a high-to-low crane shot descends to follow Metropolitan Pimen entering the cathedral for The Coronation and then continues down to let Ivan enter the shot from the other direction. The shot locates Ivan as the central figure within the huge space of the cathedral (I: 4:26).[109] Another crane down starts the next scene, again from on high, to show Ivan and Anastasia in their ritualized wedding kiss (I: 13:55). The third high-to-low shot opens the mourning scene back in the cathedral, slowly revealing Anastasia in her coffin (I: 1:19:49). The last scene of Part I begins with a tracking shot that approaches Ivan, now in retreat at Alexandrova, head down in uncertainty and despair as he waits for the people to recall him to rule (I: 1:31:38). In all four cases, the moving camera lands on a static tableau. It is impossible to know how this last unusual shot at Alexandrova was meant to be used because it directly follows the deleted scene of The Oath. In the scenario, there is a moment at the end of The Oath, where Ivan:

Looms like a black shadow
Not listening to the oath
Lost in thought
Examining his thin fingers.[110]

Each of these four, relatively lengthy shots retards the action and introduces a new scene; each acts as a kind of establishing shot. Each also depicts a moment when Ivan's interior experience is just about to give way to a transformational public performance: coronation, wedding, funeral and recommittment to the state, and recall and reassertion of power. Each therefore acts like the reverse movement that emphasizes the main movement to come and initiates transformation with accentuated movement.

FIGURE 5.5   Lost in thought. RGALI. 1923/2/137/11. Used with permission.

FIGURE 5.6   The last rites

The other two mobile camera shots occur in the deathbed scene in Part I. As Ivan begins actively begging for boyar support, a dolly back shot pulls Ivan with it toward one of the boyars, the initiation of another moment of profound revelation. The panning shot at the beginning of that scene is the oddest of all: a disorienting, quick lateral pan left to Ivan's bed from the priests singing over the Book of Gospels just before giving him the last rites (I: 45:29). The pan interrupts one of the most strikingly beautiful shot sequences in the film. The priests stand in a circle in a pitch black room, brightly lighted from the center, as if they were praying to the very word of God (who is, however, located below them). Three forward axial cuts come to rest on Pimen alone surrounded by black-shadowed figures, brilliantly lit.

The pan occurs between the second and third axial cuts, both reminding us of Ivan's presence and foreshadowing his absence after death. In this scene Ivan is poised on the brink of life and death, choices to be made for good and evil, a return from the dead as Christ and/or Lucifer. He is about to face the first open opposition to his rule. This brief, unusual panning shot gestures toward the moment's transitional significance.

In the remainder of the film, all moving camera shots concentrate on asser-tions of Ivan's power and what Eisenstein called "the bloody epic"—Ivan's murder of boyars. The Prologue opens with a close-up of young Ivan sitting alone in the dark and a dolly back from Ivan to reveal the womb-ish dark hall (II: 10:59). The Prologue closes with a pan upward as young Ivan rises to declare that he will rule without the boyars, "I will be Tsar," and tracks in to an extreme close-up of his sweet, uncertain, but assertive face (II: 17:12). A full five panning shots occur in the scene where Maliuta persuades Ivan to execute the Kolychevs and where Ivan then rises to ask "By what right do you judge, Tsar Ivan?" (II: 21:31) Two more appear in the execution scene: a tiny pan on the Kolychev neck (II: 28:51) and then an excruciatingly slow pan right as Ivan approaches the corpses, stops, points, and says "Too few!" (II: 28:54) There is another tiny pan, which comes when Pimen is trying to persuade Filipp to take revenge on Ivan, just when he says he should be excommunicated (II: 30:31). Another combination of five plus two moving camera shots appears during the next major discussion of violence: Efrosinia's attempted assassina-tion of Ivan. After Efrosinia sings her creepy lullaby, the first three panning shots show Vladimir's horrified response to Efrosinia's plan: first he shrieks when he realizes that Efrosina expects him to assassinate Ivan (II: 48:53); then when she explains that Peter will be doing the bloody deed for him, Vladimir says he will still feel guilty every time he sees Peter (II: 50:10); and finally he reacts with horror when Efrosinia explains that he won't have to feel guilty for long because they will have Peter killed after he assassinates Ivan (II: 50:30).

There are two more shots when Maliuta enters to invite Vladimir to Ivan's feast: when Efrosinia and Vladimir react to the door opening—they make a small reverse movement before the camera tracks back from the extreme closeup (II: 51:36)—and when she takes the chalice and sets her plan in motion (II: 52:55). A tracking shot follows Vladimir's procession through the cathedral to his death (II: 1:11:22); and a quick pan greets him from what looks like Peter's point of view (II: 1:11:51). There are only two other tracking shots in the film: one greets Ivan as he reenters the Golden Hall on his return to Moscow; and the other tracks in on the three boy martyrs in The Fiery Furnace just as they sing, "You will see a great miracle now," predicting—incorrectly—that the Earthly Lord, Ivan, will be chastised by the Heavenly Lord, God, through his servant, Filipp.

The concentration of these uncommon shots on the two scenes where murder (of the boyars and of Vladimir) is deviously plotted, morally resisted, and then enacted creates two related networks of images. The first network links moments when the fundamental moral question of the film is raised: when is murder justified? The second creates a network of references to Ivan's assertion of power as tsar beginning in The Prologue. Together these tracking and panning shots link murder and power, but murder doesn't justify power in these scenes; it protects Ivan's power from challenge. In Eisenstein's *Ivan*, murder is an instrument of power, not its justification.

Nikolai Cherkasov and the Determining Gesture

Eisenstein has an undeserved reputation for not caring about actors, for treating them like so much furniture. It's true that he required actors to work long hours, make unnatural movements, and hold uncomfortable poses, but it's not true that he didn't care about them or their human and emotional contributions to his films. Nor is it true that he didn't care about the inner, psychological life of his characters. In fact, Eisenstein saw the external physical gesture and internal thought and emotion to be integrally connected, and he saw his role as a director not only in purely technical or physical terms but as someone who had to "crawl into" and "crawl out of" the characters' personas and the actors' individual psyches. He thought that this kind of physical and psychological connection between director and actor was necessary for transforming his ideas and feelings into concrete physical acts.[111] Cherkasov famously complained about the difficulties Eisenstein inflicted on him when filming *Ivan the Terrible*, forcing him into contorted positions and movements. But Cherkasov credited Eisenstein with significantly broadening his view of the actor's craft, giving him a better sense of movement in space, and in general enriching his technical abilities as an actor.[112] He also wrote that Eisenstein, "infected with his own stubborn confidence, compelled us to believe in him, and we often followed along, captivated by his enthusiasm."[113] In fact, given how seriously he took the process of acting, how much he wrote about acting and actors, and given how much he liked many of the actors he knew and how much they admired and liked him, it's an odd reputation, and one that Naum Kleiman first challenged in 1968.[114] Its endurance probably has more to do with one's view of the modernist film style that gave elevated roles to set design, objects, lighting, and music equivalent to the roles of human actors, rather than the acting per se.

Acting figures in almost all of Eisenstein's writing. It was an important component of his proposed course in directing and his teaching. He also wrote about specific actors, and they wrote about him. The memoirs and interviews with those who played roles in *Ivan* form a core source on Eisenstein as a director. Like sound and color and light, he began to see the actor's movement as a significant component in creating the meaningful experience of viewing dramatic arts, therefore acting holds a prominent place in *Method* and *Nonindifferent Nature* as well.[115]

Eisenstein's early writing on acting is worth examining to place the subject in the overall trajectory of his theory and practice. As is well known, approaches to acting in the twentieth century have been divided between those who believe that feeling originates in the body and is best conveyed by movement, contour, and pose and those who believe that feeling is rooted in the psyche, and therefore a character is best inhabited by an actor who can tap into relevant memories, experience, and other psychological resources. In Russia, these positions were associated with Vsevolod Meyerhold and Konstantin Stanislavsky, respectively. As is also well known, Stanislavsky's psychological model has been far more influential in mainstream theater and film acting all over the world. Eisenstein, however, like much of the 1920s avant garde, fell firmly in the Meyerhold camp, with his emphasis on the body moving in space. Unlike many of his Constructivist contemporaries, however, he never dismissed feeling. This is an important corrective: Eisenstein didn't discover emotions in 1929 amid the general rise of interest in *pathos*, feeling was there at the beginning: the body is a machine, but its actions are stimulated by instincts and emotions. "The question here is one of approach. Just as there is a back door and front door, one can reach the unity of psychological and motor phenomena by one staircase, or one can come at it from the other side."[116] In practice, though, the body came first. Eisenstein didn't ignore the emotional and psychological, but he was known to mock efforts by Stanislavsky-trained actors who sought their characters' interior emotional core (*zerno*). As Pavel Kadochnikov remembered, Eisenstein would have lengthy conversations with the actors about the intellectual and emotional profile of their characters, but he would elicit the psychologically meaningful through physical pose and body movement.[117] He was not alone in his effort to understand the intersection of body, mind, feeling, and sensation in Russia in the 1920s. But those ideas remained a major preoccupation for him throughout his career, even when, as Widdis shows, Soviet Socialist Realist cultural ideology shifted its valorization of the body to prioritizing the psychological.[118]

Much of Eisenstein's early writing on acting was inspired by his encounter with Jean d'Udine, whose work was translated into Russian in the 1910s by Sergei Volkonsky, who also popularized the works of Émile-Jacques Dalcroze and François Delsarte, foundational thinkers for the entire Russian performing arts avant garde.[119] Writing retrospectively in 1939–1940, Eisenstein says d'Udine gave him two sets of ideas in the 1920s, both of which still interested him: synesthesia and gesture. He saw gesture as "that very originary embryo of expressive form, in which emotion is poured," and in which audiovisual synesthesia could be embodied.[120] In 1923, Meyerhold asked Eisenstein to write an article explaining his school of "expressive movement." The article, co-authored with Sergei Tretyakov, remained unpublished, but part of it found its way into the 1924 "Montage of Film Attractions" (also unpublished at the time), and many of its precepts found their way into his teaching and writing in the mid-1930s. Like everyone else in the theatrical avant garde, Eisenstein studied Delsarte and Dalcroze,[121] but it was Rudoph Bode and Ludwig Klages who provided him with a typology of physical movements and a set of psychological ideas that he would spend the rest of his life developing. In the 1923 essay, the authors adapted Klages's and Bode's theories of movement, which were physiological and psychological, to theatrical performance. Bode believed that each body movement was the result of both unconscious and conscious impulses. Instincts and reflexes were as important in producing movement as consciousness and will.[122] Eisenstein and Tretyakov were attracted to Bode's understanding of fundamental physical conflicts between, for example, the pull of gravity and the body's resistance to gravity, and the tension between the body's center of gravity and its extremities. Like Meyerhold and many others writing about movement and performance in Russia in the 1920s, their primary goal was understanding and reproducing movements that would arouse reflexological, sensory-emotional responses in their spectators. Their view of acting as linking feeling and physiology was also based on their reading of James's counterintuitive thoughts about the primacy of the body, often paraphrased as: we do not cry because we are sad, we're sad because we cry. But they saw that arousal was possible only when actors fully embodied the tensions between conscious motivation and unconscious impulse.[123] For Eisenstein, the tension between opposing impulses was key. Oksana Bulgakowa has recently shown that the underlying dualism Eisenstein discovered in his work on acting was the origin of his interest in the dialectic of pre-logical and logical.[124]

In the 1930s, while teaching at VGIK and beginning work on the pre-logical with the psychologists Lev Vygotsky and Alexander Luria, Eisenstein expanded and complicated his understanding of the reflexological process of communicating with and stimulating audience response by giving it dialectical form. He revised James to say that, for the actor, it doesn't matter whether we are sad because we cry or cry because we are sad: "we are not at all concerned with the primacy of one or the other of them. In the complex as a whole, you have an indivisible unity."[125] The actor, however, must fully embody the *tension* between these and other opposites in order to create that "indivisible unity" necessary to generate expressive movement that then can have a Jamesian impact on the audience, who reproduce in their own bodies the movement they see in order to "enter into that emotional state which the actor is demonstrating to it."[126]

Several texts written in 1939–1940, on the eve of making *Ivan the Terrible*, expound on the foundational role of gesture and movement in creating the synesthetic and pre-logical.[127] "Expressive Movement," in *Method*, is the first of a series of chapters on the ways the pre-logical is experienced in the body and on the specific dialectical form that inner conflict takes in body movement. He begins with a typically historical-autobiographical return to his 1923 discussion of Bode and Klages in order to revise his earliest ideas about the relationship between conscious and unconscious impulses. Bode and Klages understood the tension between conscious and unconscious motives underlying movement as nothing more than the will inhibiting the instinct: consciousness acts as a brake on the unconscious. Biomechanics made the same mistake, according to Eisenstein, by treating the two as canceling each other out rather than forming a productive dialectic.[128] Only when movement embodies internal contradictions working interactively with one another can an actor powerfully and accurately convey feelings and ideas. The whole body, from the core to the tips of the fingers, must function as a "unity of opposites." Eisenstein was at pains to distinguish between the false "totality" of expressive movement in the body, understood as the representation of one impulse inhibiting another, and his own dialectical "unity of opposites," in which the poles of interior conflict are in constant interplay, their roles and degrees of power constantly shifting in a dynamic dialectical process. When actors can master the gestures of dialectical conflict, they can arouse the proper feelings in their spectators.[129] The rest of this section of *Method* explores the international and historical rituals that successfully move people into states of pre-logical receptiveness through coordinating the conflicts taking place within body movement, where involuntary bodily functions like heartbeat and breathing combine with external stimuli such as sound, color, and spatial organization. The correct "totality" is the complex, unified organization of multiple dialectical oppositions occurring within the body to produce the correct effect on feeling, sensation, and thinking.

In "The Determining Gesture," another essay written in 1939–1940, Eisenstein claimed a central role for gesture as a medium capable of conveying more than mere language. Gesture is both the "originary, determining impulse toward the construction of the image" and "the key for the construction of synesthetic unity between depiction and sound."[130] The gesture is the first organizing element to project the author's intentions on the screen and everything else is determined by it. The visible contour of movement, "the geometric trace of the gesture," makes all the other elements—such as melody, rhythm, and setting—more tangible to the audience, initiating dialectical synesthesia and making the unified, generalizable image available for viewers to sense.

Eisenstein argued that because the gesture is the initial, "determining" element in a scene, the director must begin with specific, carefully thought-out movements when constructing a scene. The gesture in this case can be almost anything positioned in space—on a stage or in a film frame—as long as it is in motion. Eisenstein gives examples that range from the flourish of an actor's limb to an opening door or the shifting arrangement of groups of actors. But, he asked, how does a filmmaker decide what those initial gestures should be? In his 1948 text, "'Mise en Jeu' and 'Mise en Geste,'" Eisenstein turned to focus on the practical steps that precede the "determining gesture." First comes the transmutation of the filmmaker's idea into specific actions demanded by the plot—mise en jeu—and then come the specific gestures or movements characters perform—mise en geste. In both cases, the director must devise movement, actions, and gestures that make the characters' inner conflicts "tangible" and "palpable" for the audience.[131] Eisenstein's prescriptions, always introduced with great fanfare, often sound simplistic or naive or purely theoretical and impossible to put into practice. But these are the methods that he used in *Ivan the Terrible*—with unforgettable results.

Among his favorite gestures are his version of the Hegelian-Marxian "negation of a negation," especially the "reverse movement."[132] Eisenstein traced the uses of this dramatic gesture to various historical and international theatrical traditions and used it widely in his own work. The reverse movement was so important to him for making ideas tangible because it paralleled his belief that all processes of change (individual, social, historical) and all artistic structures contained some version of the dialectical collisions of opposites, often represented by simultaneous psychological (or historical or biographical) movement backward and forward. In *Method*, he showed the structural similarities he found in stage movement across time and cultures: in early modern European, Japanese, Chinese, and Native American performance arts. All these show him that logical, rational, commonsense ideas about linear movement forward are limited, even false, unless they contain some element of nonlogical, sensory thinking, which is translated into gesture as the counterintuitive reverse movement. In Dostoevsky's *Idiot*, for instance, when Rogozhin threatens Prince Myshkin with a knife, Eisenstein would not have Myshkin recoil in fear. He would direct an actor playing Myshkin to lean in to Rogozhin, a countermove that expresses the contradiction inherent in what he says in the novel: "You wouldn't," or literally, "I don't believe." The lean in, along with some equally dialectical zigzag gestures involving the knife in Rogozhin's hand, bring the two men even closer together immediately preceding the moment when Myshkin falls backward, down a flight of stairs, in an epileptic fit.[133]

Gesture in Eisenstein is never meant to be merely symbolic. Movement enacted on the screen must enable spectators to reproduce in their own bodies the sensations of physical act they see. In this sense, gesture plays the same role as music and lighting: it creates a nonverbal memory or shape that emerges from the unconscious and can be reassembled with the other sensory-emotional and intellectual cues through montage. In *Nonindifferent Nature*, Eisenstein shows a similar principle at work in the theatrical tradition least associated with him—and yet prominent in *Ivan the Terrible*—melodrama. A long passage on the great nineteenth-century melodramatic actor Frédérick Lemaître focuses on the actor's use of whispering to intensify the impact of events that would make anyone want to cry out to express strong emotions.[134] In his discussion of *The Idiot* in "'Mise en Jeu' and 'Mise en Geste,'" Eisenstein linked the actor's gesture to another fundamental concept, the montage image. The depiction of the leaning in, the zigzag, and the falling back is more than an intellectual exercise. When the various, multilayered dialectical conflicts were tangibly felt and embodied by the audience, spectators would be able to make the leap from quality to quality, experience *ekstasis*, and reach the deeper, higher generalized understanding of the montage image that the author intended.[135] In Eisenstein's thinking about acting, the reverse movement and the dialectics of expressive movement and gesture are dynamic structures that parallel the dynamic dialectics of the spiral and the fugue, the music of landscape and the tonalities of light.

Eisenstein's further ideas about the practices of acting can be found in his writings about specific actors. One of his first publications was a 1926 article in *Kino* about the actress Alexandra Khokhlova.[136] Khokhlova—a tall, lanky, unconventional beauty—was best known for her role in Lev Kuleshov's *The Extraordinary Adventures of Mr. West in the Land of the Bolsheviks* (1924). Eisenstein thought Khokhlova represented the future promise of Soviet acting, but he believed her greatness was unappreciated because people wouldn't go to films if the actresses didn't conform to generic formulas of beauty. In this article we can see the germ of many of the themes that would reappear later in his writing about acting. Eisenstein praised Khokhlova for her ability to use gesture and movement as a conduit for feeling and meaning. She challenged traditional, stereotypical gender roles, and she made it possible to look at women differently and thereby enable a fresh view of the rest of the world. At the other end of his life, in 1947, Eisenstein wrote a short appreciation of the ballerina Galina Ulanova, who he hoped would play Anastasia. Ulanova, he wrote, had the surprising ability to embody synesthesia. Eisenstein praised Ulanova's performance in *Romeo and Juliet* for the same reasons he praised Khokhlova: her ability to suggest melody in the graphic lines of her movements.[137]

In March 1947, Eisenstein wrote his longest article about an individual actor: his friend, Iudif Glizer, who was married to his oldest friend, the actor Maksim Shtraukh. The article contains an appreciation for the kind of qualities Eisenstein originally saw in Khokhlova and developed through the years in his work on biomechanics and "expressive movement." In her first Proletkult role twenty years earlier, Glizer had displayed "love for the strict contour of movement, precision of the graphic image, and clarity of the internal process of the role."[138] And "[Glizer] . . . is always original. Her acting technique is perfect . . . her manner of moving is precise, like a mathematical formula; her mastery of rhythm is flawless, like the verse of a first-rate poet." Plus she was funny and ironic. And always authentically, directly alive.[139] In contrast, some actresses tormented him with their "cottony details and velvety depths," or there were those who "adorn themselves in the tail feathers of the heavenly birds of their imagination."[140] Not Glizer though: she worked by "engaging with the *faktura* and tempo of the material itself."[141] Eisenstein associated her style with modernism. He wrote that one remembers not Glizer's eyes but her gaze (*vzgliad*)—that is, her eyes in motion, her eyes at work. Glizer conveyed character, idea, and feeling not by opening a "window to the soul" but by movement, action, line, and the way she used her whole body to contain and convey the meaning and feeling that came organically from within.[142]

Another way to look at Eisenstein's direction of actors was provided by the great animator Yuri Norshtein in a series of lectures he gave in Japan in 2002. Norshtein argued that the acting in *Ivan the Terrible* is modeled on animation. In animated films, persona is revealed by distilling it into a single conventional gesture or "look," and often that gesture is zoological. Norshtein's concept of animation here is similar to *pars pro toto*, in which the detail or fragment is taken for the whole. It is also related to the "types" in plays by Kyd and Jonson, or the masks used in *commedia dell'arte* or the conventions used in kabuki— all of which Eisenstein knew, studied, admired, and incorporated into his direction practice in *Ivan the Terrible*.

In *Ivan the Terrible*, Eisenstein wanted to show Ivan as both internally divided and in conflict with others, a double dialectic we saw in his spiral biography and fugue social life. Eisenstein's direction of Cherkasov aimed to bring together his thinking about the dialectical structures for conveying ideas and feelings through acting and the version of those structures that he found in Shakespeare and his contemporaries: Shakespeare's ability to dramatize inner conflict and the interplay of externalized physical conflicts that made Kyd's *Spanish Tragedy* the most popular play of its time. Eisenstein modeled his construction of Ivan's relationships with the characters around him on one of his favorite early modern plays, Ben Jonson's *Volpone*.[143] Relevant here is that he showed Ivan's transformation from vulnerable child to bloodthirsty tyrant through a succession of dialectical conflicts between Shakespearean inner conflict *and* a *Volpone*-like collision of multiple characters "ecstatically exploding into each other," to evoke *pathos*, high tension, and, most important, moments of transformation.[144] Acting, then, was another site for the dialectical division into, and merger of, opposites; as he wrote in *Nonindifferent Nature*: "one of the main signs of the *pathos* method [and] one of the essential features of creating *pathos* in general."[145]

In the passage in *Nonindifferent Nature* on Frédérick Lemaître, Eisenstein connected Shakespearean bifurcated, and Jonsonian multifaceted, disassembly and reassembly with specific processes of transformation performed by great actors. He elaborated three kinds of dialectics not as simple contrasts but as dynamic processes of unity, fusion, transition, and interpenetration, and he specifically linked these dynamics to *Ivan the Terrible*. These were, first, the collision of opposite inner conflicts or qualities (the Shakespearean); second, an instantaneous switching among a variety of possible qualities (the Jonsonian); and third, this double dialectic (the inner conflict of ideas and feelings projected onto external actions in conflicts with others) that produced the synthetic unity and a transition to a new, higher quality.[146] At times, we see Ivan change through scenes in which these three processes are enacted sequentially. One of the things that makes Nikolai Cherkasov's performance as Ivan the Terrible so remarkable is that he manages to embody, repeatedly, this very complicated three-part dialectical process of transformation.[147]

Cherkasov had the uncanny ability to visibly convey Ivan's inner conflicts— as collision and fusion, as multifaceted switching, and as synthetic merger or interpenetration—in movement and gesture as well as in more conventional facial expressions. Sometimes he conveys Ivan's various clear-cut "inner conflicts" fused within himself into an "organic whole." He stretches out while cringing inside, as when imploring the boyars to support him. He recoils from the implications of his actions while stretching up to new heights, as when he asks, "Who has the right to judge?" He leans back or crouches over when making his most powerful pronouncements such as "Too few!" He whispers (like Lemaître) in response to explosive revelations, as when he discovers that Vladimir Staritsky "wants it." Cherkasov's physical versatility was remarkable, and throughout the film he performed in a variety of acting styles: dramatic, comedic, even melodramatic. At other times Cherkasov swiftly transitions between conflicting moods. With Maliuta and Fedka, Ivan is friendly *and* angry; at his coronation, he was defiant *and* vulnerable; with Kurbsky and Filipp he switches from sentimental to strategic. He doubles down on this kind of unity of opposites by shifting between poses that both correspond to his words and undermine them, as when dealing with Maliuta and the rabble who break into the palace during his wedding.

One of the hallmarks of Cherkasov's Ivan, noticeable in each of these examples, is his ability to capture Ivan's inner conflicts by switching between the appearance of self-conscious performativity and naturalistic authenticity. All the world's a stage, nowhere more than in Stalinist Russia. Cherkasov repeatedly interrupts what seems to be a show of genuine feeling—fear, loneliness, vulnerability, grief—with direct address to the camera or with a brief shift to hyperawareness when he steps out of himself to see what everyone else is doing and how his behavior is being received. This effect is amplified by the exaggerated, physical-visual, centrifugal "expressive movement" that Cherkasov uses to display inner conflict. These breaks continually remind us that Ivan is performing the role of tsar, that being tsar *is* a role, that he is divided between his private self and his public role. Compare, for example, his performative kiss at the beginning of The Wedding scene, a public display of affection (I: 14:10), with his confession of loneliness to Anastasia just before she is poisoned (I 1:15:38). Even the more genuine expression of sadness is lined with a patina of artifice, of exaggeration that signals the performative.

Artifice plays such a large part in all the actors' performances that it is again tempting to label it camp. Cherkasov's performance becomes increasingly "stony," devoid of human feeling, but never completely. His moments of relevation—when he sees the Kolychev corpses, when he accepts Efrosinia's responsibility for poisoning Anastasia, when he realizes that Vladimir likes being tsar—combine strangely exaggerated or melodramatically unnatural poses with piercingly natural human expressions. The playful and ironic never quite dethrone the serious because the artifice never completely eradicates the kernel of genuine feeling: the scared child in the dark hall, the all-seeing ruler lurking in the shadows.

The short but remarkable scene in Part II when Ivan confronts Filipp in the Golden Hall illustrates Cherkasov's development of such gestures of contradiction into Eisenstein's three-part dialectic. With precise gestures Cherkasov enacts the bipartite, Shakespearean inner struggle, the fracturing into a multitude of colliding and intersecting possibilities modeled on Jonson, and the ultimate transformation of interpenetration and a leap to a higher, more complex image of Ivan. This is a transformative moment in Ivan's effort to balance the personal and the political. At first he still hopes he can persuade his friends to join his political campaign or, at least, that he can maintain friendships with men who object to his political project. When Filipp stands on principle, Ivan tries to elicit his compassion and reason; when that fails, Ivan corrupts him. Both are transformed by the exchange.

There are thirty shots in the scene, excluding the flashbacks to The Prologue, for just under five minutes of screen time. How does Cherkasov's performance add to what we learn from the dialogue discussed in chapter 4 in relation to the fugue? Eisenstein wanted this scene to be psychologically authentic. Ivan was to feel "very emotional. I am alone, alone."[148] But the loneliness was only half the equation here: he wanted to show Ivan's dawning recognition of the tradeoff between the personal and the political, the emotional and the rational: *"John in all his power, and in all his forces, feels himself miserable and alone. . . ."*[149]

Cherkasov gives an astonishingly nuanced, meticulous performance here. Let's look at the ways this scene corresponds to Eisenstein's writing about transformation: inner conflict, multiple collisions, and interpenetration at a higher level.

In the first four shots, Cherkasov enacts inner division with gestures (II: 9:54). He sits back, then leans forward; leans back, throwing up his hands, and moves forward to greet Filipp; there's a little up and down business with Filipp's crozier—Filipp raises it (in anger), Ivan lowers it back down, while telling him to quiet down; and then, while Ivan leads Filipp out of the hall off screen right, he turns and looks back left at Maliuta, who returns his look in

FIGURE 5.7   *"Philipp and John. John in all his power, and in all his forces, feels himself miserable and alone. . . ."* RGALI, 1923/2/1680/4 [Feb 21, 1942]. Used with permission.

the next shot, when Ivan is off screen. Cherkasov's voice in these shots begins in anger (at the interruption of his speech) and switches first to the stagey, hearty greeting—"Fedor Kolychev!"—and then to a warm, almost conspiratorial, whisper as if to say, let's take this inside and chat like friends. In the next shot (II: 10:16), Filipp, instead of accepting Ivan's friendly invitation, turns and steps away, standing resolutely facing away from Ivan, with his robes dramatically but statically draped. In this shot Cherkasov drops all signs of Ivan's official role, circles around behind Filipp and informally, almost anachronistically, looks him up and down. This is the first time Ivan has seen Filipp since he went off and entered the church, and Ivan is frankly checking out his old friend's new persona. Their eyes meet briefly—almost imperceptibly—and Filipp immediately turns away again, slightly startling Ivan. Cherkasov adopts a thoughtful look. That interaction takes all of five seconds. Ivan backs up and turns to sit on the throne, but the cut keeps us from seeing his reaction to this unfamiliar, stiff-backed priest Filipp and to whatever he saw in Filipp's eyes.

In all these first shots we see binaries: Ivan moves back and forth or switches between roles: tsar making a speech, tsar managing the sudden appearance of political opponent. This sets up the inner divisions: the costs of the clash between the personal and the political. After the cut we see two sequences that show a multiplicity of feelings all competing with each other (II: 10:24). Cherkasov moves backward into the throne, slouching, not very tsar-ish, and his face shifts registers several times: from perplexed (mouth slightly open, eyebrows slightly raised, eyes focused on Filipp) to fatigued (eyes lowered, body a little slumped), then a harsher look (with eyes focused), then introspective (face soft and eyes staring in a way that suggests reflection). His voice also switches but with more nuances, and words don't always synchronize with tone of voice. Softly, genuinely, he asks, "Why are you so severe with me, Fedor Kolychev?," a political question still with a trace of the personal. Then switching to a more resolute tone, still appraising Filipp, and in a louder, harder voice, "Why are you so cruel?" Through all this, and through most of the scene, Filipp remains stiff as a mannequin, unchanging as a mask, and now reminds Ivan of the stakes here: I'm not your friend; I serve God, not the tsar. Ivan gives this short shrift because now he has a plan. To make Filipp understand and sympathize, Ivan shows him a couple of clips of boyar perfidy from his tragic childhood. He leans forward and raises his hand in a gesture that often signifies the Great Cause, and he takes us into the flashback to The Prologue, to his childhood fear and suffering.

Two sequential structures of thought and feeling are being enacted here. On one hand, there is Ivan's inner conflict coming to the surface with Filipp's reappearance: Ivan has to realize that he is in danger of losing his last old friend by establishing the oprichnina, alienating the boyars, and moving ahead with his mission to establish one-man rule and the Great Russian State. At the beginning of this scene, he is a bundle of binary contradictions—he wants his personal and his political life—these desires are fused within him. The determining gestures of these first shots—back and forth, up and down movements—establish that binary dynamic. But when Ivan begins to realize that he can't have the personal and the political lives he wants, the range of Ivan's responses to Filipp, registered in a variety of facial expressions—naturalistic and masked—exhibit the many different centrifugal directions that are pulling at Ivan. Thoughts, feelings, memories—Ivan tries on each fragment like a mask.

We see this overlapping of the dialectic inner conflict and centrifugal multifaceted conflict in the weird, extreme close-up shot (II: 11:59) that separates the two parts of the flashback (the murder of Ivan's mother and the selling of Russia to foreigners that leads the young Ivan to assert his power as tsar for the first time). Yuri Tsivian describes Moskvin's use of lighting here and the sudden turn of Ivan's head to create a transition from the sympathetic to the diabolical.[150] But in between those poles, Cherkasov conveys a number of different responses with multiple, conventional facial expressions. At first in the grip of memory as he emerges from the flashback, he looks resigned and sad (head lowered, eyes unfocused), he moves away from memory to anger (I was orphaned). Then he turns his head as if startled, though the only cause of surprise here is the unmotivated direction and intensity of the lighting. His face registers surprise and fear, and then switches to anger, when his memory shifts from his vulnerability to anger at the boyars' treason and greed. At the same time, his voice shifts from a kind of sing-song, far-off remembering tone to the louder, harsher tone of present-felt anger. Cherkasov's tone of voice here lags behind the meaning of his words and the expression on his face, as if he's stuck in the past and only slowly coming out of his reverie to register what he's feeling. The harsh, diabolical lighting clashes with the soft tone of voice and the woe-is-me memory of childhood suffering. The score reinforces the complexity of these divisions with the lyrical version of the tsar's leitmotif, which we remember from the stateroom when he was meditating on the conflict between personal desire and political ambition, just before Anastasia was killed. This temporal displacement and trace of the past is Cherkasov embodying in acting those components of Eisenstein's spiral theory of history and biography. In this case, it is a kind of complex "reverse movement" or spiral circling back, a multifaceted collision of multiple possibilities, just before a major transition to a new, more complex dialectic inner conflict. After the second flashback, the action—and the argument—is repeated.

First we see Ivan in side-angle close-up working it out: alternating between everything he's done to make Russia great (I have power, the people, the oprichniki [II: 17:45]) and everything he's lost (no friends, cut to Filipp in medium close-up, attentive), back to Ivan, more naturalistically as he turns again to the personal: grief (Anastasia) and anger (Kurbsky) drop him to sit on the floor in front of his throne. As in the first binary shots, the dialogue here is reinforced by body movement: Ivan moves his head up and down in close-ups, then moves his body up and down. Filipp slides his eye sideways. Five shots restate Ivan's commitment, angering Filipp, who finally moves, only to form another static tableau of beautifully arranged sacred and royal robes, defending traditional boyar power. Reverse-angle long shots then show Filipp striding off, arguing (II: 19:19). Ivan sits back on the throne, gets up, moves laterally on the dais, then moves forward, chasing Filipp. From the back, only their robes visible, they move like little animals, Ivan appraising before pouncing.

But instead of pouncing, Cherkasov falls to his knees, Ivan in utter despair. As so often in this film, change is preceded by absolute despair or a reduction to nothing, rebirth preceded by a kind of death. And then all those complicated feelings that surfaced with Filipp's return and the resurrection of memory are again reduced to the conflict between friendship and duty, but now with a twist.

Cherkasov does three things here in succession (II: 19:37). In this final sequence the shots are all medium shots, so we register body movement more than facial expression. First, with a melodramatic gesture of defeat "crushed by the burden of being tsar," he grabs Filipp's robes and begs him once more to be his friend.

Filipp pulls as hard as he can to get away from Ivan, inadvertently pulling Ivan up and back to himself (perhaps an echo of that rare dolly back shot when Ivan was first begging the boyars to support him). Ivan sits down again and with a stronger voice, his head thrown back with the faraway stare he uses for important state pronouncements, again asks Filipp, despite everything, to join him in building the Great Russian State. When that doesn't work, he puts his hand on his heart and offers Filipp the metropolitanate. Filipp, for the first time, drops his own mask. When Filipp accepts, though, Ivan has lost for winning. Cherkasov crumples: shoulders rounded over, he curves his back and falls to the floor. Filipp too, though, has won only a pyrrhic victory. He lifts Ivan, embraces him, kisses him, and they walk off together—synthesis and transformation. But they have made an impossible compromise: Ivan won't be willing to do what he must do to retain Filipp's friendship (refrain from punishing those who oppose him), and Filipp won't be willing to do what he must do to support Ivan as metropolitan. Now both Ivan and Filipp struggle with inner divisions but at a higher, more complex level than at the beginning of the scene, when Filipp was single-minded in his opposition and Ivan hoped

FIGURE 5.8   "Crushed by the burden of being tsar"

he could have his cake and eat it too. Now each has "dabs of complementary tones from opposite palettes." Filipp has given in to ambition with the false hope of being able to continue to challenge Ivan's assault on the boyars, and Ivan has traded (only temporarily as it turns out) his full commitment to his political mission to hang on to his last friend. The clash inside Ivan between personal desire and political responsibility produced external conflict between Ivan and his friend-turned-enemy, which led to actions with consequences (promises and promotions) and new, more complex double dialectics—inner struggles and exterior conflicts.

If Eisenstein was right about the ways in which the film director could convey ideas and feelings through images, music, light, and gesture; if he was right about the ways we reproduce in our own bodies what we see on screen, then this scene should have given viewers a strong emotional experience of *pathos*, of empathy for Ivan's struggles, and both resolution and foreboding about what was coming next.

Did It Work?

Polyphonic montage—the weaving of audio, visual, sensory, and intellectual voices in every frame—was meant to intensify the dialectic of pre-logical and logical responses to film by arousing synesthesia, by alternating the differentiation and merging of sensations, by creating ever more dense networks of associations, and then by producing an out-of-body leap to a new awareness. In *Ivan the Terrible*, Eisenstein wanted the polyphonic to create new forms for exploring the patterns he had discovered in human psychology and history and the production and reception of art. He wanted to create a new cinematic landscape that invested the movement of people and objects in space with feeling and meaning—*pathos*. He wanted music and lighting to trace the contours of the landscape of the shot to add to the store of nonverbal memories produced by images, things, and gestures that increased *pathos* and produced the generalizable, montage image through *ekstasis*. Ironically, Eisenstein's effort to amplify every sensory, emotional, and intellectual trigger had for some people a prohibitive, alienating effect that left viewers immune to the film's sensory-emotional side. Pauline Kael, unwittingly echoing many Russian critics of the 1940s, wrote that *Ivan* was "so lacking in human dimensions that you may stare at it in a kind of outrage. True, every frame in it looks great—it's a brilliant collection of stills—but as a movie, it's static, grandiose, and frequently ludicrous."[151] That's not really what Eisenstein was going for.

Eisenstein's attempt to produce *pathos* and *ekstasis* in the viewer with polyphonic montage was also thwarted by timing. In 1945–1946, when Part I was released in the Soviet Union and abroad, and in 1958, when Part II was released globally, most people approached *Ivan the Terrible* through a strong ideological filter. Was it favorable to Stalin or not? Was it politically conformist or subversive? Until decades later, even those who wrote about form did so only after staking out a political and ideological position on the film. Even when that political filter was invoked to dismiss politics altogether it often muted sympathetic responses to Eisenstein's efforts to evoke feeling. The intellectual, logical side of Eisenstein's dialectic—whether political or formalist—dominated and distorted responses to *Ivan* by shifting attention away from its sensory-emotional impact. The film's apparent stylistic departure from Eisenstein's early films, for those with a narrow understanding of montage, also blinded viewers to the ways in which Eisenstein expanded the uses of montage to create intellectual and sensory-emotional effects. And as a method for moving viewers into a pre-logical state of receptiveness that would ultimately enable strong feeling and transformation—*pathos* and *ekstasis*—polyphonic montage and the exaggerated intensity of sound and image gave the film an artificial quality that precluded, for some viewers, the kind of unconscious engagement audiences expect from realistic cinematic storytelling or less radical denaturalization. Yet many viewers at the time who criticized *Ivan* on such terms also found that the film moved them in unexpectedly unforgettable ways. Ben Maddow, another prominent American reviewer, wrote that for all its failures as a film, *Ivan's* images stuck in his mind and continued to return days and weeks later.[152]

As I argue throughout this book, it is possible to begin to understand Eisenstein's achievement in *Ivan the Terrible* only by approaching it through the intellectual and the sensory-emotional at the same time, through the artistic and the political together, through form and content in dialogue with each other. In both the United States and the Soviet Union in the 1940s, these dialectics were still partially hidden in the mortar. The complexity of Eisenstein's experimental approach to filmmaking together with the highly charged political topic and the historical moment in which *Ivan* appeared meant that its reception was shaped by the world in which it was made. Even people who were emotionally moved by the film found it difficult to understand or acknowledge that experience. The publication of *Method* together with *Nonindifferent Nature* have changed that. They have helped make it clear that Eisenstin anticipated much of the interdisciplinary literature published since the 1990s on affect, objects, landscape, and sensory perception, all of which make his broader goals more visible to us today.

Eisenstein understood that spectators respond to every element in every frame at various levels of conscious and unconscious awareness. Polyphonic montage was intended to disassemble those elements and offer them to viewers to reassemble in ways that would sharpen focus and increase disorientation at the same time. He created an expanded sensory kind of "unity in variety," giving us fragments—close-ups, sounds, things, movement, lighting, facial expressions—underlining their fragmentariness and tempting us with the promise of unities. The number of effects that appear before us on screen taking place at the same time is extraordinary. Axial editing moves us in until the detail overwhelms us, or out so we can see (or can't see) into the smoky depths. Shifting camera placement gives us a muliplied perspective, making us wonder what we are seeing and opening fissures that let us feel Ivan's despair from the inside. Camera mobility and immobility plant information and networks of images in our sensory memory, including the dialectic of movement and stillness. Extravagant lighting shifts and flickering shadows break down and flow over surfaces, fragmenting and connecting them, in the same ways that small musical motifs take on shapes in the space of the set, moving through and around people and even pulling and pushing us into following them through space. Conventional associations with color and chord play against their unconventional opposites to move us toward and pull us away from dialectical resolution. The constant switching between exterior and interior (an exterior conflict with an interior that is itself divided), between Shakespeare and Jonson, thought and action, tragedy and melodrama, Meyerhold and Stanislavsky—Cherkasov's ability to play Hamlet *and* Volpone—show us that powerful art doesn't have to be about only subtle nuances of subjectivity, but that sometimes what's important are big juggernaut personalities, ideas, institutions, and fates colliding to tranform the world and our reactions to the world. Eisenstein wanted us to feel Ivan's pain in order to understand his actions ("to explain the most atrocious things"), and he wanted us to ask if Ivan's grief justified his actions, but he didn't want to give us an easy path to (fake) empathy. Polyphonic montage appealed to the unconscious but was intended to make us aware of the disassembling-reassembling process moving through the film and piecing together the generalizable montage image of Ivan.

Eisenstein used disorientation, movement away, shapeshifting, unnatural gestures, and the "ironic-sarcastic-sardonic" line to puncture the ease of conventional feelings, to kick you out of the womb (and make you long for it). He knew how to write fulsome, one-dimensional praise for the ruler, he knew how to put that sort of ruler on film and why people would like it, but in *Ivan the Terrible* he wanted us to feel the good in every villain, the nightmare in every humanist, the heart in the traitor, the wavering among the faithful, the teaspoon of ambition in the innocent, and for that he needed Van Gogh's yellow trees. He thought that every one of his own methods was drawn from nature and that by showing us nature's secrets and surprises, he could make us feel something real, "not as an imitation of reality, but as its *dynamic reconfiguration*," as Marie Rebecci reminds us.[153]

Eisenstein wasn't interested in engaging viewers by immersing them in a story or by creating characters to identify with. His camera doesn't stand in for our eye; his editing violates every convention of realism; his score doesn't trigger conventional feelings; his actors don't look like people we know. He wanted to stir something more primal in us—he wanted to stir everything primal in us—our deepest feelings and highest mental abilities—because that's what his subject and his medium and the world he lived in demanded.

CHAPTER 6

The Official Reception

Ivan *as Triumph and Nightmare*

When *Ivan the Terrible*, Part I, opened in Los Angeles in 1946, American critics reacted with stunned outrage. *Variety* said that the film had "the usual quota of Soviet propaganda that is so obvious it screams its meaning." For the *New York Times*'s Bosley Crowther, the film's "conception of Ivan . . . is conspicuously totalitarian."[1] These ideologically oriented views dominated the first interpretations of *Ivan the Terrible* in the United States, and they have had extraordinary longevity. Almost fifty years after Crowther reviewed *Ivan*, the musicologist Richard Taruskin denounced the film (and its Prokofiev score) as a "blatant piece of Stalinist triumphalism."[2] Popular twenty-first century views in the United States still often approach the film's politics with simplistic binaries that make the narrative incomprehensible and emphasize the alienating style in order to signify Eisenstein's fall from the greatness of *Potemkin*. In 2012, Roger Ebert confessed that *Ivan* inspired "visual fascination," but he found the film hard to like and called it "reluctant hagiography for a madman."[3] Andrew Grossman's 2011 review on the *Senses of Cinema* website presents *Ivan* as simple Socialist Realist nationalism, and the author assumes that Eisenstein was forced to abandon montage.[4] David Ehrenstein wrote that "while his theories of 'montage' have kept theorists busy for decades, they were merely matters of convenience to him—abandoned by and large by their 'master' when sound arrived with *Alexander Nevsky* and *Ivan the Terrible*, with spectacle films becoming his abiding interest."[5] The failure of *Ivan the Terrible* to meet these American viewers' political and formal expectations made it hard for audiences to experience the film as Eisenstein wished. This is not the place for a full reception history of *Ivan the Terrible*, but I offer these US responses as a point of contrast. Soviet audiences who saw Part I in 1945 and Part II in 1946 also filtered their responses through a political lens but were not so often fooled by the surface narrative. There are some notable exceptions, but while viewers differed in their appreciation for the film's formal experimentation and sensory-emotional appeal, many viewers immediately recognized the political challenges each part of the film presented. The recorded responses at official screenings show the ways that expectations and political context shaped the film's reception.

Some writers continue to think that *Ivan the Terrible*, Part I, was showered with praise and universally well received in the Soviet Union.[6] If *Ivan*, Part I, were indeed the Great Totalitarian Epic or if the party *apparat* simply controlled the film industry, we would expect to find consistent praise for the film beyond official published reviews: in screening discussions, prize committees, and in public recognition of the film in the Soviet Union in 1945 when it was released. But we do not. Soviet film critics, industry insiders, professional historians, and ordinary filmgoers responded to *Ivan*, Part I, with ambivalence, outright criticism, and plain bewilderment. The primary function of Socialist Realist art as propaganda required clear messages, unambivalent lessons, identifiable heroes, and accessible themes. Even when artists found room to modify these conventions, they couldn't stray too far from the master narrative.[7] Apart from reviews in the official state media, recorded responses to *Ivan the Terrible* failed to recognize *Ivan the Terrible* as "conspicuously totalitarian" or "Stalinist triumphalism," nor do they resemble anything like the official rhetoric that one might expect to hear in this period. More often than not, responses to the film show surprise at the *absence* of official narratives and orthodox politics in Eisenstein's portrait of the powerful ruler and founder of the centralized state. Responses to *Ivan the Terrible*, Part I, were complicated and varied, reflecting the complexities of the film itself and the context in which it was made and released. In 1945 and 1946, however, when Parts I and II were initially screened, no one was talking about *pathos* and *ekstasis*, at least not out loud.

Understanding the reception of *Ivan the Terrible* has been further complicated by the fact that Part I received the Stalin Prize a year after it was completed, and a month later Part II was banned by the Central Committee. Very few people saw Part II until it was released to the public in 1958, which led many to draw the conclusion that Part I was politically tame and Part II politically subversive. The artists and arts administrators whose job it was to approve the films for release and decide on nominations for the Stalin Prize were suspicious of the political message both films sent and they expressed their suspicions, though at times quite cautiously. There was some disagreement on these committees over the artistic achievement of the films, but very few people saw Part I as a triumphant propaganda epic or even as a positive portrait of the tsar, and Part II was sharply criticized for departing from the expected political message. In fact, nothing makes clearer the chasm between Eisenstein's view of the project and official government expectations than the prescreening discussions of Parts I and II.

Throughout the production process, Eisenstein sent rushes to Mosfilm, where they were consistently approved by Bolshakov or his direct assistants. There is no record of official discontent with the film, although as I've mentioned, there were efforts to control the story at the scenario stage, and then there was concern about how long the film took to finish. In August 1944, the Mosfilm Artistic Council viewed an edited version of Part I for the first time. The film produced a great deal of confusion: Was Ivan dead or alive after confronting the boyars on his sickbed? Why did the people come to recall Ivan to Moscow? There were complaints about the acting, which many found cold, and about the style, which some found overly cerebral.[8]

On October 28, a complete Part I was viewed by the newly formed Artistic Council of the Committee on Cinema Affairs.[9] The Artistic Council did not immediately agree to release Part I after that screening. Mikhail Romm said later that everyone at Mosfilm had been ecstatic about the rushes Eisenstein sent during production but that they were disappointed with the finished film.[10] It was at this point that Eisenstein was required to cut The Prologue, to replace the titles at the beginning of the film to shift attention to Ivan's national achievements, and to counter the sinister image of the oprichniki with titles introducing The Oath of the Oprichniki, explaining their "social and historical significance."[11] Bolshakov later claimed that the removal of The Oath made it possible for the council to agree to release Part I.[12]

The film studio artistic councils were set up in 1940–1941 to counterbalance the weight of political monitoring with professional, artistic assessment of films, but already by 1943, they had little political autonomy. They continued to screen and discuss films before their release, but often decisions were made without their advice. The central Artistic Council of the Committee on Cinema Affairs, formed in September 1944, was made up of prominent directors, actors, and writers as well as ideologically "reliable" figures chosen by Bolshakov.[13] The Artistic Council's assessment of Ivan the Terrible, Part I, was typically wide-ranging, going far beyond the film's adherence to political orthodoxy or correspondence to the goals of Socialist Realism. The discussion is extremely interesting, both for what committee members said and for what they didn't say. Although the participants were remarkably frank in both their praise and criticism, this was less a discussion than a series of speeches, made after all the editing and revising decisions had been made and after numerous previous discussions where many of the same issues had been raised. Since the council members were voting to release or shelve, they needed to defend their positions with overall assessments of the film. And we need to read them from several different points of view as the participants were speaking to a number of audiences. Council members needed to give opinions that would be heard by the studio going forward with Parts II and III and by Eisenstein, who was listening for artistic as well as political judgments, and no one involved could forget that Stalin was especially interested in the projects he had commissioned on Ivan the Terrible and would have the final word.

Efim Levin, who first wrote about the discussion, said the council members were unable to shed their expectation that Eisenstein's Ivan would be Stalin's Ivan; that Eisenstein would follow the state's commission "to exonerate Ivan the Terrible, to show that the blood was not spilled in vain."[14] No one would expect the Artistic Council to address contemporary political implications directly even if they did see them, but it is striking that the required revisions following the October screening and statements about specific historical and political content of the film made at the December meeting clearly show that the council viewers saw the divergence of the Ivan of Part I from the official expectations and a tacit recognition of Eisenstein's flouting of the very premises of the state's commission. Each of the three scenes that were removed—the original titles, the Prologue, and the Oath—were damaging to Ivan's image in political terms that had modern resonance. All three highlighted the violence of Ivan's reign, indeed of Ivan's own psyche, in ways that went beyond the direct actions of the oprichniki.

Most members of the Artistic Council were either troubled or confused by characterizations of the tsar, his mission, and the other principal characters. The Oath of the Oprichniki was criticized because members of the Artistic Council were uncomfortable with its derogatory portrayal of Ivan as a demagogue who required the absolute loyalty of his servitors. As the director of popular tractor romances, Ivan Pyriev, stated, "The oath lowered the figure of the ruler and his great significance."[15]

The Prologue was removed in part because council members found it too gloomy, even psychopathic, and because it demeaned the image of the tsar who founded the Great Russian State and defeated Kazan.[16] The actor and director Aleksei Diky found the film historically confusing. He objected that the historical Maliuta had been an "intelligent, significant" figure but here he was "just a pretty stupid guy [*prosto glupovatym parnem*]." As for Ivan, Diky stated simply that, based on Part I, it was hard to judge Ivan's historical role.[17] M. R. Galaktionov stated even more clearly that while the film was an artistic masterpiece (transcending debates about formalism and realism), it failed to meet its own goal in depicting the tsar: "Ivan the Terrible should be portrayed as a ruler; however, in this film, that is not accomplished." Eisenstein should have explained the tsar's cruelty as a legitimate political response to the enemies who opposed his "great, mighty, rule." But instead, we get melodrama: "the same old poison, the coffin, [and] the enemy [Efrosinia] is just some Baba-Yaga, not a representative of a social issue." The oprichniki too, were "completely unsuccessful," contributing to Galaktionov's judgment of the film as "unfaithful" (*neverno*), "not in some trivial sense," but in "diminishing this great figure . . . and his entire cause." Galaktionov wanted to reconsider releasing the film at all.

The young director, Igor Savchenko, also found Ivan's "wicked, cruel, degeneracy," to be unmotivated in the December 7 cut, and he did not see any redeeming features in the tsar's portrait. "Without The Prologue . . . Ivan is, from the very first episode, immediately evil, he's 'Terrible' and why he's so 'terrible' is incomprehensible."[18] Boris Gorbatov was disappointed that Eisenstein only portrayed Ivan as an autocrat, that the plot revolved around the struggle for power, rather than showing how much the historical Ivan accomplished for Russia, "the people he is fighting for, the reforms, the progressive ideas, the oprichnina, the 'window on Europe,' the broadening of ties . . . he's a little one-dimensional." Gorbatov also said, "It is not important to us, who he is struggling against, but what he is struggling for. . . . It is important to show that the idea for which Ivan the Terrible was struggling was emotionally close to the people . . . a very difficult task for Ivan the Terrible."[19] Eisenstein, who was present at the discussion, couldn't resist piping up here to say, "Even harder for me!"[20] Last but not least, Vsevolod Pudovkin defended the film, but not by refuting the political suspicions raised by other viewers. He never said that Eisenstein's Ivan is a great hero or progressive for his time; he defended *Ivan*'s artistic complexity and asked those present to view the film as a great chess match, complicated and with various possible outcomes.[21]

There was a great deal of artistic criticism as well, but it tended to be general in nature. Konstantin Simonov, among others, strenuously criticized Part I for what he saw as its overly cerebral quality, its failure to touch the heart.[22] Boris Babochkin (the actor most famous for his role as Chapaev) found the acting atrocious and the film as a whole "very tiresome."[23] But while some of these viewers denounced the film's "formalism," most of them, even those critical of its historical or political presentation, took pains to praise formal aspects of the film's style and, as Diky put it, to deflect any possible criticism of "formalism" and defend it against "formophobia." Savchenko went so far as to say that *Ivan* would be an immensely influential work and that all his own future films would reflect the impact of Eisenstein's innovation in *Ivan the Terrible*, Part I. But he did not go into much detail.[24]

From this discussion, it should be clear that Part I failed to adhere to the politically shaped expectation that Eisenstein would present a conventional "positive hero" or an accessible, heroic, historical chronicle, with clear lessons about both the past and the present. Instead film industry viewers, speaking in a closed forum, said that they found its *historical* Ivan a confusing mass of contradictions, anachronisms, and forthright distortions and its *political* Ivan dangerously somber, manipulative, and unheroic. Although these first viewers may not have articulated their criticism in explicitly political terms, their criticism of its historical rendering alongside their acceptance of its artistic vision suggests, at the very least, that they did not see the film as a celebration of Ivan's achievements or a triumph of Stalinist propaganda. Ironically, then, the efforts by the Artistic Council to sanitize and clarify Eisenstein's portrait of Ivan only further complicated an intentionally difficult film. Although their editing may have prevented the film from exposing an even darker image of tyranny, it was still not enough to make *Ivan* useful propaganda or Socialist Realism.

Bolshakov, always a champion of *Ivan the Terrible*, wrote an executive summary that represented the discussion in the best possible light, with ample if obscure forewarning of its challenges.[25] "*Ivan the Terrible*, Part I, is a significant artistic work of Soviet film art, in its original, creative interpretation of the deeply and innovatively revealed complex theme of the historical role of Tsar Ivan IV in founding the united powerful Russian state." While praising the mastery of the director, as well as Moskvin, Tisse, Prokofiev, and Cherkasov, Bolshakov included mention of its "schematic" depiction of some characters, its insufficient treatment of the people, and its excessive display of religiosity—all the subjects he had criticized from the very beginning of the negotiations over the scenario. Finally, and only on the insistence of some of the Artistic Council members, Bolshakov included a statement calling for the restoration of The Prologue.

We can partially gauge Eisenstein's reading of this official reception of Part I because we have his notes from the discussion. He underlined a number of comments, including Simonov's criticism of the film's lack of feeling: "it is antagonistic with its lack of humaneness and its absence of love for people."

He also noted Diky's comment that the film's depiction of Russia seemed "foreign," and Babochkin's irritation at the interminable length of some scenes. About Ivan as a character, he marked Galaktionov's complaint that "we don't see Ivan as a ruler," and Gorbatov's that, in comparison with *Alexander Nevsky*, *Ivan the Terrible* is harder to understand; we don't see enough of Ivan as either a ruler or as a man.[26] Eisenstein must have been disappointed that his effort to evoke both feeling and thought had left many of these viewers unmoved. It's hard to know how he responded to the comments about Ivan's politics. On one hand, he had to be pleased that *Ivan the Terrible* didn't seem "too pale," as he had feared. But he also had to be pleased that *Ivan* didn't seem too dark either. We don't know how he felt about the surprise removal of The Oath of the Oprichniki, but we do know that he readily rewrote the opening titles. We also know that he was sanguine about the loss of The Prologue, perhaps because there was considerable support for including it. At the end of the discussion on December 7, Bolshakov asked if Eisenstein still wanted The Prologue in Part I, but he declined, perhaps feeling confident that it could be added to Part II as a flashback.

The best evidence for understanding Eisenstein's reading of the official response can be found in the work he did on Part II in the year following the Artistic Council's assessment and release of Part I. He certainly did not try to make Russia look any more familiar visually or to tone down the stylized sets, acting, and editing that made the film's visual style seem so "un-Russian" and depart so far from realism, socialist or any other kind. If anything, he heightened the stylization of the characters' emotions. Several scenes, such as Kurbsky's treasonous pledge of loyalty to Sigismund and The Dance of the Oprichniki, approach satire in their costumes, gestures, speech, and set design, which both contrast and mix foreign and Western elements.

The debates in the Artistic Council over Part I show that there were limits to official toleration for variability in Socialist Realism and mutability of its conventions. The published official reviews of *Ivan*, Part I, suppressed all the questions raised by the Artistic Council, but there was some uncertainty up until the last minute about which direction those reviews would take. We know now that Vsevolod Vishnevsky was one of two critics asked to prepare a review of *Ivan the Terrible*, Part I, for *Pravda*, and that his more positive assessment of the film was chosen only at the last moment, after a final Kremlin screening.[27] Vishnevsky's review and another one in *Izvestiia* praised *Ivan* for its presentation of the progressive establishment of central state power, imperial expansion, and the support Ivan enjoyed among the people.[28] Vishnevsky explained that Eisenstein justified executing boyars as enemies of the people, but he downplayed the violence and did not emphasize the political lessons of the film. Following directly the specific points addressed in the opening titles, Vishnevsky praised Eisenstein for offering an "historically accurate" portrait of Ivan as a "progressive leader," who, with the support of the people, struggled against greedy boyars at home and cruel Germans in the Baltic region to unite the country and expand it to its historical territorial borders. However doubtful or reprehensible the justifications for these events, Vishnevsky related them dispassionately or, more important, without any effort to make claims for the film's quality as propaganda or its resonance with contemporary politics. He did not neglect to mention Eisenstein's supposed justification for centralized power, but at the same time he made an effort to emphasize the essential historicity and complexity of Ivan's persona, as well as the aesthetic qualities of Eisenstein's treatment of Ivan, rather than the film's contemporary political relevance or its lessons for moviegoers of the 1940s. Vishnevsky stated the official line, as was his task—and we know that he genuinely liked the film—but he explicitly resisted endorsing Eisenstein's treatment of its political themes, its justification of terror, or its use as propaganda.

The film's limits as propaganda directly surface in ordinary viewers' responses. There are not enough letters in Eisenstein's archive to provide more than a sketch of viewer response, but those that exist are exceptionally revealing.[29] We know from other studies of letters during this period that despite the heavy penalties for expressing dissenting views on any subject in the 1930s and 1940s, millions of Soviet citizens nonetheless wrote letters to officials and official publications to complain, to question public policies, and to hector public officials.[30] On one hand, we would not expect the letters to Eisenstein and *Pravda* to address the Ivan/Stalin metaphor directly, so its absence is not surprising. On the other hand, no one wrote solely to congratulate the director for *Ivan the Terrible*, as they had done for *Alexander Nevsky*. The letters are passionate, heartfelt, and informed (either aesthetically or historically). They come from all over the country, from Moscow and from small-town Siberia, and from a variety of backgrounds. But the one feature that almost all the letters about *Ivan* share is an astonished bewilderment in the face of the film's unexpected historical narrative.[31] Whether they praise or admonish Eisenstein for departing from Socialist Realist convention, letter writers emphasize *Ivan*'s narrative murkiness. And most of the letters, while paying lip service to the film's "achievement," questioned the meaning and purpose of its portrait of the tsar. One viewer wrote to explain that the film would never "enjoy great success among the majority of the population" because the historical events and their purpose are hard to understand and barely explained. "I loved the scenario," but the movie is disappointing.[32] Another self-described "friend of cinema" wrote to congratulate the director on his next step forward in the annals of film art. The writer goes on to say, "I don't want to speak about the historical-political meaning of the film—it is entirely obvious, in that you refute the *vulgar* understanding of the role of this tsar as the unifier of Rus and clearly prefer his qualities as servant of the people." But the writer then adds that "the only thing, that one might like to see clarified in the next Part II, is the *narod*, the Russian people. How the people felt and acted in that epoch."[33] In other words, this viewer found that Eisenstein depicted Ivan as the people's tsar but failed to make their support for the tsar comprehensible. This is typical of the kind of confusion Eisenstein created with his contradictory and elastic use of official symbols and rhetoric. A number of correspondents took it on themselves to correct Eisenstein's historical mistakes in the film. One professor was offended at the erroneous images appearing in the fabricated frescoes decorating the Kremlin and cathedral walls, and at the fact that Eisenstein placed Anastasia's coffin in the Dormition Cathedral, when historically corpses were never allowed there, and so on. "The things you make up, like Staritsky's death, aren't secondary things, but serious distortions, which mislead our youth, who believe everything they see on the screen."[34]

As if in rebuttal, one extensive and thoughtful letter from a student (who claimed to speak for many others) at the Moscow Institute for Engineers of Communal Construction, shows that there was plenty of robust critical thinking among young people who saw *Ivan*. This student was disappointed by the film and baffled by the *Pravda* review. "The audience expects to see a film of great transformation and reform." But what appeared on the screen was more or less incomprehensible: Ivan was shown "as far too long-suffering, when he should be more energetic." Kurbsky appears to be "nothing more than a man suffering from his illicit love for the wife of another and dreaming of the tsar's crown," his political relationship with the tsar subsumed by melodrama.

> We could not figure out who the boyarina leading the opposition was
> . . . Events in the film were hardly connected and seemed to develop
> independently of one another . . . The passage of time was revealed
> only by the growth of Ivan's beard . . . And what became of the cam-
> paign against Livonia after Kurbsky's betrayal? The answer to this is
> known only to Ivan the Terrible and the director of the film, but Ivan is
> dead and the director does not want to say, so the audience is forced to
> fill in the blanks with imagination.[35]

"In general," the letter concluded, as many of these comments did, "the film is tiresome, instead of exciting. The next part could be much improved if you take into account some of what I've written."[36]

Whether letters like these were political in intent or not, their historical significance for us is politically eloquent. If these letters convey anything, it is the inconclusive impression made by the image of Ivan and confusion about his historical mission. The film that for so many later and foreign viewers *proved* Eisenstein's entrapment in the Kremlin propaganda machine was found by contemporary viewers to lack even the basic ingredients necessary for propagating state-generated mythology and political imagery.

The Stalin Prize

The same kinds of criticism that the Artistic Council made resurfaced when *Ivan the Terrible*, Part I, was nominated for a Stalin Prize in the spring of 1945. That process was complicated by Stalin's personal role in the deliberations, first as a shadow over the discussions, then as probable final arbiter of the prize in his name. The fact that Part I did win a Stalin Prize and Part II was banned and publically abhorred by Stalin has often been evoked as evidence of a vast political difference between the two parts. But Eisenstein wanted to win the Stalin Prize and hoped to win it for Part II after winning the first one.[37] More important, few people realize that Eisenstein came very close to *not* receiving the Stalin Prize for *Ivan the Terrible*, Part I. It was rejected at every level of the nomination process, even though Bolshakov personally and vigorously promoted it. At the first stage of deliberation, the Film Section of the Stalin Prize Committee refused to confirm its nomination, preferring to put forward more conventional and popular wartime dramas.[38] Bolshakov, nonetheless, got it on the short list and insisted that its nomination be discussed at the plenum meeting of the Prize Committee with the other nominees as if the Film Section had sent it forward. Despite all that pressure from above, the Plenum also voted against recommending it further up "to the highest level."[39]

The plenum discussion, though carefully coded to avoid all direct political speech, is as interesting for its absences as for its denunciations. At the plenum meeting on March 29, 1945, the chair, Solomon Mikhoels, presented the Film Section's nominees, listing the other films in order.[40] Only then did Mikhoels add that there was another candidate, "which had provoked debate on matters of principle in the section meeting . . . this film is Eisenstein's *Ivan the Terrible*. . . . No one said that the film isn't appealing [*ne tianet*] or that its craftsmanship is on an inferior level . . . but matters of principle and aesthetic positions, its methods, etc., called forth considerable objections."[41] This reluctance to make a decision for a prize bearing Stalin's name, on a film commissioned by Stalin, and clearly about Stalin is telling. Although almost everyone present agreed that *Ivan the Terrible*, Part I, was the work of a master craftsman, Film Section members were too uncomfortable with matters both aesthetic and political to agree even to nominate the film. They must have assumed that Stalin would not like it.

Bolshakov opened the plenum discussion with a stirring piece of circumlocution justifying his nomination of *Ivan the Terrible*: "A monumental work, in fact a unique work . . . every element of this film represents a new direction in cinema." He conceded that the music and the acting provoked disagreements, and that Eisenstein was "more a rationalistic than an emotional artist," and he insisted that the greatest achievement of the film was that Eisenstein "correctly conveyed the image of Ivan the Terrible." Bolshakov did not elaborate on this unambiguous pronouncement, but his next comment suggests that his criteria for promoting the work were more aesthetic than historical or political, perhaps to circumvent criticism on such sensitive issues: "Cherkasov's extraordinary acting created the image that we will now associate with Ivan. And therefore we consider that this film undoubtedly represents a major event."[42]

Plenum members were not persuaded by Bolshakov's speech or cowed by his authority. After Bolshakov spoke, the playwright A. E. Korneychuk declared that he loathed *Ivan*. "Eisenstein did nothing new in this film . . . individual frames are remarkable, but the film is cold, a rationalist film, which audiences will not understand." Then Korneychuk attacked Eisenstein directly: "this is formalism by a master who has made no forward progress but who, from our point of view, has only deepened his errors, . . . he has nothing to teach young artists. He is very far from realism. If he must be allowed to continue to make films . . . we do not need to honor him with a Stalin Prize." The specific causes of Korneychuk's outrage suggest that rationalism alone was not the problem. "Let's look at the funeral. The coffin stands there. But you need a ladder to get close enough to see it. . . . There are no people anywhere, there's very little of the epoch, the real Russia—I don't see it. . . . And Cherkasov here—this is a man in a fidget. All I remember is how he turns his head. He is not capable of touching anyone." Korneychuk concluded by challenging Bolshakov's assertion that Cherkasov's Ivan was historically or politically appropriate, hinting at his discomfort with the film's politics. "It has been said here that [Eisenstein] is the first to show Ivan the Terrible relatively faithfully according to the way he is seen today. But how does philosophical, historical thought see this period? Eisenstein was unable to depict the truly disturbing [*volnuiushchie*] images, and I am opposed to giving him the Stalin Prize."[43]

The leading art historian Igor Grabar picked up on the historical objections raised by Korneychuk. Like many historians then and now, Grabar was angered by factual inaccuracies in historical films and like many such critics, he invoked the filmmaker's failure to represent the past in its proper complexity as a cover for political disagreement.[44] The historical errors in the film infuriated Grabar particularly because "the author could have avoided [them] if he had only consulted with historians more, but Sergei Mikhailovich Eisenstein was so sure of his own competence that he never did that." In his outrage, Grabar recounted a telling anecdote from another film, "I once said to him in regard to *Alexander Nevsky*, 'How could you have Buslaev say, "Well this is a serious business" [*Nu, eto delo ser'eznoe*], in the thirteenth century, when the word *ser'eznoe* did not appear until the time of Anna Ivanovna,' . . . And Eisenstein had the nerve to reply, 'I did it on purpose.' Only children speak that way," Grabar remonstrated to the plenum. "This is trivial, of course, no one noticed, except us, poor sinners who know the Russian language and how it developed and so on, but permit me to tell you . . ." and he went on to list several more anachronisms Eisenstein allowed to slip into *Ivan*.[45] Other opponents of the film rose to add their voices to this particular choir. Vera Mukhina, the prominent sculptor, noted numerous mistakes in costuming and sets and protested Eisenstein's characterization of Anastasia as an "empty space," when she had been a bright, positive influence on the historical Ivan.[46] The architect A. G. Mordvinov said that his colleagues were all deeply disappointed to find that the film departed so egregiously from the style of the epoch, and that many of them approached him to ask incredulously if this film was really going to receive the Stalin Prize.[47]

It is obviously impossible to draw definitive conclusions from such an elliptical conversation, but it is just as obviously hard to believe that *Ivan the Terrible* was to be denied the Stalin Prize because of trivial anachronisms. One waits in vain for a discussion of the film's merits or of its value as a representative of the national canon. But those who attacked the film on artistic grounds went no farther than to say that the film was, in Grabar's formulation, "cold, cerebral, from the mind and not the emotions of the artist, and everything is done for the sake of effect, not for truth."[48] Or as Mukhina lamented, "in this film everything is from the head and nothing from the heart," but also, she claimed, there is very little of Russia here: "it is almost like a *Ring of the Niebelungs*. Ivan's dress in the final scene is practically Parsifal, this isn't Russian, and there is a great deal that is foreign in these things."[49]

When someone finally did speak out in defense of the film as art, it was none other than the director Mikhail Chiaureli, who was not known to be a supporter of Eisenstein's. Claiming to speak for other Russian filmmakers, Chiaureli proclaimed *Ivan the Terrible*, Part I, "such a great film, it should not be passed over." In comparison with other historical films, he said, *Ivan* was great, not because it was a monumental work or because it depicted important events, but "because here we see the magnificent [*grandioznyi*] taste of an artist, the gigantic, fascinating contours of an artist. . . . We can't always understand the leading artists of our time, who," he continued, "don't want to follow tradition, but who try to do something new, different, and perhaps stronger and more persuasive. He is driven by a desire to liberate us from tradition and make something interesting."[50]

No one on the committee recommended the film as an epic of Stalinist triumphalism. No one sang the praises of its Socialist Realist overcoming of obstacles on the path to national greatness or its defense of national unity. No one lingered on its meaningful rendering of Russia's heroic past or Ivan's progressive achievements. Given the film's complexity, perhaps this is not surprising. But no one *attacked* the film for failure to meet these conventional expectations either. Given that we are examining a roomful of people who wanted to deny the film a prize that carried immense political importance, this lack seems especially significant. It should have been easy to criticize *Ivan the Terrible* for failing to embody even the basic requirements of Socialist Realism, or for tarnishing Russia's historical legacy, or even for portraying the ruler in any of a number of less than glorious ways. Other works received exactly this sort of treatment, but in regard to *Ivan*, the committee studiously avoided all substantive political, artistic, and historical issues.

In the end, Mikhoels offered the thinnest but probably the most honest justification for nominating *Ivan the Terrible*: it was clearly superior to some of the other nominees. He conceded that the historical experts had found errors in the film, but that these were just "pretexts [*poiski*]." By any standards, it made sense at least to nominate *Ivan* and allow the members to vote on it.[51] At the end of the day, everyone agreed to put the film to a vote. Then twenty of the thirty-two voting members of the committee voted against the film.

In all fairness, even the humorless hacks on the Stalin Prize Committee were not alone in their resistance to *Ivan*'s power and *pathos*. But except for Korneychuk and Mordvinov, who seemed adverse to all complexity, the other viewers seemed more stunned than confused by the film's ambiguities. At the very least, their avoidance of either conventional defense or substantive attack reinforces the impression that *Ivan* was seen as a complex and ambivalent work, one with no clear message in a period when some degree of clarity was required both as an aesthetic principle and a ticket to political survival.

The avoidance of direct attack cannot be attributed to Eisenstein's stature or international renown. Throughout his career he had been the subject of criticism and controversy. While he enjoyed great prestige in the early 1940s, with his Stalin Prize for *Nevsky* and his high post at Mosfilm, he had been just outspoken enough to make his position still vulnerable. Meanwhile, the priority status Eisenstein received for this project may have engendered or inflamed considerable jealousy. The star director of Soviet cinema, the current favorite of Kremlin patronage, Eisenstein was granted more time, money, and attention for *Ivan the Terrible* than other film projects of the period. Yet what did he produce? A film that seemed to condemn tyranny while flattering the tyrant, a film no one could be sure he or she understood, a film that many considered to be "un-Russian."

This last charge—*Ivan*'s foreignness—is important. The film is obviously international in its borrowings and adaptations, and in the 1940s such a charge could be dangerous by itself. But comments made two years later after a number of people had seen Part II make it clear that complaints about cultural "un-Russianness" signified suspicions of political "anti-Russianness" and suggest how personal animosity overlapped with political criticism. In March 1947, Vishnevsky wrote a long critical review of Part II (that remained unpublished, to Eisenstein's great relief!), in which he wrote that Eisenstein "is too *western*, . . . He has forgotten about Rus[sian] nature, language, spirit, manner, Rus[sian] passions."[52] A few weeks later, in April 1947, Vishnevsky reported that Alexander Dovzhenko also disliked *Ivan*, Part II, and considered it un-Russian. He told Vishnevsky that "Eisenstein is a great talent, up to his neck in the debris of the library, in western aesthetics. . . . He will never return. . . . And also, he is always ironical, cynical. . . . Somewhere over the yawning *abyss*."[53] Then as if to clarify for himself where all this had led, at the end of April Vishnevsky recorded a single comment about Eisenstein made by Petr Pavlenko, a party member who had worked with him on *Nevsky* and on some of his unrealized projects in 1939–1940: "Pavlenko is critic[al] of Eisenstein: 'He sees history through irony. Inside, he is not one of us.'"[54] Or, as Korneychuk put it at the Stalin Prize plenum: "Yes, this is a big work, Eisenstein is an exacting artist, but his manner, his style are too far from everything we maintain about art."[55]

The question remains, however, why attacks on the film had to be so indirect and coded. Bolshakov's nomination of *Ivan* offered Stalin Prize committee members an easy choice, which almost no one took. As the official state representative in the film industry and as the individual responsible for

arranging Kremlin screenings of new Russian films, his statement supporting *Ivan* should have been taken as the official state-sanctioned position. It
was well known that Stalin had supported the project throughout. He personally approved the screenplay, he approved the release of Part I, and he
probably authorized Vishnevsky's positive review. Had anyone seen the film
as conformist or orthodox, as a film Stalin was likely to approve, committee
members could have saved themselves the trouble of an independent opinion
by affirming the nomination in the terms Bolshakov set out. Alternatively,
and perhaps more dangerously, they could almost as easily have rejected the
nomination by claiming that Eisenstein's film failed to live up to Bolshakov's
description of it and Stalin's expectations for it. So why did they resort to
coded, ambiguous, and trivial arguments? One can only conclude that viewers
either hated the film for its formal experimental style or feared it for its ambiguous politics. If they had seen *Ivan the Terrible*, Part I, as patriotic, heroic, or
tragic, they would have said so. But if they did not, that put them in a difficult situation. Knowing that Stalin had supported the film up until now but
seeing nothing acceptable about its content or style left them without a safe
response. And although Stalin had approved the film up through its release,
he was known to be terrifyingly capricious and manipulative. If viewers saw
the film as (at the very least) contradictory and ambiguous, foreign and cold,
it would have been safer to neither approve nor reject the film in clear terms
but to bury it in obfuscation.

The final and perhaps most vexing question is not why the committee
did not give Eisenstein a Stalin Prize, but why that decision was reversed. It
has always been assumed that Stalin made this final decision, but there is no
evidence to confirm this point, and it seems quite possible that Bolshakov
played a much larger role than anyone has suggested. He would have needed
Stalin's ultimate approval, of course, but he did not need to report to Stalin
all the obstacles the prize committee put in the way. It was not unusual for
the plenum's nominees to fail to win a prize in the end, and Bolshakov often
submitted additional names that had not been nominated by the committee.
In 1945, Zhdanov also actively intervened in the nomination process. Since
both Zhdanov and Bolshakov had invested their own cultural capital in Eisenstein's film, they may well have lobbied for a prize for *Ivan*, Part I.[56] Whatever
disagreements Eisenstein and Bolshakov had had during the production process, Bolshakov always spoke highly of *Ivan the Terrible*, both parts. He knew
that Stalin approved the scenario, and he knew how Stalin reacted to the film
when he viewed it because he was in the room. Did Stalin see *Ivan*, Part I, as
an ode on the order of *Alexander Nevsky*? No one else did. Perhaps Stalin was
flattered by what he saw, reading the surface narrative and none of the subtext

that other viewers could not ignore. Later Stalin told Eisenstein that he was untroubled by the demagoguery, manipulation, and violence portrayed in Part II, but in the second film, Ivan's cruelty was never properly justified or explained. One partial explanation offered by Naum Kleiman proposes that Stalin offered Eisenstein the prize as a kind of bribe: in this scenario, Stalin considered Part I to be just barely acceptable in political terms; he knew Eisenstein was finishing Part II and wanted to ensure that it would not deviate any further from Soviet aesthetic and political acceptability.[57] And Roshal' argues that Eisenstein wanted the prize for the same reason, but reversed: he wanted Stalin's approval as a kind of protection for completion of the rest of the film that he knew would be seen as more critical of the tsar.[58] Whatever the reason, Stalin gave Part I his approval—and his prize—but his response to Part II would be an entirely different matter.

This Isn't a Film—It's a @#$% Nightmare

According to Mikhail Romm, when Part II was almost finished, officials at the Ministry of Cinema called some directors together to see it, saying, "This is a problem—help us figure out what to do." After the screening, the officials said, "Give it to us straight." But Romm reports that no one dared say directly that they saw Stalin in Ivan, Beria in Maliuta, and his henchmen in the oprichniki. "And we were aware of much more we could not bring ourselves to say."[59] In early 1946, less than a week after Eisenstein sent the finished Part II to be printed, Bolshakov screened it for the Artistic Council of the Committee on Cinema Affairs. The Artistic Council had sharp criticism of Part II, and Stalin absolutely hated it.

If the Artistic Council found Part I confusing and problematic, they were outraged by Part II. The tenor of the discussion was unforgiving, though in some cases reluctantly unforgiving. The majority of council members saw the portrait of Ivan as too psychological and too cold-bloodedly violent. Many members praised the music, camerawork, acting, and direction, and they all saw it as artistically more polished and exciting than Part I, especially appreciating Eisenstein's use of color. But little detail on these topics was given. Every member who spoke criticized the depiction of Ivan as far removed from the progressive leader they expected—and they did so in damning terms. Unlike the council screenings of Part I, Eisenstein wasn't present at the discussion of Part II (he was in the hospital recovering from his heart attack), which might partially account for the harshness of the attacks. Ivan Pyriev, in particular, did not pull any punches. He went so far as to say that the film made him want to take the boyars' side against Ivan, who seemed more like a Grand Inquisitor than a

Russian tsar: "it makes me feel ashamed for our past, for the past of our Russia, ashamed for this great ruler—Ivan—who was the unifier and first progressive tsar of our Russia."[60] Romm said that while Efrosinia and Vladimir were given some human qualities, Ivan was given none at all. Romm didn't object to the theme of Ivan's loneliness, as others did, but said that Ivan should have punished the boyars only after The Fiery Furnace, a roundabout way of saying he was too cruel and too random in his retribution, having punished boyars before they did anything in opposition.[61] Galaktionov said the portrait of Ivan was too pessimistic, too Dostoevskian (not a compliment); that it offered no uplift, no way forward; it only showed the tsar's negative sides. He accused Eisenstein of using his great powers as an artist to lead people in the wrong direction.[62] Alexandrov praised the film, reminding the council members that the same group had harshly criticized Part I, but that he was happy to live in a country where a higher body could refute that criticism and grant Part I a Stalin Prize. Then he turned around and said that Eisenstein made a huge mistake in separating Part II from Part III, so that the audience doesn't get to see Ivan recover from his loneliness and justify his cruelty with the victory over Livonia and triumphant march to the sea.[63] Finally, Bolshakov intervened to say that it wouldn't be simple to brush off all this criticism, but that the criticism of Part I had led to corrections that improved the film and made its portrait of Ivan thorough and profound. Some revisions to Part II could also be made. Bolshakov emphasized the division of the scenario into three parts as the main problem and wanted the Livonian victory to be included to give purpose to Ivan's murders. Bolshakov appointed a commission to propose a plan for finishing and releasing the film.[64]

Despite the council's unrelenting criticism, Eisenstein's illness, and the uncertain postwar political situation, Bolshakov remained the consummate patron. He was hedging his bets on a deeply problematic film that had absorbed enormous resources made by one of the country's most famous artists about its most powerful figure. He developed a plan for making Part II acceptable and seems to have expected it to be completed and approved. Lev Indenbom told Eisenstein that Bolshakov had no hesitation about screening the film "further"—that is, for Stalin.[65] Bolshakov sent Eisenstein an equivocal telegram saying that the Artistic Council highly praised Ivan's artistic quality and directorial mastery and that suggestions were made regarding the presentation of Ivan as a progressive state leader.[66]

Indenbom sent Eisenstein a long, accurate description of the discussion, adding that the most hostile council members found the film gloomy and had trouble understanding what it was about. He said that he was told that Eisenstein should remain calm, that one couldn't expect anything else from Pyriev and he shouldn't let Pyriev's criticism bother him. He asked Eisenstein, apparently not for the first time, which version of the scenario for Part III he should send to Bolshakov. And then he added, "What worries me is when they said that Part II is an improvement on Part I as regards form but that Part II was worse than Part I in relation to its intellectual and political content."[67] As soon as Eisenstein recovered enough to speak, he told everyone who would listen that he was intent on screening the film for Stalin. According to Alexandrov, Eisenstein said that he fully expected Stalin to approve Part II.[68]

When Stalin sat down to watch *Ivan the Terrible,* Part II, a few weeks later, on March 2, 1946, it had been more than a year since he'd seen Part I but only a month after the Stalin Prizes had been announced. If 1944 (when Part I was completed) had been a moment when Stalin could feel cautious optimism about the victorious end to the war, early 1946 was a period of growing tensions and practical problems. The war was over, but the country was suffering from serious postwar disorders: massive destruction, demobilization, migration, hunger and famine, homelessness and displacement, and rising international tensions. Just weeks before the screening, on February 9, 1946, Stalin had given a major speech that signaled renewed militarism and hostility toward the Western powers that is considered one of the catalysts of the Cold War. Stalin was also well aware of the problems of depicting rulership in history and biography, having watched writers and artists struggle for more than a decade to produce a satisfactory biography of himself or an acceptable historical and artistic treatment of Ivan the Terrible, including Eisenstein's controversial *Ivan,* Part I.[69] Eisenstein's *Ivan,* Part II, was one of the last works on Ivan the Terrible that Stalin had commissioned before the war started.[70] It had taken a long time to complete and cost a lot of money, and Stalin was still seeing only Part II of a projected three-part film. Stalin would not have forgotten the criticism of Part I and the controversy over the Stalin Prize, and of course, his opinion of any film would determine its fate.[71] For all these reasons, when the lights went down in the Kremlin screening room, Stalin would have approached *Ivan,* Part II, with some conflicted expectations.

The explanations given for Stalin's divergent responses to Parts I and II are usually political. Stalin wasn't flattered by Eisenstein's portrait of Ivan as a ruler alternating between revenge and remorse. Political priorities had changed between 1944 and 1946, when *Ivan,* Part II, got caught up in the shift in cultural policy that revoked wartime leniency and reasserted party control. In the 1950s and 1960s, after the 1958 delayed release of Part II, many agreed with the film scholar Neia Zorkaia, quoted earlier, and Grigory Mariamov, who wrote in 1992 that Part I "did not yet touch on those scenes where the irreconcilable differences between Stalin and the director lurked."[72] In fact, as I have shown, censorship removed the most defiant scenes of Part I before it was screened for Stalin, so Part II only appeared to be more challenging and unacceptable by contrast.

These well-known factors undoubtedly played a role in Stalin's about-face, but I want to explore another, entirely overlooked possibility. There is evidence to suggest that Stalin—and Lavrenty Beria, Viacheslav Molotov, Andrei Zhdanov, and others in Stalin's inner circle who chimed in—hated *Ivan the Terrible*, Part II, for another reason altogether: its pervasive, inescapable, often humorous, and always defiant homoeroticism. I believe that the homoerotic subtext, which doesn't appear very "sub" to anyone watching Part II today, was not only legible to Kremlin filmgoers in 1946, but that it rattled Stalin and angered him. The evidence for my claim is necessarily speculative, but it is based on close reading, and rereading, of the documents that recorded Stalin's response to *Ivan*, Part II. The history of archival publication in the late and post-Soviet period is partly responsible for masking this aspect of Stalin's response. A single document, published for the first time in 1988, has come to dominate our understanding of Stalin's reaction to *Ivan the Terrible*, Part II: the transcript of the Kremlin conversation with Eisenstein that Stalin orchestrated in February 1947 and that displays him at his typically controlled and controlling. Reexamining this document and examining documents that have come to light since encourage us to reread and rethink the tenor and focus of that famous conversation. Nothing connected with the production and fate of Eisenstein's *Ivan the Terrible* was straightforward, and numerous misconceptions have accrued to its interpretation and reception history due to the typical silences and complexities of documenting the Stalin period.

First, let's remember what Stalin saw. After the opening credits and Prokofiev's majestic and ominous "Tsar Ivan" leitmotif, *Ivan the Terrible*, Part II, begins with Sigismund's Palace, where Kurbsky pledges fealty to the Polish King Sigismund in a kind of homoerotic flirtation ritual. And that's just the first scene. One might argue that since these are foreigners and traitors, neither Stalin nor anyone else would mind if Eisenstein opened his film by depicting the traitor's loyalty oath as a campy double-entendre sex scene. Politburo filmgoers might not object to momentarily superior Western power played as effeminate sexual prowess in contrast to manly Muscovy. In the scenario, which Stalin read three years earlier, Sigismund's courtiers were already identified as "effeminate," and he had not objected then.[73] But in *Ivan the Terrible*, Part II, the homoeroticism doesn't stop at the border or end with Scene 1. Sigismund's Palace is followed by one image after another of men embracing, entreating, caressing, dancing, and generally using their bodies in sexually provocative ways.

Women disappear almost completely in Part II, and almost every scene involves some form of homosociality or homoeroticism. Ivan flirts with

FIGURE 6.1   Fedka at The Dance of the Oprichniki

FIGURE 6.2   Execution as castration

his erstwhile friend, the priest Filipp, in begging for his friendship. Maliuta Skuratov caresses Ivan in a moment of the tsar's weakness, and Ivan pets Maliuta in return, in gratitude for his offer to carry out Ivan's bloody executions. Those executions are portrayed as castrations by Maliuta, who lovingly admires his sword (like Sigismund and Kurbsky). Ivan meets Fedka Basmanov in the empty bedchamber of Ivan's murdered wife, Anastasia, where Fedka attempts to transform his relationship to Ivan from son to lover and consummate that bond with words and seductive gestures. Remember that Eisenstein is explicit about their homoerotic relationship in his production notes: "He must love him."[74]

Perhaps most important, Part II as a whole, is bookended by the two most pervasively homoerotic scenes in the film: at the start, Sigismund's Palace and, at the climax, The Dance of the Oprichniki and the assassination of Vladimir Staritsky. The entire culminating sequence—the Dance and the assassination—is choreographed as a multipartnered homosocial dance orgy.[75] Ivan flirts with his banquet guests, Fedka performs in drag, and all the while, the rank-and-file oprichniki perform in a variety of dance styles, ultimately running, jumping, and piling on top of one another at Fedka's feet. A drawing of the scene is captioned *The scene that probably won't be. The appearance of the masquerade and the entrance of Anastasia.*"[76]

In the Epilogue Ivan strikes very much the same pose that Sigismund took at the beginning, but with an entirely different inflection. His knee is bent and his arm raised, but Ivan's body displays aggressive, manly force.

In his study of Kuzmin's *Wings* and Vasily Rozanov's *The Final Leaves*, Evgeny Bershtein identifies a literature that links homosexual awakening and liberation with social utopia and ideas about "the new man" of the future. He frames this literature—just as Eisenstein constructed *Ivan*, Part II—as a contest between Enlightenment rationality and Western liberationist thinking, on one hand, and a more "fragmentary, marginal, semi-confessional poetics" that celebrates "the ontological otherness of gay people and their existential marginality," on the other.[77] As discussed previously, against this lineage associating homosexuality and bisexuality with self-discovery and authenticity stands a much longer tradition of representations of Ivan the Terrible that linked homosexuality with moral degradation and used that linkage to challenge Ivan's legitimacy and authoritarianism. *Ivan the Terrible*, Part II, shows a lot of men suggestively handling their swords, flirting, dancing, petting, sulking in jealousy, hugging and kissing, castrating, and piling up on top of one another, all while Ivan becomes increasingly powerful and increasingly murderous, toying with his followers, destroying his enemies, fighting off assassins, outwitting danger, and suffering bouts of remorse. The first thing

FIGURE 6.3 *"The scene that probably won't be*. The entrance of the masquerade and the appearance of Anastasia in it ('Why did they separate me from my young girl?')" RGALI, 1923/2/1692/3 [Mar 21, 1942]. Used with permission.

Stalin saw in *Ivan*, Part II, was a *"très efféminé"* king and the last thing he saw was Ivan mimicking the king's posture. If Eisenstein was right about the way our brain processes images, Stalin would have made the connection (at least semiconsciously) between the first and last images of supreme rulers, not as a difference but as a difference *and* a sameness superimposed on one another.

These images not only raised questions about the nature of male rule, the all-male Kremlin, and the links between sexuality and power, but together they posed a fundamental challenge to Ivan's legitimacy and authority. And those connections would make any paranoid, Hamlet-hating, homophobe angry.

We have three documents that record Stalin's response to *Ivan the Terrible*, Part II. First, we have Ivan Bolshakov's testimony about Stalin's reaction to the film immediately after viewing it. As head of the Soviet film industry, Bolshakov was responsible for arranging Kremlin film screenings and was present on March 2, 1946, when Part II was screened for Stalin and some friends. Bolshakov's testimony, however, comes to us indirectly. His notes have not been made public, so the record is based on two abbreviated accounts: one by Bolshakov's assistant, Grigory Mariamov; and the other by Leonid Kozlov, who had access to Bolshakov's papers.[78]

The second document comes five months later. On August 9, 1946, Stalin gave a speech to the Central Committee that focused criticism on three films as part of the shift to the postwar cultural policy known as the Zhdanovshchina. The speech itself was published after the collapse of the Soviet Union, but in 1946 only excerpts were published in the form of a Central Committee Resolution pointing out the films' "errors." The resolution is dated September 4 and appeared in *Culture and Life* on September 10. Finally, we have the famous transcript of the conversation that took place on the night of February 25/26, 1947, between Stalin, Molotov, and Zhdanov and Eisenstein and Cherkasov. Immediately afterward, on Bolshakov's advice, Eisenstein and Cherkasov dictated a record of the conversation to their friend, the journalist Boris Agapov. Agapov typed it up, and they signed it.[79] That conversation has now been widely published, though only excerpts have been translated into English, and it forms most people's understanding of Stalin's views of *Ivan the Terrible*, Part II.

Before turning to the documents themselves, a few words on sexuality and its policing under Stalin are necessary. Stalin cultivated male camaraderie and competition in his inner circle, but he was no friend to homosexual men. Male homosexuality—legally defined as sodomy—was criminalized in 1934 after Genrikh Yagoda, deputy chief of the People's Commissariat of Internal Affairs (NKVD), brought a draft law to Stalin, ostensibly intended to eradicate public disorders connected with gay men's use of bathhouses, public toilets, and outdoor spaces. Stalin agreed that "these scoundrels must receive exemplary punishment."[80] We do not know if Eisenstein, with his cautious personality and his complicated sexuality, slipped out of his flat on Chistye Prudy to participate in the lively, semi-surreptitious queer scene that Dan Healey described going on in his neighborhood, but he was certainly aware of the law and its potential consequences for all homosexual men.[81] In 1934, after the law was passed, Eisenstein married Pera Atasheva, in what is universally assumed to have been a fictional marriage and a sign that the law was perceived as a threat that would reach beyond the circle of men meeting in bathhouses and on the streets.

Let's take the documents in chronological order, beginning with the immediate aftermath of the Kremlin viewing. Things did not go well in Stalin's
screening room that night. Mariamov reports that when Bolshakov returned
to his office, he was "unrecognizable." His face was all blotchy and one eye
was half closed, which, according to Mariamov, was a sure sign of Bolshakov's
"extreme agitation" (and which is, at the very least, ironic, given the repeated
image of a closed or covered eye in the film). Bolshakov refused to say anything about what happened that night at the screening, but eventually some
of his most trusted friends got a few details out of him and shared them with
Mariamov. He tells us that as soon as the lights came up, Stalin erupted: "This
isn't a film, it's some kind of a nightmare! [*Ne fil'm, a kakoi-to koshmar!*]."[82]
This is pure speculation on my part, but it seems likely to me, given what
came next, that that *kakoi-to* might be a sanitized version of something more
demonstrative: "a @#$% nightmare!" In any case, that outburst, according
to these sources, opened the floodgates for the other members of the select
audience to start hurling their own expletives at the film, the angriest among
them said to be Beria. Kozlov confirms Mariamov's account and gives a little
more detail, though he plays down the drama. He wrote that "both [Stalin
and Beria] were extremely aggravated by the depiction of the oprichniki."[83]
Beria likened The Dance of the Oprichniki to a *khlystovskoe radenie*, the term
used for bacchanalian gatherings of the heretical sect known as the *khlysty*.[84]
A *radenie* involved singing and twirling dances intended to produce a state
of sexual and spiritual ecstasy in believers, not unlike the dancing and singing of Eisenstein's oprichniki, as Beria observed (though without any enjoy-
ment). Translations of *radenie* have misleadingly removed all trace of its male
exclusivity, its homoeroticism, and its heresy. A *radenie* was not "a coven of
witches," as one English translation has it, or a "Witches' Sabbath," as in
another, but an all-male gathering of subversive, religious heretics, whose
swirling dances were assumed to end in all-male orgies.[85] Notice also that
it is not the portrait of Ivan that's emphasized here but the depiction of the
oprichniki, Ivan's personal army, who by Part II had taken to dressing in their
pretty, fur-trimmed outfits. Both Mariamov and Kozlov add that at the end of
the evening, just before storming out, Stalin angrily warned Bolshakov that
things were about to change: "We didn't raise a hand to you during the war,
but now we'll deal with you as necessary."[86] So Stalin's immediate response
to the film was fuming anger, a hail of expletives, and a dramatic final threat
triggered by subversive, homosexual innuendo.

Several things are worth pointing out here. It was unlike Stalin to lose control. We don't know exactly what he was thinking, but the tone suggests something more than an intellectual objection to the political and psychological

profile of Ivan and the oprichniki. We don't know exactly why Stalin reacted so emotionally, and we don't know what Beria and others were swearing about, but the emotional intensity of their reactions deserves our attention.

We have a much fuller record of Stalin's response to *Ivan*, Part II, in his speech at the Central Committee meeting in August. Here for the first time, he publicly stated the objections that would be repeated in the press in the form of the Central Committee resolution, then in Bolshakov's book about Soviet film during the war, then more expansively in the conversation with Eisenstein and Cherkasov the following year, and then everywhere after the transcript of that conversation was published.[87] Despite the similarity of the specific criticisms, the two documents are different in significant ways.

In the speech Stalin accused Eisenstein of three errors. First, the director failed to prepare sufficiently for making the film because he failed to study history properly (criticism Eisenstein correctly foresaw in trying so insistently to publish his Historical Commentary in 1943 in order to forestall it). Stalin accused all three films of this lapse and used the criticism to put the filmmakers in their place. "Study takes patience," Stalin said irritably, "and some people don't have that patience, they just throw everything together and present us with a film: here swallow this just because it has Eisenstein's stamp on it."[88] In other words, because Eisenstein was too lazy to study history, his Ivan and his oprichniki failed to correspond with Stalin's view of history. Stalin saw Eisenstein's Ivan as a "weak-willed Hamlet" and the oprichniki as "degenerates, something like the American Ku Klux Klan." These criticisms line up with the official historiography on Ivan and with Stalin's response to the screenplay three years earlier. These are the three issues—the historical record and the characterizations of Ivan and the oprichniki—that Stalin repeatedly returned to and that everyone cites in discussing his attack on the film.

But what's curious here is that a careful reading of the speech, independently of what Stalin said before and afterward, raises some questions about the summaries of his views that have shaped the common wisdom about Stalin's reading of *Ivan*, Part II. Mariamov and Kozlov limit themselves to the basics in their reports of the speech: Stalin saw Ivan as weak-willed and Hamlet-like, and the oprichniki as "degenerates" who resemble the KKK. Rereading the stenogram of the speech, Stalin's attack on *Ivan* seems impetuous, almost improvised. It's oddly emotional and seems less than rational and calculating. Stalin's remarks on *Ivan*, Part II, came sandwiched between criticism of Vsevolod Pudovkin's *Admiral Nakhimov* and Leonid Lukov's *A Great Life*, and he began by saying that the shortcomings of Pudovkin's film put him in mind of *Ivan the Terrible*, Part II. "I don't know if any of you have seen it, but I have and it's an abominable thing [*omerzitel'naia shtuka*]." He goes on in a tone that is both outraged, informal, and crudely patronizing. "The guy got completely distracted from history [*Chelovek sovershenno otvleksia ot istorii*]" and depicted the oprichniki as "the worst kind of filth, degenerates [*kak poslednikh parshivtsev, degeneratov*], something like the Ku Klux Klan."

The translation in Clark and Dobrenko's edition renders *omerzitel'naia shtuka* as "a vile thing!" and "*kak poseldnikh parshivtsev, degeneratov*" as "rotten scoundrels." Neither of these, in my view, captures the sense of utter disgust expressed in the original. This is what the Multitrans online dictionary gives for *omerzitel'nii*: "abominable, detestable, loathsome, lousy, repulsive, disgusting, ghoulish, hateful, sordid, unwholesome, revolting, hideous, abhorrent, scurvy, unedifying, despicable, obscene."[89] The literary "vile" and archaic "scoundrels" lack the immediate, visceral repulsion and moral outrage in the original. And Stalin repeats "degenerate" every time he refers to *Ivan the Terrible*, as do his henchmen, usually more than once. In his speech, Stalin also seems to link Ivan to the "degeneracy" of the oprichniki. He explains to his audience that nineteenth-century historians, in their zeal to criticize the repressive regime of Nicholas II, rushed to censure the historical Ivan the Terrible for his repressive policies and his oprichniki for carrying them out. They did not understand that Russia "had to unify" in order to keep from falling back under the Tatar Yoke. He said, "How could Eisenstein not know, because there is literature, but he somehow depicted these degenerates. Ivan was a man with will, with character, but in Eisenstein he's some kind of weak-willed Hamlet."[90]

Stalin didn't use this kind of moralistic language or emotionally aggrieved tone about either of the other films discussed on that day. It may be, of course, that Stalin simply took Eisenstein's portrait of Ivan personally and didn't like being portrayed as an eccentric murderer with a conscience. But the language, scanty though it is, speaks powerfully in its repetitions and its intensity. Stalin's choice of words goes beyond deviance from the historical record to deviance from heteronormativity. Of course, "degenerate" can refer to many things: foreigners were called degenerates, as were slackers, but the word was often used to denote sexual difference. Stalin used "degenerate" and as well as *parshivets*, which I've translated as "filth," to refer to homosexuals in connection with the 1934 law.[91]

This kind of language with its excessive speech patterns is hard to explain in conventional ways. If the issues were primarily political, or primarily stylistic, or primarily what Stalin liked to call "historical," why label the oprichniki "degenerates"? Why call them degenerates repeatedly and insistently? Eisenstein's oprichniki are violent and murderous, to be sure, but Stalin doesn't object to that. And, for the most part, they display true loyalty to Ivan, an attribute Stalin valued. Eisenstein's oprichniki are, in fact, Ivan's most loyal servitors, absolutely devoted to him. They carry out his orders and act as Ivan's "effective instrument," just as Stalin explicitly wished (even those who would betray him, Aleksei and von Staden). So what is degenerate about them? Other than the nonverbal, visually depicted pleasure they take in each other, and the homosociality and homoeroticism that they consistently display, there is no marker of what Stalin labels "degeneracy" or of "filthy *parshivost'*" among the oprichniki.

The language of "weakness" also suspiciously links degeneracy to effeminacy. Those last two sentences of Stalin's remarks on *Ivan* follow one another in such a way that the degeneracy of the oprichniki seems to apply to Ivan and his weak-willed Hamletness—unmanly traits, in normative gender terms. For Stalin and his men, Ivan isn't just indecisive, he doesn't just suffer from remorse or doubt, he's weak, weak-willed, and neurotic. To me, these labels smack of discomfort, even disgust, with handsome young men dressed in velvet and furs, who hug a lot and dance with each other and gaze at each other with gestures of physical intimacy.

The extreme language and impulsive, emotional outbursts are almost entirely absent from the transcript of the Kremlin conversation, the best known of the records of what Stalin said. That conversation, which lasted just over an hour in February 1947, repeated the main subjects the earlier documents raised, stressing the notes of degeneracy and weakness, but it differs in significant ways.[92] The beginning of the conversation shows Stalin as his most composed and controlled. His comments, as well as Zhdanov's and Molotov's, seem largely planned and scripted. Almost everyone who has commented on Stalin's response to *Ivan*, Part II, focuses on this conversation rather than the two earlier, more spontaneous, and less polished statements, so the heightened emotions and tone of moral outrage apparent on those occasions and missing from the scripted Kremlin meeting have gone entirely unappreciated.

When this transcript was first published, it was a revelation.[93] As the only record we had of Stalin speaking directly about the arts, it seemed to offer rare insight into his views and into the relationship between Stalin and one of the Soviet Union's most important artists. Its undisputed value, however, should not persuade us to read it as a verbatim record. Dictated by Eisenstein and Cherkasov, it is a record of remembered, and likely self-censored, speech. The transcript is full of ellipses and elisions, and it alternates between verbatim statements and third person renderings of what was said ("And then Cherkasov discussed . . ."). Crucially, we have no idea what was left out. What, for example, was represented by the elision in this obviously important sentence: "Next Stalin made a series of remarks regarding the interpretation of Ivan the Terrible. . . ." Given that all of Stalin's other, well-known criticisms of Ivan were recorded elsewhere in the transcript (Hamlet-like, religious, neurotic, remorseful), it is not hard to imagine that this "series of remarks" concerned something different from the usual litany of complaints, and perhaps something none of these men wanted to say explicitly and in public.

One intriguing possibility appears in the archival folder holding the typed transcript of the meeting. In addition to the transcript, the folder contains two small pieces of paper with notes scribbled in Eisenstein's (and maybe Cherkasov's?) hand. In Cherkasov's memoir he says that after the conversation was over, he and Eisenstein walked around Red Square for a couple of hours discussing the conversation. It's possible that they jotted down these notes at that time.

All except one item are abbreviated references to topics that appeared in the transcript: "Kurbsky—great"; "catching the fly—good"; "Petrukha" [Stalin's name for Peter the Great]; references to God; Stalin's trivial, imperious correction of Zhdanov; and many more, all familiar from the published transcript. The one note that doesn't appear in the transcript is explicitly sexual and implicitly homosexual: "Clownish element in the dance. If [something crossed out] they went off together, and they probably went off together, then they probably went off into the shadows. [*Esli* (something crossed out) *i guliali—a guliali naverno, to naverno po t'me.*]"[94] The transcript, therefore, is not as transparent as it has been made to seem.

This was a very strange conversation by any measure. It was ostensibly called in response to Eisenstein's request for a meeting to discuss the possibility of revising Part II in order to lift the ban on its release. But Stalin seems less interested in issues of revision than in showing off his own expertise and putting the filmmaker in his place.[95] Eisenstein let Cherkasov do most of the talking, and after a while, Stalin addressed most of his comments to the actor, but I read Eisenstein's few comments as ironic and even borderline rude. Kozlov drew a similar conclusion; he noted both that Eisenstein showed none of his usual diplomatic skill during the meeting and that his behavior visibly irritated Stalin.[96] To Stalin's opening question, "Have you studied history?" he said (or he says that he said), "More or less." To Stalin's remark that the oprichniki resemble the Ku Klux Klan, Eisenstein said, "They wore white hoods, ours wore black." And to complaints about Ivan's beard, he said that when he reedited the film he would make Ivan's beard shorter. However one interprets Eisenstein's behavior, what is most striking is the difference between this conversation and the two earlier instances when Stalin spoke more spontaneously. In this context, meeting with Eisenstein in his own Kremlin office, Stalin expressed none of his earlier outrage; to do so would have given Eisenstein the tactical advantage of knowing that he had caused Stalin to lose his cool.

If we focus solely on the topics discussed, it becomes apparent that Stalin was at pains to show some new concerns. After he began the conversation by casually noting that he had received Eisenstein's letter requesting a meeting four months earlier and basically ignored it until now (a little passive aggressive power move to start things off), Eisenstein and Cherkasov dove in with a plan for reediting and reshooting Part II to "correct" it. Stalin changed the subject immediately and began telling Eisenstein and Cherkasov that history is important and they got it wrong. He said that the film's oprichniki are like the Ku Klux Klan rather than a "regular army, a progressive army," and that Eisenstein's Ivan lets other people tell him what to do; he needs to be more decisive. Stalin continued by stating that Ivan was a "great and wise ruler," whose wisdom was evident in his protection of Russia from unfavorable foreign trade and indeed from all Western influence. Ivan was, for this reason, superior to all the rulers who followed: Peter I and all the "German courts" of Catherine II, Alexander I, and Nicholas I. The xenophobia that marked the last years of Stalin's rule is a new issue, and he made a point of emphasizing it here.

After Stalin's history lesson, Zhdanov changed the subject back to Eisenstein's Ivan: he's too neurotic. Then Molotov chimed in to complain that there was too much attention to psychology and feelings. Stalin's contribution to this part of the conversation was to return to Eisenstein's historical errors: "It is necessary to show the historical figure in correct style. For example, it was not correct that in the first series Ivan the Terrible kissed his wife so long. In that period it was not permitted." He said that the historical Ivan should have killed more of the elite, and Eisenstein should not have shown the tsar as remorseful when he did. This is when Stalin told Eisenstein that Ivan's religious faith and conscience kept him from acting decisively.

The conversation turned to discussion of other historical events and other films, and Stalin reiterated the importance of history (again). Cherkasov said that he was sure corrections would make *Ivan* a better film. To this Stalin replied, "May God grant you a new year every day! (Laughs) [*Dai vam bog, kazhdyi den'—novyi god! (Smeetsia)*]."[97] In the context of the conversation, this can only be interpreted as derisive mockery—something like "Sure, why not!" or "You might as well—anything can happen. Haha." Most efforts by Eisenstein and Cherkasov to bring the conversation back to concrete plans or details were contemptuously dismissed by Stalin. The only exception is

Stalin's interest in how Part III was supposed to end. The effect was to trivialize the filmmakers' concerns and replace the ostensible purpose of the conversation—editing *Ivan*, Part II, and finishing Part III—with Stalin's own preference for pointing out the film's deficits and lecturing on history and foreign affairs. After this, the conversation began to ramble: a long digression on Czechoslovakia, the US bombing of European cities at the end of the war, the film Cherkasov was currently making, and the repetition of points made earlier. Stalin repeated, for example, that portraying the violence and cruelty of Ivan and his oprichniki was fine, but that it was necessary to explain why they had to be cruel and to show that Ivan was a nationalist who did not allow foreigners or foreign influence into the country. Finally, on taking leave of them, Stalin asked after Eisenstein's health. Although the conversation was very wide ranging, even informal at times, when it came to talking about *Ivan the Terrible*, the transcript that Eisenstein and Cherkasov dictated left out much of what was said.

Up until recently most people have assumed, even in the face of Stalin's repeated comments about Ivan's weaknesses, doubts, and remorse, that Stalin's criticism of Eisenstein's Ivan was that he was too Terrible, too cruel, too violent, and that Eisenstein's portrait was too critical of the sixteenth-century tsar. It was only in 1999 that David Brandenberger and Kevin Platt showed that Eisenstein's Ivan, on the contrary, wasn't too terrible for Stalin, but that he wasn't "terrible enough."[98] They shifted our attention from comments like Zorkaia's, quoted earlier, to Stalin's claims that Ivan should have been "more decisive" in killing his enemies and less worried about divine or other judgment. I am not suggesting that homophobia and a lack of a sense of humor about court politics are the only reasons Stalin banned *Ivan the Terrible*, Part II. But I would argue that, although political concerns underlay his criticism and these recent political interpretations are persuasive and important, they sidestep suggestions that something else was also going on here, something none of these men wanted to talk about openly. It is unlikely that we will discover hard evidence of such responses, but the difference between Stalin's initial, unguarded outbursts and the controlled performance and changed priorities in his own office are worth discussing. The fact that Stalin was most interested in exhibiting what he considered his historical expertise, that he left stylistic commentary to his advisers, and ignored or ridiculed Eisenstein's and Cherkasov's practical questions suggests that his main goal in this conversation was to assert his power over the filmmakers and remind them of the stakes involved in their work. He avoided any sign that the film upset him—that he considered it "some kind of nightmare." It is certainly possible to imagine that the unspecified "series of remarks regarding the interpretation of Ivan the Terrible" included a discussion of taboo topics, whether political or sexual and homoerotic, but Eisenstein himself was typically reluctant to put such observations on paper. Just as Stalin knew that his power lay in discipline and punishment, Eisenstein knew his own power lay in the evocative images he put on the screen.

In the year between his Kremlin conversation with Stalin and his premature death, Eisenstein made no effort to revise *Ivan*, Part II. He arranged several private showings for his friends and students and discussed the film with members of the Artistic Council who saw it in February 1946. He was upset with Vishnevsky, who wrote a fifteen-page critique of the film, and he was still annoyed when Vishnevsky phoned a couple of weeks later. But he was pleased with the friends and colleagues who seemed to appreciate the tenor of his portrait of Ivan, even if it terrified them. Years later, Romm recounted that after the secret official screening he attended, "in Eisenstein's audacity, in the sparkle in his eyes, in his evocative, skeptical smile we felt that he was acting consciously, that he decided to go for broke. It was frightening."[99]

State-sponsored memory projects succeed or fail on their appeal to a culture's needs and acceptance by a broad swath of the public. In the 1930s and 1940s, Stalin and his propagandists sought to legitimate Soviet rule by resurrecting prerevolutionary Russian leaders and giving them Soviet pedigrees. Peter the Great, as a dynamic, imperialist, and authoritarian ruler, turned out to be more appropriate to Stalinist needs and more convincing as a Soviet precursor than Ivan the Terrible. When it came time to resurrect Ivan, the artists commandeered for the project found it difficult to fulfill state requirements while crafting believable or useful narratives. All the commissioned novels, plays, and films ran into difficulties representing state-mandated themes, which proved either too complicated historically (the oprichnina) or too dangerous politically (Ivan's personality and motives). Many of the problems Eisenstein confronted plagued other projects on Ivan the Terrible during the war and other artistic works immediately after the war. Contemporary responses to Eisenstein's *Ivan the Terrible* illustrate many of the problems Stalin encountered in the campaign to create a Soviet historical memory.

The responses to *Ivan*, Parts I and II, don't change what we know about Eisenstein's goals in the film, but they do resolve some questions and correct some misinformation. No one in the Soviet Union whose uncensored opinion we have saw Part I as a straightforward depiction of Ivan the Terrible as a wise and just ruler. Opinions were divided on the film as a work of art: some found it a cinematic masterpiece, but just as many found it strange and alienating. There were no serious formal studies published at the time, so it is difficult to know what *Ivan*'s first viewers thought of its ability to effect *pathos* or *ekstasis*, but many of those who criticized the film found it cold and cerebral. We know that Artistic Council viewers felt free to praise Eisenstein's craftsmanship, though not in very specific terms, and to criticize its political liabilities, but again only in generalities. Those whom Indenbom had identified as people who kept their "noses attuned to the way the wind is blowing" clearly understood that if the portrait of Ivan in Part I had been just barely acceptable, the Ivan of Part II crossed the line. And they were right. Bolshakov and others thought Eisenstein made a mistake in ending Part II where he did, without the vindication of the victory on the sea that ends the scenario, but it is not hard to think that they were wrong. In the scenario, Part III actually multiplies Ivan's twisted cruelties, the number of his victims, and the parallels with Stalin's terror. The end is as damning as it is vindicating.

Eisenstein's diaries and the memoirs of his friends and colleagues make it clear that he cared about his audience. He wanted *Ivan the Terrible* to be seen, and he wanted people to believe that it was a great work of art. We will never know whether self-preservation, illness, writing projects, or contemporary xenophobia and nationalist politics kept him from revising Part II or trying to finish Part III, but all four surely shaped that decision. And I have to conclude that although he needed Stalin's approval during the war to keep the project going, he was not displeased to have provoked Stalin's anger. Kozlov and Kleiman both report that in February 1947 Eisenstein told a friend, "I met with Stalin. We didn't like each other."[100]

Conclusion

A cat is never on the side of power.

—Chris Marker, *Grin without a Cat*

Stalin's image was everywhere in Russia during his rule, but analytical and insightful portraits of the ruler were virtually nonexistent—and for obvious reasons. Public monuments cast Stalin as an omnipotent, beloved father figure, while censorship, terror, and mandatory conformity made it dangerous to produce a counterportrait, even for the drawer. It is deeply ironic, therefore, that the most thoughtful contemporary portrait of the Soviet ruler and the history of Russian state power can be found in a work of art from the 1940s that seems more surreal than analytical, a film that was butchered by censorship and self-censorship, that was produced under the terrible privations of war, and that was eventually abandoned unfinished by its creator. Double the irony to discover the portrait not hidden away in some long closed archive, but in a film that was commissioned directly by Stalin and rewarded with a Stalin Prize . . . and then banned by Stalin. Eisenstein wasn't a systematic political thinker, and *Ivan the Terrible* isn't a treatise. Nonetheless, the film and Eisenstein's writing about it present a coherent and compelling political narrative and a method for depicting complex issues on film that would challenge and transform its viewers.

Making *Ivan the Terrible* required Eisenstein to give serious attention to the inner workings of history and biography for the first time in his career. Character, narrative, and historical process called for new cinematic methods that expanded and enriched Eisenstein's tools for transforming the images in his head into images on film and for conveying those ideas and feelings to an audience. The need to hide his own Ivan inside a veneer of Stalin's Ivan made the process more difficult but also enabled Eisenstein to experiment with a gradual, sensory, specifically cinematic method of character and narrative construction based on sensory-emotional thinking, excavation, and reconstruction. Eisenstein reveals his Ivan and the tragedy of one-man rule incrementally, in fragments addressed to our unconscious to be collected and connected as we watch Ivan evolve. We come to understand him by constructing networks of the visual, verbal, and sensory cues linked with the picture of Ivan that we see change across the time frame of the film. The spiral, the fugue, the polyphonic montage, and the *ekstasis* of dialectical synthesis create a multifaceted, dynamic character who challenges us to continually question what we are seeing and what he is doing.

Eisenstein believed that he could make us feel Ivan's attraction to violent revenge and that we would be compelled to ask the same questions Ivan asks every time he is opposed: Is this the right path? Am I right in what I am doing? By what right do you judge, Tsar Ivan? Eisenstein used such questions to show us Ivan dealing with his inner doubts about the efficacy of centralized, one-man-rule and about the morality of the violence necessary to stay in power. He projects those inner conflicts onto Ivan's confrontations with other characters, and he uses them to model questions we can't help but ask ourselves. The answers were not predetermined by ideology or genre formula as in many other films of the Socialist Realist era. In *Peter the First* (1937), Peter overcomes various challenges to reign victorious as emperor, and in Grigory Alexandrov's *The Radiant Path* (1940), a Soviet Cinderella overcomes numerous obstacles to become a Soviet princess and win the prince and the magical car. Those outcomes were presented as inevitable and eminently good. Ivan too overcame obstacles to found the state and reach the sea, but at every point along the way, as he kills more enemies and accrues more power, Eisenstein makes the audience wonder right along with him, am I right in what I am doing? The goal is always the state-approved goal—the Great Russian State—but the obstacles are often of Ivan's own making, once he provokes the opposition into action and then eggs them on with every new outrage. Each new cycle of eye-for-eye revenge, each action and reaction, stages the impossible conflicts between private and public morality, and personal and political loyalty, which produce in Ivan (and in us) questions and self doubt. Stalin recognized this tactic and denounced it: "Ivan the Terrible should have been even more decisive."

But Eisenstein's goal was never mere critique of violence or autocratic, one-man rule. To explain *"the most atrocious things,"* one needed to explain *"the caracter that he became"*: that is, the ways in which Ivan changed over time to become the bloody, manipulative, demagogic tyrant he became. The "fugue on the theme of power" mapped onto the double historical and biographical spiral—the irresistible pull to revisit the past as we move forward in time—to demonstrate the tragic inevitability of conflict between personal and political imperatives in one-man rule and in the one-man ruler. Everywhere he looked, Eisenstein found emotions at the center of political conflicts and saw ideologies integrated into personal ones: love, loss, loyalty, rejection, jealousy, betrayal, deception, shrewdness, and lewdness. Every positive feeling in the film, such as loyalty or love, is shadowed by betrayal or deception or exploitation. Eisenstein began by linking the anguished confession of an old man who knows he's done wrong with the grief of a child whose mother has been murdered by the family's political enemies. From that conjunction, he sought the personal in the political and found a near-infinity of intersecting lines. He explored the conflict between personal and political ethics not in order to discover which one is preferable or because the exclusion of either makes for superior rulers, but rather to show that the conflict between personal and public motivation is inherent in the nature of absolute rule. He found that the personal motives for political ambition can maximize the violence involved. Revenge may seem to serve justice—one of your enemy eyes for one of my mother's or one of my wife's—but because it is, in fact, an unacknowledged attempt to alleviate the revenger's own grief as well, it can never been extinguished. But Eisenstein also found that sacrificing the personal, including especially the human need for judgment, by trying to suppress it or rise above it had even more monstrous consequences. These conflicts between ambition and ethics resonated with Eisenstein's own sense of shame and collaboration, as he revealed in his diary and memoirs.

Did he see any alternatives to absolute power? Like Shakespeare and Pushkin, Eisenstein was skeptical of democratic institutions and portrayed popular power in his notes and in the film as inevitably, inexorably giving way to corruption and demagoguery. For all three artists, the only thing capable of limiting a monarch's violence or excessive, sadistic uses of power was an awareness of some kind of judgment and a conscience. Like *Macbeth*, Eisenstein's *Ivan the Terrible* is based on the belief that "We still have judgment here, . . . this even-handed justice/Commends the ingredients of our poisoned chalice/To our own lips." But Eisenstein, like Boris Godunov and like Ivan, could not resist the call of power "which o'erleaps itself, and falls on the other."[1] Eisenstein could perhaps imagine a power that did not lead to disaster if it were restrained by judgment and remorse, but power "which o'erleaps itself"—the most dangerous thing—elicits sarcasm and irony because it is the thing that human beings can't resist.

It has become common to say that Eisenstein's Ivan is good *and* evil, a hero *and* a victim, as if Eisenstein were hedging his bets or saw in Ivan a kind of dualism that could be taken at face value.[2] But Eisenstein's dualisms were never that kind of static binary, never simply linked, but were always in dynamic interaction, as he put it in his conversation with Moskvin. And Ivan's inner divisions had content. He was conflicted about specific aspects of ruling and specific aspects of personal sacrifice and public responsibility. He had an instinct to listen to his conscience, to compromise, to resist violent retribution, but he repeatedly overrode his conscience in favor of revenge, murder, deception, and humiliation, all in the name of a higher cause. His loneliness, associated with personal abandonment and individual rule, was both a result of his public commitment, his role as tsar, and a cause of the actions he took as tsar. His remorse didn't simply evaporate in the face of his commitment to his mission; it competed throughout the film with the pre-logical instinct for revenge. Eisenstein's Ivan had to actively face and choose to reject the message of his conscience over and over again. The historical Ivan felt enough remorse at the end of his life to travel around his realm making donations and praying for those he had killed. Eisenstein extrapolated from that historical evidence, from earlier theatrical and cinematic performances of Ivan's confession, and from his own sense of shame and remorse to depict all the moral and political conflicts of Ivan's entire life. Eisenstein's Ivan hesitates in advance or regrets in retrospect exactly the kind of violence Stalin never apologized for, never regretted, and never forgave. As we watch, Ivan repeatedly does just what Eisenstein told Prokofiev: he overcomes his hesitation to follow Pushkin's Boris Godunov and reach for the highest power, only to "fall from the highest point—Irony and sarcasm flow[ing] from the tragedy." Eisenstein's portrait of Ivan is not one that combines "terror and greatness," the undeniably widespread trope that Kevin Platt discovered in his study of cultural responses to Russian historical figures, but a recognition of and challenge to that trope.[3] Ivan's reach for "greatness" is always shown to be disastrous, but his ambition, his desire, and his self-motivated selflessness are all deeply human. Ivan repeatedly strives for suprahuman greatness but, like Lucifer, is repeatedly thrown back into the pool with the rest of us sinners. This "greatness" isn't great; this is Eisenstein, following Pushkin, showing "greatness" as a state of deception, self-deception, and inevitable tragedy that "falls on the other." Not a myth, but a man.

Eisenstein's exploration of the conflicts and contradictions of one-man rule all involve the kind of dualism that attracted him to Ivan the Terrible as a character. But then, as he wrote in *Nonindifferent Nature*, his attraction to Ivan's contradictory, ambitious, remorseful, tenacious psychology is precisely what prevented him from representing Ivan as a typical Socialist Realist character who heroically overcame his inner divisions to achieve his political mission.[4] In terms of narrative and form, *Ivan the Terrible* used Socialist Realist conventions to create a surface narrative, but only in order to obliterate them. The Socialist Realist hero was a "positive hero" and a "guide to life," and the master narrative, as Katerina Clark identified it, was a tale of progress, from worse to better, from spontaneity to consciousness, from not-socialism to socialism.[5] The realistic and hyperrealistic-fantasy style of Socialist Realist art was meant to make socialism seem real. It didn't reflect or depict socialism; according to Evgeny Dobrenko's useful formulation, Socialist Realism was where socialism was performed.[6] By giving Ivan the Terrible the veneer of a "progressive hero," and by endowing Ivan's mission with a "progressive" history, Eisenstein showed just how monstrous the principles underlying those conventions were. By making a film in the style that had been explicitly rejected by the architects of Socialist Realism, by staging Ivan's biography and his ascent to the highest power as a grotesque, modernist nightmare, with all of Ivan's personal traumas and inner conflicts spilling out of his body onto the entire population around him, Eisenstein uncovers the horror show at the heart of Stalinist ideology and practice.[7] It wasn't just Ivan or Stalin or the ideal-type bloody tyrant who was a monster, but the positive hero itself, the collective hero ruling in the name of the people, revolutionary change and historical progress, individual class consciousness, hetero-normative sexuality, Soviet subjectivity, the Great Soviet Family with Stalin at its head, and the prescribed forms for embodying them that were all grotesque inversions. In that sense, *Ivan the Terrible* took Socialist Realism and the ideology that spawned it and turned them inside out.

In making *Ivan the Terrible*, Eisenstein never forgot who his first audience was. How could he? An ambitious artist, making his most ambitious film, he was playing for the highest stakes and chose to go face-to-face with the country's most powerful critic. Eisenstein was intent on making a movie "outgrowing of his own conviction" that could still win the Stalin Prize, hoping he could challenge absolute power and elude the executioner. His portrait of the ruler is no more a historian's Stalin than it was a historian's Ivan, but neither is it the one-dimensional, reductionist, Cold War portrait many expected it to be or still see in it. Eisenstein's strategy—to raise questions about numerous specific aspects of the rise of centralized power—allowed him to use the historiography about Ivan the Terrible to create a nuanced, multifaceted portrait of Ivan and any other power-hungry, power-holding authority at the same time. The answers to the questions he raised in the film refer specifically to Ivan, but they can also be applied to other rulers in any other contexts. When is murder acceptable? When is violence necessary? Do state needs supersede personal desires? What are the consequences of placing state loyalty above family love? What is the proper place of revenge? Structuring the film around such questions invites viewers to compare Ivan and his historical context with Stalin and their own historical moment. We can feel lingering sympathy for Ivan (or our fathers or mentors or anyone who shows some self-awareness or remorse), and at the same time we may feel no sympathy at all for Stalin or anyone else who never apologized and never looked back. The interrogative mode that Eisenstein used in *Ivan the Terrible* established a set of standards for judging any ruler. That's how you make a film about a bloody tyrant for a bloody tyrant.

Eisenstein's insight into the underlying conflict between the ruler's personal and political roles, which humanized Ivan, was all the more remarkable for the absence of such portraits of Stalin during his lifetime and in the historiography on Stalin that emerged in the decades after his death. The rise of the totalitarian model as an explanation for the mass violence visited by Stalin and Hitler on their own people paints them as inhuman monsters, different and separate from the rest of us, rendering their actions immune to the kind of analysis Eisenstein did. Efforts in the 1980s and 1990s to humanize Hitler and Stalin, to understand them as human beings with the ability to make choices and to participate in a political system were often criticized for supposedly minimizing the crimes of psychopathic monsters. When Soviet archives on the Stalinist period became available to researchers and when historians in the former Soviet Union acquired more interpretive latitude, studies of Stalin's persona and the political-historical context were approached with increasing nuance.[8] As J. Arch Getty wrote in 1993: "We need not turn Stalin into an omniscient and omnipotent demon in order to comprehend his evil. Indeed, making him into a superman diminishes the real horror of the period. Stalin was a cruel but ordinary mortal . . . banally human and . . . more horrifying for being so."[9] As for explaining the violence of the terror and the oprichnina, Eisenstein's understanding of Ivan's motives also anticipated the post-Soviet historiographical consensus. Two things compelled Eisenstein's Ivan to intensify the use of violence against his enemies, real and imagined: outspoken opposition to his policies and his sense that the opposition was even more widespread and dangerous than it seemed, constantly threatening to contaminate his own closest allies. Even among those historians who disagree about the extent of Stalin's power and about his role in the purges, the general consensus now is that Stalin always felt politically vulnerable. Most also agree that the mass killing during the terror was motivated by Stalin's sense of political paranoia together with his desire to exterminate any possible opposition to his power, especially as war loomed.[10]

In this context, and keeping in mind that Ivan is not an exact mirror of Stalin but an instrument for understanding Soviet rule and Stalinist violence, the dialectical portrait that Eisenstein produced looks all the more extraordinary. One could argue that Eisenstein in the 1940s predated by half a century the historical literature of the 1990s and 2000s that sought to understand the ways the individual and the institutional, historical, and ideological all interacted to shape the kind of ruler Stalin became. Eisenstein's Ivan is no totalitarian monolith; he is neither pathologically insane nor unfathomably evil. He functions as an individual with a history and a psychology, with reason and feelings, and choices that can be analyzed. Eisenstein's explanation for Ivan's murderous violence, his targeting of his closest allies, and his sadistic, demagogic manipulation of the population combines the psychological with the historical and the political. No matter how extreme, sadistic, and tragic his behavior, Ivan draws on his experience as an individual in developing strategies to deal with opposition, disloyalty, and treason. Eisenstein may have seen Stalin as lacking Ivan's capacity for remorse or as using the outdated bloody tactics of medieval princes in the twentieth century, but he saw him as a human being, making both rational and irrational choices in historical and political contexts. We do not know how much Eisenstein knew, how much he intuited, how much his Ivan = his Stalin, but his explanation of the dangers of one-man rule for both the ruler and the ruled was decades ahead of its time.

I am not suggesting that Stalin modeled his reign on Ivan's or that Eisenstein saw a direct correspondence between Stalin and Ivan. The point is that Eisenstein lived in a world that he thought resembled the world Ivan made. Both rulers destroyed revolutions that began with idealistic principles; both secured colonial empires and fought devastating wars; both unleashed inexplicable violence on their own country; and both enjoyed an extraordinary level of popular adulation. Eisenstein understood it as his job to explore the reasons why. He used the world he read about to understand the world he knew from experience, and vice versa: he used his own experience to try to understand Ivan and his actions. Many writers have noted the parallels between Eisenstein's Kremlin and Stalin's, but Eisenstein did more than simply mirror the paranoia, cruelty, and demagoguery he saw in Stalin's court, in Stalinist society, and in Soviet history. He developed an analysis and an explanation for those characteristics of Stalinist rule and its causes that historians would take decades to reach.

Eisenstein's caution was not the only reason for hiding these Stalinist allusions as ashes in the mortar. Ambiguity and contradiction provide a remarkably apt formal code for depicting everyday life in Stalinist society. Eisenstein's dense network of sensory-emotional images, confusing layers of repetition, animated objects, and expressive movement convey better than any realistic depiction what it was like to live in a world of illusion and double-speak, where official rhetoric was belied by everyday life. Several years before George Orwell's invention of dystopian Newspeak, Eisenstein understood the powers of public illusion and the sensory-emotional and cognitive struggles those illusions create. He understood that learning to "speak Bolshevik" or yearning for a genuine collective identity did not erase other, earlier modes of being or our concomitant, contradictory desires for both individual and collective identities. Eisenstein's experience of the shifting cycles of art world politics and of Stalinist terror—the arrests of his friends and his own close brush with catastrophe—showed him firsthand how brutal and unpredictable arbitrary power could be, both physically and psychologically. He saw efforts to resolve or eradicate such contradictions and inner conflicts as among the most inhuman features of Stalinist society. Dialectics, the pre-logical, and the interrogative structure both helped and hindered him in conveying this view. *Ivan the Terrible*, a film with no clear moral positions, was a genuine anomaly in Stalinist Russia. The film's emphatic contrariness, its very strangeness, made it challenging for contemporary audiences. At the same time, it asserted the artist's right to ask hard questions and convey hard truths instead of offering consoling, conformist, or generic solutions.

In his pioneering semiotic study of Eisenstein, Viacheslav Ivanov described him as a man who was "in polar opposition to the regime."[11] There was a time when I would have seen that description as too stark and one-sided, but no longer. We don't much like such binary arguments anymore and often blame the Cold War (or Russian culture itself) for producing them. The collapse of the USSR in 1991 released an abundance of new binaries in an understandably reactive post-Soviet culture and a somewhat less understandable proliferation of triumphalist narratives in the capitalist West. Then we saw a counterreaction to those initial binaries that valorizes hybridity and contingency as historical explanations. Eisenstein was far too complex a thinker and artist to be pigeonholed—for or against, conformist or subversive—and he was far too ironic for us to associate him with totalizing unities of any kind. Eisenstein's position isn't lacking paradoxes and contradictions: he clearly, explicitly admired Ivan the Terrible for what he saw as Ivan's selfless commitment, his risk taking, and his foundation of the modern Russian state as a great power in the Europe-wide project of government centralization and modern state building. But everything else about Eisenstein's work on this film, literally *everything* else, is marked by treachery, violence, trauma, tragedy, and malevolence. Every network of sensory details, every combination of shots and mise-en-scène, every lighting setup and sound synchronization and spatial composition, and every gesture and body movement is designed to show that even Ivan's triumphs, *especially* Ivan's triumphs, were motivated by illegitimate or dangerous human feelings and experiences. There is nothing unequivocally triumphalist in Eisenstein's portrait of the absolute ruler. There is no useful propaganda to be found in Ivan's victories. There is nothing inherently progressive in the regress-and-advance spiral of Eisenstein's theory of history. There is nothing especially patriotic about his references to Pushkin, Tolstoy, or Dostoevsky, when they appear alongside Machiavelli, Shakespeare, Freud, Rank, Piranesi, and Disney. There is nothing "totalizing" in Eisenstein's dialectical thinking about universality and unity. There are no heroes in *Ivan the Terrible*, where the tragedy is told with horror, melodrama, and the grotesque.

The tragedy of Eisenstein's Ivan the Terrible is that his inner conflicts had consequences: real, deadly, unambiguous consequences for the people around him. He may have remained indefinable, but the contradictions that make him so human and so universal, and that are so attuned with our desire to read contingency and ambiguity into everything, brought destruction, death, trauma, and debasement that were real. This double dialectic is at the heart of Eisenstein's work: inner contradiction, on one hand, faces off against the unequivocal, on the other. Eisenstein had a finely tuned sense of contingency and contradiction, but he also understood that while death is necessary to life, it doesn't feel that way to the dead or their children.

Readings of *Ivan the Terrible* today continue to be stubbornly ambivalent, apolitical, or doubtful about Eisenstein's position on power, so I want to state in the strongest possible terms that the evidence I have presented here shows that Eisenstein's work on *Ivan the Terrible* was radical, critical, and subversive. While Eisenstein never saw Ivan as a simple stand-in for Stalin and had much more in mind than the contemporary political themes involved in such a critique, everything that Eisenstein explored in the film—historical change over time, the way great art uses historical narratives to dramatize contemporary events, individual development, the making of a dictator, the artistic production of *pathos* and *ekstasis*, the technical details of filmmaking, the resonance with artworks of other times and contexts—all contribute to a work of art that uncovers and dissects the monstrous principles and practices of Stalinist socialism. Eisenstein used the institutions of Stalinist artistic production and a Socialist Realist narrative façade not only to expose the cruelties of Stalin and his circle but to challenge every fundamental principle of Soviet socialist ideology and artistic practice: historical progress, the positive hero, dialectical materialism, revolutionary change, class consciousness, the cult of personality, hetero-normative sexuality, and model Soviet subjectivity.

Eisenstein didn't live in a vacuum independent of Soviet culture. He developed his ideas about power through observation and survival in the world where he lived and he saw its fundamental contradictions reflected in himself. As original as his ideas were about cinematic method, many of their components—including *pathos*, depiction and generalization, expressive movement and gesture, sound and color, and of course montage—were subjects of a wider Soviet intellectual discourse. He worked within the Soviet system of film production, benefiting from it even while being tormented by it. Eisenstein wanted Soviet prizes, used Soviet language, and enjoyed Soviet privileges. But if he sold his soul for a car, a nice apartment, and a Stalin Prize, not to mention survival, he still made *Ivan the Terrible* a thoroughly anti-Soviet film.

One might reasonably conclude that the only thing Eisenstein believed in was art. And given his deeply cynical view of politics and ironic view of everything else, art offered him a lot. Those transcendent moments of *ekstasis* produced by great art gave him a sensation of freedom from the gravity of Soviet reality and from his lonely isolation. His writing about art is always about escape— from the body, from the rational mind, from loneliness, from inner division and turmoil. It is also about connection—connection with his audience and between the audience and the creators of books, paintings, architecture, theater, and films. Art offered a private world of freedom independent of the world of public responsibility and survival. Like Prospero in *The Tempest*, who cherished the books he was allowed to bring to his island exile, Eisenstein found pleasure and connection in his library and his writing. But also like Prospero, who lost his dukedom because, "rapt in secret studies," he neglected his public duties, Eisenstein accepted political authority reluctantly and fitfully. His wide-ranging reading and ironic way of thinking always sat uncomfortably in the director's chair of the state-commissioned film. Yet he had power at his disposal, and in 1941, when he was offered the chance to present the history of Russian state power and to link the past and the present, Eisenstein didn't duck the complexities of his political and historical subjects as he had done in previous films. At the end of *The Tempest*, Prospero gives up the magical powers that isolated him from other human beings, and as Greenblatt wrote in his study of power in Shakespeare, he "deliberately plunges back into the contingency, risk, and moral uncertainty that he had temporarily escaped."[12] By abandoning magic, isolation, and absolute power, Prospero reenters the world armed with the ambiguous and contradictory lessons of books and experience now joined together. Similarly, in *Ivan the Terrible*, Eisenstein embraced, for the first time, his ability to tell a complex story about Russian power based on both his work as an artist and his observations of the world. As a result, Ivan became a figure for exploring human evolution and character in universal moral terms: How do we become the people we become? Can we temper revenge with forgiveness? How are we to be judged? Who are we in our own time and place and how do we transcend our individual selves and surroundings to step outside ourselves to become someone new? The film Eisenstein made challenges us to devise a standard of moral and political judgment for behavior in a world where judgment could be arbitrary and all choices, including silence, could be interpreted as both loyalty *and* treason to an arbitrary and brutal regime. By repeatedly asking, "Am I right in what I am doing," *Ivan the Terrible* gives us the kind of individual moral accounting that we need in order to understand a society that Neia Zorkaia described as a world of "permanent moral compromise," where all public behavior was compromised and ordinarily good people could hardly avoid doing bad things.[13] Eisenstein's picture of this world draws its power from his refusal to abandon his conscience or ignore his own complicity. *Ivan the Terrible* is worth watching today not only as a cinematic masterpiece but as a moral and political challenge for all of us at any time. This thing of darkness, I acknowledge mine.

NOTES

Introduction

1. Diary entry: 2/1165/1 [Jan 2, 1941]; 1/529/1 [Dec 31, 1940]; Vishnevskii, "Iz dnevnikov," 66; the letter: Murin, "Stalin i kino," 101–2; "'. . . Iz trekh navodiashchikh strochek," *KZ*, no. 38: 138–39.

2. Vasilyeva, "Two Decades of Soviet Biographical Film"; Clark, *Soviet Novel*.

3. Platt, *Terror and Greatness*, 211–14; Platt and Brandenberger, *Epic Revisionism*, 165.

4. Eizenshtein, *Montage*, ed. Kleiman; Eizenshtein, *Metod*, ed. Kleiman; Eizenshtein, *Neravnodushnaia priroda*, ed. Kleiman; Eizenshtein, *Metod*, ed. Bulgakowa; *KZ*, no. 36/37 (1997/1998) and 38 (1998).

5. Special issue on *Ivan the Terrible*: *KZ*, no. 38 (1998); Tsivian, *Ivan the Terrible*; Nesbet, *Savage Junctures*; Kleiman, *Formula finala*; Kozlov, *Proizvedenie vo vremeni*; Lary, *Dostoevsky and Soviet Film*; Lövgren, *Eisenstein's Labyrinth*; Podoroga, *Afto-bio-grafiia*; Spring and Taylor, *Stalinism and Soviet Cinema*; Christie and Taylor, *Eisenstein Rediscovered*; Bulgakowa, *Sergei Eisenstein*; Aumont, *Montage Eisenstein*; Amengual, *Que Viva Eisenstein!*; Bordwell, *Cinema of Eisenstein*; Iurenev, *Sergei Eizenshtein*; Ivanov, "Estetika Eizenshteina"; Shklovskii, *Eizenshtein*; Thompson, *Eisenstein's "Ivan the Terrible"*; *Notes for a General History of Cinema*.

6. Bulgakowa, "From Expressive Movement to the Basic Problem"; Bulgakowa, "Uchenik charodeia"; Moore, *Savage Theory*; Tikka, *Enactive Cinema*.

7. Bartig, *Composing for the Red Screen*; Robertson, *Eisenstein on the Audiovisual;* Butovskii, *Andrei Moskvin*; Jacobs, "Lesson with Eisenstein"; Khitrova, "Eisenstein's Choreography in Ivan the Terrible"; Mar'iamov, *Kremlevskii tsenzor*.

8. Artizov and Naumov, *Vlast' i khudozhestvennaia intelligentsia*; Fomin, *Kino na voine*; Maksimenkov et al., *Kremlevskii kinoteatr, 1929–1953*.

9. Goodwin, *Eisenstein, Cinema, and History*; Perrie, *Cult of Ivan the Terrible in Stalin's Russia*; Uhlenbruch, "Annexation of History"; Platt, *Terror and Greatness*; *Notes for a General History*.

10. Iurenev, *Sergei Eizenshtein*, 2:237–67.

11. Solzhenitsyn, *One Day in the Life*, 95 (corrected translation).

12. Bulgakowa, *Sergei Eisenstein*, 219; Thompson, *Eisenstein's "Ivan the Terrible,"* 3, 65, 67; Maland, "Unpublished James Agee," 26–29.

13. *IP*, 6 vols (1964–1971).

14. *IP*, 6:548–551.

15. Kozlov, "Artist and the Shadow of Ivan," 116–17, 120–22; Kozlov, "Hypothetical Dedication."

16. Zorkaia, *Portrety*, 131.

17. For example, Karetnikova, *Seven Masterpieces of 1940s Cinema*, 80–81.

18. Goodwin, *Eisenstein, Cinema, and History*, 182.

19. Uhlenbruch, "Annexation of History," 278, Dobrenko, *Stalinist Cinema*, 43–64.

20. Skeptics include Clark, *Moscow, the Fourth Rome*, 2; Platt, *Terror and Greatness*, 237; Karetnikova, *Seven Masterpieces of 1940s Cinema*, 80; and Grossman, "Ivan the Terrible Parts I and II."

21. MacPhee, "On the Incompleteness of History," 580–81.

22. Youngblood, *Soviet Cinema in the Silent Era*.

23. Miller, *Soviet Cinema*; Belodubrovskaya, *Not according to Plan*.

24. On the *Bezhin Meadow* crisis: Maksimenkov, *Sumbur vmesto muzyki*, 241–53; Belodubrovskaya, *Not according to Plan*, 186–91; Turovskaia, *Zuby Drakona*, 185–89, 534–43; Kenez, "History of *Bezhin Meadow*," 193–206.

25. Eizenshtein, *Metod*, ed. Kleiman, 2:494–96. All citations from *Metod* that follow refer to Kleiman's edition, unless otherwise noted.

26. Kleiman, *Eisenstein on Paper*; Frank, "'Proceeding from the Heat-oppressed Brain.'"

27. "The Materialist Approach to Film Form," *SW*, 1:64; "[Ob igre predmetov]," 35.

28. I thank Ana Olenina for sharing her forthcoming works on Eisenstein's reading of Ivan Pavlov and Vladimir Bekhterev on these subjects.

29. On the importance of dialectics: Iampolski, "Point—Pathos—Totality," 365–66.

30. Aumont, *Montage Eisenstein*, 146.

31. Burliuk et al., "Slap in the Face of Public Taste," 51.

32. *Metod*, 1:89–91; Salazkina, *In Excess*, 34–37; Kleiman, "Problema Eizenshteina," 12–16; Vassilieva, "Eisenstein and Cultural-Historical Theory," 426; Bulgakowa, "From Expressive Movement to the Basic Problem," 425–32.

33. *SW* 4:350, 352.

34. Gleason, *Totalitarianism*; Kotkin, *Magnetic Mountain*; Hellbeck, *Revolution on My Mind*, esp. 9–11; Halfin, *Terror in My Soul*, 4–5.

35. 2/1167/32–39 [Sept 16, 1941].

36. Fürst, "Friends in Private, Friends in Public," 231.

37. Widdis, *Socialist Senses*; Fitzpatrick, *Tear off the Masks!*; Brooks, "Public and Private in the Soviet Press, 1921–28."

38. *SW* 3:305–16; "PRKFV," 149–67.

39. Widdis, *Socialist Senses*.

40. 1/648/1 [Nov 11, 1944].

41. Conversation with Naum Kleiman, July 2013.

42. 2/124/108 [Nov 11, 1942]. Curiously, this note was saved in one of the production folders rather than in the folder with the rest of Eisenstein's notes on working with Prokofiev on the score.

1. The Potholed Path

1. Manley, *To the Tashkent Station*; Lovell, *In the Shadow of War*.

2. Clark and Dobrenko, *Soviet Culture and Power*, x–xii; Hoffmann, *Stalinist Values*, 159–66; Brandenberger, *Propaganda State in Crisis*.

3. Miller, *Soviet Cinema*. 40, 45, 50, 101–2; Maksimenko et al., *Kremlevskii kinoteatr*, 241, 279, 482; Fomin, *Kino na voine*, 20–23, 28–30, 44–46; Belodubrovskaya challenges this characterization of film funding in *Not according to Plan*, 3.

4. On official difficulties in defining Socialist Realism, see Robin, *Socialist Realism*, 39–51.

5. Enzenberger, "'We Were Born to Turn Fairy Tale into Reality,'" 97; Von Geldern and Stites, "Ever Higher (Aviators' March)," 257–58.

6. Dobrenko, "Disaster of Middlebrow Taste," 135–64.

7. Quoted in Robin, *Socialist Realism*, 51.

8. On realism, see Johnson, "A Premonition of Victory," 408–28; Lucento, "Conflicted Origins of Soviet Visual Media," 401–28; Fore, *Realism after Modernism*.

9. Miller, *Soviet Cinema*, 1–70; Belodubrovskaya, *Not according to Plan*, 165–212.

10. On Stalin's role as film critic, see Miller, *Soviet Cinema*, 63–69; Mar'iamov, *Kremlevskii tsenzor*; and Davies, "Stalin as Patron of Cinema."

11. See, for example, Kaganovsky, "Visual Pleasure in Stalinist Cinema"; and Salys, *Musical Comedy Films of Grigorii Aleksandrov*.

12. Kaganovsky and Salazkina, *Sound, Speech, Music in Soviet Cinema*; Kaganovsky, *Voice of Technology*, Cavendish, *Men with the Movie Camera*; Butovskii, *Andrei Moskvin*.

13. Frolova-Walker, *Stalin's Music Prize*; Kachurin, *Making Modernism Soviet*; Plamper, *The Stalin Cult*; see also Fitzpatrick, *Tear off the Masks!*, 182–202; Péteri, *Patronage, Personal Networks and the Party-State*.

14. Iumasheva and Lepikhov, "Fenomen 'totalitarnogo liberalisma,'" 125–43.

15. Fomin, *Kino na voine*, 17–19, 28–30, 33–37, 48–55; Belodubrovskaya, *Not according to Plan*, 42–44; Mar'iamov, *Kremlevskii tsenzor*, 674–84.

16. "Letters from Mexico to Maxim Strauch and Ilya Trauberg," 57–58.

17. Kozlov, "Artist and the Shadow of Ivan," 113.

18. 2/1164 [Oct 4, 1940]; 2/1152/11 [Apr 1939]; also Bulgakowa, *Sergei Eisenstein*, 199.

19. Bartlett, *Wagner and Russia*, 271–81; Kleiman, "Fergana Canal and Tamburlaine's Tower," 103–22.

20. 1/565/2 [Jan 21, 1941]; 1/561/1 [Jan 23, 1941]; Iurenev, *Sergei Eizenshtein*, 2:218.

21. 1/554/62 [Jan 21, 1941].

22. 1/554/62 [Jan 21, 1941].

23. 1/530/3 [Feb 9, 1941].

24. 1/552/36 [Feb 1941].

25. 1/552/35 [Feb 10, 1941].

26. 2/1666/1–12 [Feb 2–Mar 31, 1941].

27. "Neskol'ko slov o moikh risunkakh" was first published in *Mosfil'm*, no. 1 (1959), and again in *IP*, 1:196–98; in English: "A Few Words about My Drawings," *SW* 3:240–42.

28. *SW* 3:241.

29. Eisenstein was aware that beating one's head on the floor, symbolically or literally, was a conventional gesture of subordination and supplication ("Istoricheskii kommentarii," 231).

30. *Ivan the Terrible: A Screenplay*, 225–36; that Eisenstein intended Ivan's confession to be both self-doubting and self-justifying, see 1/561/33 [Mar 5, 1942].

31. *IP*, 6:550; Lövgren, "Eisenstein's Pushkin Project," 120–33; "Stsena iz 'Borisa Godunova,'" 111–30; Bulgakova, "Uchenik charodeia, 294–96."

32. *SW*, 3:241; the manuscript notes that the event at the Bolshoi was a memorial on the anniversary of Lenin's death (*SW* 3:387); the following note, dated January 19, 1941, confirms the early timing of Eisenstein's thinking about this scene: *"The episode with the candles during the taking of Kazan. The wait for the explosion the gradual burning of the candle. Make it tense as hell."* 1/554/130 [Jan 19, 1941].

33. "Krupneishii gosudarstvennyi deiatel'," *IP*, 1:199; original publication: *Ogonek*, no. 9–10 (1945): 14.

34. 1/553/103.

35. Eisenstein, *"Ivan the Terrible*: A Film about the Sixteenth-Century Russian Renaissance," *SW*, 3:188–92; originally published in *Literatura i iskusstvo*, July 4, 1942.

36. *"Ivan the Terrible*: A Film," *SW*, 3:191.

37. 1/552/68 [c. Feb 14, 1941].

38. 2/1165/4 [Apr 4, 1941].

39. *SW*, 4:4–15, 24, 423, 453, 794–95; *NN*, 295. Two examples from his notebooks with political resonance can be found in 2/125/7–10 (Maliuta acts as a "screen" to protect Ivan from being associated with the executions he orders) and in 2/1168/3 [Feb 13, 1942] (a passage analyzing the mental and sensory qualities required by a word game in which players must guess whole words from partially visible and partially hidden letters).

40. *SW*, 4:453.

41. *Metod*, 1:349–50 [probably Feb–Mar 1944].

42. 1/561/142 [Mar 1942].

43. Iurenev, *Sergei Eizenshtein*, 2:216.

44. 1/554/6 [Apr 19, 1941]; Shklovskii, *Eizenshtein*, 251-56; Shub, *Krupnym planom*, 138.

45. 1/1350/1 [1944], cited in Roshal', "'Ia uzhe ne mal'chik,'" 151.

46. Eizenshtein, "Sozdadim fil'my dostoinye stalinskoi epokhi," *Kino*, Mar 21, 1941.

47. Eizenshtein, "Vpered," *Za Bol'shevistskii fil'm*, Mar 21, 1941.

48. Abol'nik, "Novyi istoricheskii fil'm Eizenshteina," *Ogonek*, no. 14 (1941): 19.

49. Eizenshtein, "Fil'm ob Ivane Groznom," *Izvestiia*, Apr 30, 1941: 3.

50. "The Heirs and Builders of World Culture," *SW*, 3:182; originally published in *Pravda*, Apr 30, 1941.

51. Kozlov, "Artist and the Shadow of Ivan," 114; Iurenev, *Sergei Eizenshtein*, 2:218.

52. Written May 1, 1942, and published July 4, 1942, in *Literatura i iskusstvo*, *SW* 3:188–92n382.

53. *SW*, 3:189.

54. *SW*, 3:192.

55. *SW*, 3:191.

56. Leyda, *Kino*, 365–82; Iurenev, *Sergei Eizenshtein*, 2:218–20; Fomin, *Kino na voine*, 85–96; Kadochnikov, "Stranitsy iz dnevnika aktera," 156–57; Ulanova, "Sled v zhizni," 315.

57. 2/1166/1–17 [Jul 25–Aug 16, 1941], 2/1167/14 [Aug 23, 1941]. Eizenshtein, "Voina," 157–60.

58. 2/1167/14 [Aug 23, 1941].

59. 2/1167/21 [Sep 7 or 8, 1941].

60. 1/644/1 [Oct 6, 1941]; Iurenev, *Sergei Eizenshtein*, 2:220.

61. Iurenev, *Sergei Eizenshtein*, 2:221; *SW*, 4:388; Eizenshtein, "Alma Ata," 160–61. According to Atasheva, in May 1942, when conditions in Alma Ata had been stabilized

and Mosfilm sent several trainloads of equipment, sets, costumes, and other materials, space was made for eleven boxes of Eisenstein's books (Zabrodin, "'Dorogoi starik,'" 144–45).

62. 2/1166/32 [Oct 14, 1941]. On the evacuation of Moscow, see Braithwaite, *Moscow 1941*, 235–50; and Manley, *To the Tashkent Station*, 129–32.

63. Kuznetsov, "My sporili . . . ," 340.

64. There's a sketch of his rooms in 2/1404.

65. Manley, *To the Tashkent Station*, 148–95; Budnitskii, "Great Patriotic War and Soviet Society: Defeatism," 767–97; Shostakovich cited in *Culture and Entertainment in Wartime Russia*, ed. Richard Stites, 5.

66. Shandybin, "V Alma-Ate," 381.

67. Shub, *Krupnym planom*, 139.

68. Zabrodin, "Chelovecheskii golos," 103, 105–7; Cherkasova, "Cherkasov i Eizenshtein," 325; Nazvanov, "'Prokliataia kartina,'" 1:145n.

69. Letter dated Aug 23, 1942; Zabrodin, "Chelovecheskii golos," 111–12.

70. Letter dated Aug 23, 1942; Zabrodin, "Chelovecheskii golos," 111–12.

71. Nazvanov, "'Prokliataia kartina,'" 1:145.

72. Zabrodin, "Chelovecheskii golos," 112.

73. Eizenshtein, "Alma Ata," 163–64.

74. Drawings are scattered throughout the notebooks. Some are collected in 1/576–93 and 2/1672–84; some were published in *Risunki k fil'mu "Ivan Groznyi"*; and *Risunki Sergeia Eizenshteina, 1942–44: Kollektsiia Lidii Naumovoi*. Zhakov, Kuznetsov, Shub, and others attest that Eisenstein storyboarded every shot and required actors to conform to the often contorted poses that looked so good on paper: Zhakov, "'Zakovannyi v laty,'" 335; Kuznetsov, "My sporili . . . ," 336–37; and Shub, *Krupnym planom*, 138; also Kleiman, *Eisenstein on Paper*, 202–44.

75. 1/625–41 and 2/129–59 (photographs); memos requesting books on Muscovite material culture and museum objects from that period, RGALI 2453 (Mosfil'm) 2/65/1–21 [Spring and Summer 1942].

76. 1/644/2–8 [Feb 11, 1942]; Iurenev, *Sergei Eizenshtein*, 2:223; Roshal', "'Ia uzhe ne mal'chik,'" 145–48.

77. 1/644/2–8; Roshal', "'Ia uzhe ne mal'chik,'" 146–47.

78. Cited in full in Iurenev, *Sergei Eizenshtein*, 2:223.

79. 1/644/8 [Feb 11, 1942].

80. Iurenev, *Sergei Eizenshtein*, 2:223

81. Roshal', "'Ia uzhe ne mal'chik,'" 148–49.

82. 2/1168/24 [Mar 23, 1942]; note that "from above" is underlined in the original and "of both!" is in English.

83. 2/1169/35–38 [May 10, 1942]; 44 [May 17, 1942]; and 1/570/1–14, 37–63.

84. 1/644/9–10 [Jun 1942].

85. 1/652/9–11 [Sep 5, 1942].

86. The screen tests can be viewed on *Eisenstein: The Sound Years* (Criterion Collection, DVD).

87. 2/1749/3 [Sep 15, 1942].

88. 1/652/9–11 [Sep 5, 1942].

89. These sources are included in the Historical Commentary ("Istoricheskii kommentarii," 199–200, 203–5).

90. 1/644/12–16 [Sep 1942].

91. These and other deleted scenes are on Criterion's *Eisenstein: The Sound Years*.

92. 2/124/6 [Apr 9, 1942].

93. 1/553/64.

94. *IP*, 6:495 [Apr 1, 1942].

95. 1/552/21, cited in Iurenev, *Sergei Eizenshtein*, 2:225.

96. 2/1169/15 [Apr 7, 1942]. Cherkasov received a written invitation from Eisenstein on April 15. The letter is published in Cherkasova, "Cherkasov i Eizenshtein," 324.

97. 2/127/1 [Mar 31, 1942]. An article about these two casting decisions was published in *Komsomol'skaia pravda*, May 28, 1942; a rare note about culture in a newspaper dominated by war news.

98. Nazvanov, "'Prokliataia kartina,'" 1:138; Cherkasov, *Notes of a Soviet Actor*, 103.

99. *SW*, 4:236.

100. Mgrebov, "Emu ia obiazan zhizn'iu," 329–30; Nazvanov, "'Prokliataia kartina,'" 1:147.

101. Kuznetsov, "My sporili . . . ," 336–37.

102. Ulanova, "'Khochu chtoby bylo chisto, blagorodno, i muzykal'no . . . ,' 69.

103. Roshal', "'Ia uzhe ne mal'chik,'" 155–62; Kozlov, "Eshche o 'Kazuse Ranevskoi,'" 168–72.

104. 1/644/20.

105. Birman, "Life's Gift of Encounters," 109.

106. Birman, "Life's Gift of Encounters," 110–11; *SW* 3:307.

107. Morrison, *People's Artist*, 235–36. The letter dated in December reached Prokofiev only in March; Levaco, "Eisenstein-Prokofiev Correspondence," 1–16.

108. Bartig, *Composing for the Red Screen*, 135; Morrison, *People's Artist*, 235–41.

109. 2/1168/30, 33, 73 (Chaplin and Prokofiev); 2/1165/42 [Oct 2, 1942] (Van Gogh, Balzac); 2/1168/26 [Oct 4, 1942] (Le Bon); 2/1165/44 [Oct 29, 1942] (Steinbeck); 1/568/38 [Nov 14, 1942] (music); 2/1168/36, 46, 48 [Nov 29–Dec 5, 1942] (Van Gogh, El Greco, Daumier); 2/1168/42 (Shakespeare, Holbein).

110. 2/1168/44 [Nov 29, 1942].

111. 2/1168/57 [Dec 6, 1942]; 2/1168/71 [Dec 9, 1942].

112. 2/1168/34–35, 55–56 [Nov 5 and Dec 6, 1942].

113. 2/1168/78 [Dec 17, 1942]; 2/1170/2 [Dec 20, 1942].

114. 2/1749/3 and 6.

115. 1/1624/28.

116. Shub, *Krupnym planom*, 138; also Butovskii, *Andrei Moskvin*, 191.

117. 1/1520 (to Tisse), 1/1503 (Moskvin); Butovskii, "Perepiska A. N. Moskvina i S. M. Eizenshteina," 296–313.

118. 2/1167/31 [Sep 1941].

119. 2/1749/8.

120. Vishnevskii, "Iz dnevnikov, 1944–1948 gg.," 68 [Jul 7, 1946].

121. Mgrebov, "Emu ia obiazan zhizn'iu," 331.

122. Kuznetsov, "My sporili . . . ," 338.

123. Zhakov, "Zakovannyi v latu," 335. Even Kuznetsov appreciated Eisenstein's skill with a joke ("My sporili . . . ," 340).

124. Cherkasova, "Cherkasov i Eizenshtein," 326–28.

125. Shub, *Krupnym planom*, 139.

126. Birman, "Neotpravlennoe pis'mo," 355–56.

127. Nazvanov, "'Prokliataia kartina,'" 1:143, 144, 145, 147; 2:130, 131; Birman, "Life's Gift of Encounters," 106–18.

128. Nazvanov, "'Prokliataia kartina,'" 2:131.

129. Nazvanov, "'Prokliataia kartina,'" 2:133; Cherkasov, *Zapiski sovetskogo aktera*, 134; Nazvanov, "'Prokliataia kartina,'" 2:134; 1:142; 146; 2:129–30.

130. Nazvanov, "'Prokliataia kartina,'" 2:135.

131. Nazvanov, "'Prokliataia kartina,'" 2:147.

132. Nazvanov, "'Prokliataia kartina,'" 2:129.

133. Nazvanov, "'Prokliataia kartina,'" 2:138. On being divided: Nazvanov, "'Prokliataia kartina,'" 2:129, 137–38. On unfamiliar style: 1:143, 2:130. On frustration with everything: 1:146. Marvelous: 1:147, 2:135, 2:136. On Eisenstein's ego: 2:130, 138, 318.

134. 1/652/14 [Feb 6, 1943].

135. Roshal', "'Ia uzhe ne mal'chik,'" 162–63; a draft of Eisenstein's letter is in his archive, 1/657/3–4, and is discussed in Iurenev, *Sergei Eizenshtein*, 2:233–35; and Roshal', "'Ia uzhe ne mal'chik,'" 162–63; another copy of the letter, published in *Kremlevskii kinoteatr*, 690–91 [Jan 20, 1944], comes from the Politburo collection in the Presidential Archive of the Russian Federation and displays a stamp showing that it was sent, received, and registered in the Special Section of the Central Committee on January 31, 1944.

136. Mar'iamov, *Kremlevskii tsenzor*, 70.

137. Maksimenko et al., *Kremlevskii kinoteatr*, 690–91 [Jan 20, 1944].

138. Nazvanov, "'Prokliataia kartina,'" 1:146.

139. Kozlov, "Artist and the Shadow of Ivan," 116.

140. Kozlov, "Artist and the Shadow of Ivan," 116–22.

141. Nazvanov, "'Prokliataia kartina,'" 2:133.

142. 1/1511/3.

143. 1/554/61ob. [1942]; 2/124/79 [May 23, 1942]. On permission to make a trilogy, see 1/646/21 [May 5, 1944].

144. Eizenshtein, "Istoricheskii kommentarii," 173–246.

145. 2/1171/26 [Dec 6, 1943]. See also discussion of this passage in Kleiman, "Problema Eizenshteina," *Metod*, 1:5–7.

146. Nazvanov, "'Prokliataia kartina,'" 1:144–45.

147. 1/645/3 [Apr 3, 1944]; 1/646/21–23 [May 15, 1944, and undated letter between May 14 and Jun 25].

148. 1/646/21–21ob. [May 15, 1944].

149. 2453/2/65/22 [Jul 22, 1944].

150. Manley, *To the Tashkent Station*, 253–64.

151. Levaco, "Eisenstein-Prokofiev Correspondence," 13–14.

152. 2/1749/9 [Spring 1944]; Nazvanov, "'Prokliataia kartina,'" 2:131.

153. Butovskii, "Perepiska A. N. Moskvina i S. M. Eizenshteina," 301; Nazvanov, "'Prokliataia kartina,'" 1:147.

154. Iurenev, *Sergei Eizenshtein*, 2:247.

155. 2/1749/9 [Spring 1944].

156. Iurenev summarizes the international response without paying attention to the politics of the reviews (*Sergei Eizenshtein*, 2:250–53); for more on foreign responses, see Neuberger, "Politics of Bewilderment," 227–28.

157. 2453/2/65/105; 87–95; 76–77, 81 [Apr 19, 1945]; 86 [May 14, 1945]; 87–88 [May 23, 1945], 95 [Jul 10, 1945].

158. 2453/2/65/95 [Jul 10, 1945], 97 [Jul 17, 1945], 106–7 [Dec 20, 1945].

159. Levaco, "Eisenstein-Prokofiev Correspondence," 14–15.

160. Bartig, *Composing for the Red Screen*, 136; 107–8 [Dec 20, 1945].

161. 2453/2/65/101 [Nov 14, 1945].

162. 2453/2/65/105–10 [Dec 20, 1945].

163. 2453/2/65/103–4 [Dec 21, 1945].

164. 2453/2/65/111–12.

165. Rostotskii, "Na ulitse Eizenshteina," 299–300.

166. Romm, *Besedy o kino*, 91.

167. Butovskii, "Perepiska A. N. Moskvina i S. M. Eizenshteina," 305–7.

168. Eizenshtein, "'. . . Iz trekh navodiashchikh strochek . . . ,'" 138–39.

169. Butovskii, "Perepiska A. N. Moskvina i S. M. Eizenshteina," 298.

170. As recorded by Kleiman in 1967 (*Formula finala*, 302, 318n.).

2. Shifts in Time

1. Iurenev, *Sergei Eizenshtein*, 2:211–13; Kleiman, "Kommentariia," in *IP* 6:548; Andronikova, *Ot prototipa k obrazu*, 55–58; Shklovskii, *Eizenshtein*, 251–52.

2. Conversation with Leonid Kozlov, Moscow, 1997.

3. The 2016 publication of *Notes for a General History of Cinema* makes much of Eisenstein's post-*Ivan* historical writing available and includes essays by Antonio Somaini, Luka Arsenjuk, Mikhail Iampolski, and others who address the multilayered, bidirectional sense of time embedded in Eisenstein's theory of history. Many of the historical ideas found in the *Notes* were, in fact, worked out in the making of *Ivan the Terrible* and the writing that accompanied it.

4. Goodwin, *Eisenstein, Cinema, and History*, 186–95; Dobrenko, *Stalinist Cinema*, 1, 4, 7, 45; Platt, *Terror and Greatness*, 237, 244, 247.

5. 2/1170/13 [May 18, 1945].

6. Perrie, *Cult of Ivan the Terrible*; Platt and Brandenberger, *Epic Revisionism*, 157–89; Uhlenbruch, "Annexation of History"; Plamper, *Stalin Cult*.

7. Perrie, *Cult of Ivan the Terrible*, 78–102; Platt and Brandenberger, *Epic Revisionism*, 157–62, 179–89.

8. 1/624/1–2; *SW* 4:24, 34, 566.

9. Brandenberger, "Stalin's Rewriting of 1917."

10. Iurenev, *Sergei Eizenshtein*, 2:214; Clark, *Moscow, the Fourth Rome*, 318; Zholkovsky, "Eisenstein's Poetics"; Platt and Brandenberger, *Epic Revisionism*, 166.

11. Eizenshtein, "Istoricheskii kommentarii," 173–246.

12. Eizenshtein, "Istoricheskii kommentarii," 173; Andronikova, *Ot prototipa k obrazu*, 58 (cited in "Istoricheskii kommentarii," 174).

13. 2/119/3 and 4–5.

14. 2/119/3 [Jan 1942].

15. 1/624/1–135; Iurenev, *Sergei Eizenshtein*, 2:213.

16. In the 1970s, the most important original documents from this period came under suspicion when Edward Keenan labeled them forgeries in *The Kurbsky-Groznyi Apocrypha*. Intensive research since has largely reaffirmed their authenticity, but

Eisenstein, of course, knew nothing of the controversy. On debates over the veracity of foreigners' accounts, see Poe, *"People Born to Slavery"*; and Kivelson, "How Bad Was Ivan the Terrible?"

17. 1/561/17; Vipper, *Ivan Groznyi* (1922), 109. On Vipper, see Perrie, *The Cult of Ivan the Terrible*, 12–20, 92–99.

18. 2/1165/15 [Oct 5, 1941].

19. 2/1714/7 [May 7, 1942]; 1/552/27 [Feb 7, 1941]; 1/553/9 [Jan 19, 1941]; 1/561/32 and 35; 1/570/14–17 [Aug 10–11, 1942]; 2/128/31ob. [Oct 16, 1943].

20. 1/561/143 [Mar 10, 1942] and 1/553/26 [Feb 20, 1941], for example.

21. Film industry leaders and Central Committee agitprop officials attended these conferences, where they came up with yearly thematic filmmaking plans; see Miller, *Soviet Cinema*, 93–94.

22. Eisenstein, "Problems of the Soviet Historical Film," *SW* 3:129.

23. Eizenshtein, *Montazh*; Eisenstein, *SW* 2 (*Towards a Theory of Montage*). On depiction and image in painting during this period: Plamper, *Stalin Cult*, 194–96.

24. *Metod*, 2:112–131; *SW* 3:224–38.

25. 1/561/143 [Mar 10, 1942].

26. Salazkina, *In Excess*, 16–17, 162–63.

27. 1/565/2–4 [Jan 21, 1941].

28. The most authoritative recent history in English is Madariaga, *Ivan the Terrible*; a shorter survey focusing on politics is Pavlov and Perrie, *Ivan the Terrible*; a study of specific relevant aspects of Ivan's reign is Kollmann, *Crime and Punishment*.

29. 1/530/1 [Jan 26, 1941].

30. Like other Muscovite rulers, when Ivan decided to marry, virgin daughters of noblemen were summoned to court to be displayed before the tsar; Madariaga, *Ivan the Terrible*, 53–55; Martin, *A Bride for the Tsar*; originally Eisenstein considered including this scene to contribute to themes of jealousy, preference, and revenge; 1/552/29 [Feb 8, 1941].

31. Iurenev, *Sergei Eizenshtein*, 2:214. Iurenev repeatedly quotes passages from the documents in truncated form or out of context, often significantly distorting the text.

32. Kozlov, "Artist and the Shadow," 114–15.

33. 1/530/2 [Jan 26, 1941]. "**Vidimo. Der gang ist Folgender . . . ? tverdoe gosudarstvo vnutri—baza tverdogo gosudarstva mezhdunarodnogo. Togda, nado konchat' Livoniei— vykhodom k moriu**." Iurenev, typically, quotes only the aphorism about the state.

34. Madariaga, *Ivan the Terrible*, xii–xiii.

35. Madariaga, *Ivan the Terrible*, 122–34, 336–40.

36. 1/561/3 [Feb 17, 1941].

37. 1/552/41 [c. Feb 8, 1941].

38. 1/552/35, 41 [c. Feb 8, 1941]; 1/553/5 [c. Feb 17, 1941]; 1/553/28 [Feb 20, 1941].

39. Madariaga, *Ivan the Terrible*, 63–64, 68–71.

40. 1/570/30 [Jan 18, 1941]; 1/552/41 [Feb 1941]. "Should make *three* friends in youth. Ivan, Kurbsky, and Kolychev (the future Filipp). Valishevskii, p. 316," 1/554/1 [Feb 3, 1941].

41. Critics have often described Eisenstein's Ivan as "insane" or "mad," but Eisenstein does not: see *IP*, 6:499. For example, see Ramsey, "Keepers of a Flame," 14; Thompson, *Eisenstein's "Ivan the Terrible*," 85; Goodwin, *Eisenstein, Cinema, and History*,

186; and Lövgren, *Eisenstein's Labyrinth*, 109. The scenario published in *IP* begins with an epigraph from Seneca: "There is no great spirit without a dash of insanity," but the scenario published in *Novyi mir* in Eisenstein's lifetime doesn't include the epigraph: *IP*, 6:199; see also *NP*, 2:126.

42. On the role of foreign affairs in the scenario: Perrie, *Cult of Ivan the Terrible,* 150, 153–54.

43. 1/553/52.

44. "PRKFV," *IP*, 5:468–69; *Notes of a Film Director*, 161–62.

45. Valishevskii and Soloviev are first mentioned on the busy day of January 21, 1941; 1/554/72.

46. 1/624/40.

47. Perrie, *Cult of Ivan the Terrible*, 8; Crummey, "Ivan the Terrible," 54–88.

48. Platonov, *Ivan Groznyi (1530–1584)*; Indenbom writes: "Platonov correctly defined the oprichnina as an attack on the appanage aristocracy but was wrong to see an ideal democratic character in the so-called constitution of the autocracy" (1/624/40).

49. 1/570/14 [Aug 10, 1942].

50. Ustrialov, *Skazaniia kniazia Kurbskago*, originally published in 1833, republished in 1842 and 1868; translated in Fennell, ed. and trans., *Correspondence between Prince A. M. Kurbsky and Tsar Ivan IV of Russia*, 69–77; Eisenstein gave incomplete titles for chronicles, most of which seem to be included in the massive publication project *Polnoe sobranie russkikh letopisei*, 43 vols. (Moscow: Nauka, 1846–2004); see also 1/561/70ff, 102–10.

51. 1/552/55 [Feb 1941].

52. 1/552/53–54 [Feb 1941].

53. 1/552/35 [Feb 8, 1941].

54. Madariaga, *Ivan the Terrible*, xiv.

55. 1/531/2 [Mar 9, 1941].

56. Notes on Kurbsky and Anastasia: 1/530/3 [Feb 9, 1941]; 1/553/1 [Feb 17 1941]; 1/553/71–77 [Feb 1941]. On homoeroticism among the men: 1/552/26 [Feb 7, 1941]; 1/552/31 [Feb 8, 1941]; 1/553/1 [Feb 17, 1941]; 1/553/91 [Feb 12, 1941]; 1/569/78 [Apr 1942]. On Fedor Basmanov: 1/554/43 [Feb 1941]; 1/569/45 [Aug 23, 1941]; 2/1666/7 [Feb 15, 1941]. On the historical evidence, see Platt, *Terror and Greatness*, 44–48; Rowland, "Did Muscovite Literary Ideology Place Limits on the Power of the Tsar," 133–34; and Kurbsky's first letter to Ivan, where he links moral decline to political overreach. Ustrialov, who published the correspondence for the first time, linked Ivan's immorality with Fedor Basmanov, see "Pervoe poslanie Kurbskogo Ivanu Groznomu." I thank Kevin Platt for sharing his unpublished article on earlier films, in particular *Wings of a Serf* (1926), from which Eisenstein quoted extensively in The Dance of the Oprichniki.

57. 2/1165/4 [Apr 4, 1941].

58. 2/1165/5 [Apr 16, 1941].

59. Masefield, *William Shakespeare*, 109; 2/1165/5 [Apr 16, 1941].

60. 2/1165/5–6 [Apr 16, 1941].

61. 2/1165/6 [Apr 16, 1941].

62. 2/1167/42, 49 [Sep 22, 1941]

63. 2/1167/49 [Sep 22, 1941]

64. 2/1167/42–49 [Sep 22–23, 1941]; journal entries dated Aug 23–Sep 24: 2/1167/15–59 and 1/1415/24–25.

65. 1/1415/25 [Sep 25, 1941].

66. 2/124/1 [Sep 8, 1941].

67. For examples: 1923/2/128/31–32 [Oct 16, and Nov 23, 1943]; 1923/2/1166/42–43 [Nov 14, 1943]; 1923/554/61ob. [Nov 1942]; *SW* 4:604–15.

68. 1/624/40. Additional comments on Karamzin can be found in 2/1168/20 [Feb 24, 1942]; on Kliuchevsky and Platonov in 1923/1/561 and 1923/1/570.

69. 1/624/17, also cited in *NN*, 105; see also "Istoricheskii kommentarii," 230.

70. 2/1166/44–46 [Oct 1943].

71. Platt and Brandenberger, *Epic Revisionism*, 180–81.

72. Here Eisenstein is copying A. A. Kizevetter's summary of Kliuchevsky's views; notes on Kliuchevsky appear in 1/569/59–60.

73. 1/570/7 [Feb 2, 1942]; also 1/570/72–78, 82 [Apr 18, 1942].

74. 1/569/61–61ob.

75. Kollmann, *Kinship and Politics*; Getty, *Practicing Stalinism*.

76. 1/570/7 [April 28, 1942].

77. 2/125/19 [early 1942]; also Eizenshtein, *IP*, 6:503.

78. 2/1169/43 [May 17, 1942]; Eizenshtein, *IP*, 6:511.

79. 1/569/45 [Aug 23, 1941]; 1/561/14 [Aug 10, 1942]; 2/1168/21 [Feb 24, 1942]; 2/1686/1–6 (drawings) [Mar 11, 1942].

80. 1/552/55 [Feb 1941].

81. 1/561/24–25, 60–61 (Lecture 26); also 1/561/74; 1/561/117 (Lecture 21) [Mar 1942]; 2/124/30–31 [Mar 1942]; 2/124/109–10; Kliuchevskii, *Kurs russkoi istorii*, 199–200, 201; Fennell, *Correspondence between Prince A. M. Kurbsky and Tsar Ivan IV*, 75–77.

82. 2/1172/66 [May 14, 1944], *Metod*, 1:278–95.

83. "From Saturn to Dionysus," 2/1172/18ff [Jan 7, 1944]; 2/1168/11.

84. Eisenstein also copied this one out twice: 1923/1/561/65 and 133.

85. 2/1172/8ob. [Jan 7, 1944].

86. Varia was the daughter of the director Sergei Vasiliev and the actor Varvara Miasnikova; 2/1172/8 [Jan 7, 1944].

87. 2/1172/8–8ob [Jan 7, 1944]; *SW* 4:429; "[Disnei o totemizm]," in *Metod*, ed. Bulgakowa 3:845–87; "Imitation as Mastery," in *Eisenstein Rediscovered*, 66–71.

88. *Metod*, 1:46, 82–85, 195–97.

89. 2/1172/9ob. [Jan 1944].

90. *SW* 4:436–37, 487–566; *Metod*, 1:275.

91. 1/561/67, emphasis added.

92. 1/569/44 [probably late 1941].

93. He found references to the oath in von Staden, Taube and Kruse, and Kurbsky's *Istoriia o delekh*; see "Istoricheskii kommentarii," 209–10.

94. 1/569/44, 45 [Aug 23, 1941], 46 [Nov 4, 1941].

95. 2/1168/6 [Feb 13, 1942].

96. 1/569/37 [Feb 13, 1942].

97. 2/1168/2–5 [Feb 13, 1942].

98. Eisenstein is not entirely consistent on this point: at times he says that the oprichniki become worse than those they had overthrown and at times they merely replaced and imitated the old elite (2/1168/8–14 [Feb 13, 1942]).

99. "Istoricheskii kommentarii," 238.

100. 2/1168/7 [Feb 13, 1942].

101. Getty, *Practicing Stalinism*, 147.

102. Fitzpatrick, *Everyday Stalinism*, 181, 95–106. Additional examples: Akosh Siladi, "Ten' Ivana v trekh ottenkakh," *KZ*, no. 38 (1998): 334.

103. Fitzpatrick, *Everyday Stalinism*, 105–6.

104. 2/1168/4–5 [Feb 13, 1942].

105. 2/1168/7–11 [Feb 13, 1942].

106. Swoboda, "Furnace Play," 220–34.

107. 1/570/11 [c. Jul 29, 1942].

108. 2/1168/7 [Feb 13, 1942].

109. *NN*, 104.

110. Clark, *Moscow, the Fourth Rome*, 3, 321–23; Shmulevich, "'Ivan Groznyi' i Stalin," 189–96.

111. Shmulevich, "'Ivan Groznyi' i Stalin," 189–96.

112. 1/570/28; 1/561/110. As far as I can tell, Eisenstein got this quote from Kizevetter and never read Kavelin. See 1/553/43; 1/554/28; 1/569/22; and *NN*, 323.

113. 1/561/28. On Machiavelli in Eisenstein's notes: 2/1166/19–25 [Oct 8, 1941]; 1/561/4 [Mar 9, 1941]; 1/561/28, 30–35ob. [Aug 1942]. See also Villari, *Life and Times of Niccolo Macciavelli*.

114. Machiavelli, *Prince*, chapters VIII and XVII.

115. 1/570/27.

116. 2/1166/26 [Oct 8, 1941], citing Villari, *Life and Times of Macciavelli*, 205.

117. 2/1166/23 [Oct 8, 1941], citing Villari, *Life and Times of Macciavelli*, 217.

118. 2/1166/22–23 [Oct 8, 1941].

119. 2/128/33 [Nov 23, 1943]

120. Villari, *Life and Times of Machiavelli*, 218; 2/1166/24.

121. Cherniavsky, "Ivan the Terrible as Renaissance Prince," 208–9.

122. Cherniavsky, "Ivan the Terrible as Renaissance Prince," 211.

123. *SW* 4:437; 2/1174/21–22 [Mar 12, 1946].

124. 2/1169/35–38 [May 10, 1942]; 2/1170/4–5 [Jan 1, 1943]; Willis, "Gnawing Vulture," 23.

125. For a different interpretation of much of the same evidence: Clark, "Sergei Eisenstein's *Ivan the Terrible*," 63–67; Lary, "Eisenstein and Shakespeare," 140–50.

126. 2/1169/5–6 [Apr 2, 1942]; 2/1170/4–6 [Jan 1, 1943].

127. *Metod*, 1:251.

128. *Metod*, 1:252.

129. *Metod*, 1:253.

130. *Metod*, 1:46n1 [Oct 16, 1944]. *Chuvstvennoe myshlenie* is almost always translated as *sensuous* or *sensual thinking* or sometimes even *sensuous thought*, all of which are fundamentally misleading for three reasons. Eisenstein saw sexuality as only one component of the pre-logical or of *chuvstvennoe myshlenie*, so *sensuous* with its erotic connotations in English is inaccurate. Second, *chuvstvennoe* can mean "sensory" or "emotional"; it can also be "sensory" *and* "emotional." Third, *myshlenie* is the dynamic process of thinking, not the static body of thought. I translate it as "sensory-emotional thinking."

131. *SW*, 3:38.

132. *Metod*, 1:256–61, 260, 272–73, 479n279.

133. These studies began even before Eisenstein went to Mexico: Bulgakowa, "From Expressive Movement to the Basic Problem," 425–26; Vassilieva, "Eisenstein and Cultural-Historical Theory," 421–25; Widdis, *Socialist Senses*, 36–40, 194–96.

134. *Metod*, 1:274–76. On Eisenstein's uses of Rank and birth trauma, see Lövgren, *Eisenstein's Labyrinth*.

135. *Metod*, 1:324; "Speeches to the All-Union Creative Conference of Soviet Film-workers," *SW* 3:24–38; Lövgren, *Eisenstein's Labyrinth*, 32–34, 67–82; and the concise treatment by Tsivian, *Ivan the Terrible*, 77–80.

136. *Metod*, 1:279; also 1:316–18, 479n279; and "The Psychology of Composition," 211–336.

137. *Metod*, 1:278–79.

138. On Hegel, Lenin, and the historical spiral: Salazkina, *In Excess*, 160, 163–69; Nesbet, *Savage Junctures*, 82–93; and *IP*, 4:665–67. On the spiral among the avant garde: Bulgakowa, "Spiral, Sphere, Circle: Forms and Meanings."

139. *Metod*, 1:282, 316–17.

140. 1/644/12ob. [Jun 1942]; *Metod*, 1:181, 317, 324; see also Somaini, "Cinema as Dynamic Mummification," 44.

141. *Metod*, 1:272; *NN*, 11, 265, 284.

142. *Metod*, 2:362 [Nov 15, 1941].

143. *NP*, 2:125.

144. *Metod*, 1:253. Eisenstein began this chapter by saying that until working on *Ivan*, he had not given direct attention to narrative and character, but that now the "infection" of his theorizing had extended to these features as well as form and in relation to form. On Shakespeare, 1:257–83.

145. 2/1169/38; 2/1170/5; *NN*, 104–6.

146. *Metod*, 1:257–60.

147. 2/1170/5.

148. 2/1169/38 [May 10, 1942], *NN*, 374–75. Eisenstein was delighted that Shakespeare used a seemingly passive character to represent the overcoming of passive, instinctive reflex by "humanism."

149. *NN*, 375.

150. *Metod*, 2:362–65.

151. On Eisenstein and Jonson, see Rumiantseva, "'Ne darom ia bredil Jonson'om,'" 234–41; and Kleberg, "Ivan Aksenov, Shakespeare, and Ben Jonson," 179–96.

152. *NN*, 105–6. The discussion of masking, change, and comparison with Shakespeare is on 103–6.

153. Smith, "Not Shakespeare: *The Spanish Tragedy*" (podcast), iTunes, 17:43.

154. Willis, "Gnawing Vulture," 32.

155. 2/1170/6; also *Metod*, 1:322–25.

156. On Shakespeare and *Ivan* in this context: *Metod*, 1:282–83; 1:322–23.

157. Kyd, *Spanish Tragedy*, 2:1.

158. 2/1702/6–9 [Apr 3, 1942].

159. Kleiman, "Formula finala," 102–3 (citing Eisenstein's notebooks in 1/552 and 2/243).

160. Tsivian, "Cinema and Aristotle," 407–20.

161. Nesbet, *Savage Junctures*, 210.

3. Power Personified

1. 2/1168/28 [Oct 1942]. In his influential article, Kozlov misinterprets the word "good" in this passage to refer to Eisenstein's opinion of John/Ivan as a *person* as opposed to his assessment of John/Ivan the *film*: "Artist and the Shadow," 116.

2. Uhlenbruch, "Annexation of History," 274–81; Neuberger, *Ivan the Terrible*, 78–80; Dobrenko, *Stalinist Cinema*, 49–60.

3. Fitzpatrick, *On Stalin's Team*.

4. Harris, *Great Fear*; Getty and Naumov, *Road to Terror*.

5. Djilas, *Conversations with Stalin*, 76, 102–7, 149–61; Montefiore, *Stalin*, 519–24; see also the brilliant parodies by Fazil Iskander, including "Belshazzar's Feasts," in *Sandro of Chegem*.

6. Levin, "Istoricheskaia tragediia," 87.

7. *NN*, 324.

8. 2/1168/5 [Feb 13, 1942].

9. Eizenshtein, "Avtor i ego tema," 96–97 (notes by Kozlov); also Kleiman, "Foreword," 16–17.

10. 2/128/32–33 [Nov 23, 1943]; Forsdick and Hobsbjerg, "Sergei Eisenstein and the Haitian Revolution," 157–85; Nizhny, *Lessons with Eisenstein*, 22–92.

11. "Lzhe-Neron," 1/405 [Feb 1937]; Bulgakowa, *Sergei Eisenstein*, 208.

12. 2/1164/38–39 [Sep 2, 1940]; 2/1168/20–22 [Feb 24, 1942]; Lövgren, "Eisenstein's Pushkin Project," 126–39; Goodwin, *Eisenstein, Cinema, and History*, 179–80; "Stsena iz 'Borisa Godunova' v raskadrovke S. Eizensteina," 111–30; Kleiman, "Nachnem s Pushkina," 65–74; *SW* 4:712–14; Kleiman, "Tri zhesta," 114.

13. Kozlov, "Hypothetical Dedication," 65–92; Bulgakova, "Uchenik charodeia," 286–306; *SW* 4: 264–70, 274–78, 446–50; 2/1749/2 [Jul 1, 1942].

14. Eizenshtein, *Memuary*, 1:28.

15. Gould, *Ontogeny and Phylogeny,* 13; Somaini, "Cinema as 'Dynamic Mummification,'" 38–39.

16. 2/1172/9–10 [Jan 7, 1944]; *NN*, 287.

17. *Metod*, 2:255 [Nov 16, 1941].

18. *Metod*, 2:261–63 [Sep 21, 1940].

19. Moore, *Savage Theory*, 123, 125–29.

20. *Metod*, 2:265; *Disney*, 15.

21. Nesbet, *Savage Junctures*, 157–84; *Disney*, 127–44.

22. *Metod*, 2:256 [Nov 16, 1941].

23. Nesbet, *Savage Junctures*, 191–93.

24. Tsivian, *Ivan the Terrible*, 49–51, 77–78; Iampolski, "Drawing as Will and Representation," A16–17; Nesbet, *Savage Junctures*, 201.

25. *Disney*, 66–67, 122; *Metod*, 2:514–19 [Dec 2, 1943].

26. 2/1172/8–8ob. [Jan 7, 1944]; see also *Disney*, 102–3.

27. 2/1172/9–10 [Jan 7, 1944].

28. *Metod*, ed. Bulgakowa, 3:887 [Jan 19, 1944]: "*Licht eindringen in dieses Eingeweide* [*svet, pronikaiushchii v etu utrobu*]"; this edition translates "*Eingeweide*" as "womb."

29. 1/572/36.

30. Spurgeon, *Shakespeare's Imagery*, 324–27.

31. "Otkaznoe dvizhenie," *Metod*, 1:200–205; Eisenstein, "On Recoil Movement," in *Meyerhold, Eisenstein and Biomechanics*, ed. Law and Gordon, 192–204. There is no

easy translation of this phrase; often translated as "recoil movement," the gesture Eisenstein describes and directs always *precedes* the main movement (rather than recoiling or reacting to something), so I have opted for the more neutral, descriptive "reverse movement."

32. *Metod*, 1:472.

33. 1/552/36 [Feb 1941].

34. The clips of Foma and Erema can be seen on the Criterion DVD of *Ivan the Terrible* (2003).

35. 1/570/15 [Aug 11, 1942].

36. 1/570/15–16 [Aug 11, 1942].

37. *NN*, 298–305, 310–27. Eisenstein analyzed this scene to show the evolution (and continuity) of his use of montage since *Potemkin*.

38. Roberge, *Eisenstein's Ivan the Terrible*, 61–68.

39. Thompson, *Eisenstein's Ivan the Terrible*, 150–52.

40. 1/561/94–94ob. (notes on Fedor Basmanov as a "demon" and on monks as fallen angels); 1/570/38; *Ivan the Terrible: A Screenplay*, 258.

41. On foreigners: Pavlov and Perrie, *Ivan the Terrible*, 115–16. On Albert Schlicting: "Istoricheskii kommentarii," 225; Flier, "Iconology of Royal Ritual." On Eisenstein's notes on monks as "literally fallen angels": 1/561/94ob., citing *Posobie k izucheniiu ustava Bogosluzheniiu*, 68. On jesters: "Kompozitsiia," 243.

42. Upper-case in the original, "Ivan Groznyi: Kino-stsenarii," 80–81.

43. In most versions of Part II released in the United States before the 2003 Criterion DVD, the lyrics in this scene went untranslated, so the content of the oath was unknown to many earlier commentators.

44. *Ivan the Terrible: A Screenplay*, 135; Ermolaev, "Liturgical Borrowings as Film Music."

45. On the sources: "Istoricheskii kommentarii," 209–10. On the oath in historical context: Kivelson, "How Bad Was Ivan the Terrible?," 67–84.

46. "Istoricheskii kommentarii," 209–10; Kurbsky, "Istoriia o velikom kniaze Moskovskom," cited in Kivelson, "How Bad Was Ivan the Terrible?," 76.

47. Kivelson, "How Bad Was Ivan the Terrible?," 78.

48. Kivelson, "How Bad Was Ivan the Terrible?," 78.

49. 1/155/94 [Jul 4, 1942]; 2/1168/5–7, 10–11 [Feb 13, 1942].

50. 2/124/83.

51. Kleiman, "Tri zhesta," 111–12.

52. Clark, *Soviet Novel*, 115; Günther, "Wise Father Stalin," 178–90; Brooks, *Thank You, Comrade Stalin!*, 84–89; Davies, "Cult of the 'Vozhd,'" 131–47.

53. Slezkine, *House of Government*, 96–97, 254–67, 560–62, 228–29.

54. *IP*, 6:513; 1/570/27.

55. *IP*, 6:513.

56. 1/570/27 [Apr 8, 1942].

57. 1/570/23; 2/1172/9 [Jan 7, 1944]

58. *Ivan the Terrible: A Screenplay*, 201–3.

59. *Metod*, 2:528 [Jul 8, 1946].

60. Eizenshtein, "Pushkin i Gogol'," 181–82.

61. Esfir Tobak, *Ivan's* editor, wrote that Eisenstein shot the scene for Part III but decided to append it to Part II: "Moi Gigant," 136.

62. Kleiman, "Tri zhesta," 93–118.

63. Tsivian, *Ivan the Terrible*, 37.

64. 2/1169/8 [Apr 2, 1942]

65. Thompson, *Eisenstein's Ivan the Terrible*, 202.

66. 2/1169/7–10 [Apr 2, 1942].

67. Kiaer, *Imagine No Possessions*; Widdis, *Socialist Senses*, 128–29, 145–46, 155–57, 181–96; Room, "Moi kinoubezhdenie," 5.

68. "[Ob igre predmetov]," *KZ*, no. 36/37 (1997/1998): 35.

69. "Psychology of Composition," 226n2.

70. "Psychology of Composition," 231.

71. "Psychology of Composition," 211.

72. "Psychology of Composition," 214–16.

73. *SW*, 2:128.

74. *SW*, 2:129; *SW*, 2:82 105.

75. *SW*, 2:123, translation corrected; *Montazh*, 175.

76. *SW*, 3:30; also "Psychology of Composition," 237.

77. *SW*, 3:32.

78. On these investigations: Fernández, *Beyond Metaphor*, 131–39.

79. "Psychology of Composition," 219.

80. *Disney*, 44.

81. Bennett, *Vibrant Matter*, vii.

82. Auslander, "Beyond Words," 1018–19; see also Mitchell, *What Do Pictures Want?*; Elkins, *Object Stares Back*.

83. MacDonald, *H Is for Hawk*, 55, 83, 85, 209, 211.

84. *NN*, 257–58.

85. Moore, *Savage Theory*, 73–83.

86. On the emotional power of close-up: *Metod*, 2:53–112; *SW* 4:461–78; *NN*, 48–49; 2/128/25. On William Wyler's 28mm lens in *Little Foxes* 2/128/19 [Apr 7, 1943]; Bordwell, "Eisenstein, Socialist Realism, and the Charms of Mizantsena," 24–36.

87. For a good example of analysis of repetition, connection, and allusion, see Khitrova, "Eisenstein's Choreography in *Ivan the Terrible*," 55–71.

88. Tsivian, *Ivan the Terrible*, 44–46; Clark, "Sergei Eisenstein's *Ivan the Terrible* and the Renaissance," 53–56.

89. 2/1176/51–54 [Oct 19–20, 1946].

90. *NN*, 103.

91. Bulgakowa, "Spiral, Sphere, Circle," A19–25.

92. Nesbet, *Savage Junctures*, 209–14.

93. "[Ob igre predmetov]," *KZ*, no. 36/37 (1997/1998): 35.

94. On the "axial" camerawork and the emotional intensity it produces: Bordwell, "Eisenstein, Socialist Realism, and the Charms of Mizantsena," 13–37.

95. In Roland Barthes's famous article on excess, he argues that the many ambiguous physical details in *Potemkin* and *Ivan the Terrible* functioned like trauma, blocking language and defeating efforts to derive meaning ("The Third Meaning," 52–68).

96. "Montage 1938," *SW* 2:300.

97. 2/124/30 [Mar 30, 1942].

98. Neuberger, "Eisenstein's Angel," 374–406.

99. 2/124/28 [Mar 30, 1942].

100. 2/124/28 [Mar 30, 1942].

101. 2/127/9 [Mar 30, 1942]; *IP*, 6:496. The comment is embedded in notes on Ivan's inner conflicts.

102. Rowland, "Biblical Military Imagery," 89, 195; Flier, "Semiotics of Faith," 123; Uspenskii, *Semiotics of the Russian Icon*, 16, 21n17.

103. Rowland, "Biblical Military Imagery," 195.

104. Zabrodin, "Neizvestnye stranitsy tsenariia," 253–61; "Istoricheskii kommentarii," 233.

105. Lincoln, *Between Heaven and Hell*, 46–47.

106. Zabrodin, "Neizvestnye stranitsy tsenariia," 254.

107. *Metod*, 2:501–4; Tsivian, *Ivan the Terrible*, 60–73.

108. Thompson, *Eisenstein's Ivan the Terrible*, 189–90. On the Apocalyptic Angel: Tsivian, *Ivan the Terrible*, 29–36.

109. Muratov, "Russkaia zhivopis'," 328. To some extent, Eisenstein anticipated recent scholarship on the role of the Apocalypse in Muscovite political culture during Ivan's reign: Flier, "Til the End of Time," 127–58; Mneva, "Monumental'naia i stankovaia zhivopis'," 310–15, 324–26, 329; Iurganov, *Kategorii russkoi srednevekovoi kul'tury*; Halperin, "Cultural Categories, Councils, and Consultations," 653–64; and Hunt, "Ivan IV's Personal Mythology," on the unity of opposites in Ivan's day.

110. Alpatov, *Pamiatnik drevnerusskoi zhivopisi*; Kachalova et al., *Blagoveshchenskii sobor*; Bocharov and Vygolov, *Aleksandrovskaia sloboda*; Mneva, "Monumental'naia i stankovaia zhivopis'," 313, 323–25, 329.

111. Muratov, "Russkaia zhivopis'," 328–29; Neuberger, "Eisenstein's Angel," 396.

112. *NN*, 310.

113. "Stalin, Molotov and Zhdanov," *SW* 3:300–301. Perrie cites evidence to suggest that Stalin's opinion of Ivan was known prior to the conversation that Eisenstein recorded in 1947 (*Cult of Ivan the Terrible*, 86–87).

114. Neuberger, *Ivan the Terrible*, 80–96; Kleiman calls *Method* "an autobiographical story" (*Metod*, 1:18); Kozlov, "Tvorchestvo i biografiia," 93–97; Podoroga, *Afto-bio-grafiia*.

115. *SW* 4:16–24.

116. *SW* 4:126.

117. 1/554/31 [Feb 21, 1942]; 2/1172/9ob. [Jan 7, 1944]. On the Freudian and Oedipal nature of this relationship and its social analogies, see also Ivanov, *Ocherki po istorii semiotiki*, 98.

118. 2/1168/22 [Feb 26, 1942].

119. It was much more common then for fathers to retain custody of children after a divorce, so the arrangement shouldn't be seen as a social aberration even if Eisenstein painted it as a painful separation.

120. *SW* 4:125.

121. *SW* 4:505–6.

122. *SW* 4:16–17, 23, 36, 101.

123. *SW* 4:126.

124. Podoroga, *Avto-bio-grafiia*, 58.

125. Podoroga, *Avto-bio-grafiia*, 60, 63, 70.

126. *Metod*, 2:429 [Nov 28, 1947].

127. *SW*, 4:739–42.

128. *Kremlevskii kinoteatr,* 758–61.

129. *SW* 4:742.

130. *SW* 4:739.

131. 2/1167/32–39 [Sep 16, 1941].

132. *Metod,* 1:274–75; and in his discussion of Freud's relationship with his students, "The Oedipus complex which has been blown up out of all proportion to its place in Freud's teachings," *SW,* 4:105.

133. *SW,* 4:105; *Disney,* 117; 2/1172/8–9 [Jan 7, 1944].

134. Eagleton, *Sweet Violence,* 1–3; also Booth, *King Lear, Macbeth, Indefinition, and Tragedy.*

135. *Metod,* 2:389.

136. *SW,* 4:24.

137. Greenblatt, "Shakespeare and the Ethics of Authority," 74.

138. Levin, "Istoricheskaia tragediia," 83.

139. *IP,* 6:378–87.

140. Greenblatt, "Shakespeare and the Ethics of Authority," 81.

141. Willis, "Gnawing Vulture," 23.

142. Eagleton, *Sweet Violence,* 233–34.

143. *SW,* 4:24–26.

144. Belsey, *Subject of Tragedy,* 42.

145. Tsivian, *Ivan the Terrible,* 49; see also *SW,* 2:185–93, for Eisenstein's discussion of Shakespearean dismemberment and reassembly.

146. Smith, "Character in Shakespearean Tragedy," 103.

4. Power Projected

1. *NN,* 279.

2. 1/552/37 [Feb 10, 1941]; also 2/124/1 [Nov 8, 1941].

3. *NN,* 284.

4. *NN,* 286; *SW,* 4:8–9, 27–29. Eisenstein liked this anecdote so much that he decided to make it stand for his first glimpse of polyphonic construction, even if he wasn't sure he remembered it correctly: 2/1173/45 [Nov 8, 1945].

5. 2/128/32 [Nov 1943].

6. 2/1172/90 [Aug 1944].

7. Iampolski, "Theory as Quotation," 65–67; Zholkovsky, "Eisenstein's Poetics," 254–55.

8. "Dickens and Griffith," *SW,* 3:193.

9. *NN,* 279; also "Dickens and Griffith," *SW,* 3:224–35.

10. *SW,* 4:26.

11. *SW,* 4:28.

12. Bulgakowa, "Evolving Eisenstein," 39–42.

13. 2/1169/5 [Apr 2, 1942].

14. *NN,* 298–302.

15. 2/1169/5–6 [Apr 2, 1942].

16. *NN,* 284.

17. *NN,* 323.

18. *NN,* 284.

19. *NN*, 323; also 284–85, 324.

20. 2/124/56–57 [Sep 16, 1941]; written the same day Eisenstein wrote his *"Book of Shame."*

21. Iurenev, *Sergei Eizenshtein*, 2:214–15; Kozlov, "Artist and the Shadow," 113; Bulgakowa, *Sergei Eisenstein*, 212.

22. 2/124/57 [Nov 15, 1941].

23. 2/124/13 and 56–57 [Sep 16, 1941].

24. 1923/2/1168/24 [Mar 24, 1942].

25. "Fil'm etot o cheloveke/kotoryi v XVI stoletii vpervye ob"edinil nashu stranu/iz otdel'nykh razobshchennykh i svoekorystnykh kniazhestv sozdal edinoe moshchnoe gosudarstvo/O polkovodtse, kotoryi vozvelichil voennuiu slavu nashei rodiny na vostoke i na zapade/O gosudare/kotoryi dlia resheniia etikh velikikh zadach vpervye vozlozhil na sebia/venets tsaria vseia Rusi." The inscription does not appear in the original screenplay (see S. M. Eizenshtein, "Ivan Groznyi: Kino-stsenarii," *Novyi mir*, nos. 10–11 [1943]: 61–108) or in the collected works, *IP*, 6:202; but it is printed in the English translation of the transcript of the two finished parts of the film, *Ivan the Terrible*.

26. Il'ia Smirnov, "Mezhdu dvumia tiranami," 14; also Iurenev, *Sergei Eizenshtein*, 2:237.

27. 1/548/1–8 [Nov 28, 1944].

28. "Ivan Groznyi: Kino-stsenarii," 62; translated in *Ivan the Terrible: A Screenplay*, 24–25.

29. *SW*, 3:188–92.

30. Clark, *Moscow the Fourth Rome*, 318–24. The notes on looks and costume: 1/554/86 [Feb 18, 1941] and 1/572/35–36.

31. *NN*, 106.

32. *NN*, 375.

33. Eisenstein mentions visiting the National Gallery twice in his memoirs and noted that he saw Holbein's *The Ambassadors* among other paintings there (*SW*, 4:77, 300).

34. *Ivan the Terrible: A Screenplay*, 45.

35. *NN*, 324 (translation slightly revised).

36. "Istoricheskii komentarii," 181–84.

37. *Ivan the Terrible: A Screenplay*, 54–55; see also *IP*, 6:464–65 and 484–85, for Eisenstein's notes on Pimen's and Efrosinia's reactions to the speech.

38. See, for example, Madariaga, *Ivan the Terrible*, xii; and Bordwell, *Cinema of Eisenstein*, 229.

39. 1/554/102 [probably Feb 1941].

40. *IP*, 6:460–61.

41. 1/552/36 [Feb 10, 1941].

42. 1/554/103 [Feb 1941]; *IP*, 6:460–61.

43. 1/570/11.

44. 1/561/15 [Aug 10, 1942]; *IP*, 6:462–63.

45. 1/561/17 [Aug 10, 1942].

46. *IP*, 6:498.

47. 1/570/3, 27; 2/124/8 [Nov 16, 1941]; *IP*, 6:513.

48. The original is found in 2/126; there are charts (*ankety*) for Efrosinia, Kurbsky, Filipp (Fedor Kolychev), Pimen, and Aleksei Basmanov ("Basmanov the father"). The

charts were published in *IP*, 6:460–93; Ivan's chart was translated and published in Lary, *Dostoevsky and Soviet Film*, 240–43.

49. 1/569/59–61ob.

50. 1/554/43 [surrounding notes are from January and February 1941].

51. 1/531/2 [Mar 9, 1941].

52. 1/554/28 [Apr 6, 1941]. See also 2/1165/5 [Apr 16, 1941].

53. 2/1166/23 [Oct 8, 1941].

54. 1/569/50 [Feb 2, 1942].

55. Eisenstein especially liked it that all the conflicts between Kurbsky and Ivan take place remotely, without physical proximity (1/570/18).

56. *IP*, 6:480–81; earlier notes on Filipp's opposition: 1/552/41; 1/553/28 [Feb 20, 1941]; 1/553/57–58 [Feb 1941], 1/554/3.

57. 1/569/22 [Feb 10, 1941?]; 1/554/3; *IP*, 6:481–83.

58. 2/124/6 [Apr 9, 1942].

59. *IP*, 6: 494–513; Lary, *Dostoevsky and Soviet Film*, 242–54.

60. The end of this scene, showing the new army of oprichniki, was not included in early 35mm prints of the film or early videos distributed in the United States.

61. 2/124/95 [Apr 4, 1942]

62. 2/1684/3 [caption to drawing, Mar 6, 1942].

63. 2/124/87 [Mar 1942].

64. 2/124/83 [Mar 1942].

65. *IP*, 6:511.

66. 2/1169/43 [May 1942].

67. For more on this passage, see Tsivian, *Ivan the Terrible*, 60–72; and Sultan Usu-valiev, "The Godfathers of Mikhail Kuznetsov," 184–99.

68. *IP*, 6:503, 512.

69. 1/520/35, cited in Tsivian, *Ivan the Terrible*, 89; 1/565/37 [Mar 11, 1942].

70. *IP*, 6:503, 512.

71. 2/124/96 [Apr 7, 1942].

72. *IP*, 6:503–4.

73. Based on the screenplay. Parts of this scene were filmed, but the footage has not survived. A series of drawings depict close-ups of Fedor and Aleksei and several other shots, including Ivan's despair at the end (2/1686/1–5 [Mar 11, 1942]; 2/1727/4 [Nov 10, 1942]; and 2/1723/12 [July 27, 1942]).

74. *IP*, 6:505.

75. 1/565/27 [Mar 4, 1942].

76. *IP*, 6:513 and 2/124/78 [May 28, 1942].

77. *IP*, 6:513.

78. These notes were also published in *IP*, 6:494–503. Tsivian draws his excellent discussion of Maliuta and Fedor Basmanov from this text and related archival materials, which I follow, but with different emphases.

79. This reminded Eisenstein of Grigory Kozintsev's dog (*IP*, 6:494 [Mar 31, 1942]).

80. 1/565/23 [Feb 27, 1942].

81. *IP*, 6:513.

82. *IP*, 6:498–99; 2/124/6 [Apr 9, 1942].

83. 2/1166/21–22 [Oct 8, 1941].

84. *IP*, 6:495; 1/570/41.

85. 1/570/43 [Mar 10, 1942]; 2/128/31 [Oct 1943].

86. *IP*, 6:495–96 [Mar 31, 1942].

87. *IP*, 6:495 [Apr 1, 1942].

88. The scene was intended to precede The Fiery Furnace. As Ivan enters the cathedral for the play, he is laughing at Maliuta for letting Efrosinia defeat him; see "The Staritskys' Palace," *IP*, 6:496.

89. 2/128/31 [Oct 16, 1943]; "Charlie the Kid," *SW*, 3: 243–67; "Komicheskoe," *Metod*, 1:420–431; "Misteriia tsirka: Struktura kak siuzhet," *Metod*, 1:431–40; "Disney," *Metod*, 2:264–95 and 494–529. See also *IP*, 4: 448–535; 1/570/40, 45, 62 [Mar 10, 1942]; and 2/1165 [May 7, 1942].

90. Rabelaisian humor finds its way into Eisenstein's notes on the shift between laughter and fear, but there is no evidence that he knew Bakhtin's work (1/570/45; *Metod*, 1:463n).

91. 2/1175/6–6ob. [Apr 18, 1946].

92. *IP*, 6: 510.

93. Zabrodin, "Neizvestnye stranitsy stsenariia," 247.

94. 1/554/30 [Nov 4, 1941].

95. 1/554/6 [Apr 19, 1941].

96. A. N. Veselovskii, "Skazki ob Ivane Groznom," *Sobranie sochinenii*, 16 (1876):146, 149, cited in 1/561/46.

97. Perrie, *Image of Ivan the Terrible*, 90–96.

98. 1/554/11, 15; 1/561/43, 45, 46; "Istoricheskii kommentarii," 208–9, 212–13.

99. "Istoricheskii kommentarii," 213; Perrie, *Image of Ivan the Terrible*, 17.

100. *IP*, 6:549–50.

101. 2/124/8.

102. *IP*, 6:495.

103. 1/652/9 [Sep 5, 1942].

104. The deleted scenes may be viewed on *Eisenstein: The Sound Years*.

105. 2/1175/6 [Apr 18, 1946].

106. Zabrodin, "Neizvestnye stranitsy stsenariia," 246–53; "Istoricheskii kommentarii," 212.

107. 2/128/1 [Feb 18, 1943].

108. 2/128/1 [Feb 18, 1943], written before Birman was cast.

109. 1/552/67 [Feb 1941].

110. 1/552/68 [Feb 1941]; 1/554/5 [Feb 5, 1941].

111. 2/124/26 [Feb 20, 1942]; *IP*, 6:465.

112. "Istoricheskii kommentarii," 232.

113. *IP*, 6:466–67.

114. 1/552/68 [probably Feb 1941].

115. *IP*, 6:470–71.

116. *IP*, 6:470.

117. *IP*, 6:471.

118. *IP*, 6:460.

119. Nesbet, *Savage Junctures*, 195–97.

120. 2/1172/36 [Jan 30, 1944].

121. 2/1169/19 [Apr 20, 1942].

122. 2/128/3–4 [Apr 4, 1943]; published in *IP*, 6:514 (Conversation with Pavel Kadochnikov, Apr 4, 1943).

123. Eisenstein, who loved visual rhymes, positions Sigismund in the same slouch used in a scene in *October* that was then also replicated by Eisenstein himself, on set in the same cross-throne pose. And of course it recalls the young, vulnerable Ivan on the throne and the about-to-be-murdered Vladimir Staritsky in tsarist costume on the throne. In his diary, Eisenstein recalled that the idea for this set of associations was a farce he had seen in 1916 (2/1169/19 [Apr 20, 1942]).

124. The dialectic as division and interpenetration or conflict and synthesis is discussed throughout *Method*, but in "Chet-Nechet: Razdvoenie edinogo," Eisenstein focuses on the ways these patterns appear in non-European cultures and function in composition: *Metod*, 2:151–91, 457–63; see also Neuberger, "Cosmopolitan Kremlin," 89–91.

125. *Metod*, 2:528.

126. Brzezinski, *Polish Winged Hussar*.

127. Bershtein, "Englishman in the Russian Bathhouse," 75–87.

128. 2/1677/5 [Feb 2, 1942].

129. On drag and its many resonances in *Ivan the Terrible*, see Nesbet, *Savage Junctures*, 194–97.

130. Sontag, "Notes on Camp," 275–92.

131. *NN*, 279–80.

132. *IP*, 6:322.

133. 2/1168/21 [Feb 2, 1942].

134. Platt, *Terror and Greatness*, 45–46.

135. Moss, "Underground Closet," 229–51. Moss includes one film, but his discussion addresses only its narrative and textual, rather than visual, elements.

136. Moss, "Underground Closet," 235–36.

137. 2/1169/20–23 [Apr 20, 1942].

138. 1/570/30 [Jan 18, 1941?].

139. *Ivan the Terrible: A Screenplay*, 238–44. Notes on reading about salacious activity in Elizabeth's court: 1/561/5 [Oct 1, 1941]. Reference to *Shakespeare's England*, vols. 1–2 (1916); also Aksenov, *Shekspir*, 1:24. On bawdy songs transformed by the Church into hymns: *Metod*, 2:376–77; *Risunki Sergeia Eizenshteina, 1942–44*.

140. 1/552/26 [Feb 7, 1941].

141. *Metod*, 2:528.

142. *Disney*, 96, 102–4, 109–10, 114, 119.

143. *Metod*, ed. Bulgakowa, 3:882; *Disney*, 118.

144. 2/1170/6 [Jan 1, 1943].

145. *Disney*, 93–94, 96.

146. *Disney*, 110.

147. *Metod*, ed. Bulgakowa, 3:872; *Disney*, 106–7.

148. *NN*, 282.

149. *SW*, 3:38; see also "Kino totalitarnoi epokhi," *IK* no. 2 (1990): 114.

150. *Disney*, 108.

151. *Disney*, 114–15.

152. *Disney*, 114.

153. *Metod*, 1:5; 2/1171/26 [Dec 6, 1943]. Italicized text translated from German. Kleiman uses this diary passage in the introduction to his edition of *Metod*.

154. *Metod*, 1:251, 477; 2/252/1–12, 52 [Dec 1943–Jan 1944].

155. Aumont, *Montage Eisenstein*, 159–61; "Notes for a Film of 'Capital,'" 3–26; Michelson, "Reading Eisenstein Reading 'Capital,'" 29.

156. "Psychology of Composition," 211.

157. Groys, *Total Art of Stalinism*.

158. Zholkovsky, "Eisenstein's Poetics," 254.

5. How to Do It

1. Dobrenko, *Stalinist Cinema*, 44–45; Bordwell, "Eisenstein, Socialist Realism, and the Charms of Mizantsena," 14–23.

2. Iampolski, "Theory as Quotation," 54.

3. *NN*, 291–93; *Metod*, 1:251.

4. *NN*, 385.

5. Parts of *NN* were published in 1939 and 1940 and parts were translated into English in *Film Sense* (1942) and *Film Form* (1949); Eisenstein conceptualized the book as a discrete text in 1945, and one version of that manuscript was published in his collected works in 1964 (*IP*, 3:33–432); this is the text Marshall used to translate *NN* into English but with passages omitted (1987); in 2004–2006 Kleiman published another, more complete version of the text with a second volume of related materials (*NP*); on the complicated publication history of *Nonindifferent Nature*: *NP*, 1:613–15. The best introduction to *Nonindifferent Nature* is Kleiman, "Pafos Eizenshteina," *NP*, 2: 5–32; and Herbert Eagle's introduction to *NN* (vii–xxi).

6. *NN*, 36.

7. *NN*, 8–9, 28–29, 35–36.

8. Iampolski, "Theory as Quotation," 56–59.

9. 2/1171/10 [Feb 22, 1943]; *SW*, 3:309–10.

10. Bulgakowa, *Sergei Eisenstein*, 65; *NN*, 28; 2/1173/33 [1945]. I thank Ana Olenina for sharing her forthcoming articles on Pavlov and Bekhterev, which inform this discussion.

11. *SW*, 3:319.

12. *SW*, 4:500.

13. Cited by Eisenstein in *NN*, 326; originally published as "Dalekoe i blizkoe," *Iskusstvo*, Feb 6, 1945.

14. *NN*, 168.

15. *SW*, 4:498.

16. *NN*, 27, 29, 31, 35–36.

17. *NN*, 36.

18. On reflexology: Sirotkina, "Ubiquitous Reflex," 70–81. On links between physiology and psychology: Widdis, *Socialist Senses*, 1–26; Olenina, "Engineering Performance," 297–336; Bulgakowa, "From Expressive Movement."

19. Bulgakowa, "From Expressive Movement," 427.

20. *NN*, 28–29.

21. *NN*, 4.

22. *NN*, 3–4.

23. *NN*, 11–12.

24. *NN*, 10.

25. *NN*, 295–96.

26. *NN*, 349.

27. "Opredeliaiushchii zhest," *NP*, 1:165, 633.

28. Synesthesia makes an appearance in "An Unexpected Juncture" (1928), *SW* 1:115–22; polyphony is discussed in "The Dramaturgy of Film Form," and "The Fourth Dimension in Cinema" (both 1929), *SW*, 1:161–80.

29. *NN*, 297.

30. *NN*, 140.

31. *NN*, 140–41.

32. *NN*, 84–85.

33. Nesbet, "Gogol, Belyi, Eisenstein, and the Architecture of the Future," 505–7.

34. *NN*, 147, also 151.

35. *NN*, 152. Bordwell describes deep-space framing in the same terms (*Cinema of Eisenstein*, 244–48).

36. *NN*, 152.

37. *NN*, 217.

38. *NN*, 217; 2/1169/44 [May 21, 1942].

39. Salazkina, "Introduction," in *Sound, Speech, Music*, 6.

40. Criticisms cited in Brown, *Overtones and Undertones*, 134–45.

41. Hubbert, "Eisenstein's Theory of Film Music Revisited," 125–47.

42. *NN*, 339–40, translation corrected (*NP*, 446).

43. On continuities with earlier montage essays: Kozlov's notes in the first publication of *Neravnodushnaia priroda* in *IP*, 3:635–36. Many of the ideas that would form *Nonindifferent Nature* arose during Eisenstein's year in Mexico in 1931: Salazkina, *In Excess*; Robertson, *Eisenstein on the Audiovisual*, 82–105.

44. *NN*, 305.

45. Synesthesia is a widely researched condition, although recently studies are changing the ways in which it is understood, not as a discreet condition unique to a small number of individuals but as a common component of sensory perception; see Hubbard and Ramachandran, "Neurocognitive Mechanisms of Synesthesia," 509–20.

46. *NN*, 302.

47. *NN*, 281.

48. *NN*, 281.

49. "P-R-K-F-V," 159; *IP*, 5:468. There is some ambiguity in the Russian: *obraz* can mean "image" in the literal sense, but it is also the word Eisenstein uses in the phrase "montage image" to refer to the generalized, more abstract understanding of a subject. Here I'm not sure which sense he intends: the emotional montage image or the hybrid emotional-visual that Eisenstein identifies in *Potemkin* as the "music of landscape."

50. Brown, *Overtones and Undertones*, 136.

51. *NN*, 335.

52. Bartig, *Composing for the Red Screen*; Morrison, *People's Artist*; see also Egorova, *Soviet Film Music*.

53. *NN*, 256–57.

54. "P-R-K-F-V," 163; *IP*, 5:464, 470.

55. "P-R-K-F-V," 162; *IP*, 5:468.

56. "P-R-K-F-V," 162; *IP*, 5:468.

57. "P-R-K-F-V," 162; *IP*, 5:469.

58. "From Lectures," *SW*, 3:329.

59. "P-R-K-F-V," 162, *IP*, 5:469.

60. Kleiman, *Eisenstein on Paper*, 159, 164–65, 193–95.

61. Kleiman, *Eisenstein on Paper*, 166.

62. *NP*, 444 (*NN*, 338).

63. *NN*, 336.

64. *NN*, 351.

65. On Eisenstein and Wagner: Bartlett, *Wagner and Russia*; "Voploshchenie mifa," *Metod*, 2:192–225.

66. Bartig, *Composing for the Red Screen*, 134; Brown, *Overtones and Undertones*, 13; Thompson, *Eisenstein's Ivan the Terrible*, 217–23.

67. Brown, "How Not to Think Film Music," 10.

68. Bartig, *Composing for the Red Screen*, 139–147.

69. Brown, "How Not to Think Film Music," 7; Bordwell, *Cinema of Eisenstein*, 185–90, for the criticism and the defense.

70. Jacobs, "Lesson with Eisenstein, 24–46; *NN*, 348–54.

71. *NN*, 332–33.

72. *NN*, 350.

73. *NN*, 351–53.

74. The main example Eisenstein uses to explain polyphony in *Nonindifferent Nature*, Ivan's mourning at his wife's coffin, is oriented toward showing how the structures of counterpoint and polyphony serve to bring out the basic idea of the scene: "The basic theme is Ivan's despair. . . . The *theme of despair* grows into the *theme of doubt*." *NN*, 310; also 321.

75. For cutting rhythm for the rest of the "pleading" scene, see Jacobs, "Lesson with Eisenstein," 41–42.

76. Jacobs, "Lesson with Eisenstein," 42.

77. Tsivian, *Ivan the Terrible*, 40–41.

78. *NN*, 336.

79. *IP*, 6:462–63.

80. *IP*, 6:513.

81. "P-R-K-F-V"; *IP*, 5:470.

82. *NN*, 281.

83. Cavendish, *Men with the Movie Camera*, 110–14.

84. Butovskii, *Andrei Moskvin*, 189.

85. Bordwell, "Eisenstein, Socialist Realism, and the Charms of Mizentsena," 13–37.

86. *NN*, 147–49.

87. "P-R-K-F-V," 159.

88. Butovskii, *Andrei Moskvin*, 189–90.

89. Fomin, *Kino na voine*, 82–84.

90. Butovskii, *Andrei Moskvin*, 48–114; Cavendish, *Men with a Movie Camera*, 196–240.

91. Vishnevskii, "Iz dnevnikov," 68.

92. Butovskii, *Andrei Moskvin*, 190–91; Cavendish, *Men with a Movie Camera*, 200–201.

93. 2/1166/41.

94. 2/1166/42.

95. 2/1166/41.

96. 2/1166/42.

97. 2/1166/43; *NN*, 306–8.

98. 2/1166/43 (my emphasis).

99. For example: "The scene between Filipp and Ivan is perhaps not historically accurate; however, it is psychologically faithful" (1/561/143 [Mar 10, 1942]).

100. 2/1166/43.

101. 2/1166/43.

102. 2/1166/44.

103. 2/1166/45.

104. 2/1166/45.

105. *NN*, 283, 295, 281.

106. Butovskii, *Andrei Moskvin*, 206–7.

107. *NN*, 147–48.

108. According to the database on the website Cinemetrics, there are 1,535 total shots in Ivan, Parts I and II, http://www.cinemetrics.lv/database.php.

109. On sightlines and other methods for placing Ivan at the physical and metaphorical center, see Thompson, *Eisenstein's Ivan the Terrible*, 114–29.

110. "Ivan Groznyi: Kino-stsenarii," 81.

111. *NN*, 344.

112. Cherkasov, *Zapiski sovetskogo aktera*, 237.

113. Cherkasov, *Zapiski sovetskogo aktera*, 135.

114. Kleiman, "Kak Eizenshtein rabotal s akterami," 125–46.

115. Eisenstein and Tretyakov, "Expressive Movement," 173–92, written 1923, unpublished; "'Mise en jeu' i 'mise en geste,'" *NP*, 1:386–440, 1:656–57n, written January 1948. *Directing* was to have a chapter on expressive movement and gesture, "Opredeliaiushchii zhest." "Vertical Montage" was to have a passage on expressive movement and gesture, which became a chapter in *Method* ("Vyrazitel'noe dvizhenie," *Metod*, 1:169–83). See also "Volki i ovtsy: Rezhisser i akter," *IP*, 2:304–6.

116. "Lecture on Biomechanics," in *Meyerhold, Eisenstein, and Biomechanics*, ed. Law and Gordon, 207. On approaches to expressive movement and acting in Russia before Meyerhold: Iampolski, "Kuleshov's Experiments," 31–50.

117. Kleiman, "Kak Eizenshtein rabotal s akterami," 129–30; Leyda, *Kino*, 327–34, on acting in *Bezhin Meadow*.

118. Widdis, *Socialist Senses*, 19–20, 40, 258.

119. Iampolski, "Kuleshov's Experiments," 31–50; Olenina, "Psychomotor Aesthetics"; Widdis, *Socialist Senses*, 157–60.

120. *NP*, 1:174. I thank Ana Hedberg Olenina and Irina Schulzki for sharing the prepublication draft of their editorial article, "Mediating Gesture in Theory and Practice."

121. Iampolski, "Kuleshov's Experiments," 31–35; Hubbert, "Eisenstein's Theory of Film Music Revisited," 125–47.

122. Eisenstein and Tretyakov, "Expressive Movement," 173, 175, 185.

123. "Notes on Biomechanics," 164–65; "Lecture on Biomechanics," 207–9.

124. Bulgakowa, "From Expressive Movement," 432; Vassilieva, "Eisenstein and Cultural-Historical Theory," 421–42.

125. "Lecture on Biomechanics," 207.

126. "Lecture on Biomechanics," 208.

127. *Metod*, 1:160–83, 468n; *NP*, 1:164–199, 633n. Eisenstein apparently intended to publish another version of "Expressive Movement" in 1945, updated after making *Ivan*. On the history of the text, see *Metod*, 468n.

128. *Metod*, 1:178–80.

129. *Metod*, 1:170, 174, 177.

130. *Metod*, 1:175, 179; also 177, where Eisenstein attributes the idea to Jean d'Udine; see also 1:633, on the essay's dating and provenance.

131. *NP*, 1:391.

132. "Recoil Movement," 192–204; *IP*, 4:81–90; "Otkaznoe dvizhenie," *Metod*, 1:200–205 (also 129–39); *NP*, 1:389–90; *NN*, 200–215.

133. *NP*, 1:392–410.

134. *NN*, 92–102; also 104, 357–59, 360.

135. *NP*, 1:408–10.

136. "Kak ni stranno: O Khokhlovoi," first published in the journal *Kino* (Mar 30, 1926); subsequently appeared as the first half of a pamphlet co-authored with Viktor Shklovskii, published later in 1926.

137. "Ne povtorimost' Galiny Sergeevny Ulanovoi," *IP*, 5:474–79, 480 [Jul 1, 1947].

138. "Iudif'," *IP*, 5:366.

139. "Iudif'," *IP*, 5:367–68, 386–87, 395–96.

140. "Iudif'," *IP*, 5:375.

141. "Iudif'," *IP*, 5:375.

142. "Iudif'," *IP*, 5:381–82.

143. 1/552/37. On Jonson, see Vera Rumiantseva, "'Ne darom ia bredil Jonson'om . . . ,'" 234–41; and *SW*, 2:185–93.

144. *SW*, 2:192.

145. *NN*, 102.

146. *NN* 102.

147. On the three kinds of "unity of opposites" discussed here and below, see *NN*, 102.

148. 1/556/41 [Feb 21, 1942].

149. 2/1680/4 [Feb 21, 1942].

150. Tsivian, *Ivan the Terrible*, 37–38.

151. Kael, *Kiss Kiss Bang Bang*, 288–89.

152. Maddow, "Eisenstein and the Historical Film"; 2/1174/7 [Jan 15, 1946].

153. Rebecchi, "Cinema as Architectural Art," 318.

6. The Official Reception

1. Leyda, *Kino*, 382; *Variety*, March 19, 1947; *New York Times*, March 10, 1947. See also the review in *Time Magazine*: "bold, fascinating to look at. But . . . as Eisenstein tells it, this vindication of Ivan becomes, by many parallels, a vindication of Stalin and his regime" (April 14, 1947, 104–5).

2. Richard Taruskin, "Great Artists Serving Stalin Like a Dog," *New York Times*, May 28, 1995.

3. Roger Ebert, http://www.rogerebert.com/reviews/great-movie-ivan-the-terrible-parts-i-and-ii, dated January 19, 2012.

4. Andrew Grossman, http://sensesofcinema.com/2011/cteq/ivan-the-terrible-parts-i-and-ii/, dated March 2011.

5. David Ehrenstein, "Bezhin Meadow," *Senses of Cinema*, no. 23 (December 2002), http://sensesofcinema.com/2002/cteq/bezhin/.

6. Clark and Dobrenko, *Soviet Culture and Power*, 436.

7. Clark, *Soviet Novel*; Tertz, *On Socialist Realism*; Kenez, *Cinema and Soviet Society*, 157–85; Robin, *Socialist Realism*.

8. Eisenstein's notes on the discussion: 1/642/4–14 [Aug 10, 1944].

9. On the formation of the Artistic Council of the Committee of Cinema Affairs: Levin, "Sovet da liubov'," 82–87; Fomin, *Kino na voine*, 430–33.

10. "Zasedanie khudozhestvennogo soveta," 286.

11. 1/648/7 [Nov 11, 1944].

12. "Zasedanie khudozhestvennogo soveta," 305.

13. Miller, *Soviet Cinema*, 134–37.

14. Iurenev, *Sergei Eizenshtein*, 2:244; Levin, "Istoricheskaia tragediia," 84, 87. Both Iurenev and Levin cite passages from the transcript of the discussion but they both tend to avoid comments about Ivan as a ruler.

15. RGALI, 2456 (Mosfil'm) 1/957/10 [Dec 7, 1944].

16. Iurenev, *Sergei Eizenshtein*, 2:258.

17. 2456/1/957/2–4 [Dec 7, 1944].

18. 2456/1/957/26–27 [Dec 7, 1944].

19. 2456/1/957/34 [Dec 7, 1944].

20. 2456/1/957/34 [Dec 7, 1944].

21. 2456/1/957/18 [Dec 7, 1944].

22. 2456/1/957/13 [Dec 7, 1944].

23. 2456/1/957/6 [Dec 7, 1944].

24. 2456/1/957/31 [Dec 7, 1944].

25. 2456/1/957/50–51; summarized in Iurenev, *Sergei Eizenshtein*, 2:247.

26. 1/642/14–21; Iurenev, *Sergei Eizenshtein*, 2:249–50.

27. Vishnevskii, "Fil'm 'Ivan Groznyi,'" *Pravda*, Jan 28, 1945; Vishnevskii, "Iz dnevnikov," 65–67. A critical review written by Petr Pavlenko got as far as galley proofs: Kozlov, "Artist and the Shadow of Ivan," 124; Iurenev, *Sergei Eizenshtein*, 2:249.

28. Romashov, "Fil'm 'Ivan Groznyi,'" *Izvestiia*, Feb 4, 1945.

29. I do not know how the letters were collected, selected, or preserved. Some are copies of letters sent to *Pravda* in response to Vishnevskii's review, others were sent directly to Eisenstein and are preserved in his archive (1/2289).

30. Fitzpatrick, "Supplicants and Citizens," 78–10; Davies, *Popular Opinion in Stalin's Russia*.

31. The one exception, the only purely positive assessment of the film, was a long typed letter from a fan who hoped Eisenstein might jumpstart her career in theater (1/2289/108 [Apr 11, 1945]).

32. 1/2289/109.

33. 1/2289/112–13 [Apr 10, 1945].

34. 1/2289/117.

35. 1/2289/126–127 [Jan 2, 1945].

36. 1/2289/126–127 [Jan 2, 1945].

37. 2/1170/12–14 [May 18, 1945].

38. RGALI, 2073 (Komitet po Stalinskim premiiam v oblasti iskusstva i literatury); the nominations: 2073/1/15/72 [Mar 28, 1944]; the plenum discussion: 2073/1/12/31 [Mar 29, 1945].

39. 2073/1/14/67 [Mar 29, 1945].

40. 2073/1/11/150–51 [Mar 29, 1945].

41. 2073/1/11/150 [Mar 29, 1945].

42. 2073/1/11/151 [Mar 29, 1945].

43. 2073/1/11/152 [Mar 29, 1945].

44. See, for example, historians' reviews of Oliver Stone's films *JFK* and *Nixon*: "AHR Forum"; Hoff.

45. 2073/1/11/153 [Mar 29, 1945].

46. 2073/1/11/154 [Mar 29, 1945].

47. 2073/1/11/153–55 [Mar 29, 1945].

48. 2073/1/11/153 [Mar 29, 1945].

49. 2073/1/11/154–55 [Mar 29, 1945].

50. 2073/1/11/156 [Mar 29, 1945].

51. 2073/1/11/157 [Mar 29, 1945].

52. Vishnevskii, "Iz dnevnikov," 74 [Mar 30–31, 1947].

53. Vishnevskii, "Iz dnevnikov," 75 [no date, Apr 1947].

54. Vishnevskii, "Iz dnevnikov," 75 [Apr 25, 1947].

55. 2073/1/11/152 [Mar 29, 1945].

56. Frolova-Walker, *Stalin's Music Prize*, 19, 22, 34, 253; Johnson, "Stalin Prize and the Soviet Artist," 831–33.

57. Conversation with Naum Kleiman, June 1998.

58. Roshal', "Ia uzhe ne mal'chik," 163–64.

59. Romm, *Besedy o kino*, 91.

60. "Zasedanie khudozhestvennogo soveta," 285.

61. "Zasedanie khudozhestvennogo soveta," 288–89.

62. "Zasedanie khudozhestvennogo soveta," 301.

63. "Zasedanie khudozhestvennogo soveta," 302–3.

64. "Zasedanie khudozhestvennogo soveta," 305–7.

65. 1/646/27 [undated but after the Artistic Council screening and before the Kremlin screening].

66. 1/652/34.

67. 1/646/27.

68. Clark and Dobrenko, *Soviet Culture*, 438 (Letter from Alexandrov to Stalin, Mar 6, 1946, the day Stalin watched Part II).

69. Brandenberger, "Stalin as Symbol"; Plamper, *Stalin Cult*.

70. Perrie, *Cult of Ivan the Terrible*, 149.

71. Miller, *Soviet Cinema*, 61–66; Belodubrovskaya, "The Jockey and the Horse, 29–53.

72. Mar'iamov, *Kremlevskii tsenzor*, 72.

73. *Ivan the Terrible: A Screenplay*, 118.

74. *IP*, 6:511.

75. Khitrova, "Eisenstein's Choreography in *Ivan the Terrible*," 55–71.

76. 2/1692/3 [Mar 21, 1942].

77. Bershtein, "Englishman in the Russian Bathhouse," 84–85.

78. Mar'iamov, *Kremlevskii tsenzor*, 74; Kozlov, "Artist and the Shadow of Ivan," 127.

79. The speech: Maksimenkov et al., *Kremlevskii kinoteatr*, 758–61. The CC Resolution: Maksimenkov et al., *Kremlevskii kinoteatr*, 763–67. The conversation: 1/1375/1–24; Mar'iamov, *Kremlevskii tsenzor*, 84–91. Translations of excerpts from Stalin's speech, the CC Resolution, and the conversation: Clark and Dobrenko, *Soviet Culture and Power*, 440–45, 447–54. On the Cold War context, see Davies, "Soviet Cinema in the Early Cold War."

80. Healey, "Homosexual Existence," 362.

81. Healey, "Homosexual Existence," 364.

82. Mar'iamov, *Kremlevskii tsenzor*, 74.

83. Kozlov, "Artist and the Shadow of Ivan," 127.

84. Kozlov, "Artist and the Shadow of Ivan," 127.

85. For "a coven of witches," see Clark and Dobrenko, *Soviet Culture and Power*, 440; for "Witches Sabbath," see Kozlov, "Artist and the Shadow of Ivan," 127.

86. Mar'iamov, *Kremlevskii tsenzor*, 74; "Artist and the Shadow of Ivan," 127.

87. Bolshakov, *Sovetskoe kinoiskusstvo v gody Velikoi Otechestvennoi voiny*, 80–84.

88. Maksimenkov et al., *Kremlevskii kinoteatr*, 759.

89. Multitrans: http://www.multitran.ru/c/m.exe?l1=2&l2=1&s=%EE%EC%E5%F0%E7%E8%F2%E5%EB%FC%ED%FB%E9

90. Maksimenkov et al., *Kremlevskii kinoteatr*, 759, 763–67.

91. Harry Whyte, a British Communist working for the English-language *Moscow Daily News*, wrote to Stalin in May 1934, asking him to justify the new law. He asked Stalin, "Can a homosexual be considered a person fit to become a member of the Communist Party?" Stalin scrawled across the letter, "An idiot and a degenerate. To the archives" (cited in Healey, "Sexuality and Gender Dissent," 157).

92. Eisenstein and Cherkasov wrote that the conversation started precisely at 11 p.m. and ended at ten past midnight; according to the Kremlin log, Eisenstein and Cherkasov entered Stalin's office at 11:15 on the twenty-fifth and left at 12:05 on the twenty-sixth (Artizov and Naumov, *Vlast' i khudozhestvennaia intelligentsia*, 612).

93. "Groznogo teni 1947 goda." *Moskovskie novosti*, August 7, 1988.

94. 1/1375/24.

95. Stalin's behavioi in this conversation seems similar to the role he played in mediating postwar debates in the sciences and social sciences, as discussed in Pollack, *Stalin and the Science Wars*.

96. Kozlov, "Artist and the Shadow of Ivan," 129.

97. "Laughs" was a handwritten addition to the transcript (1/1375/7).

98. Platt and Brandenberger, "Terribly Romantic, Terribly Progressive, or Terribly Tragic," 635–54; Platt and Brandenberger,*Epic Revisionism*, 157–78.

99. Kozlov, "Artist and the Shadow of Ivan," 129–30; Romm, *Besedy o kino*, 91.

100. Kozlov, "Artist and the Shadow of Ivan," 129; Kleiman confirmed this in conversation, June 2016.

Conclusion

1. Greenblatt, "Shakespeare and the Ethics of Authority," 84–85.

2. Lincoln, *Between Heaven and Hell*, 351; Platt, *Terror and Greatness*, 246.

3. Platt, *Terror and Greatness*.

4. *NN*, 104–5.

5. Clark, *Soviet Novel*, 3–24.

6. Dobrenko, *Political Economy of Socialist Realism*, 16–17.

7. Dobrenko, *Political Economy of Socialist Realism*, 23.

8. Davies and Harris, *Stalin*, 1–17; Priestland, *Stalinism and the Politics of Mobilization*, 3–5; Harris, "Introduction," in *Anatomy of Terror*, ed. Harris, 1–8.

9. Getty and Manning, *Stalinist Terror*, 62.

10. Harris, *Great Fear*; Rittersporn, *Anguish, Anger, and Folkways in Soviet Russia*.

11. Ivanov, "Estetika Eizenshteina," 148.

12. Greenblatt, "Shakespeare and the Ethics of Authority," 81–82.

13. Zorkaia, *Portrety*, 118.

Bibliography

Archives

Rossiiskii gosudarstvennyi arkhiv literatury i iskusstva (RGALI)
  Fond 1923. Sergei Mikhailovich Eizenshtein
  Fond 2073. Committee on the Stalin Prize in Literature and Art
  Fond 2453. Moscow Film Studio "Mosfil'm"
  Fond 2456. Moscow Film Studio "Mosfil'm" (*Ivan the Terrible*)
  Fond 2758. Maksim Maksimovich Shtraukh and Iudif' Solomonovna Glizer
Rossiiskii gosudarstvennyi arkhiv sotsial'no-politicheskoi istorii (RGASPI)
  Fond 17. Tsentral'nyi komitet KPSS (Opisi 116, 125, 127)

Works by Eisenstein

Collections

Eisenstein, Sergei M. *The Eisenstein Collection*. Edited by Richard Taylor. Oxford: Seagull Books, 2005.

——. *Risunki k fil'mu "Ivan Groznyi."* Moscow: Soiuz kinematografistov SSSR, Biuro propagandy sovetskogo kinoiskusstva, 1967.

——. *Risunki Sergeia Eizenshteina, 1942–44: Kollektsiia Lidii Naumovoi*. Moscow: Iskusstvo, 2004.

——. *Selected Works*. 4 vols. Edited by Richard Taylor and translated by Richard Taylor, Michael Glenny, and William Powell. London: British Film Institute, 1988–1996.

Eisenstein: The Sound Years. Criterion Collection, DVD boxed set. 2001.

Eizenshtein, S. M. *Izbrannye proizvedeniia v shesti tomakh*, 6 vols. Moscow: Iskusstvo, 1964–1971.

Kinovedcheskie zapiski, no. 36/37 (1997/1998) and no. 38 (1998). Special issues on Eisenstein.

Works Published in Russian: Selected Books

Eizenshtein, S. M. *Memuary*. 2 vols. Edited by Naum Kleiman. Moscow: Muzei kino, 1997.

——. *Metod*. 2 vols. Edited by Naum Kleiman. Moscow: Muzei kino, 2002.

——. *Metod*. 4 vols. Edited by Oksana Bulgakowa. Berlin: Potemkin Press, 2008.

——. *Montazh*. 2 vols. Edited by Naum Kleiman. Moscow: Muzei kino, 1998–2000.

——. *Neravnodushnaia priroda*. 2 vols. Edited by Naum Kleiman. Moscow: Muzei kino, 2004–2006.

Works Published in Russian: Selected Articles

Eizenshtein, S. M. "Alma Ata." *KZ*, no. 49 (2000): 160–64.

——. "Avtor i ego tema: Genezis 'Ivana Groznogo.'" With notes by L. K. Kozlov. *KZ*, no. 38 (1998): 96–97.

——. "Fil'm ob Ivana Groznom." *Izvestiia*, April 30, 1941.

——. "'. . . Iz trekh navodiashchikh strochek . . . .'" *KZ*, no. 38 (1998): 133–41.

——. "Istoricheskii kommentarii k fil'mu 'Ivan Groznyi.'" *KZ*, no. 38 (1998): 173–246.

——. "Iudif'." In *IP*, 5:364–96.

——. "Ivan Groznyi: Kino-stsenarii." *Novyi mir*, nos. 10–11 (1943): 61–108.

——. "Kak ni stranno: O Khokhlovoi." *Kino*, March 30, 1926.

——. "Kompozitsiia i izobrazitel'nost': K graficheskomu tsiklu 'Ubiistvo korolia Dunkana.'" *KZ*, no. 36/37 (1997/1998): 242–49.

——. "Krupneishii gosudarstvennyi deiatel'." *Ogonek*, no. 9–10 (1945): 14. Republished in *IP*, 1:19.

——. "Ne povtorimost' Galiny Sergeevny Ulanovoi." In *IP*, 5:474–79, 480 (July 1, 1947).

——. "[Ob igre predmetov]. *KZ*, no. 36/37 (1997/1998): 34–38.

——. "P-R-K-F-V," *IP*, 5:457–73.

——. "Pushkin i Gogol'." *KZ*, no. 36/37 (1997/1998): 180–220.

——. "Sozdadim fil'my dostoinye stalinskoi epokhi." *Kino*, March 21, 1941.

——. "Voina." *KZ*, no. 49 (2000): 157–60.

——. "Vpered." *Za Bol'shevistskii fil'm*, March 21, 1941.

Translated Works

Eisenstein, Sergei. *Disney.* Edited by Oksana Bulgakowa and Dietmar Hochmuth. Translated by Dustin Condren. San Francisco: Potemkin Press, 2013.

——. "A Few Words about my Drawings." In *SW*, 3:240–42.

——. "The Heirs and Builders of World Culture." In *SW*, 3:182. Originally published in *Pravda*, April 30, 1941.

——. "Imitation as Mastery." In *Eisenstein Rediscovered*, edited by Ian Christie and Richard Taylor, 66–71. London: Routledge, 1993.

——. "Ivan the Terrible: A Film about the Sixteenth-Century Russian Renaissance." In *SW*, 3:188–92. Originally published in *Literatura i iskusstvo*, July 4, 1942.

——. *Ivan the Terrible.* Translated (from French) by A. E. Ellis. London: Faber and Faber, 1989.

——. *Ivan the Terrible: A Screenplay.* Translated by Ivor Montagu and Herbert Marshall. New York: Simon and Schuster, 1962.

——. "Lecture on Biomechanics. March 28, 1935." In *Meyerhold, Eisenstein, and Biomechanics: Actor Training in Revolutionary Russia*, edited by Alma Law and Mel Gordon, 204–23. Jefferson, NC: McFarland, 1996.

——, "Letters from Mexico to Maxim Strauch and Ilya Trauberg." Translated by Tanaquil Taubes. *October*, no. 14 (1980): 57–58.

——. *Nonindifferent Nature: Film and the Structure of Things.* Edited and translated by Herbert Marshall. Cambridge: Cambridge University Press, 1988.

——. "Notes for a Film of 'Capital.'" Translated by Maciej Sliwowski, Jay Leyda, and Annette Michelson. *October*, no. 2 (1976): 3–26.

——. *Notes for a General History of Cinema.* Edited by Naum Kleiman and Antonio Somaini. Amsterdam: Amsterdam University Press, 2016.

——. "Notes on Biomechanics." In *Meyerhold, Eisenstein, and Biomechanics: Actor Training in Revolutionary Russia*, edited by Alma Law and Mel Gordon, 164–67. Jefferson, NC: McFarland, 1996.

——. "P-R-K-F-V." In *Notes of a Film Director*, edited by R. Iurenev, translated by X. Danko. New York: Dover, 1970: 149–67.

——. "The People of One Film." In *SW*, 3:305–16.

——. "The Problems of the Soviet Historical Film." In *SW*, 3:126–41.

——. "The Psychology of Composition." In *EC*, 211–336.

——. "On Recoil Movement." In *Meyerhold, Eisenstein and Biomechanics: Actor Training in Revolutionary Russia*, edited by Alma Law and Mel Gordon, 192–204. Jefferson, NC: McFarland, 1996.

——. "Wolves and Sheep: The Director and the Actor." In *SW*, 3:48–49, and *IP*, 2:304–6.

Eisenstein, Sergei, Vsevolod Pudovkin, and Grigorii Aleksandrov. "Statement on Sound." In *The Film Factory: Russian and Soviet Cinema in Documents, 1896–1939*, edited by Richard Taylor and Ian Christie, 234–35. Cambridge, MA: Harvard University Press, 1988.

Secondary Sources

Abol'nik, O. "Novyi istoricheskii fil'm Eizenshteina." *Ogonek*, no. 14 (May 1941).

Agee, James. "The Unpublished James Agee: Excerpts from Complete Film Criticism. Reviews, Essays, and Manuscripts." Edited by Charles Maland. *Cineaste* 41, no. 4 (2016): 26–29.

"AHR Forum [on Oliver Stone's film JFK]." *American Historical Review* 97, no. 2 (1992); 486–511.

Aksenov, Ivan. *Shekspir*. Moscow: Gospolitizdat, 1937.

Alpatov, M. V. *Pamiatnik drevnerusskoi zhivopisi kontsa XV veka: Ikona Apokalipsis Uspenskogo sobora Moskovskogo kremlia*. Moscow: Iskusstvo, 1964.

Amengual, Bartelemy. *Que Viva Eisenstein!* Lausanne: L'âge d'homme, 1980.

Andronikova, M. I. *Ot prototipa k obrazu*. Moscow: Nauka, 1974.

Artizov, Andrei, and Oleg Naumov, eds. *Vlast' i khudozhestvennaia intelligentsia: Dokumenty TsK RKP(b)-VKP(b), VChK-OGPU-NKVD o kul'turnoi politike, 1917–1953*. Moscow: Mezhdunarodnyi fond "Demokratiia," 1999.

Aumont, Jacques. *Montage Eisenstein*. Paris: Albatross, 1979.

Auslander, Leora. "Beyond Words." *American Historical Review* 110, no. 4 (2005): 1015–45.

Barna, Yon. *Eisenstein*. Translated by Lise Hunter. Bloomington: Indiana University Press, 1973.

Barthes, Roland. "The Third Meaning." In *Image/Music/Text*, translated by Stephen Heath, 52–68. New York: Hill and Wang, 1977.

Bartig, Kevin. *Composing for the Red Screen: Prokofiev and Soviet Film*. New York: Oxford University Press, 2013.

Bartlett, Rosamund. *Wagner and Russia*. Cambridge: Cambridge University Press, 1995.

Bazin, André. *What Is Cinema?* Translated by Hugh Gray. Berkeley: University of California Press, 1967.

Belodrubovskaya, Maria. "The Jockey and the Horse: Joseph Stalin and the Biopic Genre in Soviet Cinema." *Studies in Russian and Soviet Cinema* 5, no. 1 (2011): 29–53.

——. *Not according to Plan: Filmmaking under Stalin and the Failure of Mass Cinema.* Ithaca, NY: Cornell University Press, 2017.

Belsey, Catherine. *The Subject of Tragedy: Identity and Difference in Renaissance Drama.* London: Methuen, 1985.

Bennett, Jane. *Vibrant Matter: A Political Ecology of Things.* Durham, NC: Duke University Press, 2010.

Bershtein, Evgeny. "An Englishman in the Russian Bathhouse: Kuzmin's *Wings* and the Russian Tradition of Homoerotic Writing." In *The Many Facets of Mikhail Kuzmin: A Miscellany,* edited by Lada Panova and Sarah Pratt, 75–87. Bloomington, IN: Slavica, 2011.

Birman, Serafima. "Life's Gift of Encounters." Translated by Margaret Wettlin. *Soviet Literature,* no. 3 (1975): 74–119.

——. "Neotpravlennoe pis'mo." In *Eizenshtein v vospominaniiakh sovremennikov,* edited by R. N. Iurenev. Moscow: Iskusstvo, 1974.

Bocharov, G. N., and V. P. Vygolov. *Aleksandrovskaia sloboda.* Moscow: Iskusstvo, 1970.

Bol'shakov, I. G. *Sovetskoe kinoiskusstvo v gody Velikoi Otechestvennoi voiny, 1941–1945.* Moscow: Goskinoizdat, 1948.

Booth, Stephen. *King Lear, Macbeth, Indefinition, and Tragedy.* New Haven: Yale University Press, 1983.

Bordwell, David. *The Cinema of Eisenstein.* Cambridge, MA: Harvard University Press, 1993.

——. "Eisenstein, Socialist Realism, and the Charms of Mizantsena." In *Eisenstein at 100: A Reconsideration,* edited by Al Lavalley and Barry P. Scherr, 13–37. New Brunswick, NJ: Rutgers University Press, 2001.

Braithwaite, Rodric. *Moscow 1941: A City at War.* New York: Vintage, 2007.

Brandenberger, David. *Propaganda State in Crisis: Soviet Ideology, Indoctrination, and Terror under Stalin, 1927–1941.* New Haven: Yale University Press, 2011.

——. "Stalin as Symbol: A Case Study of the Cult of Personality and Its Construction." In *Stalin: A New History,* edited by Sarah Davies and James Harris. Cambridge: Cambridge University Press, 2005.

——. "Stalin's Rewriting of 1917." *Russian Review* 76, no. 4 (2017): 667–89.

Brooks, Jeffrey. "Public and Private in the Soviet Press, 1921–28." *Slavic Review* 48, no. 1 (1989): 16–35.

——. *Thank You, Comrade Stalin! Soviet Public Culture from Revolution to Cold War.* Princeton, NJ: Princeton University Press, 2000.

Brown, Royal S. "How Not to Think Film Music." *Music and the Moving Image* 1, no. 1 (2008): 2–18.

——. *Overtones and Undertones: Reading Film Music.* Berkeley: University of California Press, 1994.

Brzezinski, Richard. *Polish Winged Hussar 1576–1775.* Oxford: Osprey Publishing, 2006.

Budnitskii, Oleg. "The Great Patriotic War and Soviet Society: Defeatism, 1941–42." *Kritika: Explorations in Russian and Eurasian History* 15, no. 4 (2014): 767–97.

Bulgakova, Oksana. "Uchenik charodeia, ili troinoi portret Meierkhol'da." In *Mejerkhol'd, rezhissera v perspective veka: Materialy konferentsii*, edited by Beatris Pikon-Vallen and Vadim Sherbakov, 286–306. Moscow: OGI, 2001.

Bulgakowa [Bulgakova], Oksana. "The Evolving Eisenstein: Three Theoretical Concepts." In *Eisenstein at 100: A Reconsideration*, edited by Al Lavalley and Barry P. Scherr, 38–51. New Brunswick, NJ: Rutgers University Press, 2001.

——. "From Expressive Movement to the Basic Problem: The Vygotsky-Luria-Eisensteinian Theory of Art." In *The Cambridge Handbook of Cultural-Historical Psychology*, edited by Anton Yasnitsky, René van der Veer, and Michel Ferrari, 423–48. Cambridge: Cambridge University Press, 2014.

——. *Sergei Eisenstein: A Biography*. San Francisco: Potemkin Press, 2002.

——. "Spiral, Sphere, Circle: Forms and Meanings." *The Body of the Line: Eisenstein's Drawings. Drawing Papers*, no. 4 (2000): A19–20.

Burliuk, David, et al. "Slap in the Face of Public Taste." In *Russian Futurism through Its Manifestos*, edited by Anna Lawton, 51. Ithaca, NY: Cornell University Press, 1988.

Butovskii, Ia. L. *Andrei Moskvin: Kinooperator*. Moscow: Dmitrii Bulanin, 2000.

——. "Perepiska A. N. Moskvina i S. M. Eizenshteina." *KZ*, no. 38 (1998): 296–313.

Cavendish, Philip. *The Men with the Movie Camera: The Poetics of Visual Style in Soviet Avant-Garde Cinema of the 1920s*. London: Berghahn Books, 2014.

Cherkasov, N. K. *Notes of a Soviet Actor*. Moscow: Foreign Languages Publishing House, 1957.

——. *Zapiski sovetskogo aktera*. Moscow: Iskusstvo, 1953.

Cherkasova, Nina. "Cherkasov i Eizenshtein." In *Eizenshtein v vospominaniiakh sovremennikov*, edited by R. N. Iurenev, 319–29. Moscow: Iskusstvo, 1974.

Cherniavsky, Michael. "Ivan the Terrible as Renaissance Prince." *Slavic Review* 27, no. 2 (1968): 195–211.

Christie, Ian. "Soviet Cinema: Making Sense of Sound." *Screen*, no. 23 (1982): 34–49.

Christie, Ian, and David Elliot, eds. *Eisenstein at Ninety*. London: British Film Institute, 1988.

Christie, Ian, and Richard Taylor, eds. *Eisenstein Rediscovered*. London: Routledge, 2005.

Clark, Katerina. *Moscow, the Fourth Rome: Stalinism, Cosmopolitanism, and the Evolution of Soviet Culture, 1931–1941*. Cambridge, MA: Harvard University Press, 2011.

——. "Sergei Eisenstein's Ivan the Terrible and the Renaissance: An Example of Stalinist Cosmopolitanism?" *Slavic Review* 71, no. 1 (2012): 49–69.

——. *The Soviet Novel: History as Ritual*, 3rd ed. Bloomington: Indiana University Press, 2000.

Clark, Katerina, and Evgeny Dobrenko, with Andrei Artizov and Oleg Naumov, eds. *Soviet Culture and Power: A History in Documents, 1917–1953*. New Haven: Yale University Press, 2007.

Crummey, Robert. "Ivan the Terrible." In *Windows on the Russian Past: Essays on Soviet Historiography since Stalin*, edited by Samuel H. Baron and Nancy Whittier Heer, 54–88. Columbus, OH: American Association for the Advancement of Slavic Studies, 1977.

Davies, Sarah. "The Cult of the 'Vozhd': Representations in Letters, 1934–1941." *Russian History* 24, no. 1–2 (1997): 131–47.

——. *Popular Opinion in Stalin's Russia: Terror, Propaganda, and Dissent, 1934–1941*. Cambridge: Cambridge University Press, 1997.

——. "Soviet Cinema in the Early Cold War: Pudovkin's *Admiral Nakhimov* in Context." In *Across the Blocs: Cold War Cultural and Social History*, edited by Patrick Major and Rana Mitter, 49–70. London: Frank Cass, 2004: 49–70.

——. "Stalin as Patron of Cinema: Creating Soviet Mass Culture, 1932–1936." In *Stalin: A New History*, edited by Sarah Davies and James Harris, 202–25. Cambridge: Cambridge University Press, 2005.

Davies, Sarah, and James Harris, eds. *Stalin: A New History*. Cambridge: Cambridge University Press, 2005.

Djilas, Milovan. *Conversations with Stalin*. New York: Harcourt, Brace, 1962.

Dobrenko, Evgeny. "The Disaster of Middlebrow Taste, or Who 'Invented' Socialist Realism?" In *Socialist Realism without Shores*, edited by Thomas Lahusen and Evgeny Dobrenko, 135–64. Durham, NC: Duke University Press, 1997.

——. *The Political Economy of Socialist Realism*. New Haven: Yale University Press, 2007.

——. *Stalinist Cinema and the Production of History: Museum of the Revolution*. New Haven: Yale University Press, 2008.

Eagle, Herbert, ed. *Russian Formalist Film Theory*. Ann Arbor: Michigan Slavic Publications, 1981.

Eagleton, Terry. *Sweet Violence: The Idea of the Tragic*. Wiley-Blackwell, 2002.

Ebert, Roger. "Ivan the Terrible Parts I and II." http://www.rogerebert.com/reviews/great-movie-ivan-the-terrible-parts-i-and-ii, dated January 19, 2012.

Elder, R. Bruce. *Harmony and Dissent: Film and Avant Garde Art Movements in the Early Twentieth Century*. Waterloo: Wilfred Laurier University Press, 2008.

Egorova, Tatiana. *Soviet Film Music: An Historical Survey*. Australia: Harwood Academic Publishers, 1997.

Ehrenstein, David. "Bezhin Meadow." *Senses of Cinema*, no. 23 (2002). http://sensesofcinema.com/2002/cteq/bezhin/.

Elkins, James. *The Object Stares Back: On the Nature of Seeing*. New York: Simon and Schuster, 1996.

Enzenberger, Maria. "'We Were Born to Turn Fairy Tale into Reality': Grigori Alexandrov's *The Radiant Path*." In *Stalinism and Soviet Cinema*, edited by Derek Spring and Richard Taylor, 97–108. London: Routledge, 1993.

Ermolaev, Katya. "Liturgical Borrowings as Film Music in Eisenstein's *Ivan the Terrible*." Paper presented at American Association for the Advancement of Slavic Studies Convention, Washington, DC, November 2006.

Fennell, J. L. I., ed. and trans. *The Correspondence between Prince A. M. Kurbsky and Tsar Ivan IV of Russia, 1564–1579*. Cambridge: University Press, 1955.

Fernández, James W. *Beyond Metaphor: The Theory of Tropes in Anthropology*. Stanford, CA: Stanford University Press, 1991.

Fitzpatrick, Sheila. *Everyday Stalinism: Ordinary Life in Extraordinary Times. Soviet Russia in the 1930s*. New York: Oxford University Press, 1999.

——. *On Stalin's Team: The Years of Living Dangerously*. Princeton, NJ: Princeton University Press, 2016.

——. *Stalin's Peasants: Resistance and Survival in the Russian Village after Collectivization.* New York: Oxford University Press, 1994.

——. "Supplicants and Citizens: Public Letter-Writing in Soviet Russia in the 1930s." *Slavic Review* 55, no. 1 (1996): 78–100.

——. *Tear off the Masks! Identity and Imposture in Twentieth-century Russia.* Princeton, NJ: Princeton University Press, 2005.

Flier, Michael. "The Iconology of Royal Ritual in Sixteenth-century Moscovy." In *Byzantine Studies: Essays on the Slavic World and the Eleventh Century*, edited by Speros Vryonis Jr., 53–76. New Rochelle, NY: Arastide D. Caraztas, 1992.

——. "The Semiotics of Faith in Fifteenth-century Novgorod: An Analysis of the Quadpartite Icon." *Canadian-American Slavic Studies* 1–4 (1991).

——. "Til the End of Time: The Apocalypse in Russian Historical Experience before 1500." In *Orthodox Russia: Belief and Practice under the Tsars*, ed. Valerie A. Kivelson and Robert H. Greene, 127–58. University Park: Pennsylvania State University Press, 2003.

Fomin, V. I., ed. *Kino na voine: Dokumenty i svidetel'stva.* Moscow: Maternik, 2005.

Fore, Devon. *Realism after Modernism: The Rehumanization of Art and Literature.* Cambridge, MA: MIT Press, 2012.

Forsdick, Charles, and Christian Hobsbjerg. "Sergei Eisenstein and the Haitian Revolution: 'The Confrontation Between Black and White Explodes Into Red.'" *History Workshop Journal* 78, no. 1 (2014): 157–85.

Frank, Hannah. "'Proceeding from the Heat-oppressed Brain': Thinking through Eisenstein's Macbeth Drawings." *Critical Quarterly*, no. 59 (2017): 70–84.

Freud, Sigmund. *Beyond the Pleasure Principle.* Translated by James Strachey. New York: W. W. Norton, 1990.

——. *Totem and Taboo.* Translated by James Strachey. New York: W. W. Norton, 1990.

Frolova-Walker, Marina. *Stalin's Music Prize: Soviet Culture and Politics.* New Haven: Yale University Press, 2016.

Fürst, Juliane. "Friends in Private, Friends in Public." *Borders of Socialism: Private Spheres of Soviet Russia*, Lewis Siegelbaum, 229–49. New York: Palgrave Macmillan, 2006.

Getty, J. Arch. "The Politics of Repression Revisited." In *Stalinist Terror: New Perspectives*, edited by J. Arch Getty and Roberta T. Manning, 40–62. New York, Cambridge University Press, 1993.

——. *Practicing Stalinism: Bolsheviks, Boyars, and the Persistence of Tradition.* New Haven: Yale University Press, 2013.

Getty, J. Arch, and Roberta T. Manning, eds. *Stalinist Terror: New Perspectives.* New York, Cambridge University Press, 1993.

Getty, J. Arch, and Oleg V. Naumov, eds. *The Road to Terror: Stalin and the Self-Destruction of the Bolsheviks, 1932–1939.* New Haven: Yale University Press, 1999.

Gleason, Abbott. *Totalitarianism: The Inner History of the Cold War.* New York: Oxford University Press, 1995.

Goodwin, James. *Eisenstein, Cinema, and History.* Champaign: University of Illinois Press, 1993.

Gould, Stephen Jay. *Ontogeny and Phylogeny.* Cambridge, MA: Belknap, 1977.

Grabar', Igor' E. *Istoriia russkogo iskusstva.* 6 vols. Moscow: I. Knebel', 1909–1914.

Greenblatt, Stephen, "Shakespeare and the Ethics of Authority." In his *Shakespeare's Freedom*. Chicago: University of Chicago Press, 2010.

Grossman, Andrew. "Ivan the Terrible Parts I and II." http://sensesofcinema.com/2011/cteq/ivan-the-terrible-parts-i-and-ii/, dated March 2011; republished December 2017.

Groys, Boris. *The Total Art of Stalinism: Avant Garde, Aesthetic Dictatorship and Beyond*. Translated by Charles Rougle. New York: Verso, 2011.

"Groznogo teni 1947 goda." *Moskovskie novosti*, August 7, 1988.

Günther, Hans. "Wise Father Stalin and His Family in Soviet Cinema." In *Socialist Realism without Shores*, edited by Thomas Lahusen and Evgeny Dobrenko, 178–90. Durham, NC: Duke University Press, 1997.

Halfin, Igal. *Terror in My Soul: Communist Autobiographies on Trial*. Cambridge, MA: Harvard University Press, 2003.

Halperin, Charles J. "Cultural Categories, Councils, and Consultations in Muscovy." *Kritika: Explorations in Russian and Eurasian History* 3, no. 4 (2002): 653–84.

Harris, James, ed. *The Anatomy of Terror: Political Violence under Stalin*. Oxford: Oxford University Press, 2013.

——. *The Great Fear: Stalin's Terror of the 1930s*. Oxford: Oxford University Press, 2016.

Healey, Dan. "Homosexual Existence and Existing Socialism: New Light on the Repression of Male Homosexuality in Stalin's Russia." *GLQ: Journal of Lesbian and Gay Studies* 8, no. 3 (2002): 349–78.

——. "Sexuality and Gender Dissent: Homosexuality as Resistance in Stalin's Russia." In *Contending with Stalinism: Soviet Power and Popular Resistance in the 1930s*, edited by Lynne Viola. Ithaca, NY: Cornell University Press, 2002.

Hellbeck, Jochen. *Revolution on My Mind: Writing a Diary under Stalin*. Cambridge, MA: Harvard University Press, 2006.

Hoff, Joan. Review of Oliver Stone's *Nixon*. *American Historical Review* 101, no. 4 (1996): 1173–74.

Hoffmann, David L. *Stalinist Values: The Cultural Norms of Soviet Modernity, 1917–1941*. Ithaca, NY: Cornell University Press, 2003.

Hubbard, Edward M., and V. S. Ramachandran, "Neurocognitive Mechanisms of Synesthesia." *Neuron* 48, no. 3 (2005): 509–20.

Hubbert, Julie. "Eisenstein's Theory of Film Music Revisited: Silent and Early Sound Antecedents." In *Composing for the Screen in Germany and the USSR: Cultural Politics and Propaganda*, edited by Robynn Stilwell and Phil Powrie, 125–47. Bloomington: Indiana University Press, 2008.

Hunt, Priscilla. "Ivan IV's Personal Mythology of Kingship." *Slavic Review* 52, no. 4 (1993): 769–809.

Iampolski, Mikhail. "Drawing as Will and Representation." *The Body of the Line: Eisenstein's Drawings. Drawing Papers*, no. 4 (2000).

——. "Kuleshov's Experiments and the New Anthropology of the Actor." In *Inside the Film Factory*, edited by Richard Taylor and Ian Christie, 31–50. London: Routledge, 1991.

——. "Point—Pathos—Totality." In *Notes for a General History of Cinema*, edited by Naum Kleiman and Antonio Somaini, 357–73. Amsterdam: Amsterdam University Press.

——. "Theory as Quotation." *October*, no. 88 (1999): 51–68.

Iskander, Fazil. *Sandro of Chegem*. New York: Vintage, 1983.

Iumasheva, O. G., and I. A. Lepikhov. "Fenomen 'totalitarnogo liberalisma,'" *KZ*, no. 20 (1993/1994): 125–43.

Iurenev, R. N., ed. *Eizenshtein v vospominaniiakh sovremennikov*. Moscow: Iskusstvo, 1974.

——. *Sergei Eizenshtein: Zamysli, fil'my, metod*. 2 vols. Moscow: Iskusstvo, 1985–1988.

Iurganov, A. L. *Kategorii russkoi srednevekovoi kul'tury*. Moscow: Institut "Otkrytoe obshchestvo," 1998.

Iuzovskii, Iosif. "Eizenshtein." In *Eizenshtein v vospominaniiakh sovremennikov*, edited by R. N. Iurenev, 397–413. Moscow: Iskusstvo, 1974.

Ivanov, V. V. "Estetika Eizenshteina." In *Izbrannye trudy po semiotike i istorii kul'tury*. Moscow: Shkola "Iazyki russkoi literatury," 1998.

——. *Ocherki po istorii semiotiki v SSSR*. Moscow: Nauka, 1976.

Jacobs, Lea. "A Lesson with Eisenstein: Rhythm and Pacing in *Ivan the Terrible*, Part I." *Music and the Moving Image*, 5, no. 1 (2012): 24–46.

Johnson, Oliver. "'A Premonition of Victory': *A Letter from the Front*," *Russian Review* 68, no. 2 (2009): 408–28.

——. "The Stalin Prize and the Soviet Artist: Status Symbol or Stigma?" *Slavic Review* 70, no. 4 (2011): 819–43.

Kachalova, I. Ia., N. A. Maiaisova, and L. A. Shchennikova. *Blagoveshchenskii sobor Moskovskogo kremlia: K 500-letiiu unikal'nogo pamiatnika russkoi kul'tury*. Moscow: Iskusstvo, 1990.

Kachurin, Pamela. *Making Modernism Soviet: The Russian Avant Garde in the Early Soviet Era, 1918–1928*. Evanston: Northwestern University Press, 2013

Kadochnikov, Pavel. "Stranitsy iz dnevnika aktera." *Prostor*, no. 2 (1983): 145–64.

Kael, Pauline. *Kiss Kiss Bang Bang*. Boston: Little Brown, 1968.

Kaganovsky, Lilya. "Visual Pleasure in Stalinist Cinema: Ivan Pyr'ev's *The Party Card*." In *Everyday Life in Early Soviet Russia*, edited by Christina Kiaer and Eric Naiman, 35–61. Bloomington: Indiana University Press, 2006.

——. *The Voice of Technology: Soviet Cinema's Transition to Sound, 1928–1935*. Bloomington: Indiana University Press, 2018.

Kaganovsky, Lilya, and Masha Salazkina, eds. *Sound, Speech, Music in Soviet Cinema*. Bloomington: Indiana University Press, 2014.

Karetnikova, Inga. *Seven Masterpieces of 1940s Cinema*. Portsmouth, NH: Heinemann, 2006.

Kater, Michael H. *Twisted Muse: Musicians and Their Music in the Third Reich*. New York: Oxford University Press, 1997.

Keenan, Edward L. *The Kurbskii-Groznyi Apocrypha: The 17th-century Genesis of the "Correspondence" Attributed to Prince A. M. Kurbskii and Tsar Ivan IV*. Cambridge, MA: Harvard University Press, 1971.

Kenez, Peter. *Cinema and Soviet Society, 1917–1953*. Cambridge: Cambridge University Press, 1992.

——. "History of *Bezhin Meadow*." In *Eisenstein at 100: A Reconsideration*, edited by Al Lavalley and Barry P. Scherr, 193–206. New Brunswick, NJ: Rutgers University Press, 2001.

Khitrova, Daria. "Eisenstein's Choreography in *Ivan the Terrible*." *Studies in Russian and Soviet Cinema* 5, no. 1 (2011): 55–71.

Kiaer, Christina. *Imagine No Possessions: The Socialist Objects of Russian Constructivism.* Cambridge, MA: MIT Press, 2005.

Kivelson, Valerie A. "How Bad Was Ivan the Terrible? The Oprichnik Oath and Satanic Spells in Foreigners' Accounts." In *Seeing Muscovy Anew: Politics—Institutions—Culture. Essays in Honor of Nancy Shields Kollmann*, edited by Michael S. Flier, Valerie Kivelson, Erika Monahan, and Daniel Rowland, 67–84. Bloomington, IN: Slavica, 2017.

Kleberg, Lars. "Ivan Aksenov, Shakespeare, and Ben Jonson." In *The Flying Carpet*, edited by Joan Neuberger and Antonio Somaini, 179–96. Paris: Éditions Mimésis, 2017.

Kleiman, Naum. *Eisenstein on Paper.* London: Thames & Hudson, 2017.

——. "Fergana Canal and Tamburlaine's Tower." *Studies in Russian and Soviet Cinema* 5, no. 1 (2011): 103–22.

——. "Foreword." In *Notes for a General History of Cinema*, edited by Naum Kleiman and Antonio Somaini, 13–17. Amsterdam: Amsterdam University Press.

——. *Formula finala: Stat'i, Vysstupleniia, Besedy.* Moscow: Eisenstein Center, 2004.

——. "Kak Eizenshtein rabotal s akterami." *Iskusstvo kino*, no. 1 (1968): 125–46.

——. "Nachnem s Pushkina." *Iskusstvo kino*, no. 2 (1987): 65–74.

——. "Pafos Eizenshteina." In *Neravnodushnaia priroda*, edited by Naum Kleiman, 1:5–32. 2 vols. Moscow: Muzei kino, 2004–2006.

——. "Problema Eizenshteina." In *Metod*, edited by Naum Kleiman, 1:5–30. 2 vols. Moscow: Muzei kino, 2002.

——. "Tri zhesta Ivana Groznogo." *Ot slov k telu: Sbornik statei k 60-letiiu Iuriia Tsiv'iana*, edited by Aleksandr Lavrov, A. L. Ospovat, and R. D. Timenchik, 93–118. Moscow: Novoe literaturnoe obozrenie, 2010.

Kliuchevskii, Vasilii O. *Kurs russkoi istorii.* Moscow: Gosudarstvennoe sotsial'no-ekonomicheskoe izdatel'stvo, 1937.

Kollmann, Nancy S. *Kinship and Politics: The Making of the Muscovite Political System, 1345–1547.* Stanford, CA: Stanford University Press, 1987.

——. *Crime and Punishment in Early Modern Russia.* Cambridge: Cambridge University Press, 2012.

Kotkin, Stephen. *Magnetic Mountain: Stalinism as Civilization.* Berkeley: University of California Press, 1995.

Kozlov, L. K. "The Artist and the Shadow of Ivan." In *Stalinism and Soviet Cinema*, edited by Derek Spring and Richard Taylor, 109–30, 243–48. London: Routledge, 1993.

——. "Eshche o 'Kazuse Ranevskoi,'" *KZ*, no. 38 (1998): 168–72.

——. "A Hypothetical Dedication." In *Eisenstein Revisited: A Collection of Essays*, edited by Lars Kleberg and Håkan Lövgren, 65–92. Stockholm: Almqvist & Wiksell International, 1987.

——. *Proizvedenie vo vremeni.* Moscow: Eizenshtein tsentr, 2005.

——. "Tvorchestvo i biografiia." In *Proizvedenie vo vremeni*, 93–97. Moscow: Eizenshtein tsentr, 2005.

Kuznetsov, Mikhail. "My sporili . . . ." In *Eizenshtein v vospominaniiakh sovremennikov*, edited by R. N. Iurenev, 335–41. Moscow: Iskusstvo: 1974.

Kyd, Thomas. *The Spanish Tragedie*. Project Gutenberg, no. 6043, 2009, updated 2013. https://www.gutenberg.org/files/6043/6043-h/6043-h.htm.

Lahusen, Thomas, and Evgeny Dobrenko, eds. *Socialist Realism without Shores*. Durham, NC: Duke University Press, 1997.

Lary, N. M. *Dostoevsky and Soviet Film: Visions of Demonic Realism*. Ithaca, NY: Cornell University Press, 1986.

——. "Eisenstein and Shakespeare." In *Eisenstein Rediscovered*, edited by Ian Christie and Richard Taylor, 140–50. London: Routledge, 1993.

Law, Alma, and Mel Gordon, eds. *Meyerhold, Eisenstein, and Biomechanics: Actor Training in Revolutionary Russia*. Jefferson, NC: McFarland, 1996.

Levaco, Ronald. "The Eisenstein-Prokofiev Correspondence." *Cinema Journal* 13, no. 1 (1973): 1–16.

Levin, Efim. "Istoricheskaia tragediia kak zhanr i kak sud'ba." *Iskusstvo kino*, no. 9 (1991): 83–92.

——. "Sovet da liubov'." *Iskusstvo kino*, no. 10 (1991): 82–87.

Leyda, Jay. *Kino: A History of the Russian and Soviet Film*. Princeton, NJ: Princeton University Press, 1983.

Leyda, Jay, and Zina Voynow, eds. *Eisenstein at Work*. New York: Methuen, 1982.

Lincoln, W. Bruce. *Between Heaven and Hell: The Story of a Thousand Years of Artistic Life in Russia*. New York: Viking, 1998.

Lovell, Stephen. *In the Shadow of War: Russia and the USSR, 1941 to the Present*. London: Wiley-Blackwell, 2010.

Lövgren, Håkan. *Eisenstein's Labyrinth: Aspects of a Cinematic Synthesis of the Arts*. Stockholm: Almqvist & Wiksell International, 1996.

——. "Eisenstein's Pushkin Project." In *Eisenstein Rediscovered*, edited by Ian Christie and Richard Taylor, 120–33. London: Routledge, 1993.

Lucento, Angelina. "The Conflicted Origins of Soviet Visual Media." *Cahiers du monde russe* 56, no. 2–3 (2015): 401–28.

Macdonald, Helen. *H Is for Hawk*. New York: Grove Atlantic, 2015.

Machiavelli, Niccolo. *The Prince*. Translated by Tim Parks. New York: Penguin Books, 2009.

MacPhee, Graham. "On the Incompleteness of History: Benjamin's Arcades Project and the Optic of Historiography." *Textual Practice* 14, no. 3 (2000): 579–89.

Madariaga, Isabel de. *Ivan the Terrible: First Tsar of Russia*. New Haven: Yale University Press, 2005.

Maddow, Ben. "Eisenstein and the Historical Film." *Hollywood Quarterly* 1, no. 1 (October 1945): 46–30.

Maksimenkov, Leonid. *Sumbur vmesto muzyki: Stalinskaia kul'turnaia revoliutsiia, 1936–1938*. Moscow: Iuridicheskaia kniga, 1997.

Maksimenkov, Leonid V., and Kirill M. Anderson, with Liudmila P. Kosheleva and Larisa A. Rogovaia, eds. *Kremlevskii kinoteatr, 1929–1953: Dokumenty*. Moscow: Rosspen, 2005.

Manley, Rebecca. *To the Tashkent Station: Evacuation and Survival in the Soviet Union at War*. Ithaca, NY: Cornell University Press, 2007.

Mar'iamov, Grigorii. *Kremlevskii tsenzor: Stalin smotrit kino*. Moscow: Kinotsentr, 1992.

Martin, Russell E. *A Bride for the Tsar: Bride-Shows and Marriage Politics in Early Modern Russia*. DeKalb: Northern Illinois University Press, 2012.

Masefield, John. *William Shakespeare*. New York: Henry Holt and Co., 1911.

Mgrebov, Aleksandr. "Emu ia obazan zhizn'iu." In *Eizenshtein v vospominaniiakh sovremennikov*, edited by R. N. Iurenev, 329–34. Moscow: Iskusstvo, 1974.

Michelson, Annette. "Reading Eisenstein Reading 'Capital.'" *October*, no. 2 (1976): 27–38, and no. 3 (1977): 82–89.

Miller, Jamie. *Soviet Cinema: Politics and Persuasion under Stalin*. London: I. B. Tauris, 2010.

Mitchell, W. J. T. *What Do Pictures Want? Essays on the Lives and Love of Images*. Chicago: University of Chicago Press, 2004.

Mitry, Jean. *Eisenstein*. Paris: Éditions universitaires, 1956.

Mneva, N. E. "Monumental'naia i stankovaia zhivopis'." In *Ocherki russkoi kul'tury XVI veka*, edited by A. V. Artsikhovskii, 310 51. Moscow: Moskovskii universitet, 1977.

Montefiore, Simon Sebag. *Stalin: The Court of the Red Tsar*. New York: Knopf, 2003.

Moore, Rachel. *Savage Theory: Cinema as Modern Magic*. Durham, NC: Duke University Press, 1999.

Morrison, Simon. *The People's Artist: Prokofiev's Soviet Years*. Oxford: Oxford University Press, 2008.

Moss, Kevin. "The Underground Closet: Political and Sexual Dissidence in East European Culture." In *Postcommunism and the Body Politic*, edited by Ellen E. Berry, 229–51. New York: New York University Press, 1995.

Muratov, Pavel. "Russkaia zhivopis' do serediny 17-go veka." In *Istoriia russkogo iskusstva*, edited by Igor' E. Grabar', 6: 5–408. Moscow: I. Knebel', 1909–14.

Murin, Iu. G. "Stalin i kino." *Iskusstvo kino*, no. 3 (1993): 101–2.

Nazvanov, Mikhail. "'Prokliataia kartina': Pis'ma k Ol'ge Viklandt so s"emok fil'ma 'Ivan Groznyi.'" *Iskusstvo kino*, no. 1 (1998): 138–47 and no. 2 (1998): 129–39.

Nesbet, Anne. "Gogol, Belyi, Eisenstein, and the Architecture of the Future." *Russian Review*, no. 65 (2006): 491–511.

——. *Savage Junctures: Eisenstein and the Shape of Thinking*. London: I. B. Tauris, 2007.

Neuberger, Joan. "Eisenstein's Angel." *Russian Review* 63, no. 3 (2004): 374–406.

——. "Eisenstein's Cosmopolitan Kremlin: Drag Queens, Circus Clowns, Slugs, and Foreigners in *Ivan the Terrible*." In *Insiders and Outsiders in Russian Cinema*, edited by Stephen M. Norris and Zara M. Torlone, 81–95. Bloomington: Indiana University Press, 2008.

——. "*Ivan the Terrible* as History." *Journal of Modern History* 86, no. 2 (2014): 295–334.

——. *Ivan the Terrible: The Film Companion*. London: I. B. Tauris, 2003.

——. "The Music of Landscape." In *Sound, Speech, Music in Soviet Cinema*, edited by Lilya Kaganovsky and Masha Salazkina, 212–29. Bloomington: Indiana University Press, 2014.

——. "The Politics of Bewilderment: Eisenstein's *Ivan the Terrible* in 1945." In *Eisenstein at 100: A Reconsideration*, edited by Al Lavalley and Barry P. Scherr, 227–52. New Brunswick, NJ: Rutgers University Press, 2001.

——. "Strange Circus: Eisenstein's Sex Drawings." *Studies in Russian and Soviet Cinema* 6, no. 1 (2012): 5–62.

Neuberger, Joan, and Antonio Somaini, eds. *The Flying Carpet: Studies on Eisenstein and Russian Cinema in Honor of Naum Kleiman*. Paris: Éditions Mimésis, 2017.

Nikol'skii, Protoperiia Konstantin. *Posobie k izucheniiu ustava bogosluzhenie Pravoslavnoi tserkvi*. St. Petersburg: n.p., 1907.

Nizhny, Vladimir, ed. *Lessons with Eisenstein*. Translated and edited by Ivor Montagu and Jay Leyda. London: Allen and Unwin, 1962.

Oeler, Karla. *A Grammar of Murder: Violent Scenes and Film Form*. Chicago: University of Chicago Press, 2009.

——. "Of Cats and Men: Eisenstein, Art, and Thinking." In *The Flying Carpet: Studies on Eisenstein and Russian Film in Honor of Naum Kleiman*, edited by Joan Neuberger and Antonio Somaini, 279–94. Paris: Éditions Mimésis, 2017.

Olenina, Ana Hedberg. "Engineering Performance: Lev Kuleshov, Soviet Reflexology, and Labor Efficiency Studies." *Discourse: Journal for Theoretical Studies in Media and Culture* 35, no. 3 (2013): 297–336.

——. "Psychomotor Aesthetics: Conceptions of Gesture and Affect in Russian and American Modernity." PhD diss, Harvard University, 2012.

Olenina, Ana Hedberg and Irina Schulzki. "Mediating Gesture in Theory and Practice." "Mise en geste: Studies of Gesture in Cinema," edited by Ana Hedberg Olenina and Irina Schulzki. Special issue of *Apparatus: Film, Media and Digital Cultures in Central and Eastern Europe*, no. 5 (2017). DOI:http://dx.doi.org/10.17892/app.2017.0005.100.

Oudart, Jean-Pierre. "Sur *Ivan le Terrible*." *Cahiers du cinéma*, no. 218 (1970).

Pavlov, Andrei, and Maureen Perrie. *Ivan the Terrible*. London: Routledge, 2003.

Perrie, Maureen. *The Cult of Ivan the Terrible in Stalin's Russia*. Basingstoke: Palgrave, 2001.

——. *The Image of Ivan the Terrible in Russian Folklore*. Cambridge: Cambridge University Press, 1987.

"Pervoe poslanie Kurbskogo Ivanu Groznomu." In *Perepiska Andreia Kurbskogo s Ivanom Groznym*, with a commentary by Ia. S. Lur'e and Iu. D. Rykova. St. Petersburg: Institut russkoi literatury [Pushkinskii Dom] RAN, © 2006–2011. http://lib.pushkinskijdom.ru/Default.aspx?tabid=9105.

Péteri, György, ed. *Patronage, Personal Networks, and the Party-State: Everyday Life in the Cultural Sphere in Communist Russia and East Central Europe*. Trondheim Studies in East European Cultures and Societies, no. 13 (March 2004).

Plamper, Jan. *The Stalin Cult: A Study in the Alchemy of Power*. New Haven: Yale University Press, 2012.

Platonov, S. F. *Ivan Groznyi (1530–1584)*. St. Petersburg: Brockhaus and Efron, 1923.

Platt, Kevin. *Terror and Greatness: Ivan and Peter as Russian Myths*. Ithaca, NY: Cornell University Press, 2011.

Platt, Kevin M. F., and David Brandenberger, eds. *Epic Revisionism: Russian History and Literature as Stalinist Propaganda*. Madison: University of Wisconsin Press, 2006.

——. "Terribly Romantic, Terribly Progressive, or Terribly Tragic." *Russian Review* 58, no. 4 (1999): 635–54.

Podoroga, Valerii. *Afto-bio-grafiia*. Moscow; Logos, 2001.

Poe, Marshall T. *"A People Born to Slavery": Russia in Early Modern European Ethnography, 1476–1748*. Ithaca, NY: Cornell University Press, 2000.

Pollack, Ethan. *Stalin and the Science Wars*. Princeton, NJ: Princeton University Press, 2006.

Priestland, David. *Stalinism and the Politics of Mobilization*. Oxford: Oxford University Press, 2007.

Ramsey, Nancy. "Keepers of a Flame That Burned for Russia," *New York Times*, July 5, 1998.

Rebecchi, Marie. "Cinema as Architectural Art: Eisenstein, Ragghianti, and Le Corbusier." In *The Flying Carpet: Studies on Eisenstein and Russian Film in Honor of Naum Kleiman*, edited by Joan Neuberger and Antonio Somaini, 313–23. Paris: Éditions Mimésis, 2017.

Rittersporn, Gábor T. *Anguish, Anger, and Folkways in Soviet Russia*. Pittsburgh: University of Pittsburgh Press, 2014.

Roberge, Gaston. *Eisenstein's Ivan the Terrible: An Analysis*. Calcutta: Chitrabani, 1980.

Robertson, Robert. *Eisenstein on the Audiovisual: The Montage of Music, Image, and Sound in Cinema*. London: I. B. Tauris, 2009.

Robin, Régine. *Socialist Realism: An Impossible Aesthetic*. Stanford, CA: Stanford University Press, 1992.

Romashov, B. "Fil'm "Ivan Groznyi." *Izvestiia*, February 4, 1945.

Romm, Mikhail. *Besedy o kino*. Moscow: Iskusstvo, 1964.

Room, Abram. "Moe kinoubezhdenie." *Sovetskii ekran*, no. 8 (1926): 5.

Roshal', L. M. ""Ia uzhe ne mal'chik i na avantiuru ne poidu . . .": Perepiska Eizenshteina s kinematograficheskim rukovodstvom." *KZ*, no. 38 (1998): 142–68.

Rostotskii, Stanislas. "Na ulitse Eizenshteina." In *Eizenshtein v vospominaniiakh sovremennikov*, edited by R. N. Iurenev, 284–302. Moscow: Iskusstvo, 1974.

Rowland, Daniel B. "Biblical Military Imagery in the Political Culture of Early Modern Russia: The Blessed Host of the Heavenly Tsar." In *Medieval Russian Culture*, edited by Michael S. Flier and Daniel B. Rowland, 2: 182–212. Berkeley: University of California Press, 1994.

——. "Did Muscovite Literary Ideology Place Limits on the Power of the Tsar (1540s–1660s)?" *Russian Review* 49, no. 2 (1990): 125–55.

Rumiantseva, Vera. ""Ne darom ia bredil Jonson'om."" *KZ*, no. 110 (2015): 234–41.

Salazkina, Masha. *In Excess: Sergei Eisenstein's Mexico*. Chicago: University of Chicago Press, 2009.

Salys, Rimgaila. *The Musical Comedy Films of Grigorii Aleksandrov*. Bristol: Intellect, 2009.

Schama, Simon. "Clio at the Multiplex." *The New Yorker*, January 19, 1998.

Scherr, Barry. "*Alexander Nevsky*: A Film without a Hero." In *Eisenstein at 100: A Reconsideration*, edited by Al Lavalley and Barry Scherr, 207–26. New Brunswick, NJ: Rutgers University Press, 2001.

Schutzki, Irina. "From Sensation to Synesthesia: The Aesthetic Experience and Synesthesia in Film and New Media." Unpublished paper.

Shandybin, Gleb. "V Alma-Ate." In *Eizenshtein v vospominaniiakh sovremennikov*, edited by R. N. Iurenev, 378–84. Moscow: Iskusstvo, 1974.

Shklovskii, Viktor. *Eizenshtein*. Moscow: Iskusstvo, 1973.

Shmulevich, Eric. ""Ivan Groznyi i Stalin: Makivellievskoe prochtenie istorii." *KZ*, no. 46 (2000): 189–96.

Shub, Esfir. *Krupnym planom*. Moscow: Iskusstvo, 1958.

Siegelbaum, Lewis, and A. Sokolov, eds. *Stalinism as a Way of Life*. New Haven: Yale University Press, 2000.

Siladi, Akosh. "Ten' Ivana v trekh ottenkakh." *KZ*, no. 38 (1998): 328–38.

Sirotkina, Irina. "The Ubiquitous Reflex and Its Critics in Post-Revolutionary Russia." *Berichte zur Wissenschaftsgeschichte* 32, no. 1 (2009): 70–81.

Slezkine, Yuri. *The House of Government: A Saga of the Russian Revolution*. Princeton, NJ: Princeton University Press, 2017.

Smirnov, Il'ya. "Mezhdu dvumia tiranami." *KZ*, no. 38 (1998): 13–20.

Smith, Emma. "Approaching Shakespeare." Podcast.

——. "Character in Shakespearean Tragedy." In *The Oxford Handbook of Shakespearean Tragedy*, edited by Michael Neill and David Schalkwyk, 89–103. Oxford: Oxford University Press, 2016.

——. "Not Shakespeare: *The Spanish Tragedy*. Podcast.

——. "Shakespeare and Early Modern Tragedy." In *The Cambridge Companion to English Renaissance Tragedy*. Edited by Emma Smith and Garrett A. Sullivan Jr., 132–49. Cambridge: Cambridge University Press, 2010.

Solov'ev, Sergei M. *Istoriia Rossii s drevneishikh vremen*. St. Petersburg: Obshchestvennaia pol'za, 1894–95.

Solzhenitsyn, Alexander. *One Day in the Life of Ivan Denisovich*. New York: Bantam Books, 1963.

Somaini, Antonio. "Cinema as 'Dynamic Mummification,' History as Montage: Eisenstein's Media Archeology." In *Notes for a General History of Cinema*, edited by Naum Kleiman and Antonio Somaini, 19–105. Amsterdam: Amsterdam University Press, 2016.

Sontag, Susan. "Notes on Camp." In her *Against Interpretation and Other Essays*, 275–92. London: Penguin, 2013.

Spring, Derek, and Richard Taylor, eds. *Stalinism and Soviet Cinema*. London: Routledge, 1993.

Spurgeon, Caroline. *Shakepeare's Imagery and What It Tells Us*. Cambridge: Cambridge University Press, 1935.

"Stsena iz 'Borisa Godunova' v raskadrovke S. Eizenshteina." *Iskusstvo kino*, no. 3 (1959): 111–30.

Stites, Richard, ed. *Culture and Entertainment in Wartime Russia*. Bloomington: Indiana University Press, 1995.

Swoboda, Marina. "The Furnace Play and the Development of Liturgical Drama in Russia." *Russian Review* 61, no. 2 (2002). 220–34.

Taruskin, Richard. "Great Artists Serving Stalin Like a Dog." *New York Times*, May 28, 1995.

Taylor, Richard. *The Politics of Soviet Cinema, 1917–1929*. New York: Cambridge University Press, 1979.

Taylor, Richard, and Ian Christie, eds. *The Film Factory: Russian and Soviet Cinema in Documents, 1896–1939*. Cambridge, MA: Harvard University Press, 1988.

Tertz, Abram. *On Socialist Realism*. New York: Pantheon Books, 1960.

Thompson, Kristin. *Eisenstein's Ivan the Terrible: A Neoformalist Analysis*. Princeton, NJ: Princeton University Press, 1981.

Tikka, Pia. *Enactive Cinema*. Saarbrücken: Lambert Academic Publishing, 2010.

Tobak, Esfir'. "Moi Gigant." *Kinotsenarii*, no. 6 (1997): 126–44.

Tsivian, Yuri. "Cinema and Aristotle: Visualizing Naum Kleiman's 'Formula of a Finale.'" In *The Flying Carpet: Studies on Eisenstein and Russian Film in Honor of Naum Kleiman*, edited by Joan Neuberger and Antonio Somaini, 407–19. Paris: Éditions Mimésis, 2017.

——. *Ivan the Terrible*. London: British Film Institute, 2002.

Tsukerman, Vladislav. "Dvoinaia 'myshelovka,' ili samoubiistvo fil'mom." *Iskusstvo kino*, no. 9 (1991): 93–102.

Turovskaia, Maia. *Zuby Drakona: Moi 30-e gody*. Moscow: Corpus, 2015.

Uhlenbruch, Bernd. "The Annexation of History: Eisenstein and the Ivan Grozny Cult of the 1940s." In *The Culture of the Stalin Period*, edited by Hans Günther, 266–87. London: Palgrave Macmillan, 1990.

Ulanova, Galina S. "'Khochu chtoby bylo chisto, blagorodno, i muzykal-no . . .' Zapisal V. Kiselev." *Sovetskaia muzyka*, no. 1 (1980).

——. "Sled v zhizni," In *Eizenshtein v vospominaniiakh sovremennikov*, edited by R. N. Iurenev, 315–19. Moscow: Iskusstvo, 1974.

Uspenskij [Uspenskii], Boris. *The Semiotics of the Russian Icon*. Edited by Stephen Rudy. Lisse: Peter Rudder, 1976.

Ustrialov, Nikolai, ed. *Skazaniia kniazia Kurbskago*. 3rd ed. St. Petersburg: Tipografiia Imperatorskoi akademii nauk, 1868.

Usuvaliev, Sultan. "The Godfathers of Mikhail Kuznetsov." *Studies in Russian and Soviet Cinema* 8, no. 3 (2014): 184–99.

Vasilyeva, Elena. "Two Decades of Soviet Biographical Film: From Revolutionary Romanticism to Epic Monumentalism (1934–1953)." PhD diss., University of Southern California, 2009.

Vassilieva, Julia. "Eisenstein and Cultural-Historical Theory." In *The Flying Carpet: Studies on Eisenstein and Russian Film in Honor of Naum Kleiman*, edited by Joan Neuberger and Antonio Somaini, 421–41. Paris: Éditions Mimésis, 2017.

Veselovskii, A. N. "Skazki ob Ivane Groznom." In *Sobranie sochinenii Aleksandra Nikolaevicha Veselovskogo*, 16: 309–12. Moscow-Leningrad: Izdatel'stvo Akademii nauk SSSR, 1938 [1876].

Villari, Pasquale. *The Life and Times of Niccolo Macciavelli*. Translated by Linda Villari. New York: T. Fisher Unwin, 1892.

Vipper, R. Iu. *Ivan Groznyi*. Moscow: Del'fin, 1922. 2nd ed., Tashkent: Gosudarstvennoe izdatel'stvo UzSSR, 1942. 3rd ed., Moscow: n.p., 1944.

Vishnevskii, Vsevolod. "Fil'm 'Ivan Groznyi.'" *Pravda*, January 28, 1945.

——. "Iz dnevnikov, 1944–1948 gg." *KZ*, no. 38 (1998): 64–80.

Von Geldern, James, and Richard Stites, eds. "Ever Higher (Aviators' March)." In *Mass Culture in Soviet Russia: Tales, Poems, Songs, Movies, Plays, and Folklore, 1917–1953*, edited by James Von Geldern, 257–58. Bloomington: Indiana University Press, 1995.

Von Shtaden, Genrikh [Heinrich von Staden]. *O Moskve Ivana Groznogo: Zapiski nemtsa-oprichnika*. Translated with an introduction by I. I. Polosin. Leningrad: Izdanie M. i S. Sabashnikovykh, 1925.

Vygotsky, Lev. *The Psychology of Art*. Cambridge, MA: MIT Press, 1971.

Widdis, Emma. *Socialist Senses: Film, Feeling, and the Soviet Subject, 1917–1940.* Bloomington: Indiana University Press, 2017.

Willis, Deborah. "'The Gnawing Vulture': Revenge, Trauma Theory, and "Titus Andronicus.'" *Shakespeare Quarterly* 53, no. 1 (2002): 21–52.

Wollen, Peter. *Signs and Meaning in Cinema.* Bloomington: Indiana University Press, 1969.

Youngblood, Denise. *Soviet Cinema in the Silent Era, 1918–1935.* Austin: University of Texas Press, 1991.

Zabrodin, V. V. "Chelovechskii golos ili 'posledniaia zhertva': Pis'ma E. S. Teleshevoi S. M. Eizenshteinu, 1941–1942." *KZ,* no. 74 (2005): 70–119.

——. "'Dorogoi starik': Pis'ma Peroi Atashevoi Sergeiu Eizenshteinu, 1942–44." *Iskusstvo kino,* no. 6 (2015): 142–71.

——. "Neizvestnye stranitsy tsenariia." *KZ,* no 38 (1998): 246–61.

"Zasedanie khudozhestvennogo soveta pri Komitete po delam kinematografii: Prosmotr i obsuzhdenie vtoroi serii kinokartiny 'Ivan Groznyi' rezhissera S. Eizenshteina (7 fevralia 1946 goda)." In *Zhivye golosa kino: Govoriat vydaiushchiesia mastera otechestvennogo kinoiskusstva (30-e–40-e gody). Iz nepublikovannogo,* edited by L. Parfenov, 276–307. Moscow: Belyi bereg, 1999.

Zhakov, Oleg. "'Zakovannyi v laty.'" In *Eizenshtein v vospominaniiakh sovremennikov,* edited by R. N. Iurenev, 334–45. Moscow: Iskusstvo: 1974.

Zholkovsky, Alexander. "Eisenstein's Poetics: Dialogic or Totalitarian?" In *Laboratory of Dreams: The Russian Avant Garde and Cultural Experiment,* edited by John E. Bowlt and Olga Matich, 245–57. Stanford, CA: Stanford University Press, 1996.

Zorkaia, Neia. *Portrety.* Moscow: Iskusstvo, 1966.

INDEX

Abrikosov, Andrei, 19
actors and acting, 152, 286–300, 308
Agapov, Boris, 326
agency, 87–88, 91, 119, 162, 173, 180, 184, 200–201, 215, 217–19; objects and, 164–66
Alexandrov, Grigory, 11, 252, 320–21; *The Radiant Path*, 241, 337
Alexandrova (*Aleksandrovskaia Sloboda*), 22, 106, 140–41, 143, 204
Alma Ata (Almaty), 19, 26, 44, 56, 64–65
Androgyny. *See* B.S. (bisexuality)
Antokolsky, Mark, 40
apocalypse, 148, 150, 167–74
armillary sphere, 159–62, 174
Artistic Council of the Committee on Cinema Affairs, 23, 65, 306–10, 319–21, 334–35
Artistic Council, Mosfilm, 65, 306
Atasheva, Pera, 12, 45, 51, 56, 66, 126, 326
atavism, 92–93, 99–101, 104, 107, 117–18, 148
avant garde, 5, 14, 57, 114, 239, 253, 287–88
axial editing, 263, 266, 274, 285, 302

Babochkin, Boris, 308
Bach, J. S., 90, 187, 246
Bakhtin, Mikhail, 5, 213
Basmanov, Aleksei, 22, 24, 49, 85,
Belinsky, Vissarion, 76, 90–91
Benjamin, Walter, 5, 9, 128
Beria, Lavrenty, 319, 322, 327
biography, 132–52, 186; spiral form of, 127–29, 132, 135, 137–38, 146–49, 151–52, 168–69, 175, 265, 338; tragedy and, 175, 184;
biopic, 4, 105, 241
Birman, Serafima, 19, 55–56, 58
Blount, Charles, 230–31
Bode, Rudolph, 288–89
body and body movements, 132–35, 137, 140–41, 146–53, 158–59, 168, 204, 215, 219, 224, 228, 246, 261–66, 287–300, 303, 344; dialectics and, 287–91, 293–94; emotions

and, 287–94; spiral and, 298. *See also* acting; gesture; reverse movement
Bolshakov, Ivan, 30, 47–53, 55, 61, 65–67, 75, 136, 216, 222, 306, 309, 313–14, 318, 320, 326–28, 335
books, love of, 16, 44, 72, 179, 345
Bordwell, David, 241, 274
Bororo, of Brazil, 156
bricklaying, 254, 259–69
B.S. (Bisexuality), 12, 161, 163, 171, 206–8, 222–30, 324
Buchma, Amvrosii, 204

camp, 50, 223–29, 295, 322
Carpenter, William, 245
Cathedral, Dormition (Uspensky), 59, 281; Anastasia's coffin in, 139, 205, 283; confession in, 24, 35, 183; coronation in, 196, 283; Fiery Furnace in, 102–3, 149, 202, 280–81; frescoes in, 166–67, 281, 312; Vladimir's death in, 24, 143, 150, 168, 282; as womb, 150, 163, 224, 233
cathedral, Gothic, 248–49, 251, 274
censorship, 5, 6, 9, 20, 28–30, 336; deleted scenes, 63, 95, 321
chalice, 139, 146, 162–66, 174, 270, 338
Chaplin, Charlie, 11, 56, 149, 213
Cherkasov, Nikolai, 20, 35, 53–54, 59–60, 139, 243, 286–87, 293–300, 309, 314, 326, 330–33
Cherkasova, Nina, 59
Cherniavsky, Michael, 107–8
Chiaureli, Mikhail, 316; *Georgi Saakadze,* 241
childhood and children, 95–96. 101, 108, 132, 169, 173, 181, 202, 220–22, 239; Fiery Furnace and, 102, 148–49; memories of, 33, 38, 52, 80, 84–85, 146, 257, 295, 298; Oath of the Oprichniki and, 144, 209; pre-logical and, 156–57, 163; spiral return to, 128–29, 131, 133, 137–39, 146–49, 165, 168, 174, 233, 238, 265; trauma and, 38, 81–82, 85–87, 95, 104, 114, 118, 137, 181, 198;